Transactions of the Royal Historical Society

SIXTH SERIES

XIII

CAMBRIDGE
UNIVERSITY PRESS

Flash of consonants
Cleaving the line.[1]

Seamus Heaney's *North* will do very well as an introduction to the sources of modern conceptions of Vikings. The scop's twang in the song and story of the North was what inspired the construction of the Vikings in nineteenth-century England. William Morris set out for Iceland in 1871, a copy of *Njal's Saga* in hand to guide him from Svinafell to Bergthorshvoll. Morris had succumbed long since:

O South! O sky without a cooling cloud;
O sickening yellow sand without a break
. . .
I cannot love thee, South, for all thy sun
. . .
But in the North forever dwells my heart. . .[2]

Similar sentiments inspired the aged Gladstone: 'When I have been in Norway, or Denmark, or among Scandinavians, I have felt something like a cry of nature from within, asserting (credibly or otherwise) my nearness to them.'[3]

Maybe the sort of Scandinavians Gladstone met were like the Stockholm bourgeois fancy-dressed Vikings of 1869 in a photograph that has achieved a certain éclat through recent reproductions.[4] Helmets notwithstanding, these are distinctly domesticated gentlemen – and ladies. By the time Gladstone wrote about nearness (credibly or otherwise), the Vikings had been part of English culture for the best part of a century. The word is first recorded in modern English, though in the not fully anglicised form vikingr, in a historical compendium published in 1807.[5] Soon, the malleable North was on the way to becoming a mirror and model to the nineteenth-century present. All that was needed was for pagans to be pursued as converts and vices could turn into virtues – or rather, excesses once pruned, vices could *be* virtues, and necessary ones, to check the malign propensity of the

---

[1] S. Heaney, *North* (1996; first pub. 1975), 'Viking Dublin: Trial Pieces', 14–15, and 'Bone Dreams', 20. I should like to thank the following friends and colleagues for offprints, papers in advance of publication, advice and criticism: David Bates, Simon Coupland, Michael Gelting, Neils Lund and especially Stéphane Lebecq, whose maps I have anglicised.

[2] A. Wawn, *The Vikings and the Victorians* (Cambridge, 2000), 249–57.

[3] Wawn, *The Vikings*, 312, 330–1: Gladstone was here enthusing in a letter to Paul du Chaillu whose *Ivar the Viking: A Romantic History Based upon Authentic Facts* (1893) he had just read.

[4] *Social Approaches to Viking Studies*, ed. R. Samson (Glasow, 1991), 60; P. Sawyer, *The Oxford Illustrated History of the Vikings* (Oxford, 1997), 241.

[5] G. Chalmers, *Caledonia: Or, an Account, Historical and Topographic, of North Britain* (3 vols., 1807–24), I, pt III, iii, 341.

English (especially the southern English) to effeminacy and corruption from the Continent. No wonder men felt stronger and purer for a blast of northern winds. By 1883, Stubbs had coined Vikingism – signifying a peculiarly muscular form of muscular Christianity.[6] The Vikings have been celebrated more recently too. In the USA, at the New York exhibition marking the millennium of America's discovery by Leif Eriksson, Hillary Clinton affirmed Americans' pride in their 'Nordic roots', for America, 'like the Vikings, gave the world new ideas', while longships were 'the Internet of the year 1000'. In Novgorod, Mr Putin applauded archaeologists' success in discovering more evidence of Viking settlements – the sort of evidence long denied in the Soviet period: post-1989, Russians acknowledge with pride their ninth-century Scandinavian ancestors, the Rus.[7]

But in England, nearness has never excluded Otherness. Otherness is what was stressed in many nineteenth-century representations of the North, from Thomas Carlyle's 'Heathen, Physical-Force, Ultra-Chartists, otherwise known as Danes'[8] to W.G. Collingwood's 'bearsark' men of 'rapine and massacre'.[9] Echoing still in scholarly analysis and school-book story is J.R. Green's bloodcurdling evocation, which links the ninth century's experience firmly with that of the fifth:

> The first sight of the northmen is as if the hand on the dial of history had gone back three hundred years ... There was the same wild panic as the black boats of the invaders struck inland along the river-reaches, or moored around the river islets, the same sights of horror, firing of homesteads, slaughter of men, women driven off to slavery or shame, children tossed on pikes[10] or sold in the market-place, as when the English invaders attacked Britain.[11]

The modern dictionary translates the horror-story into a prosaic definition: 'viking: one of those Scandinavian adventurers who practised piracy at sea, and committed depredations on land, in northern and

---

[6] W. Stubbs, *Seventeen Lectures on the Study of Medieval and Modern History and Kindred Subjects Delivered at Oxford 1867–1884* (Oxford, 1886), 222: Robert Curthose saw the First Crusade as 'a sanctified experiment in Vikingism'.

[7] 'Die Wikinger. Eroberer, Barbaren, braune Kultfiguren', *Der Spiegel*, 32 (2000), 184–98. For recent archaeology in Russia, see *Les centres proto-urbains russes entre Scandinaveie, Byzance et Orient*, ed. M. Kazanski *et al.*, Realités Byzantines 7 (Paris, 2000).

[8] T. Carlyle, *Past and Present* (1843), 112.

[9] Collingwood, quoted in Wawn, *The Vikings*, 339, and see further 335–41, in *The Bondwoman: A Saga of Langdale* (1896), 100–1, contrasted the bearsark days with 'the time of our story', i.e. the tenth century.

[10] Green had read his *Landnámabók*.

[11] J.R. Green, *A Short History of the English People* (1874). I cite from the second edition of 1878, 45. For Green's context and influence, see P. Mandler, *History and National Life* (2002), 38–42, with, 141–2, a note of scepticism on the recipe's appropriateness now.

western Europe from the eighth century to the eleventh'.[12] Externality, lawlessness and violent expropriation remain the key ideas here. And in popular usage, where the Vikings tend to be plural and homogeneous, savagery has always been to the fore. In *Alfred the Great*, written for primary school children in the mid-1950s, the ahistorical horned helmets betoken Otherness.[13] In museums and on television, the message has hardly changed. Think Vikings, think 'rape and pillage', or – deliciously ambiguous – 'the Blood of the Vikings'.[14]

Does the blood of those migrant blood-spillers course now in English veins? Which English? Cumbrians, Yorkshiremen and Hampshiremen have answered variously, and still do. Such variousness subverts modern simplicities. Nineteenth-century Scottish nationalists found Teutonist ethnology inhibiting because far from opposing Scots to English, it linked them together.[15] Confronted by Vikings, the English, ancient and modern, have oscillated between repulsion and association. English identity has been constructed against a Viking Other, as a narrative of shared victimhood and resistance, personified by King Alfred the Great.[16] Yet it has been constructed, too, on an assimilationist paradigm,

---

[12] *Oxford English Dictionary*, 2nd edn, ed. J.A. Simpson and E.S.C. Weiner, XIX (Oxford, 1989), 628.

[13] L. Du Garde Peach, *King Alfred the Great* (1956), 7, 25, 27, 35, with 31 for the (equally ahistorical) winged helmet variant.

[14] This was the title of a recent TV series presented by the archaeologist Julian Richards: it was among the most widely watched History programmes of 2002. In its earlier years, the Jorvik Museum at York greeted visitors with a large display panel on 'rape and pillage' but it has since been replaced (if not consigned to the dustbin of museology). On the question of Viking rape, see J.L. Nelson, 'The Vikings in Francia', in *The Oxford Illustrated History of the Vikings*, ed. P. Sawyer (Oxford, 1997), 47, which represents an arguable position more fairly than that parodied (with some justification) by D.N. Dumville, 'The Churches of North Britain in the First Viking-Age', Fifth Whithorn Lecture (Stranraer, 1997), 9–10. The saga material is thoughtfully, but inevitably inconclusively, considered by W.I. Miller, *Bloodtaking and Peacemaking: Feud, Law and Society in Saga Iceland* (Chicago, 1990), 208–9.

[15] C. Kidd, 'Teutonist Ethnology and Scottish Nationalist Inhibition', *Scottish Historical Review*, 74 (1995), 45–68.

[16] S. Trafford, 'Ethnicity, Migration Theory, and Historiography', in *Cultures in Contact: Scandinavian Settlement in England in the Ninth and Tenth Centuries*, ed. D.M. Hadley and J.D. Richards (Turnhout, 2000), 17–39, at 28–30. For perspectives on the constructedness of national identity, see the seminal paper of P. Wormald, 'Bede, the *Bretwaldas*, and the Origins of the *Gens Anglorum*', in *Ideal and Reality in Frankish and Anglo-Saxon Society*, ed. P. Wormald *et al.* (Oxford, 1983), 99–129; P. Wormald, '*Engla Lond*: The Making of an Allegiance', *Journal of Historical Sociology*, 7 (1994), 1–24; S. Reynolds, '"Anglo-Saxon" and "Anglo-Saxons"', *Journal of British Studies*, 24 (1985), 395–414, repr. in S. Reynolds, *Ideas and Solidarities of the Medieval Laity* (Aldershot, 1995), ch. III; and S. Foot, 'The Making of *Angelcynn*: English Identity before the Norman Conquest', *Transactions of the Royal Historical Society*, sixth series, 6 (1996), 25–50. For Alfred, see J.L. Nelson, *Rulers and Ruling Families in Early Medieval Europe* (Aldershot, 1999), chs. I–VI; and cf. K. Davis, 'National Writing in the Ninth Century', *Journal of Medieval and Early Modern Studies*, 28 (1998), 611–37.

in which the Vikings, like those of Collingwood's saga of Langdale, become no longer 'them' but 'us'. The passage from Green I quoted a moment ago continues: 'But when the wild burst of the storm was over, land, people, government reappeared unchanged. England still remained England; the conquerors sank quietly into the mass of those around them.' Green's explanation was twofold. First,

> the battle was no longer [as in the fifth century] between men of different races. It was no longer a fight between Briton and German ... The life of these northern folk was in the main the life of the earlier Englishmen. Their customs, ... their social order, were the same; they were in fact kinsmen bringing back to an England that had forgotten its origins the barbaric England of its pirate forefathers.

Second, religion: 'Woden yielded without a struggle to Christ.' Today, most of us would abjure the vocabulary of race, but happily use, instead, that of culture and acculturation. Today, whistle-blowers among the archaeological fraternity are drawing attention to prejudice that obscures evidence for (im)migration, and signalling new ways in which 'situational "ethnicities"' can be read in burials.[17] If scholars working in this country are in the forefront, that is because here the question of identity has mattered and matters again. For multiple reasons, 'Peoples are back on the historian's agenda.'[18] But back on historians' agenda, too, is religion, and its capacity both to mark difference and to promote sentiments of transcendent community. Conversion as social adaptation rather than individual 'reorientation' raises important questions of chronology and process.[19]

In the single ninth-century manuscript of the 'Alfredian' *Anglo-Saxon Chronicle*, MS 'A', the main source for ninth-century England south of the Humber, Vikings are hard to find. Just three groups are so designated and the term, *wicenga*, may denote some authorial particularity.[20] Otherwise, a group of 'Danes' is usually designated collectively as a *here*, an 'army'. Sometimes they are called 'Danishmen',

---

[17] H. Härke, 'Archaeologists and Migration: A Problem of Attitude?', *Current Archaeology*, 39 (1) (1998), 19–45; G. Halsall, 'The Viking Presence in England? The Burial Evidence Reconsidered', in *Cultures in Contact*, ed. Hadley and Richards, 259–76.

[18] R.R. Davies, 'The Peoples of Britain and Ireland, 1100–1400', *Transactions of the Royal Historical Society*, sixth series, 4 (1994), 1–20.

[19] See L. Abrams, 'Conversion and Assimilation', in *Cultures in Contact*, ed. Hadley and Richards, 135–53.

[20] J. Bately, ed., *The Anglo-Saxon Chronicle: A Collaborative Edition*, general eds. D. Dumville and S. Keynes, III: *MS A* (Cambridge, 1986) [hereafter *ASC*], s.a. 879 and 885, 51 (on hloþ wicenga), 52 (.xvi. scipu wicenga... hie micelne sciphere wicenga), trans. G. Garmonsway, *The Anglo-Saxon Chronicle* (1975), 76, 78 ('pirates').

and very occasionally 'heathen'.[21] But a more insistent Otherness has been back-projected. In 1955, Dorothy Whitelock's translation added clarificatory references to 'Danes' and 'English' where few or none were present in the original's account of two types of armies, *here* and *fyrd*, so that Alfred's battles became international ones, trials through which England was formed and united.[22] In the translation of Asser's *Life of Alfred* by Simon Keynes and Michael Lapidge, Asser's *pagani* become, consistently, 'the Vikings', despite clear evidence in the same text that the term (with or without any religious significance) had become a synonym for Danes, as when Asser refers to *pagani* in Alfred's retinue or at one of his monastic foundations.[23] An alternative and still more insidious Othering was effected by twelfth-century churchmen who, in ivied Latin, blamed the flaws and gaps of pre-reformed monasticism on Viking destruction three centuries before. The *Liber Eliensis*, c. 1170, described the Vikings' arrival at St Æthelthryth's shrine at Ely, in or about 870:

> When the mob of evil ones reaches the monastery of virgins which Æthelthryth the glorious virgin and bride of Christ had built, alas, it invades, pollutes the holy things, tramples and tears (*contaminat, ... conculcat et diripit*). The sword of the madmen is stretched out over the milkwhite consecrated necks (*Protenditur rabidorum gladius in lactea sacrataque colla*).

Julia Barrow's fine translation does full justice to the original.[24] For critical historians, lurid, even faintly salacious, stories are no substitute for contemporary evidence – of which there is none. True, some prominent convents are unrecorded in the post-Alfredian period, before being 'restored' later, in the tenth or eleventh centuries, but to impute the caesura to Viking activity may be a methodological bridge too far, when other endogenous reasons for convents' fortunes (so often tied to

---

[21] See Bately's Index of people-names, 117, s.v. *Denisc, þa Deniscan, Denescan*. For *heþne men, heþen here*, see *ASC* 855, 865, 45, 46.

[22] *ASC* 865–96, trans. D. Whitelock, *English Historical Documents*, I, 2nd rev. edn (1979), 191–206 (using MS B as her base-text but with 'A' variants noted). In the single annal for 893, Professor Whitelock added no fewer than seven 'Danes/Danish' or 'English' identifiers.

[23] Asser, *De Gestis Ælfredi Regis*, ed. W. Stevenson (Oxford, 1904; repr. with introduction by D. Whitelock, 1959), cc. 76, 94, pp. 60, 81, trans. S. Keynes and M. Lapidge, *Alfred the Great* (Harmondsworth, 1983), 91, 103.

[24] J. Barrow, 'Survival and Mutation: Ecclesiastical Institutions in the Danelaw in the Ninth and Tenth Centuries', in *Cultures in Contact*, ed. Hadley and Richards, 155–76, at 155, translating *Liber Eliensis* I, c. 41, ed. E.O. Blake, Camden third series, 92, Royal Historical Society (1962), 55.

royal and aristocratic family fortunes) are not hard to find.[25]

Further, MS 'A' does not record a single case of the destruction of a church by the Vikings. Canterbury can be inferred to have suffered, and apparently the community 'by the 870s' found it hard to field a single competent scribe.[26] If so, it may be hasty to infer that the Vikings alone were to blame. As earlier in the century, those in charge of the church of Canterbury may have seen their chief problem as royal seizures of church property rather than the attacks of external enemies which simply allowed kings to seize more windows of opportunity.[27] At York, the establishment of Viking lordship from 867 does not seem to have led to the wholesale destruction or dispersal of the cathedral library – which makes you wonder how far you can generalise from Canterbury.[28] Asser, pondering in 893 the question of responsibility for the state of monasteries among the English, was inclined to blame 'that people' themselves rather than the Vikings.[29]

It is worth comparing the ways in which *les Normands* have been represented in both French and Belgian historiography in the nineteenth and twentieth centuries. In brief, Northmen were assigned relatively limited historical significance.[30] In neither case did historians trying to explain the decline and fall of the Carolingian Empire give pride of place to external forces; and in neither case did the (re)formation of national identity depend on a Viking Other. True, there were local variations on the Norman theme – most evidently in Normandy, famously founded in *c.* 911 by the Danish warlord Rollo and his followers.[31] But increasingly this is a story re-presented by historians in terms of institutional and sociological continuities with Frankish Neustria

[25] S. Foot, *Veiled Women: The Disappearance of Nuns from Anglo-Saxon England* (2 vols., Aldershot, 2001), 71–84, gives a carefully nuanced version of the 'caesura' story; but see the review by P. Stafford in *Early Medieval Europe*, 10 (2001), 287–8, and P. Stafford, 'Queens, Nunneries and Reforming Churchmen: Gender, Status and Reform in Tenth-and Eleventh-Century England', *Past and Present*, 163 (1999), 3–35.

[26] N. Brooks, *The Early History of the Church of Canterbury: Christ Church from 597 to 1066* (Leicester, 1984), 167–74, offering a rather different perspective from that of Brooks, 'England in the Ninth Century: The Crucible of Defeat', *Transactions of the Royal Historical Society*, fifth series, 29 (1979), 1–20; cf. Foot, 'Violence against Christians? The Vikings and the Church in Ninth-Century England', *Medieval History*, 1 (1991), 3–16.

[27] J.L. Nelson, '"A King across the Sea": Alfred in Continental Perspective', *Transactions of the Royal Historical Society*, fifth series, 26 (1986), 45–68, at 58–9; G. Halsall, 'Playing by Whose Rules? A Further Look at Viking Atrocity in the Ninth Century', *Medieval History*, 2 (1992), 2–12.

[28] M. Lapidge, 'Latin Learning in Ninth-Century England', in M. Lapidge, *Anglo-Latin Literature 600–899* (1996), 409–54, at 426–32.

[29] Asser, *De Gestis ælfredi Regis* c. 93, p. 81, trans. 103.

[30] This did not exclude, of course, a large amount of interest on the part of literary savants and scholars: see T.J. Beck, *Northern Antiquities in French Learning and Literature* (2 vols., New York, 1934); R. Boyer, *Le mythe viking dans les lettres françaises* (Paris, 1991).

[31] D. Bates, *Normandy before 1066* (1982), 8–9.

and the ecclesiastical province of Rouen.[32] A generation or two ago, the silence of the late ninth- and tenth-century sources on Bordeaux was imputed to Viking destruction, and that scenario was extended to Aquitaine as a whole.[33] Yet recent researchers have put more stress on endogenous forces: the extension of the lordship of the dukes of Gascony south-west of the Garonne, and over Bordeaux itself from 887, and further inland, the entrenchment of aristocratic and ecclesiastical power at Limoges, Angoulême and Périgueux.[34] In the regions of northern and north-west Francia, French historians used to argue for the Vikings' crucial, if indirect, role in weakening the monarchy, since only regional aristocrats could mount effective defence: hence the famous rise of princely powers.[35] More recently, though, there has been a clearer recognition of continuities between the structures of Carolingian government and the 'new' principalities of the tenth century.[36] In the ecclesiastical historiography of Lotharingia and the regions that were to become Belgium, plentiful allegations of Viking responsibility for monastic poverty and decline drew on the propagandistic chronicles of monasteries restored by the great reformers of the tenth, eleventh and twelfth centuries. Some thirty years ago, a major piece of revisionist scholarship convincingly demonstrated the minimal trace of Scandinavian impact in the documentary record.[37] More recently, in French and Belgian historiography (and in general parlance), *les Normands* have become *les Vikings*. But I do not think this denotes any francophone embrace of generalised Othering. Normandy apart, the Vikings themselves had always remained marginal, even exotic, in relation to modern French and Belgian identities; and if the overnight transformation of

---

[32] J. Yver, 'Les premières institutions du duché de Nomandie', in *I Normanni e la loro espansione in Europa nell'alto medioevo*, Settimane di Studi sull'Alto Medioevo XVI (Spoleto, 1969), 299–366; D. Bates, 'The Northern Principalities', in *The New Cambridge Medieval History*, ed. T. Reuter, III (Cambridge, 1999), 398–419, at 404–6; cf. D. Barthélemy, *L'an mil et la paix du Dieu* (Paris, 1999), 241–8 (reconstruction rather than continuity).

[33] C. Higounet, *Bordeaux pendant le haut moyen âge* (Bordeaux, 1963), 41, relying on letters of Pope John VIII, which in turn relied on letters of Charles the Bald; J.M. Wallace-Hadrill, 'The Vikings in Francia', in J.M. Wallace-Hadrill, *Early Medieval History* (Oxford, 1976), 228–30.

[34] M. Zimmerman, 'The Southern Principalities', in *The New Cambridge Medieval History*, ed. Reuter, III, 420–55.

[35] M. Bloch, *La société féodale* (2 vols., Paris, 1939–44), I, trans. J. Anderson (1961) as *Feudal Society*, 56, and cf. 53: 'The problem, in short, was the very same one which French officers encounter today when they try to maintain security on the Moroccan borders on in Mauretania – made ten times worse, needless to say, by the absence of any higher authority capable of exercising effective control over vast areas.'

[36] Bates, 'The Northern Principalities', 398–419.

[37] A. d'Haenens, *Les invasions normandes en Belgique au IXe siècle: le phénomène et sa repercussion dans l'historiographie médiévale* (Louvain, 1967); A. d'Haenens, 'Les invasions normandes dans l'Empire franc au IXe siècle: pour une renovation de la problématique', in *Settimane di Studi sull'Alto Medioevo*, XVI (Spoleto, 1969), 235–98.

Rollo and company from scourges to 'serviteurs de la civilisation' is seen nowadays in terms of more complicated and protracted processes, there is scholarly agreement on the definitiveness in the long run of the Normans' reconstruction as *Franci*.[38] Thus for the French and the Belgians, the Viking impact has hardly seemed problematic, as it has in England and, for some different reasons, in Scotland. In Britain, philology conditioned the roles of the Vikings in modern nation-building, and still has something to answer for in terms of constructional weaknesses in Britishness.[39]

In the rest of this essay, I want to concentrate on ninth-century evidence, and look first at Francia. Paradoxically, where the Anglo-Saxon sources suggest co-existence, some Frankish ones present dramatic Othering. The contemporary entry in the Annals of St-Vaast, Arras, for 884 gave a lurid account of corpses of clergy and lay, nobles and others, women, young men and babies lying about *per omnes plateas* – 'in every square'.[40] The shrill voice of Ermentar, the monk of St-Philibert de Noirmoutier, famed not least because Marc Bloch cited him in *La société féodale* vol. I, reached a crescendo in describing events *c.* 855:

> the innumerable multitude of the Northmen grows incessantly. On every side, Christians succumb to massacres, acts of pillage, devastations, burnings whose manifest traces will remain as long as the world endures. They seize every city they pass without anyone offering any resistance: they seize Bordeaux, Périgueux, Limoges, Angoulême and Toulouse. Angers, Tours and Orleans are laid waste ... Thus has been realised the threat uttered by the Lord through the mouths of his Prophets: 'A scourge from the North will extend over all those who dwell in the land.'[41]

The St-Vaast annalist and Ermentar, both in fact atypical among ninth-century monastic writers in such lurid accounts of atrocity, had their own agendas, naturally. The annalist implicitly disapproved of the abbot of St-Vaast for cutting a protection deal with a Viking leader called Alsting (we will meet him again) which failed to work quite as

---

[38] Contrast J. Calmette, *Le monde féodal* (Paris, 1934), 26, with current debates over the intricacies of the Normans' journey towards assimilation as appraised by E. Christiansen, *Dudo of St Quentin, History of the Normans* (Woodbridge, 1998), xvii–xxix.

[39] Kidd, 'Teutomist Ethnology'; and cf. P. Geary, *The Myth of Nations: The Medieval Origins of Europe* (Princeton, 2002), esp. 27–40.

[40] *Annales Vedastini*, ed. B. von Simson, Monumenta Germaniae Historica [hereafter MGH] (Hannover, 1909), 54. See H. Zettel, *Das Bild der Normannen und der Normanneneinfälle in westfränkischen, ostfränkischen, und angelsächsischen Quellen des 8. bis 11. Jahrhunderts* (Munich, 1977).

[41] Ermentar, *De translationibus et miraculis Sancti Philiberti Libri II*, ed. R. Poupardin, Monuments de l'histoire de l'abbaye de Saint-Philibert (Paris, 1905), 60–1.

intended, but St-Vaast's worst experience of these years ('an evil such that recovery from it was impossible' (*malum tale quod inrecuperabile est*)), as it turned out, was no Viking attack but a terrible fire in 892 as a result of which 'all the saint's relics were stolen from us, and the whole of the monastery's fortification was burned down'.[42] As for Ermentar, his string of different verbs to denote the Northmen's activities do not need to be read as carefully calibrating different types of violence.[43] This is just ivied Latin. And while it may be a shade unfair to claim that Ermentar's sole motivation was a desire 'to escape [his] Atlantic backwater and travel in the glamorous circles of the most powerful men of the Carolingian world',[44] there was collective self-interest in the community's appeal to King Charles the Bald to give St Philibert a refuge in Burgundy that was not just safe but lavish. Curiously, both St-Vaast and St-Philibert in fact came rather well out of the ninth century. But Marc Bloch, in reading Ermentar straight, and offering him as key witness to a 'catastrophic scenario'[45] of Viking destruction and disruption, wanted to make a much bigger point: it was the historiographic point I discussed in my lecture last year, about ends and beginnings. Bloch's Vikings neatly exploded the Carolingians' last chance of restoring continuity with the Roman Empire. Feudal society, and *Feudal Society*, thus had to start with Vikings signalling at once nadir and new start.[46] French ecclesiastical historians, like English ones, followed the lead given by medieval monastic writers themselves – writers not of the ninth century but of the eleventh and twelfth. In many cases, it was only when the cartulary habit, that is, the practice of collecting and copying into one big book the documents of institutional memory, charters along with charter-based history, that communities, or at least their memorialists, became aware of a gap, and an apologetic deficit.[47] Late ninth- and tenth-century monasteries seemed to later reformers to have fallen into the clutches of lay noblemen, who were

[42] *Annales Vedastini* 890, 69 (Alsting), 892, 71 (the burning down of St-Vaast).

[43] *Pace* Wallace-Hadrill, 'The Vikings in Francia', 222.

[44] F. Lifshitz, 'The Migration of Neustrian Relics in the Viking Age: The Myth of Voluntary Exodus, the Reality of Coercion and Theft', *Early Medieval Europe*, 4 (1995), 175–92, at 191–2.

[45] Lifshitz, 'The Migration of Neustrian Relics', 191, referring to Bloch, *Feudal Society*, 54–5.

[46] J.L. Nelson, 'Ends and Beginnings', *Transactions of the Royal Historical Society*, sixth series, 12 (2002), 4. Behind Bloch, there is a long French tradition, from Michelet, and even Voltaire, of emphasising the late ninth- /tenth-century watershed: Barthélemy, *L'an mil*, 58–64.

[47] P. Geary, *Phantoms of Remembrance: Memory and Oblivion at the End of the First Millennium* (Princeton, 1994); D. Barthélemy, *La société dans le comté de Vendôme, de l'an mil au XIVe siècle* (Paris, 1993), 19–83; J. Nightingale, *Monasteries and Patrons in the Gorze Reforms: Lotharingia c. 850–1000* (Oxford, 2001), 3–21.

also the patrons and providers of monastic personnel. Though the charter-draftsmen themselves scarcely ever referred to Viking or any other destruction,[48] authors of monastic narratives evaded a dilemma by casting the Vikings as destroyers of a regular monastic life.[49] Once that image had been established, modern ecclesiastical historians until recently were more than happy to go with their sources in depicting 'the Church in the clutches of the laity'.[50]

Othering Vikings was under way in southern England just as soon as Others were on hand to blame for monastic shortcomings. Asser says in his *Life of Alfred* that (I quote Keynes and Lapidge's translation)

> for many years past, the desire for the monastic life had been totally lacking in that entire race ... I am not sure why: either it is because of the depredations by foreign enemies whose attacks by lands and sea are very frequent and savage (*saepissime ... hostiliter irrumpunt* ['savage' is the translators' interpolation – I am not sure why]) , or else because of that people's enormous abundance of riches of every kind, on account of which I think this sort of despicable monastic life (*id genus despectae monasticae vitae*) became much more prevalent.[51]

(I wonder if Asser had been reading Bede's Letter to Egbert?) As I noted earlier, Asser himself did not subscribe to blaming dark foreign forces. He was a foreigner himself, of course – and a Welshman.

Blame-displacement, in the ninth century and later, has required a bit more Othering of the Vikings, though. Calling them heathen, *pagani*, was one obvious tactic.[52] Calling their attacks 'savage' may be classed as another – if English attacks are never so described. Vikings have been quite systematically Othered by modern historians, by allegations of peculiar traits ranging from a kinship system that was one of large descent-groups rather than families, to distinctively elaborate arrangements for feuds and feuding,[53] to ruthless slave-trading, to a

---

[48] 'Why should they?', was the riposte (to d'Haenens's painstaking demonstration) of Wallace-Hadrill, 'The Vikings in Francia', 230.

[49] Nightingale, *Monasteries and Patrons*, pp. 10–11. See also with similar conclusions A. Dierkens, *Abbayes et chapîtres entre Sambre et Meuse (VIIe–XIe siècles)* (Sigmaringen, 1985), 330–1; A.-M. Helvétius, *Abbayes, évêques et laïques: une politique du pouvoir en Hainaut au moyen âge (VIIe –XIe siècles)* (Brussels, 1994), 208–9.

[50] E. Amann and A. Dumas, *L'église au pouvoir des laïcs, 888–1057* (Paris, 1943).

[51] Asser, *De Gestis Ælfredi Regis* c. 93, p. 81, trans. 103.

[52] Above, p. 6.

[53] For fine critical overviews of the historiography on descent-groups and feuds: E. Christiansen, *The Norsemen in the Viking Age* (Oxford, 2002), 38–52, and M. Gelting, 'Odelsrett – lovbydelse – bödsrätt – retrait lignager: Kindred and Land in the Nordic Countries', in *Family, Marriage and Property Devolution in the Middle Ages*, ed. L.I. Hansen (Tromsø, 2000), 133–66; cf. on historiography based on saga material, W.I. Miller, *Bloodtaking and Peacemaking: Feud, Law, and Society in Saga Iceland* (Chicago, 1990), 139–220.

bizarre disposition to atrocity (blood-eagle sacrifices and all that), to exceptionally large bones, and hence large limbs – a race of giants, to a diet that resulted in farting on a heroic scale.[54] A lot of historians from Peter Sawyer onwards have rebutted or qualified those allegations so enthusiastically that they have provoked a lively counter-industry of neo-Othering. Rebuttal is only the half of a needful response. The other half entails acknowledging the sprawlier aspects of Frankish or Anglo-Saxon family consciousness; observing Frankish and Anglo-Saxon processes that involved what modern legal anthropologists (and sometimes the Franks) call feud (Frankish-Latin *faida*); admitting evidence (though frankly rather little) for Frankish slave-traders;[55] re-emphasising violence as what Peter Sawyer thirty years ago labelled 'normal Dark-Age activity'; recognising in Tim Reuter's inimitable phrase that 'for most of Europe in the eighth and ninth centuries, it was the Franks who were the Vikings';[56] or even noting that high-status Franks too could have large bones, or that farting was a major medieval monastic anxiety – hence rude monastic humour on the subject.[57]

So far I have looked at fantasies of Viking nearness and no less fantastic visions of their Otherness (a word whose Anglo-Saxon roots commend it rather than 'alterity', preferred in American academe). It is hard to say which is the more inimical to good history. Ancestral recognition can be more dangerous than denial if it ends in obliterating completely not only the Otherness of the Vikings but the Otherness of their ninth-century contemporaries in England and on the Continent. I should stress at this point that I am not for one moment denying that the Vikings were perceived, initially, as different, from those they encountered in England or Francia, different above all because of their sometimes considerable numbers, and violently disruptive impact in the short term. I am affirming, though, that that was a difference within a broader similarity – and a difference that progressively weakened in

---

[54] Slaving and atrocity: A. Smyth, *Scandinavian Kings in the British Isles* (Oxford, 1977); bones: M. Biddle and B.K. Biddle, 'Repton and the Vikings', *Antiquity*, 66 (1992), 36–51, and the same scholars' contributions to a BBC Timewatch programme on the Vikings, screened in 1995; farting: Christiansen, *Norsemen*, 202.

[55] Families: R. Le Jan, *Famille et pouvoir dans le monde franc* (Paris, 1995), 381–426; feud: G. Halsall, 'Introduction', in *Violence and Society in the Early Medieval West*, ed. G. Halsall (Woodbridge, 1998), 1–45, at 19–29; Frankish slaving: M. McCormick, *Origins of the European Economy: Communications and Commerce AD 300–900* (Cambridge, 2002), 733–52.

[56] P. Sawyer, *The Age of the Vikings* (1962; 2nd edn 1971), 203; T. Reuter, 'Plunder and Tribute in the Carolingian Empire', *Transactions of the Royal Historical Society*, fifth series, 35 (1985), 75–94, at 91. The present essay can be thought of as an extended footnote to these two works of two inspirational scholars. It has been written in the shadow of Tim Reuter's death.

[57] J.L. Nelson, *The Frankish World, 750–900* (1996), 214–15.

contemporary perceptions. I want to consider a variety of evidence for those strange people, your and my ancestors, Anglo-Saxon and Frankish and Viking as well. The ninth century saw both the first construction of the Viking Other, and the beginning of its end, through economic, social and political contacts, through recognisably similar rites and relationships. Comparing evidence from England and the Continent seems a promising approach – though it must be said that few have seriously tried it.[58] The historiographies of Vikings in England and on the Continent have been, for the most part, victims of double, because mutual, neglect: ships that pass in the night with no means to grapple each other. But I want to stress how much extraordinarily good research, and interdisciplinary research, has been done recently by British scholars on Vikings in England and Britain.[59] If I say more about Francia than England, that is because there is more to be said, and a balance to be redressed.

Christianisation can mean a number of things – from participating in Christian cult to founding, or joining, an institution that Asser would have recognised as a monastery. Christianisation is obviously process rather than event. How easily it goes, and how long it takes, depend, amongst other things, on how resistant to christianity are the people on the receiving end.[60] That means also paying attention to where contacts occur. Edges become as important as centres. The *Life of Anskar*, a missionary saint active in the 840s depicts some Scandinavian merchants who frequented Dorestad in Frisia as having converted to Christianity, thereby gaining some protection on their travels back to Birka.[61] Their faith may also have been traded as a matter of place. The ninth-century Frankish evidence does not leave the impression of strong or exclusive adherence to Viking paganism, nor of resistance to Christianity. Frankish annals present a number of cases of convert chieftains and warriors for whom, it is clear, conversion was the price

---

[58] For discussion of some forays, see Nelson, *Rulers and Ruling Families*. Ireland has had to be excluded from consideration here, but see now C. Etchingham, *Viking Raids on Irish Church Settlements in the Ninth Century: A Reconsideration of the Annals* (Maynooth, 1996). Arguing from Ireland (or anywhere else) to anywhere else requires a great deal of care. J. Kocka, 'The Uses of Comparative History', in *Societies Made Up of History*, ed. R. Björk and K. Molin (Edsbruck, 1996), 197–209, points out the exceptional value, but also the difficulties, of historical comparison.

[59] Let *Cultures in Contact*, ed. Hadley and Richard, stand as an outstanding example.

[60] Invaluable now are R.A. Fletcher, *The Conversion of Europe: From Paganism to Christianity 371–1386 AD* (1997), esp. 5–9, 369–416 (with rich comparative material), and Abrams, 'Conversion and Assimilation'.

[61] Rimbert, *Vita Anskarii* c. 24, ed. G. Waitz, MGH Scriptores rerum Germanicarum in usum scholarum (Hannover, 1884), 53. See I. Wood, 'Christians and Pagans in Ninth-Century Scandinavia', in *The Christianization of Scandinavia*, ed. B. Sawyer, P. Sawyer and I. Wood (Alingsås, 1987), 36–67, esp. 52–5, and now I. Wood, *The Missionary Life: Saints and the Evangelisation of Europe 400–1050* (2001), 123–41.

required for acceptance into alliance and service with a Frankish king or lord. Equally, there were Vikings who for decades showed no propensity to convert, yet with whom Christian kings wheeled and dealt. Take the case of Roric. Between *c.* 840 and the early 870s, this Northman of Danish royal blood became the faithful man, in turn, of no fewer than five Carolingian rulers.[62] His centre in Francia was the border-place of Dorestad, known in the ninth century as a *wic* or *vicus* or *emporium*. Roric was in charge of it on and off for most of his thirty years' recorded activity. A contemporary annal-writer having reached Roric's dealings with Carolingian number 3, reported, under 850:

> He came [back] … to Dorestad, seized and held it … He was received back into fidelity on the advice of Lothar's counsellors and through mediators on condition that he would faithfully handle the taxes and other matters pertaining to the royal fisc (*ut tributes ceterisque negotiis ad regis aerarium pertinentibus fideliter inserviret*) and would resist the piratical attacks of Danes.[63]

Twice over, in the 850s, Roric spotted windows of opportunity in Denmark and returned in hopes of gaining royal power, and twice came back to Frisia when events turned against him. On the second of these attempts, 'other Danes' took advantage of his absence to storm Dorestad. But Roric returned to Frisia and in 863 defended his base there against 'other Danes' by deflecting them upriver and inland to other targets. Note the multiplicity of Danish groups: 'the Vikings', ubiquitous in the historiography, is of course an anglicism, since Latin, ivied or otherwise, knows no definite (or indefinite) articles. The groups Vikings came in were war-bands, bonded by métier, or fictive kinship, and the loyalty of followers to chief.[64]

In 863, and not before, Hincmar, archbishop of Rheims, mentioned in passing that Roric had 'recently' been baptised: in a letter, Hincmar warned him that 'now' as a Christian he must not ally with pagans against other Christians; and in a companion letter to Bishop Hungar of Utrecht, not far from Dorestad, Hincmar said that if Roric had allied with pagans, the bishop should impose penance on him.[65] Worse

[62] S. Coupland, 'From Poachers to Gamekeepers: Scandinavian Warlords and Carolingian Kings', *Early Medieval Europe*, 8 (1998), 85–114, cunningly pieces together the careers of Roric (95–101) and others.

[63] *Annales Fuldenses* 850, ed. F. Kurze, MGH Scriptores rerum Germanicarum in usum scholarum (Hannover, 1891), 39.

[64] *Annales Bertiniani*, ed. F. Grat, J. Vielliard and S. Clémencet (Paris, 1965), trans. J.L. Nelson, *The Annals of St-Bertin* (Manchester, 1991), 861, 86, trans. 96: a rare reference to these bands (*sodalitates*) as such, though both Frankish and Anglo-Saxon sources imply their existence.

[65] Hincmar of Rheims, *Epistolae*, ed. E. Perels, MGH Epistolae VIII (Berlin, 1939), nos. 155, 156.

still, Roric had offered a safe haven to an eloping couple, Judith, daughter of the West Frankish king Charles the Bald, and Baldwin, a young man in her father's entourage. This was an act of monstrous political cheek. Archbishop Hincmar duly warned Roric of royal as well as ecclesiastical wrath. But the king, who was every bit as resourceful as Roric, forgave Judith and Baldwin, allowed them to marry and set Baldwin up in Flanders as count, where his northern neighbour was none other than Roric.[66] Subsequently Roric appeared as Charles's faithful man, still running Frisia; and though Hincmar of Rheims, wearing his annal-writer's hat,[67] could not throw off the habit of referring to Roric as 'Northman', that Northman was now firmly inside the Frankish tent. Numismatic evidence presented with admirable clarity by Simon Coupland suggests that Dorestad was in decline throughout the period of Roric's career.[68] It need not follow, though, that Dorestad's concession was no great loss to the Frankish rulers concerned. Dorestad may indeed have been reduced to insignificance, because of the gradual silting of the river Waal, but Frisia was another story. Athwart the Rhine estuary, it retained its strategic importance to rulers in the Rhineland and the Meuse–Moselle region. But conceding Dorestad was clearly not a zero-sum game: both parties could profit when Roric kept his side of the bargain as a faithful Northman.

Dorestad's control was sufficiently important for the emperor Charles the Fat to arrange for a Danish successor to Roric: this was Godfrid *rex Danorum*, one of those Viking leaders who left England in 879, pushed by diminishing prospects on that side of the Channel, pulled by news of conflict between the West Franks following the death of King Louis, successor of Charles the Bald, on 10 April 879.[69] Charles the Fat, who despite his unfortunate sobriquet (a twelfth-century one, in fact) was a lithe political mover, planned to end Carolingian intra-familial conflict by allying with his cousin Hugh, who still hoped to inherit the kingdom of his father Lothar II (who had died in 869), and at the same time to ally with Godfrid and use him as a buffer against other Vikings' attacks. These objectives were to be linked by a Carolingian woman, Gisela, Hugh's sister and thus the emperor's cousin too.[70] Once Godfrid had accepted Christian baptism with the emperor

---

[66] S. Reynolds, 'Carolingian Elopements as a Sidelight on Counts and Vassals', in *The Man of Many Devices who Wandered Full Many Ways …: Festschrift in Honor of János M. Bak*, ed. B. Nágy and M. Sebök (Budapest, 1999), 340–6.

[67] Hincmar wrote the 861–82 section of the *Annales Bertiniani*, where Roric appears in 870 and twice in 872, 168, 184–5, 188,   trans. 165, 177, 180, as 'the Northman'.

[68] S. Coupland, 'Trading Places: Quentovic and Dorestad Reassessed', forthcoming in *Early Medieval Europe* (2003).

[69] *Annales Vedastini* 879, 44.

[70] J.L. Nelson, 'Messagers et intermédiaires en Occident et au-delà à l'époque car-

himself standing godfather, Gisela was given to him to marry and Frisia to rule – perhaps this region was understood as Gisela's dowry. Conversion and spiritual kinship played a part, to be sure; but no less clear are the parts played by other rites and relationships: personal commendation, and the gift of a bride.[71]

In the years between 858 and 862, no fewer than three Scandinavian war-leaders are documented as joining Charles the Bald's service: Bjørn, Weland and Aslak. Their careers have recently been studied severally and collectively.[72] There may have been a fourth, who has attracted no attention from this point of view. His name, or the name the Franks called him by, was *Northmannus*: Northman, or more colloquially Norman.[73] Perhaps in 858, he had received a benefice and a countship from the king in the Tardenois near Rheims, and in 860, was allowed to keep it when the king negotiated terms of tenure with the recently appointed bishop of Laon, Hincmar, nephew of his famous namesake. The bishopric received extensive royal lands on condition that the king could determine which militarily useful men would be assigned them. Among them was Norman, thus faithful man of both king and bishop. By 868, Norman the count was a respectable local worthy: his military household had been given *beneficia* of their own on Norman's estates; and Norman had a manor-house (*mansus*) where he had settled down with his wife, and eventually children, and accumulated 'gold, silver, clothing, cloth, corn, wine and movables of various kinds and both sexes'. In 868, the king and the bishop fell out. Norman, and still more so his wife, got a terrible shock when the bishop turned up with *plurimi*

---

olingienne', in *Voyages et voyageurs à Byzance et en Occident du VIe au XIe siècle*, ed. A. Dierkens and J.-M. Sansterre (Geneva, 2000), 397–413, at 412–13.

[71] 'Godofridus rex ... ad eum [imperatorem] exiit', *Annales Vedastini* 882, 51; 'christianum se fieri polliceretur, si ei munere regis Fresia provincia concederetur, et Gisla filia Lotharii in uxorem daretur', Regino of Prüm, *Chronicon* 882, ed. F. Kurze, MGH Scriptores rerum Germanicarum in usum scholarum (Berlin, 1890), 120. For analysis of these and other contemporary sources, see S. MacLean, 'The Reign of Charles III the Fat (876–888)' (Ph.D. thesis, University of London, 2000), of which a revised version will shortly be published by Cambridge University Press.

[72] Coupland, 'From Poachers to Gamekeepers'.

[73] Norman's career can be reconstructed from (i) a dossier presented by the gout-afflicted and therefore absent Hincmar Senior to the Council of Attigny, June/July 870, ed. W. Hartmann, MGH Concilia IV, no. 33, pp. 392–3 (ii) a fragmentary formal complaint by Charles the Bald against Hincmar of Laon presented to the Council of Douzy, Conc. IV, no. 37, pp. 417–18 (iii) the *acta* of the Council of Douzy, August/September 871, Conc. IV, no. 37, pp. 437–8, 444, 468 (iv) the bishops' responses to the dossier, Conc. IV, no. 37, pp. 494–5 (v) the council's report to Pope Hadrian II, Conc. IV, no. 37, p. 525 (with the details about Norman's personal life). The hypothesis that Norman was a Northman is unprovable, of course; but in context, not improbable. The name-elements could be Frankish, but the name itself is unattested in Francia at this period. Otherwise the name might have to be interpreted as a nickname. Cf. J. Devisse, *Hincmar, Archevêque de Reims 845–882* (3 vols., Geneva, 1975–6), II, 730–1, 772–7.

armati homines and a *permixta multitudo vulgi* ... *cum gladiis et fustibus* ('a motley crowd of common people with swords and clubs') – at the very moment when Norman's wife was in childbirth *more femineo*. The family were driven out (what happened to mother and baby is not recorded) and all the movables seized *quasi per forciam non per justitiam*.[74] Poor Norman! Poor Mrs Norman! Fortunately, the king stood by them, and made the bishop return everything and the land as well. If Norman's wife was a Frank, the case would be comparable to that of Rollo in 911, marrying in to the local officialdom of north-west Francia through a local aristocratic bride.[75] But if Norman was a Northman why do Hincmar and company not say so in so many words? One answer might be: because labouring Norman's origin was irrelevant in the context of the story that, in the version as we have it, centred on a bishop behaving badly to his man. The man himself was assimilated, deeply implicated in a Frankish political system that had always had room for *extranei*. In terms of the secular everyday, ethnicity is as ethnicity does. Norman could be Frank. This Viking had merged so thoroughly into a Frankish landscape that he became invisible.

To get a sense of further personal networks, voyage to Quentovic, that is, the *wic* on the river Canche (see Map 1). It was sacked by Northmen in 842 in a raid that got noticed in Wessex as well as Francia: exceptional. 'They plundered it and laid it waste, capturing or massacring the inhabitants of both sexes. They left nothing in it except for those buildings which they were paid to spare.'[76] Yet Quentovic before 842 as well as after, so Simon Coupland now argues from the numismatic evidence, was no more than a minor mint, and, hence, was no wealthy emporium.[77] Its story was not one of decline, as previous historians have alleged, for here there had been no Carolingian apogée to decline *from*. In this period, Quentovic was not a place frequented by traders and payers of tolls. By contrast, from in or around 864, Quentovic's mint moved into overdrive, and this large output, Coupland invites us to think, both stimulated and reflected an 'economic boom'.

Though impressed by Coupland's expertise, I am not entirely convinced by either part of his equation. Quentovic, like Hamwic, must

[74] MGH Conc. IV, no. 37, p. 495.

[75] The hypothesis of Rollo's having married into an indigenous noble family is convincingly argued by Pierre Bauduin, 'La frontière normande aux Xe–Xie siècles: origine et maitrise de la frontière sur les confins de la Haute Normandie (911–1087)' (Thèse de doctorat, University of Caen, Basse-Normandie, 1997–8), soon to be published.

[76] *Annales Bertiniani* 842, 42, trans. 53, and Nithard, *Historiarum libri IIII*, IV, c. 3, ed. and trans. P. Lauer, *Histoire des fils de Louis le Pieux* (Paris, 1926), 124–5; *ASC* 839 (*recte* 842), 43, trans. 64.

[77] Coupland, 'Trading Places'.

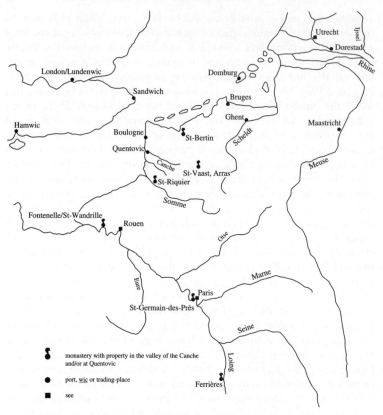

Map 1   Regions and connections of the Channel coast in the mid-ninth century

have had lootable wealth to make it an attractive target in 842. On the bluff overlooking the valley of the Canche, and hence overlooking the 35–hectare site identified in the early 1990s by David Hill and his team as Quentovic,[78] was a dependent cell, St-Josse, which belonged to the monastery of Ferrières in the diocese of Sens. Both Ferrières and its dependent cell were *de facto* in the king's gift: a highly suitable gift, Charlemagne thought, for his Anglo-Saxon court scholar Alcuin, since St-Josse was the first port of call for travellers from England, and

[78] R. Hodges, 'Trade and Market Origins', in *Charles the Bald: Court and Kingdom*, ed. Gibson and Nelson, 202–23, at 212–13, 216; D. Hill *et al.*, 'Quentovic Defined', *Antiquity*, 64 (1990), 51–8; S. Lebecq, 'Quentovic: un etat de la question', *Studien zur Sachsenforschung*, 8 (1993), 73–82; R. Hodges, *Towns and Trade in the Age of Charlemagne* (2000), 88, 118, 122. Still worth citing (and not just for its title) is K. Maude, 'Quentovic: Dark Age Europort', *Popular Archaeology* (Aug. 1986), 10–16.

presumably profited from English alms.[79] King Charles the Bald, after giving Ferrières and its cell to the learned abbot Lupus, had been forced by circumstances – the need to recruit and retain supporters – to grant St-Josse to a lay aristocrat in 842. In 845, Lupus wrote to the king to complain about the consequences for Ferrières:

> the servants of God, who assiduously pray for you, for three years now have not received their accustomed clothing, and so what they are forced to wear are garments worn and darned in many places; and they have to live on bought vegetables, and very seldom have the consolation of fish and cheese.[80]

Lupus indicates what kinds of commodities were imported through the *wic* (and thence brought the further 280 km to Ferrières): the kind of commodities, incidentally, that leave no trace in the archaeological record. In 852, when the king had returned St-Josse to Ferrières, Lupus wrote requesting Felix, the Frankish chief notary of King Æthelwulf of Wessex, and a man whom Lupus knew personally, to urge his lord to send some lead to repair the roof of the monastery church at Ferrières: could it be delivered at Etaples, please?[81] Lupus's huge efforts to recover this monastic outlier, and huge relief when he succeeded, surely indicate an economic importance that depended on St-Josse's being deeply implicated in cross-Channel communications, commercial, or religious, or both at once.[82] To these snippets can be added documentary evidence for Quentovic's place in a network of exchanges involving at least six major West Frankish monasteries: St-Vaast Arras, St-Riquier, Ferrières, St-Germain-des-Près, St-Wandrille and St-Bertin – all attested at various dates between 770 and 850 as what we might call Quentovic's stake-

[79] Lupus of Ferrières, Ep. 11, *Epistolae*, ed. P. Marshall (Leipzig, 1984), 20; cf. Ep. 53, 62.

[80] Lupus, Ep. 71, 74–5.

[81] Lupus, Ep. 14, 22–3. Cf. Ep. 13, 21–2, sent at the same time to Æthelwulf himself, promising that, though the brethren were anyway lively intercessors for him, they would be 'alacriores ... si munus acceperimus' ('livelier still ... if we receive a gift'). For the campaign to recover St-Josse, see Lupus, Epp. 11, 20; 88, 67–8; 64, 71; 92, 90. For the contacts of 852, see P. Stafford, 'Charles the Bald, Judith, and England', in *Charles the Bald: Court and Kingdom*, ed. Gibson and Nelson, 139–53.

[82] Lupus, Ep. 61, 67 and 62, 68 are a second pair of letters dispatched to York at the same time as Lupus contacted the West Saxon court. Ep. 62, to Abbot Altsig, reveals the existence of a scriptorium at St-Josse, and, in the person of the scribe Lantramn (?kinsman of the like-named archbishop of Tours), previous close contacts between St-Josse and York. The prayer-association mentioned in Ep. 61, to Archbishop Wigmund, continued one already lively in Alcuin's time: Alcuin, *Epistolae*, ed. E. Dümmler, MGH Epistolae IV (Berlin, 1895), no. 210 (probably sent in 800), 350–1, asking the patriarch of Jerusalem for prayers for himself and his *familia* and also for Archbishop Eanbald II of York. Alcuin, Epp. 175, 176 (July 799) suggest the importance of St-Josse/Quentovic as a listening-post at a critical moment.

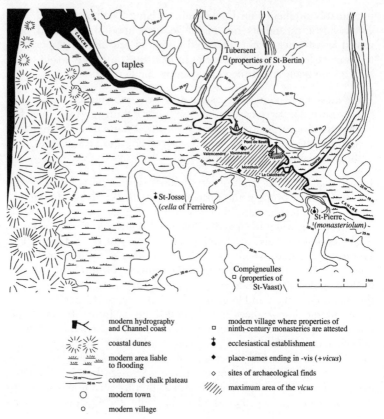

Map 2   Quentovic and its environs

holders, that is, holding land near or actually in the *wic*, or benefiting
from trade passing through it.[83] In the mid-ninth century, two little
farms at Tubersent just north of Quentovic belonging to St-Bertin were
in the hands of Saxger and Alfward respectively, the second of them
formally labelled *ille Saxo* (that Saxon man), Anglo-Saxons, surely?[84] In

---

[83] See Maps 1 and 2: St-Bertin, St-Vaast, St-Riquier, Ferrières, St-Germain-des-Près,
St-Wandrille. The documentary evidence is admirably discussed by Lebecq, 'Quentovic',
77–9.
[84] *Le polyptyque de l'abbaye de Saint-Bertin (844–859): édition critique et commentaire*, ed. F.-L.
Ganshof *et al.* (Paris, 1975), 23 (*brevis* of Tubersent), with commentary, 123. Lebecq,
'Quentovic', 78, notes two Anglo-Saxon names among Quentovic moneyers. An 'ethnic
factor' here was explored by M. Rouche, 'Les Saxons et les origines de Quentovic', *Revue
du Nord*, 59 (1977), 457–78.

857, St-Bertin also received from one of the region's fairly substantial landowners 'one tenement (*mansus*) in Quentovic'.[85] Quentovic's economic importance before *c.* 864 seems inescapable. Negative numismatic evidence may not always translate easily into slump.

Any resolution of this conundrum must be reconcilable with the coin evidence for Quentovic's new importance as a mint from *c.* 864 onwards.[86] This was an economy in which markets could be accommodated (Lupus of Ferrières mentions one, otherwise undocumented, at Chappes far inland in the modern department of Aube, which attracted Viking interest[87]) but it was not a market economy. If Quentovic was a port, it was also a royal centre of operations, to which came commercial agents of the king, and of the great monasteries under royal protection. Many exchanges may not have involved money at all. Conversely, large volumes of coins minted may not translate into boom. They could just as easily reflect royal requirements, in this case for the pay of hired troops, or the interests of a local strong man in charge of the mint in securing cash for similar purposes. In the eight or nine decades before 864, there's intermittent evidence for a political and military authority at Quentovic: an authority that could be seen as royal but which at the same time was vested in and wielded by a magnate with power on the spot. How else to explain the 'payment' to the Vikings to spare buildings at Quentovic in 842? How explain Viking avoidance of Quentovic *after* 842? Just as Roric protected Frisia, someone protected Quentovic. He might, *c.* 860, be identified as the aptly-named Grippo, identified in a contemporary miracle-collection as *prefectus emporii*.[88] Did his job extend to running the mint? Again, Grippo's tenure of this post coincides with other textual evidence for the region's political importance at that point. The contemporary Annals of St-Bertin show that these northern coasts suffered most intensely from Viking raids during the years 857 to 865, but also that these years, especially from 861, were those in which Charles the Bald started to implement effective strategies for containing and repelling attackers – strategies that included large pay-offs.[89] The coinage reform of 864 comes in the midst of these efforts. Two stories in miracle-collections, the sort of ninth-century sources that need to be taken with

---

[85] *Diplomata belgica ante annum millesimum centesimum scripta*, ed. M. Gysseling and A.C.F. Koch (Brussels, 1950), no. 33, pp. 56–7, the gifts of Gundbert, with Abbot Adalard's *Brevis* of 867, no. 37, p. 67.

[86] The case is made by Coupland, 'Trading Places'.

[87] Lupus Ep. 125, 118: 'sedes negotiatorum Cappas'.

[88] *Miracula Sancti Wandregisili* II, c. 15, ed. O. Holder-Egger, MGH Scriptores xv (i) (Hannover, 1887), 408.

[89] J.L. Nelson, *Charles the Bald* (1992), 186–8, 193–4, 202–8, 212–13.

pinches of salt, are too circumstantial to be wholly invented.[90] First, the Miracles of St-Wandrille, recorded when this community, after repeatedly suffering Viking attacks on its vulnerable location near the mouth of the Seine, decamped to – of all places – Quentovic, in 858. This needs to be set against another story in the same collection, describing how Grippo, the *prefectus* in charge of Quentovic, threatened by drowning at sea while returning from a mission on King Charles's behalf to the king of the English, prayed to St Wandrille promising gifts if he came safe to shore, escaped and fulfilled his promise.[91] Grippo's personal commitment to St Wandrille, and his local power at Quentovic, make the St-Wandrille monks' choice of refuge entirely comprehensible. A second story, this time from the Miracles of St-Riquier, does not specifically mention Quentovic but does mention another cross-Channel voyager on King Charles's business: Aslak was a Dane who converted and joined the king's military household, subsequently negotiated on Charles's behalf with Vikings in England, escorted the hired troops to the king, visited St-Riquier en route back to the sea and 'at the coast', perhaps at Quentovic, witnessed a miracle that happened to a pagan Dane whom the saint first punished for lack of respect in church, and then cured, so that three days later, he was quite fit again for his line of business (*ad omne sui operis negotium*). The date must be 862–3. In this story of varied contacts between Franks and Danes, in a place that can be seen as on the edge but also as a hub, there is a lot more transacting than Othering.

Comparable to Quentovic as a place where Vikings and others met and did business was London. In the 870s, coins (again thank the numismatists) constitute most of the evidence, but they show, at the very least, a more complicated political state of affairs than the one that until very recently we thought we knew, namely, that London was in Viking hands from 871 until 886, when Alfred captured it. The coin evidence does more than complicate: it allows and provokes reflection on the political aims and expectations not only of London's rulers but of London's inhabitants (or perhaps their leading men) who for the first time appear under a collective name *burgware*.[92] The problem becomes less lack of evidence than anachronistic interpretation. On one rather

---

[90] Not all *miracula* can be relied on, even cautiously. Cf. N. Lund, 'Horik den Førstes udenrigspolitik', *Historisk Tidsskrift*, 102 (2002), 1–22, at 9–13, effectively undermining the credibility of the *Miracula Sancti Germani* as a source for the Viking attack on Paris in 845 (which could remove, incidentally, the only specific case of atrocity attributed by a contemporary text to the Vikings in Francia: the hanging of 111 Frankish captives in full view of Frankish observers).

[91] See n. 86 above.

[92] *ASC* 893, 56, trans. 86.

older view, London in these years was 'a species of "open city"':[93] shades of Danzig after 1919 – or a really rather interesting possibility? More recent scholarship rejects that, on the assumption, apparently, that at this period any ruler worth his salt would seek a monopoly of control. Following Mark Blackburn's clever reconstruction, 'from ca 875/6 until ca 879/80, ... London was in Anglo-Saxon rather than Viking hands', in other words, while 'the Vikings were not in control of London during the later 870s and early 880s', Alfred took 'control' of London (and other Mercian mints) from the early 880s on.[94] I am not entirely happy with that word 'control' any more than I am when historians talk about 'control' of their evidence (though it is understandable that talk of coinage should evoke 'control' vocabulary, whereas other, vaguer, words are used in discussion of political matters generally).[95] In my view a humbler posture is appropriate, perhaps one of indulgence in 'controlled' speculation. In such a spirit, A.P. Smyth takes full account of the fact that the Mercian king Ceolwulf was called by the Alfredian author of the *Anglo-Saxon Chronicle* 'a foolish king's thegn' (some modern historians have characterised him as 'a puppet ruler':[96] shades of Quisling?) and infers that the Danes were in overall control of London when coins were minted at London in Ceolwulf's name.[97] Smyth concludes that if Ceolwulf was a Viking subsidiary, then, logically, Alfred when *he* issued coins at London in the 870s was 'tributary to the Danes'. Smyth continues:

> for Alfred, such an arrangement may not have been as humiliating or as economically disadvantageous as modern political commentators might imagine. He may have benefited from access to the lucrative London market and he must have availed himself of Danish supplies of silver ... [while] the Danes ... stood to gain tribute and taxation.

So far, so conceivable. When Smyth writes confidently that 'the people in London' could have had no part in choosing their ruler(s), or that

[93] M. Dolley and C. Blunt, 'The Chronology of the Coins of Ælfred the Great', in *Anglo-Saxon Coins: Studies Presented to F.M. Stenton on the Occasion of his 80th Birthday*, ed. M. Dolley (1961), 77–95, at 80–1.

[94] M. Blackburn, 'The London Mint in the Reign of Alfred', in *Kings, Currency and Alliances*, ed. M. Blackburn and D.N. Dumville (Woodbridge, 1998), 105–23, at 120, and see 120–3.

[95] S. Keynes, 'Alfred and the Mercians', in *Kings, Currency and Alliances*, ed. Blackburn and Dumville, 1–45: in this fine paper, compare the terms used at 12–14, 30, 35, where coinage is in question, with discussion elsewhere.

[96] H.R. Loyn, *Alfred the Great* (Oxford, 1967), 22; E. Roesdahl, *The Vikings* (1991), 237; but cf. the more understanding tone of Whitelock, *English Historical Documents*, I, 30; and R. Abels, *Alfred the Great* (1998), 144–7.

[97] A.P. Smyth, *King Alfred the Great* (Oxford, 1995), 49.

'Alfred was most likely free to monitor the activities of his die-cutters and their mints',[98] lurking assumptions need to be tested. Smyth deserves all credit for thinking the unthinkable: that is, contemplating an Alfred who, early in his royal career, was, like Ceolwulf, a Danish sub-king. Yet this scenario sits oddly with Smyth's otherwise strong vision of Viking Otherness (witness his many index references to 'Vikings, destructive effects of, aggressive or conspicuous paganism of') and his still stronger image of Alfred as straightforwardly heroic, that is, as much a national English leader as almost everyone else's Alfred. The coins do not lie; but that is because, to paraphrase Philip Grierson on the archaeologist's spade, speaking is not their strong suit. What historians need to do with this as with all evidence is ponder something Tim Reuter wrote not long ago:

> the constraints on medieval politicians and polities were more extensive [than on modern ones], the expectations lower, and the objectives not shaped by the same calculus of means and end. Their aims and priorities have to be carefully mined from their actions, rather than being projected on to them through the lens of supposedly timeless assumptions about the nature of the state and of politics.[99]

As a small essay in mining, excavate another London episode, this time in 893. It involved Hastein, alias the Northman Alsting documented on the Loire in 882, and thence induced by a Carolingian king to move to the Channel coast and further raiding interspersed with wheeling and dealing.[100] In autumn 892, Hastein was evidently among those Northmen who 'seeing the whole realm worn down by famine, left Francia and crossed the sea'[101] to England, where as 'Hæsten' he appears in the *Anglo-Saxon Chronicle* for 892 and 893, the only Viking leader named in its 892–6 section.[102] Alfred swiftly came to terms with him, and Hastein's two sons were christened (had Hastein himself perhaps adopted Christianity in Francia?), with Alfred and Ealdorman Æthelred of the Mercians as respective godfathers; Hastein gave 'hostages and oaths'; Alfred 'made him generous gifts of money'.[103] Hastein

[98] Smyth, *King Alfred*, 48–9.

[99] I quote from unpublished work by Tim Reuter, left in draft at his death, which will be seen through to publication in 2004.

[100] *Annales Vedastini* 882, 890, 52, 68–9.

[101] *Annales Vedastini* 892, 72.

[102] *ASC* 892, 893, 55–8, trans. 84–7. See J.L. Nelson, 'Hastein', in *The New Dictionary of National Biography* (forthcoming).

[103] When all this occurred is debatable: the obvious reading of *ASC* suggests early 893 (or perhaps late 892), but an earlier occasion is just possible: Æthelweard, well-informed author, *c.* 980, of a Latin version of the *ASC*, *Chronicon*, ed. A. Campbell (1962), says, 44–5, in a passage missing from all other *ASC* versions, that some Vikings came over to Kent from the Continent late in 884, and made a fort at Benfleet. If Hastein was part

then 'made a fort' at Benfleet in Essex, and 'immediately went harrying in that very province which Æthelred, his son's godfather, was in charge of', leaving wife and sons at Benfleet with 'a great army in occupation'. In Hastein's absence, a small contingent of West Saxons, augmented by Mercian troops from London, 'stormed the fortification at Benfleet, captured all that was in it, goods, women and children', and carried all these off to London, along with some ships. Hastein now met Alfred a second time in the same year, and this second encounter perhaps occurred at London. Alfred, mindful of their spiritual kinship, 'restored his wife and sons to [Hastein]'.[104] This was an act of royal *miltse* (mercifulness) indeed, acting out a quality to which Alfred consistently attached importance, a blend of personal humility and official power.[105] In summer 896, 'the army dispersed, some to East Anglia, some to Northumbria, and those that were moneyless (*feohleas*) got themselves ships there and sailed south across the sea to the Seine'.[106] Since Hastein does not reappear in any of the sources, we can imagine him ending his days moneyed and settled in England with his family, resident perhaps within the lordship of one or other of his *compatres*, Alfred or Æthelred. His personal journey from raiding to settlement may have typified one kind of late ninth-century Viking trajectory.

In this essay, after acknowledging the rhetorical effectiveness of images, whether medieval or modern, of the Vikings as Other, I have tried to get behind and around them to consider some of the scattered evidence for the acculturation of Viking individuals and groups in northern Francia and, more briefly, in England in the ninth century. But after some qualifying, even minimising, of Viking Otherness in the perceptions of Franks and English, I want briefly to reflect on how representations of the Vikings as Other were deployed in the formation of ninth-century regnal politics and identities.[107] In the successor-kingdoms of the divided Carolingian Empire, and a divided Francia, Frankishness could no longer make the large contribution to regnal identity that it may have done in the reigns of Pippin, Charlemagne

---

of that group, his sons might have been baptised in 885. On the whole, the association of Alfred and Æthelred in that event points to 893 rather than 885.

[104] *ASC* 893, 57, trans. 86–7.

[105] P. Kershaw, 'The Alfred–Guthrum Treaty: Scripting Accommodation and Inter-action in Viking Age England', in *Cultures in Contact*, ed. Hadley and Richards, 43–64, at 49–50.

[106] *ASC* 896, 59, my trans. Regino of Prüm, *Chronicon*, 867 (*recte* 866), 92, mentions 'Hastingus' as 'commander of Northmen' active on the Loire in 867 (*recte* 866) and 874 (*recte* 868). If this is the same Hastein (and not a kinsman), his uniquely well-documented career spanned three decades.

[107] For the very useful term 'regnal', see S. Reynolds, *Kingdoms and Communites* (2nd edn, Oxford, 1997), 254 and ch. 8, *passim*.

and Louis the Pious.[108] From 840, there were plural Frankish kingdoms, as there had been in Merovingian times. Regnal identity, now as then, had to rest on territorial definition and on political coherence, that is, positively, the obligation of faithful men to come to assemblies when summoned, negatively, their obligation not to migrate without royal permission to another royal lord.[109] In the edict he issued from an assembly at Pîtres on the Seine not far upstream from Rouen in June 864, Charles the Bald represented himself as successor to the Christian Roman emperors of late Antiquity. He did so, thanks to his adviser Hincmar of Rheims, by stuffing his edict with material from the fifth-century Theodosian Code.[110] After some introductory prescriptions about law and justice, the first main cluster of themes (cc. 8–24) was a revaluation of the coinage, strict penalties for counterfeiters or rejecters of the new coins and regulations of weights and measures: here the stress lay on territoriality, that is, on the obligations of all inhabitants within the kingdom's boundaries, whether 'regions follow Roman Law', or some other customary law. Charles then borrowed fifth-century Roman prohibitions on the export of military matériel (*c.* 25), replacing the distinction here between 'barbarians' and 'Romans' with one between *gentilitas*, gentiledom and *christianitas*, christendom. A seller of mail-coats, weapons or horses to Northmen was 'a traitor to the fatherland and a betrayer of christianity to paganism and to perdition', and would be condemned to death. In the years just preceding 864, Charles had been recruiting Northmen to his service, into his own military household, even, perhaps, into comital office. For those Vikings, Christianity was the route to assimilation. Charles had also been giving new articulation to ideas of reciprocal obligation binding faithful men to faithful king, that is, a king bound to treat subjects according to law and justice. In the regions, obligations were regularly affirmed in oaths of fidelity sworn by men resident in counties (*pagenses*). At regnal level, assemblies no less regularly both demonstrated, ritually and practically, the existence of a political community, and kept it functioning. Northmen if pagans were excluded: Northmen converted, willing to settle on condition they accepted the obligations and benefits of fidelity, could become insiders. The Vikings in question were of course noble warriors:

[108] For some limits to Frankishness in this sense even in its alleged heyday, see M. Garrison, 'The Franks as the New Israel? Education for an Identity from Pippin to Charlemagne', in *The Uses of the Past in the Early Middle Ages*, ed. Y. Hen and M. Innes (Cambridge, 2000), 114–61.

[109] T. Reuter, 'Assembly Politics', in *The Medieval World*, ed. P. Linehan and J.L. Nelson (2001), 432–50.

[110] Edictum Pistense, ed. A. Boretius, MGH Capitularia regum Francorum II (Hannover, 1897), no. 273, pp. 310–28. See J.L. Nelson, 'Translating Images of Authority: The Christian Roman Emperors in the Carolingian World', in Nelson, *The Frankish World*, 89–98.

traits of status and occupation assured an entrée into equivalent peer-groups among Franks, Burgundians or Aquitanians. The *sodalitas* had much in common with the *comitatus*.

In Alfred's case, Asser's evidence is unequivocal: the royal entourage included men owning more than half-a-dozen ethnic labels, signifying, surely, that ethnicity had little to do with inclusion.[111] Alfred, drawing on a large legacy from Bede, worked hard to recreate what *looked like* an ethnic identity for his men to inhabit: its name was Englishkind. But Alfred's treaty with Guthrum assigned men to distinct territories, divided by a boundary. If English residing in East Anglia were to be categorised as Danes, Danes residing west of the rivers Lea and Ouse, in London, for instance, would be categorically English. The way was open for the assuming, more or less rapidly, of appropriate new identities by individuals on both sides. Alfred's self-appointed task was to construct an effectively new regnal identity on the twin bases of territorial habitation, and, at higher social levels where men shared the king's *familiaritas*, on sworn commitments, practical fidelities and good lordship involving the receipt of *woruldsaelda*, worldly goods, as well. Within the community of those who shared the lord's love, there were *geferscipas*, groups of companions, and shire- or *burh*-based groups of followers or thegns. But there was nothing like racism here (the word 'race' should no longer be used to translate *gens*). How would Hastein, or any of the *pagani* in Alfred's household, have identified himself? And how would such men have identified themselves with others as a group, assimilating themselves into a wider collectivity? Not, certainly, as *wicenga*. Not yet as *Angelcyn*; but as the faithful followers – thegns, or perhaps *fas(s)elli* – of one shared 'guardian of wealth and friendship' (I quote King Alfred, not Seamus Heaney).[112] Whatever rivalrous flytings resounded in it, there was no place in Alfred's hall for Otherness. Perhaps what *did* resound in Alfred's hall were the strains of *Beowulf*, an epic tale in which Danes, not least the wise king Hrothgar, figured largely, and genealogical recitations crediting Alfred with Danish ancestors, on the spear side Scyld and Scef, on the distaff side, Stuf and Wihtgar.[113] Such incorporation of Danes into Alfred's own lineage,

[111] Asser, *De Gestis Ælfredi Regis* c. 76, p. 60, trans. 91.

[112] *King Alfred's Version of Augustine's Soliloquies*, Book I, ed. T. Carnicelli (Cambridge, MA, 1969), 62, trans. S. Keynes and M. Lapidge, Alfred the Great, 141. For *fas(s)elli*, see Asser, *De Gestis Ælfredi Regis* cc. 53, 55, pp. 41, 44.

[113] A.C. Murray, 'Beowulf, the Danish Invasions, and Royal Genealogy', in *The Dating of Beowulf*, ed. C. Chase (Toronto, 1981), 101–11; J.L. Nelson, 'Reconstructing a Royal Family: Reflections on Alfred from Asser Chapter 2', in *People and Places in Northern Europe, 500–1600: Essays in Honour of Peter Hayes Sawyer*, ed. I. Wood and N. Lund (Woodbridge, 1991), 47–66, at 51–2.

and into the traditions celebrated at his court, would have accorded with the king's own welcoming of Danes into his entourage and his friendship. The publicising – and where better than in the vernacular *Chronicle* and in *carmina saxonica*? – of Anglo-Danish associations of blood and of culture showed the malleability of identities, including that of Englishkind, and Alfred's personal commitment to an open-door policy.

Finally, to end where I began, reflecting on the Vikings' role as Others in the construction of modern national histories, you might say that if the Vikings had not existed they would have had to be invented. Or you might say that the Vikings *had not* existed before the nineteenth century, but had to be invented then. That is when their history begins. In the historic ninth century, there were indeed Northmen who threatened and damaged the people they encountered in England and on the Continent. But there were also Northmen that opted in. The ties that bound were not age-old inborn solidarities but man-made lordship and fidelity which worked in ways best understood in terms of layers, that is, of differentiated levels of social power and of rank and status, and shares, that is, partnerships of mutual interest. Such layers and shares help explain the particular stories of Roric and Hastein, of Quentovic and London. They help explain, too, the formation, in the ninth century, of new identities in both England and Francia. They explain why Northmen, even some ex-*wicenga*, could be readily assimi-lated, could feel, as the OE expression had it, *æt ham* – 'at home' – in Alfredian *burhs* and palaces. Do the Vikings have a future? Yes, maybe, in terms of harmless cultural props, like horned helmets worn by Scandinavian football fans or IKEA publicity girls. Yes, certainly, as inspirational themes for *scops* past and present. Yes, again, as fit subjects for historians, especially if the histories are comparative. But ready-made, hand-me-down Others, totemic props to chauvinism, we can do without. In that sense, the twenty-first century should see the last of the Vikings.

Transactions of the RHS 13 (2003), pp. 29–54 © 2003 Royal Historical Society
DOI: 10.1017/S0080440103000021   Printed in the United Kingdom

'ACCORDING TO ANCIENT CUSTOM': THE RETURN OF ALTARS IN THE RESTORATION CHURCH OF ENGLAND*

By Kenneth Fincham

READ 18 JANUARY 2002

ABSTRACT. Despite its association with the ill-fated reforms of Archbishop Laud in the 1630s and its dubious legality, the railed altar re-appeared in parish churches in the years after 1660. Initially only a handful of parishes and a minority of bishops backed so controversial a change, but the reconstruction of the city churches in London after the fire of 1666 popularised the railed altar, which was adopted elsewhere, particularly during the tory reaction of the 1680s. Studies of two urban parishes in the early 1680s indicate how struggles between dissenters and zealous anglicans could extend to disputes over worship. By 1700, what had been new and contested in the 1630s was becoming widely accepted, which may point to the powerful legacy of Laudian ideals in the restoration church.

Our understanding of the restoration church of England is distinctly uneven. We know a good deal about the formal re-establishment of the church in 1660–3[1] and the character and changing fortunes of protestant dissent across the reigns of Charles II and James II.[2] There are numerous episcopal biographies, yet few illuminate much beyond their subject, and we still lack satisfactory studies of Archbishops Sheldon

---

*I am very grateful to Andrew Foster, Peter Lake, Stephen Taylor and Nicholas Tyacke for their comments on an earlier version of this essay.

[1] R.S. Bosher, *The Making of the Restoration Settlement: The Influence of the Laudians 1649–1662* (1951); A.O. Whiteman, 'The Re-establishment of the Church of England, 1660–1663', *Transactions of the Royal Historical Society*, 5th series, 5 (1955), 111–31; I.M. Green, *The Re-establishment of the Church of England 1660–1663* (Oxford, 1978); R. Hutton, *The Restoration* (Oxford, 1985), 143–8, 171–80; P. Seaward, *The Cavalier Parliament and the Reconstruction of the Old Regime, 1661–1667* (Cambridge, 1989), esp. 162–95.

[2] Among much else, see C.R. Cragg, *Puritanism in the Period of the Great Persecution* (Cambridge, 1957); C.E. Whiting, *Studies in English Puritanism from the Restoration to the Revolution, 1660–1688* (1931); D.R. Lacey, *Dissent and Parliamentary Politics in England 1661–1689* (New Brunswick, NJ, 1969); M.R. Watts, *The Dissenters: From the Reformation to the French Revolution* (Oxford, 1978); J.D. Ramsbottom, 'Presbyterians and "Partial Conformity" in the Restoration Church of England', *Journal of Ecclesiastical History*, 43 (1992), 249–70. See also *The Compton Census of 1676: A Critical Edition*, ed. A. Whiteman (1986).

and Sancroft.[3] Nor has religious thought been thoroughly explored, though doctrinal developments at the universities are now receiving welcome attention.[4] We possess some useful general surveys of the period,[5] but more detailed studies tend to separate off theology from administration, and much remains obscure, or unconsidered. In particular, the institutional life of the anglican church has been largely neglected.[6] Episcopal government of the dioceses, the dominant style of churchmanship among bishops and parish clergy, the popularity of the established church in the parishes and the legacy of Laudianism for doctrine, ceremony and ecclesiastical politics are all issues about which we generalise at our peril. The only modern synthesis, by John Spurr, concentrates on religious ideals rather than on religious practice. He presents a strong case for seeing the restoration church as a united, broad church, whose consensual character was only broken by the revolution of 1688–9.[7] What follows engages with this historiography in several ways. First, it takes a single theme of religious practice – the return of railed altars to parochial churches – across the forty years after 1660, in order to explore aspects of religious politics in their provincial, diocesan and parochial contexts, and to assess the influence of Laudian ritualism and devotion to 'the beauty of holiness' in parochial

---

[3] Among the more helpful are H. Carpenter, *The Protestant Bishop: Being the Life of Henry Compton 1632–1713, Bishop of London* (1956); C.E. Whiting, *Nathaniel Lord Crewe Bishop of Durham (1674–1721)* (1940). The best remains unpublished: E.A.O. Whiteman, 'The Episcopate of Dr Seth Ward, Bishop of Exeter (1662 to 1667) and Salisbury (1667 to 1688/89)' (D.Phil. thesis, University of Oxford, 1951). See also R.A. Beddard, 'Sheldon and Anglican Recovery', *Historical Journal*, 19 (1976), 1005–17.

[4] J. Spurr, *The Restoration Church of England* (1991), chs. 3–7; M. Goldie, 'The Theory of Religious Intolerance in Restoration England', in *From Persecution to Toleration*, ed. O.P. Grell, J.I. Israel and N. Tyacke (Oxford, 1991), 331–68; on doctrine, see N. Tyacke, 'Arminianism and the Theology of the Restoration Church', in *The Exchange of Ideas: Religion, Scholarship and Art in Anglo-Dutch Relations in the Seventeenth Century*, ed. G. Groenveld and M. Wintle, Britain and the Netherlands 11 (Zutphen, 1994), 68–83, reprinted in N. Tyacke, *Aspects of English Protestantism c. 1530–1700* (Manchester, 2001), 320–91; *idem*, 'Religious Controversy', in *The History of the University of Oxford Volume IV: Seventeenth-Century Oxford*, ed. N. Tyacke (Oxford, 1997), 569–619.

[5] See R.A. Beddard, 'The Restoration Church', in *The Restored Monarchy 1660–1688*, ed. J.R. Jones (Basingstoke, 1979), 155–75; J. Spurr, 'Religion in Restoration England', in *The Reigns of Charles II and James VII and II*, ed. L.K.J. Glassey (Basingstoke, 1997), 90–124; J. Miller, *After the Civil Wars: English Politics and Government in the Reign of Charles II* (Harlow, 2000), ch. 8.

[6] For some exceptions, see N. Sykes, *From Sheldon to Secker: Aspects of English Church History 1660–1768* (Cambridge, 1959); J.H. Pruett, *The Parish Clergy under the Later Stuarts: The Leicestershire Experience* (Urbana, IL, 1978); *The Politics of Religion in Restoration England*, ed. T. Harris, P. Seaward and M. Goldie (Oxford, 1990), chs. 2, 7–8; D. Spaeth, *The Church in an Age of Danger: Parsons and Parishioners, 1660–1740* (Cambridge, 2000); and numerous important essays by Robert Beddard, many of them listed in Spurr, *Restoration Church*, 419.

[7] Spurr, *Restoration Church*.

worship in the restored church of England. The topic also provides a useful counterbalance to Spurr's emphasis on consensus, since after 1660, as it had been before 1640, the railed altar was deeply contentious, and, as we shall see, became a battleground for rival versions of anglicanism. Thus it provides a vehicle with which to examine some of the tensions and divisions within the restoration church. Finally, here is an opportunity to suggest some tentative links between theological currents and administrative practice.

Developments after 1660 should be understood in the light of events in the 1630s. The most controversial ecclesiastical reform of that decade had been the 'altar policy' enforced by Archbishop Laud. Communion tables were moved back to the east end of churches and turned 'altarwise' so that the short ends faced north and south; rails were constructed across the chancel, or around three sides of the table, at which communicants were encouraged or compelled to resort at the administration of communion; sometimes the chancel floor itself was raised, and the railed altar placed at the top of newly built steps; and the congregation in some parishes were urged to bow towards the holy table on entering church. These moves had been widely resented, on the grounds of their illegality, their cost and above all their alleged popery, as an attempt to undermine protestant practice and doctrine and to usher in the Roman mass. With the collapse of the personal rule in 1640, altars, rails and chancel steps were destroyed in campaigns of popular and then officially sponsored iconoclasm.[8]

The years after 1660 witnessed the return of the railed altar. Currently we know little about when it occurred, for what reasons and who initiated the changes.[9] It is intriguing that the most obvious sources are largely silent on the subject. Visitation articles regularly issued by bishops, archdeacons and other ordinaries habitually ignore the topic, and there is no printed debate in the copious literature of the period. Yet change was afoot, since by the early eighteenth century the railed

---

[8] P. Lake, 'The Laudian Style: Order, Uniformity and the Pursuit of the Beauty of Holiness in the 1630s', in *The Early Stuart Church 1603–1642*, ed. K. Fincham (1993), 161–85; J. Davies, *The Caroline Captivity of the Church* (Oxford, 1992), ch. 6; K. Fincham, 'The Restoration of Altars in the 1630s', *Historical Journal*, 44 (2001), 919–40; D. Cressy, 'The Battle of the Altars: Turning the Tables and Breaking the Rails', in his *Travesties and Transgressions in Tudor and Stuart England* (Oxford, 2000), 186–212; M.C. Fissel, *The Bishops' Wars: Charles I's Campaigns against Scotland 1638–1640* (Cambridge, 1994), ch. 7; *The Journal of William Dowsing: Iconoclasm in East Anglia during the English Civil War*, ed. T. Cooper (Woodbridge, 2001); J. Spraggon, *Puritan Iconoclasm during the English Civil War* (Woodbridge, 2003).

[9] For some comments, see J.H. Overton, *Life in the English Church (1660–1714)* (1885), 199–200; G.H.O. Addleshaw and F. Etchells, *The Architectural Setting of Anglican Worship* (1948), 148–55; N. Yates, *Buildings, Faith and Worship* (Oxford, 1991), 32; Spurr, *Restoration Church*, 362–3 and n. 160; Miller, *After the Civil Wars*, 139.

altar was evidently to be found in many, if not most, parish churches.[10] Moreover, its return was often contested. In 1664 William Abbott, churchwarden of All Saints Colchester, was reported for stating that 'it is superstition to place the communion table at the east end of the chancel'.[11] In about 1683 the churchwardens of North Walsham in Norfolk set up rails 'as anciently they had been' only to find that 'the said rails were afterwards removed riotously and without any order, in the night time by rude and disorderly persons'. Also in 1683, the communion table in one Dover parish was moved to the top of the chancel in the teeth of parochial opposition, and six years later the protesters removed it back into the body of the chancel.[12]

This essay attempts to chart, and to make sense of, the restoration of the railed altar in parish churches. The material is drawn from eight of the twenty-seven dioceses of England and Wales, and includes a study of both the episcopal hierarchy and parish activists, lay as well as clerical, with the intention of demonstrating links between developments at national, diocesan and parochial levels. One disclaimer is necessary at this point: I offer here mere preliminary findings, intended to open up not close down the subject. They will be refined by further research, and will eventually be incorporated into a book I am writing with Nicholas Tyacke entitled *Altars Restored*, which examines the changing character of religious worship from about 1547 to 1700.

I

In 1662 the churchwardens of Allington, Wiltshire, reported that they were uncertain if their communion table was correctly positioned or not.[13] Their doubts are understandable, for legal precedents were confused, if not contradictory. The Elizabethan prayer book and the Elizabethan injunctions, both of 1559, pointed in different directions: the first sanctioned late Edwardian practice, with the table placed

[10] Addleshaw and Etchells, *Architectural Setting*, 154–5; F.C. Mather, 'Georgian Churchmanship Reconsidered: Some Variations in Anglican Public Worship 1714–1830', *Journal of Ecclesiastical History*, 36 (1985), 264.

[11] Guildhall Library [hereafter GL], MS 9583/2 iii, fo. 130r; for the context, see J. Champion and L. McNulty, 'Making Orthodoxy in Late Restoration England: The Trials of Edmund Hickeringill, 1662–1710', in *Negotiating Power in Early Modern Society*, ed. M. J. Braddick and J. Walter (Cambridge, 2001), 234–5.

[12] Norfolk RO [hereafter NRO], DN/FCB/1, fo. 114r; for St Mary's Dover, see below, pp. 47–8. See also the comment of Humphrey Prideaux, archdeacon of Suffolk, that the erection of rails 'is a matter which often raiseth great contests and disturbances in parishes among weak and scrupulous persons': Humphrey Prideaux, *Directions to Churchwardens for the Faithful Discharge of their Office: For the Use of the Arch-deaconry of Suffolk* (Norwich, 1701), 9.

[13] Spaeth, *Church in an Age of Danger*, 68.

longways or 'tablewise' in the chancel or church at communion, while the second, by contrast, ordered the table to stand 'altarwise' where the old catholic altar had stood, except at time of communion when it could be moved into the chancel. Canon 82 of 1604 followed the prayer book rather than the injunctions, omitting any specific reference to the table's position outside communion, and stating that at the celebration of the sacrament it should be placed in the chancel or church, according to the convenience of communicants. Whether or not the Elizabethan injunctions had been superseded by the canons of 1604 was a moot point in law, though in the 1630s Laud made selective use of the Elizabethan injunction on the table – that out of time of communion it stood where the altar once had – to defend his requirement that communion tables be permanently placed altarwise at the east end of chancels.[14] These ambiguities should have been resolved by canon 7 of 1640, which gave retrospective approval to the altarwise table placed at the top of the chancel, surrounded by a rail, at which parishioners were to be encouraged to receive the sacrament. However, the canons were condemned by the house of commons in December 1640, and were not revived in a statute restoring church courts of 1661.[15] On the other hand, the long parliament's moves against the railed altar had little legal standing. In September 1641 the commons singlehandedly had ordered that communion tables be moved from the east end of chancels and the rails about them taken away, which was later incorporated into an ordinance of August 1643; this and all other ordinances were swept away by the convention parliament in 1660.[16] Thus 'ancient custom' relating to the correct placing of the communion table, as defined by the formularies and practice of the first century of protestantism, was fraught with inconsistencies and open to rival interpretations.

At the restoration of the monarchy in 1660, communion tables were again placed altarwise in the chapels royal, as they had stood since the accession of Elizabeth I, and many cathedral chapters quickly erected a railed altar.[17] However, few parochial churches in the 1660s followed

[14] Public Record Office [hereafter PRO], SP 16/499/42; W. Laud, *Works*, ed. J. Bliss and W. Scott (7 vols., Oxford, 1847–60), IV, 121, VI, 60.

[15] *The Anglican Canons 1529–1947*, ed. G. Bray, Church of England Record Society, VI (1998), 569–71; *Commons' Journal*, II, 51–2; 13 Car. II c. 12 para. 5. See C. Russell, *The Fall of the British Monarchies 1637–1642* (Oxford, 1991), 231–4; Seaward, *Cavalier Parliament*, 167–8.

[16] *Commons' Journal*, II, 279; *Acts and Ordinances of the Interregnum 1642–1660*, ed. C.H. Firth and R.S. Rait (3 vols., 1911), I, 265; see also the ordinance of May 1644 (*ibid.*, 425).

[17] P.E. McCullough, *Sermons at Court* (Cambridge, 1998), 14–15; *Anglican Canons*, ed. Bray, 570; Bosher, *Restoration Settlement*, 59; Bodleian Library [hereafter Bodl.,] Sancroft MS 11, p. 64. For cathedrals, see examples at Canterbury, Chichester and Oxford: M. Sparks, 'The Refitting of the Quire of Canterbury Cathedral 1660–1716: Pictorial and Docu-

suit. In most the communion table remained where it had been placed in the 1640s and 1650s, usually lengthways in the lower chancel or nave, sometimes with communion seats around three or all four sides. Occasionally it was put elsewhere in the nave: in 1664 the table in the godly church of St Anne's Blackfriars stood at the entrance to the north door where the old font had been before 'the times of trouble'.[18] In most churches, significant changes in furnishings and vestments were visible by 1662: the king's arms were again displayed, surplices and prayer books were purchased and the font rebuilt in stone. Only a tiny minority of parish vestries went further, and in 1661–2 voluntarily agreed that the communion table should be placed back at the east end and surrounded by rails; sometimes, the ground under it was raised and steps constructed. The city of London provides some evidence of this process, which usually turned on parish politics. At St Dionis Backchurch, the vestry agreed on a railed table in April 1661, probably with the backing of the conformist parson Nathaniel Hardy, who had just become dean of Rochester.[19] A group of anglican parishioners of St Giles Cripplegate petitioned in 1660 for 'an orthodox and godly divine' to replace the intruded presbyterian minister Samuel Annesley, and named Bruno Ryves, the royalist divine and propagandist. Annesley was ejected in 1662 under the act of uniformity, and was replaced by John Dolben, impeccable royalist and future archbishop of York, and he and leading parishioners then supervised the reconstruction of the chancel. The ground was raised, and the table was placed upon a black marble step and railed in.[20] An open struggle between zealous anglicans and nonconformists occurred at St Sepulchre's Holborn, where the presbyterian vicar, William Gouge, persuaded the vestry to block the election of William Rogers as churchwarden in April 1662, on the grounds that 'he would bring in the common prayer and set the communion table altarwise'. After his appeal to the privy council, Rogers was confirmed as churchwarden, and wasted little time in

---

mentary Evidence', *Journal of the British Archaeological Association*, 154 (2001), 7; West Sussex RO, Cap.1/23/4 fo. 315r; R.A. Beddard, 'Restoration Oxford and the Remaking of the Protestant Establishment', in *Seventeenth-Century Oxford*, ed. Tyacke, 827–8. See also Zachary Crofton, *Altar Worship, or Bowing to the Communion Table Considered* (1661), 114; Edmund Hickeringill, *The Ceremony-Monger, his Character in Five Chapters* (1689), 18, 29. I owe my knowledge of this latter work to Susannah Abbott.

[18] Bodl., MS Rawlinson B 375, fos. 230r, 307v, 310v, 328r; GL, 9583/2 I, fo. 4r.

[19] GL, MS 4216/1 (St Dionis Backchurch Vestry Minute Book 1647–73), p. 163; MS 4215/1 (St Dionis Backchurch Churchwardens' Accounts 1625–1729), p. 119. Shortly afterwards Hardy resigned the cure, and his successor was instituted on 7 June 1661.

[20] *Calendar of State Papers Domestic 1660–1* [hereafter *CSPD*], 232–3; A.G. Matthews, *Calamy Revised* (Oxford, 1934), 13; GL, MS 6048/1 (St Giles Cripplegate Vestry Minute Book 1659–1808), fo. 10r; MS 6047/1 (St Giles Cripplegate Churchwardens' Accounts 1648–69), fo. 147.

purchasing prayer books, acquiring a surplice, paying over £27 to 'Mr Harlow the joiner' for communion rails among other items and even paying for church bells to be rung on the eve of St Batholomew, no doubt in celebration of the imminent departure of Gouge, who refused to accept the act of uniformity and was duly ousted.[21] Several historians have noted the significance of popular lay anglicanism at the Restoration, and these and other cases indicate that it could represent more than a dislike of the sectaries and yearning for the old liturgy, and extend to re-establishing the Laudian altar of the 1630s. Its return was a potent and provocative symbol of the restoration of the old order in parish worship.[22]

Just as few parishes voluntarily adopted the railed altar in the 1660s, so we find few among the hierarchy of bishops prepared to address the issue, let alone enforce it. In 1661 two opportunities arose to clarify the legal position of the communion table, but neither was taken. Among the many proposals submitted for revising the prayer book was one from John Cosin and Matthew Wren that the rubric should state that the table should 'always' stand in 'the upper part of the chancel', but this was not adopted. In October 1661 southern convocation received permission to consider the revival or amendment of some of the canons of 1640, but little headway was made, and it is not even clear whether the contents of canon 7 on the railed altar were ever under serious consideration.[23] In the dioceses, Bishop Matthew Wren was initially a lone voice championing the railed altar. At his visitation of Ely diocese in 1662 he deliberately emphasised the continuity with the pre-war church by issuing a set of visitation articles which were, but for some minor modifications, identical to those he had last used in 1638. In them he enquired whether the communion table stood altarwise at the east end, approached by 'steps or ascents' and protected by 'a decent rail of wood...near one yard high' to which communicants should

[21] PRO, SP 29/53/103; GL, MS 3149/1 (St Sepulchre's Vestry Minute Book 1653–62), pp. 259, 262, /2 (Vestry Minute Book 1662–83), p. 10; MS 3146/1 (St Sepulchre's Churchwardens' Accounts 1648–64), fo. 137; Matthews, *Calamy Revised*, 229.

[22] J. Morrill, 'The Church in England, 1642–9', in *Reactions to the English Civil War 1642–1649*, ed. J. Morrill (1982), 89–114; T. Harris, *London Crowds in the Reign of Charles II* (Cambridge, 1987), ch. 3. For other examples, see the cases of Farmingham in Kent and Axbridge, Churchill and Monksilver in Somerset: Lambeth Palace Library [hereafter LPL], MS 1126 fo. 56a; Somerset RO, D/P/ax/4/1/1 [unfol.: 1660–1], D/P/Chl/4/1/1 [unfol.: 1659–60], D/P/mon/4/1/2 [unfol.: 1661]. I owe the Somerset references to Nicholas Tyacke. St Giles Cripplegate may have possessed a railed altar since the later sixteenth century, in which case conformists there were resuming long-established parochial arrangements. See N. Tyacke, 'Lancelot Andrewes and the Myth of Anglicanism', *Conformity and Orthodoxy in the English Church, c. 1560–1660*, ed. P. Lake and M. Questier (Woodbridge, 2000), 19–21.

[23] C.J. Cuming, *The Durham Book: Being the First Draft of the Revision of the Book of Common Prayer in 1661* (1961), xxii–xxiii, 132; Sykes, *From Sheldon to Secker*, 37–40.

draw near to receive. The surviving answers indicate a wide variety of practice. In the puritan parish of Dry Drayton, for example, the table was positioned longways in the body of the church, which the churchwardens justified by a pointed reference to the prayer book principle of 'convenience' for communicants, and added that the rail had been demolished 'in the time of rebellion'. Wren was probably here trumpeting his own beliefs rather than initiating a crackdown, since the admittedly thin records do not indicate any sustained campaign for railing in the tables once the visitation was over.[24] In Rochester diocese, Archdeacon John Warner, nephew and namesake of the Laudian survivor Bishop John Warner (d. 1666), presided over a drive in 1670 to clear seats from the east end of chancels and replace them with communion tables set up and railed 'as formerly'. It may not be a coincidence that his new bishop was the same John Dolben who had supervised the elaborate changes at St Giles Cripplegate eight years before.[25] A year later, in 1671, Bishop William Lucy of St David's asked in his visitation articles if the communion table stood altarwise and railed, and churchwardens' presentments suggest that this enquiry may have been enforced.[26] These early developments at Rochester and St David's were unusual, and elsewhere official action on the railed altar was infrequent and limited.

There were good reasons why the episcopate should concentrate on other issues in the 1660s. The disastrous results of twenty years of pro-scription, division and schism had to be addressed. The re-established church had to recover its powers, status and influence in local society by asserting its jurisdictional rights and privileges, reviving the machinery of office, instance and probate business of its courts, securing co-operation

---

[24] *Articles of Enquiry (with Some Directions Intermingled) for the Diocesse of Ely* (1662), 4, 7, 22; *Articles to be Inquired of within the Dioces of Ely* (1638); Cambridge University Library [hereafter CUL], EDR B/9/1, nos. 8, 15, 52 and *passim*, some of which are transcribed in W.M. Palmer, 'Episcopal Visitation Returns, Cambridgeshire 1638–1662', *Transactions of the Cambridgeshire and Huntingdonshire Archaeological Society*, 4 (1915–30), 404, 408, 410–11; see also the parochial visitation book of 1665 which focuses on other issues of fabric and furnishings: EDR B/2/59; and below, p. 40.

[25] Centre for Kentish Studies [hereafter CKS], DRa/Vb6, fos. 27rff. Warner's earlier visitation of 1663 contains a handful of orders on the table and rails: *ibid.*, fos. 15, 16r, 17r, 23r, 25v, 26r. The whole volume has been transcribed in 'Dr John Warner's Visitations of the Diocese of Rochester, 1663 and 1670', ed. F. Hull, *A Seventeenth-Century Miscellany*, Kent Records, new series, 1 (1994), 102–204. On Dolben, see R.A. Beddard, 'The Character of a Restoration Prelate: Dr John Dolben', *Notes and Queries*, 215 (1970), 418–21.

[26] *Articles of Visitation and Enquiry ... within the Diocese of Saint David, in the Triennial Visitation of ... William ... Lord Bishop of Saint David* (1671), 2. Lucy's articles of 1662 do not contain this clause, though it is possible that it appeared in his sets for 1665 or 1668, neither of which is extant. For presentments, see National Library of Wales, SD/CPD/ 21, no. 14 (1674); CD/CPD/25, nos. 39, 44 and 47, all of 1672, refer to 'the altar'.

from county leaders and borough elites and confronting the threat from clerical and lay dissent. The character, conduct and conformity of the anglican ministry needed careful supervision and the fabric and furnishings of cathedrals, churches and chapels demanded immediate attention. At an ordination in Christ Cathedral, Oxford, in 1661, the pre-war canopy over the altar collapsed during the service, which nonconformists naturally interpreted as a providential warning against the episcopalian church![27] Presentments reveal that in the 1660s parochial churches often had no fonts, prayer books, surplices or communion vessels: churchwardens had be chivvied into action, and a settled, ordered routine of worship re-created.

But the reasons for official inaction over the railed altar surely run deeper than this. Quite apart from the dubious legal basis for the railed altar, there were plenty of laity, clergy and some bishops who had conformed in the Cromwellian church of the 1650s and did not wish to embrace a rather discredited and controversial change. Moreover, prayer book ceremonies such as kneeling at communion were points of real difficulty between the established church and moderate dissenters, and those anglicans who hoped that presbyterians in particular might be absorbed back into the episcopalian church at the price of a few concessions appreciated that the re-erection of altars would widen not narrow the breach. Indeed, after the traumatic experiences of the 1640s and 1650s, the newly restored hierarchy of bishops had every reason to proceed cautiously, and cement its alliance with anglican royalists in the cavalier parliament, in the face of a good deal of lay hostility and repeated attempts by the supreme governor to secure religious tolerance for both catholics and dissenters.[28] Archbishop Sheldon's approach exemplifies this prudence. That he supported the railed altar is clear from his visitation of Dulwich College in 1664, when he insisted that the communion table should stand altarwise and railed at the east end of the chapel, but he chose not to enforce similar moves on the wider church. His copious correspondence with suffragan bishops indicates the much tighter control that Lambeth exercised over the bench of bishops in the restoration church, compared to the time of Archbishops Abbot and Laud, but Sheldon himself was patiently rebuilding the fortunes of the church at national and local level, and probably judged that a provincial campaign to impose the railed altar

[27] *The Life and Times of Anthony Wood*, ed. A. Clark, Oxford Historical Society (5 vols., Oxford, 1891–1900), I, 388.

[28] *The Diary of Samuel Pepys*, ed. R. Latham and W. Matthews (11 vols., 1970–83), I, 259, II, 57, III, 255, 271, 303, VIII, 532, 585, 596, IX, 1–2, 73, 485; Spurr, *Restoration Church*, 42–61; M. Goldie, 'Danby, the Bishops and the Whigs', in *The Politics of Religion*, ed. Harris, Seaward and Goldie, 75–105.

would provoke acrimony and division, and perhaps jeopardise other, hard-won, achievements.[29]

From the 1670s, however, developments in London diocese helped to precipitate change elsewhere. The decision to rebuild fifty-one of the eighty-six parish churches destroyed in the fire of 1666 provided an unparalleled opportunity to revisit the issue of where the table should be placed. According to the 1670 act for rebuilding the city churches, the commissioners would only pay for the fabric of each new church, so that the cost of the furnishings, such as the communion table or pulpit, would be borne by the parish. This might imply that the positioning of the table and the provision of rails would be left to the discretion of each parish vestry.[30] In fact, the detailed accounts approved by the commission indicate that the arrangements at the east end of each church followed a standardised format: the communion table was to stand on a black and white marble floor, resting on a black marble step, sometimes with a second plain step; the shallow depth of these ascents meant that the table could only be placed on them altarwise not tablewise. All were also railed, and most backed by an altarpiece, which usually contained the ten commandments, creed and Lord's prayer, and sometimes paintings of Moses and Aaron.[31]

Who was responsible for this decision to adopt the railed altar in the fire churches? One obvious candidate was their architect. Sir Christopher Wren was the son and nephew of distinguished Laudian churchmen, and had intimate links with other members of the restored hierarchy, including Gilbert Sheldon and William Sancroft, who were among the earliest of his architectural patrons. In his design of city churches, Wren aimed, when he could, to create an 'auditory', where the congregation could both see and hear the sermon and service, including the celebration of communion. Tables set on an ascent or two, usually placed against a flat east wall or a very shallow chancel, gave architectural expression to this premium on sight and audibility.[32] Nevertheless Wren was surely guided in so sensitive an issue by the

---

[29] LPL, Sheldon Register II, fos. 379v, 380r, 383r; for Sheldon's correspondence, see A.E.O. Whiteman, 'Two Letter Books of Archbishops Sheldon and Sancroft', *Bodleian Library Quarterly*, 4 (1952–3), 209–15; many letters indicate the bishops' willingness to implement Sheldon's instructions on visitation (see, for example, Bodl., Tanner MS 42 fos. 25r, 121r, 123r, 125r). For Sheldon's priorities, see Beddard, 'Sheldon and Anglican Recovery', 1005–17; and for Canterbury diocese, see the visitation charge of Sir Leoline Jenkins, Sheldon's commissary, spelling out the duties of ministers, schoolmasters and churchwardens, printed in William Wynne, *The Life of Sir Leoline Jenkins* (2 vols., 1724), I, lxxiii–lxxvi.

[30] P. Jeffrey, *The City Churches of Sir Christopher Wren* (1996), 152–3.

[31] GL, MSS 25,539/1–4; see *The Wren Society*, x (Oxford, 1933), 15–44, 93–124, XIX (Oxford, 1942), 2–56.

[32] *The Wren Society*, IX (Oxford, 1932), 15–18.

three churchmen who exercised jurisdiction over the rebuilt churches in the city of London: the local bishop, Humphrey Henchman, the archbishop, Gilbert Sheldon, and the dean of St Paul's, William Sancroft. Henchman and Sheldon were the two permanent commissioners supervising the rebuilding of the churches. Henchman himself had been something of a Laudian enthusiast in the 1630s, complaining to Laud about the lack of altar ornaments at Salisbury cathedral, and as bishop of London in the 1660s worked closely with Sancroft. All three churchmen, in fact, were advocates of the railed altar.[33] Their joint decision, if that is what it was, appears not to have survived, but we do possess an important precedent relating to Shadwell church. In 1669 the burgeoning London suburb of Shadwell became an independent parish by act of parliament, and the chapel built there in the Interregnum was consecrated in March 1671. Prior to the consecration, Henchman ordered that the east end be re-arranged: seats 'in and about the chancel' were to be removed, and an altarwise and railed table was to be installed under the east window, set 'on a platform raised two steps' above the floor.[34] There is no mention here of black and white marble, with which to distinguish the sanctuary, but in other respects this may have been the template on which the three churchmen and Wren drew a year or so later as the rebuilding of the city churches got underway.

Given that very few city parishes had voluntarily re-erected the railed altar at the Restoration, its appearance in their newly built churches must have produced some resentment and opposition. There is little trace of this except in the parish of St Magnus Martyr, where the vestry in May 1678 voted to remove the new ascent to the communion table, which was 'to be set in the body of the church or chancel according to the rubric of the Church of England'. Having earmarked some funds and appointed some workmen to level the chancel, the vestry then prudently added the caveat 'so far as it may be lawfully done'. In the event, Wren or

[33] Jeffrey, *City Churches*, 27; Historical Manuscripts Commission, *Appendix to the Fourth Report*, 127–30, a reference I owe to Nicholas Tyacke; British Library [hereafter BL], Harleian MSS 3784–5, contains the extensive Henchman–Sancroft correspondence. See also Henchman's occasional directions on the railed altar in the 1660s as bishop first of Salisbury and then London: *Churchwardens' Accounts of S. Edmund and S. Thomas Sarum 1443–1702*, ed. H.J.F. Swayne, Wiltshire Record Society (Salisbury, 1896), 228; H. Smith, *The Ecclesiastical History of Essex under the Long Parliament and Commonwealth* (Colchester, 1933), 71. For Sheldon's view, see above p. 37, and for Sancroft, see below p. 42.

[34] M. Power, 'Shadwell: The Development of a London Suburb Community in the Seventeenth Century', *London Journal*, 4 (1978), 29–46; GL, MS 9531/16, fos. 194v–198r; London Metropolitan Archives, DL/C/345, fo. 83v. I owe the latter reference to Stephen Taylor.

the bishop must have intervened, and it appears that table and step remained undisturbed.[35]

The relative lack of opposition to the appearance of railed altars in Wren's churches may have encouraged some of the hierarchy to contemplate its enforcement elsewhere. In London, Bishop Henchman died in 1675 and was succeeded by Henry Compton. Eventually, in the mid-1680s, the railed altar was imposed on the remainder of London diocese – by Compton himself in Middlesex archdeaconry, and by William Beveridge and Thomas Turner in Colchester and Essex archdeaconries.[36] Much the same action was undertaken in other dioceses in the early 1680s: in Bristol by Bishops Gulston and Trelawny,[37] in Chichester by Bishops Carleton and Lake,[38] in Norwich by Bishops Sparrow and Lloyd[39] and in Ely by Bishop Turner.[40] While these bishops did not constitute a single party, they occupied rather similar political and theological ground.

Politically, most were devoted servants of the house of Stuart: Carleton and Lake were former royalist soldiers, while Sparrow had suffered for his loyalism during the 1640s and 1650s; most were active opponents of the exclusionists in the early 1680s, and two (Lake and Turner) owed their promotion to James duke of York's personal backing.[41] Three of them (Turner, Lake and Lloyd) were to refuse to

[35] GL, MS 1183/1 (Orders of the Committee of St Magnus Martyr and St Margaret Fish Street 1677–1744), fo. 4r; but see fo. 3r, a contradictory order of six months before, which suggests that the parish itself was divided on the issue; MS 1179/1 (St Magnus Martyr Churchwardens' Accounts 1638–1734), pp. 333–4.

[36] GL, MS 9537/20, pp. 70–137; Bodl., Rawlinson MSS B 375, fos. 213–352v, C 983, fos. 72r–84v; the originals of much of this, at Essex RO, with additional material, was edited by W.J. Pressey and printed in *Transactions of the Essex Archaeological Society*, new series, XIX (1930), 263–76, XX (1933), 217–42, XXI (1937), 100–19, 306–26, XXII (1940), 114–25, 316–29, XXIII (1942–5), 147–64.

[37] *Articles of Enquiry ... within the Jurisdiction of ... William ... Lord Bishop of Bristol* (168[4]), sig. B2r; Bodl., Tanner 30, fos. 49r–50r.

[38] West Sussex RO, Ep.I/18/57, fos. 24v, 39r, Ep.II/15/4, fos. 42v, 68r, II/15/6, fo. 6v, II/15/7, fos. 6v, 9v, 15v, 25r, 29v, 32r, II/9/29, fos. 33r, 35r, II/9/31, fos. 10r–15r; *Chichester Diocesan Surveys 1686 and 1724*, ed. W.K. Ford, Sussex Record Society, LXXVIII (1994), 23–54, Bodl., Tanner MS 124, fos. 172r–173r.

[39] NRO, DN/FCB/1, fos. 100r, 114r, 121r, 131r, ANW/4, nos. 58–9, 67, 69. The railed altar was largely introduced in Norwich archdeaconry through the annual inspections of Archdeacon John Conant. Conant was a former presbyterian, ejected in 1662, and resident in Northampton not Norwich, so it is plausible to see the initiative lying with Sparrow and Lloyd, or with Andreon Hughes, their commissary who was also Conant's official. For the bishops' criticism of Conant, see Bodl., Tanner MS 39, fos. 125r, 134, fo. 27r; for Conant's earlier career, see Beddard, 'Restoration Oxford', 851–2.

[40] CUL, EDR B/2/59a, fos. 14r–40r; H. Bradshaw, 'Notes of the Episcopal Visitation of the Archdeaconry of Ely in 1685', *Cambridge Antiquarian Communications*, III (1864–70), 324–61.

[41] *CSPD 1660–1*, p. 111; R. Beddard, 'The Commission for Ecclesiastical Promotions, 1681–84: An Instrument of Tory Reaction', *Historical Journal*, 10 (1967), 23–30.

recognise the change of ruler in 1689 and were deprived of their sees. Each of these bishops was a supporter of Archbishop Sancroft's push for diocesan reform, and a staunch defender of the anglican ascendancy. Dissenters in their dioceses were actively persecuted – indeed, on his death in 1685 Carleton of Chichester was dubbed *malleus schismaticorum* by one of his court officials[42] – and Lake, Turner and Trelawny were three of the seven bishops to challenge James II's declaration of indulgence in 1688, with the active support of Lloyd, who was prevented from joining them in London. The exception here is Compton, whose poor relations with the duke of York went back to the 1670s, for he was more exercised by the threat from catholicism than from dissent; in 1688 he was one of the seven signatories inviting William of Orange to intervene, and then vigorously supported the revolutionary settlement.

These moves to restore the railed altar in parish churches indicates a commitment to the reverent organisation of public worship as expressed in anglican formularies and customary practice. It is significant that usually accompanying the order for a railed altar were demands that tables be properly equipped, with patens (sometimes of silver) not trenchers, napkins to cover the elements and 'decent' offertory basins, and attention was also paid to that other sacramental site, the font.[43] Simultaneously, there were official moves to encourage more frequent communions, often aided and abetted by enthusiasts among the parish clergy.[44]

What liturgical views informed these actions? We are best informed about Sparrow's beliefs, for he was a rubrician scholar, whose *Rationale* of the prayer book, first published in 1655, was prefaced with an illustration of a priest kneeling with the congregation before a stone altar placed on three steps. The work itself presents a conventional Laudian view of that 'holy table and altar', which is 'the tabernacle of Gods glory, his chair of state', and should be placed at the upper end of the chancel, 'the highest and chief' part of the church, 'which most nearly resembles heaven'. Rails themselves he finds to be justified by the practice of the primitive church.[45] Lake was renowned as a strict observer of the canons and rubrics, preferred to a living in London in 1663 by Sheldon 'to give an example of uniformity' to that city; later, as a canon of York, Lake insisted on reverence at divine service in the

---

[42] West Sussex RO, Ep.II/9/30, fo. 80r.

[43] See, for example, NRO, ANW/4, nos. 58, 67, 69: CUL, EDR B/2/59a, fos. 14r–40v, esp. fos. 18v, 19r, 20v, 21v.

[44] Spurr, *Restoration Church*, 364–6.

[45] I have used the much expanded second edition: Anthony Sparrow, *A Rationale upon the Book of Common Prayer of the Church of England* (1657), 45–7, 273–4, 377, 379. This edition acknowledged its debt to Hooker, Andrewes and Overall, carrying a portrait of each.

cathedral which led to a riot from which he was lucky to escape unscathed.[46] Though Lake and these other bishops did not commit their thoughts on the altar to paper, it seems likely that they were influenced not merely by knowledge of the 1630s but by non-parochial practice going back more than a century. Sancroft, intimate of Lake, Turner and Lloyd, had transcribed the views of John Hayward, nephew of Bishop John Overall and friend of John Cosin, that the true meaning of the Elizabethan settlement on the position of the communion table could be observed in the arrangements of royal chapels and most cathedrals, which since 1559 had contained east-end altars. This he contrasted with the use elsewhere of what he called lengthways 'Geneva tables', which had been introduced by returning Marian exiles, 'full stufft with puritanisme and ignorance'.[47]

It is also likely that some of these churchmen did not regard canon 7 of 1640, which authorised the railed altar, as a dead letter. One reading of the statute of 1661, which Bishop Gibson in his *Codex* was later to support, was that it barred only those canons that related to political obedience, such as the notorious *etcetera* oath, and therefore other purely ecclesiastical canons remained in force.[48] Sparrow himself had no qualms about their legality, and twice republished them alongside other formularies and canons in his *Collection of Articles* in the 1670s.[49] Publicly, at least, the railed altar was often justified in terms of

---

[46] Robert Jenkin, *A Defence of the Profession which the Right Reverend Father in God, John, Late Lord Bishop of Chichester, Made upon his Death-bed ... together with an Account of Some Passages of his Lordship's Life* (1690), 3–4, 15, 60; *A History of York Minster*, ed. G.E. Aylmer and R. Cant (Oxford, 1977), 266–7. Lloyd was another stickler for the canons and ceremonies: see A.C. Miller, 'William Lloyd Bishop of Norwich, "A Very Able and Worthy Pastor"', *Norfolk Archaeology*, 39 (1987), 150–68; and the comment of Simon Patrick that over subscription Lloyd was 'a very touchy and scrupulous man' (quoted in J. Spurr, 'The Church of England, Comprehension and the Toleration Act of 1689', *English Historical Review*, 104 (1989), 939).

[47] Bodl., Sancroft MS 11, pp. 64–5. Sparrow echoed this reading of 1559: Elizabeth I had ordered that holy tables be set up in the place of Roman altars, as was confirmed by the rubric that 'chancels are to remain as in times past' (*Rationale*, 382).

[48] Sykes, *From Sheldon to Secker*, 37–8. Denis Granville, archdeacon of Durham, gave a robust defence of the canons on visitation in 1682, and threatened to censure any in his jurisdiction who disputed their legality: *The Remains of Denis Granville DD, Dean and Archdeacon of Durham*, ed. G. Ornsby, Surtees Society, XLVII (1865), 93–7. For similar views, though expressed less trenchantly, see W[illiam] B[asset], *Corporal Worship Discuss'd and Defended* (1670), 24. Archdeacon Pory of Middlesex cited canon 7 in his visitation articles of 1662, on the position of the table, though he had dropped the reference by 1669: *Articles to be Enquired of within the Archdeaconry of Middlesex ... 1662* (1662), 6; *Articles to be Enquired of within the Archdeaconrie of Middlesex ... 1669* (166[9]), 4.

[49] Anthony Sparrow, *A Collection of Articles, Injunctions, Canons, Orders, Ordinances and Constitutions Ecclesiastical ... Chiefly in the Times of K. Edward VI, Q. Elizabeth, K. James and K. Charles I* (2nd edn, 1671; 3rd edn, 1675). Significantly, the first edition of 1661 did not include the canons of 1640. I owe my knowledge of the later editions to Nicholas Tyacke.

restoration: the court books are full of phrases such as the rails should be placed 'as formerly' or 'heretofore', the table should stand 'as it ought to be' and 'as is usual'. In 1682 some parishioners of Cockfield in Suffolk objected to the erection of communion rails on the grounds that they were an innovation, and Bishop Sparrow ordered a commission to investigate the claim. The commissioners found an elderly parishioner, who had lived in the parish for nearly sixty years, who remembered that the table had been railed in until 'the late times of rebellion, [when] they were tumultuously and violently pulled up, and broken of[f] [into] pieces, by a company of profane wicked fellows, gathered together out of several towns near by'. On the basis of this testimony, Sparrow granted a faculty for the new rails to remain in place.[50] Elsewhere, the most persuasive proof that the return of rails was according to established custom was the fact that many churches still possessed pre-war rails, carefully removed but not destroyed in the 1640s, and often placed at the back of the church.[51]

It was no coincidence that this official support for the railed altar took place during the tory reaction, based on a reinvigorated alliance of crown, mitre and magistrate against the political and religious threat of whigs and dissenters. The campaign for enclosed communion tables expressed the greater self-confidence of some members of the hierarchy, probably encouraged by the small but noticeable increase of requests for railed altars from ministers and laity in the parishes.[52] The creation of altars also represented another step in abandoning hopes of comprehension with moderate presbyterians; as John Spurr has argued, the passage of time from the 1660s had diminished support for such proposals,[53] and in the view of these bishops there was little to be lost should nonconformists be offended by greater ritualism. Reunion remained possible, but on anglican terms: nonconformists should drop their objections to the church's ceremonies and liturgy.

Yet these developments of the 1680s did not constitute a thorough-going revival of pre-war Laudian 'altar policy'. Though tables were moved to the top of the chancel, turned altarwise, railed in and sometimes placed on newly constructed steps, parishioners were not dragooned up to the rails to receive communion, which had been the

[50] NRO, DN/FCP 1/7 (certificate of Thomas Milles, dated 11 June 1682), DN/FCB/1, fo. 100r.

[51] The house of commons' order of 1641, and the ordinance of 1643 (for which see above, n. 16) had merely required the removal of the rails which had often been costly to purchase and churchwardens, then and now, were often prudent stewards of church property. This helps to explain the survival of a considerable number of pre-1640s sets of communion rails, many of them listed in Pevsner's *Buildings of England* series.

[52] See, for example, the faculties granted in Norwich diocese in the early 1680s: NRO, DN/FCB/1, fos 100r, 114r, 121r, 131r.

[53] Spurr, 'The Church of England', 927–46.

most controversial and damaging feature of the Laudian reforms of the 1630s.[54] Bishops did not advocate bowing towards the altar, though it had been recommended in the canons of 1640; and ministers in most dioceses were not instructed to read the ante-communion or second service at the communion table, although a few ritualists chose to do so, and there was an exchange of pamphlets about its legality in 1683.[55]

As in the 1630s, however, not all bishops enforced the railed altar during the 1680s. An important example is Thomas Barlow, bishop of Lincoln 1675–91, who was firmly opposed to the altarwise position of the communion table and refused to accept that it was an altar, at which a commemorative sacrifice was made.[56] Barlow's influence in Lincoln diocese may be inferred from the comments of James Gardiner, his successor but one, who complained in his primary visitation of 1697 that in many churches in the diocese the lord's supper was celebrated in the nave not the chancel, even though there was less space and poorer visibility. This was partly because some chancels were dilapidated and others used as schools, but also because some parishioners 'say it is popery' to celebrate there: 'ministers that use their chancels for this office are popishly inclined'. The association of the chancel with the medieval altar, and the fears provoked by the Laudian reuse of the east end, were evidently still strong. Barlow presumably had done nothing to counter this view, and communion tables in many parishes in the diocese had remained undisturbed in the nave since the 1640s.[57]

More surprising is the fact that William Sancroft as archbishop never insisted upon the erection of railed altars in Canterbury diocese.[58] There can be little doubt that he regarded an altarwise table as correctly positioned; and when Bishop Trelawny of Bristol submitted a series of draft injunctions, headed by the demand for a railed east-end altar in each church, at which the second service should be read, Sancroft responded enthusiastically, describing them as 'so pertinent and sig-

---

[54] Fincham, 'Restoration of Altars', 570–1.

[55] R[ichard] H[art], *Parish Churches Turn'd into Conventicles ... in Particular, by Reading the Communion Service, or any Part Thereof at the Desk* (1683), O.U., *Parish-Churches no Conventicles* (1683). According to Edmund Hickeringill, 'not one in a thousand' ministers reads the second service at the table: *Works* (3 vols., 1716), II, 83. Bishops did respond to complaints about the practice: Lloyd of Norwich supported one such case of a minister reading the second service at the table, but opposed another, in view of the length of the chancel: NRO, DN/FCB/1 [Bungay: 22 Dec. 1686]; Bodl., Tanner MS 138, fo. 52r.

[56] Tyacke, 'Religious Controversy', 605; see Barlow's annotations of the fly-leaf of Sparrow's *Rationale* (Bodl., shelfmark 8° C 240 Linc).

[57] James Gardiner, *Advice to the Clergy of the Dioces of Lincoln* (1697), 21–3.

[58] Thus Tenterden did not adopt a railed altar until 1694, Cranbrook until 1709 and Biddenden until 1716: CKS, Te/ZP; P26/5/1 (Biddenden Churchwardens' Accounts, 1594–1779); Bodl., Ballard MS 15, fo. 93r. See also *ibid.*, Tanner MS 124, fo. 26r; Canterbury Cathedral Archives and Library [hereafter CCAL], Dcb/Z.3.36, p. 8.

nificant' and urged him 'go but on as you have begun and your diocese will soon be in beautiful order'.[59] Similarly, as we shall see, he supported Kentish clergy who petitioned for an altarwise and railed table, and kept an eagle eye on diocesan affairs.[60] Sancroft's reticence may represent a preference for persuasion over coercion; certainly we need not accept Burnet's allegations about his excessive prudence in public affairs.[61]

II

The 1680s also saw a number of anglican clergymen and laity restoring the railed altar in their own parish churches, without any prompting from the ecclesiastical authorities. Petitions to the bishop requesting a railed altar give an insight into the public reasons for these changes, though some of the arguments may have been chosen to please their intended audience of diocesan officials. The principle of convenience for both minister and communicants, enshrined in the book of common prayer, was often evoked: an east end dedicated to the lord's supper was more spacious and visible than a 'tablewise' position hemmed in by pews. Moreover, petitioners observed that a communion table in the middle of the chancel could be 'profaned' or turned to secular uses, something which bishops regularly inquired about in their visitation articles.[62] Parishioners at Moulton, Lincolnshire, claimed, wrongly, that celebration in the nave was 'contrary to the rubric' of the church, but more typical was an appeal to 'ancient custom' for both the return of rails and an altarwise table. Such an evocation should be placed within the broader framework of the 'politics of custom' in parochial affairs.[63] 'Ancient custom' gave legitimacy to what was often a contested change, and its use in this context illustrates the static as well as the dynamic character of the term. Communion rails had a long pre-Laudian history, going back to the 1570s, but in most parishes a permanent east-end

[59] Bodl., Tanner MS 30, fos. 49r–51r; Bristol RO, EP/A/37; M.G. Smith, '*Fighting Joshua': A Study of the Career of Sir Jonathan Trelawny, Bart, 1650–1721, Bishop of Bristol, Exeter and Winchester* (Redruth, 1985), 31.

[60] See Bodl., Tanner MSS 122–6.

[61] Gilbert Burnet, *History of his Own Time* (6 vols., Edinburgh, 1753), iii, 82–3, 282–3.

[62] CCAL, Dcb/Z.4.11, fo. 90r; Lincolnshire Archives, Add. Reg. 3, fos. 342v–343; CKS, Te/ZP; for visitation articles see another many other examples, *Articles of Visitation and Enquiry within the Diocess of Chichester* (1670), 15; *Articles of Enquiry ... within the Jurisdiction of ... Guy Lord Bishop of Bristol* (1673), 4.

[63] Lincolnshire Archives, Add. Reg. 3, fos. 306v–7r; CCAL, EF/12/1, Sandwich St Clement's/1; *The Experience of Authority in Early Modern England*, ed. P. Griffiths, A. Fox and S. Hindle (Basingstoke, 1996), chs. 1, 3 and 8 provide a useful starting-point for a consideration of 'custom'.

altar had stood for no more than five or six years in the 1630s and had then been removed.

Such views of 'ancient custom' did not go unchallenged, especially in parishes where the vestry was divided between anglican and dissenting groups. Two such parishes were St Clement's Sandwich and St Mary's Dover, and their histories reveal the ways in which the railed altar was used as a means and an end in factional parish politics in the late 1670s and early 1680s. Colin Lee has skilfully analysed urban politics in the two corporations of Sandwich and Dover, and demonstrated that the surrender of their borough charters during the tory reaction should be viewed not as heavy-handed central inference in local affairs but as a response to pressure from anglican loyalists, who were locked into a fierce struggle with rival dissenters for political control of their corporations and appealed to the crown for a remodelled charter which would remove their opponents from office.[64] His identification of rival political groups on the corporation can be extended into the parish and vestry politics of St Clement's Sandwich and St Mary's Dover. Both were town churches, where the annual election of the mayor took place, around the communion table.

At Sandwich, the principal clash was between Bartholomew Coombes, a long-established vestryman, mayor between 1680 and 1684 and leading dissenter, who was reluctant to suppress conventicles in the town, and his opponent Alexander Mills, appointed minister of St Clement's in 1680. Mills regarded Coombes as a 'constant, insupportable burthen' who was active in 'supporting and encouraging all the factious and seditious persons in this place'.[65] In 1682–3 Mills tried to ensure that Coombes was excommunicated for not receiving the sacrament, in order to prevent him standing for re-election as mayor; though Coombes was eventually excommunicated, it was only after being re-elected.[66] Mills was also a zealous ceremonialist, later accused by his parishioners of Ash of reading the second service at the communion table, too far from the congregation for any to hear him. The vestry itself contained dissenters such as Coombes as well as anglican allies of Mills, such as Stephen Hobday and John Piers.[67] The latter pair were elected churchwardens for 1682–3, and petitioned for a faculty to have the communion table moved to the east end, on grounds of convenience and to prevent it being 'turn'd to profane uses', citing canon 7 of 1640

---

[64] C. Lee, ' "Fanatic Magistrates": Religious and Political Conflict in Three Kent Boroughs, 1680–1684', *Historical Journal*, 35 (1991), 43–61.

[65] Lee, 'Religious and Political Conflict', 53–7; Bodl., Tanner MS 126, fo. 116r.

[66] Bodl., Tanner MS 33, fos. 179r, 184r, 189r, 190r, 191r; LPL, Court of Arches MSS, Process Book D 2015.

[67] Bodl., Tanner MS 124, fos. 84r, 271r; CCAL, U3/172/4/1 (St Clement's Sandwich Churchwardens' Accounts 1667–1724 and Vestry Minutes 1668–1724), p. 90 and *passim*.

and 'ancient custom' as their justification. The faculty was granted, and that summer nearly £20 was spent on placing the table against the east wall, on an ascent of five steps, with a 'comely' rail placed before it, and the wall behind being wainscotted.[68] Mills then mobilised his extensive contacts among the ecclesiastical hierarchy, including Archbishop Sancroft,[69] to prevent the election of the mayor taking place, as usual, at the communion table around which, he reported, in previous years, the jurats had sat 'as at an alehouse bench', smoked, drank and 'committed some other filthy things I abhor to mention'. Mills was successful: a royal order was obtained by Secretary Leoline Jenkins, endorsed by Sancroft and read out in church on 2 December 1683 by Mills. Echoing Mills's complaint, it referred to 'several horrid inconveniences committed in the chancel of the said church, and even upon and about the communion table itself' before requiring that the election of the mayor be moved to the Guildhall, and urging that any parish meeting in the church 'be there held with all decency and due reverence to the place'.[70]

At St Mary's Dover, divisions can be traced back into the 1670s. The dissenting interest contained both dissenters and anglican sympathisers, and was led by Nicholas Cullen and William Stokes, both of them vestrymen and successively mayors of Dover in the early 1680s; pitched against them were anglican loyalists in the vestry led by George West, a jurat of the town,[71] and backed by John Lodowick, the minister. From the mid-1670s Lodowick fought hard against Stokes and others for the right to nominate one of the two churchwardens at their annual election each April. Lodowick presented his case to the consistory court in 1676 and lost, but triumphed in 1681, a vital victory for anglican loyalists in the vestry.[72] However, there is little evidence that Lodowick was an ardent ritualist, and he was in fairly regular trouble with the church courts on a number of counts.[73] In April 1683 two anglican loyalists

---

[68] CCAL, EF/12/1, Sandwich St Clement's/1; U3/172/4/1, pp. 143, 158–9.

[69] Mills was well known to Sancroft, as his curate at Ash. In 1681–3 Mills was also in touch with Sancroft's secretary Robert Thompson, his chaplain George Thorpe, who was a prebendary in Canterbury, and Richard Lloyd, the prominent civilian lawyer. Bodl., Tanner MS 124, fos. 40r, 42r; MS 126, fos. 116r, 117r; MS 33, fo. 162r.

[70] CSPD 1683–4, 88, 106; the order is entered in the churchwardens' accounts: CCAL, U3/172/4/1 (reversed and unfol.).

[71] Lee, 'Religious and Political Conflict', 45–9; West's allies were his cousin Nathaniel Denew, a common councillor, and his brother-in-law Aaron Wellard and Walter Jemmett who were both jurats; another important anglican was Richard Cooke, a former parishioner and churchwarden of St Mary's Dover.

[72] CCAL, Dcb/Z.4.11, fos. 11v, 72r–73v. Lodowick also supported a loyal address to Charles II in 1681 from a group of 'the best gentlemen and inhabitants' in Dover, by-passing the mayor, 'Stokes and that crew', who, they feared, would have opposed it: PRO, SP 29/415/158.

[73] CCAL, Dcb/Z.4.10, fos. 95r, 113v; Z.4.11, fos. 56r–57r, 71v; Bodl., Tanner MS 33, fos. 176r, 178r.

were chosen as churchwardens, and immediately requested that the consistory court allow them to re-arrange the chancel. Ever since the Interregnum the mayor and jurats had sat in a pew at the east end of the church, facing the congregation, with the communion table centrally placed in the chancel. This arrangement, the churchwardens argued, did not provide much room for the administration of communion, presumably because of the number of pews; moreover, they claimed that on one occasion when Charles II had worshipped there, he had criticised the position of the mayor and jurats' pew as 'undecent and irreverent' and had declined 'to sit above the communion table', a phrase popular in Laudian circles in the 1630s from which he may have learnt it. Counsel on behalf of the mayor and six of the jurats opposed any change, claiming that they had been placed there 'time out of mind'. The court, however, accepted the argument that church-wardens had the responsibility to organise the seating of parishioners, and it authorised the removal of the jurats' pew to the north side of the chancel, and the placing of the communion table at the east end.[74] Stokes, Cullen and their associates lost office with the grant of a new charter in 1684, but they returned to power in 1688, as beneficiaries of James II's purge of tories in the corporation. In April 1689 they pushed through the vestry an order reversing the court's decision of 1683, so that the mayor and jurats' seat was put back at the east end and the communion table placed back into the middle of the chancel. They tried unsuccessfully to pacify the minister, John Lodowick, and either he or an ally complained to the consistory court at Canterbury, which upheld the original order of 1683; once again, then, the communion table returned to the east end.[75]

At stake in these two parishes in Sandwich and Dover were several related issues. In both, anglican loyalists were concerned to protect the sanctity of the church building as well as the communion table itself. The royal order of 1683 removing the mayoral election from the church to the Guildhall at Sandwich was adopted in 1684 at Dover by the new tory corporation led by the mayor, George West.[76] A key ally of Alexander Mills at Sandwich was John Piers, churchwarden in 1683, who seems to have had a strong attachment to 'the beauty of holiness', for on his tombstone of 1693 is recorded the statement that 'he

---

[74] CCAL, Dcb/Z.4.11, fos. 90r–91r, 97v; EF/12/1, Dover St Mary/1. The two church-wardens elected in April 1683 were Nathaniel Denew and Edward Roberts, both active in reporting conventicles to the authorities. See BL, Egerton MS 2115 (Dover Sessions of the Peace, 1677–92), fos. 328, 340v, 342v.

[75] CCAL, Dcb/Z.4.11, fo. 174r; U3/30/8/1 (St Mary's Dover Vestry Minute Book and Churchwardens' Accounts 1611–97), pp. 226–7.

[76] BL, Add. MS 28037, fos. 33r, 34r, 47r. The elections were resumed at St Mary's in 1689 (ibid., fo. 53r).

understood the church which he cherished' and 'adorned' it 'as far as he was able', presumably a reference to the restraint that dissenters such as Coombes had exercised in the vestry.[77] At Dover, many of the corporation viewed the preservation of their east-end pew as a matter of aldermanic pride and status, and also an outward expression of their dominance in the town church. But the corporation was divided on this issue: West, a jurat, evidently approved of the change, for on Whitsunday 1683, about the time that the table was moved to the east end, he donated two silver plates for communion.[78] At Sandwich, by obtaining a royal order, Mills had inconvenienced his opponents and demonstrated his political connections and influence. By demanding that Coombes receive the sacrament, Mills was insisting on conformity with the law; by erecting a railed altar, Mills transformed the experience of that act of conformity, as he celebrated within the sanctuary of the rails, at which he probably administered the sacrament. The 'partial conformity' that dissenters such as Coombes practised was now coming at a higher price. Developments in both parishes demonstrate that the political and religious struggle between anglican loyalists and the dissenter interest extended into the pattern of parochial worship, and it is a measure of the militancy of local anglicans in the early 1680s that they pushed for the return of the altarwise table, in direct defiance of dissenters. In neither parish was there much sign of a willingness to indulge dissenting sensibilities, in the interests of broader protestant unity.

The active presence of dissenters in both parishes indicates the way in which they continued to regard the parish as their own, notwithstanding their attendance at religious meetings elsewhere.[79] Coombes, for example, after many years service as a vestryman, was buried in the central aisle of St Clement's Sandwich. In such polarised parishes, the erection of a railed altar can be seen as a weapon of militant anglicans to flush out such 'partial conformists' or fifth-columnists by forcing them to accept greater ceremonialism or full separation, as well as to pressurise those anglicans sympathetic to dissent to accept ritualism in public worship. The change of political climate by 1687, when James II abandoned his alliance with anglican tories in favour of dissenters, meant that in practice this strategy was only ever short-lived.

[77] 'Ecclesiam quam coluit intellexit et quoad potuit condecoravit': the inscription on the tombstone, placed in the central aisle close to that of Coombes (d. 1694), is faded but legible. I am grateful to Peter Lake for helping to find it and decipher it!
[78] CCAL, U3/30/8/1, p. 206.
[79] For similar findings, see Ramsbottom, 'Presbyterians and "Partial Conformity"', 249–70; M. Goldie and J. Spurr, 'Politics and the Restoration Parish: Edward Fowler and the Struggle for St Giles Cripplegate', *English Historical Review*, 109 (1994), 595.

As we move into the 1690s, what is striking is the increasing number of requests for faculties to remodel chancels, expressions in some cases of ritualism, but also perhaps too an indication of the increasing acceptability of the railed altar. When in 1693 Richard Busby, famed master of Westminster, offered to 'reform, adorn and beautify' the interior of Lutton church in Lincolnshire, his native parish, a commission of local clergy and gentlemen made a series of recommendations how the money might be spent, including the suggestion that the altar be railed in 'for the more decent celebration of holy communion'.[80] During the decade requests for railed altars were submitted in dioceses such as Canterbury, Lincoln and Chester where the local bishop had not issued a general order in favour of the altar.[81] If piety was one motive, fashion may have been another. Celia Fiennes in her journeys round England at the end of the seventeenth century occasionally refers to the adoption in the provinces of 'the London style' of proportioned, brick terraced housing,[82] and similarly we may propose a parallel style of church furnishings inspired by the interior of Wren's city churches, with their black and white marble flooring of the sanctuary, elaborate communion tables, richly carved straight or curved rails and altarpieces regularly using the classical vocabulary of pilasters, half-columns and segmental pediments. John Evelyn, a leading *cognoscento* of his generation, was mightily impressed with the altarpiece in Wren's church of St James Piccadilly on his first visit there in December 1684, while Narcissus Luttrell noted that 'tis finely beautified within, especially at the communion-table'.[83] With the upper classes often resident in, or passing through, London, the new built city and its churches were an obvious attraction, and were sometimes imitated in the provinces. Undergraduates at Oxford and Cambridge, among them future clergy as well as future lay patrons of livings, had experienced altarwise communion tables, often with an accompanying altarpiece, in the chapels of Oxford and Cambridge; at Oxford, for example, all but one chapel had its table set altarwise by the early 1680s.[84] Sometimes these metropolitan and Oxbridge arrangements were followed in the chapels of gentry houses, such as Belton in Lincolnshire in the later 1680s. They also made their mark on parochial churches. St John's Chester

[80] Lincolnshire Archives, Fac. 9/15.

[81] CKS, Te/ZP; Cheshire RO, EDA 2/3, fos. 220v, 250v–251r, 256v–257r; Lincolnshire Archives, Add. Reg. 3, fos. 342–3, Reg. xxxv, fos. 2v–3r. I owe the final reference to Stephen Taylor.

[82] *The Illustrated Journeys of Celia Fiennes 1685–c.1712*, ed. C. Morris (1982), 157, 160.

[83] *The Diary of John Evelyn*, ed. E.S. de Beer (5 vols., Oxford, 1952), IV, 397; Narcissus Luttrell, *A Brief Historical Relation of State Affairs from September 1678 to April 1714* (6 vols., Oxford, 1857), I, 313–14.

[84] Tyacke, 'Religious Controversy', 606.

erected an elaborate altarpiece in the early 1690s, with the ten commandments flanked by paintings of Moses and Aaron, and a prominent
gentry family employed Edward Pierce, who had often worked for
Wren in London, to carve a baroque monument to Lady Warburton
in the church.[85] In 1700 leading parishioners of Upholland, Lancashire,
sought approval for a refurbished chancel, with a railed altar standing,
Wren-style, on black and white marble with an ascent, 'to the end that
the worship of God may be there celebrated in greater order and
beauty'.[86]

III

By the end of the century, the railed altar had appeared in many but
by no means all parish churches. In 1695 a presbyterian opponent of
Bishop Burnet gleefully drew attention to the disunity of anglican
worship by noting a variety of practice, including the fact that in some
churches tables were 'rail'd about' and in 'many' others they were not.
Bishop Nicolson's survey of his new diocese of Carlisle in 1703–4
revealed much the same diversity, with the communion table in some
churches still unrailed and placed lengthways.[87] A few years later, in
1710, Dr William Nicholls reviewed the whole process since 1660:[88]

> Since the Restoration, no positive determination therein being made,
> in the review of the common prayer, the dispute has very happily
> died; and the tables have been generally set altar-wise, and railed in,
> without any opposition thereto; the generality of all parishioners
> esteeming it a very decent situation, they coming of themselves to a
> good liking of it, which they could not be brought to, by the too
> rigid methods which were heretofore used.

Nicholls was right to draw a sharp contrast between the vigorous
enforcement by Laudian bishops in the 1630s and the fabian tactics

---

[85] Cheshire RO, P51/12/2 (St John's Chester Churchwardens' Accounts 1684–1744),
unfol. [13. Dec. 1692]. The Warburton monument is illustrated in N. Pevsner, *The
Buildings of England: Cheshire* (1971), no. 60. For Pierce's career, see H. Colvin, *A Biographical
Dictionary of British Architects 1600–1840* (3rd edn, 1995), 754–5. Wren's city churches were
also described in some detail in London guide-books of the early eighteenth century,
especially in E. Hatton, *A New View of London* (2 vols., 1708), 93–579. See B. Cherry,
'Edward Hatton's *New View of London*', *Architectural History*, 64 (2001), 96–105.
[86] Cheshire RO, EDA 2/3, fos. 250v–251r.
[87] [John Chorlton], *Notes upon the Lord Bishop of Salisbury's Four Late Discourses* (1695), 25;
Miscellany Accounts of the Diocese of Carlile ... by William Nicolson, Late Bishop of Carlisle, ed.
R.S. Ferguson, Cumberland and Westmoreland Antiquarian and Archaeological Society
(1877), 3–156. I owe the first reference to Martin Jones.
[88] William Nicholls, *A Commentary on the Book of Common Prayer* (1710), commentary on
the Ornaments Rubric, quoted in Addleshaw and Etchells, *Architectural Setting*, 155.

deployed by the hierarchy after 1660. Initially Sheldon and other like-minded bishops proceeded cautiously, aware of the vulnerability of their position and the potential for division that the re-introduction of the railed altar might provoke. Sheldon himself was perhaps responsible for blocking the attempt by Bishops Wren and Cosin to modify the prayer book rubric in favour of an east-end altar, and few diocesans pushed the issue in the 1660s and early 1670s. The turning-point was the unprecedented opportunity presented by the need to rebuild the city churches after 1666. Just as London was the stage for the first moves in the destruction of catholic altars under Bishop Ridley in 1550, and provided the test-case for the Laudian altar at St Gregory's-by-St Paul's in 1633, so once again, in the 1670s, the erection of the railed altar in the fire churches under the auspices of three senior clerics (the archbishop of Canterbury, the bishop of London and the dean of St Paul's) provided a model for other dioceses and parishes to follow. In the early 1680s these diocesan campaigns gathered momentum, reaching a highwater mark in 1686–7, precisely the moment at which the tory reaction collapsed as James II turned to woo the dissenters.

But the restoration of altars was never the simple preserve of the ecclesiastical authorities. There were enthusiasts among the parish clergy and in the parish vestry for the railed altar, and sometimes they acted quite independently of diocesan officials, as in the early 1660s, and at other times, such as the 1680s, in fruitful collaboration with them. Indeed, this grassroots support in the 1680s for ceremonial change may have stiffened the resolve of some bishops to enforce the railed altar across their dioceses.

Several recent studies have demonstrated the deep divisions in local society exposed by the exclusion crisis, and perpetuated in the tory reaction which followed.[89] Alongside the well-known political struggles in the corporations and vigorous persecution of dissenters in 1681–6 should now be placed a drive for greater ritualism, imposed sometimes by the diocesan authorities and other times engineered by triumphant anglican vestrymen in the parishes. Though the railed altar could be simply another weapon against dissenters, the outlook of laymen such as George West of Dover and John Piers of Sandwich suggests that some were attached to more reverent and ceremonial worship. John Spurr has noted the deepening anglican piety of the 1680s, expressed through prayer and preparation for the sacrament, which could fit comfortably with the desire by some for greater decorum in public worship; indeed, some of the most popular treatises on the lord's supper

---

[89] Harris, *London Crowds*, chs. 5–7; M. Knights, *Politics and Opinion in Crisis, 1678–81* (Cambridge, 1994); P.D. Halliday, *Dismembering the Body Politic: Partisan Politics in England's Towns 1650–1730* (Cambridge, 1998), ch. 6.

assumed that it took place at a railed table or altar.[90] My two case-studies reveal anglican ritualists locked into conflict not just with dissenters, who regarded themselves as members of the national church, but also with the dissenters' anglican sympathisers, in a contest for parochial dominance, between rival readings of protestant religious practice: of ritual, reverence and the sanctity of place and object against a more sermon-centred, austere and evangelical tradition. This sharp polarity, of formalism versus godliness, occurred in two urban parishes, where the struggle between dissenters and anglicans was likely to be most intense, and quite possibly, studies of rural parishes in and after the 1680s may reveal a different and less confrontational pattern, where the two visions might co-exist more peaceably, and with a greater role taken by the local patron or resident squire.

Despite Nicholls's claim to the contrary, there clearly was opposition in some quarters to the return of altars, as a popish and illegal change. Both proponents and critics of the railed altar justified themselves by invoking 'ancient custom' though they appealed to different moments in the confused history of the positioning of the communion table: most commonly, the Elizabethan injunctions, Laudian practice and the canons of 1640 were invoked against the prayer book rubric and the practice of parochial churches under Elizabeth I, James I and during the 1640s and 1650s; evidence again of rival traditions within English protestantism.

Finally, should we view the return of the railed altar as primarily a Laudian triumph? Laudianism in and after 1660 is usually depicted as a political failure. Bosher's claims that Laudians had engineered the ecclesiastical settlement has been largely refuted, and the ambiguous status of the canons of 1640, the loss of disciplinary tools such as the court of high commission and the *ex officio* oath and the broad range of churchmanship among the new bench of bishops in 1660–1 have all been cited as evidence of the marginal importance of Laudianism at the Restoration. Yet the eventual return of altars provides a rather different perspective on the potency of Laudian views on worship: what had been novel and hotly contested in the 1630s was, by 1700, fast becoming normative. We need not go so far as to propose a 'Laudian' or 'post-Laudian' party in the restoration church, although it remains the case that a number of the clerical advocates of the railed altar were Laudians by background and conviction, committed to a punctilious observance of the church's formularies and canons, unyielding opponents of dissenters and also arminian in doctrine: notably the older generation of bishops, Wren of Ely, Lucy of St David's, Sparrow of

---

[90] Spurr, *Restoration Church*, ch. 7; see, for example, Lancelot Addison, *An Introductiuon to the Sacrament: Or, a Short, Plain and Safe Way to the Communion-Table* (1682), 109.

Norwich and Archbishop Sheldon himself. Their stance seems to have been shared by some of the younger generation such as Bishops Lake, Lloyd and Turner. The influence of these churchmen was the greater for being able to co-opt exponents of other views as allies, among whom Compton of London was pre-eminent. It may be equally significant that the most vocal opponent of the railed altar among the Restoration episcopate was Thomas Barlow, a leading defender of traditional Calvinist teaching. In 1668 Sir Thomas Littleton claimed in the house of commons that Laudianism was back with a vengeance: arminianism, he complained, 'is much received amongst our clergy' and 'the communion table set altar-manner'.[91] Laudianism, we may propose, was becoming a mainstream influence in restoration anglicanism, and its precise contribution invites further research.

[91] A. Grey, *Debates of the House of Commons from ... 1667 to ... 1694* (10 vols., 1769), I, 112–13. See also *The Diary of John Milward Esq ... September 1666 to May 1668*, ed. C. Robbins (Cambridge, 1938), 218. For the spread of Arminianism, see Tyacke, 'Arminianism and the Theology of the Restoration Church'.

Transactions of the RHS 13 (2003), pp. 55–77 © 2003 Royal Historical Society
DOI: 10.1017/S0080440103000033   Printed in the United Kingdom

EINHARD: THE SINNER AND THE SAINTS*

By Julia M.H. Smith

READ 15 MARCH 2002

ABSTRACT. This essay offers a major reassessment of the career of Einhard, biographer of Charlemagne, and an analysis of elite lay piety in the Carolingian era. Einhard's life (*c.* 770–840) is discussed in terms of childhood, youth, marriage and old age, with emphasis on the significance of his wife, Imma. His personal relationship with the relics which he had translated from Rome to Seligenstadt and his self-description as a 'sinner' offer insights into his religiosity. Einhard and Imma are also situated in a broader discussion of the religious activities of other elite married couples of their day. Monastic foundations, relic collecting, Christian household morality and close engagement with the Psalter characterise a distinctive conjugal Christianity in the Carolingian period.

Imma lay dying. Her husband prayed fervently to the martyrs Marcellinus and Peter to intervene and spare her life, but on 13 December 835 she passed away, leaving him inconsolable.[1] A few months later, he described his grief in a letter to a young correspondent. Recollection of her final moments constantly overwhelmed him: the wound which her death created would not heal, flaring up anew time and again. He felt her loss 'every day, in every action, in every undertaking, in all the administration of the house and household, in everything needing to be decided upon and sorted out in my religious and earthly responsibilities'. The pain was all the greater because the hope and trust he had placed in his chosen saints had not been fulfilled. Their intercession failed: Christ remained unmoved, and let Imma die.[2]

---

*I dedicate this paper with affection to the memory of Donald Bullough, whose help with an early version it is a pleasure to acknowledge. I am also grateful to Peter Brown, John Contreni, Mayke de Jong, David Ganz, Matthew Innes, Guy Halsall, Jinty Nelson, Janneke Raaijmakers, Barbara Rosenwein and Sidney Tibbetts for comments and advice. Preliminary versions of this paper were delivered at Loyola University, Chicago, and the Davis Center at Princeton University.

[1] The date is supplied by the personal commemorative calendar of Gozbald of Würzburg. Hansjörg Wellmer, *Persönliches Memento im deutschen Mittelalter* (Stuttgart, 1973), 15 at n. 11.

[2] Einhard's letter of April 836 to Lupus of Ferrières survives incorporated into Lupus's letter collection. *Servati Lupi epistolae*, no. 3, ed. Peter K. Marshall (Leipzig, 1984), 4–6. In interpreting this letter, I am much indebted to David Ganz's unpublished paper, 'Einhard, Grief and the Enigmas of Personality'. An extended analysis of the classical tropes and Christian understanding of death which Einhard balanced in it is provided by Peter von

Einhard, the grief-stricken husband, is renowned for his *Life of Charlemagne*, a text read by every generation of students and scholars from that day to this. To him we owe the compelling image of the emperor Charlemagne (768–814) as the mighty warrior king, the pious Christian who presided over a court of scholars where the learning of the Roman world was revived, the ruler on whom imperial coronation was foisted on Christmas Day, 800. Einhard's fame rests upon his ability to conjure the emperor to life in a sophisticated prose which evokes classical norms of Latin style and imperial biography: his importance as Charlemagne's courtier as well as his biographer has often been rehearsed.[3] Instead of discussing the familiar Einhard, the man famed among his contemporaries for his many talents – literary, artistic, administrative and political – this essay seeks out a more intimate Einhard: male, Christian and married. By teasing out the connections between his allegiance to the martyrs whose translation from Rome he organised, his powerful sense of sinfulness and his marriage, it takes his political and literary importance for granted to focus instead on his domestic and religious life. This exploration of his career does not track a progression to scholarly eminence or political wisdom, but frames it within the human life cycle of childhood, youth, marriage, maturity and old age, in a manner more familiar to historians of family than of politics or court culture.

Consideration of the intimate relationship between Einhard, his wife and his saints opens up a discussion of other contemporary elite households in order to situate Einhard and Imma in the context of a burgeoning aristocratic religiosity during the reigns of Charlemagne and his successor, Louis the Pious (814–40). In a reaction against the common tendency to over-emphasise the division between lay and religious ways of living in the Carolingian era, this essay puts the case for recognising both the malleability of that distinction and the ability of the Carolingian aristocracy to create for themselves forms of devotion which melded aspects of the contemplative and active lives into a

---

Moos, *Consolatio: Studien zur mittellateinischen Trostliteratur über den Tod und zum Problem der christlichen Trauer*, Münstersche-Mittelalter Schriften 3 (4 vols., Munich, 1971–2), i, 113–18.

[3] Important studies include Siegmund Hellmann, 'Einhards literarische Stellung', *Historische Vierteljahrschrift*, 27 (1932), 40–110 (repr. in *idem*, *Ausgewählte Abhandlungen zur Historiographie und Geistesgeschichte des Mittelalters* (Weimar, 1961), 159–229; Arthur Kleinclausz, *Eginhard* (Paris, 1942); Helmut Beumann, *Ideengeschichtliche Studien zu Einhard und anderen Geschichtsschreibern des früheren Mittelalters* (Darmstadt, 1962); J. Fleckenstein, 'Einhard, seine Gründung und sein Vermächtnis in Seligenstadt', in *Das Einhardkreuz*, ed. Karl Hauck (Göttingen, 1974), 96–121 (repr. in J. Fleckenstein, *Ordnungen und formende Kräfte des Mittelalters* (Göttingen, 1989), 84–111; *Einhard: Studien zu Leben und Werk*, ed. Hermann Schefers (Darmstadt, 1997); Paul Edward Dutton, *Charlemagne's Courtier: The Complete Einhard* (Peterborough, Ont., 1998).

coherent and practicable whole. In using one aristocratic married couple as a focal point, it takes as its theme conjugal Christianity – the shared religious attitudes and enterprises of aristocratic marriages in Carolingian times.

We may begin with Imma. That we know very little about her is no surprise, for most lay women of the early Middle Ages are seldom more than names to us.[4] For all his evident love for her and reliance upon her, Einhard himself never mentions her in any of his writings – until, that is, his grief broke down his usual barriers of silence. We first encounter her in a diploma by means of which Louis the Pious granted two estates in eastern Francia, Michelstadt and *Mulinheim*, 'to our faithful man Einhard and his wife Imma' on 11 January 815.[5] It is usually assumed that they had long since been married – but that is improbable, as will be seen. Her own family background is unknown. From the twelfth century until the nineteenth, she was widely believed to have been a daughter of Charlemagne; of various recent speculations, the most plausible is that she came from a local landowning family in the vicinity of these estates.[6] It could also be that she was the widow or daughter of the former holder of *Mulinheim*, Count Drogo, and that she had rights to property in the vicinity.[7]

We are equally ignorant about her age at marriage, or whether she had been married previously. Extrapolation from admittedly very scanty evidence suggests that elite women in the ninth and tenth centuries usually contracted their first marriage at or soon after puberty, occasionally as young as twelve but more commonly between fourteen and nineteen. If widowed, they might remarry; the interval between first and second marriage could be anything from two to twenty years.[8]

---

[4] Cf. Julia M.H. Smith, 'Gender and Ideology in the Early Middle Ages', in *Gender and Christian Religion*, ed. Robert Swanson, Studies in Church History, 34 (1998), 51–73.

[5] *Codex Laureshamensis* 19, ed. Karl Glöckner (3 vols., Darmstadt, 1929–36), I, 299–300. On the region in which these lands lay, see now Matthew Innes, *State and Society in the Early Middle Ages: The Middle Rhine Valley, 400–1000* (Cambridge, 2000).

[6] Wolfgang Hartmann, 'Kloster Machesbach und frühmittelalterliche Adel im Bachgau', *Aschaffenburger Jahrbuch*, 16 (1993), 137–237 at 63–4, 219–27, cf. Wilhelm Störmer, 'Einhards Herkunft – Überlegungen und Beobachtungen zu Einhards Erbebesitz und familiaren Umfeld', in *Einhard*, ed. Schefers, 15–39, with comments on Imma at 37–8.

[7] *Codex Laureshamensis* 19, I, 300.

[8] These statements are based upon information on aristocratic women's marriage patterns assembled from Karl-Ferdinand Werner, 'Die Nachkommen Karls des Grossen bis zum Jahre 1000', in *Karl der Grosse: Lebenswerk und Nachleben*, ed. Wolfgang Braunfels (4 vols., Düsseldorf, 1965–7), IV, 403–79. See also the comments of Suzanne Fonay Wemple, *Women in Frankish Society: Marriage and the Cloister, 500–900* (Philadelphia, 1981), 99; and Régine Le Jan, *Famille et pouvoir dans le monde franc (VIIe–Xe siècle): essai d'anthropologie sociale* (Paris, 1995), 346, 365–6; Janet L. Nelson, 'The Wary Widow', in *Property and Power in the Early Middle Ages*, ed. Wendy Davies and Paul Fouracre (Cambridge, 1995), 82–113 esp. 88–90.

Whether Imma was scarcely out of her teens or around thirty, she was certainly within her childbearing years, for although the couple were still childless in 819, they contemplated the possibility that they might have offspring in the future.[9] A fleeting reference indicates that they may subsequently have had a son, Vussin.[10]

When we encounter Imma in 819, she and her husband were making their will together. In it, they transferred their estate at Michelstadt to the royal monastery of Lorsch, reserving the usufruct for the remainder of their lives.[11] That Imma was named both in the imperial grant of 815 and the donation to Lorsch four years later is noteworthy. Wives only feature as co-donors in approximately 20 per cent of Carolingian charters; to be named as co-beneficiary in an imperial diploma is even more unusual.[12] Was Imma more central to local networks of property and patronage than her husband? Certainly she was his active partner. Two short letters from her survive in the same manuscript as Einhard's letter collection. These not only reveal her to have been literate, but also show her participating in regulating the affairs of the church at *Mulinheim*. In one, she intercedes with a neighbouring landlord and his wife about one of their serfs who had contracted an illegal marriage and then fled for sanctuary to the church of Sts Marcellinus and Peter; in the other, we find her hard at work negotiating and dispensing advice about a delicate but unknown issue with her son.[13]

Other hints corroborate this picture of her as a woman of wide-ranging contacts and considerable reputation. When Bernharius, bishop of Worms, lay dying in 825/6 he entrusted a final task to Einhard which he was to perform with Imma's participation, and he referred to her as his 'most beloved sister', words of affection for a woman he knew and respected. To them jointly he commended his soul.[14] Bishop Gozbald of Würzburg (842–55) kept notes of the deaths of important people connected with the royal court – rulers, bishops, a few others – whom he wished to commemorate. His list is exclusively men, except for Imma: this again suggests an unusual status as well as personal

---

[9] Cf. the grant of Michelstadt to Lorsch in 819 (*Codex Laureshamensis* 20, 1, 301–2): 'Filios quoque si nos habere contigerit, unus ex eis in eadem possessione nobis iure precario succedat.'

[10] Einhard's undated letter to the youth Vussin is usually presumed to have been addressed to a student, but the locution *mi nate* may imply a son. Einhard, *Epistolae*, no. 57, ed. K. Hampe, *Monumenta Germaniae Historica* [hereafter *MGH*] *Epistolae* [hereafter *Epp.*], v, ed. E. Dümmler, K. Hampe *et al.* (Berlin, 1899), 137–8. *Ep.* 38 (*ibid.*, 128–9) is addressed by Imma to a son or grandson (the manuscript reading is uncertain); if the latter she must have been married previously.

[11] *Codex Laureshamensis* 20, 1, 301–2.

[12] Cf. Le Jan, *Famille et pouvoir*, 351.

[13] Einhard, *Epistolae*, nos. 37, 38, ed. Hampe, 128–9.

[14] Einhard, *Epistolae*, no. 3, ed. Hampe, 110–11.

contact and esteem.[15] For a slightly fuller portrait of Imma, we are indebted to Lupus of Ferrières, to whom Einhard had poured out his grief in 836. In his reply, Lupus praised Imma as 'a most noble...[and]...memorable woman' with a man's spirit in a woman's body, whose good sense, dignity and probity (*prudentia, gravitas, honestas*) surpassed many men's.[16] Imma was evidently greatly respected by all who knew her, and we should perhaps read these tributes as an indication that she was a woman of mature years. Certainly she was, in Einhard's own words, his *fidissima coniunx*, his 'most trusted wife'.[17]

To Lupus, it seemed that their marriage was 'a great love, strengthened by long experience'.[18] To what extent Imma shared Einhard's devotion to Sts Marcellinus and Peter and participated in his promotion of their cult cannot readily be ascertained, however. But we know of several other Carolingian aristocratic couples where the acquisition of relics with which to endow a new family religious community was one in which the wife was as active a participant as the husband. Early in Charlemagne's reign, Roger, count of Poitiers, and his wife Eufrasia established the monastery of Charroux, accompanying their property donations with the gift of their very large relic collection.[19] In the central decades of the ninth century, we also meet wives negotiating for Roman relics alongside their husbands. In 846, for example, Oda travelled to Rome with her husband, Liudolf, count of Saxony, to obtain relics for their new foundation at Gandersheim, while in 863 Bertha was prominently associated with her husband Gerard of Vienne in requesting Roman relics for Vézelay and Pothières.[20] The active involvement of wives in establishing monastic relic shrines is particularly striking in the case of Imma's exact contemporary, Bilichild, the wife of Count Rorigo of Le Mans. She seems to have been far more energetic in restoring the ruined monastery of St Maur at Glanfeuil on the Loire than her husband, winning for herself the honorific title of 'abbess' (*abbatissa*).[21]   Slightly later, we also encounter Adelheid urging on her husband, Conrad count of Argengau (and uncle of Charles the

---

[15] Wellmer, *Persönliches Memento*, 20, on the very personal nature of Gozbald's commemorative notes.

[16] Lupus, *Epistolae*, no. 4, ed. Marshall, 6–12, but note that, however outstanding, she could never match Einhard in Lupus's estimation (8, lines 4–11).

[17] Einhard to Lupus: Lupus, *Epistolae*, no. 3, ed. Marshall, 4, lines 8–9.

[18] Lupus, *Epistolae*, no. 4, ed. Marshall, 10, lines 35–6.

[19] *Chartes et documents pour servir à l'histoire de l'abbaye de Charroux*, ed. P. de Monsabert, Archives historiques de Poitou, 39 (Poitiers, 1910), 53–62 with relics at 60.

[20] Julia M.H. Smith, 'Old Saints, New Cults: Roman Relics in Carolingian Francia', in *Early Medieval Rome and the Christian West*, ed. eadem (Leiden, 2000), 317–39 at 329–30.

[21] Odo of Glanfeuil, *Historia translationis S. Mauri*, praef., ch. 2, *Acta sanctorum quotquot toto orbe coluntur* [hereafter *AASS*], ed. J. Bollandus *et al.* (Antwerp and Brussels, 1634–1940; 3rd edn, Paris, 1863–70), *Jan*³ II, 334, 336–7. This account was written in 868/9.

Bald), in his enhancement of the shrine of St Germanus: she herself travelled to Auxerre to superintend the work.[22] For Imma to have been as enthusiastic as Einhard about the cult of Marcellinus and Peter is not inherently implausible.

After this sketch of Imma, let us turn now to Einhard. He is someone we think we know from his preface to the *Life of Charlemagne*: eyewitness to the events about which he writes, nurtured by the emperor to whom he became a friend and confidant, a German who had the temerity to imagine that he 'could write something correct and even elegant in Latin'.[23] We should not forget though that the *Life of Charlemagne* is, formally speaking, an anonymous work. Surviving in over one hundred manuscripts, it is highly unlikely that the author's name could somehow have dropped out of all versions of the text.[24] Although contemporary readers evidently knew who had written it, we now rely on either the dedicatory verse inscribed in Louis the Pious's court copy by Gerward, the palace librarian, or on the preface which Walahfrid Strabo (d. 848) added when he edited the work after Einhard's death.[25] Einhard's anonymity in his most famous work contrasts with his readiness to name himself in his other extended prose work, an account of the translation from Rome in 827 of the relics of Sts Marcellinus and Peter and of the miracles they worked in Francia. Introducing himself in the superscription, he styles himself *Einhardus peccator* – Einhard, the sinner.[26] The phrase is characteristic of the man: it recurs frequently in his letters, charters and other works, always in contexts associated with the worship or personnel of the Christian church; it is not confined to his dealings with Marcellinus and Peter.[27] It also evokes sixth-century

[22] Heiric of Auxerre, *Miracula Sancti Germani*, II.1, *Patrologia cursus completus, series Latina* [hereafter *PL*], ed. J.-P. Migne (221 vols., Paris 1844–64) 124, col. 1249B.

[23] *Vita Karoli*, praef., ed. O. Holder-Egger, *MGH Scriptores rerum Germanicarum in usum scholarum separatim editi* [hereafter *MGH SSRG*] (Hanover, 1911; repr. 1922), 2.

[24] The model of anonymity was followed by Thegan, the 'Astronomer', and Notker the Stammerer, subsequent ninth-century writers of royal biography. On the manuscript dissemination of the *vita Karoli*, see Matthias M. Tischler, *Einharts 'Vita Karoli'. Studien zur Entstehung, Überlieferung und Rezeption*, Schriften der Monumenta Germaniae Historica, 48 (2 vols., Stuttgart, 2001).

[25] Both preface Holder-Egger's edition at xxviii–xxix.

[26] *Translatio et Miracula SS Marcellini et Petri*, praef., ed. G. Waitz, *MGH Scriptores* [hereafter *MGH SS*] (30 vols., Hanover, 1826–1934), XV, pt 1, 239. I am much indebted to David Ganz, for letting me see his *'Einhardus Peccator'*, forthcoming in *Lay Intellectuals in the Carolingian World*, ed. P. Wormald, in advance of publication.

[27] The first datable use of the expression occurs in his will of 819: *Codex Laureshamensis* 20, I, 301–2. See also Einhard's charter for St Peter's Gent, in *Diplomata belgica ante annum millesimum centum*, ed. M. Gysseling and A.C.F. Koch (2 vols., Brussels, 1950), I, 127; the inscription on Einhard's reliquary arch, reproduced in Dutton, *Charlemagne's Courtier*, 63, 65; and his letters, nos. 4, 10, 16, 30–2, 36, 39, 42–3, 45, 49, 53–4, 63–4, ed. Hampe, 111, 113–14, 118, 124–5, 127–8, 129, 131, 132, 134, 136–7, 140–1.

precedents.[28] As he contemplated himself in relationship to God, his saints and clergy, Einhard repeatedly identified and labelled himself as a sinner. In so doing, he was expressing a deeply Augustinian outlook which regarded the human condition as essentially sinful and in enduring need of redemption.

The frequency with which Einhard insists on his own sinfulness contrasts sharply with his reticence about other aspects of his life, not merely Imma and their marriage. In particular, he tells us nothing about his family background. For Einhard, self-fashioning was self-effacing. In drawing attention to literary self-fashioning during the Renaissance, Stephen Greenblatt argued that it was especially characteristic of authors of middling origin who found themselves rising to high places and rubbing shoulders with men of great power.[29] Einhard fits this pattern. We learn from Walahfrid Strabo that he came from the Maingau – the basin of the river Main upstream from Frankfurt where *Mulinheim* lay – and that he had been sent as a child to the great monastery of Fulda to be educated.[30] We do not know for sure who his parents were, although it is widely assumed that they were the couple named Einhard and Engelfrit who gave Fulda a plot of land at Euerdorf, 50 km to the south-east, a grant documented in a charter drawn up by the young Einhard, and that their son was born *c.* 770.[31] Walahfrid was blunt in noting that Einhard was not from a particularly noble family: Matthew Innes has interpreted this as 'a well-to-do background, but no better' – modest indeed in contrast with the huge wealth of the Carolingian imperial aristocracy whom he encountered at court.[32] As we see him through his letters in the last two decades of his life, Einhard was an energetic networker, seeking or bestowing patronage and lobbying to get things done. He certainly exercised his

[28] Most notably the opening of Gregory of Tours's *Liber de virtutibus S. Martini episcopi*, where he styles himself 'Gregorius peccator'. *MGH Scriptores rerum Merovingicarum* [hereafter *MGH SSRM*], ed. B. Krusch *et al.* (7 vols., Hanover, 1884–1920), i, pt 2, 585. For other sixth-century examples, see Ganz, '*Einhardus peccator*', and for a unique female equivalent (*Radegundis peccatrix*), Gregory's *Decem libri historiarum*, ix.42, *MGH SSRM*, i, pt 1², 470.

[29] S.J. Greenblatt, *Renaissance Self-fashioning: From More to Shakespeare* (Chicago, 1980), 7.

[30] *Vita Karoli*, ed. Holder-Egger, xxviii–xxix. Maingau connections and possible familial links to members of the regional aristocracy are discussed by Störmer, 'Einhards Herkunft' (with the suggestion at 21 that Einhard may have owned land adjacent to Michelstadt before 815) and, more contentiously, by K. Brunner, *Oppositionelle Gruppen im Karolingerreich* (Vienna, 1979), 83–95.

[31] *Urkundenbuch des Klosters Fulda*, no. 240, ed. Edmund E. Stengel (2 vols., Marburg, 1956), ii, 235–6.

[32] Walahfrid, 'nobilitatis quod in eo munus erat insigne': praef., ed. Holder-Egger, xxviii; cf. Matthew Innes, '"A Place of Discipline": Carolingian Courts and Aristocratic Youth', in *Court Culture in the Early Middle Ages*, ed. C.R.E. Cubitt, York Studies in the Early Middle Ages, i (Turnhout, forthcoming).

patronage on behalf of a couple of his own young relatives,[33] but his range of useful contacts included no influential kinsmen in high places. The surviving sources suggest an Einhard who floats detached from any familial environment, in a manner more reminiscent of ecclesiastical than secular courtiers.[34]

Although educated at Fulda, there is no evidence that his parents gave him as an oblate, an infant gifted to God to be raised in purity as a monk. Fulda, as other major Carolingian monasteries, took into its schools not just oblates and novice monks, but also pupils destined for the ranks of the elite secular clergy and some lay boys too.[35] These might move on to complete their training elsewhere, sent away into the household of a bishop or secular lord. One such was Charlemagne's grandson Bernard who, after education at Fulda, returned to the court of his father, Pippin king of Italy.[36] Einhard, however, seems to have remained at Fulda as a layman for a while, probably until his early twenties. In the 780s–early 790s we know him to have drafted charters for the monastery, and to have started experimenting writing a more classicising Latin.[37] There is perhaps a physiological explanation for his failure to move on from Fulda. Einhard described himself as a 'tiny manlet' and those who knew him confirm that he was indeed 'despicable in stature': as he grew to maturity, it may have become evident that he lacked the physique to handle horses and weapons in the hunt or on campaign.[38]

Then, at some point between 791 and 796, Abbot Baugulf sent him to court as a young man whose exceptional intellectual gifts were well suited to royal service.[39] We hear nothing of the japes and mockery

[33] Einhard, *Epistolae*, nos. 43, 63, ed. Hampe, 131, 140–1. For a discussion of Einhard's networks of patronage, see Innes, *State and Society*, 85–91.

[34] Cf. Stuart Airlie, 'Bonds of Power and Bonds of Association in the Court Circle of Louis the Pious', in *Charlemagne's Heir: New Perspectives on the Reign of Louis the Pious*, ed. Peter Godman and Roger Collins (Oxford, 1990), 191–204 esp. 200 on the substitute networks of intellectual connections which had developed by the 820s.

[35] Mayke de Jong, *In Samuel's Image: Child Oblation in the Early Medieval West* (Leiden, 1996), 232–45.

[36] *Epistolarum Fuldensium fragmenta*, no. 1, *MGH Epp.*, v, 517.

[37] *Urkundenbuch des Klosters Fulda*, ed. Stengel, 1, pt 2, lxiii–lxiv.

[38] 'Homuncio tantille': Einhard to Lupus: Lupus, *Epistolae*, no. 3, ed. Marshall, 4, lines 24–5; 'homuncio, nam statura despicabilis videbatur': Walahfrid, preface to the *Vita Karoli*, ed. Holder-Egger, xxix. On his small size as a literary trope, see Dutton, *Charlemagne's Courtier*, xxxviii. Despite his stature, Einhard's normal method of travel was on horseback, except when he was so sick that he had to travel by boat. *Epistolae*, nos. 13–14, ed. Hampe, 116–17.

[39] Walahfrid, praef., ed. Holder-Egger, xxviii. The exact date of Einhard's move to court is uncertain. He was still drafting charters at Fulda in 791 (*Urkundenbuch des Klosters Fulda*, no. 189, ed. Stengel, 1, pt 2, 284–6) but had entered royal service by the time Theodulf composed his poetic epistle *ad Carolum regem* in 796, for the poet mentions his presence (see next note).

which surely attended the arrival of his dwarfish figure, but only that this tiny man scurried around like a purposeful ant, or a honey-laden bee.[40] Thereafter he remained in Charlemagne's entourage, rapidly winning both reputation and the ruler's trust, developing his mastery of a variety of cultural forms and honing his verbal and administrative skills. Einhard arrived at court about the time when it first settled regularly at Aachen (794), no longer as widely itinerant as previous years. At its core, the royal household comprised a fairly stable, compact group of members of the king's family together with his official secular and clerical personnel, but had an additional much wider and more fluctuating membership that changed according to the annual rhythm of warfare, hunting, political assemblies and major religious festivals characteristic of any medieval court. It also included an important group, permanently present but of changing membership: young, unmarried male aristocrats whose parents had commended them into the household of the king or his queen, to be socialised into the manners and lifestyle of the political elite. These *pueri* – the lads – were the Carolingian equivalents of the twelfth-century knightly youths whose contribution to chivalric culture Georges Duby evoked.[41] In this sense, 'youth' formed a distinct phase in the aristocratic male life cycle, when abundant physical (and sexual) energy was not yet accompanied by the responsibilites of marriage and fatherhood, property or office. These men served Charlemagne directly: their reward would come in the form of a countship, permission to marry and set up their own lordly household.[42]

The control which the Carolingian king exercised over his courtiers' lives is particularly apparent in the occasional instances of someone wishing to leave royal service. William of Toulouse was one such: twice married and after a distinguished career as a count, he desired to retire and enter a monastery. Before he could 'change his clothes interwoven with gold for the robe of Christ', he needed to be released from royal service. Finally, the *licentia convertendi*, 'permission to convert', was forthcoming, and in 804 he retired to the monastery which he founded on his own property at Gellone.[43] When such a desire surfaced in a

[40] Theodulf, *Carmina* 25, lines 155–8, ed. E. Dümmler, *MGH Poetae Latini aevi Carolini* [hereafter *MGH PLAC*], ed. E. Dümmler *et al.* (4 vols., Berlin, 1881–1923), I, 487; Alcuin, *Carmina* 30.2, line 4, *ibid.*, 248.

[41] Georges Duby, 'Youth in Aristocratic Society: Northwestern France in the Twelfth Century', in *The Chivalrous Society*, trans. Cynthia Postan (London, 1977), 112–22.

[42] Innes, 'A Place of Discipline'.

[43] Ardo, *Vita Benedicti* 30, *MGH SS*, xv, pt 1, 211–12; charter for Gellone: Claude de Vic and Joseph Vaissette, *Histoire générale de Languedoc* (5 vols., Paris, 1730–45), I, preuves, cols. 31–2; also Louis the Pious's diploma at cols. 34–5. The formulary of Marculf, 1.19, preserves the form of words for a permit to leave court and enter the church: *MGH Formulae Merowingici et Karolini aevi*, ed. K. Zeumer (Hanover, 1886), 55–6. Royal control

younger man, imperial permission might be rather more reluctantly granted, as was the case with Aldric, future bishop of Le Mans (832–57), to whom Louis the Pious offered a military retinue of his own to induce him to remain in royal service at court rather than depart for a new life in the church.[44]

These and a handful of other instances from Charlemagne's reign hint at an atmosphere of religious anxiety among the aristocratic elite of the time. And well might they worry about their own salvation: in precisely these years not only was a programme of vigorous moral and religious reform being enunciated but also bloody, protracted warfare in the Danube valley and especially Saxony was pushing the Carolingian empire to its fullest territorial extent. The conjunction threw into high relief the question of how extremely wealthy and powerful warrior aristocrats might exercise their ascendency in a Christian manner. Several of them turned to the Anglo-Saxon courtier-scholar Alcuin for advice. He replied with letters and, in one case, a full treatise, in the process working out a practical morality. Re-interpreting the late antique literature of Christian masculinity, he offered reassurance that the lay condition and the exercise of power were not incompatible with achieving salvation. The correct use of power and wealth combined with appropriate self-control sufficed.[45] Here is how Alcuin distilled his advice to one correspondent: 'be agreeable in counsel, strong in action, a peacemaker at home, prudent as an envoy, kind towards the poor and afflicted, just in giving judgement, generous in alms-giving in order that out of your temporal wealth you may win eternal riches in heaven'.[46] To another, he spelled out the sexual implications of the code of ethical self-restraint: 'He who has a legitimate wife should have sexual relations with her legitimately and at the appropriate times so that he may deserve to receive the blessing of children from God. Let

---

of courtiers' marriages was nothing new: see Gregory of Tours, *Decem Libri Historiarum*, IV.46, *MGH SSRM*, I, pt I², 181.

[44] *Gesta Aldrici Cenommanicae urbis episcopi* I (*MGH SS*, xv, pt I, 308). For an outline of Aldric's career, see Philippe Depreux, *Prosopographie de l'entourage de Louis le Pieux (781–840)* (Sigmaringen, 1997), 97–9.

[45] Donald Bullough, 'Alcuin and Lay Virtue', in *Preaching and Society in the Middle Ages: Ethics, Values and Social Behaviour*, Proceedings of the Twelfth Medieval Sermon Studies Conference (Padua, forthcoming). On Alcuin's sources, see Liutpold Wallach, 'Alcuin on Virtues and Vices: A Manual for a Carolingian Soldier', *Harvard Theological Review*, 48 (1955), 175–97. The importance of the Christian reformulation of the classical ethic of civic masculinity is emphasised by Kate Cooper and Conrad Leyser, 'The Gender of Grace: Impotence, Servitude and Manliness in the Fifth-Century West', *Gender and History*, 12 (2000), 536–51.

[46] 'Esto in consilio suavis et in opere strenuus; pacificus in domo, prudens in legationibus; pius in pauperes et miseros, justus in judiciis, largus in eleemosynis; ut ex temporalibus divitiis tuis aeternas tibi merearis in caelis.' Alcuin, *Epistolae*, no. III (to Megenfrid), ed. E. Dümmler, *MGH Epp.*, IV, ed. E. Dümmler (Berlin, 1895), 159–62, quotation at 161.

no man say he is unable to keep himself from fornicating.'[47] The layman who lived up to these exhortations would be 'wise in heart, albeit a soldier with his hands'.[48]

Other moralists sounded the same note and, in the early part of the ninth century, developed it into a full code of aristocratic ethical self-discipline and sexual restraint.[49] This was the code of conduct into which the *pueri* at court were to be socialised so that, once established as counts and heads of household in their own right, they in their turn would act as models of good conduct. Through self-discipline, they might learn wisdom, honesty and discretion in every aspect of life, the qualifications for becoming trusted and faithful courtiers.[50]

Into this world of power and its perils, Einhard arrived. He came to know Alcuin – whose esteem for him is well known[51] – and had surely met the courtiers who converted to the religious life. He must have been roughly the same age as many of the *pueri*, and he most certainly enjoyed a similarly close relationship to his royal 'lord and nurturer' as they did.[52] Yet his career trajectory differed in one crucial respect: he neither converted to the religious life nor was sent off to form his own domestic-cum-military household and administer a county. He was evidently too useful to be returned to the localities. In this context, we may consider the question of the date of marriage of this man who had no powerful relatives to argue that he should be released and endowed.

Charlemagne is famous – or notorious – for retaining his daughters at court, unmarried but free to engage in informal sexual liaisons; the rationale for this seems to be that they functioned as a collective substitute for the queen after the death of his fourth and last wife in 800.[53] Like Charlemagne's daughters, Einhard probably had to wait until middle age to escape the exceptionally prolonged 'youth' which imperial patronage brought in its wake: for Einhard, as for the new emperor's sisters, the accession of Louis the Pious in January 814 brought great changes. Scarcely ten years older than Louis, Einhard

---

[47] *Liber de Virtutibus et Vitiis*, written at the request of Count Wido of the Breton march, *PL* 101, col. 627: 'Qui mulierem habet legitimam, legitime utatur ea temporibus opportunis, ut benedictionem mereatur filiorum a Deo recipere. Nemo dicat a fornicatione se custodire non posse.'

[48] Alcuin, *Epistolae*, no. 136, ed. Dümmler, 205.

[49] Smith, 'Gender and Ideology'; Katrien Heene, *The Legacy of Paradise: Marriage, Motherhood and Women in Carolingian Edifying Literature* (Frankfurt am Main, 1997), 68–113.

[50] Innes, 'A Place of Discipline'.

[51] Alcuin, *Epistolae*, no. 172, ed. Dümmler, 284–5 at 285; *Carmina*, nos. 26, 30, ed. Dümmler, 245, 248.

[52] *Vita Karoli*, prologue, ed. Holder-Egger, 1.

[53] Janet L. Nelson, 'Women at the Court of Charlemagne: A Case of Monstrous Regiment?', in *eadem*, *The Frankish World* (London, 1996), 223–42.

was unusual in managing to remain influential in the new regime, which rapidly established itself as very different in personnel, politics and moral tone from the old emperor's court.[54] For him personally, 814 seems to have been a year of transition to both the role of 'elder statesman' and full social adulthood. From this moment, clear evidence of property, wealth and marriage accumulates. In January 815 came the gift of the estates of Michelstadt and *Mulinheim*, by which date Einhard and Imma were married. Perhaps, even, without an imperial gift of property, Einhard lacked adequate means with which to give his bride a dowry – if so, this would explain Imma's unusual prominence in the documentary record.[55] From 815 onwards, several rich abbeys to administer on the emperor's behalf were an additional recognition of Einhard's position. He derived further wealth and influence from their lands, and brought to these institutions the energy to reform them in line with imperial expectations.[56] The tradition of imperial control of courtiers' marriages combines with the pattern of the evidence for Einhard's career to suggest that he was only given permission to marry in 814.

Einhard might thus have been aged about forty-five when he finally married; Imma must have been anything from ten to thirty years younger. We should also note that the extant corpus of Einhard's writings, literary and documentary, only dates from after 814. Immediately, the burden of sin is present. When he drafted the will by which ownership of Michelstadt was given to Lorsch in 819, he opened with a comment that Christ's mission had been to a 'humankind besmirched by various filthy sins'. Declaring their 'equal devotion', he and Imma made the transaction together 'for the abolition of our sins, and for pursuing the rewards of the blessed, perpetual life'; his autograph signature on the engrossed copy read 'I, Einhard, sinner and donor'.[57]

Notwithstanding the donation to Lorsch, Einhard – and Imma? – set about developing both their estates. To supplement the simple pre-existing churches, new churches were built at Michelstadt and *Mulinheim*, while at the former, Einhard also erected a splendid large basilica, designed in a manner that fully reflected the most up-to-date imperial ideas on liturgy and sacred space. By 827, building work must have

---

[54] The court purges and changes of personnel are summarised by Egon Boshof, *Ludwig der Fromme* (Darmstadt, 1996), 92, 94, 105.

[55] For the conventions governing dowry in the ninth century, see Régine Le Jan-Hennebicque, 'Aux origines du douaire médiéval (VIe–Xe siècles)', in *Veuves et veuvage dans le haut moyen âge*, ed. Michel Parisse (Paris, 1993), 107–22.

[56] F.J. Felten, *Äbte und Lainenäbte im Frankenreich* (Stuttgart, 1980), 283–6.

[57] *Codex Laurehamensis* 20, 1, 301–2. Einhard signed thus: 'Ego Einhardus peccator et donator recognovi et manu propria subscripsi.'

been effectively finished, for he was pondering which saint to select as its dedicatee.

This is the opening point of the narrative of his *Translation and Miracles of the Martyrs Marcellinus and Peter*. This tells how Einhard sent his personal notary, Ratleic, to Rome where, with the connivance of one of the city's deacons, he robbed a catacomb and returned to Germany with the relics of the third-century martyrs Marcellinus and Peter. In November 827, Einhard installed them at Michelstadt, possession of which would revert to Lorsch after his and Imma's deaths. But the saints made it known that this was not their chosen resting place, so in January 828 he yielded to their instructions and moved them instead to *Mulinheim*. He then returned to court, only to learn that, en route from Rome, Ratleic had been robbed of part of the relics by a cleric of Hilduin, abbot of Saint-Denis (Paris) and Saint-Médard (Soissons), who had travelled with him. Only after considerable bargaining did Einhard succeed in recovering the stolen portions of the bodies. Restored to wholeness and installed at *Mulinheim*, the martyrs transformed themselves into miracle-workers. Here, at Aachen, and elsewhere, healings, reconciliations and exorcisms occurred. The purpose of the *Translation and Miracles* was to authenticate the relics, proclaim their shrine as a centre of exemplary Christianity in the midst of a corrupt empire and praise God's greatness.[58]

A strong association between the martyrs' relics and Einhard's sense of both his own sinfulness and that of the empire at large runs throughout the years after 828. He declared that he did not know why these powerful saints had deigned to take up residence with him, the 'sinner', but he rose to the challenge wholeheartedly, determined that they should receive 'fitting honour'.[59] In Marcellinus and Peter, Einhard found both patrons and clients, for just as he sought their intercession in heaven, so he fostered their cult and reputation on earth. In addition to commemorating in prose the saints' journey to their new, northern home and publicising their miracles, he decided to build them another new basilica, this time exactly modelled on the most recent architectural designs which Ratleic would have observed in Rome. The decision to build the new church was made in principle by the spring of 830, and composition of the *Translation and Miracles* completed that autumn.[60] By

---

[58] Cf. Julia M.H. Smith, '"Emending Evil Ways and Praising God's Omnipotence": Einhard and the Uses of Roman Martyrs', in *Seeing and Believing: Conversion in Late Antiquity and the Early Middle Ages*, ed. Kenneth Mills and Anthony Grafton (Rochester, NY, 2003), 189–223.

[59] Both quotations from *Epistolae*, no. 10, ed. Hampe, 113–14.

[60] *Epistolae*, no. 10, dated by Hampe to April 830, notes the decision to build a new church. On the date of the *Translatio et miracula*, see Martin Heinzelmann, 'Einhards *Translatio Marcellini et Petri*: eine hagiographische Reformschrift von 830', in *Einhard*, ed. Schefers, 269–98 at 278 and n. 43.

then, however, Louis's empire was convulsed by political crisis and his court riddled with corruption. In this environment, it proved hard for Einhard to acquire the necessary resources, material and political, necessary to get the church built. At the very least its east end, with its apsidal relic crypt and founders' burial vault, must have been completed by the time of Imma's death in December 835 and the visit the following year of Louis the Pious (perhaps to attend the church's consecration).[61] Completion of the rest presumably followed shortly thereafter, although interior decorations were still being commissioned in 847.[62]

The final decade of Einhard's life (830–40) has sometimes been construed either as a political retirement or a religious conversion.[63] Let us see what Einhard himself says. He opens the *Translation and Miracles* looking back to his days in permanent service at court: 'When I was resident at the palace and occupied with the business of the world, I used to give much thought to the leisure I would one day enjoy.' His vocabulary here is the traditional Ciceronian juxtaposition of *negotium* – *otium*, of business and responsibility juxtaposed with time apart to cultivate country estates, friends and the mind.[64] In reading this, we should bear in mind that Louis the Pious's court included all those in royal service and forwarding royal interests, whether or not they were in immediate attendance on the emperor.[65] Einhard certainly remained a member of this broad court circle, even if no longer present in person, for he kept in touch by messengers and letters.[66] Also, the transition from *negotium* to *otium* never implied a one-way street, even in the hands of fourth-century Christian writers.[67] This was not the language of irrevocable change, let alone of monastic or clerical

---

[61] *Annales Fuldenses*, a. 836, ed. F. Kurze, *MGH SSRG* (Hanover, 1891), 27.

[62] As Einhard's successor and abbot, Ratleic was still commissioning paintings in 847; Lupus, *Epistolae*, no. 60, ed. Marshall, 66–7.

[63] Felten, *Äbte*, 285–6, for brief summary of earlier interpretations.

[64] *Translatio et miracula*, I.I, ed. Waitz, 239: 'Cum adhuc in palatio positus ac negotiis saecularibus occupatus, otium, quo aliquando perfrui cupiebam, multimoda cogitatione meditarer, quendam locum secretum atque a populari frequentia remotum nanctus atque illius, cui tunc militaveram principis Hludewici liberalitate consecutus sum.'

[65] Airlie, 'Bonds of Power'.

[66] Letters show him recusing himself from the summons to court in the early weeks of 830 on the grounds of severe illness (*Epistolae*, nos. 13–15, ed. Hampe, 116–18). He was back at court, if only briefly, to write letters for Louis the Pious in November 832 (*Epistolae*, nos. 20–2, ed. Hampe, 120–1). The evidence does not reveal whether he attended in subsequent years, but does not allow us to assume that he never returned.

[67] Cf. Jean-Marie André, *L'Otium dans la vie morale et intellectuelle romaine des origines à l'époque augustinienne* (Paris, 1966); José Oroz Rota, 'L'Otium chez Saint Augustin', in *Les Loisirs et l'héritage de la culture classique: actes du XIIIe Congrès de l'Association Guillaume Budé*, ed. J.-M. André, J. Dangel and P. Demont, Collection Latomus, 230 (Brussels, 1996), 433–40. I owe these references to Susanna Elm.

conversions such as those of William of Gellone or Aldric of Le Mans. Rather, Einhard deployed this vocabulary for its resonances of public service, landed property and educated reflection upon the human condition. It marked a life in which secular and divine responsibilities were complementary not antithetical.

Einhard's actions after 830 evince neither political retirement nor religious conversion. Instead, we can see most clearly firm devotion exercised within a domestic environment, combined with a continuing concern for the welfare of the empire. He was the martyrs' political spokesman, identifying closely with their cause, dedicating himself to their service in his old age and confiding his private thoughts to them.[68] In promoting them, he was doing his best to combat the sinful corruption which he believed pervaded the empire.[69] Although in a letter to Louis the Pious in April 830, he had pleaded to be allowed to serve his saints 'freed from secular responsibilities' and declared that his intention was to spend his final years in the company of his saints, praying, reading and meditating upon scripture,[70] he nevertheless continued to run his estates, developing them energetically yet perhaps also applying that same ethical use of power which Alcuin had advocated.[71] He also maintained his place in the web of patronage that spread outwards from the royal court, putting in a good word for one man here, interceding for another there, garnering political and practical support for his martyrs. The proximity of *Mulinheim* to the newly enlarged palace complex at Frankfurt will have made it extremely easy for Einhard to retain his place in imperial networks of communication.[72] Indeed, serving Marcellinus and Peter drew upon his accumulated political and managerial skills, and led him to voice scathing criticism of the sinful state of the empire.[73] His last recorded contact with Louis the Pious came in 837, when he explained to the aging emperor that the recent appearance of Halley's comet portended disasters which could only be averted by turning to the remedy of penance and beseeching divine mercy.[74] All this was quite compatible with his own

---

[68] *Epistolae*, nos. 10, 18, for the language of *obsequium, servitium* to the martyrs; *Epistolae*, no. 16, invoking them as knowing truly his innermost thoughts; ed. Hampe, 113–14, 118, 119.

[69] *Epistolae*, nos. 10, 33, ed. Hampe, 113–14, 126.

[70] 'A curis saecularibus absolutum': *Epistolae*, no. 10, ed. Hampe, 114.

[71] *Epistolae*, no. 50, on acquiring *mancipia* for the estates; nos. 37, 46, 47, 48, 49, interceding for clemency for fugitives from lordly jurisdiction who had sought sanctuary at the martyrs' shrine; ed. Hampe, 128, 133–4.

[72] Matthew Innes, 'People, Places and Power in Carolingian Society', in *Topographies of Power in the Early Middle Ages*, ed. Mayke de Jong and Frans Theuws with Carine van Rhijn (Leiden, 2001), 397–437 at 422.

[73] *Translatio et miracula*, III.13–14, ed. Waitz, 252–4.

[74] Einhard, *Epistolae*, no. 40, ed. Hampe, 129–30.

life of prayer and meditation: in the year before the comet, we find him seeking consolation after Imma's death by reading Cyprian, Augustine and Jerome in an effort to understand mortality and eternal life.[75] When Einhard himself died on 14/21 March 840,[76] he was laid to rest in the same tomb as Imma, in close proximity to his beloved martyrs.[77] The epitaph displayed nearby praised equally his service to the emperor and to Sts Marcellinus and Peter. His life had been spent in the service of patrons both human and heavenly, in *diuinum uel humanum officium*.[78]

In religious devotions and managerial responsibilities, Imma had clearly been his partner: together they regularly attended matins and the daily mass in the martyrs' church.[79] When Einhard returned to Aachen for the winter political assemblies in 828–9–30, he travelled without her, presumably leaving the administration of the church and its property in her capable hands.[80] At precisely this time, Carolingian bishops were inveighing against the preposterousness of women who set themselves up independently as the managers and administrators of churches.[81] But to the bishops who knew her, Imma was doubtless exemplary: a married woman, firmly in her husband's shadow but his reliable partner in a shared religious enterprise (Figure 1).

In the last years of their marriage, however, its character changed. Imma was no longer Einhard's sexual partner, becoming instead his 'dearest sister and companion'.[82] Their marriage had given way to

---

[75] Einhard to Lupus: Lupus, *Epistolae*, no. 3, ed. Marshall, 4.

[76] Einhard's date of death given as 14 March in a late ninth-/early tenth-century entry to the Fulda *Annales Necrologici* (*MGH SS*, xiii, 166) and as 21 March by Gozbald of Würzburg (Wellmer, *Persönliches Memento*, 15 n. 11). The former date was also recorded in the Lorsch necrology (*Kalendarium Necrologium Laureshamense*, ed. J.F. Böhmer, *Fontes Rerum Germanicarum* (4 vols., Stuttgart, 1843–68), iii, 146).

[77] For precise location of the burial vault, see the excavation report of A. Schubert, 'La basilica dei SS. Marcellino e Pietro a *Mulinheim* sul Meno secondo i recenti scavi', *Rivista di Archeologia Cristiana*, 15 (1938), 141–6.

[78] Hrabanus Maurus, *Carmina*, no. 85, ed. E. Dümmler, *MGH PLAC*, ii, 237–8.

[79] *Translatio et miracula*, iii.4, 7, 8, 9, 10, ed. Waitz, 249, 250–1. I take Einhard's use of the plural *nos* here to mean 'we' not the formal singular other translators have assumed.

[80] Note the reversion to the singular, *ego*, each time he leaves for court: *Translatio et miracula*, iii.11, 12, 19, ed. Waitz, 251, 252, 255. Similarly, Bernard of Septimania left Dhuoda running his estates whilst he attended court. Dhuoda, *Libellus manualis*, x.4, ed. and trans. P. Riché, *Manuel pour mon fils*, Sources chrétiennes, 225bis, 2nd edn (Paris, 1997), 350–2.

[81] Council of Paris, 829, cl. 42. *MGH Concilia* [hereafter *MGH Conc.*], ii, ed. A. Werminghoff (Hanover, 1906–8), 638. On its import, see Nelson, 'The Wary Widow', 92.

[82] 'Olim fidissimae coniugis, iam nunc carissimae sororis ac sociae'; Einhard to Lupus: Lupus, *Epistolae*, no. 3, ed. Marshall, 4. Einhard must have been cruelly hurt when Lupus attempted to console him with the suggestion that perhaps God had taken Imma from

Figure 1   Einhard and Imma plan their foundation at Mulinheim (now Seligenstadt).
Mid-nineteenth-century engraving, reproduced from J. Schopp, *Der Name
Seligenstadt* (Speyer, 1965).

him in punishment for having loved her physically too much. 'Affectum uestrum in
uxoris amore forsitan subdiuisum non passus, putari potest ad se solum amandum
reuocauisse ac, si quid eius corpori intemperanter diligendo plus iusto a uobis indultum
fuerat, eiusdem corporis subtractione punisse.' Lupus, *Epistolae*, no. 4, ed. Marshall, 9.

complete sexual abstinence in a manner reminiscent of the well-attested late antique custom among pious Christian couples such as Paulinus of Nola and Therasia or Melania the younger and Pinianus as well as other members of their circles.[83] Carolingian moralists also enjoined an ethic of sexual restraint for the laity. If Imma was by this time beyond childbearing age, it would have been appropriate for the couple to heed the strictures against intercourse except for the sake of pro-creation.[84]   Even were she rather younger, they may have been mindful of the requirements of Carolingian church councils that the laity should abstain from sex before taking the sacraments: in this manner, the couple's daily attendance at mass became possible.[85]   In their last years together, Imma and Einhard shared a life of chastity, prayer and the management and promotion of the martyrs' church.

Similar patterns of conjugal piety are evident in other aristocratic couples of this period. Rorigo and Bilichild, restorers of St-Maur de Glanfeuil, were hailed as *religiosi coniuges*, 'devout spouses'.[86] Such a phrase might equally be applied to Gerald and Adaltruda: they 'held modesty and religion as if it were some hereditary dowry' of which sexual self-restraint was but one aspect, according to the hagiographer of their son, Gerald of Aurillac (born *c.* 855).[87] Similarly, Adelheid and Conrad (the benefactors of St-Germain at Auxerre) had such personal qualities that Heiric of Auxerre could scarcely decide 'which of them was more intent on devotion, more fervent in venerating the saints, more generous in attentiveness towards the poor'.[88] Such ninth-century 'holy households' could survive the death of one of the spouses.[89] For example, Gisla, the widow of the Saxon count Unwan, was another

[83] Cf. Dyan Elliott, *Spiritual Marriage: Sexual Abstinence in Medieval Wedlock* (Princeton, 1993), chs. 2–3, esp. 51–5. On fifth-century precedents for other aspects of Carolingian lay religiosity, see Martin Heinzelmann, 'Sanctitas und "Tugendadel": Zu Konzeptionen von "Heiligkeit" im 5. und 10. Jahrhundert', *Francia*, 5 (1977), 741–52.

[84] Heene, *Legacy of Paradise*, 79–89.

[85] 740x750 Council of Bavaria, cl. 6; 796/7 Council of Cividale, cl. 13; 813 Council of Chalons-sur-Sâone, cl. 46; 829 Council of Paris, cl. 69. *MGH Conc.*, ii, 52, 194, 283, 669–70.

[86] Odo of Glanfeuil, *Historia translationis S. Mauri*, ch. 2, *AASS Jan*[3] ii, 336. On *religiosus* as applied to laymen, see R. Grégoire, '*Religiosus:* étude sur le vocabulaire de la vie religieuse', *Studi Medievali*, 3rd series, 10 (1969), 415–30.

[87] *Vita prolixior*, attributed to Odo of Cluny. *Vita Geraldi*, i.1, 2, *PL* 133, cols. 642–3. The attribution of the *vita prolixior* to Odo of Cluny had recently been contested by Matthew Kuefler, 'Text and Context in the Cult of St. Gerald of Aurillac', paper presented to the Medieval Academy of America, March 2001.

[88] *Miraculi S. Germani*, ii.1, *PL* 124, col. 1247D. See further John Contreni, '"By Lions, Bishops Are Meant; by Wolves, Priests": History, Exegesis, and the Carolingian Church in Haimo of Auxerre's Commentary on Ezechiel', *Francia*, 29–1 (2003), 1–25 esp. 19.

[89] Cf. Lyndal Roper, *The Holy Household: Women and Morals in Reformation Augsburg* (Oxford, 1989).

contemporary of Imma's. She devoted her widowhood to a 'religious life', doing many good works, building churches, distributing alms, giving generous hospitality to pilgrims, offering moral advice to the new count, her son Bernhard, and fostering the piety of her surrogate daughter, the housekeeper-cum-holy woman Liutberga.[90] Hospitality to pilgrims, almsgiving, reverence to the clergy, domestic moral integrity and sexual self-discipline: these were the qualities which turned a woman's house into a 'church of Christ'.[91] We might almost add Gerald of Aurillac to this roll-call, for his monastic foundation, relic collecting and almsgiving fit the same pattern. What differentiates him is that he took sexual abstinence to the extreme of never marrying: his household was holy without being conjugal.[92]

We lose track of Einhard after Halley's comet. By then, he was in his late 60s and a widower, the male condition most invisible in the historical record.[93] His literary masterpieces had been published, but perhaps it was now that he composed his most private, heartfelt work. So private that only one manuscript is extant, Einhard's abbreviation of the Psalter is a catena of excerpts which form the prayers of a sinner meditating on his need for salvation and on the greatness of God.[94] As he explained in his preface, the complete Psalter is not suitable for

---

[90] *Vita Liutbirgae*, chs. 2, 7, ed. Ottokar Menzel, *Das Leben der Liutbirg*, Deutsches Mittelalter. Kritische Studien des Reichsinstituts für ältere deutsche Geschichtskunde, 3 (Leipzig, 1937), 11, 14–15.

[91] The phrase is that of the ninth-century hagiographer of the seventh-century saint, Sadalberga. *Vita Sadalbergae* 11, ed. Bruno Krusch, *MGH SSRM*, v, 55–6.

[92] Odo of Cluny, *Vita Geraldi*, ii.5 (founds monastery); ii.23 (relics), *PL* 133, cols. 673–4, 683.

[93] Cf. Nelson, 'The Wary Widow', 84, and on the documentary invisibility of widowers at all periods see the chapters by Julia Crick, Margaret Pelling and Pamela Sharpe in *Widowhood in Medieval and Early Modern Europe*, ed. Sandra Cavallo and Lyndan Warner (Harlow, 1999).

[94] Extant in Vercelli, Bibliotheca Capitolare MS 149 of S.ix ³⁻⁴, it is edited in full by P. Salmon under the title *Psalterium adbreviatum Vercellense* in *Testimonia orationis Christianae antiquioris*, ed. P. Salmon, C. Coeburgh and P. du Puniet, *Corpus Christianorum continuatio medievalis*, 47 (Turnhout, 1977), 37–78. Salmon has expressed doubts about the attribution to Einhard. See his 'Psautiers abrégés du moyen âge', in his *Analecta liturgica: extraits des manuscrits liturgiques de la Bibliothèque Vaticane*, Studi e Testi, 273 (Vatican City, 1974), 67–119, esp. 72–4, for his argument that since the text used is the Psalterium Romanum, no one as close to Charlemagne's liturgical reforms could have made it. This argument fails to take into account the great diversity of Bible texts in circulation in the late eighth and ninth centuries: for a conspectus, see Bonifatius Fischer, 'Bibeltext und Bibelreform unter Karl dem Grossen', in *Karl der Grosse*, ed. Braunfels, ii, 156–216. Other witnesses to the existence of an abbreviated psalter bearing Einhard's name are (i) the reference to a 'libellus Einardi de psalmis' in the tenth-century Bobbio catalogue (G. Becker, *Catalogi bibliothecarum antiqui* (Bonn, 1885), i, 72) and (ii) Sigebert of Gembloux, *De viris illustribus* 84 (ed. Robert Witte (Frankfurt, 1974), 77), where he refers to Einhard as the author of the *vita Karoli* and an abbreviated – but Gallican – psalter. See also Eligius Dekkers, 'Sigebert van Gembloux en zijn "De Viris illustribus"', *Sacris Erudiri*, 26 (1983), 57–102.

those who wish 'to invoke God and beseech him on account of their sins'. Rather, his selection of excerpts was directed towards that purpose.[95] Choosing not to open with the *beatus vir* of Psalm 1 but with the appeal to God from the psalmist beset by his enemies in Psalm 3, Einhard takes a highly selective and deeply personal course through the Psalter, omitting some psalms entirely and heavily abbreviating others. The ending is equally carefully designed: after following the psalms in sequence through to and including Psalm 144, he ends with a second set of extracts from Psalm 102, quite different in tone from the first. These closing verses are the doxology of a sinner seeking divine mercy. Here we encounter the most authentic Einhard, stripped of all literary pretension or self-fashioning: the human face to face with his God.

Einhard shared his reliance on the Psalter as an instrument of prayer with others of the Carolingian laity. Alcuin had advised Charlemagne on how the layman leading the 'active life' could nevertheless use the psalms for prayer at regular intervals throughout the day, in a simplification of the monastic office.[96] An anxious noblewoman suffering from 'various mishaps' commissioned Prudentius, bishop of Troyes (*c.* 844–61) to compile for her a series of brief and consolatory prayers based upon the Psalter. In the preface to his *Flores psalmorum*, Prudentius was explicit that it was appropriate for travellers and anyone in difficulty to recite a few short verses of the psalms instead of the entire Psalter.[97] If commissioning a personal set of psalm-based prayers was a sign of membership of the highest aristocracy, other elite lay folk might resort to borrowing a psalter: three women – a wife, a widow and a lady (*domna*) – availed themselves of copies lent by the monastic library at Weissenburg.[98] The handful of extant Carolingian wills also tell us of lay ownership of psalters and books containing both psalms and prayers, and there is even some evidence that the Psalter may have been the primer for teaching lay boys to read, just as it was in monastic schools.[99] Through the Psalter and prayers derived from it, pious Carolingian laymen and women could draw on the rhythm of monastic worship

---

[95] *Psalterium adbreviatum Vercellense*, 55.

[96] Alcuin, *Epistolae* 304, ed. Dümmler, 462–3. For the prayers of another ninth-century king, see Paul Kershaw, 'Illness, Power and Prayer in Asser's *Life of King Alfred*', *Early Medieval Europe*, 10 (2001), 201–24.

[97] Ed. Salmon, 'Psautiers abrégés du moyen âge', 93–119, with full text of preface available in *MGH Epp.*, v, 323.

[98] The tenth-century list of borrowers on the flyleaf of Wolfenbüttel, Herzog August Bibliothek MS 4119 (= Codex Weissenburgensis 35), is edited and discussed by Otto Lerche, 'Die älteste Ausleihverzeichnis einer deutschen Bibliothek', *Zentralblatt für Bibliothekswesen*, 27 (1910), 441–50.

[99] The evidence is assembled by Rosamond McKitterick, *The Carolingians and the Written Word* (Cambridge, 1989), 217–18, 246–8.

yet tailor their own devotional life to suit individual needs. Einhard shows how personal such usage was.

The account I have just sketched invites us to consider how fluid the early medieval boundaries between lay and religious life could be.[100] Einhard was not only a courtier, but became a married landowner and probably a father. He promoted the cult of his chosen martyr relics even more vigorously than anyone else of his time and turned his household into a 'church of Christ'.[101] He was also deeply religious in his reading, his thinking and his perception of a world permeated by sin. Much of this locates him securely within an emerging culture of elite, conjugal Christianity, in which codes of moral conduct first articulated at court in the years around 800 became domesticated in some magnates' households. This is not to argue that the sample of pious households discussed here is representative of the Carolingian aristocracy as a whole, for that would be to ignore compaints about wanton violence against women and church property or about inappropriate uses of wealth.[102] Nevertheless, there is enough evidence to indicate that we do not have to wait until the high Middle Ages to find expressions of lay piety that are actively pursued and distinctive in their modalities. André Vauchez once declared that one of the 'novel characteristics' of the eleventh–thirteenth centuries was 'the ability of lay people to create autonomous forms of piety which. . .succeeded in reshaping the religious message disseminated by the clergy to meet their feelings and specific needs'.[103] He was, of course, talking of large-scale religious movements and enthusiasms but nevertheless his sense of novelty was misplaced. *Mutatis mutandis*, the same comment holds true for the conjugal endeavours among the Carolingian aristocray which I have outlined. Ninth-century lay initiative created articulate, self-conscious forms of devotion which met the needs of personal salvation and familial identity whilst remaining fully orthodox.

There remains, though, something singular about Einhard. If he and Imma seem to have had more refined religious sensibilities than most of their contemporaries, it is in part because of the almost unparalleled first-hand evidence they have left us. Rather than being reliant upon the passing laudations of hagiographers, we have their own writings to

---

[100] As pointed out by Eva Synek, '"*Ex utroque sexu fidelium tres ordines*": the status of women in early medieval canon law', *Gender and History*, 12 (2000), 595–621.

[101] Cf. n. 91 above.

[102] Smith, 'Gender and ideology', 60, and *eadem*, 'Religion and Lay Society', in *New Cambridge Medieval History*, II: *c. 700–c. 900*, ed. Rosamond McKitterick (Cambridge, 1995), 664–5, for further references.

[103] A. Vauchez, *The Laity in the Middle Ages: Religious Beliefs and Devotional Practices*, trans. J. Schneider (Notre Dame, IN, 1993), 265.

hand. No one else explains their personal devotion to saints with an enthusiasm equal to Einhard's, and only in one other instance can we gain an equally privileged insight into the spirituality of the lay elite – Dhuoda, who nevertheless evinces no particular interest in the cults of saints. Concerned for the spiritual and moral welfare of her son, now enrolled in the ranks of the *pueri* at court, Dhuoda outlined in 841–3 a programme of penance, prayer, moral integrity and chastity for her fifteen-year-old son. In language suffused by the Psalms, her *libellus* reproduced in loving terms the aristocratic ethic which Alcuin had formulated half a century earlier.[104] Einhard and Imma would have wholeheartedly approved.[105]

Of the couple, Imma is easier to locate in her social and historiographical context. Poorly documented, like all lay women, but probably the transmitter of important property rights, she has much in common with other devout, capable women of the Carolingian lay elite. It is Einhard who remains distinctive. Uniquely, his prominence was not based upon military distinction, a successful career in the ecclesastical hierarchy or large-scale land ownership. Whether by marriage or birth, all the other lay aristocrats mentioned belonged to the ranks of the imperial 'super-aristocracy', whose wealth, power and privilege far exceeded that of Imma and her husband. Einhard had used his many abilities and his command of the Latin language to overcome the disadvantages of his tiny stature. Through his years at court, those talents had propelled him from the ranks of minor, local landowners into the circle of the *Reichsaristokratie*. Prolonged attendance at court had turned Einhard into the courtier par excellence; his aptitudes and closeness to two successive emperors combined to bring him status and contacts quite atypical of the local elites of the Maingau. Yet it seems that only marriage, when it finally happened, gave him his own place among the landed aristocracy.

After his youthful, monastic years, Einhard lived a life among the powerful, amidst all the temptations and corruptions of the court. He had married and been sexually active within his marriage. He had been in attendance upon Charlemagne in exactly those years when lay courtiers were most anxious about their chances of salvation, and upon Louis the Pious when his empire seemed on the point of collapse from external attack and internal moral corruption. Perhaps any or all of these circumstances sharpened his persistent sense of being a sinner; perhaps his minute frame seemed the living embodiment of Christian belief that, despite being created in the image of God, humankind was

---

[104] *Manuel pour mon fils*, ed. Riché, 27–37, for discussion of her sources.
[105] Cf. the similar but very brief advice addressed by Imma to her son (or grandson). Einhard, *Epistolae*, no. 38, ed. Hampe, 128–9 and n. 10 above.

deeply flawed. His inner meditations on his own sinfulness went to the grave with him: but he died as he wished, in the service of Sts Marcellinus and Peter.[106]

---

[106] Cf. *Epistolae*, no. 14, ed. Hampe, 117: 'timeo me aliubi quam velim at aliut agentem, quam sanctis Christi martyribus servientiem, esse moriturum'.

Transactions of the RHS 13 (2003), pp. 79–104 © 2003 Royal Historical Society
DOI: 10.1017/S0080440103000045   Printed in the United Kingdom

MIGRANTS, IMMIGRANTS AND WELFARE FROM THE OLD POOR LAW TO THE WELFARE STATE

By David Feldman

READ 19 APRIL 2002 AT THE UNIVERSITY OF MANCHESTER

ABSTRACT. Under the Old Poor Law internal migrants moved from one jurisdiction to another when they crossed parochial boundaries. Following the Poor Law Amendment Act of 1834 central government took an enlarged and expanding part in welfare. As it did so, the entitlement to welfare of immigrants from overseas was scrutinised at a national level in a way that was analogous to the manner in which the status of internal migrants had previously been scrutinised at a parochial level. Having established this analogy, the essay asks whether the entitlement to welfare of outsiders improved or deteriorated over time and seeks to account for the broad trends.

I

Welfare systems have never been universal in their reach. But who specifically has been included within the compass of collective solidarity, and who left out? Limitations can be set in a number of ways; they can be set categorically, for instance, by limiting support to members of a particular religion or denomination, or they can be established on a case by case basis, by means tests, for example. But entitlements have also been restricted by ruling that 'strangers' are not eligible for support. Indeed, according to Michael Walzer, welfare systems, as expressions of distributive justice, necessarily require hard lines to be drawn between insiders and strangers. He writes, 'The idea of distributive justice presupposes a bounded world within which distributions take place: a group of people committed to dividing, exchanging and sharing social goals, first of all among themselves.'[1] The starting point for this essay is an attempt to convert these general propositions into historical questions. As welfare systems have changed over time, we can ask whether and how definitions of entitlement have altered. Specifically, this essay examines the changing definitions and entitlements of strangers under successive welfare regimes in England from the seventeenth century to the late twentieth century.

From the consolidation of the Elizabethan structure in 1598 and 1601

[1] M. Walzer, *Spheres of Justice: A Defence of Pluralism and Equality* (New York, 1983), 31.

until the major reforms of the early nineteenth century, the official welfare system – the poor law – was financed and administered locally, by the civil parish. So far as welfare was concerned, internal migrants moved from one jurisdiction to another when they crossed parochial boundaries.[2] Although it was possible for migrants to acquire an entitlement in their new parishes of residence, people were able to move far more easily than their right to poor relief. What became known as the Law of Settlement and Removal, introduced in 1662, definitively removed any idea that paupers had a secure claim to relief simply on the basis of residence in a parish.[3] From the mid-nineteenth and, above all, the early twentieth centuries this situation began to change. In the century and a half following the Poor Law Amendment Act of 1834 central government took an increasingly dominant part, first, in administering and, then, financing welfare. As it did so the significance of migrants criss-crossing the jurisdictions of local authorities diminished. But as this problem dwindled, central government faced the question of how it would deal with the welfare needs of those outsiders who now came into the country in increasing numbers, in the form of immigrants from overseas – what would be their entitlement? The entitlement to welfare of immigrants from overseas thus came to be scrutinised and defined at a national level in a way that was analogous to the manner in which the status of internal migrants had been scrutinised at a parochial level.

By conjoining the histories of immigration and internal migration this essay brings together histories which customarily have been treated discretely by historians and social scientists. The distinction between an immigrant and an internal migrant is that the former crosses a state boundary and the latter does not. Once considered historically, however, the categorical force of this distinction appears to vary. Above all, this is because the powers and responsibilities of local and central authorities have changed over time. As the policy-making and administrative capacities of different units of government have altered so too has the significance of the boundaries between them. Writing in 1906 Sidney and Beatrice Webb highlighted the historical importance of local boundaries when they pointed out that

To the historian of England between the Revolution and the Municipal Corporations Act, if he is not to leave out of the account five-

---

[2] P. Slack, *Poverty and Policy in Tudor and Stuart England* (1988), 129, 194.
[3] 13 & 14 Car. II, cap. 12. Of course, even before 1662 parishes did not invariably relieve sick or unemployed migrants who, consequently, were 'much sent and tossed up and down from town to town'. However, the judiciary did try to check the practice and advised that only vagrants could be lawfully removed. M. Dalton, *The Country Justice* (1666), 115–16.

sixths of the population, the constitutional development of the parish and the manifold activities of its officers will loom at least as large as dynastic intrigues, the alternations of parliamentary factions, or the complications of foreign policy.[4]

At times, and in some respects, the local jurisdictions crossed by migrants may have held a similar significance to the boundaries crossed by immigrants. This recognition provides the ground for comparison between the welfare entitlements of internal migrants in past centuries and those of immigrants in more recent decades. Elements within this history will be well known to specialists in the history of the Old and New Poor Laws and of the welfare state. What may be less familiar, however, is the idea that these features are structurally similar and can be drawn together within a single historical narrative and analytical framework.

Beyond its intrinsic interest, this long-term perspective may prove useful because it bears on two broad areas of current historical discussion. First, it provides one way in which we can address the history of welfare and the state in a long-term perspective.[5] Much current writing on modern British history exhibits a zealous desire to disinter and destroy all remnants of the Whig interpretation of history. Not least is this the case in the history of social policy. Whereas once the welfare state stood as the triumphant telos of a process of governmental growth whose origins were placed confidently in the Victorian period, now it is surveillance not social insurance which historians often install as the archetypal practice and creation of the modern reforming state in Britain.[6] Where it has not been denounced, the influence of the state has been marginalised. In cases where it is still allowed a constructive role, in histories of public health, for example, it is local authorities not the central bureaucracy which receive attention and credit. More generally, philanthropic voluntarism, associational forms such as friendly societies and neighbourhood ties now receive

---

[4] S. and B. Webb, *English Local Government from the Revolution to the Municipal Corporations Act: The Parish and the County* (1906), 5.

[5] In recent years there have been some notable attempts to address the history of welfare over the long term. *Charity, Self-Interest and Welfare in the English Past*, ed. M. Daunton (1996); L. Lees, *The Solidarities of Strangers: The English Poor Laws and the People, 1700–1948* (Cambridge, 1998); P. Thane, *Old Age in English History: Past Experiences Present Issues* (Oxford, 2000); S. King, *Poverty and Welfare in England 1700–1850* (Manchester, 2000).

[6] For an interesting commentary see M. Wiener, 'The Unloved State: Twentieth-Century Politics in the Writing of Nineteenth-Century History', *Journal of British Studies*, 33 (1994), 283–306. Compare, for example, S. Finer, *The Life and Time of Sir Edwin Chadwick* (1952), with C. Hamlin, *Public Health and Social Justice in the Age of Chadwick, Britain 1800–54* (Cambridge, 1998). For a sceptical view of insurance see J. Macnicol, *The Politics of Retirement in Britain, 1878–1948* (Cambridge, 1948).

attention as the agents of significant and creative welfare provision.[7]

At the same time as there has been a negative reassessment of the history of the state in the nineteenth and twentieth centuries, the history of the eighteenth-century state in general and social policy in particular has been revised in the opposite direction. In this spirit, a significant body of scholarship now rescues the Old Poor Law from the opprobrium heaped upon it by nineteenth- and early twentieth-century writers.[8] This corpus of work contains two rather different claims. One claim is that eighteenth-century administration, far from being a patchwork of anomalies and absurdities, can be seen to have been both more efficient and more appropriate than its critics have allowed, once placed within its proper institutional, social and cultural contexts.[9] A second sort of claim goes further still and characterises welfare in the eighteenth and early nineteenth centuries, as inclusive and generous, and contrasts this to a subsequent deterioration.[10] In these ways, an assault upon Whiggish interpretations of the history of welfare in the eras of the New Poor Law and the welfare state has been greatly reinforced by a positive reassessment of the Old Poor Law.

A second reason for taking the long-term perspective adopted here is that the negative view of the modern state finds support in the customary pessimistic assessment of how British governments responded

---

[7] J. Cronin, *The Politics of State Expansion: War, State and Society in Twentieth-Century Britain* (1991), is critical of state policies for doing too little. Voluntaryism is celebrated in F. Prochaska, *The Voluntary Impulse* (1988), and highlighted in G.B.M. Finlayson, *Citizen State and Social Welfare in Britain* (Oxford, 1994). On local government see, for instance, S. Szreter, 'The Importance of Social Intervention in British Mortality Decline c. 1850–1914: A Reinterpretation of the Role of Public Health', *Social History of Medicine*, 1 (1988), 1–37. On working-class mutuality and association see A. Kidd, *State, Society and the Poor in Nineteenth-Century England* (Manchester, 1999).

[8] Most notably in Sidney and Beatrice Webb, *English Local Government: English Poor Law History. Part 1: The Old Poor Law* (1927).

[9] J. Brewer, *The Sinews of Power: War, Money and the English State, 1688–1783* (1989); J. Innes, 'Parliament and the Shaping of Eighteenth-Century English Social Policy', *Transactions of the Royal Historical Society*, fifth series, 40 (1990), 63–92; G. Boyer, *An Economic History of the English Poor Law, 1750–1850* (Cambridge, 1990); J.R. Kent, 'The Centre and the Localities: State Formation and Parish Government in England, c. 1640–1740', *Historical Journal*, 38:2 (1995), 363–404; D. Eastwood, *Governing Rural England: Tradition and Transformation in Local Government* (Oxford, 1994); N. Landau, 'The Laws of Settlement and the Surveillance of Immigration in Eighteenth-Century Kent', *Continuity and Change*, 3 (1988), 391–420.

[10] D. Thomson, 'The Decline of Social Welfare: Falling State Support for the Elderly since Early Victorian Times', *Ageing and Society*, 4:4 (1984), 451–82, implicitly extends the argument back to the Old Poor Law, see 452. K. Snell and J. Miller, 'Lone-Parent Families and the Welfare State: Past and Present', *Continuity and Change*, 2:3 (1987), 387–422. On the generosity of the Old Poor Law to the elderly, at least until the mid-eighteenth century, see R. Smith, 'Charity, Self-Interest and Welfare: Reflections for Demographic and Family History', in *Charity, Self-Interest and Welfare*, ed. Daunton, 37–41.

to immigration in the post-war period. Writing on immigration and public policy by historians and social scientists is dominated by the view that twentieth-century Britain witnessed the triumph of an exclusively 'white' notion of citizenship and national identity. Following from this, some have argued that the history of welfare in the century is also a history of racialized exclusions, directed at people of colour, the Irish and the Jewish poor.[11] By placing the history of immigrants alongside the history of other 'strangers', as we do in the present essay, it will be possible to re-examine the role of ideas and images of race in the formation of welfare policy.

II

With these broad considerations in mind, we shall now turn to the status of migrants in England under the Old Poor Law. By the beginning of the eighteenth century the poor law was well established. It operated as a national system, supported by compulsory, local taxation; its day to day to operations administered locally by the inhabitants of a district – overseers of the poor and justices of the peace.[12] Within this structure the question of which parish should take responsibility for which poor person was a matter of great importance. It was vital to ratepayers who wanted to limit their burdens and it was equally significant to anyone who at any time might apply for poor relief. For so long as welfare was provided locally, migration across the boundaries of one parish to enter another created a population of 'strangers' whose entitlement to poor relief in the place to which they moved was open to question. The predicament of these migrants was particularly significant because eighteenth- and early nineteenth-century England, both urban and rural, was a highly mobile society.[13]

[11] For instance, K. Paul, *Whitewashing Britain: Race and Citizenship in the Postwar Era* (Ithaca, 1997); D. Cesarani, 'The Changing Character of Citizenship and Nationality in Britain', in *Citizenship, Nationality and Migration in Europe*, ed. D. Cesrani and M. Fulbrook (1996), 57–73; P. Panayi, *Immigration, Ethnicity and Racism in Britain, 1815–1945* (Manchester, 1994); B. Carter, C. Harris and S. Joshi, 'The 1951–55 Conservative Government and the Racialization of Black Immigration', *Immigrants and Minorities*, 6:3 (1987), 335–47. On welfare specifically, see H. Dean with M. Melrose, *Poverty, Riches and Social Citizenship* (1998), 146; N. Ginsburg, *Divisions of Welfare* (1992), 153–5.

[12] J. Innes, 'The State and the Poor: Eighteenth-Century England in European Perspective', in *Rethinking 'Leviathan'*, ed. J. Brewer and E. Hellmuth (Oxford, 2000), 226–9.

[13] A. Redford, *Labour Migration in England* (1926); E.A. Wrigley, 'A Simple Model of London's Importance in Changing English Society and Economy 1650–1750', *Past and Present*, 37 (1967), 46–9; A. Kussmaul, 'The Ambiguous Mobility of Farm Servants', *Economic History Review*, 29 (1981) 222–35; *Migration and Society in Early-Modern England*, ed. P. Clark and D. Souden (1987); C. Pooley and J. Turnbull, *Migration and Mobility in Britain since the Eighteenth Century* (1998).

The terminology of 'strangers' was widely used by contemporaries. In 1698, for example, two years after its foundation, the Bristol Corporation of the Poor appointed a committee 'to consider of methods to prevent strange poor from coming into this city'. Before the end of the year Thomas Dropwell was employed to report twice each week 'what strangers are come to reside in the several parishes within this city that they may take care to have them removed or set at work according to law'.[14] Almost fifty years later, in 1747, John Wesley recorded in his journal the extraordinary generosity of a group of followers in Tetney, Lincolnshire. Their 'leader', Micah Elmoor, had explained to Wesley how 'from time to time' they 'entertain all the strangers that come to Tetney'.[15] By the beginning of the nineteenth century several large towns possessed a Strangers' Friend Society. The report of the Liverpool society for 1824 described its work on behalf of 'the poor and destitute stranger, attracted hitherto by the hope of work but disappointed in his expectation ... unentitled to legal support and reduced by misfortune, hunger and disease to a state of utter destitution'.[16] Methodists took a leading role in creating and maintaining these charities, attracted to the needs of the mobile poor, perhaps, by their own disregard for parish boundaries.[17]

The questions of entitlement to poor relief which arose from internal migration across administrative boundaries were resolved according to the Law of Settlement. This was not a single law but a complex collection of statutes and legal precedents. Taken together, they, and the justices of the peace and judges who applied and interpreted them, determined which parish was responsible for which pauper. The intention of the 1662 law, as its preamble made clear, was to sanction removal of the unsettled poor and to place an obstacle in the way of poor people acquiring a settlement in the parishes to which they migrated.[18] Two provisions constituted the root of the law. First, anyone able to rent a tenement for £10 per annum was exempt from its provisions but, second, all those who could not meet this criterion had to reside in a parish for forty days without objection if they were to gain a settlement. Changes to the law introduced in 1686 and 1691 made it still less likely that migrants would gain a settlement by forty

---

[14] *Bristol Corporation of the Poor: Selected Records, 1696–1834*, ed. E.E. Butcher (Bristol, 1932), 62–3.

[15] E.M. North, *Early Methodist Philanthropy* (New York, 1914), 34.

[16] *The Kaleidoscope or Literary and Scientific Mirror*, 3 May 1825, 372a.

[17] North, *Early Methodist Philanthropy*, 49. On the society in Manchester see G.B. Hindle, *Provision for the Relief of the Poor in Manchester 1754–1826* (Manchester, 1975), 78–89. For Leeds see R.J. Morris, *Class, Sect and Party: The Making of the Middle Class in Leeds 1820–50* (Manchester, 1990), 205–6

[18] 13 & 14 Car. II, cap. 12.

days' residence. By the latter date, in order to gain a settlement, migrants had to give notice in writing of their arrival and this, in turn, had to be read out in church and entered in the parish's poor law account book. These requirements were calculated to encourage objections. As Richard Burn noted, settlements by giving forty days' notice were 'very seldom obtained'.[19]

At the same time, the law set out the ways in which a 'stranger' might acquire an entitlement to poor relief in the parish to which he or she had migrated. By the beginning of the eighteenth century, there were a number of routes through which migrants were able to establish a new entitlement to relief. These arose as exceptions to the requirement to give notice or as ways in which the forty-day rule was deemed to have been fulfilled even though notice had not been given. Thus a settlement could be gained by someone being bound to an indentured apprenticeship, by someone being hired for and fulfilling one year's service, and upon marriage a wife acquired her husband's settlement. Apprenticeship, service and marriage were all contracts upon which the poor laws were not allowed to trespass. Likewise, anyone living on their own estate gained a settlement, because in the eyes of the law, the rights of property owners superseded ratepayer concerns. Finally, in those cases in which migrants acquired a settlement by paying parish rates or by serving for a year in an elected office, the law determined that the public nature of their action rendered formal notice super-fluous.[20] These exceptions provided a number of ways through which migrants could gain a settlement and gain access to the official network of collective solidarity within the parish. On the other hand, those migrants who stood in need of poor relief but had not gained a new settlement could be removed to their last parish of legal settlement or, if this could not be determined, their place of birth. Indeed, before 1795 it was possible for parishes, with the warrant of a justice of the peace, to expel 'strangers' merely on suspicion that at some time in the future they would apply for poor relief.

The logic of the system of settlement and removal was set by the fiscal and administrative structure which divided England and Wales

---

[19] The two statutes are 1 Jac. II, cap. 17 and 3 & 4 Will. and M., cap. 11. R. Burn, *The Justice of the Peace and the Parish Officer* (14th edn, 1780), III, 444. On the logic of the law see W. Blackstone, *Commentaries on the Laws of England* (4th edn, 1770), I, 362.

[20] See Blackstone, *Commentaries on the Laws of England*, I, 362–5, for a short summary of the law as it stood in the middle of the eighteenth century. More detailed expositions can be found in Burn, *The Justice of the Peace*, and in M. Nolan, *A Treatise of the Laws for the Relief and Settlement of the Poor* (3 vols., 4th edn, 1825). For a characterisation of how the law changed at the end of the seventeenth century which is different from the one given here see J.S. Taylor, 'The Impact of Pauper Settlement, 1691–1834', *Past and Present*, 42 (1976), 42–74.

into 15,000 thousand units. This was well appreciated by Sir William Hay MP writing in 1735.

> It is certain that the obligation on each parish to maintain its own poor, and, in consequence of that, a distinct interest, are the roots from which every evil relating to the poor hath sprung, and which must ever grow up, till they are eradicated. Every parish is in a state of expensive war with all the rest of the nation, regards the poor of all other places as aliens, and cares not what becomes of them if it can banish them from its own society.[21]

Faced with a mobile population parishes were armed to forestall an unwanted reputation that theirs was a comfortable resting place for migrants who were indigent or threatened to become so. Further, Norma Landau has shown that some parishes used their powers of examination and removal not only to determine access to the poor law but also to protect other collective resources, such as access to commons and wastes, against the predations of poor migrants.[22]

Powers under the law of settlement and removal were thus implemented by parishes eager to limit their obligations. In October 1783, for instance, the vestry at Hungerford in Berkshire ordered its overseers to summon all inhabitants likely to become chargeable and not legally settled in the parish, to determine their places of settlement and to have them 'henceforth removed accordingly'.[23] Writing about Warwickshire in 1794, John Wedge observed:

> A vast number of those who are employed in manufacturing towns are parishioners of different villages ... and whenever infirmity, age or check in trade happens, these men are not supported by those

---

[21] A Member of Parliament, *Remarks on the Laws Relating to the Poor*, cited in Parliamentary Papers [henceforth PP] 1851 xxvi, *Report on the Law of Settlement and Removal*, 296. Attributed in T. Ruggles, *The History of the Poor: Their Rights, Duties and the Laws Respecting Them* (1793), I, 217.

[22] N. Landau, 'The Regulation of Immigration, Economic Structures and Definitions of the Poor in Eighteenth-Century England', *Historical Journal*, 33 (1990), 541–71; Landau, 'The Laws of Settlement and Surveillance'. Landau's argument has been controversial. See K.D.M. Snell, 'Pauper Settlement and the Right to Poor Relief in England and Wales', *Continuity and Change*, 6 (1991), 375–415; N. Landau, 'The Eighteenth-Century Context of the Law of Settlement', *Continuity and Change*, 6 (1991), 417–39; K.D.M. Snell, 'Settlement, Poor Law and the Rural Historian: New Approaches and Opportunities', *Rural History*, 3 (1992), 145–72; R. Wells, 'Migration, the Law and Public Policy in Eighteenth and early Nineteenth-Century Southern England', *Southern History*, 15 (1993), 86–139.

[23] Berkshire Record Office, D/P 71/8/3, Hungerford Special Vestry Minutes, 19 Oct. 1783.

who have had the benefit of their labour but are sent for subsistence to their respective parishes.[24]

But in addition to wholesale purges of migrants such as these, overseers on their own initiative arranged for the examination of individuals and when necessary their removal.[25]

The economic interests of ratepayers were reinforced by a moral appraisal of different sorts of people which promoted inclusion and exclusion. The acquisition of a settlement – without formal notice – of anyone who lived for forty days on tenement rented at £10 was based not only on an economic judgement about such a person but also upon reputation. Here the double meaning of the term 'credit' was important. According to Burn, the £10 rent signalled 'the credit given to the tenant by the landlord' and 'the credit given by the legislature to a man able to stock a farm of such value'.[26] It was not only a measure of wealth and financial independence but also of reputation.

The parochial elites in town and country, among them the men who fulfilled the office of overseer of the poor, were drawn from the middling ranks of seventeenth- and eighteenth-century society. These men privileged values such as diligence, economic independence and discipline. Unwed mothers, idle and tippling incomers, itinerant labourers of all sorts, were not only a potential charge on the parish but also stood condemned by their habits in the eyes of the parochial elite.[27] In 1700 the Bristol Corporation of the Poor, created four years earlier to exercise central control over poor relief and to 'civilise' and 'purge' the poor, appointed a committee to 'Examin the cases of strangers and all other disorderly persons that come to live in this City and single women who live at their own hands that are likely to become chargeable to the corporation.'[28] The remit thus nicely elided the distinctions between all migrants, disorderly migrants and independent women, in an impressive sweep which combined moral disapprobation with parsimony. In Bristol,

[24] A.W. Ashby, *One Hundred Years of Poor Law Administration on a Warwickshire Village* (Oxford, 1912), iii, 67.

[25] *The Diary of Thomas Turner*, ed. D. Vaisey (Oxford, 1984), 80–1, 86–7, 93–6, 108–110, 139, 143, 269, 276.

[26] Burn, *The Justice of the Peace*, iii, 457–8. On 'credit' see C. Muldrew 'Credit and the Courts: Debt Litigation in a Seventeenth-Century Urban Community', *Economic History Review*, 46 (1993), 23–38.

[27] *The Middling Sort of People: Culture, Society and Politics, 1550–1800*, ed. J. Barry and C. Brooks (Basingstoke, 1994); K. Wrightson, 'The Politics of the Parish in Early Modern England', in *The Experience of Authority in Early Modern England*, ed. A. Fox, P. Griffiths and S. Hindle (Basingstoke, 1996), 10–46; S. Hindle, 'Power, Poor Relief and Social Relations in Holland Fen', *Historical Journal*, 41:1 (1998), 67–96; J. Kent, 'The Rural "Middling Sort" in Early-Modern England, circa 1640–1740: Some Economic, Political and Socio-Cultural Characteristics', *Rural History*, 10:1 (1999), 19–54.

[28] *Bristol Corporation of the Poor*, 83.

moreover, the practices vindicated by this rhetoric served to make the world conform to its image. The Corporation refused to provide for 'any casual poor who do not immediately belong to this City' and so forced them to beg in the streets, producing 'great disturbance and scandal of the inhabitants'. Here was a policy which inevitably converted 'strangers' into 'vagrants' and the Corporation's response was to pursue a more vigorous implementation of the laws against 'rogues, vagrants and sturdy beggars and idle disorderly persons'.[29] Bristol's size, as well as its position as a gateway to and from Ireland, meant that migration impinged on the city in some distinctive ways. However, as several historians have now shown, the poor law authorities elsewhere in eighteenth-century England – in rural parishes in particular – spent a great deal of time pursuing vagrants and unmarried mothers.[30] In their eyes the line between the unsettled poor and the immoral and disorderly poor was thin and permeable. Indeed, this moral feature was replicated in law. Someone who returned to a parish from which he or she had been removed was reclassified as a vagrant; their transgression transferred from the civil to the criminal law.[31]

Of course, want of an entitlement did not mean that all unsettled paupers were expelled by their parishes of residence. The force of the law was mitigated in a number of ways. Before departing, migrants could apply for a certificate from the parochial authorities. The latter, if they provided the document, recognised a continuing obligation to relieve the certificate-holder and his family and so saved them from removal until they actually became chargeable.[32] Conversely, by the late eighteenth and nineteenth centuries many parishes were allowing non-resident relief. That is to say, a migrants' home parish would send money to relieve a pauper who would not then be forced to return to his or her parish of settlement.[33] Migrants clearly knew the system well, and used this knowledge to try to extort poor relief from parishes known to allow non-resident relief. For example, in 1810 Mary Wilkinson wrote from Kendal to the overseer of Kirkby Lonsdale, her parish of

[29] *Ibid.*, 92–3.
[30] Hindle, 'Power, Poor Relief and Social Relations'; Kent, 'The Rural "Middling Sort"'.
[31] See for example Hertfordshire Record Office, PS/2/2/1, Minutes of the Proceedings at the Special Sessions Chipping Barnet, 8 Oct. 1796.
[32] There is a useful discussion of certificates in P. Styles, 'The Evolution of the Law of Settlement', in P. Styles, *Studies in Seventeenth-Century West Midlands History* (Kineton, 1978), 189–93. However, from the mid-eighteenth century there were complaints that some parishes refused to issue certificates. *Bristol Corporation of the Poor*, 117–19.
[33] J.S. Taylor, 'A Different Kind of Speenhamland: Nonresident Relief in the Industrial Revolution', *Journal of British Studies*, 30 (1991), 183–208; *Essex Pauper Letters*, ed. T. Sokoll (Oxford, 2001).

settlement, hoping that he would have the goodness to send her another shilling.

> I ham sorry that I ham oblidge to trouble you but I ham in such a Desterd situation that I cannot Help it for I have not half work and the times is so hard that it is impossible for me to gett anything for me and my Child to put on and we are all most Naked for we have neither shirt to our Back not shoes to our feet that we are allmost starved to Death.

But her supplication was joined to a commonplace threat; she added that if he did not send money, then both she and her child would 'be Oblidge to come to you'. In this case the tactic was effective.[34] Beyond the devices of certification and non-resident relief, the impact of the law was lessened by the large discretion allowed to poor law overseers. One factor that influenced local administrators was the state of the local labour market. In 1803–4, when male labour was in short supply due to the French wars, an inquiry into the poor law found that as many 194,052 individuals were being relieved by parishes to which they did not belong.[35]

But despite these qualifications, even when it did not lead to their expulsion, the Law of Settlement placed the migrant poor within a structure of uncertainty. Parishes that had once been indulgent could turn against the non-settled poor as the state of the labour market or demographic conditions altered, or as the nation's state of peace or war, or the identity of individual vestrymen, overseers and clergymen might change. The policies of even contiguous parishes could vary widely. Among the parishes in Holland Fen, for instance, the amount spent on settlement litigation varied between 0.7 per cent and 17.3 per cent in 1802–3.[36] Although the formal position of poor migrants improved after 1795 and, with the major exception of unmarried women with children, they could no longer be removed merely on suspicion

---

[34] Cumbria Record Office, Kirkby Lonsdale Township Letters, Mary Wilkinson to Stephen Garnett, 2 Jan. 1810. Pioneering work by Taylor, Sokoll and others on these letters written by migrant paupers proposes that non-resident relief was a functional adaptation which promoted the interests of migrants and both parishes involved. No doubt this was often the case but since so many pauper correspondents complain that they have not received answers to letters, that money has not been sent or that the amount they have been given does not meet their basic needs, future research might also consider to what extent these letters also reflect a system under strain. Dealing with a slightly later period, D. Ashforth draws attention to the low level of non-resident relief. 'Settlement and Relief in Urban Areas', in *The Poor and the City: The English Poor Law in its Urban Context, 1834–1914* (Leicester, 1985), 73.

[35] PP 1803–4 xiii, *Abstract of Answers and Returns. . .Relative to the Expense and Maintenance of the Poor in England*, 715.

[36] Hindle, 'Social Relations in Holland Fen', 89.

they would become a burden to the ratepayers, in practical terms their situation may have become still more precarious, for after this date removals became more frequent.[37] As the rate burden soared in the late eighteenth and early nineteenth centuries parishes, which now had their discretionary and pre-emptive sanction of removal taken away, used their remaining powers more energetically. In these years the amount spent by overseers on removals and legal costs rose at a still faster rate than the amount dispensed on poor relief.[38] Between 25 March 1827 and the same date the following year 43,677 individuals were removed from parishes in England and Wales.[39]

Migrants who fell on hard times were left with the difficult choice of being removed to their parish of settlement, of begging and cajoling in the manner of Mary Wilkinson or of trying to negotiate their misfortunes without support from the poor law. Indeed, the greatest effect of the Law of Settlement was to force the non-settled poor to survive without support from the poor law. The London Strangers' Friend Society, established in 1784, pointed out that it did not duplicate the work of parochial relief: 'The overseers ... do their duty if they receive every applicant for relief: our business is with those chiefly who do not apply.'[40] The rapid advance of urbanisation in the late eighteenth and early nineteenth centuries, which led to greater concentrations of migrants, as well as the impact of the trade cycle, rendered the resulting problems more intense, more visible and significantly different. In 1851 George Coode, in the course of his massive report on settlement and removal, observed that 'It is almost certain that of late years the settlement laws have not been retained so much to protect one parish from another, as to protect the towns and places of popular resort from the burden of the poor being born in the country.'[41] In the words of two nineteenth-century critics, the threat of removal was 'hung up *in terrorem* over the heads of the poor', to deter them from applying for relief.[42] In 1843 the Poor Law Commissioners reflected on the impact

[37] Taylor, 'The Impact of Pauper Settlement', 53; Wells, 'Migration, the Law and Public Policy', 114; Eastwood, *Governing Rural England*, 110.

[38] In 1775–6 legal expenses amounted to 2.2 per cent of expenditure on poor relief, by 1802–3 this figure had risen to 3.5 per cent. *The Relief and Settlement of the Poor, &, Second Report* (1777), 539; *Further Appendix to the Report from the Committee on Certain Returns Relative to the State of the Poor* (1787), 730–1. Both in *Reports from Committees of the House of Commons* (1803), IX. PP 1803–4 XIII, *Abstract of Answers and Returns...Relative to the Expense and Maintenance of the Poor in England*, 714.

[39] PP 1829 XXI, *Poor Rates: Abstract of Returns*, 202–3.

[40] Cited in M.D. George, *London Life in the Eighteenth Century* (1925; 1966 edn), 395 n. 140.

[41] PP 1851 XXVI, *Report of George Coode Esq to the Poor Law Board on the Law of Settlement and Removal of the Poor*, 111.

[42] E. Head, 'The Law of Settlement', *Edinburgh Review*, 87 (1848), 456; PP 1854/5 XIII, *Report from the Select Committee on Poor Removal*, 188.

of economic depression 'in the industrial manufacturing districts' as follows:

> All persons ... agree that the Irish and non-settled poor whom the fear of removal deterred from applying for relief have suffered far the most. The obligation to relieve existed on the spot but the pauper knew well that the receipt of relief would be followed up by removal, and he preferred any extremity to this result.[43]

By 1864 when, as we shall see, the scope of Law of Settlement had been greatly attenuated, 36 per cent of all expenditure on indoor and outdoor poor relief in England and Wales went on the irremoveable poor; that is to say it went to paupers who had no settlement but who could not be sent away.[44] This percentage is almost double the incidence of relief to the non-settled poor indicated by the returns to parliament for 1802–3. This huge gap is one rough and ready but highly illuminating measure of the level of effective disentitlement in the period before the Law of Settlement was reformed.[45]

III

The Poor Law Amendment Act of 1834 marks the onset of the slow and incomplete shift from local to state boundaries in determining entitlement to welfare. By imposing change upon myriad local authorities, the 1834 Act amounted to a vast and novel exercise of power by central government. Accordingly, the Act also created a central bureaucracy in the shape of the Poor Law Commission and, after 1847, the Poor Law Board, whose task was to monitor local practice and to promote uniformity conforming to minimum standards.[46]

The 1834 Act is widely regarded by historians as a calamity for the labouring poor. The imperatives of ratepayer economy, economic individualism and a punitive attitude to the able-bodied poor, they argue, now influenced policy to an unprecedented degree.[47] Nevertheless, for migrants the Poor Law Amendment Act set in motion

---

[43] PP 1843 XXI, *Ninth Annual Report of the Poor Law Commissioners*, 35; see too T. Koditschek, *Class Formation and Urban-Industrial Society: Bradford 1750–1850* (Cambridge, 1990), 405–6; Morris, *Class, Sect and Party*, 206–7.

[44] In 1855, following the introduction of irremovability after five years' residence the figure was 21 per cent. PP 1865 XLVIII, *Poor Relief*, 199.

[45] PP 1803–4 XIII, *Abstract of Answers and Returns...Relative to the Expense and Maintenance of the Poor in England*, 714–15.

[46] Lees, *Solidarities of Strangers*, 145–53, 177–229, provides a recent discussion of how far these goals were fulfilled.

[47] For recent restatements of this view see C. Chinn, *Poverty Amidst Prosperity: The Urban Poor in Nineteenth-Century England* (Manchester, 1995), 102–5; Lees, *Solidarities of Strangers*, 113–14.

changes which greatly improved their entitlements to welfare. It was parliament and the Poor Law Board that intervened repeatedly in the middle decades of the century to attenuate drastically the Law of Settlement and extend the welfare entitlements of 'strangers'.

Initially, the Poor Law Amendment Act barely tampered with the Law of Settlement. But once the New Poor Law had been established and it was apparent that not all the hopes it carried had been realised, the Law of Settlement became a renewed object of criticism. One aim of the poor law reformers when they tried to terminate outdoor relief for the able-bodied was to encourage agricultural labourers to migrate from southern counties with low labour demand to manufacturing districts in the north. The Law of Settlement now appeared to the poor law commissioners and inspectors to provide one reason why the 1834 Act had not liberated labour markets in the ways they had hoped.[48] They criticised settlement and removal not only as economic fetters but also as sources of unnecessary hardship and injustice. The law was interpreted as a bulwark of parochial selfishness: a device used to deny the poor their legal entitlement.[49] The commissioners also highlighted the hardship caused to 'poor and industrious' persons by a law which left them liable to be removed from a place they had lived for many years and to be sent to a parish where they were not known. In particular, they decried the ordeal caused to Scotch and Irish paupers by the Law of Settlement. Because the English Poor Law did not extend to Scotland and Ireland, Scotch and Irish paupers, unlike their English counterparts, were not removed to a parish but to a country. Irish paupers were landed 'at random' without reference to their place of birth or to where their families and friends resided. In these cases, moreover, there was no receiving parish to launch an appeal against an unjust removal.[50] Settlement and removal were assailed also as obstacles to moral improvement, freedom and manly independence. Settlement, according to George Coode, was a 'degrading and corrupting' tie, a form of bondage. In a small or over-populated parish the settled labourer was not a free man: 'He knows that the parish by its protection of removal has bound him to its soil ... there is no independence of either employer or labourer, ... no such feeling as grows out of connexions freely sought, freely maintained and, if unsuitable, freely abandoned.'[51]

---

[48] Public Record Office [hereafter PRO], MH/33/48, 'Report on the Details to be Observed in Conducting the Migration of Labourers to the Cotton Districts of Lancashire', July 1835; *Report of George Coode*, 127.

[49] PP 1839 xx, *Fifth Annual Report of the Poor Law Commissioners*, 55; T.M. Torrens, *The Life of Sir James Graham* (1863), II, 350–1.

[50] *Ibid.*, 36–8.

[51] *Report of George Coode*, 320–1.

The Law of Settlement had been subject to rising economic, ethical and political criticism since the late eighteenth century but it was not until the creation of the Poor Law Board that this opposition became effective. Situated at one remove from the daily pressures of poor law accounting and ratepayer politics and stimulated by crusading ideals of 'free labour' and 'justice', centrally appointed poor law officials could more easily choose to construe migrants as victims of parochial injustice, and many did so. Responding to opinion within the Poor Law Board, the home secretary, Sir James Graham, introduced legislation that gave rise to the Poor Removal Act of 1846.[52] The most important provision of the Act was that people who had been in a parish for five years and had not gained a settlement nevertheless could not be removed. A further Act in 1861 reduced the term before irremovability took effect from five years to three, and the unit for irremovability was extended from a single parish to the considerably larger unit of the poor law union. In 1865 the residency requirement was further reduced to just one year.[53] Cumulatively, parliament and the Poor Law Board caused a radical shift in the burden of relieving the migrant poor. These new acts forced urban authorities and urban ratepayers to take responsibility for the welfare of their migrant poor in ways that hitherto they had been able to evade.[54] Nationally, there were just 8,351 removals in the whole of England and Wales by 1867–8.[55]

After initial obstruction on the part of some local boards of guardians, it became clear that the settlement reform of 1846 also applied to the Irish in England. This was particularly significant since the level of Irish immigration was about to increase dramatically as one consequence of the famine. The number of Irish in Britain totalled over 400,000 in 1841 and rose to 806,000 in 1861. Irish immigrants arrived without a legal settlement and, on account of their disproportionate poverty, the great majority of them did not acquire one. A law of 1819 had allowed poor law officials to remove Irish men, women and children from England and Wales as soon as they applied to the poor law for assistance. This was a significant deterioration in their legal situation; hitherto the Irish had been sent home only if they were found committing acts of vagrancy.[56] Armed with this power, between 1824

---

[52] A. Smith, *The Wealth of Nations* (1776); Ruggles, *History of the Poor*, provides a digest attack up to the 1790s. For an account of the genesis of the 1846 Act see PP 1857/8 xiii, *Report from the Select Committee on the Irremoveable Poor*, 5.

[53] On these changes see M. Rose, 'Settlement, Removal and the New Poor Law', in *The New Poor Law in the Nineteenth Century*, ed. D. Fraser (1976) 25–43.

[54] See the recognition of this outcome in A. Prentice, *Historical Sketches and Personal Recollections of Manchester* (Manchester, 1851), 233–4.

[55] PP 1867–8 LX, *Orders of Removal*, 279.

[56] 59 Geo. III, cap. 12.

and 1831 English and Welsh parishes expelled 51,556 Irish poor back to Ireland through the ports of Liverpool and Bristol: a figure equivalent to roughly 15 per cent of the Irish population in England and Wales at the time. Although we should remember that among those removed were gangs of Irish harvest workers who used and abused the system and threw themselves on the parish to engineer a free passage home. In the face of the famine migration, between 1845 and 1849 29,079 Irish were removed from parishes in England and between 1849 and 1854 more than 50,000 Irish were sent back to Ireland from Liverpool and London alone.[57]

Early Victorian poor law guardians shared the conventional opinion of the time that the Irish in Britain were likely to contain more than their fair share of drink-sodden labourers and professional mendicants.[58] According to this view, those Irish in work were among the least likely to make prudent provision for bad times and those out of work were likely to prey on the poor rate if given the chance to do so. Many poor law guardians believed that the threat of removal to Ireland was a vital deterrent without which they would be inundated.[59] In 1852 the clerk of the Bradford Poor Law Union informed the national Poor Law Board that the guardians had 'latterly removed nearly all Irish paupers applying for relief without enquiring the length of time they have resided in the respective townships of the Union'.[60] The interventions of the Poor Law Board and of parliament meant that by the 1860s boards of guardians no longer deported large numbers of Irish paupers. In 1868 just 508 people were removed to Ireland.[61]

It is notable, therefore, that at a time when antipathy to the Irish, expressed in newspapers and political speeches, pulpit sermons and labour organisations, ballads and cartoons, was both extensive and intense, the treatment of the Irish under the poor law underwent a marked improvement. This was not because the officials of the Poor

---

[57] PP 1831–2 XLIV, *Number of Irish Poor Shipped from Bristol and Expense thereof, 1823–31*, 461; PP 1833 XXXII, *Number of Irish Poor Shipped under Passes from Liverpool to Ireland in Each Year since 1823*, 352–3; PP 1850 L, *Orders of Removal*, 31–44; PP 1854 LV, *Poor Removals*, 325.

[58] For an example of the attitudes of local officials to the Irish see J. Davis, 'Jennings Buildings and the Royal Borough: The Construction of the Underclass in Mid-Victorian England', in *Metropolis – London: Histories and Representations since 1800*, ed. D. Feldman and G. Stedman Jones (1989), 24.

[59] PP 1854–5 XIII, *Report from the Select Committee on Poor Removal*, qq. 458, 1191, 2360, 3168. At the same time, however, some authorities had given up removing the Irish because the procedure was seen to be impossible to enforce and increasingly laborious to administer. *Ibid.*, q. 1178; PP 1850 XXVII, *Report to the Poor Law Board on the Law of Settlement and Removal of the Poor*, 118, 125.

[60] Cited in D. Ashforth, 'Settlement and Removal in Urban Areas', in *The Poor and the City: The English Poor Law in its Urban Context, 1834–1914*, ed. M.E. Rose (Leicester, 1985), 82.

[61] PP 1867–8 LX, *Orders of Removal*, 279.

Law Board held a more enlightened view of the Irish than the men responsible for the daily administration of the poor law locally. Indeed, many of the most articulate and elaborate expressions of the conventional wisdom of the time, that the Irish migrants were 'demoralised', 'barbarous' and 'worthless', can be found in the writings of poor law officials. Men such as J.P. Kay and George Cornewall Lewis played an important part in instating Irish immigration as one of the main causes of the urban crisis in early Victorian Britain.[62] In other words, the case of the Irish suggests that a profoundly negative caricature of them, though almost ubiquitous, had only slight impact on the direction of poor law policy in England. Policy towards the Irish became more generous despite their negative image not because this image became more favourable. Conversely, in so far as a negative view of the Irish did influence the decisions of poor law guardians it did so in a situation in which fiscal, legal and administrative conditions made it both possible and financially beneficial to allow the Irish unequal access to the poor law. Once these conditions changed, then so too did the influence on policy of stereotypes and racial ideas.

The gains bought to English and Irish migrants by the reforms of the mid-nineteenth century were limited in two important ways, however. First, in many places the irremovable poor in general and the Irish among them in particular were treated more harshly than their settled counterparts. Some Boards of Guardians, forced to discharge their responsibility to these paupers, responded by rigidly offering nothing but admission to the workhouse.[63] Second, and more fundamentally, migrants achieved a degree of equality at the same time as levels of poor relief were subject to drastic retrenchment. In absolute terms, the levels of poor law expenditure that had prevailed during the Napoleonic wars did not return until the 1870s. This is similarly reflected in the declining proportion of national income devoted to poor relief which fell from 2.7 per cent of Gross Domestic Product in 1820/1 to 0.7 per cent in 1880.[64] Whereas institutional arrangements shifted to the benefit of migrants in the middle decades of the nineteenth century, fiscal arrangements did not.

[62] J.P. Kay, *The Moral and Physical Condition of the Working Classes Employed in the Cotton Manufacture in Manchester* (Manchester, 1832), 27; PP 1836 xxxiv, *Report on the State of the Irish Poor in Great Britain*; D.M. MacRaild, 'Irish Immigration and the Condition of England Question: The Roots of an Historiographical Tradition', *Immigrants and Minorities*, 14:1 (1995), 67–85.

[63] PP 1850 xxvii, *Report to the Poor Law Board*, 8; PP 1860 xvii, *Report from the Select Committee on Removals*, qq. 1132, 3676.

[64] P. Harling and P. Mandler, 'From 'Fiscal-Military State to Laissez-Faire State, 1760–1850', *Journal of British Studies*, 32 (1993), 57; P. Lindert, 'Poor Relief before the Welfare State: England versus the Continent, 1780–1880', *European Review of Economic History*, 2 (1998), 114.

IV

In an important sense the changes made to the Law of Settlement by parliament and the Poor Law Board were easy to prescribe, for their costs fell on local government and not upon the resources of the institutions enforcing reform. In the twentieth century the situation changed. Now central government increasingly contributed to old age pensions, health and unemployment insurance and, after 1945, to family allowances and to national assistance as well. By 1948 these measures had finally abolished the poor law and the laws of settlement.[65] Under this new fiscal and administrative regime the broad pattern we have already observed continued to operate: in those fields in which welfare was financed and administered by central government the entitlements of 'strangers' were defined more generously than where welfare was controlled and financed by local agencies. Of course, where central government intervened the definition of who was a 'stranger' also changed. In those spheres in which welfare was financed and administered on a national basis, migrants who traversed internal boundaries no longer became strangers. The problem of the stranger increasingly became identified with the problem of the immigrant.[66]

Once the central state provided benefits for its citizens it was forced to determine what, if anything, would be the entitlement of immigrants. The beginning was not auspicious and both aliens and the British wives of aliens were excluded from state old age pensions when they were introduced in 1908. Lloyd George also planned to exclude aliens from his scheme for national insurance, which passed into law in 1911. Nevertheless, a cross-party coalition of members of parliament, prompted by a campaign by the Jewish benefit societies, won large concessions for the immigrants. Lloyd George not only included aliens within the national insurance scheme but agreed that unnaturalised aliens who had been in the country for five years should receive the state's 2d per week contribution.[67] This new pattern of state provision was further developed in the inter-war years as contributory old age pensions, unemployment insurance and unemployment assistance outside of the poor law were introduced; each of these was a major and new source of support, and all were were extended to immigrants. In the case of contributory old age pensions, for instance, introduced

[65] 11 and 12 Geo. VI, cap. 29.

[66] On numbers of immigrants see C. Holmes, *John Bull's Island: Immigration and British Society, 1871–1971* (1988); C. Peach, V. Robinson, J. Maxted and J. Chance, 'Immigration and Ethnicity', in *British Social Trends since 1900*, ed. A.H. Halsey (1988), 561–615; D. Coleman, 'UK Immigration Policy: "Firm but Fair", and Failing?', *Policy Studies*, 17 (1996), 195–214.

[67] See D. Feldman, *Englishmen and Jews: Social Relations and Political Culture* (1994), 370–8.

in 1925, a two-year residence requirement was explicitly applied to British subjects and aliens alike.[68]

Similarly, after the war, the 1948 National Insurance Act explicitly made 'no distinction on grounds of nationality'. The free treatment of all comers under the National Health Service was also vigorously defended by Aneuran Bevan in the face of a Conservative party campaign which claimed that the young service was being overwhelmed by entrepreneurial Egyptians coming to the United Kingdom to procure free National Health Service spectacles and prostheses and selling them across the length and breadth of Arabia.[69] Crucially, the introduction of National Assistance, which directly terminated the poor law, was broadly and simply conceived 'to assist persons in Great Britain who are without resources to meet their requirements'.[70] Accordingly a Department of Health and Social Security memorandum issued in 1970 declared that 'health and welfare services and social security benefits are available to all people in this country irrespective of race, colour or origin'.[71] Under the Social Security Act of 1966 supplementary benefit was available to anyone in Great Britain, irrespective of origin and regardless of the time spent in the country, subject to the normal rules such as the requirement to register for employment if they were fit for work and under pensionable age. Groups of immigrants, such as asylum seekers and overseas students, whose terms of entry to the country did not allow them to register for work, were able to qualify for urgent needs payments.[72]

In contrast, where welfare remained a tax on local pockets and a local administrative responsibility, the characteristic pattern of the eighteenth and nineteenth centuries was maintained in the twentieth; in these cases immigrant entitlements were brought into question. We can see this, for example, in 1918 when the London County Council determined that only candidates born in Britain could apply for Council scholarships. In 1920 it banned all 'aliens' from its employ and in 1923 decided to give preference to British citizens in the allocation of accommodation on the Council's housing estates.[73] In the 1930s the Irish once again became a target for hard-pressed local authorities. In 1938 the Association of Municipal Corporations complained of the burden the Irish were placing on public assistance and all social services

[68] 15 & 16 Geo. V, cap. 70; PP 1924 xv, *Unemployment Insurance Directions to Local Employment Committees Regarding Grant of Uncovenanted Benefit*; 24 & 25 Geo. V, cap. 29.

[69] *Parliamentary Debates*, 1948–9 (457), 1015; *Parliamentary Debates*, 1948–9 (461), 2001–2; A. Bevan, *In Place of Fear* (1952), 81.

[70] PP 1947–8 IV, *National Assistance Bill*, 156.

[71] PP 1969–70 xv, *Select Committee on Race Relations and Immigration*, 380.

[72] *Ibid.*, 383–4.

[73] G. Alderman, *London Jewry and London Politics 1889–1986* (1989), 66–7.

and called for their 'compulsory repatriation'.[74] During the Second World War it was fear of the hostile reaction from local authorities and local populations that led the British government to introduce special, centrally funded, measures for the support of refugees.[75]

In the post-war period too, it has been those facets of the welfare state which have remained to a great extent the administrative and fiscal responsibility of local government – education, personal social services and, above all, housing – that have a provided a focus for anti-immigrant sentiment and in which the entitlements of immigrants have been brought into question. Many local authorities prevented new immigrants from gaining speedy access to council housing by operating a residence requirement. In other a words, a view of whether a family really 'belonged' to the authority superseded a strict assessment of housing need.[76] But a residence requirement was only the most simple means of discriminating against immigrants. For example, councils were able to omit areas with large numbers of immigrants from slum clearance and redevelopment schemes or to offer only 'short-life' properties listed for demolition to immigrant families.[77]

By 1970 Birmingham City Council was presenting the immigrants as an unwanted and expensive obstacle to the city's redevelopment programmes. In this spirit, the deputy town clerk of Birmingham complained to a parliamentary select committee in 1970:

> We just cannot house our own population there now, so one extra person brings one extra problem of housing; there is no question of that. We are paying out large sums to rehouse them virtually all over the Midlands ... Quite honestly if ten extra people came into Birmingham it would to that extent increase the problem which, as far as I am concerned, is almost insoluble at the moment.[78]

In the 'beggar my neighbour' style of eighteenth- and nineteenth-century poor law guardians, Birmingham's medical officer of health suggested that 'there are many areas of this country that do not know this problem whatsoever, and you may consider it would be quite

---

[74] S. Glynn, 'Irish Immigration to Britain, 1911–51', *Irish Economic and Social History*, (1981), 63.

[75] *Parliamentary Debates*, 1939–40 (357), 1738; PRO, AST 11/8, L.N. Ure to T.M. Snow, 14 Mar. 1941.

[76] J. Rex and S. Tomlinson, *Colonial Immigrants in a British City* (1979), 130–1; P.B. Rich, 'The Politics of Race and Segregation in British Cities: With Reference to Birmingham, 1945–76', in *New Perspectives on Race and Housing in Britain*, ed. S.J. Smith and J. Mercer (Glasgow, 1987), 74–93. As the 1969 Cullingworth Report made clear, these rules disadvantaged internal migrants as well as immigrants. J.B. Cullingworth, *English Housing Trends* (1965), 61.

[77] *Select Committee on Race Relations*, 43.

[78] *Ibid.*, 727.

reasonable and sensible and fair for immigrants to go to those areas'.[79]

This contrast between the treatment of immigrants by central government and local authorities is subject to decisive qualification only from the mid-1980s. As late as 1984, the rules for supplementary benefit were deliberately broadened to allow almost any person from abroad seeking an extension or variation of their terms of stay to qualify for an urgent needs payment.[80] Since the mid-1980s, however, a series of measures have significantly undermined the welfare entitlement of some immigrants. First, the 1988 Immigration Act extended the category of 'sponsored immigrant'. Clause 1 of this Act required the dependants of all immigrants to have a sponsor who agreed to maintain and accommodate them 'without recourse to public funds'.[81] Initially this rule was used to limit immigration by placing a means test on family unity. By the mid-1990s, however, the Department of Social Security took a growing interest in sponsorship. In 1996 its regulations for claims by 'persons from abroad' specified that 'sponsored immigrants' should not be allowed benefits unless their sponsor was dead or the immigrant acquired British citizenship.[82] The welfare entitlements of 'persons from abroad' have been diminished in other ways. The 'Habitual Residence Test' was introduced in 1994. This device requires applicants for the main means-tested benefits to demonstrate 'a genuine commitment to living in the UK'. By October 1995 over 30,000 claimants had failed the test, saving the government an estimated £7 million.[83] A further key moment came in 1996. In this year the Conservative government withdrew all benefits from asylum seekers who did not apply for asylum on arrival in the country. The cost of supporting these asylum seekers thus fell on local authorities. The 1999 Immigration and Asylum Act restored central government responsibility for these asylum seekers but did so by introducing a system of vouchers in place of cash-based welfare benefits.[84]

---

[79] *Ibid.*, 725.

[80] *Statutory Instruments*, 1984, Part II Section 1, Supplementary Benefit (Misc Amdts), Regs 8.(2).

[81] 36 & 37 Eliz. II, cap. 14. This is what had been intended in 1971 but following a campaign against this rule Reginald Maudling, the home secretary, exempted the wives and children of commonwealth immigrants who were settled in Britain before the 1971 Immigration Act came into force.

[82] C. Vincenzi and D. Marrington, *Immigration Law: The Rules Explained* (1992), 39–40; *Welfare Rights Bulletin*, February 1996, 10.

[83] House of Commons, 1996–7, Social Security Committee, *Inquiries not Completed*, 101; N. Harris, *Social Security Law in Context* (Oxford, 2000), 198–201.

[84] A. Geddes, 'Denying Access: Asylum Seekers and Welfare Benefits in the UK', in *Immigration and Welfare: Challenging the Borders of the Welfare State*, ed. M. Bommes and A. Geddes (2000), 134–47.

V

In this essay I have suggested that immigrants in twentieth-century Britain presented policy makers and officials with problems that were structurally similar to those presented by internal migrants in the eighteenth and nineteenth centuries. The overarching lesson to be learned from taking this long-term perspective is that until the 1980s, when localities bore the financial burden of welfare the entitlements of 'strangers' were usually less secure than those of people who 'belonged'. Welfare reforms introduced by central government in twentieth-century Britain have served to include immigrants within the practices of collective solidarity. Where local autonomy has retained a significant fiscal and administrative role, as in the case of housing, the rights of 'strangers' have been insecure. This does not mean that we cannot find examples of eighteenth-century parishes which treated their non-settled poor generously. Neither does it mean that immigrants to post-war Britain always received their full entitlement from benefit offices.[85] It does suggest, however, that the framework within which particular decisions were made shifted over time and that, with the growth of central government, until the mid-1980s, it shifted to the advantage of migrants and immigrants: they became more likely to be included within systems of collective provision.

With this long-term perspective we can now return to some of the historiographical and interpretive issues raised at the beginning of this essay. The treatment of the non-settled poor does not directly contradict the claim that the Old Poor Law, when seen in its appropriate contexts, was more efficient, responsive and appropriate than its critics have allowed. But it is also clear that the Old Poor Law privileged the sedentary and settled portions of the labouring population. Individuals and families who took to the road, if only to go to a nearby parish, may well have taken a less positive view of how appropriately and responsively the Old Poor Law attended to *their* needs. Moreover, the notion that the eighteenth or early nineteenth centuries marked a golden age of transfer payments, followed by a deterioration in the nineteenth and twentieth, finds no confirmation from the changing treatment of migrants and immigrants.

The history presented here is still less compatible with the customary pessimistic assessment of how the British state responded to immigration in the post-war period. Certainly, exclusive ideas concerning English and 'white' identity have played a role in the evolution of British immigration policy.[86] But if we look beyond immigration policy to the

---

[85] See, for example, National Association of Citizen Advice Bureaux, *Barriers to Benefit* (1991).

[86] However, even this has been questioned in R. Hansen, *Citizenship and Immigration in Post-War Britain: The Historical Origins of a Multicultural Nation* (Oxford, 2000).

changing structure of welfare entitlements, its causal contribution appears less significant. The reflex of racial thinking and the force of negative stereotypes cannot account for the patterns of disadvantage over the long term which this essay has revealed. The most vulnerable group we have considered has been composed of the internal migrants in England who, before 1795, could be ejected from a parish merely on the basis of a fear that they might, one day, become a charge on the rates. It was not racism that disadvantaged these paupers. Further, we saw that Irish migrants were cruelly denigrated both by those who changed the law in their favour in the nineteenth century, as well as those who operated the vagrancy and settlement laws to remove them. Neither was it a racial characterization of the Irish that determined the outcome here. When we look at post-war Britain we are forced to account for the more favourable welfare entitlements of immigrants at a national level and their discriminatory treatment at a local level. Plainly, racism encouraged and could be used to justify local practices. But it would be difficult to argue that local policy makers were collectively more hostile to the immigration of people of colour than their counterparts at a national level. Beyond the realm of immigration policy itself, the presence or absence of racialized attitudes among politicians and officials in themselves predict little in the way of policy outcomes.

What, then, did generate the pattern of entitlements documented here? In a preliminary way, this essay has drawn attention to how the fiscal and institutional system established a framework of possibilities and constraints within which policy choices were made. Welfare systems pool and redistribute wealth. The funds for this transfer have been raised in part or in their entirety by taxation. It is easy to understand, therefore, why parishes and their ratepayers and the state and its taxpayers have sought to place limits on their financial responsibility for the poor. One way they have done so has been by ruling that 'strangers' are not eligible for support. The fiscal incentive for them to do this, however, has been weakest where the cost of supporting these 'strangers' has been diffused through the nation as a whole and has not fallen on particular localities. This was the situation so far as the benefits provided by national government were concerned. As the Treasury pointed out in 1961, the impact of immigration upon the benefit system was negligible.[87]

At a local level, of course, the situation could be very different. This was particularly the case since immigrants and migrants have never been evenly distributed across the country. For example, the impact of the Irish in Liverpool, of Russian Jews in the East End of London or

---

[87] PRO, DO 175/54, Report to Ministerial Committee, 5.

of Asians and West Indians in Birmingham was greater than their representation in the population as a whole. For welfare that was funded locally, therefore, immigration and internal migration could have a significant impact upon local welfare services and local taxation – above all upon changes in the rate of local taxation. For instance, even after the famine crisis years the Irish accounted for a large part of the cost of the poor in some northern cities. In Liverpool in 1854 the Irish poor added 3 5/8d in the pound to the rates, whereas the English poor cost 7 7/8d; in Manchester the equivalent figures were 5 1/2d and 8 3/4d, and in Bradford 5 5/8d and 1s 2 1/2d in the pound in the same year.[88] Similarly, we can point to the enormous stress borne by the local tax base in the post-1945 period. While the proportion of local authority expenditure drawn from the rates fluctuated mildly between 1950–1 and 1970–1 from 48 per cent to 41 per cent, the total sum being raised from the rates increased more than five fold in the same period.[89] These are circumstances in which the additional demands on local services presented by immigrants could be made to appear especially unwelcome. The fiscal system presented a structure within which individuals made choices concerning the extent of collective solidarity. These issues were not faced in an intellectual and cultural vacuum. This essay has highlighted the moral disdain for the migrant poor in the eighteenth century, the passion for justice and uniformity expressed by poor law inspectors, as well as the narrow and racially inflected circle of community erected by some local politicians and officials in post-war Britain. These ideas, and others, gave shape to the problems of governance. They also provided a vocabulary which could be utilised by politicians and officials to persuade themselves and others that their actions were necessary and just. But if we look at the tendency of policy in the long run, fiscal and institutional considerations exerted a powerful influence, both on decisions which diminished the entitlements of migrants and immigrants and on those which extended them.

As we have seen the mid-1980s, there has been a change of direction. This requires an explanation, for these same years did not witness any reduction in central fiscal and institutional controls; rather, the reverse was the case. The historic shift of policy in these years, however, can be explained in part by the changing composition of benefits within the welfare state and to the changing political language of the immigration debate. In this way, the deterioration in immigrant entitlements can be placed in the context of wider changes introduced by Con-

---

[88] PP 1854–5 XIII, *Appendix to the Report of the Select Committee on Poor Removal*, 349–53; see too F. Neal, *Black '47: Britain and the Famine Irish* (Basingstoke, 1998), 256–62.

[89] P.G. Richards, 'The Recent History of Local Fiscal Reform', in *The Reform of Local Government Finance in Britain*, ed. S.J. Bailey and R. Paddison (1988), 32.

servative governments after their electoral victory in 1979. For in these years governments engineered a major shift in the balance between different sorts of benefit within the welfare state. Whereas in 1979 just 4.4 million people received supplementary benefit in 1995 9.8 million – one sixth of the population – were on income support.[90] Accordingly fewer benefits were distributed on the contributory principle and thus received as the proper receipt for social insurance in which all pooled their risks, and more people received benefits as a system of handouts. The emphasis of the benefit system moved from a contractual one, in which the boundaries of collective solidarity were porous – anyone could benefit, so long as they contributed – to one that was more limited in conception because it depended more heavily on handouts raised by taxation. In this circumstance it was possible to draw the boundaries of collective solidarity more tightly. As Douglas Hurd, the home secretary, told parliament in support of his Immigration Bill in 1988, 'It is no service to community relations here if they [dependants] are then homeless or destitute. It is fair and reasonable that people should not come here without having somewhere to live and some means of support without recourse to public funds.'[91] A fundamentally similar point was made by Teresa Gorman MP when she expressed her sympathy 'with the feelings of the citizens of this country who believe that people can arrive here and climb on to a raft of welfare benefits for which the indigenous population has already paid out of its earnings'.[92]

Having surveyed four centuries of history, we can now return to our more general starting point. Does this history confirm the claim that 'distributive justice presupposes a bounded world within which distributions take place'?[93] If this were so, the recent erosion in Britain of the welfare entitlements of asylum seekers would appear as the culmination of an historical trend. This argument could be supported, perhaps, by the contrast between the treatment of the unsettled and settled poor in the eighteenth century. The vulnerability of strangers and outsiders may have been a counterpart to relative generosity towards those who were acknowledged to 'belong' to the parish.[94] But in other respects, the evidence produced here suggests that the opposite

[90] A. Walker, 'The Strategy of Inequality', in *Britain Divided: The Growth of Social Exclusion in the 1980s and 1990s*, ed. A. Walker and C. Walker (1997), 3.

[91] *Parliamentary Debates*, 1987–8 (122), 705.

[92] *Ibid.*, 837. Over the twentieth century as a whole, it has been the contributory components of the welfare system which have been most open to immigrants. Thus in 1908 aliens were not allowed non-contributory age pensions but three years later they were included within the scheme for national insurance.

[93] See n. 1

[94] Hindle, 'Power, Poor Relief and Social Relations in Holland Fen'.

of Walzer's claim may be closer to the truth. For example, improvements in the welfare entitlements of the Irish arose in the nineteenth century when there was a complete absence of state controls on their entry to the country. Similarly, immigration law was more relaxed between 1948 and 1966, when immigrants gained their greatest welfare entitlements, than in the subsequent decades, during which time entitlements have been questioned and removed. A historical perspective, therefore, suggests the novelty, not the inevitability, of recent developments. The current moment is distinguished by the combination of an unprecedentedly energetic attempt to regulate entry to the country, alongside its humiliating failure to do so. Asylum seekers, who entered Britain at the rate of 4,000 per year between 1985 and 1988, do so at the time of writing at a rate of 100,000 per year. The contemporary assault on the welfare entitlements of asylum seekers will be misunderstood if we regard it as a culmination of an historical trend or as an exemplification of a philosophical truth. In this case, history underscores the novelty, as well as the moral and political challenge, of the present.

Transactions of the RHS 13 (2003), pp. 105–29 © 2003 Royal Historical Society
DOI: 10.1017/S0080440103000057   Printed in the United Kingdom

JACK TAR AND THE GENTLEMAN OFFICER: THE ROLE OF UNIFORM IN SHAPING THE CLASS- AND GENDER-RELATED IDENTITIES OF BRITISH NAVAL PERSONNEL, 1930–1939*

The Alexander Prize Lecture

By Quintin Colville

READ 17 MAY 2002

ABSTRACT. Rather than examining the navy as a professional fighting organisation, this essay approaches the institution as one in which a range of masculine identities and lifestyles were constructed. From this perspective, its focus is on the material culture of naval uniform, and the function of uniform in defining and communicating particular understandings of class and masculinity. It demonstrates that the respective uniforms of various ranks associated their wearers with specific clusters of stereotyped socio-cultural qualities and characteristics, and indeed with substantially different incarnations of masculinity. The essay also relates the design of naval uniform to much wider class- and gender-related debates within British society during the period.

The overriding concern of most of the existing academic literature on the Royal Navy in the twentieth century has been to assess the organisation's performance of its stated duties: the protection of British interests and sovereignty in peace and war.[1] The doctoral research from which this essay is drawn insists, however, that the navy can also be approached as an institution within which a range of predominantly masculine identities and lifestyles were assembled, promoted and

* I would like to record my gratitude to my supervisors, John Styles and Professor Penny Sparke; to the Arts and Humanities Research Board and the Institute of Historical Research for funding my doctoral research; and to the many retired servicemen from the HMS Ganges Association whose generous assistance made this work possible.

[1] See, for instance: Correlli Barnett, *Engage the Enemy More Closely: The Royal Navy in the Second World War* (1991); Eric Grove, *Vanguard to Trident: British Naval Policy since World War II* (1987); Stephen Roskill, *Naval Policy between the Wars* (1976). Notable contributions to the social history of the navy in this period include: Anthony Carew, *The Lower Deck of the Royal Navy, 1900–1939: The Invergordon Mutiny in Perspective* (Manchester, 1981); Christopher McKee, *Sober Men and True: Sailor Lives in the Royal Navy, 1900–1945* (2002).

protected.[2] From this perspective, its aim has been to explore the role of material culture in shaping the social and cultural identities of male naval personnel, examining a range of primary sources from naval training establishments to warship interiors. The focus of this essay, though, is on one single aspect of that material culture: naval uniform. Its primary contention is that uniform was of crucial significance in defining the understandings of class and masculinity held by servicemen of all ranks. From this starting point, it demonstrates that the respective uniforms of the 'gentleman officer' and the 'Jack Tar' associated their wearers with specific clusters of stereotyped qualities and characteristics. In this respect, uniform did not simply convey a particular vision of class stratification within the navy, but presented these different class groupings as substantially different incarnations of masculinity. Nor does the essay view the design of naval uniform as representing solely intra-institutional concerns surrounding class and gender, but instead regards it as both responding and contributing to much wider debates within British society. Indeed, much of uniform's power to communicate socio-cultural information derived from its close linkage to civilian models of fashion and display. The first half of the essay will concentrate on naval officers, dealing in turn with uniform and class, and uniform and gender. The second half examines the navy's lower ranks in similar terms.[3] More generally, the essay hopes to bring the realm of material culture centre stage within an enquiry into the formation of historical identities. In so doing it will address a situation in which the rich visual and material dimensions of class and gender have often been omitted from historical analysis, or have been only fleetingly assessed.

Throughout this period class divisions were deeply embedded within the navy. Although a comprehensive survey has not yet been undertaken, the best available evidence indicates that, from the later Victorian era onwards, the great majority of naval officer cadets were the sons of civil servants, doctors, lawyers, clergy, bankers and businessmen, and belonged within a social fraction variously termed the 'upper middle class', or the 'public school middle class'.[4] To the parents of these boys a career as a naval officer promised some financial security, a clearly defined ladder of promotion and advancement and above all mem-

---

[2] Quintin Colville, 'The Role of Material Culture in Constructing Notions of Class among Male Royal Naval Personnel, 1930–1960' (Ph.D. thesis, Royal College of Art/Victoria & Albert Museum, forthcoming).

[3] For reasons of space, the navy's middling ranks – petty officers, chief petty officers and warrant officers – will not be touched upon here.

[4] See Ross McKibbin, *Classes and Cultures, England 1918–1951* (Oxford, 1998), 35; David Cannadine, *The Decline and Fall of the British Aristocracy* (1996), 273–5; McKee, *Sailor Lives*, 47.

bership of a solidly respectable professional occupation, conferring considerable social status. As a recruiting pamphlet from 1935 entitled *How to Become a Naval Officer* rather complacently (but not altogether fancifully) put it: 'Holding the King's commission ... [an officer] has the *entrée* to every club in the world.'[5] By contrast, the navy's lower ranks – termed ratings – came overwhelmingly from the various gradations of the British working class.[6] Only a very small percentage of this grouping was permitted to rise through the ranks to reach the status of commissioned officer, and from this tiny minority only a handful ascended to the navy's highest levels.[7]

The direct consequence of the upper-middle-class monopoly of officer rank was that the socio-cultural values and attributes of this grouping became indistinguishable from the desired qualities, professional and otherwise, of the naval officer. Though rarely subjected to any exhaustive definition at the time, these idealised upper-middle-class characteristics can perhaps best be summarised as duty, self-control, discipline, conformity and leadership ability, in combination with a specific set of social skills (including a knowledge of dress) loosely labelled 'good manners'. Taken together, these components formed the blueprint of what Harold Perkin has described as a specifically upper-middle-class reconfiguration of the concept of the gentleman.[8] Frequently referred to as 'character', the Admiralty, and to a considerable extent British society as a whole, commonly portrayed this re-formed gentlemanliness as somehow congenital in the offspring of a certain section of the population, and absent among the rest.[9] However, it was of course a learned identity; and in its desire to reproduce class divisions, the way of life the Admiralty held out to its thirteen-year-old officer cadets and their families tacitly extended a tuition in gentlemanly attributes; the way of life it held out to ratings tacitly withheld that. As a result, the navy's officer cadre became, to a large extent, a social and cultural caste.

Uniform played a crucial role in this process. First, its expense was used to exclude the sons of the poorest sections of society from contention. Uniform accounted for more than a quarter of the total cost to parents of a son's cadet training; and largely because of the need to purchase new

[5] Commander E.W. Bush, *How to Become a Naval Officer* (1935), 3–4.
[6] See McKee, *Sailor Lives*, 13–15.
[7] See *ibid.*, 47–8; Carew, *Lower Deck*, 47–53.
[8] Harold Perkin, *The Rise of Professional Society: England since 1880* (1990), 83–4, 121, 368.
[9] In the words of one admiral: 'The young, dashing Lieutenant of most ships wants to entertain and to have a good time; he wants to open the doors of hospitality. The Warrant Officer [a rating risen through the ranks to commissioned status]...will not want to do that. I am not blaming him for it; it is quite natural that he should not want to.' Public Record Office [hereafter PRO], ADM 116/5496, 'Committee on Warrant Rank', verbal evidence of Admiral Sir Geoffrey Layton, 25 July 1946.

items of uniform, an officer could not expect to be financially self-sufficient on his naval salary until about the age of twenty-one – nine years into his career.[10] This, however, was only the crudest aspect of uniform's ability to define social identity. Its main function was as an active component in the creation of the gentleman officer.

From the first day at Britannia Royal Naval College, Dartmouth, uniform set this process in motion (or rather took up where parents had left off) by enfolding an officer cadet in the basic vestimentary emblems of a gentleman: a suit, collar and tie. As the captain of the college put it in 1949:

> Every cadet from the earliest stage in his career must be taught the essence of good manners befitting his position as a naval officer, and the necessity for correct behaviour and dress...The suit remains a definite requirement, not only to preserve the standard of smartness of young officers...but also as an essential part of their upbringing.[11]

Writing of his departure from Dartmouth to join his first ship, Captain Augustus Agar wrote of the transformation those early years had wrought: 'We felt instinctively that we were at last "somebodies"...and certainly our parents thought so when looking at their sons in their smart uniforms.'[12]

Cadets such as Agar went on to join the fleet as midshipmen. After approximately two years, their sea-going education was considered complete, and they became commissioned officers with the rank of lieutenant. At this point their wardrobes swelled to include the range of uniforms that (with periodic alterations in rank markings) would accompany them through the rest of their careers. Although it is not possible here to explore them in detail, a progression of ever more formal costumes was matched to a series of occasions of increasing social and ceremonial significance. The most everyday rig was the double-breasted reefer jacket and trousers. Then came mess undress, mess dress, frock coat dress, frock coat dress with epaulettes, ball dress and finally full dress. This scheme was then repeated with white uniforms for wear in the tropics (see illustration 1).[13]

Though frequently presented as part of the navy's cherished corporate

---

[10] See anon., *How to Become a Naval Officer, and Life at the Royal Naval College Dartmouth* (1935), 12. According to this volume the average officer would require £900 in financial assistance from his entry as a cadet until reaching the rank of lieutenant.

[11] PRO, ADM 1/21404, 'Kit List for Cadets at the Royal Naval College, Dartmouth – Proposed Amendments', letter from Captain N. Vincent to the secretary of the Admiralty, 13 Dec. 1949.

[12] Captain Augustus Agar, *Footprints in the Sea* (1959), 19.

[13] See Admiralty, *Uniform Regulations for Officers* (1893, 1924, 1937).

Illustration 1. *These officers' uniforms, taken from the 1893 edition of the Admiralty's* Uniform Regulations, *remained largely unchanged until after the Second World War: reefer jacket and trousers (top left); mess dress (top right); ball dress (bottom left); and full dress (bottom right).*

traditions, this elaborate scheme of uniforms had in fact been codified and standardised during the 1880s and early 1890s.[14] In terms of their design the key point is that, beneath the gold braid and insignia, they were exact copies of the range of gentleman's suits that had become *de rigueur* for civilian members of the upper middle class at comparable social functions over the same period. By these visual means, the Admiralty silently but compellingly broadcast the class-related identity of the naval officer, and elided professional and socio-cultural spheres. Beyond this, the suit (in its many forms) was also the building block of a sartorial code to which men who occupied positions of power and prestige in British society during this period invariably conformed, whether members of parliament or consultant physicians. Grant McCracken has written that over time these sober, tailored garments of the male establishment came to signify that

> the wearer exercised special powers of self-control, that his emotional and intellectual life had special qualities of rigor and discipline, that this was a man who was fully in control of his faculties and fully in possession of himself...[with the implication that] here is a man who is entitled to dominion over others.[15]

In other words, the suit had come to communicate those key upper-middle-class qualities of leadership ability, self-discipline and restraint, and thereby operated as a passport to the public sphere of government and authority. In making gentlemanly dress the template for naval uniform, officers were therefore not only broadcasting their socio-cultural allegiances, but were also consolidating their grasp of positions of authority within the navy.

That the designs of naval uniforms had evolved in accordance with social usages as much as the utilitarian necessities of the profession is further demonstrated by the Second World War. In June 1939, with conflict anticipated, an Admiralty official wrote: 'To prevent a heavy liability for compensation for expensive articles of uniform lost through the sinking of ships...ceremonial dresses, which will not be needed while hostilities last, are to be landed at the first opportunity.'[16] Officers

---

[14] See Paymaster Lieutenant-Commander E.C. Talbot-Booth, *All the World's Fighting Fleets* (1937), 202: the author notes that 1891 was the year in which ball dress, mess dress and mess undress were introduced. This is corroborated in Commander R.N. Suter, 'Costume Past and Present', paper given at the Royal United Services Institute, 26 Jan. 1921 [hereafter Suter, 'Costume'], a copy of which can be found in PRO, ADM 116/2092, 'Uniform Regulations, Reprint Approved', 1920–4.

[15] Grant McCracken, 'The Voice of Gender in the World of Goods', in *The Material Culture of Gender: The Gender of Material Culture*, ed. K. Martinez and K.L. Ames (1997), 452.

[16] PRO, ADM 1/21255, 'Wartime Regulations Covering the Wearing of Officers' Ceremonial Dress', memo from the head of Naval Law, June 1939.

duly landed between eight and ten of their twelve uniforms, and the few costumes that were left also proved far from practical.[17] Nor is it entirely convincing to claim – as the Admiralty often tried to do – that officers' finery was demanded by their frequent peacetime duties entertaining distinguished foreigners at home and abroad.

Uniform also consolidated officers' socio-cultural status by insulating them from the possible social pitfalls of exercising individual choice in dress. Although it can be misleading to extrapolate trends in social behaviour from etiquette manuals, the avalanche of such volumes dealing with men's dress published in the first half of the century surely attests to the centrality of clothing in contemporary struggles for social status.[18] At the heart of them all is a preoccupation with defining the so-called 'correct' dress of the gentleman, along with advice on the avoidance of dress 'errors'. With uniform, the colour and absence of pattern of the cloth were givens, and uniform regulations prevented any hazardously individualised statements in cut or fit. 'Errors' were, therefore, avoided at an institutional level. The brass buttons with their anchor motifs, the cap badge and the rank markings further distanced uniform from connotations of individual expression. While in uniform, therefore, officers could side-step the minefield of good taste. And in this way uniform was made to seem not a personal claim to status but an official authentication of status.

This system could only succeed, however, if the officers' uniforms prescribed by the Admiralty did, indeed, broadcast a gentlemanly *persona*. In this connection it is not surprising to discover that the navy forged strong links with a number of tailoring establishments. In particular, the first half of this century saw the growth of a close working partnership between the navy and Gieves Ltd. The benefits to naval officers of this relationship were enormous. First, through generous credit, personal service and general ambience, Gieves added a few vital pieces to the jigsaw of gentlemanliness. In the words of Richard Walker:

[17] In May 1942, for example, an exasperated officer wrote: 'The reefer jacket and trousers have proved themselves under conditions of modern warfare to be unsuitable and unpractical...The smartness of naval uniform soon wears off when it is worn continuously...Gold braid deteriorates and to prevent their expensive suits wearing out too quickly, young officers are constrained to patch their reefers at the elbow, pockets and cuffs with leather.' PRO, ADM, 1/12726, 'Proposals that Naval and Fleet Air Arm Officers be Allowed to Wear Battle Dress', letter from the commanding officer, Naval Air Stations, Lee-on-Solent, to the secretary of the Admiralty, 28 May 1942.

[18] See, for instance, Edgar Woods and Diana Woods, *Things that Are not Done: An Outspoken Commentary on Popular Habits and a Guide to Correct Conduct* (1937); also, anon., *Clothes for the Occasion: A Work of Reference to Guide the Discerning in their Choice of Dress for Every Walk of Life* (1932).

Gieves sent congratulatory telegrams to the homes of successful candidates for the Royal Naval College, and followed up with a personal visit by a Gieves emissary in frock coat and silk hat, to discuss the boy's prospects – and clothing needs – with the proud parents.[19]

Gieves's premises, described by Walker as 'furnished with all the staid grandeur of a London club',[20] also both flattered and fostered an officer's sense of belonging to the establishment. Gieves, moreover, extended the social divisions of dress into the realm of shopping, by rarely if ever selling ratings' uniforms.[21] But above all, the firm made itself indispensable through its tailoring expertise. For example, whenever the Admiralty republished its hefty tome of officers' dress regulations, the draft went to Gieves for checking.[22] And when, in between editions, the regulations began to lag behind civilian fashions, Gieves could be relied upon to ensure that officers, while perhaps old-fashioned in their dress, could seldom be described as actually unfashionable. In other words, shifts in the wider sartorial definition of gentlemanliness were monitored by Gieves and replicated in uniform. Officers, of course, were deeply implicated in this process themselves. In 1928, in reply to an Admiralty enquiry regarding the design of reefer jackets, Gieves wrote back: 'Few officers, if any, today would accept a strictly regulation coat.'[23] A poem from a 1940 cadet magazine both illustrates and parodies the centrality that Gieves came to assume within the experience of being an officer:

Some talk of Alexander,
And some of Dudley Pound,
Of Cunningham and Harwood,
And other names renowned.
But the man who runs the navy,
And keeps the fleet afloat,
Is Gieve of Piccadilly,
And Bond Street, too, please note.[24]

---

[19] Richard Walker, *Savile Row: An Illustrated History* (1989), 91–2.

[20] *Ibid.*, 102.

[21] This practice also persisted long after the Second World War. As one retired rating (born 1958, questionnaire response received 31 Jan. 2000) commented: 'Officers used Gieves...Ratings were not encouraged to shop outside of their station. Nothing official on this was ever said, it was just understood.'

[22] See PRO, ADM 1/8974, 'Officers' Uniform – Proposals of Captain, H.M.S. Excellent'; and PRO, ADM 116/2092, 'Uniform Regulations, Reprint Approved'. These dockets contain a run of correspondence between the Admiralty and Gieves Ltd clarifying the information to appear in the 1924 edition of the Admiralty's *Uniform Regulations for Officers*.

[23] PRO, ADM 1/8974, letter from Gieves Ltd to Richmond Walton, Naval Law Department, 18 May 1928.

[24] Quoted in Robert Hughes, *In Perilous Seas* (Tunbridge Wells, 1990), 148.

However, the ultimate contribution of officers' uniform to the gentlemanly status of its wearers lay in the fact that only officers could own it. In civilian society, anyone with money could purchase gentlemanly attire, and could usually buy access to the right places to display it. Moreover, by the 1930s the fifty-five shilling lounge suits and seventy-five shilling dinner suits offered by multiple tailors such as Burton's were well within the budgets of many working-class consumers. Within the navy, though, the unattainable nature of officers' trappings subtly suggested to ratings that there was indeed something intrinsic and unlearnable about the qualities of the gentleman officer. The retention into the 1930s of an outmoded item such as the frock coat also suggests a desire on the part of the Admiralty to maintain the crisp Edwardian visual delineation of class and status that had by then begun to blur in civilian life.[25]

There was also one further, and significant, aspect to the role of officers' uniform in realising the class divisions of naval hierarchy. Whether ashore or afloat, every officer could invariably call on the services of a rating to act as a valet. David Phillipson recalled that on a typical evening, after running his lieutenant's bath he

> laid out his evening dress…mess jacket and trousers freshly brushed and draped on the bunk; boiled shirt on top, dress-studs inserted, wing-collar and black tie; evening shoes dusted and placed side-by-side on the deck with silk socks tucked in; cummerbund ready to hand.[26]

Social position was consequently expressed not only in the form of clothing but in the relationship to clothing.

The cultural currency of the navy, and its popular representation as a timeless and quintessentially British institution, encouraged officers (and also ratings) to portray the social divisions of their organisation as natural and unarguable. As Captain Bernard Acworth wrote in 1935: 'The navy is, when all is said and done, a very perfect mirror of the country which it so loyally and devotedly serves.'[27] However, the socio-cultural stratification of the navy represented a system of social arrangement, not the expression of organic social realities. Through uniform the nexus of values that underwrote the status of the gentleman officer could be both inculcated in the individual and transmitted to the wider community. And through uniform every single naval officer could be made a propagandising instrument for the realisation of their corporate desire for socio-cultural status.

*

[25] See Christopher Breward, 'Manliness and the Pleasures of Consumption: Masculinities, Fashion and London Life, 1860–1914' (Ph.D. thesis, Royal College of Art/Victoria & Albert Museum, 1998), 50.

[26] David Phillipson, *Band of Brothers* (Stroud, 1996), 128.

[27] Captain Bernard Acworth, *The Restoration of England's Sea Power* (1935), 285.

The idealised persona of the male officer promoted so successfully through uniform was not, however, delineated solely in contradistinction to men from different socio-cultural backgrounds. It was also defined against contemporary constructions of femininity (and also of homosexuality). Although the Admiralty was obliged to rely on female recruits for the performance of many essential functions during both World Wars, they were organised as a separate body, the WRNS,[28] and their numbers were rapidly reduced when hostilities ceased. Moreover, at all times, combat and military command remained male preserves. In this way, the navy reflected and perpetuated the notion that leadership, worldly responsibility and military affairs were the natural remit of men.

Clothing played a crucial role in substantiating these assumptions. However, in order to illuminate its significance it is necessary to look briefly beyond the adult officer to the realm of contemporary childhood. After all, as Nigel Edley and Margaret Wetherell have written, most people 'become expert in gender roles long before they are in a position to reflect upon the process'.[29] To begin with, throughout this period middle- and upper-class parents dressed their offspring in gender-specific costumes from their earliest years. More importantly still, the different clothing of boys and girls was made to represent and entrench the power differential between men and women. For instance, the supposed girlish infatuation with fashion was conceptually linked with the trope of female frivolity, decorativeness and irrationality. At the same time, boys' clothes, though at least as prone to fashion change, were purged of the feminine connotations of fashion through their association with stereotypically masculine activities such as sport, scouting and military service. In the words of Ethyle Campbell, a brilliant but little known fashion writer from the 1930s:

The perennial jibe of the small boy...is that the small girl is always wanting to dress up, disregarding completely the fact that the urge to dress up is infinitely stronger in him. But when the small boy dresses up it is called by another name...The sporting of his football colours, and his cricket blazer isn't dressing up. These are in the sacred name of sport. The boy scout's uniform isn't dressing up. It isn't dressing up when he swaggers about in his Territorial Sam Browne, the shining of which and his boots required several hours of earnest application. No! That is patriotism, which is something else again.[30]

---

[28] The Women's Royal Naval Service, frequently termed the 'Wrens'.
[29] Nigel Edley and Margaret Wetherell, *Men in Perspective: Practice, Power and Identity* (1995), 74.
[30] Ethyle Campbell, *Can I Help You, Sir?* (1939), 4.

Rather than frivolity and vanity, therefore, the values communicated by boys' clothing were those same upper-middle-class masculine qualities of patriotism, leadership ability and self-discipline. The notion that all normal boys from this social fraction shared this identity was further entrenched by the insistence of preparatory and public schools (powerful seminaries of upper-middle-class values in so many ways) that their pupils should wear uniform. Statements of gender-related non-conformity, or at least their visual expression, were thereby made extremely difficult. In part through clothing, therefore, this conglomeration of socio-cultural characteristics was made to appear a male birthright. In the process, the authority of the male establishment could be endlessly re-justified, while at the same time the claims of women could be endlessly devalued, as *their* clothing communicated the supposition that they inherently lacked those same characteristics.

A consideration of youth and schooling is all the more relevant here given that most naval officers, as we have seen, began their careers as thirteen-year-old cadets. The college in which they were trained also shared the public schools' emphasis on strict adherence to uniform.[31] The following passage from the 1934 *Dartmouth General Order Book* could, for instance, have been taken directly from the regulations of Rugby, Harrow or Marlborough: 'The clothing of cadets must be of the uniform pattern and no other will be allowed. Should a cadet bring clothing which is not uniform it will be returned to his parent or guardian.'[32] Parades and daily inspections made a boy's conformity to the structures of uniform and kit a still clearer index of his conformity both to the institution as a whole, and to its image of the masculine ideal.[33] Failures to meet standards of 'smartness' were viewed as evidence of incomplete identification with the organisation, and reprobates were forced into line through penalties that often involved corporal punishment.[34] Inevitably, in this environment, cadets rooted out or suppressed aspects of their personalities that did not accord with the gendered identity represented by their uniforms. In the words of one officer: 'The Service does its training young, on the principle of flog a dog while it's a puppy. And if you get through that stage – well, you're

---

[31] See Colville, 'Material Culture'. Britannia Royal Naval College, Dartmouth, was in many ways designed to replicate public school practice.

[32] Britannia Royal Naval College archive, *General Order Book* (1934), ch. 3, para. 5.

[33] As one officer remembered: 'Socks, with toes facing east, had to be laid across folded vests; combs had to be placed on upturned hair-brushes, in a north and south direction; and tooth-brushes, with bristles facing west, had to be displayed on top of tooth mugs.' Sam Lombard-Hobson, *A Sailor's War* (1983), 15.

[34] One cadet, for example, was beaten for having his toothbrush 'pointing east instead of west' on top of his tooth mug. Commander Henry de Chair, *Let Go Aft: The Indiscretions of a Salt Horse Commander* (Tunbridge Wells, 1993), 4.

probably shaped to the mould like the Chinese women's feet, and you forget.'[35]

For naval officers the process of defining masculinity as the absence of femininity and effeminacy, thus begun during childhood, continued throughout their careers in relation to dress. Even the partial and mediated integration of uniformed women into the institution consequently proved profoundly troubling to them. Given the Admiralty's authority in this area, it is not surprising that WRNS uniforms – though conceding an air of professionalism – remained highly feminised.[36] Senior officers also frequently encouraged servicewomen to appear at mess dinners and other military functions in their civilian clothes – occasions where men invariably wore uniform.[37] The commander-in-chief of the Mediterranean Fleet wrote approvingly in 1944 that the women under his command showed 'a feminine delight in wearing a dress of different colour and material on gala occasions', adding that it 'confirms one's hopes that service life has not robbed the women of Britain of their natural feminine instincts'.[38] Any disruption of the gendered construction of uniform, and in particular female appropriation of military dress, could therefore pose a direct threat to male authority. In fact, contact of whatever kind between officers and women was frequently seen as corrosive of maleness. For example, one officer wrote that after shore leave his captain would drive the ship especially hard, 'To get the canker out of the system, planted there by over-caring mothers and too-demanding wives.'[39]

However, the fixing of an ideological template to human identity can only ever be partially successful. Paradoxically, given its use in concretising the mutual exclusiveness of male and female roles, naval material culture also gives an excellent demonstration of Michael Kimmel's contention that: 'The stricter the separation of spheres, the more deeply each gender yearns to appropriate the material and

---

[35] Charles Morgan, *The Gunroom* (1919), 5.

[36] The Admiralty's discussions in 1950 regarding the design of a new evening dress for female officers are a case in point. The Commodore of the Royal Naval Barracks, Portsmouth, described the blouse and long skirt that were chosen as 'essentially feminine, while remaining unmistakably uniform...It successfully avoids the pitfall...of arraying young ladies in quasi-masculine attire.' PRO, ADM 1/26660, 'Evening Uniform Dress for WRNS Officers', letter to the commander-in-chief, Portsmouth, 25 Nov. 1950.

[37] As one 'Wren' wrote from Malta in 1944: 'All the naval officers...are most insistent that one wears evening dress...It has been decided that the Wrens must wear plain clothes in officers' messes and at the Union Club.' PRO, ADM 1/15101, 'Wearing of Uniform and Plain Clothes by Naval Personnel', letter to the director of the WRNS, 18 Mar. 1944.

[38] *Ibid.*, letter from the commander-in-chief, Mediterranean, to the Admiralty, 24 Sept. 1944.

[39] Lombard-Hobson, *War*, 56.

cultural artefacts of the other.'[40] For instance, with women themselves excluded from shipboard life, naval personnel went to extraordinary lengths conceptually to feminise their environments. Describing the rescue of a group of survivors from a merchant ship torpedoed during the Second World War, Sam Lombard Hobson noted how:

> When the seamen came to remove the oily mess left on deck ... it was noticed that there was a clearly defined outline of ... [a] girl's shoulders and buttocks, imprinted in oil on the grey paint where she had leaned against the superstructure. They chose to leave this as it was; and in a short while, the impression hardened. The ship's joiner was commissioned to cut a frame with a glass front, and secure it ... over the picture in oil...[it] remained for the rest of the ship's life.[41]

Clothing played a particularly important role in mediating this largely subconscious longing for feminine presence and feminised expressiveness. For instance, in the privacy of their cabins, some officers indulged in lemon, pea-green or violet pyjamas with matching bed-sheets.[42] On board the Royal Yacht Britannia, certain days were reserved for wearing what was called 'Bula rig' – which involved officers vying with each other for possession of the brightest and loudest shirts; and one admiral apparently took advantage of the greater informality of life at sea to wear a feather boa while on the bridge.[43] Frequent shipboard theatricals also allowed men to cross-dress within (to para-phrase Angus McLaren's work) a controlled and legitimated context.[44]

Officers' uniform itself, and in particular their full-dress uniform, represents these ambivalences, and the uneasy compromises that were reached. The use of colour, the elaborate embroidery, the rich silks, satins and velvets, the ribbons and sashes and the glittering orders, decorations and medals all spoke of an urge to express, and had to be exhaustively ideologically camouflaged to prevent them blurring gender boundaries or rupturing the paradigm of male sartorial restraint. By and large this was achieved by taking much of the choice in the appearance of costumes out of the hands of individuals, and reserving it for Admiralty decision. In this way an officer's painstaking attention to his dress could be placed within the unproblematic envelope of

---

[40] Michael Kimmel, 'The Power of Gender and the Gender of Power', in *Gender*, ed. Martinez and Ames, 4.

[41] Lombard-Hobson, *War*, 68–9.

[42] See Vice-Admiral Sir John Hayes, *Face The Music: A Sailor's Story* (Edinburgh, 1991), 41.

[43] *Ibid.*, 14.

[44] Angus McLaren, *The Trials of Masculinity: Policing Sexual Boundaries, 1870–1930* (1997), 214. Here it is worth mentioning that in his 1952 volume *Sexual Anomalies and Perversions*, Magnus Hirschfeld found that transvestitism was over-represented in the ranks of the military. Cited in *ibid.*, 220.

obedience to authority. In the case of medal ribbons, for example, Admiralty officials devised an exact order of precedence in which they were to be worn, and officers had no latitude as to how or where they were attached.[45] A further line of defence was the insistence that specific occasions demanded specific costumes, and that officers were duty bound to comply with these conventions whatever their personal feelings.[46] These conventions had, however, been created in the late nineteenth and early twentieth centuries precisely by male institutions such as the navy, in order to authorise masculine display.

Therefore, within the policed and protected boundaries of the institution, clothing did allow a certain, if highly orchestrated, expressiveness. However, the possession of even the highest honour or most distinguished decoration ironically still drew an officer ever closer to the ultimately impersonal ideal of the military hero. An attempt to use clothing to achieve a more individualised masculinity can be detected in officers' invariable preference for made-to-measure rather than ready-made uniform. In the words of the head cutter of a West End tailoring firm in the 1930s:

> Men like to believe that they are in some way unique, and that there is something which sets them apart from other men. We have to foster that belief, which I can assure you is not easy since the general style of men's clothes is so uniform.[47]

It was also tacitly accepted that officers might ask for minor modifications in, say, the cut of the lapels or the spacing of a jacket's buttons. It is typical of the multi-faceted nature of material culture that uniform could, in this way, sustain a dream of individuality while otherwise working to erase it.

Within the organisation, uniform was consequently used to articulate, propagate and defend the hegemony of a specific male identity. However, the immense amount of time and energy devoted by the Admiralty to describing and enforcing this identity also reveals its extraordinary fragility. The military masculinity that was supposedly biologically innate could, in fact, be compromised by a colourful cuff link, or a polka-dot handkerchief protruding from a uniform pocket.

However, the meanings represented by naval uniform could only achieve full expression, and can only be comprehensively understood,

---

[45] See, for instance, PRO, ADM 1/21309, 'Officers − Introduction of Interim Dress and the Wearing of Orders, Decorations and Medals', 1948–9.

[46] The *Navy List*, for example, printed elaborate tables detailing particular events and the versions of uniform required to attend them.

[47] Campbell, *Help*, 228.

in the relationship between officers' uniforms and those of ratings. In an attempt to bring those meanings into sharper focus, the remainder of the essay will concentrate on the role of uniform in moulding the identities of naval ratings.

In turning to the class-related implications of ratings' dress, we should avoid characterising ratings as simply the passive victims of an oppressive upper-middle-class regime. Ratings, as much as officers, frequently displayed great attachment to the navy's ordered, secure and conservative socio-cultural world; and it was only in the later 1940s and 1950s that the Admiralty began to experience difficulties in recruiting and retaining lower deck personnel. Ratings' generic cultural persona – the Jack Tar or matelot – was consequently not just imposed from above; it was also inhabited and exploited by working-class men as a source of social kudos and esteem. At the same time, the consensual, deferential and patriotic identity that it involved (though representative of a great swathe of British working-class opinion)[48] could also be employed by officers to suppress any disruptively independent working-class consciousness. Ratings' uniform illustrates both sides of the coin. Ratings used it to stake a claim in the cultural landscape. The Admiralty used it as an instrument of control, subordination and even de-humanisation.

The most culturally redolent and institutionally significant of the various uniforms worn by ratings was 'square rig' (see illustration 2). Examining first what ratings stood to gain from uniform, it is clear that this costume – and with it the image of the Jack Tar – offered an array of positive associations. To begin with it broadcast job security and a wage for life – considerable assets in the precarious economic climate of the thirties. But beyond this, the *persona* of the Jack Tar, and in particular its suggestion of foreign travel, were glamorous; and to many boys seemed to offer far more than the dull monotony of factory work. As one rating commented: 'You were seen as being someone who had seen a bit of the world...[which] before foreign holidays were enjoyed by everyone meant you were also a character to be envied.'[49] Ratings who had served in the Far East exploited this by having red Chinese dragons sewed to the underside of their jumper cuffs, which they then turned back when ashore on leave. Moreover, the uniform also reflected the cultural status of the navy, and its global profile as a cornerstone of imperial power, and associated these qualities with the wearer.[50]

The fact that ratings modified their square rig uniforms to bring

[48] See, for instance, Robert McKenzie and Allan Silver, *Angels in Marble: Working-Class Conservatives in Urban England* (1968).

[49] Retired rating, born 1946, questionnaire response received 6 Feb. 2000.

[50] In the words of another retired rating (born 1950, questionnaire response received 12 Jan. 2000): 'Square rig...provided a superb level of identity and [the sense of] "belonging" to an elite class of people, namely the Royal Navy.'

Illustration 2.   Four examples of 'square rig' uniform: as worn by ratings c. 1930 (top left); an R.N.V.R. recruitment poster from the early 1950s; the future Lord Louis Mountbatten photographed in 1905 with his father and elder brother (bottom left); a rating in square rig from the turn of the century (bottom right).

them closer to the ideal of the Jack Tar, also testifies to their willing and eager engagement with the image.[51] Autobiographies and oral testimonies reveal that many young seamen bleached their blue jean collars to a lighter shade, to signify that they were old hands.[52] Others wore wider than regulation bell-bottoms, and some sewed coins into the turn-ups of their bell-bottoms to accentuate their swing.[53] It seems likely, therefore, that the uniformed naval rating often enjoyed considerable regard within working-class communities. As another rating remembered: 'You got away with murder in a naval uniform...if Jack went and did something and then a civvy went and did the same thing, the civvy would get hammered, but they'd say "He's a matelot, Jack ashore." '[54]

At the same time, however, ratings' alterations to their uniform also indicate a more troubled and ambivalent relationship with the square rig. For instance, from the end of the First World War, ratings were paid a kit upkeep allowance that allowed them to replace worn items of uniform with new ones at regular intervals. Admiralty records show that in 1930 high-ranking officers became concerned that only a tiny fraction of this allowance was being spent on the navy's own stocks of ready-made square rig uniform.[55] In the previous financial year, for example, ratings had bought 353,000 pairs of socks, 219,000 towels and 133,000 tooth-brushes from naval stores, but only 231 square rig jumpers.[56] The explanation was that ratings had turned to private outfitters for their uniform requirements.[57]

---

[51] A questionnaire circulated by the author among members of the HMS Ganges Association in Jan. 2000, and responded to by 135 retired ratings (who had joined the navy between 1935 and 1960), revealed that 106 had modified their uniform to enhance its smartness. The alterations mentioned most frequently included: giving the cap a 'bow wave' by flattening its sides and pushing up the centre front and back; wearing longer tapes; wearing thinner lanyards; altering the cap tally bow, and wearing it over the eye rather than the ear; wearing the cap on the back of the head; making alterations to the silk; and cutting the collar so that it entered the jumper at a sharper angle. See also John Douglas, *H.M.S. Ganges, Tales of the Trogs* (Penmarth, 1995), 47–8.

[52] See Godfrey Winn, *Home from the Sea* (1944), 40–1.

[53] One retired rating (born 1938, questionnaire response received 12 Jan. 2000) commented that he 'added ball bearings within the bottom seam to help make the swing of the walk more emphasised (rough seas = tough sailor = image)'.

[54] Retired rating, born 1937, oral testimony, 20 Sept. 2000.

[55] See PRO, ADM 116/2092, *Uniform Regulations, Reprint Approved*. In a memo of 25 Aug. 1930, the director of victualling gave a breakdown of the kit upkeep allowance and how it was spent. Of the £134,000 specifically earmarked for ratings to spend on replacement square rig jumpers and trousers, only £1,400 had been used to purchase ready-made jumpers and trousers from service sources.

[56] Statistics taken from PRO, ADM 116/2824, 'Statement Shewing [sic] the Quantities of the Principal Items of Clothing, &c., Issued on Repayment During the Year Ending 31 March, 1930'.

[57] See PRO, ADM 116/2092, *Uniform Regulations*: in a memo of 3 Sept. 1930, an

To understand why, it is necessary to look to the wider context of working-class dress in the inter-war period. In general terms, the use of clothing to achieve and consolidate status was far from just a middle-class phenomenon. As briefly touched upon, the rapid expansion of multiple tailors such as Burton's represented, above all, the engagement of the working classes in this process, facilitated both by cheaper goods, and the rising wages of those in work. Ratings did not want to be left behind. And just as Gieves had profited from its association with naval officers, companies such as Greenburgh's, Cooper's and Bernard's of Harwich expanded their operations during the twenties and thirties by catering for and interpreting ratings' desires for socio-cultural status. As was the case with officers, this included creating a flattering environment in which to shop. The bleak, barrack-room atmosphere of the naval clothing store could not compete.

The great majority of suits sold by the multiple tailors were made-to-measure, and this, too, was copied by ratings' outfitters. A ready-made, square-rig uniform quickly became the mark of a raw recruit and through made-to-measure uniform, ratings moved as close as they could to the lounge suit designs of the civilian 'fifty shilling' tailors. This is particularly clear in the small but significant stylistic changes that appeared in square rig during these years. The deepening of the jumper's 'V' neck, its tailored fit at the waist and its figure-hugging shape around the hips, all paralleled contemporary fashions in suit jackets, and occurred without explicit Admiralty authorisation.

However, in defining the meanings of ratings' uniform, officers' institutionalised powers could exert considerable influence. Revealingly, the essentials of the design were only finally settled and standardised by the Admiralty in 1891 – around the same time that officers were reformulating their own dress to maximise its class-related associations.[58] It is in this context that we should view the square rig's crucial lack of jacket, collar or tie. At the same time, in a complex process whereby late Victorian society seized on the navy as the lynchpin in Britain's triumphal progress to global dominance, the uniform was mythologised, projected back in history and associated with the glories of the Nelsonian era. So, too, was the rating. For example, an unvarying theme in the

Admiralty official noted that 'the outfitting of the naval rating after he has passed the recruit stage, i.e. when he is in a position to choose for himself, is to a great extent in the hands of the private outfitter as regards uniform suits'.

[58] A standardised uniform was first introduced for ratings in 1857, consisting of a blue cloth jacket, blue cloth trousers, duck frock, duck trousers, serge frock, pea jacket, black and white hats and badges (as agreed upon in Suter, 'Costume'; Petty Officer Writer Robert Burgess and Leading Writer Roland Blackburn, *We Joined the Navy: Traditions, Customs and Nomenclature of the Royal Navy* (1943), 58; Talbot-Booth, *Fighting Fleets*, 186). According to Burgess and Blackburn, however, the blue cloth jacket was dropped in 1891.

vast literature on the Royal Navy from this period was the notion that the modern-day rating was somehow the same in spirit as his Nelsonian predecessor.[59] The invariably middle-class authors of these works thereby blotted out the transformations that had occurred in working-class lives – the improved standards of living, the growth of unionised labour and the rise of socialist politics – in favour of a potentially manipulative stereotype. The Admiralty did all it could to fuel this popular ideology, along with the docile, unthreatening working-class identity it propagandised.[60]

Consequently, ratings were never fully in possession of their collective cultural persona, the Jack Tar. The identity it represented had, to a considerable extent, been delineated to keep working-class men in their place, and served also to accentuate the socio-cultural gulf between them and their upper-middle-class officer superiors. The nature of the class-related dynamic involved here is encapsulated in that first visit of the Gieves's emissary to the home of a future officer cadet. What it represented was the parents' and the Admiralty's shared investment in gentlemanliness and its transmission through clothing. By contrast, the Admiralty had only limited interest in the socio-cultural aspirations of ratings' families. For instance, when a boy stepped through the gates of one of the navy's ratings' training establishments during the 1930s, 1940s or 1950s, he was probably wearing a shirt and tie, a 'V' neck jumper, a sports jacket, a pair of flannel trousers and black or brown Oxford-style shoes.[61] Once inside, however, one of the first things to happen to him was that those clothes – along with the personal and familial status claims they represented – were boxed up and posted back to his home.[62] He was then presented with a full set of ratings' uniform and kit and was made to spend much of the next two weeks sewing or stamping his name on to all seventy-four items[63] – symbolising the sublimation of his personal identity within the stereotyped cultural identity of the Jack Tar.

During the year of training, the Admiralty also used every device at its disposal to indoctrinate boys in the belief that deviations from the

[59] See, among many others, Reverend James Baikie, *Peeps at the Royal Navy* (1913), 88: 'Each age has brought its own changes. Only one thing has remained the same through all the centuries – the cool, steady courage of the men who manned the ships and fought the battles for the sake of the land they loved. That, we are sure, remains as unquestionable today as it was when Nelson led his ships into action at Trafalgar, or when Grenville in the little "Revenge" defied the whole fleet of Spain.'

[60] See Colville, 'Material Culture'.

[61] As can be seen in a short film entitled 'Sam Pepys Joins the Navy', produced during the Second World War by the National Savings Committee and the Admiralty, a copy of which is held by the Imperial War Museum.

[62] As recorded in Phillipson, *Brothers*, 60.

[63] Douglas, *Trogs*, 93.

prescribed way of wearing the uniform were indications of a flawed personality. Pride in the self, and pride in the navy and its traditions, were treated as interchangeable concepts.[64] And as with officer cadets, conformity to the rigmaroles of kit musters and parades was made to operate as a metaphor for conformity to the institution as a whole. For officers, however, conformity was a prelude to power. For ratings, the process was a theatrical legitimation of their powerlessness. The smallest defects in the presentation of uniform or kit (an off-centre cap tally, a less than pristine lanyard, a smudge of blanco on a belt buckle) were made punishable offences, which often meant beatings.[65] Even in the 1950s and 1960s, boys deemed particularly untidy sometimes had their entire kit thrown in a dustbin and covered with water, or even buried in the ground with the instruction that every item had to be washed, dried and ironed by the next morning. The most recalcitrant cases were occasionally stripped naked, thrown out into the open and scrubbed down with yard brooms and fire hoses.[66] The training was also used to inure boys to a menial relationship with their clothing, far removed from the world of officers and their valets.

Nor did the use of square rig as an instrument of control end with training. For instance, from the end of the First World War to the start of the Second there is much evidence to suggest that while ratings were happy with the uniform as a ceremonial and shore-going rig, they found it highly impractical as a working dress.[67] But because of its profound importance to the socio-cultural configuration of the navy, the Admiralty was extremely reluctant to make any changes; and because officers by definition monopolised positions of authority in the organisation, they were able to stave off reform year after year. The way the Admiralty operated is illustrated by the records of a committee that was set up in 1931 to explore the issue of square rig. Even before it had begun to take evidence, the committee members – who were all officers – had agreed that 'no change in the general design of uniform is contemplated'. Forty-five ratings were then interviewed, each of whom had previously been instructed by an officer to avoid 'contentious matter from the point of view of discipline', an injunction interpreted

[64] As the trainees' handbook put it: 'Each individual must be dressed smartly so that he is a credit both to himself and to the Service. Slovenliness in dress is a sure reflection of slackness in character and is therefore discouraged.' *Admiralty Manual of Seamanship* (1950), 29.

[65] See Douglas, *Trogs*, 147–86.

[66] See Phillipson, *Brothers*, 23–4.

[67] The contents of PRO, ADM 1/15725, 'Admiralty Uniform and Clothing Committee Recommendation No. 4 – Working Dress for Ratings', reveal that considerable discontent over the square rig as a working dress had existed among ratings from at least the end of the First World War, a particular bugbear being the tropical white version.

as ruling out any calls for substantial alterations to square rig design.[68] At the end of the proceedings, the committee complacently reported back to the Admiralty that 'no wish for any radical change in uniform was expressed'.[69]

Beyond this, ratings in square rig were consciously employed by the Admiralty to maintain the cultural visibility of the Jack Tar, with the aim of influencing future generations of boys. A memo from the Director of Naval Recruiting written in 1958 reads: 'From the recruiting angle, the more that naval uniform can be seen ashore, the more it helps to keep the navy in the public eye and the better it is for recruiting.'[70] Partly with this in mind, ratings' lockers on board warships, unlike officers' relatively spacious wardrobes, were designed so that they could not hold civilian clothes as well as uniform.[71] Most ratings managed to secrete a few items of casual dress, but they were not allowed to wear them when either leaving or returning to the ship. In this and other ways, ratings were frequently treated as objects – moved, positioned and displayed in accordance with agendas defined and controlled by officers.

Nonetheless, although the lifestyle of ratings was, in the words of A.H. Jones, frequently 'demeaning and wretched',[72] this seems only to have strengthened ratings' attachment to the persona of Jolly Jack Tar. David Phillipson recalled that after a morning spent laboriously scrubbing the deck of the officers' wardroom he:

> Wondered, not for the first time, if my naval career was to be all skivvy-like servitude. I felt cheated – none of the Navy's recruiting posters had shown Jack on his knees, wringing out a grubby deck-swab. He was shown astride a 14-inch gun barrel, wearing snow-white tropical ducks and a cheery grin...against a background of swaying palms.[73]

But rather than rejecting the image, he and so many others seem to have internalised it still more comprehensively. That they did so is

[68] See PRO, ADM 116/2092, AFO 262/31, 'Committee on Uniform – Visit to Devonport', 17 Feb. 1931.
[69] PRO, ADM 116/2092, 'Report on Uniform of Petty Officers, Men and Boys', 17 Apr. 1931.
[70] PRO, ADM 1/27011, 'Privilege of Wearing Plain Clothes when Proceeding on or Returning from Leave from H.M. Ships – Extension to Leading Rates and Below', memo from the director of recruiting, 10 Mar. 1958.
[71] See *ibid.*, memo from the Director of Welfare and Service Conditions, 4 Mar. 1958: 'Although additional stowage space is not provided, it is evident that nearly all ratings contrive to keep some plain clothes on board.'
[72] Albert Jones, *No Easy Choices: A Personal Account of Life on the Carrier H.M.S. Illustrious, 1940–1943* (Worcester, 1994), 26.
[73] Phillipson, *Brothers*, 127.

hardly surprising. Among the general public during this period, the square rig represented a charismatic and attractive (though not necessarily respectable) working-class identity. And, within the navy itself, the positive and picturesque connotations of the uniform could soften the contours of an often harsh and thankless profession.

Focusing once again on uniform and gender, it is clear that there was considerable common ground between officers' and ratings' constructions of masculinity and their representations in clothing. The pan-cultural resonance of military masculinity during this period – illustrated in a range of media from juvenile literature, to cigarette cards, packaging designs, theatre and film[74] – meant that the uniformed male had become an exemplar for all classes. Equally, there is no evidence to suggest that the poorer sections of British society were any less keen than the middle classes to define masculinity as the absence of femininity and effeminacy. The stereotypical manliness of military masculinity was consequently just as appealing to them. Nonetheless, there are a number of clues to suggest that, once within the institution of the navy, the gender of officers and ratings was, in fact, constructed very differently. In this respect, too, clothing was of key importance.

Here we must first return to the Admiralty's careful selection of the gentleman's suit – with its connotations of socio-cultural and professional authority, self-discipline and responsibility – as the model for officers' uniform. By contrast, square rig was designed along quite separate lines. The unmistakable implication of this division (and one inevitably internalised by ratings themselves) was that ratings intrinsically lacked those same gentlemanly qualities. Through the medium of clothing, therefore, the Admiralty propagandised the view that the categories of officer and rating represented not merely different social classes, but in fact qualitatively different incarnations of masculinity with differing abilities.

The Admiralty also used a number of other vestimentary devices to entrench this notion of the differentiated masculinity of officers and men. It has already been mentioned that this period frequently witnessed the operation of a binary system that equated masculinity with empowerment and femininity with dis-empowerment; and that, within this context, officers had eradicated or disguised expressions in their dress that might connote femininity. From the upper-middle-class perspective of officers, however, the meanings broadcast by ratings' uniforms were altogether more ambiguous. For instance, the neckline of the square rig, along with its flapping tapes, silks and ribbons could

---

[74] See John MacKenzie, *Propaganda and Empire: The Manipulation of British Public Opinion, 1880–1960* (Manchester, 1985).

all be seen as highly feminised (and were indeed incorporated into female fashions). Nor did the uniform as a whole do anything to counter this impression of unorthodox expressiveness – its tight fit at the hips and arms and the flaring bell-bottoms gave a very different profile from the officer's reefer jacket and trousers.[75]

To middle-class observers (though of course not necessarily to ratings themselves) square rig thus visually defined ratings as a dilution of the notionally 'pure' masculinity of officers. In the process, ratings were associated with feminised qualities such as a love of domesticity, sentimentality, emotional spontaneity and immaturity; connotations further borne out by the requirement of ratings to wash and repair their own clothes. It is no coincidence, therefore, that whereas officers' attentiveness to their dress was portrayed as commendable obedience to the customs of the institution, ratings' concern with their appearance was frequently characterised as fashion-consciousness or a love of personal adornment.

There was one further dimension to officers' apparent willingness to inflect ratings with connotations of an 'inferior' masculinity. As a consequence of the cultural linkage drawn between femininity and the use of dress as a mode of sexual attraction, officers appear to have been reluctant to use dress for any overt expression of sexual identity. In fact, as Angus McLaren has written in connection with male exhibitionism, a dominant discourse of the period held that: 'The parading of one's sexuality was an infantile preoccupation embraced by women, children and perverts, but spurned by mature males.'[76]

At the same time, however, the Admiralty continued to feed the mythology of the bawdy, womanising rating. This is not to say that ratings did not willingly contribute to the persona. Oral testimonies, for instance, suggest that most were convinced of the sexual attractiveness of their uniform to women, and were pleased with the roguish quality it conferred. As one retired rating put it: 'I liked the uniform very much, but it was a bit impractical when you needed to dress quickly, especially at such times as rapidly exiting via the bedroom window when the husband came home unexpectedly.'[77] Nonetheless, from the middle-class perspective of officers, the sexualised associations of their uniforms carried ratings still further from the self-control and reserve of the gentlemanly masculine ideal.

As Angus McLaren's comment begins to suggest, ratings' overt sexuality also contributed to an appreciation of them as childlike beings

---

[75] Many ratings, however, considered officers' tailoring and body posture to be stiff and formal, cultivating instead a jaunty aspect and a rolling gait. See John Douglas, *H.M.S. Ganges, Roll on My Dozen* (Penmarth, 1997), 58; Douglas, *Trogs*, 89.

[76] McLaren, *Trials*, 206.

[77] Retired rating, born 1954, questionnaire response received 17 Feb. 2000.

who required the fatherly guidance and discipline of adult officers. And, indeed, a strong vein of paternalism did run through every level of interaction between officers and ratings.[78] This was also transmitted by other aspects of uniform. For instance, although both officers and ratings used alterations in dress to signify progress towards a male ideal, one thing that officers left behind forever with their scouting uniforms was the good conduct badge. However, in the form of chevrons, this concept was applied to ratings throughout their careers. A maximum of three could be awarded – one after three, one after eight and one after thirteen years service – to men who had conducted themselves with 'sobriety, activity and attention',[79] and each was accompanied by a small rise in pay. Anything deemed to constitute misconduct could also result in their forfeiture. The badges therefore played their part in holding ratings in a semi-childlike relationship to authority; and they also allowed officers to assume the identity of part parent, part school-master. A passage from the 1942 memoir of Admiral Sir Ernest Chatfield illustrates the relish with which some officers accepted the role:

> [Ratings are] a special breed...simple, good-tempered, cheerful and optimistic...It is an absorbing interest to command them and to make them what you wish them to be...[they] like a firm but just hand over them, the unruly punished, the well-conducted rewarded.[80]

Uniform was consequently deeply implicated in a process that differentiated between officers and ratings at the most fundamental levels of gender. The connotations of powerlessness and childishness that adhered to ratings' uniform are, perhaps, precisely what endeared its facsimile, the sailor suit, to middle- and upper-class parents. However, when male children from these social strata reached adolescence and set out on their own struggles for socio-cultural power, those same connotations became anathema. The sailor suit was sent to the attic, and the preparatory school Eton collar suit made its first appearance.

In conclusion, it would probably be accurate to say that the relationship between people and clothing always narrows the range of possible personal expression. This process is, however, an essential part of orienting the individual from childhood onwards to the context of the time and place in which he or she lives. In terms of this period, however, the experience of naval uniform was different in two main

---

[78] As one newspaper commented: 'We have treated you [ratings] like naughty boys, while demanding from you the best work of a man', *Daily Express*, 9 Sept. 1912, quoted in Carew, *Lower Deck*, 46.

[79] Admiralty regulations quoted in Burgess and Blackburn, *Traditions*.

[80] Admiral of the Fleet Lord Chatfield, *The Navy and Defence: The Autobiography of Admiral of the Fleet Lord Chatfield* (1942), 78.

respects. The first lies in the institutionalised intensity with which it was used to narrow identity. The second can be perceived in the relationship of naval uniform with the marketplace. With regard to clothing (and indeed the entire material configuration of the navy), once within the institution, the external civilian worlds of consumption and display were substantially suspended. Statements of individualised expression became considerably harder to achieve. It is, perhaps, this quality that gave uniform such power to communicate and entrench generalised, and often stereotypical, socio-cultural understandings. Officers and ratings could mediate uniform regulations in the informality of the mess, and exercise more individualised choices when buying their civilian clothes; but few, if any, could cast off the influence of uniform on their early training and their early selves.

At the same time, the meanings ascribed to naval uniform both reflected and consolidated the linkage of the institution to far wider socio-cultural worlds. Through uniform naval officers could proclaim their membership of the professional upper middle class. Equally, the nature of the control they exercised over ratings' dress can be seen as one component of the contemporary middle-class desire to differentiate itself from working-class people and working-class lifestyles. The identity of the Jack Tar, too, had much in common with civilian working-class culture. The conservative, consensual and deferential identity articulated by square rig was, after all, in keeping with the outlook of many working-class people much less directly exposed to the gaze and influence of authority. Finally, during the 1930s the exclusion of women from professional employment and the conceptualisation of working-class people as immature, irresponsible and in need of guidance were hardly confined to the Royal Navy. As this essay demonstrates, the construction of these linkages between the naval and the civilian, the professional and the socio-cultural owed much to the material culture of uniform.

Transactions of the RHS 13 (2003), pp. 131–62 © 2003 Royal Historical Society
DOI: 10.1017/S0080440103000069   Printed in the United Kingdom

WRITING FORNICATION:
MEDIEVAL LEYRWITE AND ITS HISTORIANS*

The Prothero Lecture

By Judith M. Bennett

READ 4 JULY 2002

ABSTRACT. Leyrwite was a fine for fornication levied on the bondwomen of many medieval English manors. This essay traces the distinctive chronological history of leyrwite (it flourished especially *c.* 1250–1350), its regional distribution (leyrwite was levied only in England and only in some regions of England), its socio-economic implications (leyrwite was directed especially at the poor and more at bastardy than fornication) and, most of all, the significance of its focus on women (leyrwite served as one means of regulating poor women and their families).

In 1086, when the clerks of William the Conqueror wrote the customs of Broughton (Hunts.) into the Domesday Book, they used a word that appears only once in the many folios of that survey. The sokemen of Broughton had told the Domesday officers that their privileges included freedom from any obligation to pay a forfeit to Ramsey Abbey, which held the manor, whenever one among them committed a petty assault, minor theft or an offence they called leyrwite.[1] This single reference to leyrwite in Domesday Book is also its first extant reference; whatever its pre-Conquest uses, leyrwite first appears to us as an Anglo-Saxon loan word in a post-Conquest, Latin text.

This essay will examine leyrwite as it exists in medieval documents, as it has been understood by historians and as it can be usefully

---

*I am grateful to Sandy Bardsley, Barbara Harris, Cynthia Herrup, Maryanne Kowaleski, Christopher Whittick and the members of the North Carolina Research Group on Medieval and Early Modern Women for their comments on drafts. I thank Blain Roberts, Brandon Hunziker and Kristin Dachler for their help as research assistants. Some people who answered my questions about leyrwite are acknowledged in specific notes below, but others are not, and I am none the less grateful for their generosity of time and thought. The errors and infelicities that remain are my own.

[1] *Domesday Book*, I, 204b. Jean Scammell has claimed that leyrwite 'is recorded, well-established, in the mid-eleventh century in a context which shows it profitable to lords and of intense concern to villeins', but she offered no references to support this statement. I have found none before 1086. See Jean Scammell, 'Wife-Rents and Merchets', *Economic History Review*, 2nd series, 29 (1976), 487–90, at 488.

reinterpreted as a *gendered* fine. The term itself has been usually understood as a manorial fine levied for fornication, and its history has been usually placed within two complementary frames: the moral teachings of the medieval Church and the dynamics of lordship and serfdom on medieval manors.[2] I will suggest today that the medieval meanings of leyrwite must also be seen within a third frame: the lives of peasant women in the half-century before the Great Plague of 1348–9.[3]

Leyrwite was an obscure fine levied on obscure people a long time ago. But its history still echoes in England today, where single mothers number among the poorest of the poor and the powers-that-be bemoan the seemingly numberless children of those who must rely on charity and state support. And its history also illustrates the essential place of gender in 'Rewriting the Past', the project of this year's Anglo-American conference. As we shall see, leyrwite has been often understood as a fine for fornication, but it is much better understood as a fine for fornication *by women*.

The word 'leyrwite' has many variants in medieval records, but it is composed of two Anglo-Saxon elements, *leger* for 'lying down' and *wite* for 'fine': it was, literally, a 'fine for lying down'. Although *leger* often signified a sickbed or even a grave, it was also linked with sexual bedding. Of its original Anglo-Saxon meaning, we cannot be sure, given its late attestation in Domesday Book. There, and then again in its next occurrence (in the early twelfth-century *Leges Henrici Primi*), leyrwite was twinned with bloodwite, a fine for drawing blood in a

---

[2] Penalties for leyrwite moved freely between two sorts of payments made in manorial courts: *fines* offered to a manorial lord or lady in return for a favour, such as being allowed to enter a tenement, and *amercements* paid as a result of being placed 'in mercy' for an offence. Leyrwite was sometimes treated as a fine and sometimes as an amercement. For examples of both within one manorial jurisdiction, see the court rolls of Worlingworth (Suffolk), Suffolk Record Office (Ipswich) [hereafter SRO-I], especially S1/2/1.2. I thank Larry Poos for suggesting that I look at this collection. Because *fine* is a more familiar word for modern readers, I will use it throughout.

[3] The term 'leyrwite' was not invariably applied to all manorial fines for illegitimate sexual intercourse, pregnancy or birth; some were labelled as 'childwite' and others were merely described. The distinction between illegitimate sexual activities identified as leyrwite/childwite and those not so identified seems to have had no importance. See, for example, British Library, Additional Roll [hereafter BL, Add. Roll] 39465, where two women in Broughton were fined, the first because she was pregnant outside marriage ('est pregnans extra matrimonium, ideo etc. 6d.') and the next for the same offence but with the term 'leyrwite' used ('est convicta de eodem, ideo pro leyrewyta 12d.'). Both cases, and others like them, are considered in this essay. Interestingly enough, the only exception to the unimportance of the 'leyrwite' label might be cases of male sexual misconduct, for sometimes courts and their clerks seem to have avoided applying the term to men. In Broughton, for example, leyrwite was never used when men were charged and fined for sexual offences.

violent assault, and this association suggests that leyrwite might have once been linked with violence as well as with sexual intercourse – that is, with rape.[4] In any case, in both Domesday Book and *Leges Henrici Primi*, leyrwite was treated as a minor manorial incident, a fine that was bundled with other similar forfeitures and conceded back to the tenants, usually in return for a single annual fee.[5]

Leyrwite first appears in an English-language text in an early thirteenth-century defence of holy virginity usually known today as *Hali Maidenhad* (c. 1210–20). The anonymous author of this ill-tempered harangue against not only sex but also marriage, men and children advised young women to resist sexual desire by answering back to the devil, 'You crafty demon, all for nothing you incite me to commit sin, and forgo bliss upon bliss, the crown upon crown of a virgin's reward, and cast myself wretchedly of my own accord into your *leirwite*.'[6] Here, clearly, no rape was involved, nor was there a manorial context of lords and ladies profiting from the sexual or violent misbehaviours of their serfs. To the author of *Hali Maidenhad*, leyrwite signified simply lechery (with all the degradation it implied) or perhaps a devilish punishment for fornication.

Within a few decades of *Hali Maidenhad*, the term began to appear in abundance in the original context suggested by Domesday Book and *Leges Henrici Primi* – that is, in the manorial records that began to proliferate in variety and volume from the middle of the thirteenth century.[7] In Broughton, it was being imposed by the 1290s on bondwomen for having been convicted of fornication in an ecclesiastical court (*convicta est in capitulo super fornicationem*), for being pregnant (*est pregnans*), for giving birth to a bastard child (*peperit extra matrimonium*) or simply as an offence itself (*pro leyrwita sua*).[8] In Broughton and elsewhere,

[4] *Leges Henrici Primi*, ed. L.J. Downer (Oxford, 1972), cap. 23.1 and 81.3. I am grateful to Ian McDougall for this observation about the possible implications of leyrwite's association with bloodwite. In 1974, Jean Scammell claimed that leyrwite had 'no implication whatsoever of violence', but she offered no explanation of this judgement: see her 'Freedom and Marriage in Medieval England', *Economic History Review*, 2nd series, 27 (1974), 523–37, at 526.

[5] For a further instance of such compounding, see *Charters and Custumals of the Abbey of Holy Trinity, Caen*, ed. Marjorie Chibnall (1982) [hereafter *Holy Trinity, Caen*], 91 and xlvii–xlviii.

[6] I have relied on the edition and translation found in *Medieval English Prose for Women: Selections from the Katherine Group and the Ancrene Wisse*, ed. Bella Millett and Jocelyn Wogan-Browne (Oxford, 1990) [hereafter *Hali Maidenhad*], 42–3.

[7] For leyrwites levied as early as 1237, see British Library, Additional Manuscript [hereafter BL, Add. MS] 40625 (Court Book for Park). It might be telling that I could find no references to leyrwite or childwite in a survey of Ely manors undertaken in 1222 (BL, Cotton Tiberius B II), but that both fines were common in a similar survey undertaken a generation later in 1251 (BL, Cotton Claudius C XI).

[8] These examples are taken, respectively, from BL, Add. Rolls 34304 (1308), 39465

these levies had a distinct chronology: they first began to appear in the middle of the thirteenth century; they became much more common by the end of the century; they waned a bit after the Great Famine of 1315–22; they nevertheless continued until the Great Plague of 1348–9; and they disappeared quickly thereafter.[9] Leyrwite, then, was a minor Anglo-Saxon forfeiture; it was one of the few wites that did not disappear in Anglo-Norman England; by the late thirteenth century, it was imposed especially on never-married bondwomen, for sexual activity or the reproductive results thereof; it flourished particularly between 1250 and 1350; by the late fourteenth century, it had disappeared from all but the most conservative of estates; and in 1500, it was everywhere in England a matter of memory, not practice.

We can know more about leyrwite than fornication, in part because

---

(1316), 39468 (1329) and 39459 (1307), but they can be found throughout the Broughton rolls. One woman in Broughton was even fined because she had borne one child and was already pregnant with another: 'peperit et iterum impregnata extra matrimonium', BL, Add. Roll 34913 (1301).

[9] Five examples will suffice to show the trend. (1) At Halesowen, there were few leyrwites in the 1270s, an increasing number from 1280, a decline with the Great Famine and a rise again *c.* 1330. See Margaret Spufford, 'Puritanism and Social Control?', in *Order and Disorder in Early Modern England*, ed. Anthony Fletcher and John Stevenson (Cambridge, 1985), 41–57, at 55. (2) On the St Albans manor of Park (Herts.), the pattern was: two in 1230s, two in 1240s; three in 1250s; two in 1260s; none in 1270s (the gap runs from 1264/5 to 1288–9); one in 1280s; two in 1290s; seven in 1300s; three in 1310s; four in 1320s; two in 1330s; none in 1340s; one in 1350s, one in 1360s; four in 1370s; none for the rest of the century. BL, Add. MS 40625. (3) In Broughton, there were twelve fines for sexual misbehaviour in the 1290s; thirty-four in the half-century before the Great Plague, and only two in the second half of the fourteenth century. My figures differ from those given by Edward Britton in *The Community of the Vill: A Study of the Family and Village Life in Fourteenth-Century England* (Toronto, 1977), 34 and 250–1n. I relied on Britton's citations in tracking occurrences of sexual misbehaviour before 1348, since I could not, of course, replicate the full analysis on which his book was based. But I have excluded some of Britton's cases as the entries are not explicit about the sexual nature of the offence (these note merely chattels lost in chapter court); I chanced on a few others that Britton seems to have missed; I read a few others differently from Britton; and, in a few cases, the rolls are now so fragile that I relied on Britton's account without rereading myself. All told, this new count relies on but substantially modifies Britton's early work. These figures include two men in the 1290s (each was presented for having sex with a 'certain woman of Walton'), and three more men fined later, each for adultery; none of these men was explicitly charged with leyrwite. The male partners of many women presented for sexual offences were named, but not fined. For the late fourteenth century (which is not covered in Britton's book), I read through all extant rolls; the two leyrwites are found in BL, Add. Roll 39472 (1360), and BL, Add. Roll 34815 (1391). (4) For the manors of Spalding Priory, see Table I in E.D. Jones, 'The Medieval Leyrwite: A Historical Note on Female Fornication', *English Historical Review*, 88 (1992), 945–53. (5) For Cottenham (Cambs.) see Table 4.3 in Jack Ravensdale, 'Population Changes and the Transfer of Customary Land on a Cambridgeshire Manor in the Fourteenth Century', in *Land, Kinship and Life-Cycle*, ed. Richard M. Smith (Cambridge, 1984), 197–225.

we simply have more documentation for the fine than for the offence. In the middle ages, 'fornication' was a catch-all term applied to a variety of sexual errors, including adultery, clerical concubinage, proscribed sexual positions and even marital sex, if husband and wife enjoyed themselves too much or sought to avoid pregnancy. But 'fornication' most commonly described vaginal intercourse between an unmarried man and an unmarried woman. This was the least of all sexual sins according to medieval churchmen and so minor a misdeed, in the eyes of the laity, that they needed constant reminders of its sinfulness.[10]

We know precious little about the sexual practices of medieval people, much less medieval peasants. Pastoral guides tell us more about what worried priests than about what people actually did. Medical writers offer extensive but abstract commentary on sexual matters. Artistic representations are little help. And although contemporary ballads and carols say a great deal about love and sex, they rarely describe sexual acts. When they do, the descriptions are conventional. As one maiden sings of her plans for a day off work:

> Sone he wole take me be the hond,
> And he wole legge me on the lond,
> That al my buttockus ben of sond
> Opon this holyday.[11]

Medieval people expected women as well as men to take pleasure from sex. In medieval songs, some maidens report merely that they allow a lover to 'have his will', but others sing about their lovers in highly flattering terms; one remembers her encounter as 'the murgust nyt [merriest night]' she had ever known, and another reports of her lover, 'Fayne wold I haue hem bothe nyght and day.'[12] Such praise might reflect more the egos of the men who probably authored these songs (most are anonymous) than the actual experiences of women, but such praise was, at least, plausible to medieval audiences. As to the circumstances of fornication, for some couples in these songs, sexual encounters include the comforts of shelter and bed; for many others, fornication occurs out-of-doors and on the ground; and for most, these

---

[10] See especially Ruth Mazo Karras, 'The Latin Vocabulary of Illicit Sex in English Ecclesiastical Records', *Journal of Medieval Latin*, 2 (1992), 1–17, and *idem*, 'Two Models, Two Standards: Moral Teaching and Sexual Mores', in *Bodies and Disciplines: Intersections of Literature and History in Fifteenth-Century England*, ed. Barbara A. Hanawalt and David Wallace (Minneapolis, 1996), 123–38.

[11] *The Early English Carols*, ed. Richard Leighton Greene (2nd edn, Oxford, 1977) [hereafter *Carols*], item 452. I am grateful to Judith Ferster for her assistance in interpreting this carol (which survives in a single, fifteenth-century text).

[12] *Carols*, items 453 and 456.1.

sexual missteps happened during festivals, holidays and other public revelries. In such situations, discovery and public knowledge must have been common risks.

In theory, all instances of fornication were reported to the Church which enjoyed jurisdiction over sexual offences. For peasants, this jurisdiction was exercised through rural chapters – that is, courts convened by archdeacons and rural deans.[13] To judge from the few records that have survived from such courts, fornication was a major concern, indeed, *the* major concern. In the rural deanery of Wych (diocese of Worcester) in 1300, for example, the docket consisted of six cases of adultery, two of extra-marital pregnancy, one of a husband abusing his wife and forty-six of fornication.[14] Corporal punishment – usually a highly ritualised public whipping – was the standard penalty imposed on fornicators, but this was sometimes avoided by payment of a monetary fine.[15] Church courts did not capture more than a 'modest' proportion of offenders, but they punished many more fornicators than those who paid the manorial fine of leyrwite.[16]

In fact, jurisdiction over leyrwite netted so few offenders and so little profit that, on leyrwite's evidence alone, we would conclude that most peasants either did not fornicate or did not get caught.[17] In the six

---

[13] Jean Scammell, 'The Rural Chapter in England from the Eleventh to the Fourteenth Century', *English Historical Review*, 338 (1971), 1–21.

[14] F.S. Pearson, 'Records of a Ruridecanal Court of 1300', in *Collectanea*, ed. Sidney Graves Hamilton (Worcestershire Historical Society, 1912), 69–80. See also *Lower Ecclesiastical Jurisdiction in Late-Medieval England: The Courts of the Dean and Chapter of Lincoln, 1336–1349, and the Deanery of Wisbech, 1458–1484*, ed. L.R. Poos (Oxford, 2001) [hereafter *Lower Ecclesiastical Jurisdiction*] ; Nigel Tringham, 'The Parochial Visitation of Tarvin (Cheshire) in 1317', *Northern History*, 38 (Sept. 2001), 197–220; and the other printed sources cited in Tringham, 'Tarvin', n. 2.

[15] Payment to avoid punishment was common, for example, in the Tarvin visitation (Tringham, 'Tarvin'), but it was never noted in the records of John Trefnant's visitation of his diocese of Hereford in 1397 (Hereford Cathedral Archives, MS 1779). Christopher Whittick is editing this visitation, and I am grateful to him for this information.

[16] Sandra Lee Parker and L.R. Poos, 'A Consistory Court from the Diocese of Rochester, 1363–4', *English Historical Review*, 106 (1991), 652–65, at 654.

[17] What E.D. Jones has noted for the manors of Spalding Priory is generally true elsewhere; so little was made from the levying of leyrwite that 'the Priory did not levy the fine from primarily financial motives' (Jones, 'Medieval Leyrwite', 947). In some instances, however, landowners seem to have exploited leyrwite for financial profit. See, for example, Eleanor Searle, 'Seigneurial Control of Women's Marriage: The Antecedents and Function of Merchet in England', *Past and Present*, 82 (1979), 3–43, at 28–9. The data provided in the table are inaccurate, but Searle's point about seigneurial profit nevertheless stands. Please note, however, that most of the earl of Warenne's profit came not from leyrwite fines but from fines levied for *concealing* leyrwite; a woman paid for her lapse (usually 6d. or 12d.) and her community paid for having failed to report it (usually 40d.). *Court Rolls of the Manor of Wakefield*, IV: *1315–1317*, ed. John Lister, Yorkshire Archaeological Society, 78 (1930) [hereafter *Wakefield*, IV], 53–4. Also, on some manors, the standard charge was so large that each levy constituted a tidy profit. In Worlingworth in the early

decades before the Great Plague, only some forty-six instances of fornication came before Broughton's court – that is, less than one per year.[18] The peasants of Halesowen (Worcs.) paid at a brisker rate, but still only 117 leyrwites over seventy-eight years.[19] And peasants on some other manors rarely endured the fine; in the large and populous manor of Wakefield (Yorks.), several years often passed between the recording of one leyrwite and its next occurrence.[20] Similarly, in Sutton (Lincs.), only forty-eight leyrwites were recorded in 180 years.[21] Such paltry returns prompted H.E. Hallam to conclude in 1981 that 'the medieval peasant did not have sex on the brain'.[22] Perhaps so, but as we shall see, it is more plausible that only *some* instances of fornication were written into the documentary record as leyrwites.

As leyrwite faded into memory in the fifteenth and sixteenth centuries, it took on new life as a subject of history. When Thomas Blount published his monumental *Ancient Tenures* in 1679, he took what had by then become a standard interpretation: he conflated leyrwite with merchet (a fine for the marriage of bondwomen) and described both as payments whereby bond tenants avoided the 'first nights lodging with the Bride, which the Lord anciently claimed in some mannors'.[23] This myth of what has been variously labelled *jus primae noctis, droit de*

---

fourteenth century, childwite charges rose from 6d. or 12d. to 2s.8d.: SRO-I, S1/2/1.1. And, as discussed below, on many manors after 1348, a single leyrwite could yield 5s. or more. Yet, despite the profit to be made in such instances, exceptional numbers of fines were not then levied. Indeed, after 1348, very few leyrwites were levied at all. In sum, profit seems to have been a weak motive for the levying of leyrwite or childwite.

[18] Similarly, for the three Cambridgeshire manors of Crowland Abbey taken together, F.M. Page noted that leyrwite 'was incurred, upon an average, only twice a year'. F.M. Page, *The Estates of Crowland Abbey* (Cambridge, 1934), 133.

[19] Zvi Razi, *Life, Marriage and Death in a Medieval Parish: Economy, Society and Demography in Halesowen, 1270–1400* (Cambridge, 1980), 65.

[20] This pattern can be found in all the printed extracts from the Wakefield rolls, but see, for example, *Court Rolls of the Manor of Wakefield*, II: *1297–1309*, ed. William Paley Baildon, Yorkshire Archaeological Society, 36 (1906), where the numerous courts for 1306–9 yield only two such fines (found on 57 and 93).

[21] Jones, 'Medieval Leyrwite', 950. Although none of these manors boasts today a perfect run of records, the figures for Sutton are drawn from a fifteenth-century compilation that might accurately represent the annual incidence of leyrwite. For discussion of this source, see E.D. Jones, 'Going Round in Circles: Some New Evidence for Population in the Later Middle Ages', *Journal of Medieval History*, 15 (1989), 329–45; Mark Bailey, 'Blowing up Bubbles: Some New Demographic Evidence for the Fifteenth Century', *Journal of Medieval History*, 15 (1989), 347–58; and E.D. Jones, 'A Few Bubbles More: The Myntling Register Revisited', *Journal of Medieval History*, 17 (1991), 263–9.

[22] H.E. Hallam, *Rural England, 1066–1348* (Brighton, 1981), 262–3.

[23] Thomas Blount, *Fragmenta Antiquitatis: Ancient Tenures of Land and Jocular Customs of Some Mannors Made Publick for the Diversion of Some, and the Instruction of Others* (1679), 145 and 159. The conflation of merchet and leyrwite, marriage and fornication, was not new in the sixteenth century. For an early fourteenth-century example, see case 25 in *Year Books of the Reign of King Edward the Third, Year XV*, ed. Luke Owen Pike (1891), 332–5.

seigneur and *droit de cuissage* has produced some stirring scenes in opera (*The Marriage of Figaro*) and cinema (*Braveheart*), but as Alain Boureau has recently established, the right of a lord to deflower his bondwoman on the night of her marriage is powerful polemic, enduring myth and bad history.[24] There is no doubt that medieval lords fathered bastards from their female servants and tenants; Helena Graham has found, for example, at least two and possibly five bastards of Philip de Somerville living on his manor of Alrewas (Staffs.) in the fourteenth century.[25] But there is also no doubt that the sexual expression of the social power of lords was buttressed by neither law nor custom. Lords could intimidate, cajole, threaten and take; they could not command sexual intercourse with their bondwomen as a matter of seigneurial right. The link between leyrwite and right-of-the-first-night is the oldest and most enduring of its histories, but it is also its most misinformed.

Perhaps because leyrwite was already tainted by this antiquarian interpretation or perhaps because of Victorian prudery, the earliest generations of professional historians downplayed leyrwite or even ignored it. Yet even in their brief comments on the fine, Frederic Maitland and Paul Vinogradoff set the two themes – moral offence and seigneurial power – that have dominated leyrwite's study ever since. To Maitland, this 'trifling' fine addressed a moral error, which raised for him a jurisdictional problem, namely why secular courts punished a transgression that should properly have been adjudicated by an ecclesiastical tribunal. Maitland found the answer in the legal principle that serfs owned no property of their own; since serfs who paid ecclesiastical fines therefore alienated manorial property, manors, he concluded, took leyrwite in retribution.[26] To Vinogradoff, a different explanation for leyrwite made sense, but it also wove together morality and lordship. Assuming that a woman sexually active before marriage was so morally tarnished that no man would ever marry her, Vinogradoff understood leyrwite as a seigneurial compensation required because 'the lord loses his merchet from women who go wrong and do not get married'.[27]

[24] Alain Boureau, *The Lord's First Night: The Myth of the Droit de Cuissage* (Chicago, 1998).
[25] Helena Graham, 'A Social and Economic Study of the Late Medieval Peasantry: Alrewas, Staffordshire, in the fourteenth century (Ph.D. thesis, University of Birmingham, 1994), 95–9.
[26] Frederick Pollock and Frederic William Maitland, *The History of English Law before the Time of Edward I* (2 vols., Cambridge, 1911), II, 543; *Select Pleas in Manorial and other Seigneurial Courts*, ed. Frederic William Maitland, Selden Society, 2 (1888), 98; *The Court Baron*, ed. Frederic William Maitland and William Paley Baildon, Selden Society, 4 (1890), 102 and 104. For a recent elaboration of this interpretation, see Tim North, 'Legerwite in the Thirteenth and Fourteenth Centuries', *Past and Present*, 111 (1986), 3–16.
[27] Paul Vinogradoff, *Villainage in England* (Oxford, 1892), 154. For a more recent reiteration of this interpretation, see Chris Middleton, 'Peasants, Patriarchy and the

In the century since, historians have added new twists and turns to the history of leyrwite: leyrwite as a seigneurial reaction to the freedom that bastards born to bondwomen could sometimes claim;[28] leyrwite as an instance in which the patriarchal interests of rich and poor men worked in tandem;[29] leyrwite as a form of social control;[30] and even leyrwite as a historian's tool (tried, but then rejected) to measure demographic trends.[31] The interpretations of these historians have been new, but their assumptions have echoed those of Maitland and Vinogradoff; in essence, leyrwite was a response to moral lapse and a manifestation of seigneurial power. They have also mostly followed Maitland and Vinogradoff in recognizing, but not investigating, the fact that leyrwite was, in essence, a woman's fine.[32] The documentary record makes this very clear: aside from the unusual case of Cornwall, only a handful of men were ever presented for leyrwite, and although a few more were named as partners of women who paid leyrwite, they were not themselves fined.[33] For most historians, leyrwite's relentless

---

Feudal Mode of Production in England: 2 Feudal Lords and the Subordination of Women', *Sociological Review*, 29:1 (1981), 137–54, at 144–6.

[28] Rodney Hilton, 'Peasant Movements in England before 1381', originally published in 1974, but reprinted in his *Class Conflict and the Crisis of Feudalism: Essays in Medieval Social History* (1985), 122–39, at 125. The legal status of bastards varied from manor to manor. In Ingoldmells (Lincs.), for example, a bastard born of a freeman and a bondwoman was considered to be unfree; see *Court Rolls of the Manor of Ingoldmells in the County of Lincoln*, ed. W.O. Massingberd (1902) [hereafter *Ingoldmells*], 69 (for a related custom, see also 111). In Cottenham (Cambs.) in 1346, some women tried to avoid leyrwite by claiming that they were bastards and therefore free of the fine (Cambridge University Library, Dd1).

[29] Middleton, 'Feudal Lords: 2', 145–6.

[30] Spufford, 'Puritanism'. See also Britton, *Community*, 51–4, and Sherri Olson, *A Chronicle of All that Happens: Voices from the Village Court in Medieval England* (1996), 215.

[31] L.R. Poos and R.M. Smith, ' "Legal Windows into Historical Populations"? Recent Research on Demography and the Manor Court in Medieval England'; Zvi Razi, 'The Use of Manorial Court Rolls in Demographic Analysis: A Reconsideration'; L.R. Poos and R. M. Smith, 'Shades Still on the Window: A Reply to Zvi Razi'; Zvi Razi, 'The Demographic Transparency of Manorial Court Rolls', all originally published in 1984–6 but reprinted in *Medieval Society and the Manor Court*, ed. Zvi Razi and Richard Smith (Oxford, 1996), 298–368.

[32] A good example is North, 'Legerwite', in which the fine's focus on women is treated in a single paragraph. Despite this brief treatment, North's argument stands or falls on his assertion that women more frequently than men avoided corporal punishment by paying fines in ecclesiastical courts.

[33] For Cornwall, see appendix. For men presented for leyrwite elsewhere in England, see: (1) *Court Roll of the Manor of Downham 1310–1327*, ed. M. Clare Coleman, Cambridgeshire Records Society, 11 (1996), 20 (item 15); (2) BL, Add. MS 40625 (Court Book for Park), fos. 12v and 96; (3) Ada Elizabeth Levett, *Studies in Manorial History* (Oxford, 1938), 235. For customs that state that men should pay leyrwite, see *Lancashire Inquests, Extents, and Feudal Aids*, Part III: *1313–1355*, ed. William Farrer, Lancashire and Cheshire Record Society, 70 (1915) [hereafter *Lanchashire Inquests*], 122 and 132. In Crowle (Lincs.), men were often named as partners of women presented for leyrwite, but were not presented themselves (Lincolnshire Archive Office [hereafter LAO], CM I/1–8).

focus on women has seemed a fact of almost timeless meaning, not a phenomenon worthy of historical interpretation.

All women were not everywhere at equal risk of leyrwite. It was, to begin with, a peculiarly English fine. On the continent, there remain the merest hints of seigneurial fines for female fornication (*bedemund*) in some districts of Germany, but otherwise a rather remarkable silence.[34] In Wales, the English imported leyrwite in the thirteenth century, where it merged with an earlier Welsh fine, *amobr* (Latin: *amobragium*). The pre-Conquest purpose of *amobr* is not entirely clear, but it seems to have been a 'maiden fee' paid by free and unfree when a young woman married or cohabited for the first time. Perhaps because the English could not comprehend Welsh customs of marriage or perhaps as a sort of post-Conquest insult, *amobr* was more often assimilated into the English fine for fornication (leyrwite) than the English fine for marriage (merchet).[35] In Ireland, there was no native equivalent to leyrwite, and the English never imposed it on the otherwise much oppressed *betaghs* – that is, Irish villeins – on their estates.[36] And in Scotland neither native

---

[34] Bedemund was most commonly a marriage due, not a fine for fornication: s.v. bedemund, *Lexikon des Mittelalters*, ed. G. Droege (Munich, 1980). See also Jörg Wettlaufer, *Das Herrenrecht der ersten Nacht: Hochzeit, Herrschaft und Heiratszins im Mittelalter und in der frühen Neuzeit* (Frankfurt, 1999), 177–84. G.G. Coulton adduced several continental analogues of leyrwite, but none could be verified through his references; see *The Medieval Village* (1935; republished New York, 1989), 477–8.

[35] *Amobr*/leyrwite/merchet was more lucrative in Wales than in England, and it survived into the sixteenth century (see, for example, the Kidwelly reference s.v. legerwita in *Dictionary of Medieval Latin from British Sources*); its history merits more careful study. For recent, but brief, comments see Llinos Beverley Smith, 'Towards a History of Women in Late Medieval Wales', in *Women and Gender in Early Modern Wales*, ed. Michael Roberts and Simone Clarke (Cardiff, 2000), 14–49, at 17 and 31; Huw Pryce, *Native Law and the Church in Medieval Wales* (Oxford, 1993), 95, 110, 218–20; R.R. Davies, *Lordship and Society in the March of Wales 1282–1400* (Oxford, 1978), 136–8; Dafydd Jenkins and Morfydd E. Owen, *The Welsh Law of Women* (Cardiff, 1980), esp. 73–5. The merging of *amobr* with leyrwite and merchet can be clearly seen in *Survey of the Honour of Denbigh, 1334*, ed. Paul Vinogradoff and Frank Morgan (1914), e.g., 150–1 (this source also illustrates the value of the fine; in the commote of Kaymergh, for example, it was valued at £4 per year). See also: *The Black Book of St. David's*, ed. J.W. Willis-Bund (1902); *The First Extent of Bromfield and Yale, A.D. 1315*, ed. T.P. Ellis, Cymmrodorion Record Series, 11 (1924) [hereafter *Extent of Bromfield*]; and *Registrum vulgariter nuncupatum 'The Record of Carnarvon'*, ed. H. Ellis (1838). Eventually English queens claimed the income from 'amobrages'; see Hilda Johnstone, 'The Queen's Household', in *Chapters in the Administrative History of Medieval England*, ed. T.F. Tout (6 vols., Manchester, 1920–33), v, 231–89, esp. 264–7.

[36] I am grateful to Bruce Campbell for his advice on Irish manorial history and to the Royal Irish Academy for access to their excellent library. See especially, Edmund Curtis, 'Rental of the Manor of Lisronagh, 1333, and Notes on "Betagh" Tenure in Medieval Ireland', *Proceedings of the Royal Irish Academy*, 43, section C (1935–7), 41–77; J. Otway-Ruthven, 'The Organization of Anglo-Irish Agriculture in the Middle Ages', *Journal of the Royal Society of Antiquaries of Ireland*, 81 (1951), 1–13; and G.J. Hand, 'The Status of the Native Irish in the Lordship of Ireland, 1272–1331', *Irish Jurist*, new series, 1 (1966), 93–

custom nor English influence have left any traces of leyrwite in the sparse medieval archives of that nation.[37]

Only in England, then, did lords and ladies take a profit from the fornication of their bondwomen – and only in some parts of England. Except for Cornwall, evidence of leyrwite is difficult to find along most of the south coast. But the fine was familiar to the peasants who lived in the East and West Midlands, as well as to those in Lincolnshire, Yorkshire, Lancashire and even farther north.[38] It was also common in East Anglia, although in Norfolk and Suffolk leyrwite was sometimes replaced by a related fine childwite which, as its name suggests, was levied when childbirth followed fornication. (Leyrwite and childwite were mutually exclusive. Some manors levied leyrwite; others levied childwite.[39]) Even within regions where such fines were known, they were not universal. A mid-thirteenth-century survey of the Ely estates, for example, reveals some manors with no custom of leyrwite; some in

---

115. T.P. Ellis (in his *Extent of Bromfield*, 34) linked the traditional Irish fine of *coibche* to leyrwite, merchet and *amobr*, but, if so, it was more related to marriage than to fornication: s.v. coibche in *Ancient Laws of Ireland* (6 vols., Dublin, 1865–1901), vi (glossary).

[37] I am grateful to Elizabeth Ewen for her advice on Scottish manorial history, where the earliest manorial court records survive from the early sixteenth century. It was in Scotland that the myth of the *jus primae noctis* began when, in 1526, Hector Boece told in his *History of Scotland* of how Malcolm III had eliminated the pagan customs of his predecessors, including that 'the lord of the ground sall have the madinheid of all virginis dwelling on the same'. Thanks to the pious efforts of King Malcolm and his queen Saint Margaret, the nobility agreed, Boece said, to revoke this right in return for a golden penny 'callit the marchetis' paid when virgins married. This potent brew of aristocratic power, sex and Celtic barbarism soon became standard history, and within a few centuries, apparent analogs had been found in such conveniently rough places as Ireland, Wales, Frisia, Mexico and Libya. Boureau, *Lord's First Night*, 17–24. See also Raphael Holinshed, *The Historie of Scotlande* (1577), 257; and John Anderson, 'Enquiry into the Origin of *Mercheta Mulierum*', *Transactions of the Society of Antiquaries of Scotland*, 3 (1831), 56–73.

[38] See the appendix for information about my search for leyrwite in southern counties. I have not found evidence of leyrwite along the Welsh marches, but my search there was limited to (1) 'A Transcript of "The Red Book", a detailed account of the Hereford Bishopric Estates in the Thirteenth Century', ed. A.T. Bannister, *Camden Miscellany*, 15 (1929), 1–36, and (2) my own work with selected pre-1348 courts of the Hereford manors of Norton Canon, Preston-on-Wye and Woolhope (Hereford Cathedral Library, R892, R908, R824, R833, R747 and R756). The counties where leyrwite flourished roughly correspond to the Danelaw, but there is, to my knowledge, no Scandinavian antecedent for Anglo-Saxon leyrwite.

[39] The one exception I have found is Worlingworth where the first extant fine was 'leyerwyta' but all subsequent fines were some version of 'cheldwyte'. See SRO-I, S1/2/1.1. Although the terms were mutually exclusive, they did not necessarily refer to different circumstances. Some leyrwites were levied for fornication alone, but others were, like childwite, directed at illegitimate childbirth. See, for example, entry for Chalgrove, *Rotuli Hundredorum* (2 vols., 1812–18), ii, 768–70. See also the various descriptions of leyrwite in the Ely survey of 1251 (BL, Cotton Claudius C xi).

which leyrwite was levied for fornication; and some in which leyrwite was replaced by childwite.[40]

On a manor whose customs included leyrwite or childwite, it usually fell, as we have seen, on women only. But not all women. With few exceptions, these fines targeted bondwomen, not women of free birth and not women of no fixed abode.[41] Never-married bondwomen were most at risk, especially on those manors where leyrwite specifically punished loss of virginity before marriage (e.g., *quia deflorata est*). On other manors, the usual formula for leyrwite stressed fornication more generally (e.g., *pro fornicatione*), so the fine could also capture wives and widows, as well as repeat offenders among singlewomen. On still other manors, the link of leyrwite or childwite with illegitimate birth (e.g., *quia peperit extra matrimonium*) limited its reach to singlewomen and widows and its applicability to a much smaller group of offenders. (Richard Smith has estimated that it would often have taken more than a year and a half for a woman engaged in regular sexual intercourse to give birth to a child.[42])

Even those at highest risk – that is, unmarried bondwomen – usually avoided the fine, especially if they came from better-off families within their villages. As Zvi Razi has shown for Halesowen before 1348, only

[40] BL, Cotton Claudius C XI. For examples of each, see respectively Hatfield (Herts.), fo. 160; Leverington (Cambs.), fo. 83; Pulham (Norf.), fo. 211.

[41] There are, of course, exceptions. On the Ely manor of Bramford (Suffolk), it was specified that any stranger who came to the manor and gave birth to an illegitimate child had to pay 2s. or a better-quality piece of cloth ('superiorem pannum') as childwite: BL, Cotton Claudius C XI, fo. 315v. On some of the manors of the Ely estates, freewomen were as liable as bondwomen for the levy: see, for example, Doddington (Cambs.), fo. 63v. E.A. Kosminsky noted that both free and unfree paid leyrwite in Northumbria: E.A. Kosminsky, *Studies in the Agrarian History of England in the Thirteenth Century* (Oxford, 1956), 135. Sometimes freewomen who held unfree land were assessed; see, for example, *The Court Rolls of Walsham le Willows 1303–1350*, ed. Ray Lock, Suffolk Record Society, 41 (1998) [hereafter *Walsham*], 332; and cases from Worlingworth given in *Select Cases in Manorial Courts, 1250–1550: Property and Family Law*, ed. L.R. Poos and Lloyd Bonfield, Selden Society, 114 (1998), item 170.

[42] R.M. Smith, 'Marriage Processes in the English Past: Some Continuities', in *The World We Have Gained: Histories of Population and Social Structure*, ed. L. Bonfield *et al.* (Oxford, 1986), 43–99, at 92. Some three decades ago, Jean-Louis Flandrin suggested that medieval peasants might have employed a variety of non-procreative sexual practices and that single persons, eager to avoid pregnancy, might have been particularly creative in this regard: Jean-Louis Flandrin, 'Contraception, Marriage, and Sexual Relations in the Christian West', originally published in 1969, but reprinted in *Biology of Man in History*, ed. Robert Forster and Orest Ranum (Baltimore, MD, 1975), 23–47. His suggestions have since been buttressed by: (1) J.M. Riddle who has established the efficacy of many drugs then used as contraceptives or abortifacients, see *Contraception and Abortion from the Ancient World to the Renaissance* (Cambridge, MA, 1992); and (2) Peter Biller who has exhaustively traced clerical anxiety about the laity engaging in sterile forms of sexual intercourse (an anxiety that was especially strong, interestingly enough, around 1300), see *The Measure of Multitude: Population in Medieval Thought* (Oxford, 2000), 135–212.

about one of every six young women was ever fined for leyrwite. Poor
bondwomen paid leyrwite two to three times as frequently as their
better-off contemporaries. One in four daughters among the poorest
families paid the fine; only one in twenty daughters among the best-off
tenants.[43] For late thirteenth-century Rickinghall (Suffolk), Richard
Smith has described the women fined for childwite as 'landless or land
deficient individuals'.[44] And for Horsham and Salle (Norf.), Elaine Clark
has concluded that unwed mothers consistently 'numbered among the
village poor'.[45] In other words, leyrwite and childwite were not fines
for offences per se, but fines for offences committed by poor bondwomen. On these women in particular fell punishment for extra-marital
fornication, pregnancy and childbirth.[46]

Poverty is, of course, a relative concept, and it is well to remember
that these poor bondwomen were poor by the standards of a generally
impoverished peasantry. All medieval peasants lived hard lives, but
their lot was especially difficult in the late thirteenth and early fourteenth
centuries – the heyday of leyrwite – when population growth had finally
outstripped economic resources. Good land was scarce in 1300; well-
paid work scarce too; and hunger a constant threat. At the time, about
one in four peasants held enough land to hope, but not too confidently,
for a surplus at harvest-time; another quarter held sufficient land to
squeeze by, if they were lucky; and about half of all peasants held so
little land that they had to juggle agricultural work with wage-labour,
service, trade, gleaning, charity, pilfering and other expedients.[47]

The burden of leyrwite fell most heavily on women in this poorest
but largest group of medieval villagers: female servants, female wage-
labourers, female cottagers and, since poverty was partly a life-cycle
phenomenon, women among the landless young.[48] In most cases, these

---

[43] Razi, *Life, Marriage*, Table 12.

[44] Richard M. Smith, 'Appendix on the Bastardy Prone Sub-Society', in *Bastardy and
its Comparative History*, ed. Peter Laslett *et al.* (1980), 240–6, at 245.

[45] Elaine Clark, 'Mothers at Risk of Poverty in the Medieval English Countryside', in
Poor Women and Children in the European Past, ed. John Henderson and Richard Wall (1994),
139–59, at 151.

[46] Edward Britton (*Community*, 53–4) and Sherri Olson (*Chronicle*, 215–16) found that
leyrwite was particularly directed at daughters from better-off families in Broughton and
Upwood respectively. Perhaps there was something peculiar about the manors of the
Ramsay estate, but the observations of Britton and Olson are based on questionable
methods of social reconstruction applied to communities that are not especially well
documented for the fourteenth century.

[47] For the details that lie behind this general summary, see especially Christopher Dyer,
Standards of Living in the Later Middle Ages: Social Change in England, c. 1200–1520 (Cambridge,
1989), 109–50.

[48] The youthfulness of most women who paid leyrwite can be deduced from their
identification as daughters, a generally reliable indicator of not-married status. Other
evidence suggests, albeit anecdotally, the family and personal circumstances of these

poor women actually paid the fine themselves. Fathers were sometimes told to pay leyrwites for daughters who still lived at home, and male partners were occasionally expected to pay, *if* they could, part or all of the leyrwites imposed on their female companions.[49] But in most courts most of the time, the fine was levied on the woman herself and, as best we can tell, paid by her as well.[50]

These women who paid leyrwite grew up in a world where sexual liaisons were often publicly pursued and publicly known; where bastardy was not uncommon and, in any case, might bring freedom for the bastard child born of a bondwoman; where the Church's definitions of marriage – none too clear themselves – were only just beginning to take hold; where daughters (and sons) often left home and supported themselves before marriage;[51] where rape was a common menace; and where poverty, hunger and landlessness plagued an overpopulated countryside. In this world, the imposition of leyrwite on fornicating women doubtless pleased moralizing churchmen and added to the profits that manorial stewards reported in their Michaelmas accounts, but it also negotiated the hard realities of women's lives, especially the three hazards of marriage-making, sexual violence and poverty.

As a fine for illegitimate sexuality, leyrwite operated, of course, within the context of legitimate sexuality – that is, what did and did not

---

young women. (1) Some paid fines with their sisters: for example, see payment by Catherine Fyokewornger and her sister Margaret in Sutton, Public Record Office [hereafter PRO], DL 30/85/1159. (One young woman even paid a leyrwite at the same time as did her mother: see Joan Wenington and her daughter in Upwood, BL, Add. Roll 34850.) (2) Some paid leyrwite at the same time as their sisters married: see the marriage of Agnes Reeve and the leyrwite of her sister in Crowle, LAO, CM 1/19. (3) Some themselves married in conjunction with leyrwite: see case of Cicely Saleman of Cottenham in *Select Cases*, ed. Poos and Bonfield, item 141. (4) Some inherited or received land from parents: see Cecilia Pudding in *Walsham*, 37, 107, 117, 122. Others argued with siblings about inheritance: see Agnes Bond of Chatteris in *Court Rolls of the Abbey of Ramsey and of the Honor of Clare*, ed. Warren Ortman Ault (New Haven, 1928) [hereafter *Ramsey*], 274–6. (5) Some worked as servants: see Alice servant of Big John and Margery servant of the hall in *Halmota Prioratus Dunelmensis*, ed. W.H. Longstaffe and J. Booth, Surtees Society, 82 (1889) [hereafter *Halmota Dunelmensis*], 13 (and many others in later pages).

[49] On the Ely estates in 1251 (BL, Cotton Claudius C xi), it was sometimes specified: (a) that parents paid leyrwite for daughters: see, for example, Willingham (Cambs.), fo. 113, (b) that the male lover paid, or if he defaulted, the woman: see, for example, Tyd (Cambs.) fo. 87 or (c) that the father paid, if his daughter still lived with her, but if not, that either the woman herself or her lover paid: see, for example, Colne (Hunts.), fo. 99v. A custumal for Lessingham (Norf.) specified that male partners should pay all or part of the fine, *if* they could: see *Select Documents of the English Lands of the Abbey of Bec*, ed. Marjorie Chibnall, Camden Society, 3rd series, 73 (1951) [hereafter *Abbey of Bec*], 113.

[50] This has been noted, for example, by Jones, 'Medieval Leyrwite', 949. The only exception might be Cornwall, where Duchy account rolls indicate that more men than woman paid leyrwite there. See the appendix.

[51] On this, see especially H.S.A. Fox, 'Exploitation of the Landless by Lords and Tenants in Early Medieval England', in *Medieval Society*, ed. Razi and Smith, 518–68.

constitute a marriage, and what the 'twilight area' between the two meant for women, especially poor women.[52] For us today, marriage is an event that happens at a certain time: hence, wedding anniversaries. For medieval peasants, marriage-making was a *process*, a sometimes lengthy process that blurred the line between marriage and cohabitation and that, if derailed, could render legitimate sexual intercourse illegitimate. By the late thirteenth century, the Church was asking its faithful to publicise marriages in advance, to contract them in public and to sanctify them before priests. But it also acknowledged that, because the essence of marriage was free consent, two people who pledged marriage *ipso facto* were married, even if no witnesses could testify to their vows. This theological concession coincided neatly with secular customs of trothplight, whereby a couple exchanged vows, usually before friends and family, and could thereby be considered married, even without formal sanctification in church. Trothplight-as-marriage was straightforward, inexpensive and therefore well suited to the poor; so too was simple cohabitation, with or without the benefit of betrothal.[53]

Medieval peasants understood well these ecclesiastical rules and secular customs, but they could also disagree about when exactly a marriage had been made. To some, sexual intercourse and childbirth after trothplight were legitimate; to others, neither was legitimate until a marriage was sanctified in church.[54] Many women found themselves caught in the gap between these two understandings of marriage – and paid leyrwite as a result.[55] This is what happened, for example, to

[52] Smith, 'Marriage Processes', 57.

[53] Informal cohabitation was so common that English synods introduced in the thirteenth century a practice whereby couples convicted of habitual fornication were told that any future sexual intercourse between them would create a legal marriage. See R.H. Helmholz, 'Abjuration *sub pena nubendi* in the Church Courts of Medieval England', published in 1972, but reprinted in his *Canon Law and the Law of England* (1987), 145–56. For the process of marriage-making in medieval England, see especially: Smith, 'Marriage Processes', and Christine Peters, 'Gender, Sacrament and Ritual: The Making and Meaning of Marriage in Late Medieval and Early Modern England', *Past and Present*, 169 (2000), 63–96.

[54] We can see such disagreements most clearly when a younger brother challenged the legitimacy (and hence, inheritance claims) of an older brother. See, for example, cases cited by Smith, 'Marriage Processes', 57. For lay knowledge of canon law, see especially Frederik Pedersen, *Marriage Disputes in Medieval England* (2000), 59–84. Note, however, that lower ecclesiastical courts had no jurisdiction over marriage disputes, and in the higher courts that judged such cases, serfs did not participate as either witnesses or litigants. See R.H. Helmholz, *Marriage Litigation in Medieval England* (Cambridge, 1974), 160.

[55] Church courts had similar difficulties. Of the fifty-four couples charged with fornication in the Rochester consistory court between 1347 and 1348, ten stated that they had contracted to marry. Andrew John Finch, 'Sexual Morality and Canon Law: The Evidence of the Rochester Consistory Court', *Journal of Medieval History*, 20 (1994), 261–75, at 267. Manors often tried to distinguish between leyrwite and merchet. It was stated in 1251 that on the Ely manor of Ditton (Cambs.) a woman who paid leyrwite and later

Matilda Catte of Ingoldmells (Lincs.); she and Ralph Lamb agreed to marry in March 1319, and although they eventually did, they were considered to have fornicated in the interim; in January 1320 she had to pay a leyrwite of 6d.[56] Agnes Everard of Broughton fell similarly foul of the process of marriage-making; in 1297, she paid 5s. for both leyrwite and permission to marry.[57] And so too did women such as the unnamed *concubina* of John Taillour of Whitburn (Durham) in 1350; because the two of them had cohabited in an informal union, she was charged with leyrwite.[58]

In addition to negotiating this twilight area between marriage and fornication, leyrwite also could also fall on women whose conjugal agreements had gone wrong.[59] Because canon law stipulated that valid vows did not require witnesses, a woman and man could later disagree about the meaning of their sexual encounter. To one, it could have seemed casual fornication preceded by meaningless talk; to the other, it could have seemed sexual intercourse legitimated by prior marriage vows. Bishops and priests had no doubt that men exploited this uncertainty to trick women into fornication. The early thirteenth-century statutes of Richard Poore, bishop of Salisbury, admonished men not to weave straw rings on the hands of young women just 'in order to fornicate more freely with them'. [60] And Robert Mannyng, a Gilbertine canon who wrote a penitential guide for laity in the early fourteenth century, criticized men who sought

---

married her lover did not have to pay a fine for marriage (BL, Cotton Claudius C xi, fo. 117). In Worlingworth in 1319, jurors issued a judgement that carefully distinguished between liability for purchase of marriage licences and liability for leyrwite (see Poos, *Select Cases*, 120–1). In Crowle in 1314, it was ordered that payment of leyrwite did not preclude subsequent payment of merchet (LAO, CM 1/3).

[56] *Ingoldmells*, 70 and 75. See the similar case of Mabel Springold in *Walsham*, esp. 176 and 178.

[57] PRO, SC2 179/9. Cases of simultaneous fines for fornication and marriage are common. For other examples, see (1) *Halmota Dunelmensis*, 1, 60, 87, 108, 126, 134 and 180; (2) the St Albans manor of Park, where many early fines for fornication were combined with licences to marry (BL, Add. MS 40625, fos. 1v, 2, 5v, 37v); (3) Sybil Sklacter of Chester-le-Street in 1350 (PRO, DURH 3/12, fo. 43v); (4) Cecilia Saleman in Cottenham in 1290 (Poos, *Select Cases*, item 141).

[58] PRO, DURH 3/12, fo. 43.

[59] It might be telling, in this regard, that two case studies have suggested that leyrwites were especially common in times when marriage was difficult to achieve. Razi, *Life, Marriage*, 64–71, 138–9; and Miriam Müller, 'Rural Politics and Peasant Ideology in the 14th Century: The St Albans' Manor of Winslow, A Case Study' (M.Phil. thesis, University of Cambridge, 1997), 80–1. I am grateful to Miriam Müller for sharing this information with me.

[60] *Councils and Synods with Other Documents relating to the English Church*, II: *1205–1313*, ed. F.M. Powicke and C.R. Cheney (2 parts, Oxford, 1964), 1, 87.

To begyle a womman with wordys;
To gyve here trouþë but lightly
For no þyng but for lygge here by
With Þat gyle þou makest here asent.[61]

Poore, Mannyng and other churchmen were right to worry that many men cared more for sex than marriage; it was, in fact, women who predominated among those who went to ecclesiastical courts to force lovers to honour commitments made and then broken.[62] The complexities of judging such 'he said/she said' disputes explains the evidence that puzzled Maitland so long ago – that is, why so many leyrwite entries refer to prior conviction by ecclesiastical authorities. For manorial jurors, a conviction in an ecclesiastical court cut through all the uncertainties about what did and did not constitute marriage or, by marriage's absence, fornication. No matter what misunderstandings might have precipitated a woman's plight, an ecclesiastical conviction rendered absolute her guilt as a fornicator; she could be presented for leyrwite and fined without further ado.[63]

---

[61] *Robert of Brunne's 'Handlyng Synne'* A.D. 1303, ed. Frederick J. Furnivall, Early English Text Society, original series, 119 (1901), 265 (lines 8394–8).

[62] Charles Donahue, Jr, 'Female Plaintiffs in Marriage Cases in the Court of York in the Later Middle Ages: What Can We Learn from the Numbers?', in *Wife and Widow in Medieval England*, ed. Sue Sheridan Walker (Ann Arbor, 1993), 183–213. One unusual solution to premarital sexual relations was described in a case heard in East Grinstead (Sussex) before the King's Bench in 1276. When the friends of one Matilda caught her in fornication, they gave her lover Simon three choices: he could promise to marry her, lose his life or kiss her backside ('vel ipsam affidare, vel vitam suam amittere, vel ipsam Matillidem retro osculare'). Simon chose to plight his troth to Matilda, but in the end, he never actually married her. See *Select Cases in the Court of Kings Bench under Edward I*, ed. G.O. Sayles, Selden Society, 3 vols., 55 (1936), 57 (1938), 58 (1939), I, 27–9.

[63] The difficulties of proving fornication led Razi to conclude that virtually all leyrwites were occasioned by physical proof thereof – that is, pregnancy or childbirth. Richard Smith and Larry Poos have effectively questioned this assumption in their debate with Razi, 'Legal Windows'. In some cases, common fame might have sufficed; on this, see especially, L.R. Poos, 'Sex, Lies, and the Church Courts of Pre-Reformation England', *Journal of Interdisciplinary History*, 25 (1995), 585–607. But in other cases, neighbours were genuinely uncertain about what had transpired; see cases from Church courts described in Helmholz, 'Abjuration', 148–50. The Broughton court rolls provide a good example of how prior conviction in Church courts worked as a substitute for the physical evidence of pregnancy or childbirth. Most women in Broughton were presented for either pregnancy or illegitimate birth, and in these instances of obvious culpability, prior conviction in Church courts was seldom mentioned. Yet when the women or men were presented for fornication or adultery – that is, cases harder to prove – prior conviction in a Church court was a customary part of the presentment. For examples of both sorts of presentments from one Broughton court session, see PRO, SC2 179/20. The same pattern can be observed in the courts of Houghton (Hunts.); see, for example, PRO, SC2 179/13. And it can also be traced in the selected court rolls printed in *Ramsey*. Prior-conviction-as-evidence might also explain a phrase that recurs in the 1251 survey of the Ely estates: that a leyrwite is levied if a woman fornicated 'et inde sit attincta'. For

The hazards that informal and uncertain marriage posed for young bondwomen were exacerbated by the risk of rape. Sometimes it was difficult for young women (and young men) to distinguish fornication, marital intercourse and rape – and it is harder still for us to sort the evidence today. In 1288, Emma, daughter of Robert Clerk, complained to the Broughton court that William Gilbert had raped her as she harrowed the land of Agnes Gilbert (who was probably William's mother). William denied the charge, claiming he had enjoyed Emma of her own free will on that day as on many occasions in the previous three years. Both Emma and William sought an inquiry, and twenty-five men judged the case. Perhaps rape had punctuated a long-term but casual liaison; perhaps Emma had thought they were betrothed and considered herself to have been raped when she found William had a different view; perhaps William, probably the son of Emma's employer, had repeatedly forced himself on Emma over several years. The jurors of Broughton negotiated these and other possibilities with care, finding in favour of William but imposing no penalties – for either false claim or leyrwite – on Emma.[64]

For us today, the uncertainty of what 'really' happened in a case like this is further complicated by the varied meanings of *raptus* in medieval law; this term encompassed not only forced sexual intercourse but also abduction, sometimes abduction to achieve a marriage desired by both principals.[65] The law's mingling of rape, courtship and marriage had parallels in other media, including medieval songs which sometimes

---

examples, see BL, Cotton Claudius C xi, fos. 83, 87 and 117. If ecclesiastical conviction functioned as evidence, then leyrwite cannot be understood as a fine levied for the alienation of seigneurial property in ecclesiastical courts. North's argument in this regard hinges on the assumption that women more often than men paid money to commute the corporal punishments levied in ecclesiastical courts (North, 'Legerwite'); I have found no evidence in support of this point. See, for example, not only the records cited by North in support of his contention (Pearson, 'Ruridecanal Court'), but also the cases in Tringham, 'Tarvin', and *Lower Ecclesiastical Jurisdiction*.

[64] *Ramsey*, 200. The jurors found William innocent of the charge, presented Emma for false claim and forgave her fine with the standard excuse of poverty. They did not present Emma for leyrwite. For another case that linked forcible intercourse, courtship and marriage, see Pedersen, *Marriage Disputes*, 63–5.

[65] See especially, J.B. Post, 'Ravishment of Women and the Statutes of Westminster', *Legal Records and the Historian*, ed. J.H. Baker (1978), 150–64; Sue Sheridan Walker, 'Punishing Convicted Ravishers: Statutory Strictures and Actual Practice in Thirteenth and Fourteenth-Century England', *Journal of Medieval History*, 13 (1987), 237–50; Christopher Cannon, '*Raptus* in the Chaumpaigne Release and a Newly Discovered Document concerning the Life of Geoffrey Chaucer', *Speculum*, 68 (1993), 74–94, and the response by Henry Ansgar Kelly, 'Meanings and Uses of *Raptus* in Chaucer's Time', *Studies in the Age of Chaucer*, 20 (1998), 101–65. For recent literary studies, see Corinne Saunders, *Rape and Ravishment in the Literature of Medieval England* (Woodbridge, 2001); and *Representing Rape in Medieval and Early Modern Literature*, ed. Elizabeth Robertson and Christine M. Rose (New York, 2001).

describe courtship in terms of forced sexual intercourse. One song, for example, tells of a young daughter courted and then raped while working at home; another tells of a woman raped by a man with whom she engages in witty repartee; and a third tells of a maidservant raped at a village festival who later accepts her rapist as her lover.[66] Indeed, rape is so much an ordinary part of courtship in these songs that modern scholars have often missed or misread the violence they contain; in 1980, for example, one literary critic cheerfully described one of these songs as 'a merry example of the battle of the sexes'.[67]

More than sixty years ago, Ada Elizabeth Levett first linked leyrwite and rape, but there are, as I read the documents, no entries that unequivocally tie leyrwite to forced sexual intercourse.[68] Rape is as elusive in leyrwite as in law and literature. But maidservants were sometimes presented specifically for fornication with their employers, a classic form of sexual intercourse inflected by economic or physical coercion, if not outright rape.[69] And some women paid leyrwites that

[66] *Carols*, item 456; Frederick Morgan Padelford, 'Liedersammlunger des XVI Jahrhunderts, besonders aus der zeit Heinrichs VIII, IV. 7. The Songs in Manuscript Rawlinson C. 813', *Anglia*, 31 (1908), 309–97, at 380–1; John Stevens, *Music and Poetry in the Early Tudor Court* (1961), 339–40.

[67] David C. Fowler, 'XV.Ballads', in *A Manual of Writings in Middle English 1050–1500*, ed. Albert E. Hartung (10 vols., New Haven, 1967–98), VI, 1773. Protection from rape might also lie behind the custom of Singleton (Lancs.) where singlewomen and widows – that is, women who lacked a man's protection – paid each year to place themselves under the protection ('advocatio') of the lord. See *Lancashire Inquests*, 128.

[68] Levett, *Studies*, 235. Levett noted that on the manors of St Albans the fine was paid by fathers for guarding their daughters badly ('pro filia sua male custodita'), and she linked leyrwite to instances of rape which were, as she put it, 'dealt with by a light fine, paid apparently by the woman'. Levett's understanding of leyrwite-for-rape hinged on 'violata est' (see BL, Stowe MS 849, fo. 12v), a phrase as hard to pin down in medieval Latin as in modern (or Middle) English.

[69] For an example see: *Halmota Dunelmensis*, 27. Because of the greater detail recorded in Church courts, they provide more instances of sexual relations between female servants and masters or sons. For examples, see cases 2, 67, 89 and possibly 90 in Tringham, 'Tarvin'; and also cases 30, 32, 73, 76 and 81 in Parker, 'Diocese of Rochester'. A related problem was incest, usually involving stepfathers and stepdaughters: see case 52 in Parker, 'Diocese of Rochester'; cases involving Blaunkenay (68 and 79), Bunting (213) and Marabel (220) in *Lower Ecclesiastical Jurisdiction*; and examples given in Karras, 'Vocabulary', n. 6. The possibility of illegitimate sexual relations between persons living in the same household was so acute that apprenticeship contracts sometimes set heavy penalties for such behaviour. For an example from the early fourteenth century, see the contract of Robert Sharp and Richard ate Grene, as reported in *Year Books of Edward II, 22: 11 Edward II (1317–1318)*, ed. John P. Collas and William S. Holdsworth, Selden Society, 61 (1942), 126–30, at 127. The more extensive evidence of master–servant sexual relations in the early modern era leaves no doubt about the sexual vulnerability of female servants. For the best discussions, see Laura Gowing, 'Ordering the Body: Illegitimacy and Female Authority in Seventeenth-Century England', in *Negotiating Power in Early Modern Society: Order, Hierarchy and Subordination in Britain and Ireland*, ed. Michael J. Braddick and John Walter (Cambridge, 2001), 43–62; Tim Meldrum, 'London Domestic Servants from

were described in terms that suggest violence. In Halesowen, for example, the clerks usually described leyrwites laconically as *pro fine leyrwyte* or *deflorata per leyrwyte*, but in 1301, a clerk was moved to unusual language: Agnes Hulle had to make amends because *violata est per carectarium de Blakeley*.[70]

Women like Agnes Hulle faced not only uncertain paths to marriage and the dangers of rape; they also faced the special vulnerabilities of poor women in an over-crowded land. About 6 million people lived England in 1300 – that is, more people than England would again support until after 1750, by which time agrarian and industrial changes would have enormously expanded the productive capabilities of town and country.[71] As Margaret Spufford first pointed out some twenty years ago, the heyday of leyrwite coincided with this extraordinary crisis in the English countryside; wages were paltry, land and food were expensive and villages were crowded with idle and hungry people.[72] In such a context, a poor woman who produced a bastard child was especially unwelcome, although not so much to churchmen and land-owners as to her better-off neighbours. These tenants, a well-off but embattled minority, shouldered most of the burdens that manor, crown and Church placed on their communities, and they also bore some – perhaps most – of the burden for poor relief. We would like to know more about the alleviation of rural poverty in the century before the Great Plague, but as the studies of Christopher Dyer and Elaine Clark have particularly shown, it is clear, first, that monasteries, hospitals,

---

Depositional Evidence, 1660–1750: Servant–Employer Sexuality in the Patriarchal Household', in *Chronicling Poverty: The Voices and Strategies of the English Poor, 1640–1840*, ed. Tim Hitchcock, Peter King and Pamela Sharpe (Basingstoke, 1997), 47–69; and Paul Griffiths, *Youth and Authority: Formative Experiences in England, 1560–1640* (Oxford, 1996), 267–89. See also the subtle analysis of this problem in a US context by Darlene Clark Hine, 'Rape and the Inner Lives of Southern Black Women: Thoughts on the Culture of Dissemblance', in *Southern Women: Histories and Identities*, ed. Virginia Bernhard, Betty Brandon, Elizabeth Fox-Genovese and Theda Perdue (Columbia, MO, 1992), 177–89.

[70] *Court Rolls of the Manor of Hales, Part 3*, ed. Rowland Alwayn Wilson, Worcestershire Historical Society, 41 (1933), 155. In some cases, this phrase should not be interpreted as entailing violence (see, for example, Poos, *Select Cases*, case 115, or the Crowle courts where it was the most common verb used in leyrwite presentments, LAO CM I/1–8). When the phrase is used infrequently, however, 'violata est' might signify rape. The two cases cited by Levett, for example, are unique uses of the phrase in the Codicote courts of their time. I found no other leyrwites or similar fines levied for ten years thereafter; the only earlier instance (fo. iv) states that a woman 'pro leyrwit' dat 2s' (24 Henry III). One other clue: it might be telling that in the court of Elton (Hunts.) in 1279, entries about a case of attempted rape are preceded and followed by fines for out-of-wedlock births. See *Elton Manorial Records, 1279–1351*, ed. S.C. Ratcliff (Cambridge, 1946), 3–4.

[71] Richard M. Smith, 'Demographic Developments in Rural England, 1300–48: A Survey', in *Before the Black Death: Studies in the 'Crisis' of the Early Fourteenth Century*, ed. Bruce M.S. Campbell (Manchester, 1991), 25–77.

[72] Spufford, 'Puritanism'.

almshouses, fraternities and other institutional remedies were insufficient and, second, that the rural poor were therefore a local problem. Poor villagers were a particular responsibility for their better-off neighbours who not only saw this poverty on a daily basis but also had the food, employment and money that could ease it.[73]

It was men from these better-off families who predominated on the juries that reported whether there were leyrwites to be collected; they decided whether to report all offenders, only a few, or none at all.[74] These well-off men usually chose to name poor women, and since they also usually set fine amounts, they not only named these women but also burdened them with especially heavy charges. By the late thirteenth centuries, many manorial amercements were just a few pennies: 3d. was most common. Leyrwites and childwites were usually more, often much more. In the midst of the Great Famine, for example, Alice Becket of Worlingworth (Suffolk) paid what had by then become the customary fine for childwite in her village: 2s.8d.; the other fines collected on that day were 3d. (seven instances), 6d. (three instances) and 12d. (one instance).[75] High charges such as this are easily found for

---

[73] When the Statute of Cambridge first articulated an English poor law in 1388, it readily assumed – presumably because of long custom – that beggars would be supported either by the communities in which they lived or the communities of their birth. 12 Richard II, c. 7: *Statutes of the Realm*, II (1816), 68. No relevant parish records survive before 1348. Parish priests were expected to support the poor, and this expectation, whether met or not, might be the root of later parish-based poor laws. For the theory of this form of parochial relief, see Brian Tierney, *Medieval Poor Law: A Sketch of Canonical Theory and Its Application in England* (Berkeley, CA, 1959), esp. 89–109. As Christopher Dyer has concluded, formal charities alleviated so little poverty that self-help and community assistance must have filled the gap: Dyer, *Standards of Living*, 254–6, but also 234–57 more generally. See also Elaine Clark, 'Mothers', and 'Social Welfare and Mutual Aid in the Medieval Countryside', *Journal of British Studies*, 33 (1994), 381–406; Marjorie K. McIntosh, 'Local Responses to the Poor in Late Medieval and Tudor England', *Continuity and Change*, 3 (1988), 209–45; and Judith Bennett, 'Conviviality and Charity in Medieval and Early Modern England', *Past and Present*, 134 (1992), 19–41. There is no reason to assume that better-off tenants viewed their lesser neighbours altruistically; some, possibly most, used their social power to personal advantage. See Christopher Dyer, 'The English Medieval Village Community and its Decline', *Journal of British Studies*, 33 (1994), 407–29. Still, these people lived in such small communities that most were forced to heed Walter of Henley's advice to 'have the love of your neighbors, for whoever has a good neighbor has a good morrow' (as cited in Clark, 'Social Welfare', 401).

[74] Jurors were often fined for concealing leyrwites: for examples, see *Wakefield*, IV, 53–4; *Ingoldmells*, 107; Crowle rolls, LAO, CM I/3. Some women contested jurors' presentments, claiming they were unfair or ill-informed. For an example, see *Manorial Records of Cuxham, Oxfordshire, circa 1200–1359*, ed. P.D.A. Harvey, Oxfordshire Record Society, 50 (1976) [hereafter *Cuxham*], 611. In Minchinhampton (Glos.), these challenges were to be judged by five women; see *Holy Trinity Caen*, 61 and 73. Some women resisted leyrwite and childwite by refusing to pay it. For examples see *Walsham*, 91–5 (Alice daughter of Simon Kembald).

[75] SRO-I, S1/2/1.2.

leyrwite and childwite.[76] The most common charge for leyrwite was more modest (just 6d.), but even this hurt more than most other fines. For a female wage-labourer who could earn ¾d. or 1d. a day it would have taken a week or more to earn this sum, *if* she could find the work; for a brewster, 6d. would have consumed most profit from several brewings; for a woman lucky enough to hold a bit of land, 6d. could have taken all the money needed for a year's rent on an acre of good arable. Moreover, some communities supplemented leyrwite with further penalties, sometimes seizing the landholdings of women and sometimes simply expelling them.[77] For village elites in the hard times of the late thirteenth and early fourteenth centuries, control of the proliferating poor was a survival strategy in which leyrwite and childwite were very useful tools.

Nothing proves this more clearly than the historian's best friend, chronology. As we have seen, leyrwite and childwite were most common at the peak of population pressure, *c.* 1300; they waned a bit after the famine of 1315–22 eased that pressure; and they disappeared from most manors after the Great Plague of 1348–9 replaced over-population with under-population.[78] Other seigneurial levies also faded in the later

---

[76] For examples of pre-plague customary fines set at high levels, see: 'An Extent of Langar and Barnstone, c. 1340', ed. L.U.D. Owen, *Thoreton Society*, 11 (1943–5), 158 (5s.4d.); *Holy Trinity, Caen*, 61 and 73 (10s.); *Abbey of Bec*, 113 (2s.8d.); *Walsham* (2s.8d.); courts rolls of Crowle, LAO, CM I/3 (40d.). Sometimes such fines exhibit strong regional patterns: for example, a fine of 2s.8d. was standard in the East Anglian communities of Worlingworth, Walsham and Lessingham, even though these manors were held by different lords. Such patterns suggest that regional custom more than manorial regime determined the charges for leyrwite. I am grateful to John Hatcher and, through him, Mark Bailey, for drawing my attention to this.

[77] For seized landholdings, see Poos, *Select Cases*, cases 92, 170; *Cuxham*, 609; Homans, *English Villagers of the Thirteenth Century* (1941; repr. Cambridge, MA, 1970), 438 n. 14; Clark, 'Mothers', 150; Page, *Crowland*, 109. For expulsions, see Clark, 'Mothers', 151. On the manor of Swainston (Isle of Wight), a bondwoman guilty of illegitimate birth became *ipso facto* a forced servant of the manor, although most women seem to have avoided this by payment of a fine; see *Registrum Johannis de Pontissara, 1282–1304*, Surrey Record Society, 6 (1924), 674.

[78] The last leyrwite that I have found for England was levied in Ingoldmells in 1492: *Ingoldmells*, 282–3. But leyrwite had long been rare even there; the penultimate leyrwite noted in this edition was levied in 1424 (*Ingoldmells*, 263). Leyrwite also survived into the fifteenth century on the estates of the bishop of Durham: see PRO, DURH 3/14. As leyrwite waned after 1348, its charge often increased to 5s. or more. Charges of 5s.1d. were common in Cornwall before 1348, but uncommon elsewhere until after the Great Plague. For examples: (1) a leyrwite of 5s.4d. was recorded in Ingoldmells in 1424 (*Ingoldmells*, 263); (2) a fine of 5s.1d. was levied in Werrington, Devon, in the late fourteenth century, but see the appendix on the likely Cornish antecedents of this fine (Devon Record Office, W1258M/D70); (3) fines of 5s. to 5s.4d. became customary in Cottenham in the 1350s (Ravensdale, 'Population Changes', 211); and (4) 5s. was levied at Sutton in 1410 (Jones, 'Medieval Leyrwite', 946). In 1391, a leyrwite on the three Cambridgeshire manors of Crowland Abbey was stated to cost 5s. *and* a purse ('bursa') worth ½d.

middle ages, but leyrwite was already a memory in many places where such servile fines as merchet and heriot still flourished in the late fourteenth century. After the Great Plague, wages were high, land was cheap, the standard of living was better than ever before and neither fornication nor illegitimate birth caused much worry to English villagers. James Thorold Rogers called these years the golden age of labourers; perhaps it was also a golden age for unwed mothers.[79] When population pressure renewed towards the end of the late fifteenth century, rural communities would begin again to punish fornicators and expel unwed mothers. But by that time, the decline of manorialism had changed the mechanisms at their disposal; instead of leyrwite, early modern villagers relied on village by-laws and parish government.[80]

For medieval bondwomen, then, leyrwite was a punitive fine that fell particularly on those ensnared by the hazards of marriage-making, rape and poverty. Yet this does not exhaust leyrwite's meanings, for, as Maitland and Vinogradoff saw so long ago, leyrwite was also a fine for immorality and a source of manorial profit. Not quite, however, in the ways that once seemed so obvious. In leyrwite's history, neither morality nor lordship look the same when viewed through the prism of gender.

As we have seen, the Church had no doubt about the immorality of sexual intercourse outside marriage. Yet there was a critical distinction between the Church's punishment of fornication and similar punishments in manorial courts: the Church punished *male* fornicators as well as female ones, sometimes even punishing men more harshly than women.[81] Medieval villagers marched to a different drum. They knew well the public and humiliating rituals through which churchmen punished fornicators: offenders stripped to their underclothes, bare-footed and bare of head too, subjected to public whipping and paraded through churchyards or marketplaces. But when the same villagers who

(Cambridge University Library, QC4/Ad23). As Michael Camille has noted in *The Medieval Art of Love: Objects and Subjects of Desire* (1998), 64, the purse is 'one of the most charged signs in medieval art', but its meaning in Oakington remains obscure. North has implausibly speculated that these expensive leyrwites suggest that, after 1348, leyrwite was only levied when the cost of meeting an ecclesiastical fine necessitated the sale of land. The explanation for leyrwite's post-1348 history of rising charges but declining incidence remains an open question.

[79] James E. Thorold Rogers, *Six Centuries of Work and Wages* (1894), 326.

[80] Ecclesiastical supervision of sexual offences continued unabated after the Great Plague. For the resumption of *local* actions against those who misbehaved sexually, see the data in Marjorie Keniston McIntosh, *Controlling Misbehavior in England, 1370–1600* (Cambridge, 1998), 69–74. I thank Marjorie McIntosh for sharing with me her list of late medieval and early modern by-laws on sexual behaviour.

[81] For an interesting discussion of ecclesiastical punishments, as well as an instance of heavier sentences imposed on men, see James Masschaele, 'The Public Space of the Marketplace in Medieval England', *Speculum*, 77 (2002), 383–421.

had witnessed these ecclesiastical punishments gathered within a few weeks at the manorial court, they reconceptualized fornication as a *female* offence, naming only women for leyrwite and usually not even bothering to mention, must less impose fines on, male partners.

They also reconceptualised fornication as an offence of the female poor, for medieval peasants seem to have been fairly tolerant even of women's sexual irregularity *except* when it was combined with poverty. After all, many women guilty of fornication or illegitimate birth were never presented at manorial courts for leyrwite or childwite.[82] And those who were so presented suffered little social ostracism in the long run. Yes, some of these women did descend into what demographers like to call a 'bastardy prone sub-society':[83] some women had several bastard children;[84] some sisters paid leyrwite together;[85] and some families produced impressive numbers of bastards.[86] But many former fornicators and bastard-bearers managed to marry. In Halesowen before 1348, for example, Razi has found that one out of four women presented for leyrwite later married; given the difficulties of tracing women's marriages in court rolls, this is a minimal figure.[87] Many, perhaps most, women who were unlucky in youth were not marked by that bad luck forever.

This 'luck' was largely a matter of economic status. Impoverished

---

[82] Since evidence from ecclesiastical courts shows that fornication was spread across the social spectrum of rural society, it is unlikely that only poor women fornicated outside of marriage. Interestingly enough, literary sources suggest a similar ambivalence, breaking across socio-economic lines, towards unwed mothers. On the one hand, Neil Cartlidge has argued that popular songs, a genre that depicts unwed mothers of low socio-economic status, are funny, catchy and generally hostile in their depictions of clumsy, vain, silly women who alone bear 'responsibility for bringing social catastrophe on themselves': Neil Cartlidge, ' "Alas, I Go with Chylde": Representations of Extra-Marital Pregnancy in the Middle English Lyric', *English Studies*, 5 (1998), 395–414, quote at 406. On the other hand, Jennifer Fellows has argued that Middle English romances, a genre that depicts women of much higher social status, 'display a good deal of sympathy towards the unmarried mothers' of their tales. See 'Mothers in Middle English Romance', in *Women and Literature in Britain*, ed. Carol M. Meale (Cambridge, 1993), 41–60, at 48.

[83] Smith, 'Appendix', has used network analysis to explore the extent to which such a sub-society can be found in late thirteenth-century Rickinghall. He concluded, albeit with considerable hesitation, that there was such a sub-society, although it might have been marked as much by poverty as by bastardy.

[84] For examples, see multiple fines paid by Isabel Fair, Matilda Lenild, Alice Anger and Matilda Becket in Worlingworth: SRO-I S1/2/1.1–1.6.

[85] Smith gives examples in 'Appendix'. See others in n. 48 above.

[86] For an example of four families in Salle that accounted for fourteen illegitimate children, see Clark, 'Mothers', 151.

[87] Razi, *Life, Marriage*, 66. Unless a marriage licence was noted in manorial records, it is very difficult for historians today to trace an individual woman's marriage; this difficulty makes it even more remarkable that so many women fined for illegitimate sexual relations are known to have later married.

unwed mothers and their children stretched community goodwill to breaking point, in part because their poverty was tainted by sin. By contemporary standards of charity, the sexual sinfulness that lay behind the plight of poor single mothers and their children rendered them unworthy of help, for giving charity to sinners encouraged more sin and, it was thought, delighted the devil.[88] Almsgiving institutions sometimes explicitly excluded unwed mothers from their rosters of worthy poor and so too, it seems, did ordinary people.[89] Even William Langland, an author who, writing after the Great Plague, expressed enormous sympathy for the poor and especially for poor mothers, had little truck with unwed mothers whose children he condemned as 'corsed wreches'.[90] It was similar reasoning that prompted the good folk of Horsham to include four poor mothers and their six small children among the twenty-one people they expelled from their community in the 1280s.[91] It seems that medieval peasants worried little about fornication, worried a bit more about women's fornication and worried most of all about the sinful poverty of unwed mothers and their children. The morality of leyrwite, then, was neither separate from nor dependent on the ideals of the medieval Church; leyrwite reflected a moral universe that did not neatly coincide with Christian teaching and law.

An attention to women also offers new ways of thinking about leyrwite as an expression of seigneurial power. Leyrwite has often been taken to epitomise the humiliating subjection of medieval serfs, a people so abject that even sexual matters were subject to seigneurial oversight (or, to put it another way, a people so abject that bondmen had ceded to others control over the sexuality of bondwomen). There is merit in this interpretation, for leyrwite clearly manifested the extraordinary powers that lords and ladies exercised over the bodies of their serfs. But women's history offers additional ways to think about the seigneurial meanings of this fine. For example, we now know that medieval women were commonly thought to take material benefit from courtship; perhaps, therefore, leyrwite was, in part, one way in which lords and ladies profited from the profit-making of their tenants. In other words,

---

[88] See especially Clark, 'Mothers', 145–7.

[89] See the charitable practices of the communities of the Hospital of St John in Cambridge and Oxford, as described in Miri Rubin, *Charity and Community in Medieval Cambridge* (Cambridge, 1987), 157–8. For the exclusion of women who were suspected of prostitution, see *The Account-Book of Beaulieu Abbey, Hampshire, 1269–70*, ed. S.F. Hockey, Camden Society, 4th series, 16 (1975), 174.

[90] *Piers Plowman: The C-Text*, ed. Derek Pearsall (rev. edn, Exeter, 1994), Passus x, line 217.

[91] See Clark, 'Social Welfare', 398. My discussion here relies particularly on Clark's insightful discussions of medieval provisions for the poor, especially in her 'Mothers', and 'Social Welfare'.

leyrwite might have been exacted, in part, because bondwomen profited from fornication or at least, so it was commonly thought. For young women in town as well as country, courtship was partly about gaining materially from the attentions of men. Men were expected to give women food, gifts and even money in return for the favour of their company – and sometimes the pleasures of sexual intercourse too. This is a common dynamic in medieval songs. In one song, a man offers a maidservant some gloves; she goes to his room to collect them; they spend a delightful night together.[92] In another, a man propositions a maiden by pulling a gold ring out of his purse and saying, 'Haue ye thys, my dere swetyng, / With that ye wylbe lemman myn.'[93] And in yet another, the material benefits of sex for women gave rise to a sacrilegious pun; as the maiden in this song tells of her lover, 'in my box, he puttes hys offryng'.[94]

Of course, songs such as these reflected practice, shaped it and even mocked it in ways that are difficult for us to discern today.[95] Yet it is not in songs alone that we can discern these assumptions about the profitability of female sexuality in medieval England. In the early thirteenth century, the author of *Hali Maidenhad* spoke baldly about the 'selling' of virginity for the economic support that union with a man might offer.[96] In the late fourteenth century, Chaucer had Absolon straightforwardly (but unsuccessfully) offer money to sleep with Alison in *The Miller's Tale*.[97] By the fifteenth century, when the English began to use a new word – singlewoman – for a never-married woman, they also began to use it as an occasional synonym for 'prostitute'. And by the next century, John Stow would describe the Southwark's burial ground for the prostitutes as 'the single womans churchyard'. As Ruth Karras has noted, this semantic equivalency of 'singlewoman' and 'prostitute' suggests that it was then difficult to imagine that a young woman would engage in extra-marital sex just for pleasure or affection; instead any woman who was sexually active outside of marriage necessarily had material gain on her mind. This does not mean that all singlewomen were prostitutes; instead, it means that courtship and sexual play were then commonly assumed to bring tangible benefits to

---

[92] *Carols*, item 453.

[93] *English and Scottish Popular Ballads*, ed. Helen Child Sargent and George Lyman Kittredge (Boston, 1904), 238–9, at stanza 5.

[94] *Carols*, item 456.1.

[95] I have discussed these songs at greater length in 'Ventriloquisms: When Maidens Speak in English Songs, c. 1300–1550', in *Medieval Woman's Song: Cross-Cultural Approaches*, ed. Anne L. Klinck and Ann Marie Rasmussen (Philadelphia, 2002), 187–204.

[96] *Hali Maidenhad*, 22–4. For this and many other examples, see Janelle A. Werner, 'Romance and Finance: Courtship, Commerce, and Female Sexuality in Late Medieval England' (M.A. thesis, University of North Carolina at Chapel Hill, 2002).

[97] *The Miller's Tale*, lines 3380–2.

women.[98] It was with this understanding that men courted and sought sex with women. As Robert Allerton explained when hauled before the London's consistory court in 1472, the gifts that had passed between him and Katherine Aber, who claimed to be his wife, were 'only because of the desire of his body and the satisfying of his lust'.[99]

For women of the mercantile and landed elites, these gifts of courtship were pleasures, not necessities. But for poor and landless women, having sex with a man might yield a night's lodging, a good meal, even, perhaps, some steady employment. In the manorial context, the benefit that bondwomen could take from their sexual liaisons might have seemed little different from the profits a brewster made in selling ale or the wages earned by a day-labourer; all were, in this thinking, rightly subject to manorial levy. When seen in this gendered context, leyrwite looks more like a run-of-the-mill manorial levy, directed not so much at the bodies of bondwomen as at the profit they took from their bodies. I do not mean to suggest here that leyrwite was strictly equivalent to fines levied on commercial brewsters or wage-labourers. Instead, I mean to suggest that it is useful to explore more fully the possible meanings of leyrwite. This fine drew clearly on seigneurial claims over the bodies of serfs. It might also have drawn on customs of courtships, ideas about profit, rules about the expected behaviour of women and men, and other aspects of manorial culture that we can

---

[98] I have relied here on the path-breaking work of Ruth Karras; see especially, *Common Women: Prostitution and Sexuality in Medieval England* (New York, 1996), and 'Sex and the Singlewoman', in *Singlewomen in the European Past, 1250–1800*, ed. Judith M. Bennett and Amy M. Froide (Philadelphia, 1999), 127–45, at 131.

[99] I have relied on the translation in Shannon McSheffrey, *Love and Marriage in Late Medieval London* (Kalamazoo, MI, 1995), 42–3. Karras cites a similar case in *Common Women*, 87. Both date from the second half of the fifteenth century, but they contain detail not available in early fourteenth-century records. In both cases, the women gave gifts to the men too, but only the men spoke of the gifts in terms of a bald exchange for sex. The link between male gifts and male sexual access to women has been explored in any other contexts. In traditional Ghanaian courtship it was expected that 'a man exchanged valued gifts in return for sexual services'; see Carmen Dinan, 'Sugar Daddies and Gold-Diggers: The White-Collar Single Women in Accra', in *Female and Male in West Africa*, ed. Christine Oppong (1983), 344–66, at 353. In early twentieth-century Chicago, working-class women partly survived by the benefits derived from dating; see Joanne Meyerowitz, 'Sexual Geography and Gender Economy: The Furnished Room Districts of Chicago, 1890–1930', *Gender and History*, 2 (1990), 274–96; and in Germany after the Second World War, women similarly found economic incentives to date soldiers in the occupying forces; see Perry Biddiscombe, 'Dangerous Liaisons: The Anti-Fraternization Movement in the U.S. Occupation Zones of Germany and Austria, 1945–1948', *Journal of Social History*, 34 (2001), 611–47. The link is perhaps most memorably phrased in the Nigerian expression 'No romance without finance', now enshrined in Gwen Guthrie's 1986 hit 'Ain't Nothin' Goin' on but the Rent'.

perceive today only by attending to the women who were the subject of this fine.[100]

Leyrwite's most recent definition in the 1997 volume of the *Dictionary of Medieval Latin in British Sources* echoes many past definitions by describing it as a 'payment for illicit sexual lying with a woman'.[101] Leyrwite was really, of course, a payment for illicit sexual lying *with a man*. This might seem a narrow point, but as we have seen today, it has broad implications. Leyrwite simply looks very different if we replace man-the-actor with woman-the-actor: its morality grows more complex, its seigneurial meanings get complicated and its usefulness in controlling poor bondwomen becomes much clearer. There is still much to investigate about this fine: how it was used by the Anglo-Saxons; why it predominated more in some regions than others; what it meant after 1348 when its imposition was rare but exceptionally costly; and, of course, the different trajectory of its history in colonised Wales. And there is still much that leyrwite, obscure fine that it was, can reveal to us about England in the time of the three Edwards: its regional distribution might help us reconstruct regional patterns of economic stress and over-population; its importation into Wales but not Ireland might offer interesting insights into medieval colonialism; its punitive intent has much to say about poverty and charity in these hard decades. But we will not effectively rewrite leyrwite's history – or, for that matter, England's history – if we rely on old assumptions and old approaches. Leyrwite was an obscure fine levied on obscure people a long time ago, but its long misunderstanding as a 'payment for illicit sexual lying with a woman' is a caution to us all.

Appendix: leyrwite in southern England

In addition to the usual archival work, I searched for leyrwite and related fines in all printed editions of primary sources in which they might plausibly have appeared – that is, in extents, surveys, terriers, custumals and manorial court rolls of the thirteenth and fourteenth

---

[100] Lords and ladies, who derived so much of their profit from control of the bodies of unfree tenants, laid different obligations on married and unmarried, young and old, male and female. As Chris Middleton has shown, they attended particularly to the *productive* labour of men in fields and the *reproductive* labour – social as well as biological – of women in cottages and farmyards. Middleton, 'Feudal Lords: 2', and 'Peasants, Patriarchy and the Feudal Mode of Production: 1: Property and Patriarchal Relations within the Peasantry', *Sociological Review*, 29 (1981), 105–35. In short, insofar as leyrwite reflects seigneurial interests, it was also one of several ways in which the *reproductive* work of *women* was a source of particular manorial attention and profit.

[101] S.v. legerwita. See also s.v. leirwite in the *Middle English Dictionary*, and s.v. lairwite in the *Oxford English Dictionary*.

centuries. For this search, I relied primarily on resources in the English Local History Room at the Institute of Historical Research [hereafter IHR] and those of the library of the Royal Historical Society as catalogued by E.L.C. Mullins. It is always difficult to prove a negative, but my comments about leyrwite in southern England reflect my findings in the lists printed below. In the interest of brevity, I have abbreviated some titles, but provided, where appropriate, the reference to fuller bibliographic information available in *Texts and Calendars: An Analytical Guide to Serial Publications*, ed. E.L.C. Mullins (2 vols., 1958–83). My regional divisions are based on those used in *The Agrarian History of England and Wales, 1042–1350*, ed. H.E. Hallam (Cambridge, 1988), 137–8. I am grateful to Harold Fox, John Hatcher, Maryanne Kowaleski and Mavis Mate for sharing with me their thoughts on leyrwite in their respective regions of southern England.

South-eastern England (Middlesex, Surrey, Kent, Sussex)[102]

- *The Domesday of St Paul's, 1222*, ed. William Hale, Camden Society, old series, 69 (1858). Mullins 31.69.
- *Custumals of Battle Abbey, 1283–1312*, ed. S.R. Scargill-Bird, Camden Society, new series, 41 (1887). Mullins 32.41.
- William Young, *The History of Dulwich College* (2 vols., 1889).
- *Court Rolls of Tooting Beck Manor, 1394–1422* (1909).
- *The Register of St Augustine's Abbey, Canterbury, Commonly Called the Black Book*, ed. G.J. Turner and H.E. Salter (2 vols., 1915–24). Mullins 11.2 and 11.3.
- *Court Rolls of the Manor of Carshalton*, ed. Dorothy L. Powell, Surrey Record Society, 2 (1916). Mullins 63.2.
- *East Kent Records*, ed. Irene Josephine Churchill, Kent Archaeological Society 7 (1922). Mullins 47.7.
- *Thirteen Custumals of the Sussex Manors of the Bishop of Chichester*, ed. W.D. Peckham, Sussex Record Society, 31 (1925). Mullins 64.31.
- *The Cartulary and Terrier of the Priory of Bilsington, Kent*, ed. N. Neilson, (1928). Mullins 11.7.
- *Lathe Court Rolls and Views of Frankpledge in the Rape of Hastings, 1387–1474*, ed. Elinor Joan Courthope and Beryl E.R. Formoy, Sussex Record Society, 37 (1934). Mullins 64.37.
- *Records of the Barony and Honour of the Rape of Lewes*, ed. Arnold J. Taylor, Sussex Record Society, 44 (1940). Mullins 64.44.
- *Some Court Rolls of the Manors of Tottenham, Middlesex 1318–1503*, ed. W. McB. Marcham (Tottenham, 1956).

---

[102] In addition to these printed sources, I consulted the pre-plague court rolls of Alciston (Sussex) in the East Sussex Record Office, SAS/G18/1–6. I am also grateful to Mavis Mate who has informed me that, in her extensive work in the manorial archives of Kent and Sussex, she found no references to leyrwite.

- *Custumals of the Sussex Manors of the Archbishop of Canterbury*, ed. B.C. Redwood and A.E. Wilson, Sussex Record Society, 59 (1958). Mullins 64.59.
- *The Chartulary of Boxgrove Priory*, ed. Lindsay Fleming, Sussex Record Society, 61 (1960). Mullins 64.61.
- *Court Rolls of the Manors of Bruces, Dawbeneys, Pembrokes (Tottenham) 1377–1399*, ed. R. Oram (Tottenham, 1961).
- *Custumals of the Manors of Laughton, Willingdon and Goring*, ed. A.E. Wilson, Sussex Record Society, 62 (1962). Mullins 64.62.
- *Two Estate Surveys of the Fitzalan Earls of Arundel*, ed. Marie Clough, Sussex Record Society, 67 (1969). Mullins 64.69.

Southern England (Somerset, Wiltshire, Dorset, Berkshire, Hampshire)[103]

- *History of the Manor and Ancient Barony of Castle Combe*, ed. G. Poulett Scrope (1852).
- *A Collection of Records and Documents relating to Crondal, Part 1: Historical and Manorial*, ed. Francis Joseph Baigent, Hampshire Record Society, 3 (1891). Mullins 43.3.
- *Rentalia et Custumaria Michaelis de Ambresbury, 1235–1252*, ed. C.J. Elton, Somerset Record Society, 5 (1891). Mullins 61.5.
- *The Manor of Manydown*, ed. G.W. Kitchin, Hampshire Record Society, 10 (1895). Mullins 43.10.
- *Two Registers Formerly Belonging to the Family of Beauchamp of Hatch*, ed. H.C. Maxwell Lyte, Somerset Record Society, 35 (1920). Mullins 61.35.
- *The Manor of Michelmersh, 1248–1331*, ed. John Summers Drew (typescript in IHR, 1943).
- *The Manor of Chilbolton*, ed. John Summers Drew (typescript in IHR, 1945).
- *Accounts and Surveys of the Wiltshire Lands of Adam de Stratton*, ed. M.W. Farr, Wiltshire Record Society, 14 (1959). Mullins 68.14.
- *The Medieval Customs of the Manors of Taunton and Bradford*, ed. T.J. Hunt, Somerset Record Society, 67 (1962). Mullins 61.67.
- *The Rolls of Highworth Hundred 1275–1287*, ed. Brenda Farr, Wiltshire Archaelogical and Natural History Society, 21 (1966) and 22 (1968). Mullins 68.21 and 68.22.
- *Court Rolls of the Wiltshire Manors of Adam de Stratton*, ed. Ralph B. Pugh, Wiltshire Record Society, 24 (1970). Mullins 68.24.

---

[103] I have also consulted the pre-plague courts rolls of: (1) Cranborne (Dorset), 1328–9 only, held by the marquess of Salisbury in Hatfield House; (2) Stockton (Wilts.) in BL, Add. Rolls 24330–84; in the Wiltshire Record Office 108/1–13 and in the Winchester Cathedral Library; and (3) Chedzoy (Somerset) in BL Add. Rolls, 15903–62.

South-western England (Devon, Cornwall)

The south-west presents a different case. Leyrwite is rare in Devon, which seems to have conformed to the general southern pattern, but leyrwite was levied, at an exceptionally high rate, in Cornwall.

The pre-plague accounts of the Duchy of Cornwall show that men and occasionally women paid a 5s.1d. leyrwite on the Cornish manors of the Duchy estate.[104] This levy is unusual in (a) its high cost (for comparison, marriage licences on these manors usually cost 2s.), and (b) its strong focus on men. But it was ordinary in one respect; as John Hatcher has noted, it disappeared from these manors after the Great Plague even though other servile exactions were still 'strictly maintained'.[105] The accounts rarely elaborate on the fine, but it was once linked with permission to enter the manor (PRO, SC6 811/4) and once with a fine to marry (PRO, SC6 811/10). As I have not found leyrwite in manorial court rolls for Cornwall before 1348, our best glimpse of what leyrwite meant in pre-plague Cornwall might come from post-plague Devon.[106] In Werrington (Devon), leyrwites of 5s.1d. were levied on pregnant bondwomen from the 1360s (when the first court rolls survive) into the 1380s.[107] On the Cornish side of the Tamar, Werrington was annexed to Devon in the 1080s; its custom of leyrwite is atypical of Devon but perhaps typical of Cornwall. If so, the focus on males-paying-leyrwite in the Duchy accounts might indicate different recording practices for different sorts of records; that is, fathers, brothers or other men might have been noted in the account rolls as paying fines that were noted in the court rolls as imposed on women. Or perhaps leyrwite was levied on men before 1348, but not by the time the Werrington courts survive. Clearly, Cornish leyrwite merits more research.

Because of Devon's proximity to Cornwall and because of the scarcity of printed sources, I searched for leyrwite in the relatively sparse pre-

---

[104] The accounts edited by Midgley happen to show only men paying this fine, but women did also pay it. For examples, see: PRO SC6 811/1 which records nine men and one woman paying the fine; 811/2 with eleven men and two women; 811/3 with fourteen men only; 811/4 with five men and two women; 811/6 with nine men and two women.

[105] John Hatcher, *Rural Economy and Society in the Duchy of Cornwall* (Cambridge, 1970), 78–9, 194–5. According to Hatcher, this fine was also levied in similar ways 'on many other Cornish manors as well as some Devon manors' before 1348. Aside from Werrington, I have found no evidence of leyrwite in Devon.

[106] I also found no references to leyrwite in (i) a 1345 survey of Tybesta and other Duchy manors which lists other servile dues (PRO, LR 2/247) and (ii) in the printed sources listed here. As Hatcher has noted, however, the Caption of Seisin and other Duchy records are poor guides to the customs of the Duchy's original Cornish manors and that 'as far as is known these [customs] were never comprehensively listed', 67.

[107] DRO, W1258M/D70.

plague manorial materials for the county.[108] I have found leyrwite only in Werrington whose custom in this regard seems to tell us more about Cornwall than Devon. I am grateful to Harold Fox who has informed me that he recalls no leyrwites in the post-1348 Devon courts he has examined (with, of course, the exception of Werrington).

- *Ministers' Accounts of the Earldom of Cornwall, 1296–1297*, ed. Margaret Midgley, Camden Society, 3rd series, 66 and 67 (1942 and 1945). Mullins 33.66 and 33.68.

- *The Cornish Lands of the Arundels of Lanherne, Fourteenth to Sixteenth Centuries*, ed. H.S.A. Fox and O.J. Padel, Devon and Cornwall Record Society, new series, 41 (2000).

- *The Caption of Seisin of the Duchy of Cornwall (1337)*, ed. P.L. Hull, Devon and Cornwall Record Society, new series, 17 (1971).

---

[108] I consulted materials for the following pre-plague manors: Yarcombe (DRO, CR 1429–30, CR 1432–5, 346 M/M1); Filleigh (DRO, 1262M/M1–M16); Halstock, Inwardleigh and Venn (DRO, W1258M/G5/18); Ogbear and Ottery (DRO, W1258M/D49/4); Willand and Middleton (BL, Add. Charter 16332); Budleigh (PRO, SC2 166/18).

Transactions of the RHS 13 (2003), pp. 163–85 © 2003 Royal Historical Society
DOI: 10.1017/S0080440103000070   Printed in the United Kingdom

RESISTANCE, REPRISALS AND COMMUNITY IN OCCUPIED FRANCE

By Robert Gildea

READ 18 OCTOBER 2002 AT THE UNIVERSITY OF WALES, ABERYSTWYTH

ABSTRACT. This essay examines the issue of armed resistance in France 1941–4 through the lens of collective reprisals inflicted on local communities as a result of armed resistance. It uses three examples from different parts of France: the north, the west and the Massif Central. It examines not only the incidents themselves and the reprisals but the way in which the local communities reacted to and commemorated the events in the years after the war. The essay concludes that local communities were at best ambivalent towards and at worst hostile to acts of armed resistance committed in their midst

In his introduction to *The Liberation of France*, Rod Kedward tells the story of the 3,000 maquisards mobilised on Mont Mouchet in the Auvergne, who repulsed a German unit on 2 June 1944, four days before the Normandy landings, descended into the village of Paulhac and at its entrance erected a banner reading 'Ici commence la France libre.' This liberation, however, was premature, and in a throwaway line Kedward says that 'Eight days later the Germans returned in force to take Mont Mouchet and exact reprisals on the surrounding villages.'[1]

This line in fact poses a whole series of questions which historians of the French resistance have not adequately addressed. Why were reprisals exacted on the surrounding villages? What kind of reprisals were they and who ordered them? Did local populations feel the same way about resistance after they had suffered the reprisals? The French resistance, so often described as the heroic endeavours of the few, needs to be put back into the context of the local community, and one way of doing this is through the lens of collective reprisals. Like all occupying powers, the Germans outlawed armed resistance by civilians, who were branded 'terrorists', and suspected that local people harboured and supported them. They held communities collectively responsible for terrorist acts committed within them, and whether they found the real culprits or not, regularly inflicted collective reprisals on those

[1] *The Liberation of France: Image and Event*, ed. H.R. Kedward and Nancy Wood (Oxford and Washington, 1995), 1.

communities. These strategies evolved in the course of the occupation, ranging from the mild to the brutal, from calibrated response to what seemed like the unleashing of blind fury.[2] Oradour-sur-Glane is the most memorable site of German atrocities, but in the summer of 1944 there were dozens of Oradour.

To analyse the relationship between resistance, reprisals and the local community, this essay will look at three different kinds of resistance in three different parts of France. The first incident was the assassination of a German officer in Nantes by a communist hit-squad on 20 October 1941. The second was the sabotage of a train bearing SS troops bound for the Normandy front, at Ascq just outside Lille, during the night of 1–2 April 1944. The third was the mobilisation of the Mont Mouchet maquis of which Kedward spoke, in June 1944, in that part of France which had remained unoccupied until the end of 1942. Each incident provoked savage collective reprisals against the local population and exposed in the raw the complex relations between the resistance and the local community. Those communities struggled to reconcile their faith in the resistance as a force that redeemed France with the tragedy that specific acts of resistance called down upon them. Some communities made a cult of the heroes of the resistance, others chose to remember the victims and martyrs. Some communities turned their anger and frustration outwards on to the Germans; others turned them inwards on those resisters they felt had provoked the reprisals. Each incident marked the community not only at the time but for long afterwards, and how they dealt with the pain over the years will be explored not least through the oral testimony of survivors.

Early in the morning of 20 October 1941 Gilbert Brustlein, a communist of Alsatian origins, who had recently come by train from Paris to Nantes to continue the campaign against German military personnel, shot dead Lieutenant-Colonel Hotz, who was no less than the Feldkommandant or military governor of Nantes, and made good his escape.[3] Returning to the scene of the crime fifty years later he claimed that his gesture was an 'act of war' that had 'unleashed armed resistance in the West of France'.[4] This may be seen as a highly contentious rewriting of history because, at the time, far from welcoming

[2] Richard Cavill Fattig, 'Reprisal: The German Army and the Execution of Hostages during the Second World War' (Ph.D. thesis, University of California, San Diego, 1980); Rab Bennett, *Under the Shadow of the Swastika: The Moral Dilemma of Resistance and Collaboration in Hitler's Europe* (Basingstoke, 1999).

[3] Louis Oury, *Rue du Roi-Albert: les otages de Nantes, Châteaubriant et Bordeaux* (Paris, 1996), 13–14, 89–93; Robert Gildea, *Marianne in Chains: In Search of the German Occupation, 1940–1945* (2002), 243.

[4] *Ouest-France*, 21 Oct. 1991.

Map 1   Sites of reprisals discussed, 1941–4

this assassination as the first step towards their liberation the population of Nantes was horrified by the assassination of its military governor.

In the first place Hotz was a German soldier in his sixties, known to the local population before the war and an official who related easily to the local authorities and notables. Edmond Duméril, German master at the Lycée of Nantes seconded during the occupation to be interpreter at the prefecture, noted in his diary,

> I have lost a sure support with the Germans. He was a just, intelligent man who was in no sense a Hitlerian, a friend of the French and particularly considerate towards me, linked to him almost daily for over fifteen months as I was. Will the Nazis replace him by some odious Prussian sabre-rattler?[5]

Second and more seriously, the Nantais feared that the German military

---

[5] Edmond Duméril, *Journal d'un honnête homme sous l'occupation* (Thonon-les-Bains, 1990), entry for 20 Oct. 1941 (p. 181).

authorities would immediately inflict collective reprisals in accordance with the ruling of Field Marshal Keitel, chief of the Wehrmacht High Command (OKW) on 16 September 1941 that for every one German soldier killed between 50 and 100 hostages would be shot. When the news reached Hitler's headquarters Keitel in fact demanded that 100 to 150 hostages be shot. Otto von Stülpnagel, the military governor in occupied France, fought to maintain some local control of the situation, accepting the execution of 100 hostages but only after three days' grace to find the killer or killers. Hitler ruled that 50 hostages must be shot at once, and 50 more in forty-eight hours' time if the perpetrators had not been found.[6]

The impact on Nantes would have been less if the hostages shot had all been communists from outside the local community. Since May 1941 over 200 communists from all over France had been held at a former POW camp outside Châteaubriant, about forty miles from Nantes, and the Vichy interior minister Pierre Pucheu put pressure on the German authorities to choose their victims from these inmates. Some German officials, however, were keen to punish a much wider cross-section of the population in order to impress the region and the nation more generally, and they focused their attention on a group of Great War veterans and notables of Nantes, of whom the most significant was Léon Jost, one leg shot away and decorated with the Legion of Honour, who had been sent to prison by a German military court earlier in the year for organising the escape of POWs still held in France. The forty-eight victims shot by the Germans on 22 October accordingly fell into three groups: twenty-seven communists from the Châteaubriant camp, sixteen prisoners in Nantes including Jost and five other veterans' leaders, and five Nantais then held at Fort Romainville in Paris.[7]

This was only the first stage: the Nantais had until midnight the next day, 23 October, to find the assassins of Hotz if another fifty hostages were to escape the firing squad. The local authorities and notables did not protest but saw the best way forward to resurrect the policy of collaboration with the Germans that seemed fatally damaged by the assassination. The prefect, mayor and bishop of Nantes called together on the new Feldkommandant to ask for mercy. The city of Nantes offered a reward of 200,000 francs and the French government a further 500,000 for information leading to the arrest of the killer. Marshal Pétain himself wanted to go to the demarcation line to surrender as a unique hostage before he was dissuaded by Pucheu and

---

[6] Gildea, *Marianne*, 246–7.
[7] *Ibid.*, 247–9.

other ministers.[8] Most poignantly of all, thirteen of the families of Nantes victims, led by the father of nineteen-year-old Jean-Pierre Glou, petitioned the Feldkommandant to say that they 'accepted with courage and resignation the cruel loss that afflicts them' and expressed confidence in the Germans' 'feelings of humanity' to call off further executions.[9]

It is difficult to assess whether it was the force of such intercessions or the persuasiveness of the argument of the military governor in France, Otto von Stülpnagel, that secured reprieve for the second batch of hostages. Von Stülpnagel, fearing that the policy of mass executions would undermine the goodwill that kept the French working for the Germans and drive them into the arms of the English, sent a famous telegram to Hitler's headquarters warning against the use of what he called 'Polish methods' in France.[10] What is clear however is that the authorities and population of Nantes were not minded to respond to General de Gaulle's call from London for a five-minute demonstration between 4 and 4.05 p.m. on 31 October as a gesture of solidarity and defiance. Similarly, when de Gaulle decided to award the Croix de la Libération to the city of Nantes on Armistice Day 1941, in recognition of its suffering and heroism, the mayor and municipal council decided not to acknowledge it for fear of upsetting the Germans who had, after all, pulled their punches. This rebuff was never forgotten by the general, who after the liberation did not visit the city to make the award in person until January 1945, and then pointedly did not call at the town hall.[11]

The second incident of resistance and reprisal took place in the far north-east of France, which under the occupation was governed directly from Brussels rather than from Paris. The small town of Ascq, just outside Lille, lay on the main railway line from Brussels to Lille and was inhabited to a large extent by railway workers. At 10.45 p.m. on the evening of Saturday 1 April 1944, a small charge exploded on the track just outside the railway station, stopping train number 649355. It was a German military train carrying troops and equipment of the 12th SS Panzer Division Hitlerjugend towards Normandy, to defend against a possible Allied landing. It was recruited from the Hitler Youth and commanded by young SS officers, many of whom had seen service on the Russian front.[12] No Germans were hurt, and the train was not even

[8] Marc Ferro, *Pétain* (Paris, 1987), 344–7.
[9] Archives Départementales [hereafter AD] Loire-Atlantique [hereafter L-A] 270w480, petition of families, 25 Oct. 1941; Gildea, *Marianne*, 248, 253–4.
[10] Bundesarchiv-Militärarchiv Freiburg RW 35/1, von Stülpnagel to Major-General Wagner, 24 Oct 1941; Gildea, *Marianne*, 254–5.
[11] Gildea, *Marianne*, 255–8.
[12] Jean-Marie Mocq, *La 12 SS Panzer-Division: Massacre: Ascq, cité martyre* (Bayeux, 1994), 41–7.

derailed, but the line was broken and the convoy could not move. Unfortunately the sabotage was catastrophic for the town. An immobilised convoy was a sitting target for Allied planes. A bottleneck would severely impede the timetable of further convoys west. There was also a sense of being stranded in enemy territory, and a fear of partisans concealed behind every wall, generated on the savage eastern front and now imported to the peaceful brick-built villages of northern France.

The initiative was taken by SS Obersturmführer Walter Hauck, aged twenty-six, who later claimed that shots had been fired on the convoy from a house adjoining the railway line. 'Get out! Action stations!' he ordered. This was generated by fear, no doubt, but was also in accordance with instructions issued on 3 February 1944 by Field Marshal Hugo Sperrle, Commander-in-Chief West. The calibrated response authorised by Hitler himself in 1941 was no longer an option in an environment where troops were exposed to attack by resistance fighters. The new instructions read:

If troops are attacked in any manner, their commander is obliged to take his own countermeasures immediately.

a. There is to be an immediate return of fire. If innocent persons are hit this is regrettable, but entirely the fault of the terrorists.

b. The surroundings of any such incident are to be sealed off immediately and all civilians in the locality, regardless of rank or person, are to be taken into custody.

c. Houses from which shots have been fired are to be burned down on the spot.

A report will not be made until these or similar immediate steps have been taken.

In judging the actions of troop commanders, the decisiveness and speed with which they act will be regarded as priorities. A slack and indecisive troop commander deserves to be severely punished because he endangers the lives of the troops under his command and undermines respect for the Wehrmacht.

Given the present circumstances measures that are subsequently regarded as too harsh cannot provide ground for punishment.[13]

The SS troops plunged into the town, searching houses and dragging out all adult males. Any who resisted or tried to flee were gunned down on the spot. The vicarage was broken into and the vicar and his two lodgers killed; the curate was shot in the street as he tended to the dying. Those rounded up were marched, some in their nightclothes, to

---

[13] Hans Luther, *Der französiche Widerstand gegen die deutsche Besatzungsmacht und seine Bekämpfung* (Tübingen, 1957), 240; Otto Weidinger, *Tulle and Oradour: A Franco-German Tragedy* (n.p., n.d.), 27.

the level-crossing where the train had stopped and then taken, in three groups, to the end of the train where they were shot. The massacre went on from 11.30 p.m. to 12.30 a.m. A fourth batch, who included the mayor, were spared as the German Feldgendarmerie arrived to stop the carnage. Sixty-two men died on the railway line, another twenty-four in their homes or in the street, making eighty-six dead in all.[14]

Unlike in Nantes, the damage was done immediately and irreparably. Such good relations that existed between the French civil and ecclesiastical authorities on the one hand and the German military authorities on the other dissolved. The massacre was bad enough, but to add insult to injury Lieutenant-General Bertram, Oberfeldkommandant of Lille, issued a communiqué saying that the troops had acted in self-defence after shots had been fired from windows of houses in Ascq. It read

> The population must know that any attack on German units or individual soldiers will be responded to by all means required by the situation. The example of Ascq must be a lesson. In the nature of things it is inevitable that innocent people will suffer when such things happen. Responsibility lies with the criminals who make such attacks.[15]

The regional prefect, Fernand Carles, who until now had pursued a discrete policy of collaboration, protested in person to the Oberfeldkommandant, asserting that no shots had been fired, that the attitude of the population was blameless and that the reprisals were completely disproportionate. The Oberfeldkommandant explained that the soldiers were returning from the Russian front and their methods were explained by 'the atmosphere of danger and struggle they had endured for long months'.[16] A protest about the massacre of innocents was also lodged by the influential Pétainist archbishop of Lille, Cardinal Liénart, who had lost a vicar and curate in the massacre, and been horrified by the sight of bodies riddled with bullets. The Oberfeldkommandant, his nerve failing, expressed his fear that a 'gulf' had opened up between the Germans and the agitated local population and

[14] AD Nord 1W1505, reports of Captain Guillemain of gendarmerie of Roubaix and commissaire de police du Sûreté Lafon of Lille, 3 Apr. 1944; AD Nord Musée 355/1, enquiry of commissaire de police, affaires criminelles, Deruelle, 14 Apr. 1944; Jean-Marie Mocq, *Ascq 1944: la nuit la plus longue* (Suresnes, 1971).

[15] AD Nord 1W30, press cuttings from *Le Réveil du Nord*, 3 Apr., and *L'Echo du Nord*, 4 Apr. 1944; see also AD Nord Musée 355/1, procureur général près la cour d'appel de Douai to minister of justice, 7 Apr. 1944; AD Nord 1W1569, report of chef des renseignements généraux, Lille, 8 Apr. 1944; Canon Lucien Detrez, *Quand Lille avait faim, 1940–1944* (Lille, 1945), 322–3.

[16] AD Nord Musée 355/1, regional prefect Carles to head of government, 3 Apr. 1944.

asked the cardinal to do something to calm things down. The cardinal replied coolly that the only way to calm things was for the German authorities to punish those soldiers who had been responsible for the massacre.[17] The German authorities were manifestly embarrassed, but made their point by tracking down, arresting, court-martialling and executing on 7 June 1944 six railway workers who were held responsible for sabotaging the train. The judgement of the military court, sent to the French authorities on 16 June, developed that the argument that the massacre at Ascq had been provoked by terrorist activity and that the 'band of terrorists' had now been dealt with. Their membership of the *Voix du Nord* resistance group and involvement in train sabotage since November 1943 was carefully detailed. It also claimed that the condemned men had named thirty of those killed in the Ascq massacre as members of resistance organisations, throwing doubt on the notion that only innocent men had died.[18] For the Germans this was supposed to put an end to the matter but for the French it was out of the question. Cardinal Liénart told General Bertram flatly that he 'could not consider that this verdict was an answer to my previous protest [as] there are also German killers and they remain unpunished'.[19] Needless to say his letter received no reply.

The third resistance incident takes us back to where we started, with the gathering of a great maquis on Mont Mouchet in the Auvergne. This could scarcely be more different than the two previous examples: not the furtive activity of individual gunmen or handfuls of saboteurs – *les armées de l'ombre* – but a mass mobilisation in broad daylight of would-be freedom fighters, making their way to the rendez-vous by rail, car, truck, bicycle or on foot. Behind it lay the 'Plan Caïman' (Alligator Plan) drafted by General Billotte of the Free French in London, envisaging a mobilisation of maquisards in the Massif Central, on to which would be parachuted weapons and commanding forces, in order to keep the Germans pinned down in the south while the Normandy landings got under way. In fact the Plan was never adopted by the Allies, because the Americans had no desire to encourage a national insurrection in France, but the charismatic leader of the resistance in the Auvergne, Emile Coulaudon codename Gaspard, pressed ahead with the idea anyway after meeting a Special Operations Executive (SOE) agent Maurice Southgate on 15 April and obtaining the approval of resistance groups on 2 May. The order for the *levée en masse* was published on 20 May and volunteers made their way to Mont Mouchet,

[17] Diocesan Archives [hereafter Arch. Dio.] Lille 8M5, private report of Cardinal Liénart on the massacre of 2 Apr. 1944.

[18] AD Nord 1W1350, communiqué of Oberfeldkommandantur of Lille, 16 June 1944.

[19] As above, n. 17. This is a manuscript addition to the typed report, referring to a letter sent to General Bertram on 8 July 1944.

less from the immediate rural vicinity than from the factories of Clermont-Ferrand and Montluçon or from Strasbourg University, whose staff and students had been evacuated to Clermont in 1940.[20]

This mobilisation took place under the noses of the Germans and in spite of a curfew they imposed in the region. The first German attack, as described by Kedward, took place on 2 June. The second, more concerted, was launched on Mont Mouchet on 10 June from three sides, Saint-Flour in the west, Brioude in the north and Le Puy in the east. Some historians say there were around 12,000 Germans, others calculate a more reasonable 2,000–3,000.[21] Dislodged from the mountain, the maquisards evacuated south to a second base at Chaudes-Aigues. This was attacked by the Germans on 20 June and the maquis was finally scattered. The leaders realised that the congregation of so many forces in one place had been hazardous, and now broke their forces up into twenty guerrilla groups dispersed around four departments. The arms drop, which never arrived on Mont Mouchet, finally came on 14 July, when in Operation Cadillac swarms of American aircraft unloaded their contents.[22]

This story encapsulates the romance of the resistance but minimises the impact of such struggles on the surrounding communities. Reprisals were inflicted on neighbouring villages, as Kedward noted, and indeed on neighbouring towns. As German forces moved up from Saint-Flour to Mont Mouchet on 10 June they passed through the large village of

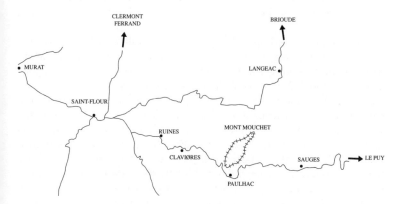

Map 2   Mont Mouchet and its surrounds, 1944

[20] Eugène Martres, *Le Cantal de 1939 à 1945: les troupes allemandes à travers le Massif central* (Cournon d'Auvergne, 1993), 353–62.

[21] Interview with Eugène Martres, Aurillac, 12 Mar. 2002.

[22] Martres, *Cantal*, 368–87, 409–16.

Ruines, a *chef-lieu de canton*. It was not a haunt of maquisards but its station had been the terminus for many going up on to the mountain. A few days before there had been an exchange of fire between a German patrol and a car-load of maquisards. Locals said that the troops who arrived in the early afternoon of 10 June were drunk and angry; though officered by Germans many had an oriental appearance and were later categorised as Azerbaijanis. What they did not know is that orders issued by Field Marshal Sperrle on 8 June, two days after the Normandy landings, said that he expected

> undertakings against the guerrilla gangs in southern France to proceed with extreme severity and without any leniency...Partial successes are of no use. The forces of resistance are to be crushed by fast and all out effort. For the restoration of law and order the most rigorous methods are to be taken to deter the inhabitants of these infested regions from harbouring resistance groups and being ruled by them, as a warning to the entire population.[23]

As at Ascq the Germans searched the houses and rounded up the adult males. Those who resisted or tried to flee were shot: these included the schoolteacher, tax collector, a lycée teacher from Montpellier and the wife of a POW. Others were taken to a footpath outside the village where machine-gunners were in place and gunned down. Altogether twenty-five men and one woman died. Houses were set on fire before cigarettes were distributed to the soldiers and the column moved off.[24]

The column moved up to Clavières, a small hillside village inhabited mainly by dairy farmers. It was, however, also an outpost of the Mont Mouchet maquis, and as at Paulhac a banner there read 'Ici commence la France libre.' A tree trunk had been thrown across the road as a barricade and maquisards opened fire on the advancing armoured column with small arms and a bazooka. The farmers had seen the smoke rising from Ruines and scampered off into the surrounding rocks and ravines, but in order to save the village from destruction the mayor, François Broncy, also a farmer but veteran of the Great War with a black handlebar moustache, donned his tricolour sash and went out to meet the Germans waving a white handkerchief. He was never seen again. The Germans set fire to the village and probably threw his body into a burning house. Nine other people died, including a bed-ridden women, Mme Johanny, her farmer husband and daughter. The death

---

[23] Luther, *Der französische Widerstand*, 247; Weidinger, *Tulle and Oradour*, 28.

[24] AD Puy-de-Dôme (P-de-D) 908w150, eye-witness accounts, notably that of Hélène Odoul, mayor of Ruines Sept. 1944, and anon. typescript 'La tragédie de Ruines: juin 1944'.

toll of the maquisards, given the battle, was much higher: sixty-four bodies which were buried by the curé and the courageous women who stayed after their menfolk had fled.[25]

While the Wehrmacht was engaged in crushing the maquis the Gestapo and Milice were involved in winkling out resisters among the civilian population. On 12 June 1944 the Gestapo chief of Vichy, Hugo Geissler, arrived at the town hall in Murat, west of Saint-Flour, to question and arrest some key individuals: the mayor, his secretaries and the wives of local resisters. As they left at 4 p.m. a group of maquisards concealed in the upper part of the town opened up with machine-gun fire, killing Geissler. Enraged and threatening to destroy the town, the Gestapo and Milice took their captives to Saint-Flour, where the previous day a number of suspects had been rounded up in the Hotel Terminus, opposite the railway station. These included the mayor, a judge, a number of police officers suspected of trying to win over Germans in a local post, Frère Gérard, director of Sacré-Coeur school, and the wife, daughter and one of the sons of a local resistance leader, Dr Louis Mallet, who was tending the wounded on Mont Mouchet. To exact reprisals for the death of their chief, they improvised a court martial in the hotel in the night of 13–14 June. At dawn the next morning twenty-five victims including sixteen-year-old Pierrot Mallet were taken by truck to a bank near the railway bridge of Soubizergues, outside the town, and shot.[26]

Military operations then took over. The Germans mounted an assault on Chaudes-Aigues on 20 June, ended the last stand of the maquis and captured Dr Mallet and his other son, whom they promptly shot. Once they had done with the maquis they returned to finish their business at Murat, where Geissler had been shot. Ten days had passed since the attack and the men who had fled the town had by now confidently returned. On 22 June the town was surrounded, houses were searched and the men were rounded up in the town hall and schools. Papers were systematically checked and those aged under sixteen or over fifty were released. The others, 115 in all, were deported to concentration camps like Neuengamme, a lingering death from which only a handful returned.[27]

[25] AD P-de-D 908w90, report of Lieut.-Col. Plantier of War Crimes service, n.d.; anon. typescript 'Clavières, 10–11 juin 1944'; 900w61, report of intendant de police of Clermont-Ferrand, 21 June 1944.
[26] AD Cantal 1w358, report of Conseiller Alfred Chardon [of Bordeaux appeal court] 'sur la violation des lois de guerre dans le Cantal, 30 Oct. 1944'; Valentin Palmade, *Sous-Préfet à Saint-Flour durant l'occupation* (Clermont-Ferrand, 1974), 136–92; Frère Gérard Mayet, *Soubizergues: terre de sang* (Clermont-Ferrand, 1956).
[27] AD Cantal 1w358, report of Conseiller Chardon; AD P-de-D 908w90, account of Henri Fournier, head of maquis of Chaudes-Aigues, n.d.; interview with Eugène Martres, Aurillac, 12 Mar. 2002; Charles Berenholl, 'Le service de santé de 'état-major des maquis

The second part of this essay is devoted to an exploration of how local communities reacted to these tragic events, both at the time and subsequently. Did they celebrate the heroes who undertook acts of resistance or only mourn the victims who had lost their lives in the reprisals? Did they direct their anger and pain outward against the Germans, or did they forgive the Germans and criticise those resisters whose brave but foolhardy gestures had brought so much suffering? How did they reconcile the tragedy that befell their own towns and villages with the joy felt after the liberation of France as a whole? To find answers to such questions I have looked at how these events have been publicly commemorated, but also at how they have been remembered privately by individuals whom I or others have been able to interview.

Only at Mont Mouchet was there a serious and sustained cult of the resistance heroes. There maquisards were deified as the incarnation of the French resistance and their armed activities were legitimated as both militarily and psychologically crucial in the liberation of France. Yet, because of the heavy losses sustained by the maquisards themselves, and even more because of the reprisals inflicted on civilians in the surrounding towns and villages, the resistance myth was never quite secure. Over time, moreover, it became even more contested.

On 20 May 1945, the first anniversary of the mobilisation order of maquis leader Gaspard, the first stone of a monument dedicated to the maquis of France was laid on the summit on Mont Mouchet by Gaspard himself.[28] There was a large official contingent, including resistance organisations, prefects, the bishop of Saint-Flour and Allied delegations, but some opposition to the ceremony was already expressed. The Liberation Committee of Cantal, whose leading light was René Amarger, the right-hand man of Dr Mallet at Saint-Flour, declined to attend the ceremony on the grounds – communicated in a private letter – that 'the operations of Mont Mouchet were a failure, in view of the lack of preparation and the lack of equipment put at the disposal of the volunteers, which resulted in considerable loss of life and the destruction of many villages and farms'.[29] The role of Gaspard was controversial, not only because of the heavy price paid for the rising but because the internal resistance was seen as acting without orders

---

d'Auvergne', in *Occupation, résistance et libération dans le Cantal*, Revue de la Haute-Auvergne, Apr.–Sept. 1994, 241–9.

[28] Serge Barcellini and Annette Wieviorka, *Passant, souviens-toi! Les lieux du souvenir de la seconde guerre mondiale en France* (Paris, 1995), 266–8; Françoise Maury-Fermandel, 'Lieu de mémoire et de commémoration: le Mont Mouchet, 1944–1989', in *De Vichy à Mont Mouchet: l'Auvergne dans la guerre, 1939–1945*, ed. André Gueslin (Clermont-Ferrand, 1991), 147–72.

[29] Martres, *Cantal*, 662.

from the Allies or the Free French in London and Algiers. When General de Gaulle visited the region in July 1945 he did not go to Mont Mouchet and at Clermont-Ferrand, as evidenced in the 1971 film, *Le chagrin et la pitié*, refused to shake Gaspard by the hand.[30] Before the unveiling of the completed monument in June 1946 there was a security alert after rumours were picked up of a plan to damage the monument because it was felt that the money raised for it would be better spent on rebuilding burned-out villages.[31] It was felt more discrete that the monument be unveiled not by Gaspard but by the widow of Dr Mallet, who had recently returned from deportation and represented the victims rather than the heroes.

The route to Mont Mouchet every June for reasons of geography followed the route of the German reprisals from Murat to Saint-Flour and on to Ruines and Clavières, each one marked by the grief of reprisals and, hidden as best it might be, by the bitterness of recrimination. Addressing the villagers of Ruines in the cemetery on 1 November 1944 the new mayor Hélène Odoul, an eye-witness of the massacre, called for unity and the forgoing of recrimination, perhaps because graffiti had appeared at one moment attacking the local resistance that was alleged to have provoked the reprisals.[32] Both Ruines and Clavières were awarded the Croix de Guerre as martyred villages on Armistice Day 1948, and Ruines unveiled a poignant monument of a woman holding two fallen children in October 1950. Clavières, which had had to bury a large number of maquisard dead, unveiled an ossuary containing the remains of eleven unknown maquisards in 1949 and a monument to Mayor Broncy, who had died trying to protect the village, and the other local victims, in 1954. In an attempt to forget its painful past Ruines voted in 1961 to rename itself more picturesquely Ruynes-en-Margeride.

Down the valley at Saint-Flour the liberation was not celebrated in 1944. The bodies of the twenty-five victims shot at the Pont de Soubizergues, and which the Germans had demanded be buried there, were disinterred and brought back to the town for a proper burial. On 12 June 1945 at 6 a.m., the hour of the mass execution, and at the same time every year since, a silent procession made its way from the town to the bridge, where in 1946 a line of stones, one for each victim, was erected. One of those was Pierrot Mallet, whose father Dr Louis Mallet gave his name to the town's monument listing those who died for France during the war and which was unveiled in 1947. A country

---

[30] Interview with Eugène Martres, Aurillac, 12 Mar. 2002.
[31] AD Cantal 1w331, report of chef des services des Renseignements Généraux, Aurillac, 5 June 1946.
[32] *La Femme de l'Auvergne*, 18 Nov. 1944.

doctor whose peasant clientèle provided a network of hiding places for Service du Travail Obligatoire (STO) refusers, who gave his medical services unstintingly to the maquis and in the process lost his own life and that of his two sons and heard of his wife and daughter deported, Dr Mallet was the generous father-figure of the resistance who, had he survived, would have been universally acclaimed mayor of Saint-Flour at the liberation.[33]

Some of those shot at Saint-Flour had come from Murat, to the west, where in reprisal for the assassination of Gestapo chief Geissler 115 men were deported. The most moving account of their suffering in German concentration camps was written by a schoolboy, Raymond Portefaix, who had only just taken his *baccalauréat* when he was deported. Published as *The Hell that Dante Did Not Foretell* in 1946, initially in René Amarger's paper *La Margeride*, he told with the guilt of the survivor of 'the shadow that all the tenderness of my own family cannot disperse. There are dead. I bring tidings of mourning. I came home but other families will cry when I speak.'[34]

The resistance lobby did not accept defeat but made a concerted effort to put across its own heroic account of events. The turning point in its fortunes was the visit of General de Gaulle, now president of the Republic, to Mont Mouchet in June 1959. Dressed in his general's uniform of 1940 he this time shook the hand of Gaspard that he had avoided in 1945 and declared that 'an insufficiently known and heroic episode of the French resistance happened here'.[35] The legitimacy cast by this visit was exploited by Gaspard himself and by his lieutenant, Gilles Lévy, who had gone from the maquis to the regular army. The argument that they developed was that the maquis was a national insurrection which was planned in London, mobilised 17,000 maquisards against 15,000–20,000 Germans who suffered heavier casualties than the French, and had the military significance of pinning several divisions down in central France at the time of the Normandy landings.[36]

The resistance story, however, did not have it all its own way. When

[33] René Amarger, *Des braises sous le cendre: souvenirs d'un résistant* (Saint-Florent, 1983), 137; *La Margeride*, 20 June 1945; *La Voix du Cantal*, 28 June 1947; AD Cantal 1W331, note on Dr Mallet by Dr Julhe for prefect, 6 June 1947. See also Julian Jackson, *France: The Dark Years, 1940–1944* (Oxford, 2001), 602.

[34] *La Margeride*, 10 Nov. 1946; René Portefaix, *L'enfer que Dante n'avait pas prévu* (Aurillac, n.d.), 227.

[35] Maury-Fernandel, 'Lieu de mémoire', 162.

[36] Gilles Lévy, 'La véritable histoire du Mont Mouchet', *Le Mur d'Auvergne*, 10 June 1956, 'Un épisode crucial de la résistance française en mai–juin 1944: la concentration des maquis d'Auvergne', *Revue Historique de l'Armée*, 24 no. 3 (1968), 43–60, and – with François Cordet – *A nous, Auvergne!* (Paris, 1974); Emile Coulaudon [Gaspard], 'Histoire du premier corps franc d'Auvergne' (*Le Mur d'Auvergne*, n.d.), and *idem*, Le *Mont Mouchet, haut-lieu de la résistance* (Clermont-Ferrand, 1971).

President Giscard d'Estaing, himself an Auvergnat from a Pétainist family who had joined the regular army to invade Germany in 1945, visited Mont Mouchet in June 1974, he broadened the list of those deserving homage from the resistance to those who died for the liberation of France as soldiers and hostages, in prisons and in deportation camps. President Mitterrand visited Mont Mouchet in 1981, anxious to drape himself in the colours of the resistance, but focused on the spiritual rather than the military value of the resistance, fighting 'Nazism, fascism, imperialism and intolerance', inspiring now as then 'a more just, more humane and more fraternal France'. Introducing Mitterrand in his capacity as president of the Comité d'Union de la Résistance d'Auvergne (CODURA) René Amarger was in sombre mood. 'We will never be able to forget our friends who died in an unequal fight', he said,

> or those who were shot or deported, hundreds of victims of Nazi barbarism, nor the mourning of so many families in this region, whose dear ones were murdered in the cruellest conditions by an uncontrolled soldiery thirsty for blood, nor the ruins of which our villages for so long have borne the stigmata.[37]

The commemoration of the fiftieth anniversary of the events on and around Mont Mouchet marked less the heroism of the resistance than the suffering of the local communities. Madeleine Mallet, daughter of the good doctor, who had been held in the hotel Terminus at Saint-Flour before she was deported to Germany with her mother, unveiled a new monument to all those who had been shot, including her twin brother Pierrot, in front of the hotel. 'The more time passes the closer the events are, she recalled. I spent three days here with my brother, in the same room of the Terminus, and I can see everything as clearly as I did then, unchanged.'[38] One of the commando group who had killed Gestapo chief Geissler and triggered the reprisals at Saint-Flour and Murat did not flaunt his resistance credentials but felt the need to justify his action. 'We answered barbarism with weapons in our hands to save what might be saved', he said. 'We acted as guarantors of democracy and not as barbarians ourselves.'[39] Gilles Lévy, who in 1956 was exalting 'the most open hospitality and the most constant support' for the resistance in the villages surrounding Mont Mouchet, in 1994 conceded that:

[37] *La Montagne*, 23 June 1974, 6 July 1981; Maury-Fernandel, 'Lieu de mémoire', 168, 172.

[38] *La Montagne*, 15 and 26 June 1994.

[39] Edmond Leclanché, 'Nous avons tué Geissler!', in *De Vichy à Mont Mouchet*, ed. Gueslin, 179–88.

For the Auvergne the real drama will always be the collective reprisals that were repeated, sometimes against localities (Saint-Flour, Murat, Ruynes, Clavières, Paulhac), sometimes against the region as a whole...the massacre of innocent civilians, the shooting of hostages, burned, sacked and depopulated villages, ill-treated and deported survivors, wounded and prisoners finished off,

although he was still reluctant to see resistance and reprisal in a relation of cause and effect.[40]

In the spring of 2002 I visited the scene of resistance and reprisal around Mont Mouchet. Eugène Martres, local historian, began our interview by talking about the repression at Murat, where he had been a boy at the time. He cited the anger of parents at resistance leaders who had recruited young men for the maquis and, disorganised as they were, led them to disaster. He recalled his friendship with his classmate Raymond Portefaix who had been deported after the roundup on 22 June. 'Murat', he said, 'never recovered. It lives but it does not prosper.'[41] I met Eugène Portefaix (no relation), a metal sculptor of Ruynes, who was a boy at the time of the massacre. He says that the maquisards, who came mainly from Clermont-Ferrand and Montluçon, did not get on well with the locals: they were 'salauds' who took everything. 'We still suffer', he confided, 'some families more than others.'[42]

In the *mairie* of Clavières I was introduced by Paul Esbrat, president of the Association de la Résistance et des Maquis du Cantal, to three locals who shared their memories of the events. In true resistance style, Paul Esbrat recounted the heroic events of the battle, although he conceded that at Ruines there had been 'rancour' towards the maquisards for a long time. Louis Bony, an old farmer, who at the age of eighteen had gone up to Mont Mouchet with twenty young men of the commune, reflected 'Perhaps we shouldn't have done it, but what were we supposed to do? We followed the crowd.' Maria Roche, thirty-three at the time, remembers that the men fled and the women were left to bury the bodies of fallen maquisards under the eye of the curé. Laurence Johanny, then twenty-four, was to marry one of the Johanny sons who were POWs in Germany. She lost her future father-in-law, future mother-in-law, bed-ridden and burned alive in her house, and her future sister-in-law, Yvonne. 'Even today, Monsieur', she says,

[40] Gilles Lévy, 'La véritable histoire', and 'Il y a cinquante ans, avril–juin 1944: pourquoi le Mont Mouchet?', in *De Vichy à Mont Mouchet*, ed. Gueslin, 199–239.

[41] Interview with Eugène Martres, Aurillac, 12 Mar. 2002.

[42] Interview with Eugène Portefaix, Ruynes-en-Margeride, 13 Mar. 2002.

'when we talk about it, we live it. It is like a nightmare that never ends.'[43]

At Ascq the first reaction to the massacre of 2 April 1944 was a wave of hatred of the Germans. The word 'atrocities' was now on everyone's lips in a way it had not been since 1914–18, and there was a sense that the barbarities of the war raging in the east were now moving to the west; Ascq was 'the copy of what was happening in Russia'. People were now prepared to believe that the massacre of Polish officers at Katyn, where their mass grave had ben discovered the previous April, was the work of Germans rather than Soviets. Maurice Schuman, de Gaulle's spokesman, went as far as to describe Ascq on the BBC on 15 April as France's Lidice, the Czech town rased to the ground by the Germans in retaliation for the assassination of Reinhard Heydrich.[44] Cardinal Liénart, who had officiated at the funeral of the victims before a crowd of 10,000–20,000 Catholic parishioners and communist workers on 5 April 1944, announced at the first ceremony after the liberation at Ascq, on 24 September 1944, that no laws of war permitted the massacre of innocents. On the first anniversary of the massacre, when Ascq was cited in the same breath as Oradour, the new vicar, Abbé Wech, who had been curate at Ascq until 1941, denounced these 'acts of barbarism' although he made a distinction between the barbarism of the Nazis and the German people as a whole. This distinction was not made by the mayor of Ascq, who had narrowly survived, and attacked 'the German people who were responsible for these atrocities...a people that committed such acts should be excluded from humanity'.[45]

The liberation meant the expulsion of the Germans but it was also a time of bitter mutual recrimination. Cardinal Liénart warned against this in his September 1944 sermon, urging that hatred and division must be countered by love and reconciliation. The fact that those who had undertaken the sabotage were local men and had been shot shortly after the massacre made it possible to remember the *massacrés* and the *fusillés* almost in the same gesture. The committee set up to help the families of those massacred decided in January 1945 to include the families of those shot.[46] On 10 June 1945 the rue de la Gare, where

[43] Interview with Maria Roche, Laurence Johanny, Louis Bony and Paul Esbrat, Clavières, 13 Mar. 2002.

[44] AD Nord Musée 355/1, reports of police commissars of Wattrelos and Roubaix, 4 Apr. 1944; *Il y a 50 ans...le massacre d'Ascq* (Ascq, 1994), 12.

[45] Arch. Dio. Lille 2Z19, cutting from *La Croix du Nord*, 25 Sept. 1944; Abbé Wech, *J'accuse...Témoignage d'un Asquois sur le massacre du 22 avril 1944 et contribution à l'histoire de la civilisation au Xxe siècle* (Ascq, 1945), 90; AD Nord Musée 355/1, cutting from *Le Nord Eclair*, 3 Apr. 1945.

[46] AD Nord Musée 355/1, minutes of meeting of Comité de répartition des secours, 20 Jan. 1945.

many of the *massacrés* died, was renamed the rue des Martyrs, and the route Nationale, where many of the *fusillés* had lived, became the rue des Fusillés.[47] When General de Gaulle visited Ascq on 29 June 1947 he unveiled a plaque dedicated to the memory of both the *massacrés* and the *fusillés*. The following month the socialist president of the Fourth Republic, Vincent Auriol, laid the first stone of the monument to the six *fusillés* next to the cemetery that was sponsored by the resistance and unveiled in October 1947, while in October 1955 an Ensemble du Souvenir, including a monument to the massacred and a clinic for the local population, symbolising new life, was inaugurated on the site of the executions by the railway line.[48]

Meanwhile with the support of resistance organisations and the widows of those massacred at Ascq the perpetrators of the massacre were tracked and brought to trial by the military court of Metz, meeting at Lille for the occasion, in August 1949. Crowds outside the Palais de Justice shouted 'A mort! A mort!'. The star of the proceedings was the gaunt-featured Walter Hauck, who commanded the SS unit on the night of the massacre. With him in the dock were eight other members of the unit, while seventeen others who had not been caught were also tried under the law of 15 September 1948 which established collective responsibility for war crimes. On 6 August 1949 all but one of the nine in court and eight others *in absentia* were condemned to death.[49]

This might have been the cathartic end of the story: a community united in mourning and satisfied that justice had been done. But it was not to be. Cracks appeared in the united front over two issues: first over whether or not to forgive the SS soldiers who had been condemned; and second as to whether the *fusillés* should bear some responsibility for provoking an avoidable massacre, a controversy that divided the families of those who had been massacred from the families of those who had been shot.

The Catholic Church under the leadership of Cardinal Liénart, who had insisted from the first that justice must be done to the guilty Germans, came to extend his gospel of love and reconciliation after the condemnation of the Germans to the Germans as well. He stopped attending the annual commemorative ceremony of Ascq after 1950 and in February 1951 attended a requiem mass for the victims of the massacre in the German town of Dortmund. In his address he said that the crime was to be condemned but not the person and that for the Christian there was 'a collective responsibility of love'. The umbrella

---

[47] Jean-Marie Mocq, *Ascq. 1er avril 1944: la longue marche du souvenir* (Dunkirk, 1984), 78.
[48] *La Voix du Nord*, 1 July 1947; Mocq, *Ascq*, 43, 77–8; Mocq, *La 12 SS Panzer-Division*, 146–56.
[49] AD Nord Musée 355/2, press cuttings from *La Voix du Nord* and *Liberté*; Mocq, *La 12 SS Panzer-Division*, 159–74.

for this reconciliation was the Pax Christi movement that had been founded in 1945 and had 10,000 followers in the diocese of Lille by 1953.[50] It linked up with a legal movement to have commuted the death sentences passed against the condemned SS men, orchestrated by Raymond de la Pradelle, who had acted as their defence counsel at Lille. He argued that the so-called 'Oradour' law of 15 September 1948 on collective responsibility under which they were condemned violated three fundamental principles of French justice: individual responsibility, non-retroactivity and innocence until proven guilty. This was eventually abrogated by parliament during the Bordeaux trial of those accused of the Oradour massacre, on 30 January 1953. Persuaded by Pradelle, Cardinal Liénart wrote to President Coty in June 1950 warning of the danger of condemning the Germans out of 'a spirit of vengeance'.[51] At Whitsun 1955 a group of widows of the massacred wrote a letter to the president of the Republic, René Coty, asking for the Germans under sentence of death to be pardoned. They asked for their names not to be published, for fear of dividing the association of widows. Many widows were not able to go along with their gesture. Madame Guer-monprez, for example, second president of the widows' association, later said that it was too early and she was not yet ready to forgive.[52] On 15 July 1955 President Coty duly commuted the death sentences and the Germans returned home at once except Hauck, who was released in 1957. The work of reconciliation was moved forward by a service of reparation held in the parish church of Ascq in March 1957, officiated by Cardinal Liénart and attended by Mgr Schoeffer, head of the German section of Pax Christi and bishop of Eichstatt in Bavaria. Finally, in April 1964, on the occasion of the twentieth anniversary of the massacre, a group of survivors and families of those massacred led by Abbé Wech went on a pilgrimage to Rome and were blessed by Paul VI. 'Happy are you', they were told, 'who have turned hate into love, vengeance into friendship and war into peace.'[53]

The public and official even-handedness of the commemoration in memory of the families of the victims of the massacre and of those who had been shot as resisters was maintained at the ceremonies which took place annually until 1969, then every five years. But privately, under the surface, there was an antagonism between the two groups

[50] Catherine Masson, *Le Cardinal Liénart: évêque de Lille 1928–1968* (Paris, 2001), 352–3.

[51] Arch. Dio. Lille 8M5, Raymond de la Pradelle to Liénart, 9 June 1950; Liénart to Coty, 10 June 1950. See also Raymond de la Pradelle, *Aux frontières de l'injustice* (Paris, 1979).

[52] France 3 Nord Pas-de-Calais, *Ombres portées* (1994), interview with Valentine Guer-monprez.

[53] Arch. Dio. Lille 2Z19, cutting from *La Croix du Nord et du Pas-de-Calais*, 19 Mar. 1957; cutting from *Ascq mon pays*, Apr.–May 1964.

because in the end it was resistance that had provoked the reprisals. When a film was made of the events in 1969 and a key role went to Edouard Lelong, a railway boilermaker who had been involved in the sabotage but escaped arrest, Madame Dewailly, who had been dragged with her two daughters to witness the first execution cried, 'Ah non, pas lui!' Rumours circulated that the saboteurs had been imprudent, that Delescluse in particular smoked English cigarettes and that the sabotage was not officially authorised.[54]

Tensions between the different families was also laid bare by an FR3 film, *Ombres portées*, on the occasion of the fiftieth anniversary of the massacre in 1994. Interviewed for it Valentine Guermonprez recalled that one of the saboteurs had continued to live in her *quartier* and said wryly, 'If I had been him, I would not have remained at Ascq.' On the question of forgiveness she said that there were not one but two groups of people who had to be forgiven: the Germans of course, but also 'those who set off the explosion so close to a town'. She said that these had been forgiven, and the widows of the *fusillés* were welcome in the widows' association, which was purely an association of war widows. How far this was so was revealed by the interview with one of those widows of the *fusillés*, Simone Gallois. Timid, burdened by sadness, she related that although her daughter had received the Legion of Honour awarded to her father at a ceremony in Lille, and although she went with her children every year to the monument to the *fusillés*, where the municipality laid a wreath and she felt she had her place, she also felt that people in the community resented her and held her husband responsible for the tragedy. 'I told myself that my husband had not done anything wrong, because there were no victims on the German convoy, and then he was obeying orders: it was for France, for his *patrie*.' She said she hoped that everything would be sorted out for the fiftieth anniversary but then choked back her tears: 'Why, why, won't they forgive me, why?'[55]

In Nantes the execution of the fifty hostages caused an immense shock, but collaboration with the Germans seemed to work in that a second batch of fifty hostages were reprieved. There was no cult of the act of resistance of the lone gunman of 20 October 1941, even by the Communist Party (PCF), which realised how unpopular his deed had been. Instead, the Party competed for the ownership of the memory of the victims of 22 October, exploiting the communist hostages shot at Châteaubriant to develop their myth of the party of the '75,000 *fusillés*' in order to regain the patriotic credentials it had lost after the Nazi–

---

[54] Interview with Jean-Marie Mocq and Gérard Chrétien (whose father was killed on 2 Apr. 1944, conservator of the Musée du Souvenir), Ascq, 18 Sept. 2001.

[55] *Ombres portées*, interviews with Valentine Guermonprez and Simone Gallois, 1994.

Soviet Pact of 1939. Their rivals were the families of those (mainly war veterans and Catholics) executed at Nantes, lead by the bishop of Nantes. He portrayed the Nantes victims as Catholic martyrs, promised to light a candle every year if a second batch of hostages destined for the firing squad were spared, and at a ceremony on 22 October 1945 declared that 'the Church would not forget them, any more than a mother could forget her children'.[56] That same afternoon communists swamped the commemoration at Châteaubriant, brandishing banners demanding 'avenge our dead' and power for the party secretary Maurice Thorez, and singing the *Internationale* to the annoyance of French officials and American officers present. The seventy-six-year-old Marcel Cachin called the PCF 'le parti des fusillés' and warned, 'Much ill has been said of the communists but in future it will be prohibited to say that communists are not loyal to France...many died for her, and their tragic fate will be mourned, but their death showed France the way.'[57]

There was, to be fair, one member of the cult of the resistance of the lone gunman of Nantes: the lone gunman himself. Gilbert Brustlein, who survived the occupation, revealed his story in the *Humanité Dimanche* in 1950.[58] He soon broke with the Communist Party, claiming that after the assassination it had instructed him to commit suicide since he was a security risk and asking how many resistance heroes had actually been shot by the Stalinist machine.[59] This led to a good deal of controversy at the fiftieth anniversary of the death of the hostages in 1991, when for the first time Brustlein returned to the scene of the action. He interrupted the speech of George Marchais, secretary-general of the PCF, at Châteaubriant, shouting that Marchais had spent the war working voluntarily in a German factory and had no right to speak for the resistance, before being wrestled to the ground by Marchais's minders. In the rue du Roi-Albert in Nantes, where he had shot Hotz, he found it difficult to convince onlookers at the spot where he had pulled the trigger that he had performed not a murder but an 'act of war' and had 'unleashed armed resistance in the West of France'.[60] Michel Jost, son of the most illustrious hostage to be shot, declared that 'Gilbert Brustlein is using the blood of the dead for publicity. This anniversary has not been organised in memory of the attack on Hotz, but in honour of the 48 dead of Nantes, Châteaubriant

---

[56] Mgr Villepelet, 'Le diocèse de Nantes, 1940–1945', entry for 22 Oct. 1945.

[57] AD Maine-et-Loire 90w4 inspecteurs du service des Renseignements Généraux, Angers, 23 Oct. 1945.

[58] *Humanité Dimanche*, 20 Aug. 1950. See file in Archives Municipales Nantes, 1134w12.

[59] Gibert Brustlein, *Le chant d'amour d'un 'terroriste à la retraite'* (Paris, 1989), 248.

[60] *Ouest-France*, 21 Oct. 1991.

and Paris.'[61] The visitor's book of the exhibition to mark the affair of the fifty hostages showed twenty-one entries critical of Brustlein and only three in favour. He was accused of shooting the German in the back, of failing to turn himself in, in order to spare the lives of the hostages and then of daring shamelessly to return to the scene of the crime.[62]

Nantes had to await the sixtieth anniversary of the events in 2001 before any reconciliation was possible. The hard work was done by Louis Oury, a former engineering worker and local writer, who committed long years to persuading the Nantais to embrace their resistance past. On 22 October 2001, in the presence of the minister of war veterans and deputy-mayor of Nantes, a plaque was unveiled in the rue du Roi-Albert commemorating the 'execution' of the Feldkommandant by a group of Communist Youth as well as the execution of the forty-eight hostages on the orders of Hitler and with the collaboration of Vichy. The authorities however refused to put the name of Brustlein on the plaque, alleging that according to 'republican tradition' only the names of the dead could be publicly commemorated in this way (despite the existence of a lycée and college dedicated to Lucie Aubrac). More eloquent still was the agreement of Michel Jost to shake the hand in public of Gilbert Brustlein, saying that Brustlein had only been obeying orders and had no idea of the consequences of his actions. That said, consensus was still lacking. Many were still horrified by the presence of Brustlein and a plaque commemorating the execution of the Feldkommandant. 'The wound remains deep in Nantes', reported L'Ouest-France, 'among the families of hostages who held the commandos responsible for the death of their loved ones.' Hostility was also expressed by twelve of the fifteen local resistance organisations which boycotted the events. Gaullist and anti-communist in sympathy, they preferred to align with the victims rather than with the gunman who for them would always remain the 'assassin'.[63]

The French resistance, seen from the perspective of the local community, was never considered either then or later as unalloyed heroism. The German practice of collective reprisals made any kind of armed resistance extremely dangerous, for the resisters themselves but even more so for the communities in which they operated. German strategy to discourage the harbouring of 'terrorists' by local communities evolved over the course of the occupation from a calibrated response decided at the highest levels to a rapid and ruthless response decided by local

[61] Presse-Océan, 23 Oct. 1991.

[62] Livre d'Or, exposition des 50 otages, Nantes, 16 Oct., 24 Nov. 1991. I am indebted to Frank Liaigre for lending me a photocopy of these entries.

[63] L'Ouest-France and Presse-Océan, 23 Oct. 2001; letter of Louis Oury to author, 18 Nov. 2001.

unit commanders. The desire to praise the resistance because it had liberated and redeemed France was undercut by the local experience of brutal reprisals which threatened to drive a wedge between armed resisters and local communities. The reactions of these communities was not everywhere the same. In the Auvergne, at Mont Mouchet, there was an explicit cult of the resistance, but even this was ambivalent, preferring to concentrate on the good doctor of the maquis rather than its hotheaded leader, and the German reprisals are still remembered as a 'nightmare' in the surrounding towns and villages. At Ascq the anger and grief of the local community was initially projected on to the Germans for their barbarism, but after the German perpetrators had been pardoned those feelings turned inwards on the resisters who had provoked the massacre, even though they were local men who had also lost their lives. At Nantes it was not the Germans who were vilified but the lone gunman from outside the community who pulled the trigger, brought untold grief to the community and had the misfortune to live to tell the tale. Even after sixty years the reconciliation between him and the families of the hostages who died was still partial and imperfect.

ARCHITECTURE AND HISTORY

A Joint Symposium of the Royal
Historical Society and the Society of
Architectural Historians of Great
Britain, Held at Tapton Hall,
University of Sheffield, 5–7 April 2002

Transactions of the RHS 13 (2003), pp. 189–97 © 2003 Royal Historical Society
DOI: 10.1017/S0080440103000082   Printed in the United Kingdom

ARCHITECTURE AND HISTORY: AN INTRODUCTION

By Clyde Binfield

I like to hear a girl in the elementary school beginning her sentences with the words 'I wonder why!'. There is all hope for a girl who wonders: 'I wonder why the arches in this old church are some of them round and some of them pointed?' You are getting ready to begin your study of English history.[1]

Of course you must know something of architecture. When you have grasped a few elementary ideas then you go out in search of a church or castle in which you can find those ideas illustrated. In process of time you will be able to read histories in stone. Everything will have a voice. You will say to your companion,

> Here such a man began to build; there he stopped. Times were bad ... there, William's monks wrought. See the chipping of their axes on the capitals of the columns! Now you may detect the influence of some stirring abbot. Restless man! He could not be content until his minister outshone all others ... And there see the out-bursting of an efflorescent mind that had not learned to worship God in the beauty of simplicity!

You can read it all.[2]

Those two quotations come from prize-giving addresses delivered in 1881 and 1883 respectively. One was called 'Taking an Interest in Work' and the other was called 'Books, and how to Read Them'. The speaker was John Smith Simon, a Wesleyan minister in his late thirties. His audience was Wintersdorf, a girls' boarding school (ages eight to twenty) run by his sister in Southport.

Readers who find comfort in simple models will already be constructing theirs. 'Boarding school' and 'Southport' announce the middle classes. The Wesleyan connection suggests that these will be more

[1] John S. Simon, *The Three Reverences and Other Addresses* (1889), 50–1.
[2] *Ibid.*, 91–3.

middle than upper middle, a case of the short 'a's and the inescapable rhythms of Lancashire and Yorkshire complicated by the gutteral implications of 'Wintersdorf'. Pugin, father and son, had over the past forty or so years burst out down the road at Scarisbrick for their landlord, but these are the daughters of rich tradesmen, prospering manufacturers and discreetly subsidised Methodist ministers. It is easy to see spheres separated, genders put in place, patriarchy confirmed. Perhaps that is what was happening. Private schools can only survive by attracting parents who wish to consolidate their families' already successful place in life. The visual, the imaginative, the intuitive, to which those two quotations attest, are the female domain. History and architecture, as seen rather than made, are eminently suitable for girls, certainly Victorian girls.

Such a model, of course, while not wholly wrong, is wrong enough. A careful reading of the artfully constructed annual prize-giving addresses delivered by that Methodist minister to his sister's pupils in the 1880s suggests the inculcation of a temper which one would crave a century and a quarter later for all university graduates let alone eight-year-old drapers' daughters. It encompasses passion reined in by intellectual discipline: passion for accuracy, passionate inquisitiveness, and then the exercise of imagination, and then of clear reflection, and then, at the last, the duty to communicate.

Most of those Southport girls were destined to become helpmeets or homemakers. In all other respects they were doomed (or privileged) to be amateurs. I have a personal reason for gratitude since my own future, now past, in History was formed by such a girl of the 1880s, educated on the south coast rather than in Southport but with the Wintersdorf frame of mind and sense of missionary responsibility. Mine was the post-war generation trained, like the generation before it, to look, feel and assemble by building blocks, Lott's Bricks, cut-out books of Cotswold villages, but also books on architecture by Maxwell Fry or on town- and village-scapes by Thomas Sharp, in preparation for the discovery of Banister Fletcher. The result was a shockingly, stimulatingly promiscuous affection for what I later realised was Arts and Crafts England slipping into the better sort of Stockbroker's Tudor England (somehow purged of subtopian ribbon development), culminating in the cold clear douche of the Modern Movement. All were enjoyed and their contexts were relished, for the promised land was none the less in view.

Then History took over. My historian contemporaries regarded such things coldly. History was Ideas, concepts shaped best by written evidence. History was Philosophy with its footing in fact. The visual was recreational but hardly foundational. I failed to realise that my contemporaries were ill at ease with the visual because they had been neither trained nor encouraged to analyse and communicate it. They were frightened by what they saw.

So much for the gift of reading 'histories in stone', of discerning such evidence as a historian might trust to explain why a particular architect adopts such and such a style, in that street, for this building. That gift, born of discipline, calls into play a serious testing of sources. It also acts as a literary test. How does one write about a building without the unconscious plagiarism which is the apprentice historian's occupational hazard? It is even easier for the tyro to use the words, rhythms, jargon and judgements of the architectural historian than it is to use those of the political historian. So how does one learn to use language freshly, freely, accurately, to describe what one feels and sees rather than what one ought to feel or see, in a way which communicates competence as well as confidence, and which demonstrates shape and proportion as well as responsibility? What still too easily eludes historians is in fact what fired that Methodist minister talking to Wintersdorf's girls in the 1880s, telling them that they were ready to begin their study of history.

John Smith Simon's mentors were predictable enough. They were Macaulay, John Richard Green and that Hon. FRIBA, Edward Augustus Freeman. Simon's views, it has to be admitted, were as likely to encourage antiquarians as historians, heirs to that English tradition whose job, as Elizabeth Williamson puts it, 'until recently has been to observe, record and classify monuments and other buildings whose chief merit has been their age or rarity.' That tradition's supreme monument, constructed in 1899, has been the Victoria History of the Counties of England which, county by county, 'took the antiquarians' task on to a national stage and applied the standards of the professional historian'.[3]

The *History*'s history is instructive. Within ten years (1908) its responsibility for the national architectural record was passed to the Royal Commission on the Historical Monuments of England and its own evolving record of buildings was caught in Ralph Pugh's directive of 1952, that 'In general, buildings are to be regarded as a type of source for economic and social history rather than for the history of art and architecture.' Elizabeth Williamson's gloss on what has actually happened is salutary: 'data has been presented almost raw, with the relationship between the histories of the settlements it has delineated and the development of the buildings it has described, left unexplained'. It has taken a further half-century for the *History* to leave the 'positivist pseudo-scientific tradition' of its formative years for 'the world of

---

[3] Elizabeth Williamson, 'After Antiquarianism: Architectural History and the Heritage Industry', 1, 2. I am indebted to Dr Williamson for her permission to use and quote from her contribution to the symposium's panel session, 'Historical and Visual Awareness'.

post-modern relativism' in which aggregated facts are turned into a comprehensible, even communicable, whole and the study of settlements and institutions is enlarged into that of communities. The *History* has returned to History.

But where does that leave the antiquarians, the gatherers of the evidence on which historians build?

> Data is what antiquarians collected ... With freedom from its former constraints, will the VCH, gorged on data, like late eighteenth-century antiquarians, be carried away by 'theory developed to the point of fantasy', to quote Stuart Piggott, or will our continuing intense scrutiny of documents and buildings together keep us firmly grounded within the communities we study?[4]

We are back to John Smith Simon, the Wintersdorf girls, their motivation and their education.

Amateurs, antiquarians, architects, both teaching and practising, joined architectural historians and such other historians as dared put their heads above the parapet for a Symposium arranged jointly by the Royal Historical Society and the Society of Architectural Historians of Great Britain at the University of Sheffield from 5 April to 7 April 2002.

The setting was appropriate: a post-Robbins hall of residence at the top of the Sheffield suburb famously praised by John Betjeman. Its aim was to explore what architectural history and other types of history have to offer and learn from each other and can offer to a wider public. Its intention was to do this from two perspectives. One is the role of architecture as evidence for a variety of other types of history – that is, the view of architecture from history in general. The other is the view of history in general from architectural history – the ways in which historical evidence contributes to the understanding of architecture and the processes of architectural change.

The sessions were carefully sequential and pretty predictable. They began with 'Approaches to History and Architecture – Some Challenges and towards Some Resolutions'. They developed from 'Architectural History and Political History' and 'Architectural History and Socio-Economic History' to 'History, Heritage and Politics'.

It was a *Symposium* – a conversation in which themes were shared, developed, frequently reworked. The rhythms of the conversation are more apparent from reading the papers than they were from hearing them, though their delivery was stimulating enough. The papers printed here are representative of the whole. They vary in length, style, focus, argument, region and period but, as in conversations when the

---

[4] *Ibid.*, 4.

participants talk, listen, share and move on, so in this symposium the papers relate unforcedly to each other: words, concepts, jump from one to another. This symposium is already a period piece. The reader will note the references to the Millennium Dome and Bridge; to a highly regarded film (*Gosford Park*) and a popular television programme (*Changing Houses*), to that already historic beast, the Mega-telly-don, and to that academic bugbear, the Research Assessment Exercise. Such clues will promote its historiographical value.

The tone was set in what estate agents would describe as a deceptively spacious manner by Eric Fernie ('History and Architectural History'), his range broad in period and region though consciously omitting antiquarians ('if anyone still answers to the term') and even-handedly concluding that 'architects bring a special expertise to bear on the subject ... Yet ... all other things being equal, the special abilities of the historian are more important for writing history than the specialist knowledge of someone working in the aspect of history in question.'

Neil Jackson and Nicola Coldstream rise to the challenge. The former ('Where Now the Architect?') urges architects to recolonise the writing of architectural history, from which they have withdrawn for the past seventy years, and reclaim it from the antiquarian (that word again) backwater into which the Modernist hegemony in architecture has relegated it. Yet his argument focuses on Modern architecture and what makes it different – the machine aesthetic, the new sense of space, the architect's ability to think three-dimensionally, to know (in Derek Linstrum's words) 'how designs evolve, how structures and materials behave' and the need for the architectural historian to communicate this. He draws on Cubism – its exploration of the time–space relationship as a paradigm. That implicitly and explicitly will reappear in other papers.

Nicola Coldstream ('The Architect, History and Architectural History') described her piece as 'a squib designed to put a few cats among pigeons'. Her squib soars from its medieval launchpad, a crisp reminder of how equivocal the contribution of architects to architectural history can be, that 'as the architect moves through history, the historian can never take him or her for granted'; that when buildings enter 'the main historical narrative', they are entering a narrative that encompasses 'far more than understanding how a building is made'; and that the 'history of architecture is a narrative of reflection on the past'.

Dr Proctor's 'A Cubist History: The Department Store in Late Nineteenth-Century Paris' is at once a tightly focused case study and an argument or, rather, the argument is the case study. The focus is the Parisian department store. Its sources dictated a post-modernist approach. Dr Proctor communicates that approach: no source is privileged; a building – or source – is a text, but it is also more than just a text; yet what that 'more' is can only be discovered through other texts. Thus a building's historian, an architectural historian, must spread the net more widely, must 'become more like a historian'. The communication of such history, however, needs something more appropriate to the reality than narrative can be. It needs a Cubist approach. Just as the Cubist focuses attention away from the painted subject towards the act of mediation (the process of observing and representing reality; the technique of collage) so a Cubist history is one in which the building is 'continuously present in different manifestations ... a rhythmic time ... parallel times, replacing the linear time of narrative based on literary realism'. That prompts a naughty question. Cubist history is certainly comprehensive. Can it be truly comprehensible?

Sean Sawyer ('Delusions of National Grandeur: Reflections on the Intersection of Architecture and History at the Palace of Westminster, 1794–1834') and Judi Loach ('The Hôtel de Ville at Lyons: Civic Improvement and its Meanings in Seventeenth-Century France') focus on famous buildings. Dr Sawyer returns us to London and the building complex which was the national focus of Britain's political (and legal) life. Their society is now in the wash of the French Revolution and the reaction and reform which it distilled. His buildings have largely vanished, indeed the most interesting of them were the most transient, yet their totality was powerfully representative of all sorts of political reality and stamped by forceful architectural personalities (few political historians of the period take due account of Soane and Wyatt). His aim – to examine public architecture with a 'nuanced understanding of the cultural, social, political and economic forces that shape both the designer and the design' – is less obvious than might appear.

Dr Loach provides an intricate case study of one building in its immediate urban, municipal, national and European context, but that immediate context could not be more far-reaching and it is multifaceted. Hers is a densely interwoven fabric, studded with cultural and political references and with a distinctively, not wholly expected, religious motif. And in exploring ways in which architectural history can be an essential tool for political historians she beats the Annalistes at their own game. She corrects an Annaliste interpretation of the history of Lyons by an approach which offers essential ingredients for fulfilling that school's purpose: the recovery of the experience of people who have not recorded it in writing.

Katie Withersby-Lench ('Investigating the Bigger Picture: A Case Study of the Jacobean Great Barn at Vaynol Park') adds a reference to Wales at a time of a rising gentry and of an anglicising Britain. Her focus is sharp rather than general. It is on the most striking (but not perhaps at first sight the most interesting) building on an estate that has recently come into public ownership. Here too is an essay on how a building-centred study, deploying the interaction of architectural, economic, socio-cultural and political history (with a strong woman yet again powerful in the not-so-distant background), can answer the historian's questions as no single type of history could.

Several of the papers are contributions to the history of gender which, here as elsewhere, tends to mean women's history. In 'Women Using Building in Seventeenth-Century England: A Question of Sources?' Anne Laurence's women are Puritan ladies, high rather than well born. For her the historian straddles 'the ground between the surviving buildings of the architectural historians and the imaginative spaces of the literary scholars', yet how literate is the historian in reading buildings as a source rather than merely using them as illustration? For the historian needs to understand how buildings reveal what the written record cannot, and to combine that with the insight of the literary scholar's new readings of old sources. Thus, here too, post-modernism creeps in.

Bill Stafford ('The Gender of the Place: Building and Landscape in Women-Authored Texts in England of the 1790s') and Rachel Stewart ('Telling Tales: Anecdotal Insights into the West End House c. 1765–c. 1785') are complementary yet contrasting. Professor Stafford takes us further into the meanings, spaces and openings of genteel if on the whole less grand houses than those of Dr Laurence and Dr Stewart. His texts are literary and women-authored although what they reveal is not solely about women. He asks what 'women- authored' texts, chiefly fictions whether by right-minded or radical women, say to architectural and other historians. Perhaps inevitably, certainly relevantly, the thrust is more on décor or ambience than architecture and the conclusion to which he tends slips free of gender: the absence of decoration may proclaim a masculine aesthetic, but for writing women at least of the 1790s it also proclaimed a female aesthetic – even, perhaps, 'an ungendered human aesthetic'.

Dr Stewart takes us to Town and returns us on the whole to grandees. Her source is that indispensably tangential factor, the anecdote, especially as gleaned from women's letters. Her object is to illuminate the town house's 'various functions as symbol, property, and commodity, as well as home'. Her justification is that although 'the body of anecdotal evidence is rarely looked at on its own terms', it can none the less help us to see such houses as functional objects in the histories of their occupants as well as entities in themselves. We are used to seeing them as the latter. We need training to understand them as the former.

The symposium demonstrated what ought to be obvious: that cultural, political and socio-economic issues may be accented, sometimes heavily so, but can never be satisfactorily separated and pigeon-holed. Stephen Caunce ('Houses as Museums: The Case of the Yorkshire

Wool Textile Industry') shows this clearly. The careful reader will find in Dr Caunce's paper the autobiographical element that historians, certainly Cubist historians, discount at their peril. Here too is architectural history (three houses are kept centre stage) as advocacy backed by argument. The general reader will be glad that the museum has been brought into the action: the symposium is already turning to the vexed, inescapable issue of heritage. This paper certainly tells a story. It has a narrative running steadily across a long (and local) chronology but, like most stories, this one proves to be many-layered. It is family history, industrial history, a community's history. It is also a story of everyday museum history, with political overtones – the constraints and (dwindling) opportunities of local government – and an unfinished agenda.

There remain the three papers on History, Heritage and Politics, taking up themes and methods already touched on in the symposium but with a powerful concluding slant. It was inevitable that the broad town-and-country-house world of the British political classes should figure throughout the symposium. Melanie Hall's 'The Politics of Collecting: The Early Aspirations of the National Trust, 1883–1913' develops this by introducing the liberal (indeed Liberal) politics of conservation, Arts and Crafts for the Reform Club. Here are men and women with an intense sense of place and race (a word they have discovered and are playing with), intelligently apprehensive of the political restructuring and social transformation to which they have contributed. Her focus is the National Trust in its suggestive but not too successful early years, with a particular eye on its Anglo-American and ideological dimensions, and its use of landscape and architecture to sustain a vision of national life and social order, high-minded, idealistic and English-speaking.

Melanie Hall's people were amateurs, great and good volunteers. Miles Glendinning ('The Conservation Movement: A Cult of the Modern Age') speaks as a professional conservator. His paper is unique, in part because it is cast as a sermon and in part because it was not delivered at the symposium. A much shorter variant was delivered at the Institute of Historic Buildings Conservation Annual School (June 2000) and reproduced in the Institute's newsletter, *Context* (2001). The present version replaces 'Sir Robert Matthew: The Modern Movement and the Politics of Conservation'. Admirers of Matthew will have to wait for Dr Glendinning's forthcoming biography. What is printed here returns us to the broader issues with which the symposium began, reminding us of their European dimension and the Modernism whence architectural historians especially are hewn. Its polemic has an immediacy for the themes of the symposium and an uncomfortable prescience, given the recent war in Iraq and assaults on conservation said to be without parallel since the Second World War. It brings home political realities from which pure historians recoil.

Robert Jan van Pelt's 'Of Shells and Shadows: A Memoir of Auschwitz' speaks for itself. The author, who was an expert witness in the David Irving trial, tells a story that could not be stronger or more subjective. Yet this narrative is a celebration of Cubist history for it is an implicit summation of all the themes, texts and methods explored in the symposium. It is also an enlargement of architectural history and, without relaxing tone or passion, it is a sharply detached take on the politics of heritage and conservation. Tourism is today inseparable from the life of Oswiecim. Professor van Pelt held captive an audience which was wholly unaware that his text and slides had been mislaid at the airport. The vigour of a map dashed on to a flipchart was assumed to be conscious method. It certainly worked. Here, in the true sense, was extempore communication. It expressed the symposium.

The organising committee – Clyde Binfield, Robert Shoemaker and Mary Vincent of the University of Sheffield, Peter Leach of the University of Central Lancashire and Chris Wakeling of Keele University – are grateful to each contributor and regret that it was not possible to include every contribution here. The three Sheffielders are conscious of the extent to which Dr Leach and Dr Wakeling were foundational to the symposium's success.

Transactions of the RHS 13 (2003), pp. 199–206 © 2003 Royal Historical Society
DOI: 10.1017/S0080440103000094   Printed in the United Kingdom

HISTORY AND ARCHITECTURAL HISTORY

By Eric Fernie

ABSTRACT. The term 'history' is confusingly ambiguous, not least in being identified both as the study of the whole of the past and only that part of the past accessible through the written record. This has an effect on those historical disciplines such as architectural history in which the study of the material evidence is inseparable from that of the documents. The paper examines how the use of texts in the study of objects can both casually mislead and powerfully explain, and equally how analyses of objects can both obscure and illuminate the textual record. Examples discussed indicate the value of stylistic analysis in the study of areas as different as African sculpture and the effects of the Norman Conquest.

'History' is a truly dreadful label. It might just be a case of the grass being greener, but I find that, while other subjects can be fiendishly abstruse, only 'history' by its very name presents completely irrelevant complexities of its own before one even starts on the problems of the material. It does this in at least four ways.

First, it means both the past *and* the academic study of the past. That is, as if the heavenly bodies were called 'astronomy' or the human race 'anthropology'.

Secondly, because of its association with written documents this academic study applies to only a tiny fragment of even the human past. This in turn leads to the absurdity of a period called 'pre-history', which is rendered doubly odd by the fact that the pre- or non-human past is referred to very properly as 'natural history'.

Thirdly, enter at this point the next villain of the piece, archaeology, the study of the material or non-documentary evidence. Its role is clear and essential, indeed heroic, but archaeologists have tended to define their contribution as a subject in its own right, a twin with history. Yet these are not two different subjects like, say, chemistry and physics or linguistics and anatomy, which, even if they overlap, really are different areas of enquiry. As the late Allen Brown eloquently put it, the past is a seamless web and archaeology simply one of the sets of techniques of the historical discipline with which it is explored.

The confusion does not end there, because, fourthly, 'history' has traditionally meant the history of power, leaving the study of other aspects of the past to be identified as such (social history, economic history, etc., each with its adjective). Braudel and others have of course taken this view to task, but it is still part of standard usage: witness a review of *Gosford Park* which compliments the scriptwriter on getting the historical and social details right for 1932, as if the social details were not historical.[1]

However much these particular variations contribute to the confusion surrounding the term 'history', it has to be acknowledged that subdivisions are none the less inevitable: because we cannot do everything, because we have different aptitudes and because our involvement always begins with curiosity about something specific. The main subdivisions are by area of human activity (political, social, economic, architectural, metrological), by period (Byzantine, Modern, the nineteenth century), by place (Latin American, Scottish, local) and by technique, for want of a better word (palaeographic, linguistic, petrological). All are capable of intersecting with the others. All have strong tendencies to separation, because of things like scholarly ambition and sociability, and because differences are exaggerated by various organisations such as learned societies like our own: what a pleasure it is to attend the annual conference, where even the sharpest disagreements have the comfort of a familiar context.

The subdivision of subjects has certainly aided the advance of knowledge, but it has also impeded it. For example, whatever the contingent reasons for the existence of our two societies, I have no doubt that, in a more ordered (though less interesting) parallel universe, the SAHGB would be a subsection of the RHS, as would the Victorian Society, the Georgian Society, the Classical Association of Scotland and so on. This is a defensible claim not only because of the over-arching 'history' label of the RHS, but also because of the strength of the case for accepting that some kinds of history are more fundamental than others. While judging what is 'fundamental' is clearly a minefield, it is easy to accept that political power has a greater impact on, say, architecture than vice versa, and therefore that it is reasonable to continue to use the term 'historian' as a shorthand for those who study that power. Usages such as this may distort our view, but there is no mileage in being a prescriptive grammarian. Hence also 'archaeologist' rather than something like 'historian of material culture'.

And what about the relationship between architectural history and the history of art in this game of Russian dolls? Architectural history is logically a part of the history of art, especially if the latter is taken to mean the fine arts, so architecture as opposed to building, but in terms of usage it is clearly something separate.[2]

---

[1] *Spectator*, 15 Feb. 2002.
[2] I discuss this question in more detail in 'The History of Art and Archaeology in England Now', in *The Art Historian: National Traditions and Institutional Practices*, ed. Michael F. Zimerman (Clark Art Institute, Williamstown, 2003), 160–6.

With those rather random remarks on the label 'history' and its subdivisions, I would like now to turn to the core purposes of the symposium, to look first at some of the ways in which architectural historians use documentary evidence, and then conversely at how the evidence of the buildings, like other objects, can be of use to other kinds of historian. But I need to stress, this complementary structure, of a–b and then b–a, is not intended to be in any way exclusive, as if only historians used documents or only architectural historians used buildings: the subdivisions of history are like Venn diagrams, a series of overlapping areas of expertise.

Architectural historians and the documentary evidence

The texts used by architectural historians are of many kinds, but among the most interesting are those which can be categorised as respectively misleading, to be taken at face value, and restrictive.

Misleading texts

The architectural historian, like everyone else, has to be careful when using documentary evidence. Taking texts at face value is a good principle, but it can mislead. I offer two examples. The Pantheon in Rome has on its façade an inscription several feet high which announces that *M[arcus] Agrippa L[uci] f[ilius] Co[nsul] tertium fecit*, which, with clear evidence for the right Marcus, dates the building to the time of Augustus, between 27 BC and AD 14. The hidden brick stamps on the contrary make it clear that it was built by Hadrian, between 118 and 125.

Next is a cartouche bearing the date 1677. This could be the date of the building to which the relief belongs, but in fact it forms part of a more recent structure, Munro Cautley's Lloyds Bank, Norwich, of the 1920s, 1677 referring to the founding of the company. In this instance, of course, we are unlikely to be misled, but in both cases the inscription refers to a concept which is more important than the specific structure.

Texts to be taken at face value

These are the reverse of misleading texts, in that they are available and clear in their meaning, but are ignored or argued away. The documentary evidence associated with the Anglo-Saxon see of the East Angles at North Elmham provides an example. After the Norman Conquest the see was moved to Thetford in 1072 and then in 1094 by Bishop Herbert to Norwich, where it stayed. The ruined masonry church at North Elmham was described as the Anglo-Saxon cathedral by all writers on the subject up to the late 1970s, including those who excavated the site. This despite the well-known statement in the First Register of the See (fo. 1) that Bishop Herbert completed the process of moving the see to Norwich, which had begun from a wooden cell (*sacello ligneo*) at North Elmham. The words *sacellum ligneum*, so glaringly at variance with the masonry ruins, were explained as intended to maximise Herbert's achievements by contrasting an unworthy structure with the magnificent cathedral which he built at Norwich. But, as Stephen Heywood has pointed out, this will not do. The First Register was written in the thirteenth century, but the section containing the quotation is an insertion from an earlier document which can be dated to the early twelfth. Thus the writer would have been asking those people who had known the site in 1072 to accept a bald lie as fact: wood for stone, and *sacellum* for a noteworthy church with a large western tower, an external cylindrical staircase, cylindrical buttresses and, to cap it all, a continuous transept, the only known example in England of the chief identifying feature of St Peter's in Rome and therefore almost certainly a reference to it. So Heywood accepted the plain unvarnished sense of the text that in 1072 the church at North Elmham was a small wooden cell, with the consequence that the masonry building on the site must have been built after 1072 and could not have been a cathedral. Instead he convincingly argued that it was a Norman bishop's chapel, a good example of an interesting building type, well worth an application of the face value rule.[3]

If Heywood is to be complimented on this example of the proper use of documentary evidence, then the American Arthur Kingsley Porter has to be described as a force of nature. In the 1920s he erupted into the study of the art of the tenth, eleventh and twelfth centuries, his wealth enabling him to send teams of researchers to comb the archives of Europe, the results of which transformed our understanding of the architecture of medieval Italy and Spain in particular. In the case of Italy, for the first time, despite at least two centuries of work, some degree of clarity was brought to the history of its architecture in the central Middle Ages.[4]

In Spain his studies of the arts of the period transformed the way the Spanish saw their history. Before Porter, Spanish Romanesque art was explained largely in terms of the influence, political, cultural and stylistic, of France. If a work in Spain had an early documentary date then the evidence was either wrong or commemorative. Porter applied the principle of accepting dates at face value, and, though not all of

---

[3] Stephen Heywood, 'The Ruined Church at North Elmham', *Journal of the British Archaeological Association*, 135 (1982), 1–10.

[4] Arthur Kingsley Porter, *Lombard Architecture* (1917; repr. New York, 1967).

them have survived reassessment, he succeeded in overturning the accepted wisdom and established the status and inventiveness of Spain in the period – an unsurprising inventiveness considering that the Christian kingdoms shared the peninsula with the cultural power of the caliphate of Córdoba. My favourite example of his work is that of the tiny village church at Iguácel in Aragon, with unsophisticated carvings and an embarrassingly early documented date of 1072, earlier even than the start of work in the great basilica of St Sernin in Toulouse, of the late 1070s.[5] Porter in fact developed something of a prejudice of his own, arguing the case for Spanish primacy beyond the call of duty. One might say that, as a North American and hence lacking a European bias of his own, he developed a sort of displaced, vicarious nationalism.

Restricted texts

Lastly there is the use of texts in ways which restrict their significance to researchers' own specialisms, as for example when they are dividing up periods. The architecture of the Anglo-Saxons again provides a good instance. The subject is traditionally divided, following the scheme devised by Gerard Baldwin Brown, into three phases, A, B and C: pre-Viking: 600–800, Viking: 800–950, post-Viking: 950–1100. The sequence begins *c.* 600, because architecture was taken to be building in masonry, the earliest Anglo-Saxon masonry structures are churches, and the churches post-date the start of the conversion in 597. But, as Richard Gem has pointed out, this ignores the documentary evidence for the arrival of the Saxons in Britain in the mid-fifth century, the proper start of the Anglo-Saxon period. As Gem argues, the architecture should be set in the context of the migration and power structures of the peoples involved, producing subdivisions of, say, period A *c.* 450–600, period B, 600–800, and so on.[6]

Another and more long-standing example is the setting up by art historians of the Renaissance, Baroque, Rococo and Neo-classical periods. It is eloquent testimony to an awareness of the clash between the different systems of structuring the past in the historical and art

[5] Arthur Kingsley Porter, 'Iguácel and More Romanesque Art in Aragon', *Burlington Magazine*, 52 (1928), 115; *idem*, *Romanesque Sculpture of the Pilgrimage Roads* (1923; repr. 1966); and *idem*, *Spanish Romanesque Sculpture* (1928).

[6] Gerard Baldwin Brown, *Anglo-Saxon Architecture* (1903; 2nd edn 1925). It is surprising that Brown invented such specifically architectural periods, as his work covered all aspects of the period. The volume preceding that on architecture in the series *The Arts in Early England*, for example, is entitled *The Life of Early England in its Relation to the Arts* (1903; 2nd edn 1926). Richard Gem, 'ABC: How Should We Periodize Anglo-Saxon Architecture?', in *The Anglo-Saxon Church: Papers in Honour of Dr H. M. Taylor*, ed. Laurence Butler and Richard Morris (1986), 143–55.

historical disciplines that many art historians who teach in these areas have recast them all into a single early modern period.[7]

The value of the evidence of the objects for other kinds of historian

While politics, economics and many other aspects of society are clearly of greater importance for the explanation of the forms of art objects than vice versa, the evidence of the objects can also be indispensable to an understanding of the past. Stylistic analysis, one of the chief art historical tools for dealing with objects, has been criticised from all sides, by documentary historians, by archaeologists, by anthropologists and (most vociferously of all) by 'new' art historians. The criticisms are largely justified. Too many art historians, especially medievalists, when dealing with undated objects, construct an ideal sequence of development and then apply it to the object in question to select a five-year slot ('carving, c. 1165–70'), like taking a reading from a Geiger-counter. An example of this is provided by the donjon at Loches in western France, a building with a documentary date in the early eleventh century which has none the less for decades been dated on stylistic grounds to c. 1120 (due no doubt to the assumption that churches must be 'ahead' of castles). The donjon has now been dated on dendrochronological evidence between 1010 and 1030.[8]

Against this criticism, however, there is a powerful consideration, namely the importance which style has for the members of a society. One need only recall from one's own experience (whether as agent or critic) the person for whom a difference of mere millimetres in width of a tie or scarf can make between the stylish and the naff, or the child who refuses to go to school because of the mortification of wearing socks a fraction too long, or the teenager who rejects a present which is exactly as ordered except for what to others is a mere nuance of colour. Direct communication with the artefacts of a society provides a means of understanding that society arguably as important as that of the written word. Of course one can be misled by it, but can one really argue that it is therefore better to ignore it?

---

[7] It is odd that for the ancient periods art historians use standard historical labels based on peoples or dynasties, as with Egyptian, Greek, Roman, Merovingian, while from the Romanesque on the style label is almost the rule (the observation is Sandy Heslop's). The reasons for this change will be more fully in considered in my chapter on Romanesque architecture in *Romanesque and Gothic*, ed. Conrad Rudolph (forthcoming).

[8] Jean Mesqui, Christian Dormoy and Philippe Durand, 'Mélanges: actualités sur le château de Loches', *Bulletin Monumental*, 154 (1996), 221–8, and Christian Dormoy, 'L'expertise dendrochronologique du donjon de Loches (Indre-et-Loire): des données fondementales pour sa datation', *Archéologie Médiévale*, 27 (1998), 73–89. Note that in *The Making of the Middle Ages* (1953), 84, Richard Southern got it right ('c. 1007').

This is especially the case where there is no written evidence whatsoever. As William Fagg has pointed out, anthropologists working on pre-modern African societies had no alternative but to use their eyes to sort the genuine from the spurious among the wooden artefacts which formed an important part of their evidence. In so doing, however, as he pointed out to his incredulous and dismayed colleagues, they were acting as connoisseurs, like Bernard Berenson.[9]

Another example of the evidence which can be derived from the style of objects is provided by the Norman Conquest and the old chestnut of change or continuity. Early writers such as Adam of Bremen, writing around 1070, present a picture of massive change ('There followed the vengeance of God and the Norman disaster and the overthrow of England') and historians up to the twentieth century largely concurred with this view. Most historians now, however, would argue, the destruction of the English land-owning classes apart, for a picture of continuity. Yet the architectural evidence makes it clear that, in some respects at least, Adam was nearer the mark. To take one indication, English medieval churches are well known for the mixture of parts of different dates and styles which they frequently contain – the Norman, Early English, Geometric, Decorated and Perpendicular – all often present in the same building. This can be contrasted with the following claim: at the time of writing no English cathedral or large monastic church is known to retain within its fabric *any* standing masonry of Anglo-Saxon date. That is, while there are remains of Anglo-Saxon plans extant beneath such Norman churches, and Anglo-Saxon masonry may have been reused in the new building, nothing of a pre-Conquest date is known to survive standing in the churches themselves. The sole possible exception is Sherborne Abbey; and while it is always possible that other examples will be found, unless there is a positive rash of them the significance of the observation will stand. It would be difficult to imagine a more graphic illustration of the imposition of one culture on another which this observation implies.[10]

Conclusion

There are many things I have not discussed. Among the most obvious, I have not considered the work of historians who have influenced architectural history, nor have I said anything about historical geography, or about antiquarians (if anyone still answers to the term).

[9] William Fagg, 'In Search of Meaning in African Art' (1973), reprinted in Eric Fernie, *Art History and its Methods: A Critical Anthology* (1995), 239–44.
[10] Eric Fernie, 'Architecture and the Effects of the Norman Conquest', in *England and Normandy in the Middle Ages*, ed. David Bates and Anne Curry (1994), 105–16.

Equally, comment would be relevant on the position of the architect in history: it is possible that architects are currently not given the prominence they deserve, due to an increase in the importance given to social and topographical contexts, so a reassessment may be warranted. And finally there is the role of architects as architectural historians: it is clear that architects bring a special expertise to bear on the subject and some of the finest and most influential architectural historians have been architects (one need think no further than Fletcher, Street and Bilson). Yet I think that, all other things being equal, the special abilities of the historian are more important for writing history than the specialist knowledge of someone working in the aspect of history in question.[11]

[11] For an example far removed from the academic world, see that of Robert Jan van Pelt, an architectural historian who appeared as a witness for the defence in a legal action brought by the historian David Irving. When van Pelt contended that the buildings housing the gas ovens at Auschwitz were designed and built for the purpose, Irving challenged his evidence on the grounds that he was not a qualified architect. The presiding judge, however, ruled that an architectural historian's view was as valid as that of an architect. Robert Jan van Pelt, *The Case for Auschwitz: Evidence from the Irving Trial* (Bloomington, IN, 2002), 441, 556.

Transactions of the RHS 13 (2003), pp. 207–17 © 2003 Royal Historical Society
DOI: 10.1017/S0080440103000106   Printed in the United Kingdom

WHERE NOW THE ARCHITECT?

By Neil Jackson

ABSTRACT. Central to the understanding of Modern architecture is the concept of
three-dimensional space and an appreciation of the nature of new materials. But
the contemporary architectural historian, denied an Architectural education,
continues to explore, often two-dimensionally, traditional structures. Conversely,
many architects, denied an education in History, have moved towards Philosophy
in the study of their own subject, alienating their discourse from much of the
profession and almost all of the public. The historical study of Modern architecture,
therefore, can never be successful until the architectural historian has learned the
process of making buildings within the language of Modernism.

On the occasion of the presentation of the Royal Gold Medal for
Architecture to Sir Nikolaus Pevsner in 1967, Sir John Summerson
made the observation: 'There was a time, still within living memory,
when all, or nearly all, architectural history in England was written by
architects; and not only by architects but by the biggest and busiest
architects ... But somewhere about 1934 the game came to an end.'[1]
What had brought the game to an end was a combination of two
things: first, the arrival from Nazi Germany, in 1933, of Fritz Saxl
and the 60,000–volume Warburg Library, of Rudolph Wittkower, of
Nikolaus Pevsner in 1934 and, a little later, of Ernst Gombrich, and
thus the importation of the new concept of *kunstgeschichte* – history of
art;[2] and secondly, the rise of the Modern movement, viewed by many,
such as Sir Reginald Blomfield in his 1934 diatribe, *Modernismus*, as
another European import and one best repelled. How shaken he must
have been, two years later, to see Pevsner's *Pioneers of the Modern Movement*
and to read that the first-named pioneer, William Morris, was as English
as he and that the last, Walter Gropius, was now living in his country.

This paper suggests that, a century or so after some of those

---

[1] *RIBA Journal*, 3rd series, 74 (Aug. 1967), 316. British architects who wrote polemical
histories in the nineteenth and early twentieth centuries included Thomas Rickman,
Augustus Welby Pugin, Sir George Gilbert Scott, George Edmond Street, Sir Thomas
Graham Jackson, Sir Reginald Blomfield, Sir Charles Reilly, Sir Albert Richardson, Sir
Banister Fletcher and Henry Goodhart-Rendel.
[2] See David Watkin, *The Rise of Architectural History* (1980), 148.

pioneering Modernist monuments illustrated by Pevsner (such as Auguste Perret's concrete-framed apartments in Paris and Peter Behrens's steel-framed Turbine Factory in Berlin) it is now high time that architects recolonised the writing of architectural history.

In a paper given at the Society of Architectural Historians of Great Britain's (SAHGB) Annual Symposium sixteen years ago, and subsequently published in the journal *Architectural History*,[3] Mark Swenarton, who with Adrian Forty ran the architectural history teaching at the Bartlett School of Architecture at University College, London, argued that, due to the Modernist hegemony in architecture, architectural history had slipped into an antiquarian backwater. His concern was that, with the then much vaunted demise of Modernism, architectural history might only emerge as a vehicle for propagandists anxious to promote the next 'ism'. With the prevalence of post-Modern historicism, he had a right to be concerned. His recommendation, as he put it, was this: 'that architectural history needs to wake up from the intellectual slumber into which it has fallen in the last forty years, take note of the advances made in the adjacent historical disciplines and do all it can to catch up'.[4] In this he has been rewarded, but the extent to which he has been rewarded with yet another 'ism' is worth considering. For books on architectural philosophy, theory rather than history – if the two are, indeed, mutually distinguishable – now pack the shelves of the architectural bookshops. One such recent volume is Daniel Libeskind's *The Space of Encounter*. Here the turn of phrase is particularly opaque. When interviewing Libeskind on Radio 4's *Start the Week*, Jeremy Paxman quoted this passage from his guest's book: 'We live in an age when economic globalisation, the market economy and technological advances make it possible for architecture to consume the immemorial.' And another: 'Architecture is the machine that produces the universe that produces the gods.' The redoubtable Paxman admitted to being slightly baffled by these assertions, yet they do imply an understanding of architectural history. Quite what that might be is difficult to say.

It is to such universal pronouncements and to writers peripheral to architecture, such as Jacques Derrida or Jean-François Lyotard that many contemporary architectural commentators turn for reference, rather than to the built product. The irony is that much of this writing is done by architects or those working within architectural education. Surely they, more than anyone, are best equipped to address the

[3] See Colin Cunningham, 'The Annual Symposium', *Society of Architectural Historians of Great Britain Newsletter*, 36 (Summer 1987), 4–5, and Mark Swenarton, 'The Role of History in Architectural Education', *Architectural History*, 30 (1987), 202–15.

[4] Swenarton, 'The Role of History in Architectural Education', 213.

building rather than the text? Complex structures, such as Libeskind's Jewish Museum in Berlin, might beg some explanation beyond the emotive if simplistic concepts upon which they are apparently based.

This leaves a vacancy to be filled. For the study of Modern architectural history is not the antiquarian pursuit described by Mark Swenarton, but rather, in a fundamentally Modernist and self-justifying way, an investigation of the *zeitgeist*.[5] For the watershed of the early twentieth century separates our age from those preceding it as much as it separates the history of the near-past from Modern History. If we are to accept Walter Gropius's Bauhaus principle of 1923, established at Weimar and developed at Dessau, that 'the character of an epoch is epitomized in its buildings. [and that] In them, its spiritual and material resources find concrete form',[6] then the architectural historian can now, so many years later, embrace the study of Modern architecture without risk of undermining, paradoxically, their Modernist position. The question then remains, what defines Modern architecture?

In the acknowledgements to his seminal study of 1960, *Theory and Design in the First Machine Age*, Nikolaus Pevsner's pupil Peter Reyner Banham credited Alan Colquhoun, an architect and a writer on architecture, with the observation that 'what distinguishes modern architecture is surely a new sense of space and the machine aesthetic'.[7] In the same sentence he thanks James Stirling, Alison and Peter Smithson, Colin St John Wilson, Peter Carter and Colin Rowe, for 'a constant view of the mainstream of modern architecture flowing on'.[8] Now all those people, except Banham himself, were architects and had been involved in making or teaching Modern architecture, as well as writing about it. Banham, who became Professor of the History of Architecture at the Bartlett, had trained in engineering at the Bristol Aeroplane Company. Thus his interest in *The First Machine Age* and, more particularly, *The Architecture of the Well-tempered Environment*, is not surprising. He was, similarly, coming from the inside.

At the Bauhaus thirty-five years earlier, Gropius's curriculum had famously precluded the study of architectural history which he feared would impede design development, yet this schism between Modernism and the history of architecture was not as complete as might be imagined. Although Gropius said, 'Concentration on any particular

[5] This reflects Fritz Saxl's comment regarding 'The Warburg Institute. . .and its methods of studying the works of art as an expression of an age', quoted in David Watkin, *The Rise of Architectural History* (1980), 149.

[6] Walter Gropius, 'The Theory and Organisation of the Bauhaus', in *Bauhaus 1919–1928*, ed. Herbert Beyer, Walter Gropius and Ise Gropius (Boston, 1952), 20.

[7] Reyner Banham, *Theory and Design in the First Machine Age* (1960), 2.

[8] *Ibid.*

stylistic movement is studiously avoided',[9] Le Corbusier, in his Modernist manifesto of 1923, *Vers une architecture*, quite consciously juxtaposed classical, medieval and renaissance buildings against images of Modernism, to give credence and credibility to the new architecture. The English reader, on opening Frederick Etchells's translation of 1927, might have been surprised to find that the path *Towards a New Architecture* was by way of the regulating lines on Michelangelo's capitol in Rome and Blondel's own notes on the Porte Saint Denis. Indeed, of the 220 or so illustrations in the 1946 edition of this book, 58 are of Le Corbusier's own designs whereas 85 (that is nearly 40 per cent) show historic buildings.[10]

What clearly alarmed Gropius, but apparently not Le Corbusier, was the threat of *style*. Had Gropius shown his students the Greek temple, they, like Schinkel or von Klenze before them, might have adopted it as a paradigm: Le Corbusier, on the other hand, would never be so fey. It could be the apparent absence of styles in Modern architecture which discourages most contemporary British art historians from studying it, Gothic or Palladian being much more accessible. Yet, as David Watkin argued in the introduction to *Morality and Architecture* twenty-six years ago, contrary to Sigfried Giedion's assertion that 'the contemporary movement is not a style', Modern architecture clearly is a style. It was announced as early as 1932 in the title of Henry-Russell Hitchcock and Philip Johnson's book, *The International Style*, and its demise was surely implied in 1977, the very same year as Watkin published *Morality and Architecture*, by Charles Jencks's supervenient *The Language of Post-Modern Architecture*. If Modern architecture is a style like any movement which preceded it, why is its history so much avoided in this country? It offers all the usual topics for discussion, such as plan forms and elevational composition, settings and ceremony, politics and patronage, documentation and discourse. So what is it about Modern architecture that makes it different?

Let us return to Alan Colquhoun's aphorism, that 'what distinguishes modern architecture is surely a new sense of space and the machine aesthetic' and consider it more carefully. The presence of the machine aesthetic in Modern architecture can be easily recognised. It was promulgated, as has been seen, through the writing of Le Corbusier who observed famously that 'la maison est une machine à habiter'.[11] Once the Bauhaus came to Dessau in 1926, Walter Gropius demonstrated its mechanistic intent with curtain walling and a concrete frame. This same machine aesthetic was expressed figuratively and

[9] Gropius, 'The Theory and Organisation of the Bauhaus', 24.

[10] In the 1946 edition of *Towards a New Architecture*, 58 illustrations were of Le Corbusier's own designs, 28 were of other Modernist buildings, 50 were of cars, ships, aeroplanes and pieces of machinery and 85 were of historic buildings.

[11] Le Corbusier, *Vers une architecture*, 2nd edition (Paris, 1924), 83.

literally from the Futurists, the Constructivists and the Expressionists, whose work straddled the First World War, to the lightweight, factory-produced California Case Study Houses which followed the Second World War. By the time Banham published his book in 1960, the machine aesthetic had become part of the new architectural language. James Stirling and James Gowan's contemporaneous Faculty of Engin-eering at the University of Leicester was as much a metaphor for itself – engineering – as it was an expression of the new architecture: in this Stirling and Gowan surely played the same game as Deane and Woodward had done at the Oxford University Museum a century before. The presence of the machine aesthetic continues in the work of high-tech architects, and the award in 2002 of the Royal Gold Medal for Architecture to the Archigram group recognised the continuing influence of those 1960s pioneers of the Plug-in City, whose work Banham promoted so enthusiastically.

It is, however, the first part of Colquhoun's aphorism which is the most interesting: that bit about 'a new sense of space'. To consider this we must return to Paris in the first decade of the last century, and briefly consider the work of the Cubists. Cubist art achieved on canvas what the early Modern architects were moving towards in their buildings, a time–space relationship. Through the incorporation of newspaper cuttings into their paintings, and the representation of different profiles within one face, Georges Braque and Pablo Picasso suggested, amongst their static *objets types*, the fourth dimension of time. The introduction of a daily newspaper marked a date, a moment in time, as surely then as it does now when used by terrorists to demonstrate that their kidnap victim yet lives. Similarly, the superimposition of two differing profiles suggests a photographic double exposure, two points in time caught, moments apart, on the same negative.

In architecture it was the fourth dimension of time which led to this 'new sense of space'. In the same way that Oscar Schlemmer's 'Dance of Circles' expressed fluid movement through a darkened room at the Bauhaus, so the Modernist's uninterrupted architectural promenade through a series of clean volumes served to express the essence of the new architecture. Although similar spatial explorations had been achieved in Baroque architecture, their effect was neither dependent upon nor encouraged by the machine, except perhaps in the theatre, whether secular or ecclesiastical. For the early Modernist, nowhere was this duality more immediately noticeable than at Le Corbusier's Villa Savoye at Poissy, built in 1929. From its D-shaped ground floor plan, where the radius of the curve was defined by the turning circle of the Voisin automobile, to the ramped progression up to the first floor reception rooms and ultimately to the roof terrace and solarium, there are a smoothness and a fluidity which almost negate all changes in direction and floor level, so much so that one can imagine the building revolving around one, over a number of minutes, rather than one walking through the building for however long it takes. This is an architect's interpretation. In the introductory essay to the catalogue of the 1987 exhibition *Le Corbusier: Architect of the Century*, William Curtis describes the building in traditional, almost pedestrian, terms, more applicable to Chiswick Villa than to the Villa Savoye. 'One approached the building along a ceremonial driveway ... [before] ... wandering through the interiors.'[12] It could be questioned whether a non-axial driveway approaching a building from the rear would be, for a designer, convincingly ceremonial, and whether the highly structured circulation routes of turning circle, ramp and helix actually allows the visitor to 'wander' through this building's interiors.

This catalogue to a major public exhibition, bought perhaps by more people than many books on Modern architecture, contained essays on Le Corbusier's buildings (as opposed to his paintings or furniture) by seven writers, four of whom – Colin Rowe, Kenneth Frampton, Sunand Prasad and Judi Loach – were trained as architects, and another, Adrian Forty, who works with architects. Only two such contributors, William Curtis and Tim Benton, were removed from the making of architecture. Yet Tim Benton's writing reveals none of the two-dimensional thinking which betrays Curtis, rather it shows an architect's perception as well as a welcome breadth of reference when it asks: 'As a sequel to Vitruvian man (the measure of humanist classical architecture), can we talk here of the Vitruvian car (the measure of machine-age man)?'[13] And when he adds that 'Le Corbusier clearly believed, with Alexander Pope, that modern patrons should be "proud to catch cold at a Venetian door" ',[14] he surely employs a wit few self-respecting architects would seriously feign.

Where the machine aesthetic, or perhaps just the machine component, has been brought to bear, the static stair has been replaced by the moving escalator and, as in the glass elevator, the user can be projected through the building without moving a muscle. The faster the machine operates, the quicker the experience of the space. The epitome of this must be the new house at Boulogne, designed by Rem Koolhaus and the Office of Metropolitan Architecture, where, as in the hydraulically operated flight-deck of an aircraft carrier, the whole living room rises through three storeys of the house so that the owner, confined to a wheelchair, can take his space with him to whichever

---

[12] William Curtis, 'Le Corbusier: Nature and Tradition', in *Le Corbusier, Architect of the Century* (1987), 18.

[13] Tim Benton, 'Six Houses', in *Le Corbusier, Architect of the Century*, 64.

[14] *Ibid.*, quoted from Alexander Pope, *Epistle to Lord Burlington on the Use of Riches*, line 36.

level he wishes to go. Ramped access, often so hard to incorporate in a building plan, will soon assume, thanks to new disabled access legislation, the significance and quite possibly the aesthetic identity previously accorded to ceremonial stairs from the pyramid at Chichen Itza to the Vatican's Scala Reggia.

The 'new sense of space' has been considered so far only in terms of the users and their progression through it. But what if the users do not move, but the building does? This can be regarded in two ways: the flexible building and the ambiguous building. In the first, the building changes shape, either to encompass space or to discard space. The earliest example of this within the Modernist vocabulary was the Schröder House, built by Gerrit Rietveld at Utrecht in 1923. Here moveable walls could redefine the first floor plan while windows opened to dissolve apparently solid corners and frame external space. Rietveld had already achieved this simple demarcation of space by floating planes in his Red and Blue Chair of 1917, where those two primary colours defined the seat and the back, and the third primary colour, yellow, pin-pointed coordinates from which the structure could be plotted in space. The conception of this floating form reflects accurately yet predates by seventy or eighty years current computer-aided design techniques which themselves have opened up a whole new exploration of architectural space.

The ambiguous building is to do with reflection, transparency and indeterminacy. New structural systems, developed in the twentieth century, encouraged the employment of new materials. Lightweight steel frames required lightweight claddings and, when combined with new attitudes towards outdoor living and a healthy life style, often resulted, when the climate allowed, in an architecture where indoor and outdoor space merged. At the Eames House, built by Charles and Ray Eames in Pacific Palisades, California, in 1949, one is rarely certain of being inside or outside. The exposed steel frame and open-web trusses provide a universal language which combines outdoor and indoor space; the profiled metal roof deck above the terrace becomes the ceiling of the main living space; and the glazed side wall reflects the hanging screen of eucalyptus leaves which form a curtain to the meadow beyond. But maybe more significant, in terms of ambiguity, is that what was intended to be a bridge-house was redesigned and built as a pavilion, not before but after the materials had arrived on site.

The new sense of space of which Alan Colquhoun spoke was largely made possible by new structural materials. In the same way that the rounded arch characterised Roman architecture and the pointed arch characterised Gothic architecture, so the use of reinforced concrete and of steel has distinguished Modern architecture and made the art of the engineer as important as that of the architect. The graphic expression of these forms is distinguished by the need to think three-dimensionally, a skill developed through the axonometric drawing rather than the perspective, and now fully available through computer modelling. Similarly, the use of the three-dimensional concept model as the design generator, whether it be a red and blue chair in Gerrit Rietveld's workshop, or an assemblage of screwed-up newspapers in Frank Gehry's studio, demands a new way of thinking.

Although Walter Gropius insisted to CIAM (the Congrès Intern-ationaux d'Architecture Moderne) that 'Three-dimensional conception is the basic architectural discipline',[15] such perceptions are not exclusive to architects, but they are perhaps more easily arrived at from their position. So why is so little Modern architectural history written by historians who are also architects or who work within that field? The duality which they can offer should provide much greater insight into the complexities of Modern architectural form and form-making. As the SAHGB's past chairman, Deborah Howard, wrote: 'Not being an architect by profession, I naturally feel that non-architects have some-thing to offer, but I also know that I have learned far more about buildings and the art of design from architects than from art-historians.'[16] Yet when, in 1966, Mark Girouard went on to study architecture at the Bartlett after taking his doctorate at the Courtauld and having worked at *Country Life* for a number of years, it was an experience which he found unrewarding. The fault appears to have been more with Professor Llewellyn Davies than the place: what he made of Reyner Banham is not recorded. But, as he says in his autobiographical introduction to *Town and Country*, 'I discovered that architects were, on the whole, better company than architectural historians.'[17] David Prichard, who was a contemporary of Girouard's at the Bartlett, recalls a pile of broken hardwood study-models of historic buildings at the foot of a stair-well. 'Such was the iconoclasm of the time', he later commented.[18]

In his reproachful paper of 1987, Mark Swenarton took the SAHGB to task, observing that 'in nearly thirty years of existence its journal has ... failed to carry a single article on architecture since 1914 (to say nothing of architecture since 1945)'.[19] In a response issued in the following volume John Newman, then retired from the editorship, pointed out that the Society had in fact published architect Jeremy

[15] Walter Gropius, 'In Search of Better Architectural Education', in *Dix ans d'architecture contemporaine / A Decade of Contemporary Architecture*, ed. S. Giedion (Zurich, 1951), 45.
[16] E-mail from Deborah Howard to Neil Jackson, 23 Sept. 2001.
[17] See Mark Girouard, *Town and Country* (New Haven and London, 1992), 8.
[18] David Prichard is now a principal with MacCormac Jamieson Prichard, architects. This comment was made at Castle Auckland, County Durham, on 14 Apr. 2002, during a conference on 'Constructing Place'.
[19] Swenarton, 'The Role of History in Architectural Education', 212.

Gould's monograph on *Modern Houses in Britain 1919–1939*, and it was so successful that it made a profit for the Society. The editorial policy of the subsequent editors Peter Draper, Christine Stevenson and Andor Gomme, has been, it would seem, to endorse the traditional strengths of the journal while at the same time extending its range both geographically and chronologically. Yet during their curatorship only fourteen articles, about 7 per cent of the total, have dealt with the Modern movement.[20] Of these, maybe three were written by architects. A recent edition, volume 44, published in 2001, was admittedly a *festschrift* for John Newman and the majority of the forty-three essays contained therein reflected, appropriately enough, Newman's more historicist interests.[21] But nobody developed the point made in the introduction, that John and Margaret Newman lived in a 1960s Span Development house at New Ash Green. Since Span made one of the more significant contributions to British post-war housing, surely an opportunity was missed here, for John Newman, apparently, is 'a passionate advocate of Eric Lyon's Span housing concept'.[22]

There must be many reasons for this continued focus on pre-Modern architecture. Perhaps a prime one is the perception of where, in the era of the Research Assessment Exercise, scholars would do their best to publish their work, and the fact that History of Art departments are much more research-active than schools of architecture whose return is made to Built Environment. This Unit of Assessment is extraordinarily wide-ranging, reaching from Construction Management and Building Services Engineering at one end to Design Theory at the other, so much so that the relative evaluation of architectural history within this Unit must be extremely difficult. Perhaps that is why no school of architecture in 2001 received a 'Five Star' and only three received a 'Five'. When the results for the schools of architecture within Unit 33, Built Environment, are compared with those for all departments listed under Unit 60, History of Art, Architecture and Design, it can be seen that almost the same percentage of returns in each group fell below the funding threshold, even though it was apparent that some schools and departments which had received low ratings in 1996 chose not to submit in 2001.[23] But if these 'Twos' and 'Threes' are discounted, on

[20] In *Architectural History* volumes 31 to 44 (1988–2000), only 20 out of 149 articles (or 13.4 per cent) have been on any subject post-dating the First World War, of which 10 are on subjects post-dating 1945.

[21] Only Roger Woodley's 'River Views: Transformations on the Thames' made any mention of Modern architecture. See *Architectural History*, 44 (2001), 121–2.

[22] Gordon Higgott, 'John Newman: An Appreciation', *Architectural History*, 44 (2001), 3.

[23] See *RAE 2001 Results*, History of Art, Architecture and Design UoA 60 (http://www.rea.ac.uk/results/byuoa/43.htm), and Built Environment UoA 33 (http://www.rea.ac.uk/results/byuoa/70.htm). Para 2.1 of the *Report on the Outcomes of RAE 2001: History of Art, Architecture and Design*, states, 'In the case of the History of Art,

the grounds that they will not receive funding anyway, then you are exactly five times *less* likely to receive a 'Five' or 'Five Star' as an architect writing on history in Unit 33, than as a historian writing on architecture in Unit 60. But as the report for Unit 60 said, 'as regards the study of Western art forms, there was more attention to the history of fine art than to the history of design, of modern architecture or of film'.[24]

Now that the discipline of Architectural History has emerged, as Mark Swenarton might have said, from its antiquarian torpor, a whole range of topics and methodologies is being employed by the contemporary architectural historian, as suggested by the variety of essays in John Newman's *festschrift*. Unexpectedly although not inappropriately, it is an essay on technical terms in English medieval architecture,[25] rather than the one on Transformations,[26] which discusses the influence of Jacques Derrida and deconstructionist philosophy. The essay on Transformations, a term topical and not without design application in schools of architecture, dwells meanwhile upon the River Thames and contrives to dismiss, as riverside buildings, both the Royal Festival Hall and the National Theatre while promoting Embankment Place and the MI6 Building. This surely undermines that essay's critical credibility, for whereas the former contain complex and stimulating internal and external spaces, the latter, like so many post-Modern buildings, are architectural one-liners.

The panoply of architecture described in that essay, 'River Views: Transformations on the Thames', reflects the breadth of 'Heritage Britain'. For like an oarsman on the Thames, we are a culture moving forward but always looking back. On television, there is no lack of popular interest in History, judging from what David Starkey was to be paid by Channel 4,[27] nor indeed in Architecture itself. Five times a week, on British television, the title sequence to *Eastenders* revolves around the Millennium Dome, but rather than being understood for what it is, a tent structure and not a dome, it remains for many an object of derision. For in Britain the serious discipline of Modern architectural history is undersold. The Millennium brought forth a flurry of journalistic reappraisals of the closing century but none that

---

Architecture and Design, there was also a tendency for those HEIs which received low ratings in 1996 either to submit to other UoAs, or not to submit at all.'

[24] *RAE 2001 Results*, History of Art, Architecture and Design, UoA 60, para. 3.3 (http://www.rea.ac.uk/results/byuoa/43.htm).

[25] E.C. Fernie, 'Technical Terms and the Understanding of English Medieval Architecture', *Architectural History*, 44 (2001), 13–21.

[26] Woodley, 'River Views: Transformations on the Thames'.

[27] It was reported in the *Sunday Times* on 3 Mar. 2002 that the historian David Starkey was to be paid £75,000 per screen-hour by Channel 4 making him the best paid performer on British television. *SALON*, the bulletin of the Society of Antiquaries of London, issue 8, 4 Mar. 2002, 4.

seemed quite as thorough as Kenneth Frampton's *Critical History of Modern Architecture*, published some years earlier and now in a new edition. In contrast, the many brightly coloured monographs which are stacked high on the bookshop counters are light on words and heavy on pictures, and are often little more than evidence of vanity publishing on the part of some young or fêted architectural practice. The result is that, in current publishing, architectural criticism is too often superficial and historical analysis, if any, both brief and shallow. That architects can write good architectural history cannot be doubted: the SAHGB has at least three times, in recent years, awarded its Alice Davis Hitchcock medallion to an architect – John Allen in 1993, Robin Evans in 1997 and Derek Linstrum in 1999. On at least one occasion, it has given its Essay Medal to an architect.[28]

Derek Linstrum, formerly deputy director of the Institute of Advanced Architectural Studies at York, and my predecessor as Hoffman Wood Professor at the University of Leeds, chaired, together with Joe Crook, that 1987 symposium in which Mark Swenarton issued his challenge to the SAHGB. Subsequently he wrote, 'For some reason his paper annoyed me.'[29] In a lecture given later that year to the Society of Architectural Historians of Australia and New Zealand, Linstrum offered his viewpoint on the uses of architectural history:

> There is a need for historians who will provide the objective facts, the truth as far as can be ascertained ... But there is also a need for architect/historians ... who know how designs evolve, how structures and materials behave, as well as being conversant with the grammar of classical composition and the well-tried theories of proportion and harmony.[30]

The grammar of classical composition, notwithstanding, the experiential or design-based approach to architectural history is a method still unknown to most architectural historians. As Walter Gropius told CIAM half a century ago: 'The visual arts are being taught by historical and visual methods of "appreciation" and "information" instead of through **direct participation in the techniques and processes of making things**' (Gropius's emphasis).[31] This raises the question, 'Where Now the Architect?' To which a second question may be added: 'Would you ask a mechanic who cannot drive to fix your car?'

[28] Neil Jackson, 1983.
[29] Letter from Derek Linstrum to Neil Jackson, 18 Mar. 2002.
[30] Derek Linstrum, 'The Uses of Architectural History Today', in *Companion to Contemporary Architectural Thought*, ed. Ben Farmer and Henty Louw (1993), 230. This essay is a revised and shortened version of the David Saunders Memorial Lecture given at the University of Adelaide in May 1987.
[31] Gropius, 'In Search of Better Architectural Education', 43.

Transactions of the RHS 13 (2003), pp. 219–26 © 2003 Royal Historical Society
DOI: 10.1017/S0080440103000118   Printed in the United Kingdom

THE ARCHITECT, HISTORY AND ARCHITECTURAL HISTORY

By Nicola Coldstream

ABSTRACT. The relation of the architect to architecture is elusive, since documentation can be scarce and the cult of the individual architect as a hero has allowed less well-recorded individuals to disappear from the narrative. The collaborative nature of building throughout history has been lost to historians. The paper considers the problems of attribution and the efforts of historians to discover architects, as well as those of architects to rewrite history to their advantage. We cannot take for granted the architect as he or she moves through history.

That an architect can make a significant contribution to the study of a building should be self-evident, and both spatial awareness and understanding of how a building is made are important critical aspects of architectural history. But it is less self-evident that education as an architect will of itself impart this understanding or that only someone with an architectural training is qualified to comment. The wobble that beset the Millennium Bridge between St Paul's and Bankside in London revealed only too pitilessly that not everyone involved understood how the structure should have been made. The scholarly interpretations of medieval architecture by the great architect-restorers of the nineteenth century created more difficulties than they solved. Viollet-le-Duc's explanations of Gothic structure look as rational as anyone could desire; but 150 years later they are still highly controversial, and, as architects, structural engineers and architectural historians contribute to the debate, it is clear that there is still no agreement on how Gothic buildings stand up.[1] August von Reichensperger, the architect who completed the building of Cologne Cathedral, followed the surviving fourteenth-century drawings for the west façade; but he also created building lodges in what he thought was the tradition of the great

---

[1] K. Alexander, R. Mark and J. Abel, 'The Structural Behaviour of Medieval Ribbed Vaulting', *Journal of the Society of Architectural Historians*, 36 (1977), 241–51; J. Heyman, *The Stone Skeleton: Structural Engineering of Masonry Architecture* (Cambridge, 1995); R. Mainstone, *Developments in Structural Form* (Oxford, 1998).

medieval building works at Cologne and Strasbourg, so that his masons could be trained in an authentic manner. Reichensperger's picture of the building lodge, the books of designs known as lodge books and the mason's training path including the so-called *Wanderjahre* – the wandering years – are merely speculations that caught on, were repeated uncritically in the literature through the generations and took such a firm hold in historiography that time has scarcely rooted them out.[2]

Architects' contributions to architectural study can, therefore, be equivocal. In any case, they need the assistance of historians since you cannot take the past out of architecture, even if a building is being created in front of your eyes. Future histories of architecture in London will not ignore the wobble in the bridge, even though it has now been cured. The history of any building starts from the moment it gleams in its designer's imagination, and much may happen even as it goes up. Major changes to the design of the Trinity chapel in Canterbury Cathedral, which were made while construction was in progress, could certainly be detected by an observant architect, but only an historian could offer an explanation for them. There the change appears to have coincided with the arrival of a new monastic prior, who brought a different attitude to the cult of St Thomas Becket.[3] In the 1840s, however, it seems to have been aesthetic and practical reasons that made Pugin alter the design of his family house, The Grange, in Ramsgate, as it was being built. Together with the additions made later by his son, Edward, these changes are part of the history of the house and add considerably to its interest.

Once a building is completed it may continue to have a personal history, but it will also enter the main historical narrative, a narrative that encompasses far more than understanding how a building is made. Some designs, notably those made for competitions, such as Scott's Gothic designs for the government buildings in Whitehall, or Zahah Hadid's design for the opera house in Cardiff, become part of architectural history without ever being built. An architectural site that has existed over many years may contain many references to its own past. Some will be forced upon it: the eastern arm of Canterbury is, except for the Trinity chapel, contained within the ground plan, crypt and lower walls of its predecessor. Likewise, the famously squat proportions of Exeter Cathedral were dictated by the partly surviving masonry of its Anglo-Norman predecessor, whose ghostly presence within the main

---

[2] A. Reichensperger, *Die christliche-germanische Baukunst und ihr Verhältnis zur Gegenwart* (Trier, 1845); L. Shelby, *Gothic Design Techniques: The Fifteenth-Century Design Booklets of Mathes Roriczer and Hanns Schmuttermayer* (London and Amsterdam, 1977); C. Brooks, *The Gothic Revival* (1999), 263–5.

[3] P. Draper, 'Interpretations of the Rebuilding of Canterbury Cathedral, 1174–86', *Journal of the Society of Architectural Historians*, 56 (1997), 184–203.

walls dictated the length, width and height of the later building.[4] What seems to reflect a conscious aesthetic choice is judicious housekeeping; by retaining some of the old masonry, the authorities at Canterbury and Exeter saved significant sums of money. But they also maintained continuity with the past. Churches with established cults did this as a way of honouring the saint and anchoring memory. History and memory affirmed both the sanctity of the site and the legitimacy of the patron's claims to the protection of the saint. The twisted columns of the Baldacchino in St Peter's, Rome, are an obvious example of such historical reference; in the twelfth-century abbey church of Saint-Denis, near Paris, capitals were carved to resemble forms in much earlier parts of the crypt.[5] In the Gothic fervour of the nineteenth century Cologne was not the only cathedral to be completed in a style that matched the medieval work: for the nave of Prague Cathedral, Kranner and Mocker paid due honour to the fourteenth-century choir and transept. Even twentieth-century buildings recognised, even saluted, earlier work. Venturi's Sainsbury Wing at the National Gallery overtly recalls the neo-classical façade of Wilkins's main structure.

Thus, no building can be divorced from history, nor, despite modernist attempts to deny the past, can the architect. The history of architecture is a narrative of reflection on the past, on drawing inspiration from it – the long twentieth-century search for new architecture to suit new materials has often produced forms and solutions that a medieval master mason would recognise – or, occasionally, rejecting it: the Renaissance rejection of Gothic was based on a perception of the past. Ever since Vasari we have become accustomed to placing the architect at the centre of the story, and although architectural history is now much more wide-ranging, the architect as hero (or villain) still dominates the headlines. Yet, as a figure in the process of design and construction the architect is not secure: the evidence is often much more ambiguous than we think, and the architect can be elusive, not always voluntarily: while medieval architects are poorly documented, modern ones may consciously seek to elude us by manipulating our responses to their work. There is also an historiographical problem of changing perceptions of the architect's role, from the medieval architect, trained on the building site to be designer, builder, engineer and often the contractor as well, to his successors who merely supplied designs for others to execute. Such

[4] N. Coldstream, 'The Great Rebuilding *circa* 1270–1390', in *Exeter Cathedral: A Celebration*, ed. M. Swanton (Crediton, 1991), 47–59.

[5] W. Clark, '"The Recollection of the Past Is the Promise of the Future": Continuity and Contextuality: Saint-Denis, Merovingians, Capetians, and Paris', in *Artistic Integration in Gothic Buildings*, ed. V. Raguin, K. Brush and P. Draper (Toronto, Buffalo and London, 1995), 95–9.

book-educated individuals as Lord Burlington are easier for modern scholars to identify as architects, while contemporary designer-builders, men such as Francis Smith, can be described as contractor, builder or architect, as appropriate.[6] Yet Smith's experience reflected medieval practice, and a medievalist would describe him as an architect or master mason. Marxist-inspired efforts to read modern conditions back into the past have postulated the existence of non-building architects as early as the thirteenth century;[7] and others have argued for the creative participation of patrons and administrators, to the extent of suggesting that they, rather than the master masons, were the true architects. One such individual is Elias of Dereham, from 1220 a canon of Salisbury and probably the clerk of the cathedral works. The notion that he was responsible for the design of Salisbury Cathedral has persisted since it was first suggested by Hamilton Thompson in 1941.[8] Medieval terminology itself creates difficulties, since the recording clerks wrote down what made sense to them and to the authorities to whom they were accountable; wording often reveals more about contemporary attitudes to masons than about masons' activities.[9] Medieval buildings, if attributed at all, were associated with their patrons or the building administrators. Thus, the Geoffroi de Noyers named as *constructor* of Lincoln Cathedral was not the master mason but almost certainly the clerk of the works.[10] To confuse things further, the term *magister operis* – master of the works – could be applied to either the clerk of the works or the master mason. The meaning of such terms is specific to a time and place, and often it has to be elucidated with the help of other evidence, which may or may not exist.

Apart from contracts, documents that name architects are uncommon. Contracts survive only from the late Middle Ages; otherwise,

[6] A. Gomme, 'Architects and Craftsmen at Ditchley', *Architectural History*, 32 (1989), 85–97, *passim*.

[7] D. Kimpel, 'La sociogenèse de l'architecture moderne', in *Artistes, artisans et production artistique au moyen âge*, I: *Les hommes*, Colloque International CNRS, Rennes, 1983, ed. X. Barral y Altet (Paris, 1986), 135–49.

[8] A. Hamilton Thompson, 'Master Elias of Dereham and the King's Works', *Archaeological Journal*, 98 (1941), 1–35; H.M. Colvin, ed., *History of the King's Works*, I and II: *The Middle Ages* (1963), I, 100 and n; T. Tatton-Brown, *Great Cathedrals of Britain* (1989), 95; V. Jansen, 'Salisbury Cathedral and the Episcopal Style in the Early 13th Century', in *Medieval Art and Architecture at Salisbury Cathedral*, ed. L. Keen and T. Cocke, British Archaeological Association Conference Transactions, 17 (1996), 33–7; N. Coldstream, 'Architectural Designers in the Thirteenth Century', in *Thirteenth Century England*, IX: *Proceedings of the Durham Conference 2001*, ed. M. Prestwich, R. Britnell and R. Frame (Woodbridge, 2003), 201–7.

[9] N. Pevsner, 'The Term Architect in the Middle Ages', *Speculum*, 17 (1942), 549–62.

[10] N. Pevsner, *The Choir of Lincoln Cathedral: An Interpretation*, Charlton Lectures on Art (1963), 5; P. Kidson, 'Architectural History', in *A History of Lincoln Minster*, ed. D. Owen (Cambridge, 1994), 43.

names may occur in fabric rolls (building accounts), but fabric rolls are rare. Masons are named in legal and property transactions; the business dealings of a successful master can be reconstructed from them, giving the illusion of a biography, but it is often difficult to associate such men with the design of an existing building.[11] Yet while the documents, with or without corroborative buildings, can often supply names, the names themselves yield limited, sometimes misleading, information. The second architect of the eastern arm of Canterbury Cathedral is described by Gervase of Canterbury as 'William by name, English by nation';[12] but his work, on the virgin ground east of the remains of the former cathedral, is quite notably French in style, more so than the parts further west, which were circumscribed by the earlier building. Was English William merely carrying out a design settled under his French predecessor, William of Sens? The first architect of Westminster Abbey, rebuilt by Henry III, was Henry of Reyns, which could stand for Rayne in Essex or Reims in France. The hybrid design of the building and its English methods of construction argue that Henry was trained in England rather than in France.[13] The origins of these men mattered far less than their training and the taste of their patrons, and the survival of their names is irrelevant to our understanding of their work.

Since master masons were almost always paid a salary as distinct from a weekly wage, their activities are seldom mentioned in fabric rolls, and there are scarcely any references to the process of design. Medieval architects designed templates for mouldings, of which drawings survive only exceptionally; they are economical of line and effectively unattributable.[14] The only drawings that can be compared to architectural drawings as understood from the sixteenth century onwards are the façade designs linked to the cathedrals of Orvieto and Strasbourg. John White suggested that the two drawings of the west front of Orvieto Cathedral, made in the early fourteenth century, were competition designs, one by Lorenzo Maitani, to whom White attributed the façade as built.[15] The late thirteenth-century drawings at Strasbourg are taken to represent ideas at the design stage, but none is attributable

[11] J. Harvey, *Henry Yevele c. 1320–1400: The Life of an English Architect* (1944); critique by A.D. McLees, 'Henry Yevele, Disposer of the King's Works of Masonry', *Journal of the British Archaeological Association*, 3rd series, 36 (1973), 52–71.

[12] R. Willis, *The Architectural History of Canterbury Cathedral* (1845), 51.

[13] J. Harvey, *English Medieval Architects: A Biographical Dictionary down to 1550*, 2nd edn (Gloucester, 1984), 251; C. Wilson, 'The Gothic Abbey Church', in C. Wilson *et al.*, *Westminster Abbey*, New Bell's Cathedral Guides (1986), 26.

[14] F. Bucher, *Architector: The Lodgebooks and Sketchbooks of Medieval Architects*, 1 (New York, 1979).

[15] J. White, 'The Reliefs on the Façade of the Duomo at Orvieto', *Journal of the Warburg and Courtauld Institutes*, 32 (1959), 254–302.

and none resembles the final realisation.[16] In 1436–7 the mason Pierre Robin left 'a complete' drawing for Saint-Maclou at Rouen, but the reference is otherwise inexplicit and the drawing has not survived.[17] Attempts to show that late medieval architects were consummate draughtsmen in the manner of their successors are unpersuasive, since neither evidence for, nor examples of, such drawings exist.

Medievalists also detect the work of specific architects through stylistic comparison, not of drawings but of elements: such large-scale designs as elevations, and small-scale details, especially mouldings. Several scholars claim success in associating particular profiles of mouldings with particular masons; or, in the absence of a name, with the same anonymous master.[18] In the past, changes to mouldings or tracery were automatically presumed to mark a change of architect. Conversely, no change to design meant no change of master mason. We are not quite so naive now: since Stephen Murray demonstrated that changes in design at Troyes Cathedral could not be correlated with the recorded arrival of new master masons, this method of attribution, always doubtful, cannot be relied upon.[19] Troyes demonstrates clearly the stylistic constraints that tradition, the unquantifiable (by us) demands of the patron and a pre-existing structure placed upon the architect. We can form some idea of these from Exeter Cathedral, which was built over several decades under the supervision of successive recorded master masons, none of whom altered the essential design once it had finally been decided. The 'signature' of the longest-serving master, Thomas of Witney, has had to be identified in such details as window tracery and door mouldings, since there was evidently no question of his making a new design for the elevation.[20]

It is reasonable to suppose that research into both the documentary record and the building fabric ought to produce definitive evidence of an architect and his style. The investigations by Maurice Hastings, John

[16] Les batisseurs des cathédrales gothiques, exhibition catalogue, ed. R. Recht, Musées de la Ville de Strasbourg (Strasbourg, 1989), 381–405.

[17] L. Neagley, Disciplined Exuberance: The Parish Church of Saint-Maclou and Late Gothic Architecture in Rouen (University Park, PA, 1998), 10–11.

[18] S. Harrison, R. Morris and D. Robinson, 'A Fourteenth-Century Pulpitum Screen at Tintern Abbey, Monmouthshire', Antiquaries' Journal, 78 (1998), 233–4; L. Monckton, 'The Late Medieval Rebuilding of Sherborne Abbey: A Reassessment', Architectural History, 43 (2000), 88–112.

[19] S. Murray, Building Troyes Cathedral: The Late Gothic Campaigns (Bloomington and Indianapolis, 1987), 36–7, 111.

[20] V. Jansen, 'The Design and Building Sequence of the Eastern Area of Exeter Cathedral, c. 1270–1310: A Qualified Study', in Medieval Art and Architecture at Exeter Cathedral, ed. F. Kelly, British Archaeological Association Conference Transactions, 11 (1991), 35–56; R. Morris, 'Thomas of Witney at Exeter, Winchester and Wells', in ibid., 57–84; Coldstream, 'The Great Rebuilding circa 1270–1390'.

Harvey and Christopher Wilson into the origins of the Perpendicular style were, admittedly, impeded by the destruction of two of the relevant buildings, St Stephen's chapel in the Palace of Westminster and the chapter house of St Paul's Cathedral. Visual records survive only in a few moulded stones and not wholly reliable drawings.[21] This may be one reason why each scholar claimed the credit of inventing Perpendicular for a different architect: Michael of Canterbury at St Stephen's (Hastings); William Ramsey at St Paul's (Harvey); and Thomas of Canterbury at St Stephen's (Wilson).[22] Yet there are difficulties even where buildings survive. Arnold Taylor's attribution of Edward I's castles in north Wales to James of St George, a mason from Savoy, was based on meticulous research into the detailed accounts of the King's Works in Wales and the comital works in Savoy; and on the fortunate survival in a reasonably authentic state of the castles in both regions. Conclusive though Taylor's reasoning ought to be, however, neither the records nor the fabric bear out his argument. The building accounts typically do not mention the design process. The type of castle built in Wales, with a trace of mural towers focused on a strengthened, towered gatehouse fronted by barbicans, was unknown in Savoy. Master James would never have seen such a castle and would not have known how to design one. His role in Wales needs to be re-examined.[23] John Maddison has discussed the contribution there of other masters, emphasising the need to be aware of architects who may vanish from history because their activities are not set down in writing.[24] Collaboration runs clear through the history of architecture from the Renaissance onwards, as witness the seventeenth-century rebuilding of St Peter's, Rome, where Borromini, among others, worked with both Maderno and Bernini. Indeed, the Baldacchino has been described as a 'team effort';[25] but tradition has ignored Borromini's contribution.[26] Contemporary architectural partnerships are likewise team

[21] J. Topham, *An Account of the Collegiate Chapel of St. Stephen, Westminster* (1834); E. Brayley and J. Britton, *The History of the Ancient Palace and Late Houses of Parliament at Westminster* (1836); F. Mackensie, *The Architectural Antiquities of the Collegiate Chapel, of St. Stephen, Westminster* (1844); W. Dugdale, *The History of St Paul's Cathedral in London from its Foundation until These Times* (1658).

[22] J.M. Hastings, *St Stephen's Chapel and its Place in the Development of the Perpendicular Style in England* (Cambridge, 1955); Harvey, *Henry Yevele*, 244; C. Wilson, *The Gothic Cathedral: The Architecture of the Great Church 1130–1530* (1990), 204.

[23] A.J. Taylor, 'Master James of St. George', *English Historical Review*, 65 (1950), 433–57; N. Coldstream, 'Architects, Advisers and Design at Edward I's Castles in Wales', *Architectural History*, 46 (2003), 19–36.

[24] J. Maddison, 'Decorated Architecture in the North-West Midlands: An Investigation of the Work of Provincial Masons and their Sources' (Ph.D. thesis, University of Manchester, 1978), 67, 125.

[25] P. Stein, in *Grove Dictionary of Art*, ed. J. Turner (1996), IV, 428.

[26] A. Blunt, *Borromini* (1979), 25; S. Burbaum, *Die Rivalität zwischen Francesco Borromini und Gianlorenzo Bernini* (Oberhausen, 1999), 11–49.

efforts. In the Middle Ages, too, collaboration was normal, especially between the master mason and the master carpenter, who needed to stabilise the action of timber roofs on masonry walls. Richard Goy's study of Ca' d'Oro in Venice has shown how the bricklayers, carpenters and marblers collaborated under the direction of the master bricklayer.[27] (The person in overall charge of such a site was the clerk of the works, or, at Ca' d'Oro, the patron, Marin Contarini.) Thus, emphasising 'the architect' diminishes the part played by other architects who were also working on a building. We must be aware of architects who, as it were, slide through the cracks to elude us. A high-profile individual may not necessarily be the person that the historian of architecture needs to seek. And by privileging such men at the expense of those who are less well recorded, we may be distorting the past even more seriously than we already do.

The problem of the elusive architect is, however, also a problem for the present: the architect who is elusive not because the record is incomplete, but because he is himself trying to reconstruct the past. Pugin published a watercolour of The Grange that subtly modified details of the design that he had come to regret.[28] And trying to rewrite history continues to this day. To take the example of Norman Foster and Richard Rogers: when their works are deemed to be successful, all is well. The roof of the Great Court of the British Museum is seen as a triumph for Norman Foster and Partners.[29] We are all fully aware that Montevetro, the block of flats that now dwarfs St Mary's church, Battersea, is a design by the Richard Rogers Partnership. When, however, a structure is seen to be a failure, something else happens. The Rogers Partnership's Millennium Dome is a structural success, but a political and cultural failure. Foster's Millennium Bridge was, if not a failure, scarcely at first a structural success. The names of the architects, engineers and – in the case of the Bridge, the sculptor – are now hardly ever, if at all, mentioned in connection with them.[30]

Since the nineteenth and twentieth centuries were well recorded, the Dome and the Bridge will be securely attributed in future without trouble; and Pugin can never have imagined that his house and his illustrations of it would be so closely scrutinised by scholars in the future. What these and earlier episodes demonstrate, however, is that, as the architect moves through history, the historian can never take him or her for granted.

---

[27] R. Goy, *The House of Gold: Building a Palace in Medieval Venice* (Cambridge, 1992), 99–260.

[28] Pointed out by Paul Drury at the Society of Architectural Historians' Study Day at The Grange, September 2000. A. Pugin, *Aerial View of The Grange and St. Augustine's, Ramsgate, with Interior Details*, shown at the Royal Academy Exhibition, 1849; repr. in *A. W. N. Pugin, Master of the Gothic Revival*, exhibition catalogue, ed. P. Atterbury (New Haven and London, 1995), no. 98.

[29] See the enthusiastic comment in *Architectural Review*, 208 (2001), 2/74–9.

[30] See the eulogies in *Architectural Review*, 207 (2000), 4/54–7, 4/106.

Transactions of the RHS 13 (2003), pp. 227–35 © 2003 Royal Historical Society
DOI: 10.1017/S008044010300012X   Printed in the United Kingdom

A CUBIST HISTORY: THE DEPARTMENT STORE
IN LATE NINETEENTH-CENTURY PARIS

By Robert Proctor

ABSTRACT. Postmodernism is now firmly established as a critique of historical
narrative; this paper looks at its implications for architectural history, where the
built object is viewed through many texts. The example of the department store
in Paris shows how the process of writing history has been simplified to serve
different purposes, while the complexity of different viewpoints and contradictions
within and between them can be restored and emphasised to give a more truthful
historical account. Cubist painting is proposed as a useful analogy for reconciling
this process of historical representation to Postmodern thought.

What seemed at its outset merely a moment of crisis in the discipline
of history has now become a thirty-year body of literature, both
academic and, more recently, popular. Once criticised as a fleeting
academic fashion, Postmodernism can no longer be so easily dismissed.
Meanwhile, architectural historians have often insulated themselves
from concerns that question the foundation of their work; but the
reflexivity of theoretical debate promoted by this symposium is one
sign that Postmodernism has now established itself in their discipline
too. Many, even when rejecting a Postmodern approach, nevertheless
realise that they must defend their rejection, since it no longer suffices
to say that history has no theory. While the potential effects of
Postmodernism on the working assumptions of historians may be
seen as a drastic threat, I believe that it offers an opportunity for
positive change. I propose an analogy to Cubism for my model of a
Postmodern history: not a perfect comparison, but a vivid and relevant
one.

In my work on the department store in late nineteenth-century Paris,
a Postmodern approach has been just about inevitable; since the nature
of the sources has largely dictated it, I will begin with them.

Historians and architectural historians have always been attentive to
the reliability and provenance of their sources. Postmodernism demands
that no source be considered as privileged in its access to reality, and
most historians would accept that all evidence is the product of

conventions or viewpoints that make it partial. The greatest trepidation has been caused by the idea that Postmodernism regards reality as non-existent, but this is to miss the point; it would be better to say that Postmodernism holds reality to be unknowable except through partial texts. This is, of course, precisely the reason that documentary research has always been essential to the practice of history. But the idea has another important consequence, which is that the texts of the past must become the subject of history, rather than the past itself. Inasmuch as buildings can be considered as texts, architectural historians find themselves at an advantage, since they already write this kind of history. Of course, a building is more than just a text, but this something more can only be discovered through other texts; thus, the architectural historian needs to look more widely for historical sources, in other words, to become more like a historian.

The department stores of nineteenth-century Paris had a material existence: they were real. But there is no way of gaining access to this materiality today. The buildings that remain have been radically altered, and occasionally halfheartedly restored. The Bon Marché, for example, was built gradually throughout the late nineteenth century and into the twentieth, four architects having worked on it before the First World War. Its interior has had a few of its glazed cast-iron atria restored, but these no longer admit daylight, and bear no relation to nineteenth-century photographs. These photographs possess no sense of scale (being mostly unpopulated), they have no colour, they disguise materials and distort perspectives, and their vantage points are selected according to artistic convention. Architectural plans may be thought to provide an objective account, but what they describe was by no means always built, and shows different aspects of the building depending on their purpose. The evidence thus is always incomplete, and the historian's task involves conjecture to recreate the fact. However, even if it were possible to reconstruct the Bon Marché exactly as it was at a particular point in its history, we would still know nothing about it: what it means to have an iron frame or a classical façade or toplighting must be discovered through other texts.

Postmodernism, drawing on structural linguistics, insists that the meaning of a sign can only be known by comparison with many others in the same system of meanings, and that meaning depends as much on its reception by an audience as on the intentions of the sign's creator. The architectural historian, then, must draw from the widest possible range of contextual sources. Here, context is not so much the 'back-ground' to architecture (in the sense that a nineteenth-century history painting possesses a background to its figures), but the field of texts which surrounds the building and actively constitutes it as an object (much as, in a Cubist painting, the hierarchy of figure and ground is

levelled through interpenetration).[1] In determining a building's meanings, the reactions of its viewers are of equal significance to a knowledge
of the intentions of its architects. That this is an opportunity rather
than a threat must be clear. In my research on the Parisian department
store, first-hand sources included feminist newspapers, a paper produced
by a union of shopworkers, women's magazines, a journal for investors
in shares and the minutes of committee meetings for the formulation
of building regulations, all with new things to say, since nobody had
previously thought to consult them on this subject.

The more sources are consulted, however, the more the physical
object breaks up, refracted through multiple viewpoints. As the department store tended to elicit extreme reactions from its contemporaries,
the evidence gives a particularly distorted representation. Even images
were often produced to serve distinct requirements: an engraving of
the Bon Marché in the 1870s, for example, has an exaggerated
perspective, and depicts an impossibly fragile structure, its interior
drenched in light.[2] This is a different impression from that given by a
contemporary photograph,[3] and supports the right-wing myth of the
store as a model of progressive capitalist concentration for the benefit
of society – a myth purveyed by Emile Zola's novel of 1883, *Au Bonheur
des Dames*, as well as by the stores themselves.[4] Architectural journals,
meanwhile, presented the buildings with greater pictorial accuracy, but,
consonant with their practical function, tended to discuss technical
advances at the expense of descriptions of architectural style or meaning,
or of the buildings' social and cultural purposes.[5] There are, then, no
objective sources; the department store is only visible to us through the
many prismatic facets of its contemporaries' minds. The image produced
by archival research may already be compared to the multiple faceted
viewpoints of single objects in the paintings of Picasso and Braque.

Perhaps none of this will be new to either historians or architectural
historians, and it is my opinion that Postmodernism describes a condition that historians have always understood. This approach to sources,
however, bears implications for the *writing* of history, which Postmodernism questions with greater urgency. Traditionally, history has
taken the form of narrative, that is, it tells a story, and the techniques
which it deploys are borrowed from literature, specifically the nineteenth-century realist novel. Descriptions of past events are informed

[1] Thomas Vargish and Delo E. Mook, *Inside Modernism: Relativity Theory, Cubism, Narrative*
(1999), e.g. 115–26.
[2] Archives de Paris, D18Z/7.
[3] Reproduced in Bernard Marrey, *Les grands magasins des origines à 1939* (Paris, 1979), 59.
[4] Emile Zola, *The Ladies' Paradise*, trans. Brian Nelson (Oxford, 1995).
[5] For example, an article on Paul Sédille's Printemps building, 'Grands magasins du
Printemps', in *L'Encyclopédie d'architecture*, 3rd series, IV (1885), 1–35.

and ordered according to conventional ideas of plot, in a linear mode which implies causality. Hayden White, in *Metahistory*, showed that the different kinds of narrative structure (whether farce, satire, comedy or tragedy) enable historians to produce different stories of the past according to their political thinking;[6] while the conventions of realism (a continuous neutral timeframe, detailed descriptions, context as background), have been seen by others as giving an illusion of truth to the historian's subjective account.[7] The past, meanwhile, eludes the narrative order that we would like to impose upon it, and so writers such as Hans Kellner have called for historians to 'get the story crooked' instead.[8] Postmodernism's insight into the nature of writing allows us to question previous accounts of our subjects by revealing their methodology, and gives us the opportunity for presenting our evidence in new ways better to reflect our understanding of human experience and activity.

Just as the condition which Postmodernism describes is emphasised by the nature of the evidence about the Parisian department store, so the secondary writing on the subject confirms Postmodernism's attitude to narrative. The department store fulfils an important role in the plots of many histories. In architectural history, Sigfried Giedion first appropriated the building type in his *Building in France, Building in Iron, Building in Ferro-concrete* of 1928, and later in *Space, Time and Architecture*.[9] In both, the department store is described as a model of positive engagement with modernity in its bold use of exposed iron and glass, and therefore as a precursor to the structural and functional aesthetic of Modernism. Giedion's aim was to show that Modernism was the result of a century of continuous evolution towards an aesthetic perfection in harmony with the spirit of the age. His representation of the department store is thus engineered to support his linear narrative. In *Building in France*, an illustration of the Bon Marché's roof shows that structural honesty was a dormant principle, while the masonry façade, acknowledged only as 'pure veneer', is not shown or discussed. Another store described is the Printemps. This building, one of three for the store before 1914, was built from 1882 to 1889 by the Rationalist architect Paul Sédille. It was taken by contemporaries as the ideal model of a department store, and was widely imitated subsequently; it also conformed more strictly to the current idea of Rationalism in architecture.

---

[6] Hayden White, *Metahistory* (1973).

[7] Thus Elizabeth Deeds Ermarth, *Sequel to History: Postmodernism and the Crisis of Representational Time* (Princeton, NJ, 1992).

[8] Hans Kellner, *Language and Historical Representation* (Madison, WI, 1989).

[9] Sigfried Giedion, *Building in France, Building in Iron, Building in Ferro-concrete*, trans. J. Duncan Berry (Santa Monica, CA, 1995); Sigfried Giedion, *Space, Time and Architecture: The Growth of a New Tradition*, 3rd rev. edn (1954).

Giedion, however, frowns upon its decorative elements; corner pavilions 'could not be abandoned' – although they were created as an essential feature of the new building type.[10]

Although Giedion's approach is easily faulted, it is unique in frankly announcing its intentions to the reader. It was imitated by Pevsner, whose *A History of Building Types* (as late as 1976) translated Giedion's enjoyable polemic into a putatively objective history concealing the motivations of its narrative.[11] His distortions are fewer, but this only heightens its apparent realism. His analysis ascribes the department store a place in an evolution of types including arcades and bazaars, their position in the sequence determined by the complexity or honesty of their iron structures. Thus, the part of the Bon Marché designed by Louis-Charles Boileau receives attention because of the architect's description of it as a 'large metallic cage', and Gustave Eiffel is assigned the role of engineer on tenuous evidence.[12] The Grands Magasins du Louvre, one of the four largest in Paris from 1855 until its demise in the 1970s, is only briefly mentioned, presumably because it had no structural innovations.[13] Perhaps it would be largely irrelevant to make any use of Giedion and Pevsner here, were it not for their overwhelming influence on subsequent writers. The Modernist narrative in architectural history has not substantially been altered; it has only gained in complexity and depth, for example in Bertrand Lemoine's erudite *L'architecture du fer*.[14]

Other forms of history have other narratives, and therefore confer different roles upon the department store. The economic history of retail embellished a consistent story for nearly a hundred years following several articles in the 1890s. The department store was first thought of as the most highly developed form of capitalist trade in a long evolutionary history, having introduced fixed marked prices, a low profit margin and a high turnover enabling economies of scale, further enhanced through concentration and centralisation of the business, and diversification of goods. The ancestry of the department store is traced from medieval fairs to eighteenth-century drapery shops. Variations on the story depend on their ending: for Georges d'Avenel in 1894, the department store was the final outcome of capitalist development;[15] in

[10] Giedion, *Building in France*, 115–19.

[11] Nikolaus Pevsner, *A History of Building Types* (1976).

[12] *Ibid.*, 268; for a revision of Eiffel's role, see François Faraut and Cloud Dupuy de Grandpré, 'Le Bon Marché: 119 rue du Bac', in *Le Faubourg Saint-Germain: la rue du Bac*, ed. Bruno Pons and Anne Forray-Carlier (Paris, [n.d.]), 79–95 (87).

[13] Pevsner, *Building Types*, 267–9.

[14] Bertrand Lemoine, *L'architecture du fer: France: XIXe siècle* (Paris, 1986).

[15] Georges d'Avenel, 'Le mécanisme de la vie moderne. 1. Les grands magasins', *La Revue des Deux Mondes*, 15 July 1894, 329–69.

the twentieth century, economic history took the retail chain as the final logical phase of development, but acknowledged the department store as essential in the transition from small-scale enterprise to national corporation.[16]

Here, then, are already two narratives incorporating the department store, and there are many others: more recently, social history, cultural history, consumption studies and the history of literature have all appropriated the department store for the invention of their own stories. Between the architectural and economic histories, there are convergences, largely due to cross-fertilisation (Pevsner, for instance, quotes d'Avenel); but there are also dissonances, as different scales of time are employed, and peaks of development are unrelated. Sometimes there are radical incompatibilities: Pevsner includes the bazaars (such as the Galeries du Commerce et de l'Industrie of 1837) as architectural predecessors of the department store; economic histories, meanwhile, describe the bazaars merely to explain their failure to develop, in telling contrast to department stores.[17] These divergences show that narrative is arbitrary, since it requires the selection of facts according to the particular story that is to be told, from the many stories that are possible. A major fault with all the histories mentioned here is their frequent use of terms such as 'evolution': causality is asserted without having to be investigated. The narrative is therefore constructed linguistically where evidence is insufficient.

The total range of sources, however, does not suggest that any particular story is truer than another, and in fact does not easily align itself to any story at all without substantial omissions. It is, in any case, improbable that life, society, events or the past should take the forms that stories take. Narrative is simply not suitable for the depiction of a complex and sometimes meaningless reality. So the task of a Postmodern history is to find a better mode of representation. I will conclude by suggesting some possibilities.

An acknowledgement of one's subjectivity is essential, and this can take the form of a continually reflexive approach: if, as Hans Kellner wrote, 'history is not "about" the past as such, but rather about our ways of creating meanings from the scattered, and profoundly meaningless debris we find around us', then this process of eliciting meaning from the evidence should always be explicit.[18] In my own history, this has meant, above all, being honest: describing the evidence within the text, rather than assigning it to footnotes; relating the

---

[16] E.g. Hrant Pasdermadjian, *The Department Store: Its Origins, Evolution and Economics* (1954).

[17] Pevsner, *Building Types*, p. 262; Georges Michel, 'Une évolution économique: le commerce en grands magasins', *La Revue des Deux Mondes*, 1 Jan. 1892, 133–56 (137).

[18] Kellner, *Language and Historical Representation*, 10.

methods by which every conclusion has been drawn; leaving conjectures as possibilities rather than statements of truth. Here, the analogy to Cubism returns: by portraying unimportant objects, Picasso and Braque focused attention away from the painted subject and towards the act of mediation, that is, the process of observing and representing reality.[19]

A possibility for structuring historical writing is suggested by the technique of collage. In Cubist painting, the collage undermined the illusionistic convention of the surface as a transparent plane, through which reality is viewed; bottles and violins were made of the newspaper which also partook of the scene as object of depiction.[20] A comparison can be made with Walter Benjamin's *Arcades Project* of 1927 to 1940, which deals with a subject close to my own, namely the shopping arcade in earlier nineteenth-century Paris.[21] Benjamin's work was unfinished, and speculation continues over his intentions; but the form in which it was recovered is revealing. Assembled into folders headed with the titles of broad themes ('Photography', 'Iron Construction', 'The Streets of Paris' and so on) are reams of quotations from many sources, both contemporary and modern, on all possible subjects of interest, juxtaposed deliberately to confer meanings upon each other, many cross-referenced to other folders, and interwoven with Benjamin's own thoughts in the form of notes. Between each note or quotation is a gap, where a narrative connection is absent, so that the whole is made up of a vast collection of fragments composed to form a kaleidoscopic image of Paris. Despite the initial effect of incoherence, each theme is found to have a linear development, perhaps suggesting that the work was eventually to be integrated as prose. Between themes, however, there are further breaks, where the viewpoint or faceted surface is shifted, and complementary or contradictory images of the arcades emerge. Tying together the whole, however, and evident throughout, is Benjamin's own subjective motivation – to explain, as a Marxist, the artificial nature of consciousness under twentieth-century capitalism.

Giedion's correspondence with Benjamin is well known, and his *Building in France* also has a montage composition (implemented by Moholy Nagy of the Bauhaus) of images and captions and bold, disconnected statements. Both Giedion and Benjamin used the technique for its persuasive 'shock', jolting the reader into a sudden

[19] Vargish and Mook, *Inside Modernism*, 81–3.
[20] Marjorie Perloff, *The Futurist Moment: Avant-Garde, Avant Guerre, and the Language of Rupture* (1986), 44–51.
[21] Walter Benjamin, *The Arcades Project*, trans. Howard Eiland and Kevin McLaughlin (Cambridge, MA, 1999); see also Susan Buck-Morss, *The Dialectics of Seeing: Walter Benjamin and the Arcades Project* (1989).

realisation of an underlying truth or reality.[22] In a Postmodern history, no such manipulation would be intended; rather, the underlying reality would be gradually perceived as complex and full of contradictions, as the historian is open to different plausible conclusions.

In approaching the Parisian department store, my first intention was to understand the meanings behind it, giving the reasons for its physical appearance, from the viewpoints of the different people and institutions involved in its creation.[23] Architects are therefore only one category; others were the owners and managers of department stores; the city, which influenced the possibilities for businesses through urban planning, and property laws, while restricting design with building regulations; technology, since engineering developments in iron, reinforced concrete and steel, as well as lifts and lighting, led to changes in meanings and the forms with which they were expressed; and the audience for the department store, subdivided into customers, workers, neighbours, other shopkeepers and various political groups.

Between each category, irreconcilable differences appeared, such as the willingness of architects to adopt certain technological features, particularly materials, but their extraordinary reluctance to use others, notably (with disastrous consequences) the improved understanding of fire precautions around 1900.[24] Further inconsistencies appeared within each category, which could be separated into strands of intention or ideology. The owners and managers of department stores, for example, inherited traditions which were at variance with the perfect economical running of the business; one such was the desire for daylight, considered necessary for the honest exposure of the quality of materials, which made the central atrium a common, though spatially inefficient, feature.[25] Architects, torn between the competing aesthetic systems of Beaux-Arts classicism, Rationalism and, later, Art Nouveau, attempted compromises with variable results: all three of these strands may be observed at once in Frantz Jourdain's Samaritaine building of 1907. Since even within a single person, conflicting ideas and motivations may coexist, there can be no simple narrative explanation for anything approaching the complexity of a building.

Thus, a Postmodern history, like a Cubist painting, can present its object of study through multiple perspectives, coexisting, though they may disagree; it represents the object as composed of different views according to the people and their texts that the historian consults, and

---

[22] See, for example, Walter Benjamin, 'Theses on the Philosophy of History', in Walter Benjamin, *Illuminations*, trans. Harry Zohn (1992).

[23] Robert Proctor, 'The Department Store in Paris, 1855 to 1914: An Architectural History' (doctoral thesis, Cambridge University, 2002).

[24] *Ibid.*, 234–40.

[25] *Ibid.*, 87.

according to the methods used to interpret them. An important consequence is that the building no longer appears situated within a linear chronological frame, or as evolving across time, but as continuously present in different manifestations. Since the history is thematic, aspects of the represented object will recur in different contexts, not unlike the recurring patterns of a Cubist painting. The effect is one of a rhythmic time, or of parallel times, replacing the linear time of narrative based on literary realism. This Cubist history then approaches more recent literary models;[26] ultimately, however, its intention remains a more truthful and realistic form of history.

[26] Elizabeth Ermarth suggests Alain Robbe-Grillet's *Jealousy*, trans. Richard Howard (1960), amongst other potential models (in *Sequel to History*, 72–84).

Transactions of the RHS 13 (2003), pp. 237–50 © 2003 Royal Historical Society
DOI: 10.1017/S0080440103000131   Printed in the United Kingdom

DELUSIONS OF NATIONAL GRANDEUR: REFLECTIONS ON THE INTERSECTION OF ARCHITECTURE AND HISTORY AT THE PALACE OF WESTMINSTER, 1789–1834

By Sean Sawyer

ABSTRACT. This paper examines the important but obscure late Georgian architectural history of the Palace of Westminster and attempts to put architectural developments in their historical contexts in order to gain insight into the dynamic relationship between public architecture, public policy and the public perception of the nation and its values. The substantial but lost work of the architects Sir John Soane and James Wyatt at the Palace form the core of the study. From this perspective, the design competition of 1835–6 was not the beginning but the culmination of four decades of intense struggle over the form and meaning of architectural interventions at the Palace.

Introduction

When Americans think of Britain a few images invariably come to mind: the Beatles, James Bond or Emma Peel (depending on one's predilections in the super spy category) and Big Ben. Of them all, that estimable timepiece stands most unmistakably as a symbol of the British nation.[1] This colossus of Britishness arose from a powerful conjunction of architecture and history.

Nowhere in Britain do the forces of history and architecture collide with such direct and widespread impact as at the Palace of Westminster, the time-honoured seat of national government and, until 1882, law. Architecturally, Sir Charles Barry and A.W.N. Pugin's inventive transposition of an ecclesiastical aesthetic on to a plan of classical clarity is widely recognised as a landmark in both the Gothic Revival and the

---

[1] Sir Kenneth Clark declared that 'we cannot rid our imagination of that extraordinary building which seems to embody all that is most characteristic and most moving in London'. Kenneth Clark, *The Gothic Revival* (Harmondsworth, 1962), 105.

evolution of modern, institutional architecture.[2] Yet to understand the full significance of their architectural accomplishment and its enduring power as *the* emblem of British national identity, one must move beyond architecture and aesthetics into the stuff of history. My goal as an architectural historian is to integrate the study of architecture and its historical contexts to produce a nuanced understanding of the cultural, social, political and economic forces that shape both the designer and the design. While this approach yields fascinating results for the study of individual architects or private architecture, it is imperative in examining public architecture where these forces are both more complex and compelling. As Victor Hugo declared in 1831:

> architecture's greatest products are less individual than social creations; the offspring of nations in labour rather than the outpouring of men of genius; the deposit left behind by a nation; the accumulation of the centuries; the residue from the successive evaporations of human society; in short, a kind of formation.[3]

Barry and Pugin's Palace of Westminster was only the last, most recent layer added to the parliamentary-judicial formation along the Thames at Westminster. The focus of my work has been those laid down between 1784 and 1834, principally by Sir John Soane (1753–1837) and James Wyatt (1746–1813), which were lost either in the fire of 16 October 1834 or to the wrecker's axe and bar as the new complex was built through the next fifty years. From this perspective, the design competition of 1835–6 was not the beginning but the culmination of four decades of intense struggle over the form and meaning of architectural interventions at the Palace. This paper examines this important but little-known chapter in the Palace's history and attempts to put architectural developments in their historical contexts with the thought that some insight might be gained into the dynamic relationship between public architecture, public policy and the public perception of the nation and its values.

The topography of the Palace of Westminster

In order to understand the architectural transformation undertaken during this period it is necessary to come to grips with the outlines of the parliamentary and judicial complex in the last quarter of the eighteenth century. The Palace consisted of five principal medieval structures ranged north to south between the east end of the Abbey

[2] *Ibid.*, 93; Henry-Russell Hitchcock, *Architecture: Nineteenth and Twentieth Centuries* (New Haven and London, 1977), 150.
[3] Victor Hugo, *Notre-Dame de Paris* (Harmondsworth, 1978), 129.

and the river: the most substantial was (and still is) Westminster Hall, a Norman great hall recast in a Gothic mode at the end of the fourteenth century, whose principal entry faces north toward Whitehall and from which palatial chambers extended southward, including – from north to south – the palatine chapel dedicated to St Stephen, the Lesser or White Hall later known as the Court of Requests, the Painted Chamber, so called for its glorious murals commissioned by Henry III, and the Queen's Chamber. By the eighteenth century Westminster Hall accommodated the High Courts of Common Law and Equity, St Stephen's Chapel was home to the House of Commons and the Lords were installed in the Queen's Chamber. The upper house transferred to the Court of Requests with the addition of Irish members in 1801.

However, these substantial masonry structures were enmeshed within a mass of smaller, largely timber-frame additions, which diminished their visibility and threatened the entire complex with destruction by fire. Two public spaces bordered the Palace: New Palace Yard on the north and Old Palace Yard on the south. Historically, access to the Palace was principally by water, and the dominant public image of the complex was the view from the Thames.

The construction of Westminster Bridge and its approaches through the 1750s dramatically reshaped the Palace's environs, removing some of the metropolis's worst slums and creating broad new streets: Bridge Street running across the north side of New Palace Yard; Parliament Street linking New Palace Yard with Charing Cross; and Abingdon Street, replacing Dirty Lane as principal access into Old Palace Yard from the south and connecting with New Palace Yard via St Margaret's Lane. The Palace was now linked to the rapidly developing urban infrastructure but remained a decrepit and incommodious mass of buildings.

The Neoclassical vision of the Palace

The reconstruction of the Palace of Westminster was, in Sir John Summerson's words, 'that project on which, all through the eighteenth century, were focused the hopes of British architecture'.[4] As the century progressed and Britain forged its first global empire, the desire to see the decrepit medieval complex replaced with a suitably magnificent structure extended beyond the architectural community to a wide spectrum of patrons and politicians. A prime opportunity for reconstructing the Palace came between 1730 and 1760 when the circle of Neo-Palladian architects and surveyors around Richard Boyle, 3rd earl of Burlington (1694–1753) advanced a series of proposals that clearly

[4] Sir John Summerson, *Architecture in Britain* (Harmondsworth, 1983), 345.

articulated a classicising vision for the site. William Kent (1685–1748) was the chief designer involved in this process, and fragments of his designs were realised by his colleague John Vardy (1718–65), from 1755 to 1770. The former clerk of parliament's residence by Vardy still stands on Old Palace Yard as a largely unrecognised testimony to this long-forgotten Neo-Palladian vision of the Palace.[5]

This vision remained the lodestone of British civic architecture as the generation of Neoclassical architects came of age in the 1760s and 1770s.[6] James (1732–94) and Robert Adam (1728–92) produced a series of designs for a Parliament House in the 1760s ranging from the fantastically impractical to the grandly possible.[7] Perhaps most influential, however, were John Gwynn's (1713–86) proposals contained in his remarkable treatise *London and Westminster Improved* of 1766.[8] Declaring that 'the English are now what the Romans were of old' and condemning the 'gloominess and horror' of Westminster Hall, he called for sweeping away all vestiges of the medieval palace, embanking the river and constructing a magnificent Classical structure that would 'preserve a character and decorum suitable to a building in which the laws of this great Kingdom are formed and executed'.[9] Gwynn's sentiments were echoed in an anonymous but widely circulated pamphlet of 1771 entitled *Critical Observations on the Buildings and Improvements of London*.[10] This distinctly Whiggish text declared that 'all public improvements must among us spring originally from the spirit of the people and not from the will of the prince' and contained a proposal for rebuilding the Palace as a 'Senate House'. This notion of civic grandeur as representative of civic virtue is also found in the polemics of John Wilkes at this time.

---

[5] The clerk's residence was constructed in 1756 and has also been attributed to Isaac Ware (1704–66). *The History of the King's Works*, gen. ed. H. M. Colvin, v (1976), 411. There is an elevation by Ware in Avery Library. John Harris, *A Catalogue of British Drawings for Architecture, Decorations, Sculpture and Landscape Gardening 1550–1900 in American Collections* (Upper Saddle River, NJ, 1971), 267, pl. 211.

[6] Summerson termed this the 'Golden Age of Georgian culture' and marked its inception to the Peace of Paris in 1763, which ended the Seven Years War and secured Britain's first global empire. John Summerson, *Georgian London* (1948), 115.

[7] For a complete analysis and description of the Adam designs for a Parliament House see Alan Tait, *Robert Adam: Drawings and Imagination* (Cambridge and New York, 1993), 55–70.

[8] John Gwynn, *London and Westminster Improved, to which is Prefixed a Discourse on Publick Magnificence* (1766). Gwynn, an intimate of Dr Johnson's in the circle of artists, designers and critics of the St Martin's Lane academy and one of the four architects among the founding members of the Royal Academy in 1768, proposed the systematic renewal and reconstruction of the metropolis, promoting public over private interests and including a series of monumental public and royal projects.

[9] *Ibid.*, 91–2.

[10] The author is now thought to have been the Scottish MP John Stewart (*c.* 1723–81). Eileen Harris, *British Architectural Books and Writers* (New York, 1990), 169.

In this context, the young John Soane's design of a British Senate House in 1778 reflects both his academic training amid the white heat of Georgian Neoclassicism and his proletarian origins as the son of a rural brickmason. His Senate House designs demonstrated what would be a lifelong commitment to the concept of a national culture and his youthful ability to design in a grand Neoclassical mode, but they bore no relation to the programmatic needs of the parliamentary complex.[11]

The transformation of the Palace, 1789–1834

Soane began to come to grips with the gritty reality of the Palace a decade later, in July 1789, when he and thirteen other eminent architects, including James Wyatt, participated in a survey of the entire complex commissioned by the House of Commons.[12] This proved to be the beginnings of fifty years of urban renewal, historic preservation and architectural intervention that would transform the decrepit medieval palatial precinct into a modern civic complex to serve the institutions of national law and government. The first phase, from 1789 to 1799, centred on the rivalry between Soane and Wyatt over who would be charged with work at the Palace and demonstrated that the politics of patronage and culture would be the determinative factors in work at the Palace. Soane held the immediate advantage in that he counted the prime minister William Pitt (1756–1806, in office 1783–1801 and 1804–6) among his private clients and had won the most recent patronage contest to become Architect to the Bank of England in October 1788.

Pitt's support would seem to have been pivotal, since the redevelopment of the Palace and its precincts may be understood as the architectural extension of his principal policy initiatives in the aftermath of the loss of the American colonies and the onset of war with Revolutionary France. Pitt advanced a sweeping programme of administrative and financial reform and suppressed dissent through parliamentary patronage and repressive legislation. On the one hand, the centralisation and professionalisation of governmental operations cast the chaotic assemblage of structures at Westminster in a harsh light

[11] They were conceived, as he later grandiloquently acknowledged, 'without regard to expense, or limits as to space, in the gay morning of youthful fancy, amid all the wild imagination of an enthusiastic mind, animated by the contemplation of the majestic ruins of the sublime works of imperial Rome'. John Soane, *Designs for Public Improvements in London and Westminster* (1828), 23.

[12] The other architects participating in the survey were: Robert Adam, Robert Browne, Charles Alexander Craig, S.P. Cockerell, George Dance, Jr, Thomas Fulling, Henry Holland, Robert Mylne, Thomas Tildesley, John Woolfe Sr and Jr and John Yenn. *Parliamentary Papers*, 1788, 62, p. 548.

and encouraged the creation of efficient, modern facilities. On the other, Pitt's method of controlling the unreformed Commons by loading the benches with rotten borough flunkies garnered from peerages given to their patrons aggrandised the House of Lords as did the agricultural boom sustained by two decades of war. Therefore, despite the ascendancy of ministerial government and the promotion of a popular civic culture, the reconstruction of the House of Lords became the government's highest priority and control of patronage shifted from minister to monarch.

However, in July 1794 Soane was able to manoeuvre around the Surveyor-General of the King's Works, Sir William Chambers, and parlay his political connections into a broadly stated commission to 'render the House of Lords ... more commodious'.[13] He produced four designs, his preferred design proposing a new Lords Chamber which projected eastward from the Painted Chamber toward the Thames. The other principal feature of this design was a grand Royal Entrance at the centre of a new south façade with a forecourt providing both access and a dramatic panorama from the river. All the designs responded to budgetary concerns by reusing the substantial masonry of the medieval chambers, but they were to be embedded within an

Figure 1   Sir John Soane, design perspective for reconstructing the House of Lords, watercolour by Joseph Michael Gandy, 1800. By courtesy of the Trustees of Sir John Soane's Museum.

[13] John Soane, *A Statement of Facts Respecting the Design of a New House of Lords, as Ordered by the Lords Committees and Humbly Submitted to the Consideration of their Lordships, by John Soane, F.A.S. Architect to the Bank of England, and Member of the Royal Academies of London, Parma & Florence* (1799), 11, footnote.

emphatically Neoclassical structure articulated by ashlar basements, giant order Corinthian columns, saucer domes and sculptural skylines. Even within, the medieval chambers were to be clad in Neoclassical garb to form a 'National Monument' for the display of patriotic painting and sculpture by British artists.

George III particularly approved of this last notion along with the grand Royal Entrance and its proposed 'Scala Regia' when Soane presented the designs at Windsor in October 1794.[14] However, the king's preference in architects was for the charmingly slipshod Wyatt rather than the ingratiatingly professional Soane. Wyatt's courtly graces had won over the king during renovations at Frogmore House for Queen Charlotte in 1793–5, and, thus, when Chambers died on 8 March 1796, Wyatt immediately succeeded him as surveyor-general and asserted his prerogative to control work at Westminster, even going so far as to represent Soane's concept of a National Monument as his own. Soane refused to submit to this *coup d'état*. From February to October 1800 he revamped his designs with his assistant, Joseph Michael Gandy (1771– 1843), who had been a pupil of Wyatt's and was sensitive to the formal innovation and decorative finesse of his mentor's designs. However, Soane and Gandy's aggrandised designs were pointless.

Between 1794 and 1800 an aesthetic revolution fuelled by socio-political concerns had overtaken Westminster. As Revolutionary France co-opted the imagery of a mythologised republican Antiquity, a reactionary and assertively monarchical Britain abandoned Neoclassicism and embraced Gothic as a more sincere and even native style. Despite Wyatt's disregard for archaeological correctness, he was renowned for his original Gothic designs and in 1796 had begun work on Britain's culminating expression of Gothicism, William Beckford's Fonthill Abbey. Thus, when formally encharged with reconstructing the House of Lords in mid-1799, Wyatt's stated objective was for 'the whole [palace] ... to assume the appearance of a large Gothic edifice'.[15]

Yet architectural innovation took backseat to the more immediate need to control public space around the Palace. Throughout the 1790s Westminster was the focus of anti-war protests and food riots, including an attack on the king's carriage during the opening of parliament on 29 October 1795. Pitt's infamous 'Two Acts' introduced in the aftermath of this event had the banning of mass meetings around the Palace as

---

[14] *Ibid.*, 15.
[15] *Times*, 23 Oct. 1806, p. 3, col. 3. Joseph Farington's diary entry for 5 July 1799 states: 'Wyatt told us it is now in agitation to have all the new buildings including the House of Lords of Gothic Architecture, so as to make a whole mass of that kind of building.' *The Diary of Joseph Farington*, ed. Kenneth Garlick and Angus Macintyre (New Haven and London, 1978–9), IV, 1591.

PART OF DESIGN FOR NEW HOUSE OF LORDS. (SIR J. SOANE 1800)

Figure 2   Sir John Soane, design perspective of the Scala Regia, watercolour by Joseph Michael Gandy, 1800. By courtesy of the Trustees of Sir John Soane's Museum.

a principal objective.[16] Pitt and succeeding governments invested heavily in the clearance and reconstruction of the network of streets and squares surrounding the Palace. From 1799 to 1815 the Westminster Improvements Commission spent over £250,000 on urban renewal

[16] In his correspondence with the home secretary, the duke of Portland, in the aftermath of 29 October carriage attack, George III was explicit about the necessity of preventing such gatherings and referred to the still potent memory of the Gordon riots: 'The

work.[17] This resulted in the clearance of the slums just north of the Abbey to create Parliament Square; the further improvement of vehicular access to the Palace by widening St Margaret's Street; and the disengagement of the Abbey, St Margaret's Church and Westminster Hall from post-medieval accretions, and the consequent restoration of the revealed medieval façades.[18] In turn, this rediscovery of Westminster's medieval monuments fuelled public interest in the Gothic and cemented its identity as *the* style of church, crown and country.

As this urban renewal work proceeded, Wyatt prepared plans for reconstructing the Palace as a Picturesque, castellated Gothic ensemble in which the original medieval structures were to be set like jewels in a crown. He shifted the architectural paradigm from one of confrontation and provocative juxtaposition with Westminster's Gothic past to one of compromise and evocation. Ultimately, Wyatt completed only two elements of his larger scheme at a cost of over £200,000: the reconstruction of the Speaker's House (1802–8) and a new range of offices along the east side of Old Palace Yard (1805–7). The latter in particular was such an unqualified aesthetic failure – it was compared to both a prison and a gentleman's lavatory in the Commons – and Wyatt's administration of the project and the Office of King's Works in general was so corrupt and slipshod that he was forced to abandon any further work. In September 1813 he died in a carriage accident on the Marlborough Downs, and in the reformation of the Office of Works that ensued Soane was named Attached Architect responsible for

---

intention of meeting in Westminster Hall or Palace Yard on Monday is so avowedly to intimidate both Houses of Parliament that I should think it highly proper for them this day to apply to the Executive power that all the avenues to Parliament may be kept clear, and that if necessary this must be enforced with those means that will effect success. I mention this more as the riot of 1780 began with an assemblage before the House of Commons which, if it had at that period been dispersed, the outrages and mischiefs of the following days would have been prevented.' *The Later Correspondence of George III*, ed. A. Aspinall (Cambridge and New York, 1962–70), II, 420.

[17] The Commission resulted from the amalgamation of two distinct urban planning efforts: the parliamentary committees to improve the approaches to the Houses of Parliament first appointed in 1792 and the commissions established in 1777, 1799 and 1804 to supervise the development of the Westminster Sessions House. Its authority was consolidated by seven acts of parliament between 1800 and 1814, and any land it purchased became crown property. Mostly high-ranking parliamentary and royal officers, the commissioners were: the lord chancellor; the speaker of the House of Commons; the lord chief baron; the dean of Westminster; the high steward of Westminster; the clerk of the parliaments; the lord great chamberlain; Earl Spencer; and Lord Auckland. Although the majority of its work was completed by 1815, the Commission was not disbanded until 1826, when its responsibilities were transferred to the Commissioners of Woods, Forests and Land Revenues. *The History of the King's Works*, gen. ed. H. M. Colvin, VI (1973), 515–56.

[18] Wyatt was responsible for restoration work at the Abbey, particularly the restoration of the exterior of Henry VII's Chapel, as Architect to the Dean and Chapter.

Whitehall and Westminster, poised at sixty years of age to realise his life's ambitions.

Soane's appointment at Westminster was supported by Robert Banks Jenkinson, 2nd earl of Liverpool (1770–1828), who became prime minister upon the assassination of Spencer Perceval in May 1812 and remained in office until 1827. Soane had undertaken alterations and additions to Coombe House near Kingston for Liverpool between 1801 and 1809, but it was his reputation as a meticulous and budget-conscious professional that earned him the prime minster's patronage.

The immediate impetus in the aftermath of two decades of war was for so-called 'economical reform' and was led by a parliamentary coterie of Whigs and Tory cross-benchers, an informal and uneasy coalition of City-minded Whigs, such as George Tierney (1761–1830), and independent-thinking Tory country gentlemen, such as Henry Bankes (1756–1834), the scion of a landed but untitled Dorset family. As the long serving chairman of the Commons' finance committee and champion of select committees, Bankes was a powerful voice for retrenchment in the post-war years and systematically opposed expenditures for both royal and public works.[19] Soane's works at the Palace of Westminster – where Bankes had a house on Old Palace Yard[20] – were the particular object of his economical and aesthetic scrutiny.

However, no work occurred in the first five years after Waterloo. Economic recession and widespread unemployment led to frequent mass protests, riots and threats to the unpopular prince regent and government ministers, including the Peterloo incident of August 1819 and the Cato Street Conspiracy, which was uncovered in February 1820.

From 1821 the British economy recovered and then surged ahead in what might be termed the first boom of the industrial era. As the standard of living rose, social and political unrest diminished almost as suddenly as it had sprung up after Waterloo, and the 1820s were a period of stability and prosperity. Gradually Liverpool realigned his cabinet to a more progressive bent by bringing in reformers such as George Canning (1770–1827) and Sir Robert Peel (1788–1850), who gradually liberalised government policy. Soane's works at Westminster were executed during the heyday of this 'Liberal Toryism' with the direct involvement of Liverpool and his cabinet and certainly reflected this atmosphere of national confidence and renewal.

Soane's first and most significant project at the Palace was the reconstruction of the Law Courts begun in 1820 and completed in

---

[19] *The History of Parliament, The House of Commons, 1790–1820*, ed. R.G. Thorne (1986), III, 132.

[20] That is according to John Thomas Smith, *Antiquities of Westminster* (1807), 125.

1826. This project had been conceived of since at least Kent's time, when he had rebuilt the Court of Common Pleas outside the west wall of Westminster Hall with a portal connecting to the Hall, and Wyatt's larger scheme had included rebuilding the Courts along St Margaret's Street. Growing reverence for the Hall was a principal factor behind Soane's commission as antiquarians called for clearing it of the court partitions that obscured its interior. Soane recounted that it was Liverpool himself who, on walking through the Hall in the summer of 1820 when it had been cleared for George IV's impending Coronation Banquet, 'was so struck with the grand effect of that unique edifice' that he ordered that the Courts be removed permanently.[21] An ulterior motive was the government's desire to circumvent the comprehensive reform of the Chancery Court by making permanent the Vice-Chancellor's Court, which had been created in 1813 as a temporary means of alleviating the chronic inefficiency of the Lord Chancellor's Court.

Driven by the precedent of Kent's Court of Common Pleas, Soane's challenge was to place seven court chambers, robing rooms and associated clerical and records offices in an irregularly shaped plot 300' long by 50' wide at its narrowest outside the west wall of Westminster Hall. In addition, the site was punctuated by the Hall's six huge buttresses and partially built up with Kent and Vardy's Neo-Palladian 'Stone Building' at its southern end. These stringent constraints inspired Soane to a feat of planning genius: he deftly inserted the court chambers between the buttresses in a sequence that demonstrated his mastery of the judiciary's logistic and hierarchical requirements and sewed the whole together with a network of corridors and interlinking offices. He created distinct architectural characters for each court, from the sober Neo-Palladian King's Bench to the awesome Greco-Gothic fusion of the Chancery Court, each an architectural jurisdiction unto itself but interrelated through shared affects of space and light.

On the exterior elevations, Soane made the Stone Building symmetrical and somewhat awkwardly extended its ashlar basement and Palladian openings on to New Palace Yard. This façade was substantially complete in early 1824 when Bankes and his fellow defenders of British virtue objected to this perceived affront to the Hall's restored Gothic glories and forced its demolition and replacement with a supposedly complementary castellated Gothic front. This dramatic episode of direct parliamentary interference in the design process festered in Soane's civic consciousness for the remainder of his life.

This dichotomy between brilliant planning and interior architecture and constrained, imitative exteriors also characterised Soane's other

[21] Sir John Soane, *Memoirs of the Professional Life of an Architect between the Years 1768 and 1835* (1835), 43.

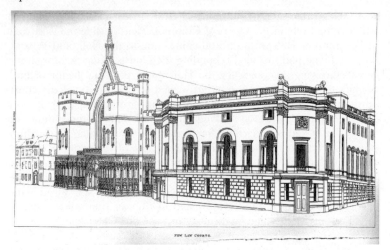

Figure 3   Sir John Soane, north Façade of the Law Courts adjacent to Westminster Hall as partially built in 1824, engraving from Soane's Designs for Public Improvements in London and Westminster *(1828). By courtesy of the Trustees of Sir John Soane's Museum.*

major work at the Palace, the new Royal Entrance to the House of Lords, completed in 1824. Here he continued the castellated mode of Wyatt's office range around the south end of the Palace to form a *porte cochere* and entrance 'cloister' leading to the Scala Regia and Royal Gallery, which were both exuberantly Neoclassical and bravado demonstrations of Soane's particular skill at creating fluid, evocative spatial sequences. The sequential nature of the Royal Entrance was a conscious affect designed to serve the ceremonial of the monarch's arrival at the Palace for the state opening and prorogation of parliament.[22] Soane even sketched an audience in several early designs and commissioned Gandy to represent the completed chambers in an almost cinematic series of perspective renderings. In this sense, the Royal Entrance directly reflected George IV's ambition to reassert the royal ceremonial presence at the Palace of Westminster. Unlike his father, he enjoyed and excelled at pageantry, and it accorded with the government's desire

[22] The state opening and prorogation of parliament had long been a principal occasion on which the monarch could demonstrate his sovereignty over parliament, as it supposedly remains today. H.S. Cobb, in his essay on surviving manuscript and printed evidence for the ceremony in the Tudor era, notes that 'throughout the Tudor period the opening of Parliament by the Sovereign provided an important occasion for political pageantry...the procession, for example, appears to have grown steadily in size and splendour throughout this period'. H.S. Cobb, 'Descriptions of the State Opening of Parliament, 1485–1601: A Survey', in *Essays Presented to Maurice Bond*, ed. H.S. Cobb (1981), 17.

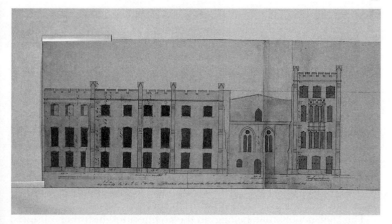

Figure 4   Sir John Soane, elevations of the House of Lords and the House of Commons office blocks as built with east end of the Painted Chamber, 1827. By courtesy of the Trustees of Sir John Soane's Museum.

to promote patriotic attachment to king and country in a time of social and economic change, particularly when the monarch posed an increasingly nominal political threat.[23]

As construction of the Royal Entrance and Law Courts concluded, Soane began work on office blocks for both Houses of Parliament, including the first purpose-built libraries for both Houses. Both blocks fronted the river and represented *ad hoc* solutions to immediate needs rather than elements of a concerted plan to reorganise and expand the complex. This was not due to any lack of trying on Soane's part. For each of his projects at the Palace summoned up copious proposals for more comprehensive and architecturally ambitious responses, but considerations of public economy thwarted the execution of any grander concept for the Palace.

Conclusion

What decades of architectural plotting had failed to accomplish, a few hours of carelessness did when overheated furnaces started a conflagration that consumed the core of the palatial complex on 16 October 1834. Although the spectacle of the fire left an indelible impression on a generation and led to the design competition and Barry and Pugin's new Palace, much of the complex, including

[23] Linda Colley, *Britons: Forging the Nation, 1707–1837* (New Haven and London, 1992), 207–16.

Westminster Hall, the Law Courts, the Royal Entrance and Lords' office block remained standing and continued to function until replaced, bit by bit, through the course of the nineteenth century. Victoria processed through Soane's Royal Entrance for the first fifteen years of her reign, and the Law Courts were only demolished in 1883 after the completion of George Edmund Street's new judicial complex on The Strand. Despite their physical survival, however, Soane's Law Courts were defunct from almost the moment of their completion, overwhelmed by the unprecedented expansion of the judicial system to meet the needs of a more populous and litigious society that began in earnest in the 1830s. Similarly, Soane's cosmopolitan subversion of the parochial Gothic mandate at Westminster through the fusion of Gothic affects with Neoclassical forms in his interior spaces garnered little admiration in an age increasingly obsessed with archaeological correctness.

This melancholy tone belongs to the architectural historian, obsessed with the architect's dreams and aspirations. The historian takes a broader, albeit colder, view and suggests that the ultimate failure of Wyatt and Soane's interventions at Westminster was due to historical forces beyond their control. On the one hand, public policy determined the nature and timing of projects. Through the nearly half-century from 1789 to 1834 civic architecture was closely linked with urban renewal as the creation of a more centralised and disciplined society prioritised the reordering of public space as a means of exerting social and political control. On the other, public opinion, as defined in the expanding public sphere, governed the form of civic architecture, or at least its outward, public appearances. George III promoted Wyatt's castellated Gothic but the public demanded something more. Soane found a productive dissonance between the Gothic Hall and the Palladian Courts but the Commons demanded conformity.

Transactions of the RHS 13 (2003), pp. 251–79 © 2003 Royal Historical Society
DOI: 10.1017/S0080440103000143   Printed in the United Kingdom

THE HÔTEL DE VILLE AT LYONS:
CIVIC IMPROVEMENT AND ITS MEANINGS
IN SEVENTEENTH-CENTURY FRANCE

By Judi Loach

ABSTRACT. This paper highlights some roles architectural history can uniquely play both *vis-à-vis* political history and/or in constructing it. Through looking at a particular city – Lyons – it suggests how the disregard both of built evidence *per se* and of its specifically architectural interpretation has distorted the conventional account of that city's history. By means of a particular case study, of perhaps the most significant single building within that city – its town hall – it indicates some of the ways in which architectural history can serve to enrich political history, and indeed why it should be considered an essential tool for such history.

The intention of this paper is to highlight roles which architectural history can play *vis-à-vis* political history. Through looking at a particular city it suggests how the disregard both of built evidence *per se* and of its specifically architectural interpretation has distorted the conventional account of that city's history. By means of a particular case study it indicates some ways in which architectural history can serve to enrich political history, and why it should be considered an essential tool for such history.

The city is Lyons, and the building its town hall, erected from 1646 onwards. Although relegated to being France's second city since the Middle Ages, Lyons remains proud of her former status as Roman capital of Gaul, and of her continuing role as ecclesiastical capital of the nation. According to the conventional account of its history, the city has enjoyed two Golden Ages, the first due to the Renaissance, the second to the industrial revolution. It has been widely assumed that the period between these two Golden Ages constituted a Dark Age.[1]

---

[1] The first work to have contested this seems to have been Thérèse Moyne's doctorate, published as *Les livres illustrés à Lyon dans le premier tiers du XVIIe siècle* (Grenoble, 1987); this, however, appeared through a small, local (yet not Lyonese) press, and has been ignored by most subsequent scholars. This alternative interpretation finds support in Olivier Zeller's socio-economic research into seventeenth-century Lyons, in particular on its demography, where the quantitative data suggests that the seventeenth century was

As far as concerns the Renaissance, during much of this period the kings of France held their court in Lyons rather than Paris, in order to benefit from its geographical position as a more convenient base from which to wage wars on the Italian peninsula.[2] Lyons profited both economically and culturally from the court's presence in its midst. Such close contact with the king facilitated further royal concessions (*privilèges*) to hold international *foires*, or wholesale markets. Situated on the major north–south axis through France, the Rhône valley, and at its confluence with the Saône, Lyons was already long acknowledged as an international trading centre, with well-established routes connecting it to the north with the low countries and northern France, to the east with the Germanic lands and the Swiss cantons and to the south with the Mediterranean; equally estabished land routes linked it, across the Alps, with the Italian peninsula, and across the coastal plain of southern France to the Iberian peninsula. It thus owed its economic pre-eminence not so much to local and regional or even to national trade – in all of which, however, its leading role was accepted – but to international trade.

It was this characteristic which attracted Florentine bankers fleeing civil war in their native city, thus leading to Lyons's rise as an international banking capital;[3] from the early sixteenth century, international exchange rates were decided here daily, and then applied as the standard throughout the known world. Lyons also enjoyed a comparable reputation as a centre of trading in textiles, progressively specialising in the luxury end of the market, and thus attracting merchants from Italian cities specialising in fancy silks and velvets.[4] Yet the range of international trading at Lyons was diverse, with considerable activity in the fields of metalworking (including armaments), printing and publishing and fine foodstuffs, notably wines. So many foreigners resided permanently at Lyons that communities (*nations*) were formed for each of the best represented foreign countries or cities

---

actually the city's period of greatest growth, in turn a consequence of contemporary economic success: *Les recensements lyonnais de 1599 à 1636* (Lyons, 1983).

[2] For Lyons in the Renaissance see *Lyon des origines à nos jours: la formation de la cité*, ed. A. Kleinclausz (Lyons, 1925); Richard Gascon, *Grand commerce et vie urbaine au XVIe siècle: Lyon et ses marchands* (Paris and The Hague, 1971); *Histoire de Lyon et du Lyonnais*, ed. André Latreille (Toulouse, 1975); J.-P. Gutton, *Les Lyonnais dans l'histoire* (Toulouse, 1985); Françoise Bayard and Pierre Cayez, *Histoire de Lyon*, II: *Du XVIe siècle à nos jours* (Le Coteau, 1990), 1–240.

[3] The Florentines were the first to organise *courriers de banque* in Lyons, and in 1543 obtained a *monopole de droit* for this (Gascon, *Grand commerce*, 180).

[4] The Florentine merchants led the trade in fine silks but the Genoese and Luccans that in fancy silks, specialising respectively in silk velvets and in damask or satin silks; the Milanese specialised in cloth of gold (or silver), but in a much lower quantity (Gascon, *Grand commerce*, 62).

(notably Germans, Florentines, Genoese, Luccans and Milanese), and these usually financed at least one Italian priest.

As the city's wealth base – and with it the number of citizens enjoying substantial disposable income – rose, an exceptionally rich intellectual and cultural life developed. No doubt the visible remains of Lyons's Roman past inspired many citizens – most notably Symphorien Champier, Pierre Sala, Claude Bellièvre, Jean Grolier and Guillaume du Choul – to pursue Humanistic research into its history, undertaking archaeological investigations and studying antique inscriptions and medals. Creative artists likewise drew inspiration from the Renaissance across the Alps, as can be seen in the work of eminent literary figures such as Maurice Scève, Louise Labé, Clément Marot and François Rabelais, whilst musicians composed and played in the same idiom. All these writers and composers saw their works brought to a wider audience by some of the foremost printers and booksellers in the land, Sébastien Gryphe, Jean de Tournes, Etienne Dolet and Guillaume Roville; Lyons acquired an incomparable reputation for illustrated editions, thanks to ambitious booksellers employing engravers of the calibre of the 'Petit Bernard' (Bernard Salomon).[5]

In architectural terms the main evidence of this cultural activity is due to the wealthy merchants and bankers (often native Italians), primarily in the body of private houses erected on the narrow strip of flat land stretching north along the Saône from the cathedral towards the Loge de Change, erected beside the stone bridge leading to the church of St-Nizier on the Presqu'île; built in stone around courtyards with balconies, open staircase towers and galleries, they evidently owed less to the French tradition of *hôtels particuliers* than to that of the *palazzi* in the Italian towns from which many of their owners had come. The same spirit prevailed in the chapels added to existing churches, being endowed by merchants and dedicated to their own dynasties,[6] for in both cases architecture was marked by inter-family rivalry and Italianate – Renaissance – taste, in form and decoration alike. Within this context, the highpoints are due to the local mason who became France's greatest architectural theoretician of the Renaissance – and thus to a Frenchman trained in Rome – Philibert de l'Orme; for he dramatically extended one of these Italianate *palazzi* – the Hôtel Bullioud – and inspired the design of the new west façade of the church of St-Nizier.[7]

---

[5] For further details see the proceedings from a conference on the subject, held in Lyons in 1972: *L'humanisme lyonnais au XVIe siècle* (Grenoble, 1974).

[6] For example, the Pazzis built a chapel at the Celestins church and their fellow Florentines the Gadagnes at the Jacobins, the Grolliers at the Cordeliers de l'Observance and the Savarons at the Augustins Déchaussés in the faubourg de la Croix-Rousse.

[7] Hôtel Bullioud, 8 rue Juiverie, built 1536; see Philibert de l'Orme, *Le premier tome de l'architecture* (Paris, 1567). From the early eighteenth century the west façade of St-Nizier

The Wars of Religion abruptly brought this Golden Age to its end. On the night of 29 April 1562 Huguenot forces from nearby Geneva suddenly captured the town. Over the following thirteen months, this venerable religious centre, and the seat of the Christian church in Gaul from shortly after the arrival of Christianity in the land, was systematically purged of all marks of established religion: the practice of the Roman Catholic religion was prohibited; clergy, monks and nuns were forced into exile or conversion; churches, monasteries and convents were closed and often demolished.

No foreign traders dared come near the city, precipitating the collapse of the city's economic base. The continuation of any cultural endeavours not only lacked resources, but also faced opposition from puritanical administrators. When the Catholics finally gained exclusive control, in 1567, they were faced not only with a city whose economic base had collapsed but also one where most of the major public buildings had been severely – often deliberately – damaged; for not only had churches and monasteries been the objects of attack, but so had most educational or welfare establishments, since these too had been ecclesiastical foundations.

To turn to the industrial revolution, the introduction of Jacquard and other mechanical looms in the nineteenth century saw the rise of what Lyonese call the Fabrique, at once an industry and a trade, producing and marketing luxury textile goods, notably varieties of worked silk cloth; this business was controlled by a few merchants, who operated as middlemen, buying the silk thread (and other raw materials) and selling the finished products, whilst their weavers (*canuts*) worked from their own homes.[8] The Fabrique thus marked the city by covering the steep Croix-Rousse hillside – the backdrop to the Presqu'île – with towering blocks of high-ceilinged, large-windowed flats, designed to accommodate tall looms and maximise the daylight by which to weave.

Meanwhile the profits from this industry enabled the rise of commercial banks, and encouraged investment in the enterprises spawned by the industrial revolution. The coalfield around St-Etienne, soon linked with Lyons by railway and canal, provided coal and coke at two-thirds the price in the Paris basin, thus supporting a move to

was attributed to Philibert de l'Orme, during his stay in his native Lyons on his way back from Italy in 1536; the archives, however, show that it dates from 1579, and that it was designed by Jean Vallet (André Clapasson, *Description de la ville de Lyon 1741*, ed. Gilles Chomer and Marie-Félice Pérez (Seyssel, 1982), 104); François-Régis Cottin, 'Philibert de l'Orme et le portail de l'église de Saint-Nizier de Lyon', *Communication au 112e Congrès national des Sociétés savantes*, Lyons, Apr. 1987.

[8] For Lyons in this period see *Lyon des origines*, ed. Kleinclausz; Maurice Garden, *Lyon et les Lyonnais au XVIIIe siècle* (Paris, 1970); *Histoire de Lyon*, ed. Latreille; Gutton, *Les Lyonnais dans l'histoire*; Bayard and Cayez, *Histoire de Lyon*, II, 1–240.

steam-powered machinery; this in turn favoured the adoption of the latest means of transportation (on river and railway alike) and the development of the iron and steel industry, for which iron ore could be obtained from the nearby Ardeche, and subsequently boilermaking and the manufacture of heavy machinery. Improved transportation with the agriculturally rich hinterland led to the industrialisation of by-products from its livestock market: candles, soap, glue and varnish; this nascent chemical industry (which also advanced the glass industry) received a further impetus with the invention of synthetic dyes, due to Lyons's leading role as a textile centre.

This time the urban fabric was most affected through speculative construction, in the form of large-scale, peripheral expansion to house the labour force attracted by industry from the countryside around; the high-rise blocks covering the Croix-Rousse to the north were paralleled by others along the main streets of the Guillotière faubourg to the east, a lower-rise, grid of streets over the Brotteaux lying in between them, and the quasi-rural, low-rise and low-density development of Vaise, to the north-west. Meanwhile, however, the successful merchant families controlling the Fabrique, but now also profiting from their investment in the new industries, set about restructuring the city centre, imposing an almost mechanical order upon its largely mediaeval fabric, so as to make it better serve the industrial age. With the rue Impériale (today's rue de la République) driven through to join the two main squares and further thoroughfares laid out to link the city centre with its burgeoning periphery (or, as on the plateau of the Croix-Rousse, to open up circulation within a new suburb), Lyons was the only city outside Paris to be 'Hausmannised'. As in the capital, the motor behind these civil engineering projects, which also included the installation of a comprehensive sewage system and the creation of a vast municipal park between the Brotteaux and the Croix-Rousse, was the *préfet*, in this case Vaisse (1852–63).

In architectural terms, however, the focus remained the Presqu'île, where buildings proclaiming civic pride were restored or erected – the Hôtel de Ville in the first instance, and the Marché des Cordeliers in the second; others arose to celebrate the ascendancy of the bourgeoisie – Opera, Stock Exchange and railway stations (first at Perrache and then at Brotteaux). In fact the new axis created by the rue Impériale led from the Opera and Hôtel de Ville, past the Stock Exchange and market, to culminate in the new square laid out in front of Perrache Station.

The standard account of Lyons's history, emphasising these two Golden Ages, is supported by much scholarly research, notably by the two eminent Lyonese socio-economic historians who first exploited the techniques of the *Annales* school – the application of quantitative analysis to archival material – to unearth the everyday living conditions of Lyons's citizens. Their magisterial studies have dominated subsequent interpretations: Richard Gascon's *Grand commerce et vie urbaine au XVIe siècle: Lyon et ses marchands* (1971)[9] and Maurice Garden's *Lyon et les Lyonnais au XVIIIe siècle* (1970).[10] In both cases extensive, detailed and meticulous research was combined with progressive historical technique. One might duly conclude that civic life had merely struggled on between these two Golden Ages. The buildings, however, tell a different, and indeed contradictory, tale. Moreover, the discrepancy between the tales presented by these two sources – paper and stone – is particularly striking in the case of buildings representing the body politic.

Lyons was divided into two electoral constituencies, Fourvière to the west of the Saône, and Presqu'île to its east, between this river and the Rhône; in turn the Saône (and, below the confluence, its continuation in the Rhône) marked the frontier between the legal jurisdiction of Paris and that of another *parlement*, Dauphiné. The district thus defined as Fourvière, effectively consisting of the narrow riverside strip beneath the eponymous hill, is today – just as it was in the seventeenth century – dominated by the cathedral of St-Jean, but otherwise largely filled by the sumptuous private houses erected by Italian bankers and other international merchants during the French Renaissance. The district's public buildings comprise the episcopal palace complex (a major seventeenth-century addition), the *mairie* (built for the Jesuits in the seventeenth century, as their second college), the city's law courts (a nineteenth-century building replacing the 1620s *tribunal*, the Palais de Roanne) and the Loge de Change (Soufflot's first major work, but again replacing its mid-seventeenth-century forebear); in fact, most civic buildings in this district were first erected in the seventeenth century.

In the larger district of the Presqu'île, the vast majority of the principal buildings also date from the seventeenth century: the town hall, the Musée des Beaux-Arts (built as the convent of St-Pierre), the town college (now the Lycée Ampère), the hospital of the Hôtel-Dieu (albeit much-extended by Soufflot a century later) and numerous churches, either restored or newly built. In addition the belltower of another hospital, the Charité – demolished in the 1930s to make way for the Central Post Office and sorting office – stands as a reminder of what was, when built in the seventeenth century, the largest hospital in all Europe. Despite nineteenth-century insertions such as the Opéra (recently eviscerated and enlarged by Jean Nouvel), the Stock Exchange and the Celestins theatre, seventeenth-century buildings and their allied urban interventions still dominate in the Presqu'île north of the Perrache district (its extension created by nineteenth-century engineering works, which physically moved the confluence further south). For most of the

[9] Gascon, *Grand commerce.*
[10] Garden, *Lyon et les Lyonnais.*

quaysides and both the two main squares – Terreaux and Bellecour – were laid out in the seventeenth century, even if the major thoroughfare linking them only dates from the nineteenth century.

What is significant is not just the quantity of buildings erected during the seventeenth century, but their overwhelmingly civic character. Obviously the Wars of Religion had left an urgent need for reconstruction. Yet the fabric which was built, far from being any short-term solution to this problem, has proved to be of sufficient quality to have endured, implying that it must have originally constituted a considerable expense. This suggests that, far from being a 'Dark Age', this period was a particularly dynamic one in the city's economic and political life; either the city as a whole became unusually self-confident, or some individual or body within it harboured exceptional ambitions for it.

The fact that the conclusions drawn from historical studies based on serious archival research – such as those of Gascon and Garden and their followers – are open to question once confronted with a genre of evidence which they neglected – namely that of built evidence – raises an important issue for historians. In the case of Lyons cited above, buildings provide evidence for political historians which supplements that available in written sources, indeed evidence essential to their completion of the picture of the period concerned, one for which a fuller record was left in stone than on paper. Conversely this points to the fact that the restricted range of sources generally used by historians, even those descended from the *Annales* school – neglecting many material, non-written sources, and most notably that of built fabric – constitutes a serious, and unnecessary, limitation.

A specifically architectural study of the built evidence – analysing plans, elevational composition, style and details – can illuminate political history. The remainder of this article is therefore devoted to such a case study, of the principal building erected in seventeenth-century Lyons, the town hall.

The Hôtel de Ville is unquestionably the most important single building from Lyons's seventeenth-century building campaign, not only for its role within the city itself but also for its part in constructing the self-portrait projected by the city to those outside it, notably in Paris and at court. In the frontispiece to *Lyon dans son lustre*, issued in 1656, the year after the completion of the building, its Terreaux façade is collaged with a lion, whose skin is imprinted with a map of the city, and whose paws bear the arms of the four consuls, whilst those of the Prévôt des Marchands appear on its forehead; in turn, the three fleurs de lys which appear in the sky above enable the composition to be read as the city's arms.[11] In another frontispiece to an official publication,

[11] Samuel Chappuzeau, *Lyon dans son lustre* (Lyons, 1656).

Les forces de Lyon, issued a couple of years later (perhaps in conjunction with a royal visit to the city), a lion strides across the square in front of the town hall whilst Renowns bearing the governor's and lieutenant's arms fly overhead.[12]

That the town hall should be the most impressive building erected by the city – and that it was therefore deliberately set back at the far end of the principal square expressly to display it to best effect – may not be surprising, since one would expect it to have been conceived as a symbol of civic authority. It is, however, worth noting that in Lyons this was the unique symbol of secular authority, due to the curious fact that this city, unlike smaller cities around (such as Grenoble) and despite its scale and (perhaps because of) its age, lacked any *parlement*, university or other such institutions. Instead Lyons lay (just) within the jurisdiction of Paris. On the one hand, the upper merchant class thus exercised greater power in Lyons than elsewhere, where its members would have competed with officers of *parlement* and other institutions. On the other hand, Lyons balked at being under the authority of its distant rival.

Under these circumstances it might seem strange that Lyons had managed without any purpose-built town hall up to the mid-seventeenth century. Until then the city had made do with the parish church of

Figure 1   The façade of the town hall, engraved by Jean Chevene after Israël Sylvestre, executed by Robert Pigout (c. 1650). Fonds Ancien, Bibliothèque Municipale de Lyon: 101.896 rés.

[12] Tristan l'Hermite de Soliers, *Les forces de Lyon* (Lyons, 1658).

St-Nizier – effectively the city's guild church, since the confraternities associated with various crafts and trades had their chapels there – for council meetings and allied civic ceremonies, whilst private houses in the central part of the Presqu'île were progressively acquired and converted to accommodate civic administration.[13]

The idea of erecting a town hall does not seem, however, to have originated with the consuls who, as economically minded merchants, were primarily concerned with preventing their city from sliding into deficit. Shortly after the completion of the building's construction the consuls would attribute the impetus for having undertaken the project (and then for carrying it through) to the provincial governor of the Lyonnais, Nicolas (V) de Villeroy (1592–1686), and to his lieutenant, his brother Camille de Neufville (1606–93).[14] The consuls had committed the city to the venture in their first meeting of 1646.[15] Nicolas had become governor of the province in 1642 and Camille lieutenant in 1645; in addition, Nicolas had been appointed Louis XIV's personal governor (in other words, tutor) in 1645. These facts lead one to suspect that the ambition inspiring the building of a town hall reflects the rising power of the local oligarchy rather than the wishes of a cautious consulate.

The extraordinary scale of the building – considerably bigger than its counterpart in Paris – is significant. The Lyonese ambition to outdo the capital, however, was to continue in an unparalleled sumptuosity of decorations and a hitherto unprecedented display of foreign – Baroque – style. As such it was evidently conceived as a political statement directed at citizens and outsiders alike; in fact it asserted Lyons's status not just as the capital's rival within the kingdom but also as an established international centre for ecclesiastical and commercial networks extending across Europe and even beyond.

On 8 March 1646 the consulate agreed to send the city's *voyer*, Simon Maupin, to Paris to consult 'the most expert architects' there[16] over the plans and drawings which he and other professionals in Lyons were to draft for this new town hall. The reason given by the consuls for consulting these Parisians was 'in order to avoid those defects and deficiencies which often occur in great buildings'.[17] It is noteworthy that no Parisian architect was invited to design the building, but simply to comment on designs already produced by the Lyonese. Furthermore,

---

[13] V. de Valous, *Les anciens hôtels de ville de Lyon* (Lyons, 1882).

[14] 'Mgr l'Archevesque, lequel avec Mgr. le Mareschal son frere a esté le principal mobile pour l'entreprise, le progrès et l'accomplissement de ce bel édifice' (consular meeting of 9 Mar. 1655: Archives Municipales de Lyon [hereafter AML], BB210, p. 106).

[15] Minutes for consular meeting of 4 Jan. 1646 (AML, BB200, fo. 9v).

[16] 'les plus expertz architectes de la ville de Paris': AML, BB200, fos. 51v–52r.

[17] 'd'avoir un desseing et un plan faict par les architectes et personnes expertes, afin d'evicter les défauts et manquemens qui arrivent souvent en des grands bastimens': *ibid.*

of the two architects in Paris actually consulted – Lemercier and Desargues – the latter had been born and bred in the Lyonnais and built at least one house in Lyons before moving to Paris; moreover, the former was probably approached less for his reputation – as architect to Louis XIII and Richelieu – than because of his close relationship with Nicolas de Villeroy, one half of the pair promoting the town hall. Presumably the Lyonese designed the initial scheme (or schemes) rapidly, since Maupin seems to have taken them to Paris by 19 April, when the consulate voted the payment of the two Parisian architects.[18] Evidently the latter played little further part in the design, since thereafter Maupin alone was paid for design work;[19] moreover, subsequent Lyonese publications never mention either as having played any part in the design. Nevertheless, later references in Parisian publications – by no less authorities than Abraham Bosse and François Blondel – attribute the main staircase to Lemercier, with Desargues refining its detailed design.[20]

The consuls' overt and pragmatic reasons for sending the designs to Paris perhaps obscure the likely, if unstated, reasons of the building's key promoters, Villeroy and Neufville. For they no doubt wanted those in the capital, or more precisely at court, to be made aware of their intentions, not least because – as they would later express more explicitly – this project formed part of their preparations for an anticipated visit to their town by the monarch.[21]

Viewing the project from this perspective, it becomes clear that it constituted the final piece in a much larger urban development scheme begun by the brothers' father, Charles de Neufville, marquis d'Halincourt, shortly after he became lieutenant in 1607, and particularly after he became governor in 1625. This included buildings to accommodate those institutions worst affected by the Wars of Religion – the town college (the Collège de la Trinité) and two hospitals (Hôtel-Dieu and Charité) – but also others symbolic of faith in economic revival – the *tribunal* and the Loge de Change. In all cases, however, the new building demonstrates a greater sense of local or regional ambition than had any previous building in the city. Moreover, they were now, at least officially, due to civic rather than ecclesiastical backing.

---

[18] AML, BB200, fo. 71; CC 1938, No. 68 (quittance pour 600').

[19] AML, BB200, fo. 186: 18 decembre 1646: 300' paid to Simon Maupin for his journey to Paris for the plans to be consulted; BB200, fo. 196: 20 decembre 1646: 600' paid to Maupin; BB201, fos. 200 and 217: 10 decembre 1647: for the engraving of a new plan by Maupin; BB202, fo. 21: 4 janvier 1648: 300' paid to Maupin for the engraving (*taille-douce*) of the plan and elevation.

[20] Abraham Bosse, *Traité des manieres de dessiner les ordres de l'architecture antique en toutes leurs parties* (Paris, 1664), Pl. xxxix; François Blondel, *Cours de l'architecture* (Paris, 1675), 696, 700.

[21] Claude-François Menestrier, SJ, *Factum Justificatif* (n.p., n.d. [Paris, c. 1694]), 67.

Yet this civic improvement scheme was more a matter of infra-structure and civil engineering: a series of new city gates; fountains installed in front of certain monumental buildings; several ports and a stone bridge; the repair and enlargement of fortification walls; piercing of new thoroughfares and improving of existing ones, not only for functional reasons but equally to open up vistas towards the most prestigious buildings; and laying out squares in front of the principal buildings for the same purpose. In seeking a model for such a com-prehensive, city-wide urban design scheme at so early a date – inte-grating utilitarian concerns with perceptual ones – one has to look abroad. The closest model might be Sixtus V's replanning of Rome, which likewise conceived the city in terms of a visitor's experience, setting up vistas articulated by fountains and other punctual monuments, always arranged so as to draw attention to key buildings.[22] One might detect parallels not only in means but also in aims, Sixtus and Neufville both pursuing such a scheme in order to affirm their city's status as a Christian capital, since throughout the seventeenth century Lyons was obliged to mount a defence of her position as primacy of Gaul against challenges from other cities.

Furthermore, the town hall itself formed but half of a more complex project, which also embraced the rebuilding of the town college – the Collège de la Trinité – which had burned down in 1644. At the time the two buildings were presented as 'twins', being 'born' together, at the same time and of the same 'parents' (the consulate).[23] Indeed it would have been much easier in seventeenth-century Lyons than today to have represented this as a single scheme since their sites would have been virtually contiguous, the buildings now separating them having been built since.

This helps to explain why the town hall was erected on the site that it was. For whilst the college was – almost inevitably – rebuilt on its

---

[22] This was well known through the sumptuous publication by Domenico Fontana (1543–1607), effectively the papal architect at the time, of a set of plates describing the transformation, under the title *Della Trasportione dell'Obelisco Vaticano* (Rome, 1590).

[23] They are specifically referred to as 'twins' in Jean de Bussières, SJ, *Basilica Lugdunensis* (Lyons, 1661), 7. This reiterates an idea already current in Lyons. For instance, on Trinity Sunday 1653 the rector of the town college, Joseph Gibalin, spoke of how the city had acquired a new Temple of Honour and Virtue, the college being dedicated to Honour, through its protection of Letters and Sciences, and the town hall to Virtue: Actes Consulaires, AML, BB 207, pp. 329–44. Likewise, on Trinity Sunday 1662 the same rector claimed that the consuls themselves referred to the Jesuit college as 'la seconde maison de la ville': Actes Consulaires, AML, BB 217, pp. 241–3. The same idea is further developed in Théophile Raynaud, SJ, 'Admonitio' to 'Oratio Triplex de S. Ignatio a Loyola aedificante Dei Domum Templo S. Sophia, Basiliadi Justinianeae & Domum Charitatis Lugdunensi, proportionalem', *Opera Omnia*, Tom. VIII, *Hagiologium Lugdunense* (Lyons, 1665), 423.

existing site, the town hall's functions were transferred from the centre of the Presqu'île, in and around St-Nizier, at the heart of the most densely populated part of the city, where they had been enacted since the origin of civic government in the Middle Ages; they were being moved eastwards, in fact to the very edge of the city. The Terreaux, as it was called, was an unlikely site for construction of any kind, let alone for anything so prestigious, since it was marshy (as the placename suggests) and had previously been used for the city's pig market and gibbet. Better building sites were available: on the Presqu'île, either further south where development was less intense, or by the Dominicans' church (Notre-Dame du Confort), by the Franciscans' (St-Bonaventure) or even by St-Nizier itself; alternatively there were sites within the Fourvière circumscription, on the other side of the Saône, for instance by the Loge de Change, thus immediately across the bridge from St-Nizier.[24] Instead this site with poor ground conditions, but virtually adjacent to the college, was chosen.

Maupin's principal façade – that carefully set up to be viewed across the Place des Terreaux, and destined to become the official image of the building, and thereby of Lyons' civic government – stood firmly within the idiom of recent French château architecture. Since the town hall was referred to not only as 'Hôtel de Ville', as it is today, but also 'Maison de Ville'[25] it is not surprising that its designers turned to the *hôtel particulier* – the private urban residence of the wealthy – for its model; this in turn derived from the *châteaux* of noble families, adapted for urban situations. The façade was thus typical of the *corps de logis* of recent French *châteaux* from the 1620s onwards. Its symmetrical character is emphasised by its central section being flanked by two higher side pavilions, and accentuated by the axial placing of such features as a flight of steps leading up to the main entrance, an ornamented tympanum over the central window at *piano nobile* level and a tower above. As regards material and decoration, the wall surface is kept smooth, formed of fine ashlar masonry, with contrasting quoins employed to articulate the harmonious relationship set up between the building's various simplified and clearly defined masses; likewise mouldings around door and window openings serve to articulate the equally careful relationship contrived between solid and void.

Likewise the usual plan for *hôtels particuliers* derived from that of *châteaux*: the *château* was habitually arranged in three wings around an open courtyard, so that the advancing service wings framed and

[24] See Simon Maupin, Plan de Lyon, 1625.
[25] It is thus labelled on at least two contemporary prints of it – by G. Mérian (1647) and Israel Sylvestre (1652) – and within the mid-seventeenth-century city plan by Séraucourt, 'Description au naturel de la ville de Lyon et paisages alentour d'icelle'.

enhanced the view of the *corps de logis* containing the main accommodation; a low wall in front of the courtyard might serve to increase the residents' privacy.[26] In moving into a more densely inhabited urban environment, this wall rose to full height, whilst remaining a single wall; meanwhile the main accommodation remained in the block situated at the far end of the courtyard. Although, as early as the late 1630s, Louis le Vau tried developing a front block immediately behind this street wall – in his Hôtel de Bretonvilliers and his Hôtel Lambert – he dropped it by the early 1640s. The practice of extending the *piano nobile* around all four sides of the courtyard did not take off until the mid-1650s, with François Mansart's Hôtel Carnavalet.

In the town hall at Lyons the building behind its typically French façade evidently drew on another tradition. For it effectively turned this plan back to front, retaining the 'U' form but planting the *corps de logis* firmly on the street front, with the side wings running back from it so as to enclose a courtyard behind, instead of in front (Fig. 2). This would have seemed less radical in Lyons than elsewhere in France, in that the Italianate *palazzi* built there in the previous century had used the block on the street front for accommodation as much as any of the three wings around the courtyard behind it. In the town hall, however, the side wings were proportionally much longer, and the courtyard was closed by a block which – being lower than the other three – played a role equivalent to that of the low front wall in a' French *château*, as if the plan had been turned back to front. In addition, being in the form of an open arcade at ground floor level, it allowed views through and beyond it from the entrance vestibule; in other words, it was conceived not as the final boundary of the property but as a screen separating the courtyard from the gardens beyond. The scheme thus betrayed its Italian inspiration, which was confirmed by the east façade of the central block containing the reception rooms, dominated by a loggia at *piano nobile* level, enabling visitors to the Grande Salle to look out over the *cortile* and gardens to the river and open country beyond.

If a single model is sought, the closest might be a generic one, that of the *palazzo* as developed by Galeazzo Alessi (1512–72)[27] in Genoa in the latter part of the previous century; here again one finds the *cortile* enclosed by long wings, framing and accentuating a vista set up to be viewed first from the entrance and then from the principal reception rooms above. Furthermore, this *palazzo* plan had subsequently been adapted in Genoa, from its original function of private residence to that of public building; the Jesuit college (now University) by Bartolomeo

---

[26] Anthony Blunt, *Art and Architecture in France, 1500–1700* (Harmondsworth, 1953; 2nd edn 1970), 120.

[27] On Alessi, see E. de Negri, *Galeazzo Alessi Architetto di Genova* (Genoa, 1957).

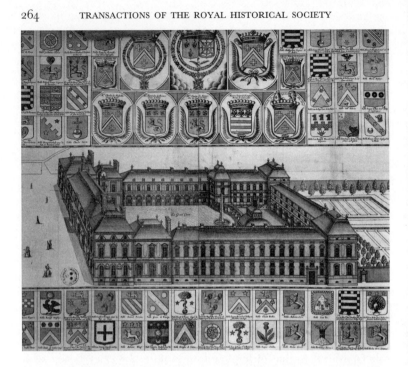

Figure 2   The new Hôtel de Ville, surrounded by the arms of past provosts and aldermen; the Place des Terreaux appears to the left of the building and the gardens to the right. Detail from Frontispiece, Jean de Bussières SJ, Basilica Lugdensis (Lyons, 1661). Fonds Ancien, Bibliothèque Municipale de Lyon.

Bianco (1590–1657), dating from 1630 onwards, is generally considered the best example.[28]

This model was well known by the time that the design of the town hall at Lyons was being considered, due to the publication of a splendid folio volume, *Palazzi di Genova*, illustrated by Rubens himself.[29] Rubens's book consisted of folio plates, prefaced solely by a letter to the reader

[28] Via Balbi. The first design dated from 1630, the executed one from 1634, the year when construction began. The judgement of its quality derives primarily from its innovatory architectural unification of vestibule and courtyard (and thus interior and exterior spaces), employing similar arcades at two levels. Via Balbi, laid out by Alessi himself (1606–18), was the epitome of this Genoese style of architecture and townscape.

[29] Peter Paul Rubens, *Palazzi di Genova* (Antwerp, 1622); a second edition was published just a few years before work began on the decoration of the town hall at Lyons, this time in two parts bound together in a single volume; *Palazzi antichi [- moderni] di Genova* (Antwerp, 1652) consists of the original book, now entitled *Palazzi antichi di Genova*, followed by an additional book *Palazzi moderni di Genova*.

('Al Benigno Lettore') and a dedication to its patron. In his introductory letter Rubens contrasted the usual plan of a palace for an absolute prince and his retinue, where extensive accommodation was arranged around a courtyard ('il Cortile in mezzo, & la fabbrica tutto attorno, di capacità commitente ad allogiar una Corte'), with that of a palace for a private gentleman and his family, where a lesser amount of accommodation was contained within a solid cube situated on the street front. Critics have observed an apparent contradiction between this statement and the related plans presented by Rubens, in that the latter include courtyards.[30] The explanation would seem to be that Rubens assumes both to be arranged around courtyards; he is instead distinguishing the Genoese courtyard *palazzi* for gentlemen, their principal reception rooms being brought forward into the street front block ('un cubo solido col salone in mezzo') whilst the side wings accommodate services, from the *palazzi* of absolute princes, in which the principal rooms were situated at the rear of a closed courtyard, a more traditional practice and therefore one less in need of explanation. Hence Rubens's assertion above – made as if to emphasise this distinction – that in the gentleman's *palazzo* one enters directly from the street into the block whose central space is that of the main reception room. In the town hall at Lyons the Grande Salle, its principal reception room, is found precisely in this position, occupying the entire central section at *piano nobile* level.

In the first edition (and thus the first part of the second edition) of his book, Rubens identifies the *palazzi* he presents by letter rather than name, supposedly because they as often change names as they change hands; yet he must surely have realised that this practice would suggest to readers that, even if these depictions represent actual *palazzi*, the abstraction due to their identification by letter alone implies that they are offered here as abstracted models for application elsewhere. In looking through the plans presented by Rubens it becomes evident that, despite a considerable degree of diversity, the *palazzo* of the Genoese gentleman can be defined as typically consisting of a main accommodation block on the street front with two colonnaded service wings behind enclosing a *cortile*. The central section of this front block contains a *portico* or *atrio* or, in the case of the larger *palazzi*, an *atrio* with a *portico* or *terrazza* behind; on entering this one would find oneself looking along the central axis across the *cortile* (or *fondighi*) to a niche containing a statue or to a fountain, centrally placed in the closing wall beyond. Above, the equivalent space was occupied by the *sala* (hall) or

---

[30] See, for instance, Alan Tait's introductory essay in the facsimile of *Palazzi antichi [-moderni] di Genova* (Antwerp, 1663; facsimile edition with introductory essay and notes, New York and London, 1968), 13.

salotto (drawing-room), usually with its own loggia, from which one could look out over the gardens beyond. The staircase leading up to the *piano nobile* is therefore displaced from the vestibule, into a side pavilion on the front block or into the side wing immediately behind that, so as to lead directly to the principal reception room, without eating into either its space or that of the vestibule below. The side wings were then filled with smaller rooms (*camere*).

This arrangement corresponds exactly with that of the town hall in Lyons, in which the vaulted *salle basse*, serving as a vestibule, takes the place of the Genoan *atrio*, which had served an equivalent function, whilst the Grande Salle above (with its loggia behind) takes the place of the Genoan *sala* or *salotto* with its loggia. As with the Genoan *palazzi*, strictly symmetrical and axial planning of building and open space alike ensures that on entering the vestibule a vista opened up, centring on a fountain in front of an open arcade, through which a garden beyond could be glimpsed (albeit framed by arcaded wings instead of col-onnaded ones); from the loggia above this axial view was recapitulated, and extended to include a fuller view of the gardens (now seen in the plural) descending to the river, with open countryside beyond. In moving the principal staircase (the Grand Degré or Grand Escalier) out of the central block into the side wing immediately behind, and in filling the side wings with smaller rooms and offices, the town hall is again adopting the plan typical of Genoan *palazzi*.[31]

Rubens's book – the first published north of the Alps to give such detailed plans of Italian buildings – exercised an enormous influence across Europe. Nevertheless, there are two reasons why it would have fallen in particularly fertile soil in Lyons, at this time. First, the style which it advocated accorded with the refined and simplified Classicism in vogue in larger French towns from the mid-1630s onwards. In his introductory letter Rubens extols the Genoese palaces as examples of truly symmetrical architecture which obeys the 'rules' of the Greeks and Romans, in opposition to the 'Barbaric', in other words Gothic, architecture which had preceded it and which it now displaced. It is significant that Rubens commends the Jesuit churches of his own Antwerp and of Brussels as exemplars of this style, given the role played by Jesuits in devising the rhetorical programme underlying the town hall at Lyons. In particular, the Jesuit playing the leading role in this,

---

[31] The closest model depicted would seem to be that of Palazzo H (figs. 50–2). Like the town hall this is oriented west–east, the principal façade facing west and the axial view through the palace and *cortile* towards the east. At *piano nobile* level the central section of the front block is occupied by the *sala* and associated loggia, whilst the main staircase is pushed to the side and backwards, adjacent to the north wing but still adjoining the loggia. The *cortile* is enclosed by long, colonnaded wings, closed by a single-storey, colonnaded terrace.

Claude-François Menestrier, promoted just such a view of correct architectural taste.[32]

Second, as Rubens again points out in his introductory letter, the Genoese *palazzi* had been designed for gentlemen rather than princes specifically because Genoa was a Republic, governed by gentlemen, as opposed to a state ruled by nobles or a prince. He thereby implies that these models are particularly relevant for his fellow citizens in Antwerp because both towns are mercantile oligarchies. This governmental parallel in turn explains why the Lyonese would also have found these models particularly apposite; moreover, Lyons, like Genoa, saw itself as a meritocracy, since it too admitted citizens to the nobility each year, notably through service as consuls.

Even if the Lyonese had not known Rubens's book they are likely to have been aware of the Genoese *palazzi* from other sources. In his widely circulated treatise, Scamozzi writes admiringly of how densely built-up Genoa has nevertheless created magnificent streets, made up of palaces. He then explains the typical *palazzo* in terms of its adaptation to such restricted sites, through its narrow-fronted deep plan, and its relatively high-rise construction, using different orders to articulate the storeys. The Genoese *palazzo* is defined by the same characteristics here as in Rubens's book: the front block containing the loggia and main reception rooms (*sale, salotti*); the side wings, consisting of series (*appartamenti*) of smaller rooms; an implied symmetry of plan, from steps in front, with views through to eyecatchers such as fountains in the gardens beyond.[33] Besides, regardless of the availability of published sources, Lyons's pre-eminence in the luxury textile trade meant that it had strong links with Genoa, where the best-quality cut velvet was woven; in addition, a community (*nation*) of Genoese merchants consequently resided in Lyons.

The plan adopted for the town hall was, as we have already noted, devised not by a Parisian but by a Lyonese. This designer was evidently looking not north to the French capital but across the national boundary, over the Alps, to Italian models. This deliberate selection of models which contrasted with those employed at the time in Paris would have struck contemporaries, and its signification would have been obvious to Lyons's higher ranking professionals and merchants, especially those

---

[32] 'à l'exemple de Bramante, qui voyant que les beaux-arts étoient comme anéantis depuis l'Empire du grand Constantin, par les inondations frequentes des Barbares, et la stupidité de dix ou onze siecles ignorans, se mit à prendre les mesures de toutes les antiques d'Italie, et rétablit de leurs debris et de leurs ruines, l'Architecture à demi perdûe en formant des dessins de ces restes de bâtiments Grecs et Romains', Claude-François Menestrier, SJ, *Des ballets anciens et modernes* (Paris, 1682), 4–5.

[33] Vincenzo Scamozzi, *L'idea della architettura universale* (Venice, 1615), Parte Prima, III, 4, pp. 241–2.

engaged in international trade, as well as to Italian merchants and clerics visiting the city.

Furthermore, this plan was devised not by an architect but by a *voyer*, an official in charge of bridges, thoroughfares and the like, someone more like a cross between a civil engineer and a surveyor today. It is therefore not surprising that this building was primarily designed in terms of functionality. It seems that the new college was likewise designed without the aid of either Parisians or professional architects, and with equally pragmatic concerns to the fore. The Jesuits, having been awarded the direction of the town college in 1565–7, had in the early seventeenth century used the Jesuit then specialising in architectural work for their order in France, Etienne Martellange (1569–1641),[34] to design at least part of the buildings which they erected in 1607–22.[35] The Jesuits' standard practice, then and thereafter, in college design throughout the world, was to erect simple, functional buildings;[36] given the prescriptions of the *Ratio Studiorum* (whose definitive version appeared in 1591), buildings were devised to accommodate the educational activities it defined and other activities supporting them:[37] college buildings were thus generally arranged around the main courtyard (*cour des classes*) whilst the Jesuit community's residential buildings were arranged around a secondary one (*cour domestique*). Such courtyard plans drew upon two relevant models simultaneously, those of the mediaeval monastery and the Renaissance *palazzo*.[38] College churches, like all Jesuit churches, were designed to ensure the congregation's optimum visibility of the mass and audibility of homilies; therefore they usually took the form of a simple rectangular box, a single nave flanked by lateral chapels, a minimal choir lacking any ambulatory or side chapels and flat ceilings throughout.[39] In Lyons, as in many other cases, the church was placed so as to separate the two courtyards whilst enabling direct access from both. Although style might vary, according to local situation, the 'Jesuit manner' (*modo nostro*) was characterised by such uniformity of plan, due in turn to common function.[40]

The merchants who constituted the consulate would have appreciated

[34] On Etienne Martellange the standard work is Etienne-Léon-Gabriel Charvet, *Etienne Martellange (1569–1641)* (Lyons, 1874); to this may be added Henri Bouchot, *Notice sur la vie et les travaux d'Etienne Martellange, architecte des jésuites ... d'après les documents inédits conservés au cabinet des estampes de la Bibliothèque Nationale* (Nogent-le-Rotrou, 1886). See also J. Vallery-Radot, *Le recueil de plans d'édifices de la Compagnie de Jésus* (Rome, 1960).

[35] Vallery-Radot, *Recueil des plans d'édifices*, 201–3.

[36] *Ibid.*, 6ff.

[37] *Ibid.*, 42.

[38] *Ibid.*, 43–5.

[39] *Ibid.*, 55–61.

[40] *Ibid.*, 19ff, 71ff.

On Etienne Martellange see n. 34. See also Vallery-Radot, *Recueil des plans d'édifices.*

the practical orientation of the town hall's design, and also the idea of money only being spent where it showed: using fine ashlar stone, left uncovered so as to display it, and applying much sculpted ornament. Yet this approach also corresponded with specifically French taste, representing a tradition of which the French were rightly proud. Whereas the paucity of good stone in parts of Italy had led to an architecture conceived in terms of simple brick or rubble stone structures to be covered with render, and to which stucco ornaments were applied, in France architecture was virtually equated with stone masonry; decoration was thus wrought in the same material as the structure itself, and even to form an integral part of it. In the Renaissance, far from discarding their tradition of virtuoso stonemasonry, in which the French believed they had outshone other nations from the Middle Ages onwards, these skills were combined with a new scientific, and in particular mathematicised, understanding of form; hence French theoreticians such as De l'Orme or Desargues were at least as interested in the development of stereotomy as in the codification of the Orders. Their architecture, derived from this long tradition of spectacular vaulted structures, depended upon architectonics rather than applied decoration.[41]

It seems that the initial intention was to decorate the building in this manner, both externally and internally. On entering, the visitor was to have been led through a rather sober entrance hall into the well-lit main stairwell (Grand Escalier), thus displaying the fine stone staircase – that designed by Lemercier and refined by Desargues – to its best advantage; this would have been ornamented by a solitary lion, carved from high-quality stone and set in place at the bottom newel.[42] From

---

[41] See the highly influential presentation of this view: Jean-Marie Pérouse de Montclos, *L'architecture à la française, XVIe, XVIIe, XVIIIe siècles* (Paris, 1982); revised edition *L'architecture à la française du milieu du XVe siècle à la fin du XVIIIe siècle* (Paris, 2001). Tellingly this originally developed from a doctoral thesis entitled 'Stéréotomie et art de la voûte'. Pérouse de Montclos reiterates these views in his more general coverage of French architecture, *Histoire de l'architecture française, de la Renaissance à la Revolution* (Paris, 1989), notably in the fourth chapter, '1540–1559: l'invention de l'architecture à la française' (91–116). In this he emphasises the influence of the Gothic masons' craft traditions upon the free interpretation of the Classical canon made by French theorists from de l'Orme onwards, claiming stereotomy to be the touchstone of the 'French manner' (and linking the rise of French vernacular language with that of a distinctly French Renaissance style). He states that the priority given to stereotomy explains the French preference for sculptural over painted decoration, and uses this to distinguish between French and Italian architecture of the period: 'Pour les Italiens, la voûte, comme le mur, est d'abord une surface à peindre ... Les Français se sont singularisés en recherchant la nudité de la pierre de taille jusque dans des espaces réputés nobles' (108).
[42] The consulate paid the sculptor Martin Hendrecy 300' 'pour le Lyon quil a faict estant au pied du grand degré du nouvel hostel de ville': AML, BB 210, fo. 208 (minutes of consular meeting); CC 2049, No. 13: payment for same.

the top of these stairs one was to have proceeded to the principal reception room (Grande Salle) where, in a similar spirit, four eight-foot-high stone figures of the cardinal virtues provided the chief ornaments; these were arranged in pairs, one pair flanking the entrance and the other the central window directly opposite, looking out over the Place des Terreaux.[43] These were probably intended to be set off against tapestries hung around the walls, as was the custom then in Lyons, and as happened in other reception rooms in the town hall.[44] The decorative scheme was completed by a mechanical clock, with its carved wooden figures of the planets.[45]

In early 1655 the consuls found themselves once more under pressure from the Neufville–Villeroy brothers – this time quite explicitly so – now to undertake the painted decoration of the town hall, beginning with its main reception room.[46] At their meeting of 9 March, despite the fact that the municipal budget had now been running at deficit for three years,[47] the consuls agreed to proceed; in fact the drawings had been prepared already, since they were attached to the contract passed with the painters the same day. In other words, the consuls had not

---

[43] On 19 Oct. 1651 the consulate commissioned four eight-foot high stone statues of the cardinal virtues from the sculptor Jacques Mimeral: AML, BB 205, p. 427; CC 2000, pièce 1. The ironwork needed to hold them in place was in position by 8 Feb. 1654: CC 2036, pièce 25. The final payment was made to Mimerel on 27 Sept. 1654: BB 208, p. 470; CC 2036, pièce 4.

[44] Hautecoeur, *Histoire de l'architecture classique*, Vol. 1, Tom. III (Paris, 1948), 828–9. Some tapestries were commissioned before 1655 to decorate the new town hall, notably for the two Chambres du Consulat (there being one for summer and another for winter). The commission to Fiacre Alleaume and Victor Prestisselly, master *tapissiers*, and François Rambaud, painter, for his oil sketches for them, was passed on on 19 Mar. 1650: AML, CC 1686, Nos. 112–15; final payment was made on 18 Sept. 1657: CC 2076, No. 7. Tapestries were procured for other rooms after 1655, for instance a series on the theme of the Story of Solomon for the Salle de la Conservation, bought from a merchant, Thomé, on 29 Dec. 1661: BB 216, fo. 150r, No. 533; CC 2137, No. 12. The decoration of the Salle d'Audience de la Conservation included paintings simulating tapestry, and thus comparable with the murals which Blanchet would paint on the walls of the Grande Salle; these were commissioned from Laurens Lagneau on 22 Mar. 1657: BB 212, fo. 156. Archival evidence for tapestries commissioned specifically for the Grande Salle is lacking, hence my deviation from the interpretation proposed by Lucy Galactéros de Boissier, *Thomas Blanchet 1614–1689* (Paris, 1991), 82.

[45] The clock was commissioned from the clockmaker Daniel Gom in 1650: AML, DD 97bis, fos. 416–18. It had been installed by 20 Mar. 1653: CC 2025, pièce 3. Its sculpted figures were in place by 31 Dec. 1655: BB 210, p. 637; CC 2049, No. 10. Nevertheless the clock does not seem to have functioned until shortly before 28 Nov. 1656: BB 217, fo. 36; CC 2064, pièces 37–40.

[46] According to the minutes of the consular meeting of 9 Mar. 1655 Camille had 'pressé lesdicts sieurs, par diverses fois, de travailler incessemment à la dicte peinture, et de ne point retarder l'entreprise d'un ouvrage si absolument nécessaire': AML, BB210, p. 106.

[47] *Lyon des origines*, ed. Kleinclausz, II, 50. This explains why the consulate passed an act on 7 Oct. 1655 forbidding any inessential expenditure: AML, BB 438, fo. 417v.

really had any choice. By the mid-seventeenth century provincial governors and lieutenants usually behaved like absentee landlords, not living in their provinces but kept at court by Louis XIV, where he could have them within sight. In 1653, however, Camille de Neufville had become archbishop of Lyons, and thus the Primat des Gaules (the head of the Catholic church in France), so that he resided permanently in Lyons. He retained his secular office of lieutenant and, in his brother's absence at court, effectively took on the governor's role too, a fact which was tacitly acknowledged through his occupation of the governor's residence during his brother's absences at court.[48] He thus now held ultimate secular and ecclesiastical powers. In 1654 he had appointed his bastard brother Antoine to the post of vicar general, and thus the *de facto* censor of the town's press, further reinforcing his own hegemony.[49] As Saint-Simon would remark, Camille was 'less a commander than a king in these provinces ... everything trembled beneath him, the city, the troops, even the intendant'.[50]

Throughout his reign over the region – which would last four decades, until his death in office – he would count Jesuit fathers from the town college amongst his chief advisors, even on political matters.[51] In the absence of any university in the city they had already acquired a reputation as Lyons's educated elite, and as such had been habitually called upon to arrange the ephemeral decorations mounted for civic festivals. It is understandable that they should now assume responsibility for devising the rhetorical programme underlying the town hall's decorative scheme.

It is perhaps from this point in time that the architectural evidence hints where the balance of power really lay, in a way that the written records cannot. For a detailed examination of the building demonstrates how Camille was not only pushing the consuls into financing a building they could ill afford, but was also controlling its character and detail, and was doing so in order to ensure that it proclaimed a message of prime concern to himself rather than to the consuls or the citizens they represented. The two roles which Camille seems to have been playing –

---

[48] On the death of their father, the governor, Camille moved out of the house he had built for himself at the Abbaye d'Aînay and into the governor's apartments, 'pour luy succeder, & exercer sa charge à l'absence, & pendant l'empéchement de Monsieur le Maréchal de Villeroy' (Germain Guichenon, *La vie d'illustrissime et reverendissime Camille de Neufville* (Trévoux, 1695), 205).

[49] Antoine de Neufville (1595–1670) was Nicolas IV de Villeroy's illegitimate son by a nun. From 1618 he had been abbé de Saint-Just.

[50] Louis de Rouvroy, comte de Saint-Simon, *Mémoires*, ed. Boislisle (1930), xiii, 484. On Camille de Neufville see also Guichenon, *La vie d'illustrissime*; Th. Malley, 'Un archevêque lieutenant du roi et gouverneur', *Revue des études historiques* (1923); Marie Emile Aimé Vingtrinier, 'Le dernier des Villeroy et sa famille', *Revue Lyonnais*, 5e série, 4 (1887).

[51] Guichenon, *La vie d'illustrissime*, 172.

politically astute oligarch and pious Counter-Reformation prelate – were in fact one, inspired by the figure of the godfather after whom he had been named, Cardinal Camillo Borghese, or Pope Paul V.[52] Born in Rome, while his father was French ambassador, Camille had later returned there to complete his studies with a doctorate in theology; consequently he was profoundly ultramontane in his beliefs and Roman in his aesthetic tastes. A painter was now summoned from Rome to translate the Jesuits' abstract rhetorical programme into visual form; when this artist died soon after arrival, he was replaced by another, trained in Rome, Thomas Blanchet.[53]

With Louis XIV's impending visit in view, the rhetorical programme devised by the Jesuits for the town hall's Grande Salle sought to gratify the monarch, with the aim of persuading him to extend existing *privilèges*. The theme chosen was the 'Le Temple d'Auguste' (the Temple of Augustus),[54] referring to the famous temple built in the city in Roman antiquity, and thereby flattering Louis by drawing a parallel between him and the Roman emperor Augustus, since the French king had recently assumed the title of 'Auguste'.[55] Nevertheless, the antique temple had also been known as 'Le Temple de Lyon' (the Temple of Lyons)[56] or 'L'Autel de Lyon' (the Altar of Lyons).[57] As a ballet under this last title, performed before Louis during his visit in 1658,[58] would explain, this was at once intended as a pun on the building's function (*hôtel de Lyon* being an alternative title for the town hall)[59] and an allusion to that Roman temple whose altar embodied Lyons's capital status within Gaul.[60]

[52] Vingtrinier, 'Le dernier des Villeroy', 35–6.

[53] Menestrier, *Factum Justicatif*, 1–2; Claude-François Menestrier, SJ, *Eloge historique de la ville de Lyon* (Lyons, Benoist Coral, 1669), Part III, ch. v (separate pagination), 8; for archival references see Léon Charvet, 'Recherches sur la vie et les ouvrages de Thomas Blanchet', *Revue du Lyonnais* (1895), 364. Bousquet provides archival evidence that Blanchet was a native Parisian who studied in Rome from 1649 to 53 (J. Bousquet, *Recherches sur le séjour des artistes français à Rome* (Montpellier, 1951; new edn 1980), 219). Sandrart, however, claims that Blanchet was already working in Lyons, and was appointed as assistant to Panthot, whom he had known in Rome: J. von Sandrart, *Academia Nobilissima Artis Pictoris* (Nuremberg, 1683), 381. The contemporary records and later accounts thus provide several conflicting versions of Blanchet's appointment. An alternative attempt to my own at reconciling these can be found in Galactéros, *Blanchet*, 79–81.

[54] Menestrier, *Eloge historique*, Part III, ch. v, 16.

[55] *Ibid.*, Part III, unpaginated section, entry for 1658.

[56] Menestrier, *Factum Justificatif*, 67.

[57] Claude-François Menestrier, SJ, *Histoire civile et consulaire* (Lyons, 1696), 69.

[58] Claude-François Menestrier, SJ, *L'Autel de Lyon* (Lyons, 1658).

[59] This pun was commonplace in seventeenth-century Lyons, due to the predominately oral nature of language. Indeed, craftsmen's accounts submitted to the consulate in conjunction with the town hall's construction inadvertently demonstrate this point; for instance, François Basset's account of 23 Dec. 1655 refers to the town hall as the 'Autel de Lyon': AML, CC 2049, pièce 51.

[60] Menestrier, *Histoire civile et consulaire*, 69.

The ceiling, however, had a complex programme of its own, entitled 'Le Soleil au Signe du Lyon' (the Sun at the Sign of the Lion),[61] thus evoking the entry staged for Louis's father in 1622.[62] As had been enunciated in the richly illustrated publication for that event, just as the sun is strongest when it enters its zodiacal house of Leo, so monarch and town alike attain their greatest splendour when the king enters his 'home' of Lyons.[63] In the wake of the Fronde this now became a not-so-veiled attempt to secure the transfer of capital status from Paris.[64]

The central panel of the ceiling depicted Apollo – the sun king – astride a lion – the eponymous city – attended by Renown and Muses.[65] Each of the principal paintings of mythical scenes surrounding this represented a zodiac sign, which in turn allegorised events in the life of the young king; thus, for instance, a picture of Chiron, representing Capricorn, alluded to the education of Louis XIV.[66]

Blanchet's translation of this rhetorical programme into painted form betrayed his Roman allegiance through its form and style. Its combination of *quadratura* – the central panel being rendered within illusory architecture – and *quadri riportati* – pictures painted like separate easel paintings, each within its own sculpted and gilded frame – was a Roman model barely known in France. This combination, pioneered by Raphael in his Vatican Loggia (1512–18), had been developed by Pellegrino Tibaldi for his Ulysses cycle in the Palazzo Poggio (now the University) in Bologna, in the 1550s.[67] The best-known example, however, and that closest in compositional terms to Blanchet's ceiling decoration of the Grande Salle, is Annibale Caracci's of the Galleria in the Palazzo Farnese at Rome (1597–1608).[68] Here, as in the Grande Salle ceiling in Lyons, the *quadri riportati* are exploited as a means of simultaneously separating various mythical scenes whilst signalling – through the repetition of frames – that they are to be understood as all belonging to the same series. In both cases *ignudi* – naked figures –

[61] Menestrier, *Eloge historique*, Part III, ch. v, 17; also Jean de Saint-Aubin, SJ, *Histoire de la ville de Lyon ancienne et moderne* (Lyons, 1666), I, 336.

[62] Anon., *Le soleil au signe du Lion* (Lyons, 1623).

[63] *Ibid.*, 2.

[64] Judi Loach, 'Lyon Versus Paris: Claiming the Status of Capital in the Middle of the Seventeenth Century', in *Lugares de Poder*, ed. Gérard Sabatier and Rita Costa Gomez (Lisbon, 1998), 260–85.

[65] Menestrier, *Eloge historique*, Part III, ch. v, 17.

[66] *Ibid.*, 19.

[67] On the early development of the combining of *quadratura* and *quadri riportati*, see Juergen Schulz, 'A Forgotten Chapter in the Early History of *Quadratura* Painting: The Fratelli Rosa', *Burlington Magazine*, 103 (1961), 90–102.

[68] See Rudolph Wittkower, *Art and Architecture in Italy 1600–1750* (Harmondsworth, 1958; integrated and revised edition with corrections, 1970), 63–8.

are used to separate further adjacent paintings from one another. In the Farnese Galleria, however, the central panel, a painting of the 'Triumph of Bacchus and Ariadne', takes the form of one – albeit the largest – of these *quadri riportati*, whilst *quadratura* is used in the spaces between it and the other *quadri riportati*.

Blanchet knew the interiors of the Palazzo Farnese well, as is proven by his use of fragments from their decorative schemes as models for his own in the town hall. First he would take a figure of 'Forza' from Salviati's frescoes in the Sala dei Farnesiani as the model for his own depiction of Alexander (cutting the Gordian knot), on the walls of the Grande Salle.[69] Then he would take the figure of Mercury offering the apple to Paris, from Caracci's depiction of the 'Amori dei Dii', within the Galleria scheme, as the model for his own Mercury in the painting of 'La Grandeur Consulaire de Lyon', on the ceiling in the town hall's Salle du Consulat.[70]

Blanchet probably exploited this scheme as a useful model for attaining coherence with such a complex programme. Although the Palazzo Farnese's Galleria had been one of the most spectacular and influential interiors at the end of the previous century, it had rapidly fallen out of fashion, and in fact had done so half a century before Blanchet began work on the Grande Salle. Therefore any reference to that scheme cannot be intended to portray Lyons as occupying a position at the cutting edge of fashion. Instead, alluding to this well-known scheme would have evoked memories of Rome, and could thus have been intended to signal the city's Roman sympathies.

Yet other decorative schemes executed more recently in Rome, whilst less closely related to Blanchet's composition in geometrical terms, continued to combine *quadratura* with *quadri riportati*, and moreover developed this composite mode so as to accentuate the overall coherence and sense of dynamism, just as Blanchet would do in the Grande Salle. One of the best-known examples was Pietro da Cortona's ceiling for the Salone of the Palazzo Barberini, dating from 1638–9 (after Maffei Barberini had become Pope Urban VIII).[71] Its celebrity is easily understood on grounds of scale alone, since it is the largest painted ceiling apart from Michelangelo's in the Sistine Chapel, and thus the largest in any secular palace.[72] Yet its fame was equally due to its architectonic and aesthetic innovation, employing a masonry vault

---

[69] Jennifer Montagu, 'Some Drawings of Thomas Blanchet in the Nationalmuseum of Stockholm', *Gazette des Beaux Arts* (July–Aug. 1965), 105–14 (106).

[70] Galactéros, *Blanchet*, 138–41.

[71] See Wittkower, *Art and Architecture*, 250–3. John Beldon Scott, *Images of Nepotism: The Painted Ceilings of Palazzo Barberini* (Princeton, 1991); Frederick Hammond, *Music and Spectacle in Baroque Rome: Barberini Patronage under Urban VIII* (New Haven, 1994).

[72] Scott, *Images of Nepotism*, 18.

instead of the usual ceiling of timber beams, which lent itself to the division into sections developed so spectacularly in the Farnese Galleria. Furthermore, the Barberini Salone was specifically designed to provide the maximum uninterrupted surface of ceiling for painting, by pushing all windows below the level of the cornice and avoiding the inclusion of stucco mouldings.[73] In both these respects the Grande Salle of the Hôtel de Ville at Lyons followed the model provided by the Barberini Salone rather than that of the Farnese Galleria. The ceiling of the Barberini Salone is almost wholly filled with a single *quadratura* painting, depicting the 'Trionfo della Divina Providenza', with the *quadri riportati* now relegated to the four corners, where they contain allegories of the pope's virtues, as epitomised by specific good deeds; meanwhile his arms and *impresa*, similarly treated within rich frames, appear attached to the cornice in the centre of the room's two short sides.

Cortona's Salone scheme in the Palazzo Barberini was well known, thanks to the publication in 1643 of a detailed description of the building by Count Girolamo Teti (*Aedes Barberinae*).[74] In this book the Salone (here referred to as 'Aula') is both the first room whose decorations are described and that for which they are described in greatest detail, filling more than a dozen pages and being illustrated in five separate plates. The account given includes a full explanation of the scheme's iconographical signification.

There was, moreover, another reason why the Palazzo Barberini might have been invoked in the Lyonese scheme. By 1658 the Jesuit responsible for overseeing the iconographical content of the Grande Salle scheme was Claude-François Menestrier, whose Jesuit uncle, Claude Menestrier, had until his death in 1639 been Maffei Barberini's librarian. In the case of the Barberini Salone, the court poet Francesco Bracciolini has been credited with composing the rhetorical programme for Cortona's decorative scheme;[75] nevertheless, given that librarians would usually be consulted over such programmes – in the case of the Farnese Galleria, the librarian Fulvio Orsini had actually been respon-

---

[73] *Ibid.*, 126.

[74] Hieronymus Tetius Perusino, *Aedes Barberinae ad Quirinalem ... descriptae* (Rome, 1642); a revised edition (by Philippe de Rubeis) was published in 1647. The text of nearly 200 folio pages was complemented by fourteen plates, engraved by J. F. Greuter, C. Cung, Cornelius Bloemart and M. Natalis, depicting the decorations by G. Ubaldo Abbatini, A. Camassei, Pietro da Cortona, Andrea Sacchi and F.F. Gagliardi. Cortona's ceiling was thus both described and illustrated (44–58 and pls. [A]–E). It is perhaps worth noting that a doctor at Lyons by the unusual name of Panthot – that of the official town painter, who assisted Blanchet in the painting of the town hall decorations – owned a copy of the revised edition: Bibliothèque Nationale, K599. It is also worth noting that the 1647 edition was dedicated to Mazarin.

[75] Wittkower, *Art and Architecture*, 252 n. 63; Scott, *Images of Nepotism*, 172.

sible for devising the programme[76] – it is likely that Claude Menestrier had some involvement, and at the very least had been aware of the programme as it was being developed.

Furthermore, the Barberini scheme was directly linked with the stylistically most Roman scheme in Paris, one devised for another Italian cardinal, Mazarin. For the Upper Gallery in the Hôtel Mazarin, dating from 1646–7, had been painted by Francesco Romanelli, one of Cortona's assistants on the Salone ceiling in the Palazzo Barberini (Romanelli being appointed only after Cortona had turned down the commission); here again the decorative scheme is a composite of *quadratura*, filling the central panel, and *quadri riportati*, arranged around it.[77] This Parisian scheme would have been well known to Nicolas de Villeroy who, as Louis's personal governor (in the sense of tutor) through the regency, maintained an intimate relationship with the cardinal, especially after being forced to flee the capital with him and the royal family, during the Fronde.

In all other respects, however, the Mazarin scheme is French in character, not Italian. The orderly arrangement of the separate paintings prevails over any sense of the ceiling as a single painted surface, whilst the *trompe l'œil* figures between them politely fade away into the background so as not to distract from or compete with the paintings themselves. Above all, the overall effect is far more stable and calm – even static – than in the Roman precedents. Blanchet's ceiling would have stood out in stark contrast, striking any contemporary visitor as more Roman in spirit than French.

Perhaps Blanchet should be understood as steering a middle course in his juxtaposition of *quadratura* and *quadri riportati*. On the one hand he gives these two types of representation virtually equal status, in that *quadratura* is kept firmly within its own frame and is hardly allowed any greater area than the larger *quadri riportati*. On the other hand, the *quadratura* occupies the central panel, the focus of the ceiling. It is possible that in thus combining references to two well-known models he was deliberately attempting to evoke Roman models in general, whilst avoiding identification with any single model in particular, in order to endow his scheme with a sense of *Romanitas*.

Blanchet would take a similar approach in designing the decorative scheme for the walls of the Grande Salle. Here individual figures in his Alexander cycle have been identified as drawing on Primaticcio's stucco-framed fresco of Alexander cutting the Gordian knot in his mural decoration at Fontainebleau and Perino del Vaga and Pellegrino

---

[76] Wittkower, *Art and Architecture*, 63.

[77] Hilary Ballon, *Louis le Vau: Mazarin's College, Colbert's Revenge* (Princeton, 1999), 20, illustration p. 21.

Tibaldi's Alexander cycle for the Sala Paolina in the Castel Sant'Angelo.[78] In fact Blanchet does not seem to have drawn on such sources to provide models for individual figures so much as to have used them as compositional models. In both cases a series of framed scenes from a legend are separated by *ignudi* and other ornaments, playing a comparable role to that taken by the *ignudi* in the ceiling decoration. Both these sources are of course due to Italian artists, even if the former was executed in France, albeit for an Italian patron (Catherine de Médicis). Nevertheless, as in the ceiling design, the Lyonese scheme resembles the French precedent less closely. For whereas the *ignudi* and allied ornaments at Fontainebleau had been executed in stucco, as three-dimensional figures, thus contrasting with the two-dimensional paintings contained within the frames, in both the Roman Sala Paolina and the Lyonese Grande Salle the *ignudi* were executed in *trompe l'œil*. To summarise, this building's decoration would have confirmed and reinforced a message of deliberate espousal of Italian models in preference to the more expected French ones; indeed, as one moves on from the architectural structure to its painted decoration this Italianisation becomes more self-conscious and more explicit.

In late 1658, Louis XIV duly arrived in Lyons, but signally failed to deliver the expected increase in *privilèges*. The decoration of the town hall and of the town college continued thereafter. Now, however, their decorative schemes no longer flattered the monarch; indeed they no longer even mentioned him. Consequently, the part already executed – the Grande Salle ceiling – was even provided with an alternative reading so as to make it fit a new rhetorical programme.

By alluding to a certain form of the city's seal, the topos of 'The Sun at the Sign of the Lion' now symbolised the establishment of the consulate (in 1372), when the citizenry was awarded autonomous powers.[79] It also (as indeed it had done a generation earlier) referred to the local oligarch as the sun,[80] thus implying that the city owed its current peace and prosperity not to Louis's presence but to Camille's. The figures of the central panel now represented 'Authority Supported by Force',[81] meaning

[78] Montagu, 'Drawings of Thomas Blanchet', 106 and n. 13. This identification has been accepted and followed by subsequent authors, notably (in this context) by Galactéros, *Blanchet*, 88–9 (illus., pp. 92–3).

[79] Judi Loach, 'The Seventeenth-Century Restoration of the Temple de Lyon', in *The Emblem and Architecture*, ed. Hans Böker and Peter Daly (Turnhout, 1999), 45–56 (47–8); Judi Loach, 'Reverses of Consular Jetons in Seventeenth-Century Lyons: Locally Specific Propaganda in Absolutist France', *The Medal*, 27 (Autumn 1995), 24–56 (40–1).

[80] François Goujon, *Parallelle de deux soleils* (Lyons, 1622).

[81] Cf. François I's hieroglyph to commemorate his victory at Marignan in which the king is represented by a crowned 'solar lion' which, following Horapollo's *Hieroglyphica*, symbolises force (or courage or vigilance) (Anne-Marie Lecoq, *François Ier imaginaire* (Paris, 1987), 254–7).

Camille supported by the citizenry, through the consulate.[82] Meanwhile, the dozen mythological scenes were reinterpreted as symbolising the city's twelve principal commerces (textiles, publishing and so on). Chiron, for instance, now represented the horse trade.[83] In the new programme, however, they simultaneously presented twelve moral lessons for its magistrates, who met in this very room;[84] here a small detail in the Chiron picture – a crown lying at the centaur's feet – becomes the pretext for admonishing magistrates to defend the rights of the crown, and to consecrate themselves to the service of their prince.[85]

Throughout the new programme, Lyons's Roman, and imperial, past was constantly underlined, and the beneficial nature of her present close relationship with Rome made explicit. The official description and explanation of the decorations published at the end of the decade portrayed Europe as a 'body', in which Rome – as its spiritual capital – served as head, directing its activities, whilst Lyons – as commercial centre – functioned as heart, pumping life through its arteries.[86]

Contemporary dramatic performances and ephemeral decorations elucidating the decorative schemes now presented Camille as a latter-day Camillus,[87] the refounder of Rome in antiquity,[88] whilst the decorations – or rather the new explanations of them – drew parallels between him and Plancus, the legendary refounder of the Roman capital of Gaul, at Lyons.[89] The overall decorative project covering both 'twin buildings' – town hall and town college – acquired further signification through the festivities mounted to enunciate their meaning on completion, in 1667; for these simultaneously celebrated the centenary of the (Roman) Catholics' reconquest of the city, now revealed

[82] Menestrier, *Eloge historique*, Part III, ch. v, 28.
[83] *Ibid.*, 30.
[84] It is worth noting that such an allegorical representation of moral lessons, simultaneously political and Christian, had a certain Jesuit tradition by this time. See, for instance, the collection of such precepts in form of devices: Diego de Saavedra Fajardo, SJ, *Idea de un Principe politico Christiano* (1st edn, Munich, 1640).
[85] Menestrier, *Eloge historique*, Part III, ch. v, 30.
[86] *Ibid.*, 36–8.
[87] One of the three principal emblems presented at the Trinity Sunday celebrations in 1657, that representing Hope, depicted a ship led by Cupids, with Hope standing on the prow holding a cruciform anchor, alluding to the anchor crosses in Camille's coat of arms. The identification of Camille with the figure of Hope was enunciated through the accompanying verse, and made explicit in Menestrier's own description of it, where he refers to 'L'allusion a l'histoire de Camille, qui delivra Rome, au nom de Monsieur l'Archevesque' (Claude-François Menestrier, SJ, *L'art des emblemes* (Lyons, 1662), 82). Other contemporaries also drew this parallel between the Lyonese Camille and the antique Roman Camillus (for example, Guichenon, *La vie d'illustrissime*, 245–6).
[88] Plutarch, *Lives: Camillus*, 7, 1–2; Livy, 5, 32, 4–7.
[89] Saint-Aubin, *Histoire*, I, 336; Menestrier, *Eloge historique*, Part III, ch. v, 21.

as their refoundation of Lyons as the Christian Roman – the Catholic – capital of the Gauls.[90] This later phase in the decorative scheme not only takes yet a stage further that Italianising tendency already demonstrated in the design of the building itself and then in the earlier phase in its decoration; it also confirms the political signification inherent in such stylistic preference.

This case study demonstrates, first, how buildings can alert us to, and then provide evidence to fill in, certain lacunae left by written sources. Secondly, an architectural reading of this evidence – including comparisons of plans, compositional schemas, style and details – can suggest how it might be interpreted so as to uncover further meaning. Architectural history can thus provide tools essential for revealing aspects of political history, hitherto withheld from us through ignoring elements over which written records pass in silence, sometimes because they are too contentious. Moreover, since such tools are applied to media other than the written word, they are working on those most likely to have coloured the perceptions of a broad range of the local citizenry of the time. The patrons and designers who originally commissioned and devised such non-verbal documents were more aware of their persuasive powers than modern historians often appear to be. This is no doubt partly due to the counter-reformation belief in the superior ability of visual images to move human emotions and therefore the will. These media are precisely those whose examination will enable us to recover the experience of people who have not recorded it in writing. This is therefore a prerequisite for fulfilling the agenda set out by the founders of the *Annales* school.

---

[90] Judi Loach, 'Charonier's Medal for "the City's Eternity" – Ephemeral Jeton or Foundation Monument?', *The Medal*, 9 (Sept. 1986), 54–78.

Transactions of the RHS 13 (2003), pp. 281–91 © 2003 Royal Historical Society
DOI: 10.1017/S0080440103000155   Printed in the United Kingdom

INVESTIGATING THE BIGGER PICTURE:
A CASE STUDY OF THE JACOBEAN GREAT BARN
AT VAYNOL PARK

By Katie Withersby-Lench

ABSTRACT. This paper seeks to examine the origins of the Jacobean Great Barn at Vaynol Park in North Wales. The evidence suggests that this barn was built to represent the status and ambitions of the owner of the Vaynol Estate in 1605. However, the barn itself poses questions about the finances of the Caernarfonshire gentry and the state of local agriculture at that time. By relating the study of its physical form to the social and economic context in which it was built, the threads of evidence create a picture of an expanding estate and substantial seventeenth-century Home Farm.

Vaynol Park has been at the heart of the Vaynol Estate for over 400 years. Situated on the banks of the Menai Straits, the Park sits confidently between the water and the mountains of Snowdonia. This location is no accident; the Park has long enjoyed the convenience of communication by road, sea and, later, rail. The weather is more clement on the coast than in the mountains, allowing the production of arable crops on this coastal plain as well as the ubiquitous cattle and sheep. This was an ideal location to establish the nerve centre of what was to become a dominant landed estate.

Following the Act of Union of Wales with England in 1536, key Welsh families seized the opportunity to consolidate the power they had been accruing in an English-ruled Wales. Power relied on land-holding, and substantial landholding at that. The shared *gwely* land system was abandoned as the Welsh gentry emulated their English counterparts in the practice of building up private landed estates. So it was with the Williams family of Cochwillan, whose scheme included the annexing of part of *Maenol Bangor* in the county of Caernarfonshire, an area of land which had previously formed part of the bishop of Bangor's home manor.

In the mid-sixteenth century Thomas Williams of Cochwillan began to style himself 'of Vaynoll'. As a younger son he did not inherit the family home, Cochwillan Hall, but amongst his holdings was this part of *Maenol Bangor*, which was becoming known as Vaynol or Vaynoll.[1] At Vaynol there was already the remains of an apparently high-status building, the foundations of which Thomas Williams reused to build his own house. An ambitious and rather ruthless businessman, Williams began relentlessly to acquire land in Caernarfonshire. This was a policy followed by his son William and for four more generations to come until the family line died out in 1696, by which time the Vaynol Estate consisted of at least 24,000 acres and was a significant player in the politics and economics of north-west Wales.

But this is not the story of the Vaynol Estate, or of Vaynol Park as a whole. The focus of this paper is the Great Barn at Vaynol Park, built by Thomas Williams's son William and his second wife Dorothy in 1605. In researching the history of this building it became obvious that in the absence of any building records, or any documents relating to its erection, a certain amount of lateral research was required. It was also apparent that in order to ascertain both a physical and contextual history there would have to be interaction between the various avenues of historical research. Architectural, economic, socio-cultural and political histories must all be tapped in order to reveal as clear a picture as possible and to suggest answers to the questions of who, why, what and when?

The Great Barn combines practicality with handsome proportions and it is clear that the construction of this building was designed to be impressively permanent. Built of local limestone, this barn has been designed by a craftsman with strict instructions to create a prestigious building. Perhaps all the more prestigious within a region that traditionally relied on pastoral farming on poor-quality land. Located on the crest of a rise, the barn faces east/west, overlooking the rest of Vaynol's Tudor Home Farm and Vaynol Old Hall itself. This barn represents physical and psychological power over some of the best-quality agricultural land in the locality. As the land falls away from the barn on either side it is obvious that the barn has also been carefully sited in a well-drained position. This site has 'location, location, location'.

Measuring 140 ft by 30 ft, the Royal Commission on Ancient and Historical Monuments survey believes this to be by far the largest stone barn in the county of its age. The roof consists of ten bays, the principal rafters of which are strengthened with collars and struts. The roof is currently slated with large nineteenth-century slates from the Vaynol Estate's own slate quarries. This is likely to have replaced a slate roof

---

[1] The most straightforward translation of *Maenol Bangor* is Bangor Manor. To say 'the Manor' in Welsh one would say *Y Faenol* – the word *Maenol* mutates to *Faenol*. *Y Faenol* in this context has been anglicised to Vaynol (or variations on this spelling, but all beginning with the 'v') since the fourteenth century.

that dated back to the building's construction. Vaynol Old Hall (Thomas Williams's home) was re-slated in 1832 with the same large slates as part of an improvement programme. However, at the Hall the remains of an earlier slate roof endure in the form of a few tiny, fish-scale-shaped slates surviving in the eaves of the later roof, possibly as packing. The Hall was undoubtedly the *pièce-de-résistance* of the Tudor Vaynol, but there is no reason why a building as impressive as the Great Barn should not also have been slated. Although the estate's quarries were not in the massive-scale production in the seventeenth century that they were in the nineteenth, it is known that slate was quarried on a more low-key basis, as it was required from the medieval period onwards. Brunskill suggests that the grade of farm building tended to follow the grade of farmhouse.[2] In this case the farmhouse was a gentry house, built by and intending to represent the noble descent and ambitious plans of the Williams of Vaynol. The threshing barn was usually given 'an architectural treatment commensurate with its import-ance as the chief storage building and most important workshop of the farm'.[3] Given the relatively sophisticated roof structure of this utilitarian building, there is no reason to doubt that the durability and exclusivity of slate would have been accorded to the Great Barn.

Over the centuries this barn appears to have been in consistent use for the processing of grain. The exterior has probably changed very little, but evidence in the interior walls and floor is testimony to the evolution of the threshing machine from hand flails to automated processes during a four-hundred-year period.

The Great Barn was undoubtedly designed to facilitate the processing of grain. The large opposing doors are designed to admit a waggon loaded with grain, or possibly two at once, where both reverse into the barn through the opposing doors. Although the back wall door is partially boarded up to create a smaller opening, the original sizes are similar enough to have been intended to be a matching pair. The doors are sited in the sixth bay (from the left) putting them slightly off centre. Over 100 years later the builders of the similar Henblas Barn,[4] which also consisted of ten bays, chose to site their doors across the fifth and sixth bays to give them a central position. We can only speculate whether the master builder in charge of the Vaynol Great Barn project sited the doors off-centre for a practical or a structural reason. That this barn is designed to receive waggon or cartloads of produce is indicative of its siting on a coastal plain with reasonable access to and from the fields from which the harvest was gathered. Lake notes that

---

[2] R.W. Brunskill, *Traditional Buildings of Britain* (1981), 27.
[3] P. Smith *Houses of the Welsh Countryside* (1975), 146.
[4] Llangristiolus, Anglesey.

carts or waggons were rarely used on hill farms and, in Wales, were more usually confined to the anglicised south and east and prosperous river valleys.[5] It is therefore pertinent to note that in 1669 Vaynol Farm possessed two 'great carts' along with a number of smaller items of equipment for carting.[6]

The 'arrow-slit' windows in the walls allow the correct ventilation to the grain without exposing the harvest to the weather or unwelcome visitors. Situated high up on the north-east gable end, the larger window offers access to owls; welcome visitors who would tackle the problem of rodents. This gable wall also has a pair of what appear to have been 'arrow-slit' windows low down at floor level, now filled in. One can only assume that these were again for ventilation. It can be further assumed that the threshing floor in this instance was sited in the draught of the two large doors, although Lake suggests that threshing floors were not always sited in this central location.[7] A probate inventory from 1669 mentions not only the equipment used for winnowing, but also 'one dozen of Oake Boards valued att 12s', stored in the Granary. Lake, who writes that 'threshing floors needed to be very clean and

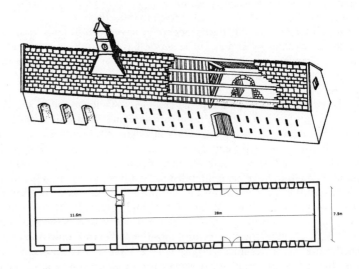

Figure 1   Vaynol Great Barn

[5] J. Lake, *An Introduction and Guide in Association with the National Trust to Historic Farm Buildings* (1989), 92.

[6] The probate inventory of Sir Griffith Williams of Vaynol, 1669, National Library of Wales.

[7] Lake, *Introduction and Guide*, 21.

were often made of one-inch thick oak planks', offers the most likely explanation for the purpose of these boards.[8]

The 1605 date-stone suggests that the main body of the barn was built on the orders of William and Dorothy Williams. A second stone records an extension to the barn by Sir Griffith and Dame Penelope Williams in the 1650s. Unless contradictory evidence comes to light this survey will assume that these two date-stones indicate build periods.

Undoubtedly this barn was built to provide the Vaynol Home Farm with a required facility. Whether this was a new or replacement build is unknown. However, this is far from being a merely functional building; it is a very large and clear statement of account. This is a message to all who see it, as clearly as if Williams had written out the worth of his estate and his noble lineage and distributed it amongst his betters, peers and underlings. The Williams of Vaynol were a powerful family in Caernarfonshire with a significant *uchelwyr*[9] lineage, ever-increasing landholdings, influential marriages and a fearless resort to litigation. Within twenty years of building this barn William Williams was in a position to purchase a baronetcy from James I. The size and construction of the barn are designed to impress, creating a building reminiscent of those 'Cathedrals of Labour', the Medieval tithe barn. Surely Tudor society was no less impressed with such a building and the power it represented than their medieval forefathers? Being located within the former manor of the bishops of Bangor there is no reason not to suggest that it might replace just such an edifice.

William Williams was not the only ambitious force in the equation. His second wife Dorothy seems to have been a determined woman, capable of managing business affairs and marrying wisely. Exactly when they were married has not yet been established, although, given the date-stone on the barn we can assume that it was either during or before 1604. A date-stone on the porch at Vaynol's St Mary Chapel records WW / E /1596, suggesting that Williams's first wife, Elin, was still alive in this year (unless it was intended to record her death) and in fact Dorothy herself was not widowed until 1598. Her first husband was Robert Wynn of Plas Mawr in the town of Conwy. Plas Mawr is itself a prominent declaration of status but one which, it has been suggested, may have crippled Wynn financially towards the end of his life. Carr argues that the provisions he made for his large family, begotten as an old man, indicate a cash flow crisis in his later years.[10] There is also evidence to propose that Dorothy managed

[8] *Ibid.*

[9] A person of high birth claiming free clan status and the forerunner of the sixteenth-century Welsh squire-gentleman.

[10] A.D. Carr, *The Affairs of Robert Wynn*, Caernarfonshire Historical Society Transactions Volume 49 (1988), 170.

Wynn's affairs during the last years of his life after a stroke rendered him incapable.[11] If this woman was capable, or learned to be capable, of managing her husband's business interests despite a lack of capital she would have made a very strong partnership with the ambitious Williams. How much money she brought to her second marriage is unclear. Although there was a protracted period of litigation regarding money held in trust for her children with Wynn, there seems to be no suggestion that Dorothy did not receive the lands or the goods and chattels earmarked for her jointure. Carr suggests that it is not inconceivable that Dorothy's reasons for marrying Williams included the very salient fact that he was a prominent figure in Caernarfonshire society who might be able to protect her cause in litigation ensuing from her previous husband's 'sharp dealings' in land acquisition.[12] We might also consider that perhaps Dorothy had no wish to remarry below the status of her previous marriage and perhaps there were qualities in Williams, which had suited her in Robert Wynn. Neither man was the type to hide his light under a bushel or to shrink from 'sharp' practice or litigation. These were men to whom the appearance of power and wealth was as if not more important than actually possessing it and it is possible that the Great Barn should be judged as much for whom it represented as what function it was designed for.

Status symbols are rarely cheap. For the Great Barn to have been built in 1605 implies that the estate's finances were in a position to support such an investment, or at least that Williams anticipated that the returns would make it worth the outlay. We can only speculate where the resources came from; perhaps the money was borrowed against land, perhaps it came from Dorothy's jointure or from land sold to raise capital. Documents have survived which demonstrate that Williams was providing land mortgages for his neighbours at this time; in 1603 for example one such deal was established at 16 per cent interest per annum. It seems that he was his father's son; a man with natural business acumen and an ability to restrain himself from giving special favours to friends, neighbours and family when it came to profit margins.

Taking factors from economic and political history at face value, this would not seem to have been an advantageous moment for British landowners to consider estate expansion. Towards the end of the sixteenth century poor weather had caused a number of harvest failures and a succession of monarchs had demanded, and continued to demand, money for loans and mises to the Crown. However, regarding these taxes payable to the Crown, it is well established that in the provincial

---

[11] *Ibid.*, 157.
[12] *Ibid.*, 171.

counties like Caernarfonshire, far from the influence of London, the gentry consistently undervalued their landholdings upon which their share of the loans and mises were based. One might add to the equation the stabilising political forces such as the establishment of the Council of Wales in 1603 and the treaty of peace with Spain signed in 1604. The seaboard counties of Wales such as Caernarfonshire had long felt themselves to be vulnerable (with good reason) to the threat of invasion and contingency plans were often drawn up amongst the gentry at times of trouble.

For the landowners the failure of harvests had perversely been something of a boon. The lack of food raised the price for which the surviving crop could be sold and this in turn raised the value of land. Additionally, in the second half of the sixteenth century the population of Britain had more than doubled, creating a greater demand for food and pushing the price up further still. Bad news for the person buying a loaf of bread, but good news for landowners who felt justified in putting up land rents in line with the rising land value. The spiralling inflation of this period favoured landowners who were in a position to take advantage of it.

Although Wales was known more for its animal rearing than for its grain production, Williams's barn shows that grain was grown wherever possible, even in these damp climates, and was probably considered all the more valuable for the difficulty in growing the crop. So few corn barns of this scale survive in north-western Wales that it seems unlikely that they were ever plentiful. However, a comparable seventeenth-century example survives on the Lleyn Peninsula at the Corsygedol Estate whose fortunes and history in the Tudor/Stuart periods were very similar to those of the Vaynol Estate.[13] The outbreak of peace and order, combined with the rising value of land might well have been a stimulant to committing money to improving estate facilities.

The building of the Great Barn at Vaynol implies that the Home Farm was producing or receiving enough grain to warrant such a large processing and storage facility. The Home Farm was one of a series of small farms on Vaynol Demesne (now Vaynol Park). These were located in an area that is amongst the most potentially productive agricultural land in the county. On this coastal plain farmers had access to natural fertilisers such as lime, shale and seaweed, all in use in Wales since at least the sixteenth century[14] and weather patterns at Vaynol Park, being

[13] P. Smith, *Corsygedol*, Journal of the Merioneth Historical and Record Society, 2 (1956), Part IV; L.W. Lloyd, *Corsygedol, Ardudwy's Principal Estate*, Journal of the Merioneth Historical and Record Society, 8 (1977), Part I.

[14] However, evidence from a late eighteenth-century survey of the Vaynol Estate suggests that tenants were reluctant to adopt improved techniques of land cultivation even at this late date.

more akin to Anglesey than Snowdonia, provided further favourable conditions for arable farming. During the nineteenth and twentieth centuries fields within the Park have been used for both grain and pasture. Similarly, a significant number of field names on an estate survey from 1777 are designated 'quillets', or strip farming, recalling an earlier time when this land was not solely dedicated to pasture as it is today.

However, it is reasonable to question whether these farms alone could warrant such a large barn. Landed estates at this point in time were not a consolidated geographical unit and the Williams of Vaynol were not content to limit their landownership to the Demesne and the mountainous areas. Unfortunately, the evidence of their landholdings and the use to which they were put is so sparse that it is difficult to build up a picture of activity, let alone formulate a theory about the extent of grain growing. The wills of the father and grandson of William Williams (barn builder and first baronet) allude to unspecified tenements owned by the estate in Anglesey. It is recognized that Anglesey is a far more productive location for arable farming than Caernarfonshire, although cattle and sheep were also a staple business. The wills, however, do not go into any kind of detail. Sir Griffith Williams's probate inventory of 1669 lists 'The old and new Hey and all the Corne at Hirdrefaig deducting therout £51 rent for the farme for the year is valued att £22.' Hirdrefaig, a farm near Llangefni on Anglesey, was obviously a mixed farm (as was customary) because the inventory also mentions cattle and sheep at the same location. However, the grain, even before the farm rent was deducted, was not worth as much as the cattle, which were valued at £110.[15]

Disappointingly the first baronet's own will refers to land left to his second son but does not detail the rest of the estate's landholdings – all of which were to go to his eldest son, Thomas. This Thomas's will does not appear to have survived, but it is possible that the lands in Anglesey continued in estate ownership during the intervening period.[16]

In 1604 William Williams must surely have commissioned the barn with an eye to further estate expansion and indeed records show him purchasing land further down the coast south of Caernarfon in 1623.[17] Furthermore, it was around the time that the Great Barn was built that Williams inherited a not inconsiderable amount of land in the

[15] Probate inventory taken on the death of *Sir Griffith Williams of Vaynol Barronett* (sic) 1669, National Library of Wales, Aberystwyth.
[16] PCC – *The Will of Thomas Willi[a]ms of Vaynoll 1592*; *The Will of Sir William Williams of Vaynoll 1625*; (Pell 288) *The Will of Sir William Williams of Vaynoll 1658*, Public Record Office, London.
[17] Baron Hill MSS 3218–28, Calendar, Vol. 2v, 1329–1752, Caernarfonshire, University of Wales, Bangor.

fertile Conwy Valley from his uncle Edward Williams of Maes y Castell. However, the condition of the roads in seventeenth-century Caernarfonshire was notoriously bad and it must be considered whether it would have been practical to transport a harvest on these roads? A detail in the building accounts of the Carreglwyd Estate on Anglesey records a cart being sent to Vaynol 'to fetch corne' in 1636.[18] A return trip from Carreglwyd to Vaynol by direct modern roads is a forty-mile journey; why this trip should have been made from the 'bread basket' of North Wales to Vaynol is another interesting question. It is of course possible that the Vaynol in question does not refer specifically to the Vaynol Estate and that the Griffiths of Carreglwyd owned land in *Maenol* (or 'Vaynol') *Bangor*.

Before the Industrial Revolution landed estates tended to rely on their land rents for a steady income. But this was not always a cash rent; in the late sixteenth century the Gwydir Estate, situated in the Conwy Valley,[19] took half their tenants' corn crop in return for two oxen and two steers as draught animals.[20] The evidence seems to suggest that more land was under tillage during the period in which the Williams family owned Vaynol than it is today. It was not until the advances in agriculture of the eighteenth and nineteenth centuries that the crop growing regions of Caernarfonshire gradually returned to pasture. Whatever the source, it stands to reason that there must have been a considerable amount of grain grown in the area and processed at Vaynol Home Farm to warrant such a building.

This volume of grain is also suggested by the seven mills listed in 'A deed to lead the uses of a fine, being also a settlement after the marriage of Sir Griffith Williams with Dame Penelope his now wife...' dated 1665.[21] Although these are not specifically identified as mills for processing grain, neither are they designated *pandy* or even the less frequently used *melin ban*, which would indicate fulling mills. Tenants were obliged to bring their grain to be ground at their landlord's mill(s) and one such mill was to be found on the Vaynol Demesne; a sea mill or *melin heli*[22] at the southern end of what is now the Park. Such a monopoly was a part of estate economic and social order within the community that landowners had inherited from the feudal system.

By the 1650s Sir Griffith Williams felt the need to extend the barn built by his grandfather. This extension appears to be the granary and upper stable mentioned in a probate inventory taken at his death in

[18] D. Knoop and G.P. Jones, *The Carreglwyd Building Account 1636*, Anglesey Antiquarian Society and Field Club Transactions (1934–5), 31.

[19] About twenty miles away from Vaynol in the Conwy Valley.

[20] E. Wiliam, *The Historical Farm Buildings of Wales* (1986), 149.

[21] Mostyn MSS 1342, Calendar, Vol. II, Nos. 1094–993.

[22] Literally 'salt water mill'.

1669. It was common agricultural practice for a granary to be built over a cart shed or stable, raising the stored grain from the potential dampness of the ground and to protect it from hungry rodents. The building has been altered to meet the changing needs of the farm; the arches of the ground floor have been blocked up and windows inserted during the nineteenth century. On the middle floor a large door has been inserted to facilitate the loading of stored grain to cart. The top floor today still contains grain bins built within the bays of the roof of this extension. These particular bins do not appear to be as old as the roof timbers, but judging by the graffiti certainly date back to the early nineteenth century. It is possible that these bins replaced earlier versions.

From his study of Caernarfonshire inventories, Gareth Williams concludes that the Home Farm at Vaynol in 1669 was one of the top-ranking farms in the community.[23] It boasted fifty-four horses and mares for a variety of purposes, two carts for farm use and even a coach for domestic use. Although this is the only inventory discovered to date for this era at Vaynol, it is unlikely that the farm had always supported this number of horses. It does appear, from studying Griffith's inventory and his father's will, that, despite the Civil War, the farm had expanded during the middle years of the century and that one result of this was the need for more equine accommodation.

Every building has a story to tell. The physical structure of Vaynol Great Barn indicates the degree of wealth and rank of these Welsh squire-gentlemen, combining utility with status. If one chooses to accept the date-stones as reliable witnesses, the building stands witness to those men who recognised and seized the opportunity to underline their position in society and in the landscape. Not only did the Williams family own this fertile land, but they could also afford to build a functional building, which visually dominated the landscape more than even Vaynol Old Hall itself. Such a building either consciously or unconsciously echoes the dominance, both physical and psychological, of the great medieval landowners, particularly the tithe barns of the Church.

To give the building a historical context, however, it was necessary to build up a picture of the social, political and economic world in which the Great Barn was erected. The fragments of information gleaned from archival sources build up a shadowy portrait of William Williams, enough at least to try and get the measure of the man, and of his wife Dorothy. Rather less can be determined about Griffith, perhaps because of his early and possibly sudden death. However, the probate inventory taken on his death provides the only physical

[23] G.H. Williams, *Farming in Stuart Caernarfonshire*, Transactions of the Caernarfonshire Historical Society, 42 (1981), 75.

information we have about the extent of the seventeenth-century farmstead and the contents of the various buildings.

That the barn exists at all allows suppositions to be made about the use of the land; one might assume that, being so near Snowdonia and owning so much mountainous land, as well as the fertile Vaynol Demesne, there would be limited need for a corn barn of this size. However, this appears not to have been the case and suggests that the Vaynol Estate owned or had the harvest from far larger areas of arable land than might have been imagined. The barn's existence also implies projected plans for the future and not just for one lifetime, but plans which would ensure the estate's continuing good fortune and be passed from father to son *ad infinitum*.

Even if full building accounts and personal testimonies from William and Griffith Williams had survived, it would never be possible to gain a complete and exact understanding of the physical and contextual evolution of the Great Barn at Vaynol. However, in order to gain any measure of the true picture the researcher cannot rely upon one avenue of history alone; the evidence of one sustains and nurtures the understanding of the others.

Transactions of the RHS 13 (2003), pp. 293–303 © 2003 Royal Historical Society
DOI: 10.1017/S0080440103000167   Printed in the United Kingdom

WOMEN USING BUILDING IN SEVENTEENTH-CENTURY ENGLAND: A QUESTION OF SOURCES?*

By Anne Laurence

ABSTRACT. Documentary sources for studying buildings commissioned by women tend to conceal their involvement in building projects. Historians could usefully give greater attention to the formal elements of women's commissions to show how women used buildings and building projects to make statements to a wider world about their wealth, ancestry, social aspirations, taste, religious preferences and their ability to deal with directing builders, managing money and the other practical details that go with building projects. Architectural historians could benefit from an understanding of buildings that do not survive and of buildings which exist in literary works which allow some reconstruction of the spaces occupied by men and women and illuminate their domestic relations.

The study of buildings commissioned by women poses particular problems, which are in part those of sources.[1] Merely identifying women's commissions is difficult, especially those of married women in the early modern period, since the presumption is always that the work was done for the husband who paid the bills. Yet it is clear that many women were responsible in their own right for ordering and directing substantial building works.

Historians are well placed to take this study further, their sources straddling the ground between the surviving buildings of the architectural historians and the imaginative spaces of the literary scholars. However, they need to refine the ways in which they use existing buildings, which they rarely do with much sophistication, tending to use surviving fabric as illustration rather than as a source itself capable

---

*I am particularly grateful to Malcolm Airs, Nicholas Cooper and Richard Hewlings for references and for the award of a Fletcher Jones Fellowship and for a Mellon Fellowship (on the British Academy exchange programme) which allowed me to work at the Huntington Library.

[1] For a discussion of the connections between the study of architecture, society, gender and culture and the role of theory, see Alice T. Friedman, 'The Way You Do the Things You Do: Writing the History of Houses and Housing', *Journal of the Society of Architectural Historians*, 58 (1999), 406–13.

of being 'read'. They are often justly suspicious of the use of imaginative space as it has been presented in recent work on space and representation, on public and private and on constructions of identity and gender, often based on the study of plays, dramatic texts which conceal much of the author's intention and about whose staging little is known.

The approaches of both architectural historians and of literary scholars have much to offer historians interested in the material world of production and consumption. Surviving buildings and objects can reveal much which the written record can not. New readings of old sources, the real significance of much recent literary work, can take historians beyond their literal readings of such documents as inventories and correspondence.[2] Both approaches, too, can help in comprehending the spaces that people occupied which have not survived, but which have left a footprint.

Surviving buildings

Studies of the built world are inevitably skewed towards what survives rather than what does not. Yet much of the built world in which historians may be interested exists only in the written record. Historians work ingeniously with these records, but their use of them is informed by what they have seen amongst the surviving buildings. Maurice Howard, in his 1998 article in *Architectural History*, emphasises the value of inventories, where the house survives in a recognisable form, to aid the study of archaeology of *existing* buildings.[3]

Four examples of women's building from surviving buildings illustrate the difficulties. Houghton Conquest, Ampthill, Bedfordshire, is, on the face of it, a fairly straightforward subject. The house was commissioned in 1617 by the widowed Mary Sidney, countess of Pembroke (1561–1621). Patron, poet, translator, member of the court where she would have seen the latest fashions in architecture, she chose to build an H-shaped house in a fashionable style, with a centrally placed hall.[4] The identity of the architect is uncertain, it may well have been Inigo Jones.[5] The original design of the house is also unclear: Nikolaus Pevsner

[2] On the use of inventories, see Maurice Howard, 'Inventories, Surveys and the History of Great Houses 1480–1640', *Architectural History*, 41 (1998), 14–29.

[3] Howard, 'Inventories', 15.

[4] Nicholas Cooper observes that two other notable houses with innovative plans featuring centrally placed through halls were commissioned by women: Hardwick Hall and Ashley Park. See Nicholas Cooper, *Houses of the Gentry, 1480–1680* (New Haven and London, 1999), 137.

[5] John Harris, Stephen Orgel and Roy Strong, *The King's Arcadia: Inigo Jones and the Stuart Court*, Catalogue of the quartercentenary exhibition held 1973, Arts Council, London (1973), 100, 109–11; John Harris and Gordon Higgott, *Inigo Jones: Complete Architectural Drawings*, the Drawings Center (New York, 1989), 84–5.

suggests that there may have been a later phase of building in the 1630s; John Harris is persuaded that the whole is by Jones; while Andor Gomme has argued that the countess employed Jones to modernise an earlier building.[6]

Lady Anne Clifford (1590–1676) is best known for the restoration of the ancestral Clifford castles in the north of England and for the monuments she erected to her parents, her tutor, her steward and herself. She also built or restored several churches, such as the plain box-shaped church at Outhgill, Westmorland, which carries a tablet saying that in 1663 she rebuilt the church, it having 'lain ruinous and decayed some 50 or 60 years'. The work, which cost £46, may have been either a restoration or a new build.[7] In one place in her diary she refers to having 'lately repaired' the church, while in another she writes of having 'caused [it] to be new-builded'.[8]

Weston Park, Shropshire/Staffordshire, was built in 1671 for Elizabeth Wilbraham (née Mitton, 1632–1705). It has been suggested that the architect was Lady Wilbraham herself. Her copy of the first English edition of Palladio's *First Book of Architecture* (1663) is heavily annotated with notes about timber and the costs of building materials.[9] Christopher Hussey, writing in 1945, devoted several paragraphs to speculating who the architect might be and suggested that Lady Wilbraham must have had some help from William Wilson (who later built the church for her) because the design of the house was so advanced for its time. Hussey then makes a point of saying how much more architecturally correct are the stable block (1688) and farm yard (1760s).[10] A more plausible suggestion is that the house was designed by William Taylor, with the active engagement of the patron.[11]

Elizabeth Wilbraham's activities extended to her husband's property

[6] Nikolaus Pevsner, *Bedfordshire, Huntingdon and Peterborough* (Harmondsworth, 1968), 40–1; Harris, Orgel and Strong, *The King's Arcadia*, 111; Harris and Higgott, *Inigo Jones: Complete Architectural Drawings*, 84–5; Andor Gomme, 'Houghton House', Proceedings of the Summer Meeting of the Royal Archaeological Institute in Bedford, *Archaeological Journal*, 139 (1982), 41–2.

[7] Richard T. Spence, *Lady Anne Clifford* (Stroud, 1997), 156.

[8] *The Diaries of Lady Anne Clifford*, ed. D.J.H. Clifford (Stroud, 1990), 168, 202, 169.

[9] *The First Book of Architecture by Andrea Palladio; Translated out of Italian, with an Appendix Touching Doors and Windows, by Pr. Le Muet; Translated out of French by G[odffey] R[ichards]; to which are Added Designes of Floors lately Made at Somerset-House, and the Framing of Houses after the Best of Manner of English Building, with their Proportions and Scantlings* (London, 1663).

[10] Hussey argued that there cannot have been an architect solely responsible because someone trained in architecture would have had a better idea of Palladian proportions, though the south face is early as 'a fully-fledged attempt at a Renaissance elevation', suggesting that the design was adapted from that of another house. *Country Life*, 9 Nov. 1945, 818–21.

[11] John Harris, 'William Taylor: Further Attributions?', *Georgian Group Journal*, 8 (1998), 14.

at Woodhey, Cheshire, where she refurbished the house (which does not survive) and built a chapel, to which she referred in her notes. This is a characteristic piece from the 1690s, plain with no chancel, and no altar, and a centrally placed pulpit, finely carved, placed between the two east windows. Such an arrangement was usual for a chapel of ease, but Elizabeth Wilbraham also preferred an unceremonial church, as evidenced by her support of nonconformist clergy in the 1660s.[12] Another very distinctive feature is the use of some Jacobean stonework for a loggia giving access from a raised terrace outside to the gallery which forms the family pew inside.

The great eighteenth-century heiress and philanthropist, Lady Betty Hastings (1682–1739), inherited her grandfather's property at Ledstone, West Yorkshire. He had been a wealthy merchant and had improved the house in the 1650s and 1660s.[13] She started her alterations in 1708, building a new entrance and installing sash windows, leaving mullion windows only in the basement, and from 1711 Ledstone Hall was her principal home. Extensive as the Hastings archive is, there is no record of the work done on Ledstone.[14] There is a reference, by the York joiner, William Thornton, to going to London with Lady Betty Hastings in 1719, presumably in connection with work on Ledstone.[15] She was proud enough of her house and gardens to commission from John Setterington, a well-known Yorkshire topographical painter, four views of the house.[16]

In each case the documentary evidence for the association of these women with their buildings is problematic, in part because of the greater scarcity of material for women. Mary Sidney was a wealthy widow, but there is little documentation for the early history of Houghton House.[17] Anne Clifford had inherited the Clifford estates in 1643 and started her building activities during the lifetime of her estranged husband, the earl of Pembroke. After his death in 1650 she devoted herself to celebrating her father's family. The evidence for her

[12] A.G. Matthews, *Calamy Revised: Being a Revision of Edmund Calamy's 'Account' of the Ministers and Others Ejected and Silenced, 1660–2* (Oxford, 1934), 103 and elsewhere.

[13] Timothy Mowl and Brian Earnshaw, *Architecture without Kings: The Rise of Puritan Classicism under Cromwell* (Manchester, 1995), 169.

[14] Hastings papers, Huntington Library, California. It is clear that Betty Hastings was a patron of the best craftsmen: the gardens were probably by Bridgeman, she bought silver plate from Paul de Lamerie in London. The association with Thornton suggests that the improvements continued during her occupation of the house.

[15] Geoffrey Beard, *Georgian Craftsmen and their Work* (1966), 49.

[16] All four are reproduced in John Harris, *The Artist and the Country House: A History of Country House and Garden Painting in Britain 1540–1870* (1979), 192–3, and three in John Harris, *The Artist and the Country House from the Fifteenth Century to the Present Day*, exhibition catalogue for an exhibition at Sotheby's (1996), 54–5.

[17] Gomme, 'Houghton House', 39–42.

building is clear enough in the commemorative stone on the church, but there are no construction accounts and little reference in her memoirs (what are loosely known as her diaries) to building. Elizabeth Wilbraham was heir to her father's estates in Shropshire, and built Weston during her husband's lifetime. The suggestion that she might have designed Weston House is purely circumstantial; her notes clearly show an interest in the building works and she may have assisted her daughter and son-in-law with their improvements at Chirk Castle. Betty Hastings was a wealthy single woman, the evidence for the nature of her work on the house is through painstaking work tracking inventories; there is no material in her own family's archive, nor did she write about it in her surviving correspondence. In all these building projects there is a substantial unknowable element, which may tempt the historian to make deductions on the basis of the surviving structures which the documentary evidence may not actually bear, but where close examination of the structures may add to the written record.

Built, but not surviving buildings

Buildings that were built or substantially altered by women but which do not survive pose a different set of problems. There is much to be learnt about vanished buildings as well as their contents from inventories and other records; work has been done on reconstructing interiors where the dimensions of the house are unknown, using inventories for spatial analysis.[18]

Probably the best-documented disappeared buildings are those of Queen Anne of Denmark (1574–1619), who was responsible for employing Inigo Jones from 1604 until her death, when he designed her hearse.[19] Apart from masque scenery and sets, he designed the Queen's House at Greenwich, did work at Somerset (Denmark) House and at Oatlands. These royal buildings are documented, though there is much that remains mysterious about them.

One of the largest buildings, and in some ways most problematic, is Belvoir Castle, rebuilt in the 1650s by the countess of Rutland (d. 1671), wife of the eighth earl. It had been a traditional medieval castle, was damaged during the civil war and was then slighted to make it indefensible. John Webb made drawings for the new house, but his scheme was never fully realised.[20] The nineteenth-century historian of Belvoir Castle tells us how the eighth earl of Rutland devoted his time

---

[18] Howard, 'Inventories', 23.
[19] Howard Colvin, *History of the King's Works* (6 vols.) (1963–82), III, 138.
[20] The house was painted in 1731 and 1744, see Harris, *The Artist and the Country House*, 167, 196.

after the Restoration to reconstructing the castle. He then cites the Pindaric ode of 1679 which records that the rebuilding was done at the wish, and to the taste, of the *countess*.[21] How far the house that was finally built diverged from Webb's scheme is unclear, because in the nineteenth century one of the duchesses of Rutland employed Wyatt to rebuild the castle.[22]

The duchess of Ormonde (1615–85), daughter of the earl of Desmond and cousin and wife of one of the great magnates and courtiers of Ireland, was responsible for remodelling Dunmore Castle, Co. Kilkenny, in the grandest manner during the 1660s, though nothing survives.[23] The size of the principal apartments has been estimated from the size of the suite of Antwerp tapestries which hung there (and which are now at Kilkenny Castle).[24] The duchess is said to have purchased for the house the marble fittings from Strafford's great palace at Jigginstown.

Historians have rarely tried to reconstruct vanished buildings from written records, rather they have used records of such buildings in exactly the same way that they use records for surviving buildings: in order to say something about the social, economic or cultural life of the period. Yet the reconstruction of the spaces which historical subjects occupied can be a worthwhile extension of their material world.

Buildings of the imagination

The term 'buildings of the imagination' is used here to refer to buildings that appear in literature and have a relationship with real places, but perhaps only symbolically. The literature informs us about the spaces occupied by women, but these cannot necessarily be identified with particular houses or with specific spaces within real houses.

One genre of writing which provides a good deal of material about women and the interiors of houses is the commemorative lives which commonly accompanied published funeral sermons in the seventeenth century. These lives, unlike the commemorative biographies of men which recount what they did during the entire span of their life, describe what the deceased did each day, where she was in the house and who she was with.[25]

---

[21] Irvin Eller, *The History of Belvoir Castle* (1841), 98.

[22] Most of the later work was by Wyatt, see Christopher Christie, *The British Country House in the Eighteenth Century* (Manchester, 2000), 64–5.

[23] Jane Fenlon, 'Episodes of Magnificence: The Material Worlds of the Dukes of Ormonde', in *The Dukes of Ormonde, 1610–1745*, ed. Toby Barnard and Jane Fenlon (Woodbridge, 2000), 142ff.

[24] Fenlon, 'Episodes of Magnificence', 145.

[25] See A. Laurence, 'Daniel's Practice: The Daily Round of Godly Women in Seventeenth-Century England', in *The Use and Abuse of Time in Christian History*, ed. R.N. Swanson, Studies in Church History 37 (2002), 173–83.

A characteristic example may be seen in the life of Lady Mary Vere: on Sundays she and her family rehearsed the sermon they had heard at church and called in the servants to give an account of what they had remembered of it. The family then prayed together in one room, and the servants in another. On weekdays, Mary Vere and her family were to be found twice a day praying together:

> Follow her up the stairs, there you should be sure to find her, twice every day, shut up some hours in her Closet (which was excellently furnished with Pious Books of Practical Divinity). Here she redeemed much pretious time, in reading the holy Scriptures, and other good Books...and every night she used...to pray with her maidens before she went to bed.[26]

Mary Vere (1581–1671) was the widow of the great military commander, Sir Horace Vere, who had died in 1635. She outlived him by more than thirty years, dying at the age of ninety at her house Kirby Hall, in Essex. She was celebrated for her godliness and was a great patron of Puritan ministers. The author of her life, William Gurnall, did not describe the interior of Kirby Hall, but did provide a vivid picture of the spaces where Mary Vere's daily devotions took her.

Inevitably, because it was generally godly women who merited such biographies, there are many references to closets as spaces in which women read, prayed, meditated and conducted their devotions in private.[27] Some were furnished, but some were little more than spaces through which there was no household traffic. An image of such a space may be seen in an imaginative construction of Bishop Lancelot Andrewes's prayer closet. Since this was produced many years after the bishop's death it can bear no relation to his actual closet, but it is suggestive of what such a space might look like.[28]

The activities represented are real activities, taking place in real space, but space that the reader has to imagine. Other kinds of space are mentioned in these godly lives. Mary Boyle countess of Warwick (1625–78), another great Puritan patron, fed the poor at the gate of her London house, where 'she built a convenient receptacle for them...to shelter them from the injury of the weather till they received their dole'.[29] They already had shelter when they came to collect their dole at her house at Great Leez in Essex.

A final example of buildings of the imagination shows the dangers of

[26] William Gurnall, *The Christians Labour and Reward* (London, 1672), 132–4.
[27] See A. Laurence, 'The Closet Disclosed: The Ambiguous Privacy of Women's Closets in Seventeenth-Century England', forthcoming.
[28] R[ichard] D[rake], *A Manual of Private Devotions with a Manual of Directions for the Sick*, by Lancelot Andrewes, late Bishop of Winchester (London, 1670), titlepage.
[29] Samuel Clark, *Lives of Sundry Eminent Persons* (London, 1683), 159–76.

relying upon literary evidence for realistic descriptions. John Aubrey, who had never visited Houghton Conquest, nevertheless described Mary Sidney's house as 'curious', designed by Italian architects and costing £10,000. He also claimed that it was built according to the design of Basilius's house in the first book of Sir Philip Sidney's *Arcadia*, yellow stone and star-shaped, a far cry from the red-brick house that stands there.[30]

Space, style and aesthetic choices

Women's use of fabric and space is of interest not simply for showing that women could control these things, but also because it adds to the history of the domestic relations of men and women. The ways in which women and men occupied their houses and the surroundings, and the allocation and arrangement of rooms all convey information about social and familial relations and daily occupations. Alice Friedman has argued that in the early modern house the master was the only person admitted to all spaces in the house, but that a female head of household lacked the control of space of a male head of house, with the result that there was a greater need for innovative planning to express her role.[31] Style, however, is a more problematic subject, not least because historians often lack the vocabulary to deal satisfactorily with it.

Architectural historians have devoted much energy to tracing the dissemination of styles and the influence of earlier models and patterns. Historians have sometimes considered the meanings of style and the extent to which it was used self-consciously in image-making by people such as Charles I and Thomas Howard earl of Arundel.[32] But historians' discussion of women and architectural style rarely goes further than saying that the idiosyncratic arrangements of the interior of Hardwick reflect the countess of Shrewsbury's role as a forceful patron or that Lady Anne Clifford's building work shows her devotion to lineage rather than to convenience or architectural aesthetics.[33]

---

[30] John Aubrey, *Brief Lives*, ed. Andrew Clark (2 vols.) (Oxford, 1898), I, 312: 'The lodge is of a yellow stone, built in the form of a star, having round about, a garden framed into like points; and beyond the garden, ridings cut out, each answering the angles of the lodge. At the end of one of them is the other, smaller, lodge, but of like fashion, where the gracious Pamela liveth; so that the lodge seemeth not unlike a fair comet, whose tail stretcheth itself to a star of less greatness.' Sir Philip Sidney, *The Countess of Pembroke's Arcadia (The New Arcadia)*, ed. Victor Skretkowitz (Oxford, 1987), Book I, 85.

[31] Alice T. Friedman, 'Architecture, Authority and the Female Gaze: Planning and Representation in the Early Modern House', *Assemblage*, 18 (1992), 57–8.

[32] Some of these issues have been addressed for the sixteenth century by an architectural historian, see Maurice Howard, 'Self-fashioning and the Classical Moment in Mid-Sixteenth-Century English Architecture', in *Renaissance Bodies: The Human Figure in English Culture c. 1540–1660*, ed. Lucy Gent and Nigel Llewellyn (1990), 198–217.

[33] Two architectural historians have considered some of these issues, see Friedman, 'Architecture, Authority and the Female Gaze'; Cooper, *Houses of the Gentry*.

Undoubtedly, however, women were making aesthetic choices about the kinds of building they wanted. They had fewer chances to see continental buildings than men did, and less access to architectural treatises; nevertheless, they had to tell their builders what they wanted and they appear to have done so self-consciously. Mary Sidney, familiar with the court, chose to build a modern fashionable house.[34] Lady Anne Clifford, however, who had lived at court and in the earl of Pembroke's new wing at Wilton, chose to rebuild her castles to emphasise the role of the Clifford family as great northern territorial magnates of ancient lineage.[35] The countess of Rutland turned to John Webb.

An intriguing example is the work of Abigail Sherard (*c.* 1600–*c.* 1657), supposedly responsible for rebuilding Stapleford Park, Leicestershire, in the 1630s after her husband's elevation to the title Baron Leitrim. The original sixteenth-century house was improved in the 1630s in a self-consciously antiquarian Gothic style, decorated with statues representing putative Sherard ancestors such as William the Conqueror and Gilbert de Clare, while an archway of the same period is correctly classical. In 1640 Abigail Sherard's husband died and in 1650 she rebuilt the south aisle of the parish church to form a family chapel. Here she erected a white marble monument to her husband with both their effigies in contemporary dress.[36] Both projects were clearly intended to connect this parvenu family with the landed aristocracy; Abigail Sherard indicated her interest in lineage elswhere by commissioning an ornamental pedigree of the family in 1653.[37]

Can there be a typology of women's building?

Conventionally both historical materials and modern historical and architectural commentaries have tended to assume that buildings were not commissioned by women unless there is compelling evidence for this. The standard of proof for a commission to have been placed by

[34] Though see Gomme, 'Houghton House', 41, 'Lady Pembroke cannot have failed to be intimately aware of Jones's pre-eminence, even though we need not assume she fully understood it.'

[35] Mowl and Earnshaw, *Architecture without Kings*, 19; Alice T. Friedman, 'Constructing an Identity in Prose, Plaster and Paint: Lady Anne Clifford as Writer and Patron of the Arts', in *Albion's Classicism: The Visual Arts in Britain 1550–1660*, ed. Lucy Gent (New Haven and London, 1995), 369. See also Helen C. Gladstone, 'Building an Identity: Two Noblewoman in England 1566–1666: Lady Anne Clifford and Elizabeth Cooke' (PhD thesis, Open University, 1989).

[36] John Nichols, *The History and Antiquities of the County of Leicester* (4 vols.) (1795–1815), II, Part i, 334, 339.

[37] Howard Colvin, *Architecture and the After-Life* (New Haven, 1991), 257; Nichols, *County of Leicester*, II, 334.

a woman, let alone the design of a building being by one, is unusually high.

It is plainly not possible to attribute commissions to women on the basis of style, but further investigation of the history and use of architectural style would be a useful tool for historians. It might be true that women were more likely to choose to build in Gothic styles when classicism was the style of the moment.[38] But the reason for this may well be less the singularity of feminine taste than the reason for which many women embarked on building projects – to commemorate a family rather than an individual – when references to an ancient past might be what was required. Such references to the past were not just for the lifetime of the builder; they were also for posterity. The countess of Oxford (1693–1755) explained that her purpose in improving Welbeck Abbey in the 1740s and 1750s was 'to incline my family to reside at the only Habitable Seat of my Ancestors'. She did much of the rebuilding in Jacobean revival style (referred to as Gothic) and assembled large numbers of family portraits there.[39]

Likewise, many women commemorated not their husband's family but their father's. This was usually because they were heiresses to their father's fortune in the absence of a male heir, so it was their filial duty to commemorate the line from which they had sprung (and which had provided the funds for building). So, Anne Clifford, heir to the Clifford estates in the north of England; Elizabeth Wilbraham, heir to the Mitton estate in Staffordshire; and Betty Hastings, heir to the Lewis fortune and estates in Yorkshire, commemorated those families, while Abigail Sherard, widow of a man who had made money during his lifetime (but heir, with her sister, to only a small estate from her father), commemorated the Sherards.

Without appropriating to women more than is their due, it is still clear from such sources as funeral sermons, monuments, church plate and charities that women engaged much more actively with building and restoration projects than the record has so far suggested is the case. Greater attention to the formal elements of women's commissions would illuminate the significance of their patronage. It would show how women used buildings and building projects to make statements to a wider world about their wealth, their ancestry, their social aspirations, their taste, their religious preferences *and* their ability to deal with directing builders, raising the money and all the other practical

---

[38] Both Andor Gomme and Ian Nairn associate the presence in a single building of both conservative and innovative elements with the patron being a women (respectively Houghton Conquest and Byfleet Manor), see Gomme, 'Houghton House', 42; Ian Nairn and Nikolaus Pevsner, *Surrey*, 2nd edn, revised by Bridget Cherry (1971), 127.

[39] Peter Smith, 'Lady Oxford's Alterations at Welbeck Abbey, 1741–55', *Georgian Group Journal*, 11 (2001), 134, 140.

details that go with building projects. It also seems evident that many of the women who engaged in such projects did so in the full knowledge of the public nature of the statements they were making.

Transactions of the RHS 13 (2003), pp. 305–18 © 2003 Royal Historical Society
DOI: 10.1017/S0080440103000179   Printed in the United Kingdom

THE GENDER OF THE PLACE: BUILDING AND LANDSCAPE IN WOMEN-AUTHORED TEXTS IN ENGLAND OF THE 1790s

By William Stafford

ABSTRACT. The paper surveys almost fifty women-authored texts of the 1790s, asking what they reveal about the gendering of space in elite houses, about the meaning of buildings and landscapes for women and about women's aesthetic preferences. They imply that elite houses had largely ungendered public, private and intermediate spaces. Castles had negative meanings for women, but not 'olden time' houses; there was some disapproval of exclusionary landscapes and an idealisation of country life (but not for hunting) and of rural cottages (but not rural villas). A neoclassical aesthetic was endorsed by women writers alongside sensibility and the picturesque.

There was a debate about women in the 1790s, to which women themselves contributed. Do their writings contain anything which might interest architectural historians? Do they agree or disagree with what historians have argued, do they offer any new insights? This paper asks three questions. First, do those writings have anything to say about the use of space by men and women in elite houses? Secondly, what do they have to say about the meaning of particular places – houses and landscapes – for women? Thirdly, do they express aesthetic preferences which represent a woman's point of view? The texts on which I draw include those by women whom we might label radical – 'unsex'd females', as a contemporary called them: Mary Wollstonecraft, Mary Hays, Eliza Fenwick, Elizabeth Inchbald, Helen Maria Williams, Mary Robinson, Catharine Macaulay, Charlotte Smith. It also notices writings by conservative or 'proper' females: Hannah More, Maria Edgeworth, Jane West, Frances Burney, Ann Radcliffe, Priscilla Wakefield, Elizabeth Hamilton.

There are obvious problems in consulting these writers to answer these questions. None of them speaks from, or very much about, the non-genteel. But are they representative of the views of gentlewomen? I have already indicated that they do not express a single political stance. But they are perhaps unrepresentative in other ways. None is aristocratic. Most come from low down on the scale of gentility; only Catharine Macaulay and Charlotte Smith came from the ranks of the landed gentry. Furthermore they are all writers, and therefore what they say is shaped by the genres and discourses within which they write. They write essays, conduct books, educational treatises, political tracts. But the bulk of their output is prose fiction, and there are special problems in using that as evidence of what women did and felt outside the bindings of novels and romances. To take an obvious example, the half-ruined castle or abbey has a scripted, clichéd, mythic role in romances which has nothing to do with the everyday experience of women. Explicit aesthetic judgements on buildings and gardens are rare: Catharine Macaulay is exceptional among them in devoting a chapter to landscape gardening in her *Letters on Education*, and Fanny Burney alone pens an extended aesthetic critique of a house. But though the sources must be used with caution, these problems do not invalidate the exercise; for the unarticulated assumptions, the things taken for granted, may reveal much about the gendering of space.

The gendering of space

In *The Gentleman's Daughter*, Amanda Vickery insists that the elite woman's house was not a private sphere. It was not only the site of intimate relations and family life: formal entertaining, the exercise of patronage, transaction of business and even the production of commodities went on within it.[1] Architectural historians have taken for granted that great and gentry houses had within them both public spaces, public even in the sense of being places for politics. If we accept as a working assumption that gentry houses were not purely private, then we can ask whether and in what way women-authored texts reveal and describe a public/private binary within the house itself, and whether any such binary is gendered. We find in the first place that they do not reveal a simple binary; rather they suggest public, private and intermediate spaces. Most obviously public is the hall, to which strangers have access, and where the tenants are entertained.[2] It is in the hall that Sir Hugh Tyrold in Fanny Burney's *Camilla* gathers his family including servants to welcome Edgar Mandelbert upon his coming of age, publicly recognising him as a suitor to Indiana Lynmere.[3] Drawing room and dining room are public also, places of genteel sociability. In these texts even quite modest gentry houses, for example Emily's family home on

---

[1] Amanda Vickery, *The Gentleman's Daughter: Women's Lives in Georgian England* (New Haven, 1998), 9, 153–4.
[2] Helen Maria Williams, *Julia* (London, 1790), I, 74.
[3] Frances d'Arblay, *Camilla, or a Picture of Youth* (1796) (Oxford, 1972), 46.

the banks of the Garonne in Ann Radcliffe's *Mysteries of Udolpho*, have separate breakfast rooms[4] which like dining room and drawing room are places where family and visitors meet.[5] In Elizabeth Inchbald's *Nature and Art*, the room where the dean has just finished breakfast is explicitly contrasted with a private apartment.[6]

The only absolutely private space is the bedchamber, and its attached closets if it has any; in the words of Mary Wollstonecraft writing about Marie Antoinette's bedroom, 'The sanctuary of repose, the asylum of care and fatigue, the chaste temple of a woman.'[7] In prose fiction texts principal members of a family each have an 'apartment' sometimes of more than one room, sometimes of one only. If there is more than one, the other is usually the dressing room. This is not private in the sense that only intimates meet there, but it is private in the sense that it is a place for private conversations, conversations that would be inappropriately overheard if they were conducted in dining or drawing room. In Jane West's *Gossip's Story*, the doomed heroine becomes an object of gossip after she quite innocently receives a man in her dressing room.[8] But Jane West appears to have been exceptionally strict about dressing-room proprieties. In Charlotte Smith's *Desmond* the heroine Geraldine Verney suffers constant intrusion in her dressing room by Colonel Scarsdale, who wishes to seduce her; the impropriety is not that he comes to her dressing room, but that he comes so often, uninvited. Geraldine is a model of virtue, but she regularly receives men in her dressing room.[9] In Charlotte Smith's *Young Philosopher*, Armitage goes for an interview with the prudish Mrs Crewkherne in her dressing room, and finds her in conclave with a methodist preacher.[10] Similarly in these texts the library functions as an intermediate space between public and private. Unlike a dressing room, it is neutral ground; it is also a place in which conversations of formal importance occur, as when Lord Elmwood in Elizabeth Inchbald's *Simple Story* confronts his nephew Rushbrook and demands to know his marriage intentions. Emma Courtney, after a quarrel with the whole family at the dinner table, asks her uncle to go with her to his library for a full, frank and formal discussion.[11] It is more private than dining room or drawing

[4] Ann Radcliffe, *The Mysteries of Udolpho* (1794) (Oxford, 1980), 4.

[5] Mary Hays, *Memoirs of Emma Courtney* (1796) (1987), 34.

[6] Elizabeth Inchbald, *Nature and Art* (1797) (1997), 21; Eliza Fenwick, *Secresy; The Ruin on the Rock* (1795) (Peterborough, Ontario, 1994), 152.

[7] Mary Wollstonecraft, *An Historical and Moral View of the Origin and Progress of the French Revolution* (London, 1794), 457.

[8] Jane West, *A Gossip's Story* (London, 1797), II, 160–6.

[9] Charlotte Smith, *Desmond* (1792) (1997), 194, 10, 140, 142.

[10] Charlotte Smith, *The Young Philosopher* (1798) (Lexington, 1999), 243.

[11] Elizabeth Inchbald, *A Simple Story* (1791) (Oxford, 1988), 286; Hays, *Memoirs of Emma Courtney*, 44.

room to the extent that romantic declarations can occur there.

Philippa Tristram argues that the Victorian great house had gendered spaces;[12] Dana Arnold maintains that space in the Georgian house was largely ungendered.[13] The texts I have examined suggest that there were vestiges of gendering, but that they were being contested by radical women writers. Occasionally the library is referred to as 'his', belonging to the male head of the house, and sometimes it doubles as his study.[14] But in general women are either described as having unrestricted access to the library, or their exclusion is protested. Mr Valmont bars his niece Sibella from his library in Eliza Fenwick's *Secresy*, but this is just one more indication of his outdated authoritarianism.[15] In Mary Hays's novel, Emma Courtney's father to her chagrin at first locks the bookcases and selects books for his daughter to read: but eventually she is given the keys.[16] In these works women spend much time in the library, or visiting it for books. We should not be surprised; as Peter Jupp has argued, elite women in this period were probably better read than elite men, because they had more time for it.[17]

Some have thought with Mark Girouard that the Georgian dining room was a masculine space, because it was the locus of male drinking at the end of dinner after the women had withdrawn.[18] Amanda Vickery by contrast thinks that the Georgian dining room was the most important social space for the gentlewoman at home, and finds a lack of evidence to show whether or not women usually withdrew at the end of dinner.[19] Women-authored texts of the 1790s imply that a woman presided at the dinner table,[20] even if she was a kept mistress,[21] and that sometimes the women withdrew while the men drank.[22] But they do not always withdraw; we do not hear of it in Fanny Burney's *Camilla* for instance and there are occasions when it is clear they do not.[23] Perhaps a separation of the sexes was less likely when dinner was *en*

[12] Philippa Tristram, *Living Space in Fact and Fiction* (1989), 59.

[13] *The Georgian Country House. Architecture, Landscape and Society*, ed. Dana Arnold (Stroud, 1998), 88.

[14] Williams, *Julia*, II, 117–18.

[15] Fenwick, *Secresy*, 157.

[16] Hays, *Memoirs of Emma Courtney*, 21, 24.

[17] P.J. Jupp, 'The Roles of Royal and Aristocratic Women in British Politics, c. 1782–1832', in *Chattel, Servant or Citizen: Women's Status in Church, State and Society*, Institute of Irish Studies, Queens University Belfast, Historical Studies 19 (1995), 103–13.

[18] Mark Girouard, *Life in the English Country House* (Harmondsworth, 1980), 205.

[19] Vickery, *Gentleman's Daughter*, 206–7.

[20] Smith, *Desmond*, 194.

[21] Mary Wollstonecraft, *The Wrongs of Woman, or, Maria* (1798) (Oxford, 1976), 111.

[22] Williams, *Julia*, I, 40; II, 205.

[23] D'Arblay, *Camilla*, 578; Inchbald, *Simple Story*, 28; Hays, *Memoirs of Emma Courtney*, 42, 55.

famille, but we read of women remaining on more formal occasions too. Miss Ardent remains to converse with her guests after the food has been cleared and the bottles placed on the table in Elizabeth Hamilton's *Hindoo Rajah*.[24] When Mary Wollstonecraft dined with the English vice-consul in Sweden, she was at table while 'the bottle was rather too freely pushed about'.[25]

Just as we find women occupying the library, so in the dining room Mary Hays protests against the 'barbarous and odious custom',[26] and in her *Letters and Essays* we hear that 'When dinner was ended, and the dessert gave place to wine, Josepha and Miss ---- retired to the drawing-room. Clermont allured by the sound of the harpsichord, and preferring the company of the ladies to the noisy toast, and bacchanalian song, soon followed them.'[27] Women writers in general disapprove of homosocial drinking. This is not because they are desperate for male company. A pervasive, half-overt, half-buried theme of this woman-authored literature is the need to reform and civilise men, to make them less brutal and more woman-friendly; disapproval of homosocial drinking is part of this campaign.

Philippa Tristram has argued that in Jane Austen's time, women were not permitted to retire to their own chambers during the day.[28] Women-authored texts of the 1790s give no indication that this was the case before the end of the eighteenth century. Sociability was compulsory at dinner, but apparently at no other time. A woman who did not come down on hearing the dinner bell would be sent for; only illness offered an excuse.[29] When Mr Valmont in Eliza Fenwick's *Secresy* abolishes the practice of meeting to dine, this is another sign of his unacceptable eccentricity.[30] Sociability in the breakfast room by contrast, though normal, was not compulsory.[31] At other times women were free to be on their own; etiquette was relatively relaxed. This accords with the easy, unceremonious politeness and sociability whose late eighteenth-century ascendancy historians of manners have observed, contrasting it with the stiff formality of the seventeenth and early eighteenth centuries. Women writers at the time notice and endorse this trend, and Helen Maria Williams in her novel *Julia* explicitly draws a parallel

[24] Elizabeth Hamilton, *Translation of the Letters of a Hindoo Rajah* (1796) (Peterborough, Ontario, 1999), 232–3.

[25] Mary Wollstonecraft, *Letters Written during a Short Residence in Sweden, Norway and Denmark* (London, 1796), 137.

[26] Hays, *Memoirs of Emma Courtney*, 116.

[27] Mary Hays, *Letters and Essays, Moral, and Miscellaneous* (London, 1793), 144 (this essay is by Hays's sister Eliza).

[28] Tristram, *Living Space in Fact and Fiction*, 183.

[29] D'Arblay, *Camilla*, 347, 363, 782–3, 811; Radcliffe, *Mysteries of Udolpho*, 145.

[30] Fenwick, *Secresy*, 103.

[31] Williams, *Julia*, I, 232.

with the contrast between older formal and modern natural landscape gardens.[32]

Places and their meanings

Are certain places presented as masculine or feminine? Are there places with which women seem to have special affinity? As Philippa Tristram has asked, are places depicted as havens or as prisons?[33] Do they enclose and disempower the women in them, or are they places of empowerment and base camps from which female activity can be launched? Are they exclusionary, with class separation intensifying female isolation?

The woman who has no secure place to go is a stock theme of prose fiction, as we might expect; it is found for example in Mary Robinson's *False Friend*, Mary Hays's *Victim of Prejudice* and in most of Charlotte Smith's novels.[34] Novels and romances put the heroine in danger so as to create suspense, and a standard way of doing this is to cut her adrift. The word 'protection' crops up constantly; women need protection at all times. But where are the safe and unsafe places?

It may be that subliminally women readers got a *frisson* out of contemplating the frightening masculine gothic castle, with its threat of brute force and rape. Overtly, the gothic castle has negative meanings for women. In 1790s woman-authored texts, castles are standard places where women are imprisoned, and 'gothic' is almost invariably a pejorative term. Classic examples are Emily's imprisonment in the castle of Udolpho, or Eliza Fenwick's *Secresy*, in which George Valmont imprisons his niece Sibella in his castle behind moat and drawbridge. Mary Robinson furnishes occasional exceptions to this rule: the castle of Vancenza is an asylum in her romance of that name, and in two of her novels 'gothic' liberties and gothic marital proprieties are favourably contrasted with the tyrannies and infidelities of her own age.[35] Castles in these texts, as Elizabeth Bohls has remarked, predominantly mean lingering feudality, reactionary tyranny and patriarchal oppression of women,[36] and this is true not only of radical writings. There are for example echoes in the novels of the conservative Jane West.[37] A stock

[32] *Ibid.*, I, 63.

[33] Tristram, *Living Space in Fact and Fiction*, 232.

[34] Mary Robinson, *The False Friend; A Domestic Story* (London, 1799); Mary Hays, *The Victim of Prejudice* (1799) (Peterborough, Ontario, 1994).

[35] Mary Robinson, *Vancenza; Or, the Dangers of Credulity* (London, 1792), I, 6; *The Widow, Or a Picture of Modern Times* (London, 1794), I, 106, II, 91; *False Friend*, I, 198.

[36] Elizabeth A. Bohls, *Women Travel Writers and the Language of Aesthetics, 1716–1818* (Cambridge, 1995), 120. For example see Mary Wollstonecraft, *A Vindication of the Rights of Men, in a Letter to the Right Honourable Edmund Burke* (1790) (Cambridge, 1995), 42, 50.

[37] Jane West, *A Tale of the Times* (London, 1799), I, 284.

theme of eighteenth-century prose fiction is the conflict between love and the arranged marriage. Several women-authored texts of the 1790s associate the castle as prison theme with the threat of a marriage for the heroine to a man she cannot love, at the behest of her patriarchal father.[38]

If the castle has negative meanings for women in 1790s texts, this is not wholly true of 'olden time' houses. In Fanny Burney's *Camilla*, the heroine visits 'the noble antique mansion, pictures and curiosities of Knowle', and admires 'the noble old trees which venerably adorn' the park.[39] Charlotte Smith's old manor house in her novel of that title symbolises an *ancien régime* in need of reform, a society in which freedom of choice in marriage is thwarted and punished. But it also symbolises a paternalism which she endorses. The tenants are received and feasted in the hall.[40] If, as Carol Gilligan has argued, there is a feminine ethic of care and concern for the welfare of others,[41] then we may say that this feminine ethic is writ large in women-authored texts of the 1790s. Almost without exception, radical and conservative women alike promote an active welfare role for gentlewomen, and through this olden time buildings with their supposedly hospitable halls acquire positive meanings. Even a castle can become a good place if it is the base camp of a caring maternalism. In Jane West's *Tale of the Times*, the heroine Geraldine turns Monteith castle in Scotland into a 'Bower of Bliss'. For she has decided to care for her husband's tenants: 'I will frequently visit them; I will be their legislator, their instructor, their physician, and their friend.'[42] She builds a model village, endows a school and sets up a carpet manufactory to provide employment.

Mark Girouard has related the building of houses in castle style in the early nineteenth century to a conservative fear of revolution and desire to exclude the mob.[43] Tom Williamson has argued that the Brownian landscape, with the house set in the centre of an extensive park, the perimeter belt and the lodge gates, was always 'the landscape of polite exclusion', a landscape moreover which clearly marked the landed from the middle classes who did not have enough land for a park.[44] Such meanings hardly ever find favour in texts of the 1790s by radical or conservative women, precisely because of the emphasis upon

[38] For example Smith's *Celestina*, *Montalbert* and *Marchmont*, Robinson's *Angelina* and *False Friend*.

[39] D'Arblay, *Camilla*, 416.

[40] Charlotte Smith, *The Old Manor House* (1793) (Oxford, 1969).

[41] Carol Gilligan, *In a Different Voice* (Cambridge, MA, 1982), 17, 159.

[42] West, *Tale of the Times*, II, 10.

[43] Girouard, *Life in the English Country House*, 242.

[44] Tom Williamson, *Polite Landscapes: Gardens and Society in Eighteenth-Century England* (Stroud, 1995), 58, 100, 102, 107, 113.

social engagement and activity. Fanny Burney certainly pokes fun at Mr Dubster's ridiculous and pretentious attempt to establish a park, with arbour, summer house, pond, island, labyrinth and grotto on a mere handkerchief of land,[45] and her *Camilla* is not free of snobbery. But this does not imply social separation; she agrees that gentlewomen should be active among the poor.[46] As Elizabeth Bohls has remarked,[47] Mary Wollstonecraft protests against exclusion:

> Every thing on the estate is cherished but man ... But if, instead of sweeping pleasure-grounds, obelisks, temples, and elegant cottages ... the heart was allowed to beat true to nature, decent farms would be scattered over the estate ... Instead of the poor being subject to the griping hand of an avaricious steward, they would be watched over with fatherly solicitude.[48]

Catharine Macaulay praises the landscape of Kent and Brown specifically because it is *not* the landscape of polite exclusion: 'When the high unsocial wall gave place to the sunk fence, the public were permitted to share in the benefits of private wealth.' She has a vision of the whole country being turned into a landscape garden, with the opulent leading the way, encouraging their humble neighbours including farmers and cottagers. 'If no relapse to barbarism, formality, and seclusion is made, what landscapes will dignify every quarter of our island.' She rejects architecture symbolic of social separation: 'There is no appearance which shocks a candid mind more, than the views of a little hovel contrasted with a princely palace' and she welcomes the social peace which makes the moated castle no longer necessary.[49]

If we are considering places as sites of female activity and empowerment, then as Amanda Vickery has insisted it is vital that we do not belittle household management.[50] Radical women such as Mary Hays and Mary Robinson, conservative women such as Jane West, Hannah More, Maria Edgeworth and Priscilla Wakefield all insist upon the dignity of household management. They sometimes draw a contrast between an ideal modern manager and the housewife of the past who engaged in lowly domestic tasks such as cooking, sewing and domestic adornment. The activity of the manager they recommend is described in ungendered or even masculine language; it is a rational activity

[45] D'Arblay, *Camilla*, 274–82.

[46] *Ibid.*, 98, 109, 574.

[47] Bohls, *Women Travel Writers*, 112.

[48] Wollstonecraft, *A Vindication of the Rights of Men*, 59.

[49] Catharine Macaulay Graham, *Letters on Education: With Observations on Religious and Metaphysical Subjects* (London, 1790), 303ff.

[50] Vickery, *Gentleman's Daughter*, 127.

of ruling, of organising and commanding servants.[51] Historians of architecture might consider how the increasing scale, and increasingly sophisticated organisation of the service areas of great and gentry houses, relate to the gentlewoman's perception of her managerial role.

From castles, great houses and landscape parks we might turn to cottages. Philippa Tristram thinks that cottages became salient in Victorian novels.[52] In fact they figure largely in 1790s women-authored prose fiction, and there is a remarkable consistency in their favourable evaluation as places of female refuge.[53] When Udolpho is beseiged, Emily is removed from her castle prison to a cottage. This is a place of confinement also, but 'Of her pleasant embowered chamber she now became fond, and began to experience in it those feelings of security, which we naturally attach to home.'[54] There are cottage refuges in Mary Robinson's *The Widow*, *Angelina* and *Hubert de Sevrac*, in Charlotte Smith's *Celestina*, *Banished Man*, *Montalbert*, *Marchmont* and *The Young Philosopher*, and in both of Maria Hays's novels. Obviously these are often *cottages ornées*. The young philosopher is able to accommodate a party of four gentlefolk, as well as his sisters and aunt, at his elegant Upwood cottage. Mrs Harley's cottage in Maria Hays's *Emma Courtney* has a breakfast room and a room 'which the servant called a library'.[55] But I think that Philippa Tristram is wrong in judging that Mr Dubster's ridiculous house in *Camilla* is a *cottage ornée*.[56] With its flight of steps rising above the threshold of the front door, its first-floor balcony and Venetian window, it is an absurd parody of a Palladian villa, a Barratt's Georgian Detached 200 years before its time.

Why are cottages idealized in these texts? An obvious answer is because of their close relationship with 'nature'. Anne Mellor has argued for a distinct female romanticism in this period, one which tropes nature as a sister or friend with whom women engage in a mutually nurturing relationship.[57] 1790s woman-authored texts lend support to this interpretation. The ideal living room in Ann Radcliffe or Mary Hays is on the ground floor with windows opening on to the garden.[58] In Eliza Fenwick's *Secresy*, Caroline Ashburn is revolted by George Valmont's castle because 'instead of smiling lawns and gay

[51] Hays, *Letters and Essays*, 28; Priscilla Wakefield, *Reflections on the Present Condition of the Female Sex* (London, 1798), 105; Hannah More, *Strictures on the Modern System of Female Education* (London, 1799), II, 5.
[52] Tristram, *Living Space in Fact and Fiction*, 66.
[53] The association of cottages with femininity is explored in Karen Sayer, *Country Cottages: A Cultural History* (Manchester, 2000).
[54] Radcliffe, *Mysteries of Udolpho*, 418.
[55] Hays, *Memoirs of Emma Courtney*, 54.
[56] Tristram, *Living Space in Fact and Fiction*, 212.
[57] Anne K. Mellor, *Romanticism and Gender* (1993), 3.
[58] Radcliffe, *Mysteries of Udolpho*, 471; Hays, *Memoirs of Emma Courtney*, 54.

parterres, without, I found moats, walls, and drawbridges, frowning battlements ... carved saloons and arched galleries, into which the bright sun of spring can only cast an oblique ray'.[59] The young philosopher's ideal cottage was remodelled by his mother who built a large conservatory into which the ground and first floor windows open, thus breaking down the distinction between inside and outer nature.[60] Improbably in *The Mysteries of Udolpho*, the enlarged cottage which is Emily's loved family home has an attached greenhouse in 1584.[61] Major approved pastimes for women in these texts are gardening and botany. The city is a dangerous place, where women need protection: but in the novels of Charlotte Smith and the romances of Ann Radcliffe we find women taking solitary walks through the countryside apparently without fear or danger. The country is hardly a private place, but it is presented here as a woman's place. So why the cottage rather than the villa? Perhaps the luxurious country retreat had ambiguous meanings for women. The marquis de Montalt's villa in Ann Radcliffe's *Romance of the Forest*, and Sir Harry Richmond's Yorkshire mansion in *The Young Philosopher* are all too obviously male places, places for the sexual abuse of women.[62] There is a class dimension to this also; middle-class women writers trade upon the clichéd association of aristocratic males with libertinism of every kind.

According to Dana Arnold, the country was generally seen as dull.[63] It was a stock joke that gentry wives panted to return to the dissipations of the town. In novels of the 1790s such women are regulars in the cast lists, but they are invariably satirised or disapproved.[64] Heroines, and approved men too, always prefer rural retirement, with its pleasures of communing with nature. Most woman-authored works of prose fiction sound this theme sooner or later, and both Fanny Burney and Jane West refer to the lines from Thompson's 'Spring':

> An elegant sufficiency, content,
> Retirement, rural quiet, friendship, books,
> Ease and alternate labour, useful life,
> Progressive virtue, and approving heaven;
> These are the matchless joys of virtuous love.[65]

In a remarkable passage in her *Historical and Moral View of ... the French*

[59] Fenwick, *Secresy*, 52.

[60] Smith, *Young Philosopher*, 32.

[61] Radcliffe, *Mysteries of Udolpho*, 3.

[62] There is a clear example of this in Amelia Opie, *Adeline Mowbray, or the Mother and Daughter* (London, 1805), I, 148–67.

[63] Arnold, *Georgian Country House*, 23.

[64] Robinson, *The Widow*, I, 3–4.

[65] West, *Tale of the Times*, III, 64.

Revolution Mary Wollstonecraft opines that in a virtuous and egalitarian republic, cities will be abandoned and Paris will decay as population spreads across the countryside.[66] But when in Scandinavia she lived in places of coarse rusticity, she began to think that the intellectual vibrancy of a metropolis had advantages after all.[67]

How are we to interpret, how much weight can we place, on the rural idyll and the ideal of a close relationship with nature in woman-authored texts? Is it just a cliché, which tells us nothing about what women actually thought and felt? Is it an aspect of an ideology asserting the superiority of middle-class lovers of nature over aristocratic urban rakes? As a normative discourse, did it perhaps bear no relation to lived reality? Does the very fact of its reiteration imply a vain protest against a general preference for town living? And does it represent a distinctively female attitude to place? After all, the rural idyll is a cliché of male-authored texts also. One aspect at least represents a point of view adopted by women authors in response to and in contradiction of men. This is their virtually universal disapproval of the use of the park and countryside for hunting. Women authors both radical and conservative sign up to a humanitarian agenda which includes this as a key item.[68] Even the exceptions prove the rule. In Jane West's *Gossip's Story*, Marianne is criticised for stopping her husband from hunting with his friends. But what she disapproves of here is Marianne's lack of wifely submission; there is no suggestion that she approves of hunting.[69] The critique of hunting, like the objections to homosocial drinking, is part of the female reformation of male manners agenda, part of the attempt to unbrutify men.

A female aesthetic?

Are places gendered in that certain styles of building can be labelled masculine or feminine? Historians of architecture and even architects have used such language, for example labelling the castle style and neoclassicism masculine, and the gothic style feminine.[70] It is tempting to dismiss such claims as subjective and flimsy. But, to move to firmer ground, are there clear and shared aesthetic preferences in these texts? The answer is yes. In none of these texts is there any commendation of original gothic interiors and furnishings. In Charlotte Smith's *Young Philosopher* for example, Medora is imprisoned in 'an old mansion house

[66] Wollstonecraft, *Historical and Moral View*, 508.
[67] Wollstonecraft, *Letters Written during a Short Residence*, 136–7.
[68] Macaulay Graham, *Letters on Education*, 6, 65, 122; Hamilton, *Hindoo Rajah*, 217.
[69] West, *Gossip's Story*, II, p. 92.
[70] Tristram, *Living Space in Fact and Fiction*, 238–9; Kenneth Clark, *The Gothic Revival* (1928) (1962), 17.

of gloomy and gothic appearance', with ghastly, moth-eaten, tapestry-hung interiors.[71] Approval is reserved for modernisations which introduce lightness and comfort, as we see in Ann Radcliffe's description of Chateau Le Blanc in her *Mysteries of Udolpho*; the ancient rooms appeal to Lady Blanche's imagination, but it is clear she would not wish to live in them.[72] And in *Julia* Helen Maria Williams approves of the modernisations introduced by Mr Clifford who

> had too much pride in his family to remove any marks of its ancient magnificence. He left, therefore, the tapestry, the massy chairs, and the family pictures, undisturbed, as useless but proud monuments in the back-ground of his apartments, while he took care to bring forward all the comforts and conveniences of modern luxury.[73]

The endorsement by women writers of sensibility and the picturesque has been widely commented upon.[74] In addition to that, and much less remarked, is a virtually unanimous preference for the simple, the undecorated, the unadorned. Most examples of this – and they are legion – are to be found in descriptions of the presentation of the female body. For example when travelling through Holstein Mary Wollstonecraft was amused to observe the 'grotesque and unwieldy' dress of the women, 'almost completely concealing the human form'.[75] Women should not ornament, or rather disfigure, their persons; the best dress is the simple garb that fits close to the shape.[76] Both Priscilla Wakefield and Mary Hays rejoice that corsets – a 'vile and unnatural mode of dress' – have gone out of fashion.[77] In Helena Maria Williams's novel the two heroines Julia and Charlotte come down to dinner dressed with graceful simplicity, while the disapproved Mrs Seymour is overdecorated.[78] Later Mrs Seymour duets with a friend, her singing 'so tricked out with ornament, and performed with such affected distortions of the lips, and apparent labour' that her doting mother alone admires it.[79] Resonances with neoclassicism are clear. Charlotte Smith contrasts the 'exquisitely simple Grecian statue' with the debauched taste for 'court figures in hoops and perriwigs'.[80] Mary Wollstonecraft refers to the body as a sacred temple, and calls for 'Not

[71] Smith, *Young Philosopher*, 312.
[72] Radcliffe, *Mysteries of Udolpho*, 471, 473–4, 479; Smith, *Young Philosopher*, 91.
[73] Williams, *Julia*, 74.
[74] Bohls, *Women Travel Writers*, 14, 101–2.
[75] Wollstonecraft, *Letters Written during a Short Residence*, 242–3.
[76] *Ibid.*, 216.
[77] Wakefield, *Reflections*, 25; *Appeal to the Men of Great Britain* (anon.; probably by Mary Hays) (London, 1798), 200–1.
[78] Williams, *Julia*, I, 145–6.
[79] *Ibid.*, II, 141.
[80] Smith, *Young Philosopher*, 352.

relaxed beauty ... but such as appears to make us respect the human body as a majestic pile fit to receive a noble inhabitant, in the relics of antiquity.' She goes on to illustrate this with reference to Grecian statues.[81] She commends the sober satisfaction which arises from the calm contemplation of proportion, simplicity and truth.[82] Women should exhibit dignity, majesty and strength. It is almost a commonplace remark in these texts that true beauty is the result of mental and moral qualities shining in the face. Catharine Macaulay and Mary Hays wish for a woman's mind and individuality to be written there and Macaulay quotes the stoic maxim that the wise man alone is beautiful.[83] She hopes that

> The inventive faculties, which are now pressed into the service of milliners and hair dressers, would be better employed; and the motley shew which society at present sets forth, would give place to a gravity and a dignity of appearance more conformable to the high ideas we have conceived of a rational nature.[84]

Likewise Mary Wollstonecraft distinguishes between pretty women and fine women, and prefers the latter.[85] She commends the beauty of older women, in whom 'vivacity gives place to reason, and to that majestic seriousness of character, which marks maturity'.[86] Miss Milner is admired in *Simple Story* when she dresses with 'dignified simplicity' and her daughter Lady Matilda is dignified too.[87] 'Proper' females can be found endorsing this aesthetic also.[88]

An obvious objection here is that there is nothing distinctively female about such aesthetic preferences: men shared them too. But an argument is possible that these aesthetic preferences had a peculiar appeal to women. Stephen Bending has argued that sensibility and the picturesque represented a democratisation of taste, modes of aesthetic appreciation available to those who lacked the knowledge of classical literature presupposed by so much post-renaissance art and enjoyed by elite males.[89] Women were obvious beneficiaries of this – though it is to be doubted that they felt themselves part of a democratic aesthetic culture. Mary Wollstonecraft, Mary Robinson, Charlotte Smith and Ann Radcliffe present sensibility and appreciation of picturesque nature as

[81] Wollstonecraft, *Vindication of the Rights of Woman*, 267.
[82] Wollstonecraft, *Vindication of the Rights of Men*, 57–8.
[83] Macaulay Graham, *Letters on Education*, 178.
[84] *Ibid.*, 299–300.
[85] Wollstonecraft, *Vindication of the Rights of Woman*, 119.
[86] *Ibid.*, 147.
[87] Inchbald, *Simple Story*, 14.
[88] Hamilton, *Hindoo Rajah*, 164, 175.
[89] Stephen Bending, 'One Among the Many: Popular Aesthetics, Polite Culture and the Country House Landscape', in *The Georgian Country House*, ed. Arnold, 63–5.

alternative status-markers, indicators of spiritual superiority which regularly elevate the sensitive and refined woman above the socially superior and classically educated male.

The resonance of a neoclassical aesthetic of plainness, dignity and unadorned simplicity for women is clear. The best-known and most explicit statement of it is the principal message of Mary Wollstonecraft's *Vindication of the Rights of Woman*, but it is present in most of these texts. Unanimously these women authors judge that a decorated and prettified woman is a diminished, trivialised woman, a woman who has been turned into a sexual object of the male gaze. If absence of decoration connoted a masculine aesthetic, then these women writers were engaged in the enterprise of capturing it for women as a female aesthetic too, or perhaps as an ungendered human aesthetic.

Transactions of the RHS 13 (2003), pp. 319–27 © 2003 Royal Historical Society
DOI: 10.1017/S0080440103000180   Printed in the United Kingdom

TELLING TALES: ANECDOTAL INSIGHTS INTO
THE WEST END HOUSE *c.* 1765–*c.* 1785

By Rachel Stewart

ABSTRACT. Anecdotal evidence is much beloved of architectural historians, particularly in their attempts to recreate the social context in which architectural practice took place. But there are dangers inherent in its use. Using examples relating to the West End house in the period *c.* 1765 to *c.* 1785, this paper argues that architectural historians should be wary of tacking on such evidence to corroborate what they read from built evidence; rather they should treat the body of anecdotal evidence as a source worth investigating in its own right. Only then will they unearth new readings and new understandings which elaborate and sometimes contradict received interpretations of architectural forms.

In 1777, Lady Sarah Lennox remarked of Lady Ilchester, new to London and to Grosvenor Square: 'I thought she had too much sense not to make a proper figure if she undertook to make any at all ... but I fancy a good House and good suppers will soon recover the faux pas of going to the Opera sans powder.'[1] A good West End house and the entertainment it facilitated could be an antidote to worse offences than that. The duchess of Devonshire was wary that people might think she shunned Lady Derby not because of the exposure of that lady's affair with the duke of Dorset, but simply because she no longer had at her disposal the use of the magnificent Derby House, also in Grosvenor Square, which had been expensively and prominently transformed by Robert and James Adam only a few years earlier. 'I have the greatest horror of her crime', the duchess wrote to her mother in 1778,

> but her conduct has long been imprudent, and yet, I have sup'd at her house ... and now it does seem shocking to me ... that at the time all her grandeur is crush'd around her, I should entirely abandon her, as if I said, I know you was imprudent formerly, but then you had a great house and great suppers and so I came to you but now that you have nothing of all this, I will avoid you.[2]

[1] British Library, Holland House papers, Add. MS 51354, Lady Sarah Lennox to Lady Susan O'Brien, 30 Dec. 1777.
[2] Amanda Foreman, *Georgiana, Duchess of Devonshire* (1999), 68–9.

Women's comments, often about other women, dominate the type of anecdotal evidence that can be used to explore the town house's various functions as symbol, property and commodity, as well as home – functions that can be obscured by the aesthetic and developmental considerations that often preoccupy architectural historians, particularly in this field. Such comments as those of Sarah Lennox and the duchess of Devonshire help us not just to answer, but to pose questions often disregarded by approaches centred on the built form or its architects. What did occupants want from their houses? What did they look for when they purchased a house, or commissioned a rebuilding or refurbishment? What factors affected their decisions? What roles did town houses play for their owners, and how were they perceived by others? Anecdotal evidence is an indispensable aid in recreating the range of motives that may have governed individuals' behaviour in respect of London houses, the physical evidence of which we see in actual or documented buildings, such as Derby House. But anecdotal evidence also poses problems for the researcher, some inherent in the material itself, and some in the way it is generally used.

In *Objects of Desire*, Adrian Forty complains that writers very often pay only lip service to architecture's social background, if they bother at all. 'Cursory references to the social context are like the weeds and gravel around a stuffed fish in a glass case', says Forty. 'However realistic these may be, they are only furnishings, and taking them away would have little effect on our perception of the fish.'[3] In practice, lip service often takes the form of anecdote used in an isolated or fragmentary way – a single apposite comment to corroborate or illustrate findings or arguments deriving principally from the buildings themselves, official or corporate papers, financial evidence or some other source. But the *body* of anecdotal evidence is rarely looked at on its own terms.

One consequent risk is that an individual example might be misleading, misunderstood or mistakenly generalised to all people for a long period of time. For example, Lawrence Stone and Jeanne C. Fawtier Stone quote César de Saussure's remark from the 1720s that 'many noblemen live in town to economize' as evidence to support an assumption that this was, in fact, the case.[4] Yet a wide study of anecdotal and other sources for the years from 1765 to 1785 offers directly contrary evidence. Many letters refer to abandoning city life for a while in order to recoup finances, a strategy verified and vindicated by financial

[3] Adrian Forty, *Objects of Desire: Design and Society 1750–1980* (1986), 8.

[4] Lawrence Stone and Jeanne C. Fawtier Stone, *An Open Elite? England 1540–1880* (Oxford, 1984), 299, 350, quoting César de Saussure, *A Foreign View of England in the Reigns of George I and George II* (1902), pp. 208–9.

evidence. Advertisements, too, give 'retiring to the country' as the reason for many house sales. The composite evidence for the period *c.* 1765–*c.* 1785 contradicts Stone and Stone's conclusions, raising the question of whether economising by living in London was ever a fact and, if so, whether the balance had changed in or by the 1770s. Certainly de Saussure's remark cannot be generalised to the whole of the eighteenth century. Moreover, the writings of such foreign visitors to Georgian London – a favourite with architectural historians – have limited use in some contexts. They might be useful for observations about a man's life in his town house, but less so about the town house in his life. And their remarks were not always as disinterested as they might have been, as contemporaries sometimes noted.[5]

There is also a tendency to rely on the same, readily accessible and admittedly highly quotable sources, such as Horace Walpole, and Lady Mary Coke. Anecdotes are made unjustifiably representative by their repetition time and again for the same purposes, exacerbating a general problem with historical writing. The tacked-on, seemingly corroborative anecdote is too easily used as a means of making truisms truer. But a broader study of anecdotal evidence can sometimes give us reason to challenge received views.

Because of its casual and repeated use, the anecdote may not be studied closely enough in itself, and may lose some of its original potency. Architectural historians regularly quote Walpole's famous comment that Derby House was 'filigreed into puerility'[6] because the adjective 'filigreed' seems to match the style of decoration shown in surviving images of and designs for the now demolished house. But the choice and force of the word 'puerility' is largely ignored. The Adams's client here, Lord Stanley, later Derby, was reportedly unrefined in both behaviour and understanding,[7] and the combination of, or perhaps fine

---

[5] See, for example, *The Town and Country Magazine*, 4 (1772), 322, where Pierre-Jean Grosley's *A Tour to London; Or, New Observations on England, and its Inhabitants* is reviewed: 'Monsieur Grosley, though he seems to have divested himself as much as possible of national prejudice, still retains such a tincture of the Frenchman, that we cannot pronounce his work an impartial disquisition on the manners and genius of the English. If we add to this the mutations of taste and fashion since the time of his writing, we shall find a very imperfect idea of our present modes and polite pursuits.'

[6] *Horace Walpole's Correspondence*, ed. W. S. Lewis *et al.* (48 vols.) (1937–83), XXXII (1965), 371, letter to Lady Ossory, 8 Aug. 1777.

[7] In *Georgiana, Duchess of Devonshire* (45), Amanda Foreman writes of the delight that Derby and his friends took 'in being overtly crude, as the following wager illustrates: "Ld Cholmondeley has given two guineas to Ld Derby, to receive 500 Gs. whenever his lordship fucks a woman in a Balloon one thousand yards from Earth"'. See, also, an open 'Letter to Lord Stanley', from 'Gentlemen of Lancashire' in *The Public Advertiser*, 24 Oct. 1775: 'Your Youth and Inexperience, in some measure, shield you from the Severity with which your conduct would otherwise be treated; but it is necessary to give a hint to your Vanity ... Your personal Character hath hardly yet budded. I wish the Twig

line between, vulgarity and the sort of display of 'taste' seen at Derby House seems to have been at the root of Walpole's criticism, in which he linked the 'filigreed' decoration which pervaded every surface with a lack of sophistication and maturity. Thus Walpole's remark is much more than a comment on excess and excessive fineness of detail. The anecdote's connections with other comments made about similar, if less high-profile town-house interiors are also ignored. The 'puerility' of indulging in such a frivolous display was not a point of view exclusive to Walpole. Mrs Elizabeth Carter, in response to a town-house room 'adorned with the utmost profusion of expensive elegance' declared she would 'as soon be tempted to cry for a doll or a coral' as to covet the overdose of ornament she beheld.[8] The fault lies not simply in the ornament, or its designer, but in the sort of person it is deemed to appeal to. The town house was particularly susceptible to associations with childish or effeminate impermanence, inconstancy, insubstantiality and intemperance, and Adam or Adam-style decoration exemplified these emasculating traits.

So, in the simple matching of remark with evidence, other subtleties may be lost. But if, rather than tacking it on, we use anecdotal evidence as a lever, we can gain new insights into subjects we sometimes believe to be adequately pinned down already. For example, we can identify and unpick the negative associations of the town house implied by Walpole and many others. Although it is too simplistic to call the country house masculine and the London house feminine, anecdotal information not only reveals but also goes some way to explaining the circle of links between women, luxury and the town house in this period.

There is abundant anecdotal evidence about the financial distress caused by purchasing or building in London.[9] When Elizabeth Montagu claimed in 1782, on settling accounts for the building of her new house in Portman Square, that 'there is … a wonderful charm in those words *in full of all demands*', she gave a hint to the modern researcher by qualifying her comment. 'I will own my taste is unfashionable', she admitted, and indeed if others concurred that 'the worst of haunted Houses … are those haunted by Duns', they certainly did not reflect

---

may be so bent, that the Tree may be well inclined. You was pruned indeed by an able Hand, but you tell us too plainly that your Uncle is not now with you.'

[8] *A Series of Letters between Mrs Elizabeth Carter and Miss Catherine Talbot, from the Year 1741 to 1770. To Which Are Added Letters from Mrs Elizabeth Carter to Mrs Vesey, between the Years 1763 and 1787; Published from the Original Manuscripts in the Possession of the Rev. Montagu Pennington, M.A. Vicar of Northbourn, in Kent, her Nephew and Executor*, ed. Montagu Pennington (4 vols.) (1809), III, 327, Mrs Carter to Mrs Vesey, 18 Jan. 1768.

[9] For more on this topic, see Rachel Stewart, 'The West End House *c.* 1765–*c.* 1785: Gamble and Forfeit', *Georgian Group Journal*, 13 (2002), 135–48, where some passages from this paper also appear.

it in their behaviour.[10] 'Executions' in town houses, through which creditors tried to recoup some of their losses by targeting the debtors' house and property, were a common topic in private correspondence and no doubt town gossip. Derby was said to have had four executions in one day at Derby House,[11] a report previously undiscovered or ignored by architectural historians, although an essential contributor to our understanding of the house's function in the dissolute peer's life.

People went to great lengths to disguise reasons for selling London houses and small wonder, as there is considerable evidence not only that people knew who was moving in or out of houses and often the sums for which they were bought and sold, but also that they freely drew their own conclusions. The duke of Manchester was rumoured to be retiring to the country and selling his house in town, and therefore supposed to be in financial distress. The duke did not care for such inferences: 'The Duke of Manchester will not now sell his house', reported Caroline Howe to Lady Spencer in 1767; 'they say he has changed his mind on hearing that everybody says he is undone'. This conclusion, erroneous or otherwise, joins other anecdotal evidence that the purchase or disposal of a town house was an indicator: on the one hand of wealth, ambition or good fortune; on the other of debt, failure or bad luck. We can note, too, in this example, how anecdote was used and abused at the time: another problem waiting to trip the researcher.

Men often cast women as the instigators of expenditure, and over-expenditure, on and in the London house, and directly responsible for moves to and within London. In 1767 Philip Francis supposed Mrs Chandler to be 'at the summit of her wishes' now that her husband had bought a house in Bruton Street, and Frederick Reynolds believed that it was his mother and aunt, 'like the compass, bent on a still farther variation to the westward', who had persuaded his father to forsake Salisbury Square for the new Adelphi.[12] The anecdotal evidence is rich in this respect, but it was not always wives who needed to be kept happy in a London house, or who were to blame for the consequent debt. In March 1778, Judith Milbanke reported that 'Lord Onslow had an Execution in his House last week for an hundred and sixty thousand pounds & is quite ruined.' Onslow allegedly tried to soften the blow to his wife, who 'knew nothing at all of his Debts', by explaining that the

[10] British Library, Montagu correspondence, Add. MS 40663, fol. 117, Elizabeth Montagu to Mrs Robinson, 9 July [1782].

[11] *The Noels and the Milbankes, their Letters for Twenty-Five Years, 1767–1792*, ed. Malcolm Elwin (1967), 103, 18 May 1778, Sophie Curzon to Mary Noel from London.

[12] *The Francis Letters, by Sir Philip Francis and Other Members of his Family*, ed. Beata Francis and Eliza Keary, with a note on the Junius controversy by C.F. Keary (2 vols.) (1901), I, 79, Philip Francis to Alexander Mackrabie, 5 Dec. 1767; *The Life and Times of Frederick Reynolds, Written by Himself* (2 vols.) (1826), I, 65.

latter were 'greatly owing to his having kept two or three Women whose expenses lay very hard on him'.[13] Again, the anecdotal evidence suggests that town houses were both the cause and the target of debt, a fact corroborated by the financial evidence, giving the historian the best of both worlds: a seductively good story, tinged with exaggeration, which nevertheless proves to hold much more than a grain of truth.

Blame for overspending on luxuries in town, including the house itself, may have been projected on to women to 'safeguard' the masculinity of men. Consumption has long been characterised as feminising, and women are certainly represented in the fictional and journalistic literature of this period as possessors of irrational desires, which lead them to drive the last remnants of consumer sanity from men's minds. But the anecdotal evidence balances its own implications of women's culpability by explaining, too, why women were so closely linked with town houses. The composite picture which we get from it reveals that both being in town, and the town house itself, were immensely important to many women, particularly elderly women and widows, seeking society, medical expertise and amusement. Caroline Howe, who spent most of her time in London, declared that she was 'never without a party of some sort or other', at least during the season.[14] Many women expressed a preference for town life either in words or action. In 1785 Judith Milbanke wrote to her aunt, Mary Noel:

> I only wish Mil [her husband] was as well satisfied with the country as I am ... certainly men have not half the resources to amuse themselves as we females. I do not carry the Joke so far as to say I prefer the Country, for to own the truth I should like to set out for the gay City tomorrow morning.[15]

Two years later her aunt was obliged to retire from London for financial reasons, but hoped by prudent living to return in a few years to 'go off at last in a blaze like a tallow candle wrapt up in brown paper'.[16] Although not all men appreciated the attractions of the country, these women, at least, certainly seem to have preferred the town.

Women often saw a town house as a means for themselves or other women to pass many leisured hours, particularly following the death of a husband. In 1759 Lady Hervey referred to her house in town as an 'amusement (for old people must not pretend to pleasures)' and busied herself in 'altering, fitting up, and completing [the] house, which

---

[13] *Noels and Milbankes*, ed. Elwin, 91, Judith Milbanke to Mary Noel, 3 Feb. 1778.
[14] British Library, Althorp papers, F 42, Caroline Howe to Lady Spencer, 29 Dec. [1772].
[15] *Noels and Milbankes*, ed. Elwin, 258, letter of 28 Jan. 1785.
[16] *Ibid.*, 317–18, Mary Noel to Judith Milbanke, 2 Feb. 1787.

[was] no small affair'.[17] Twenty years later Sarah Lennox pitied David Garrick's widow because not only had her *raison d'être* disappeared with the death of the actor and the loss of her role in his social life, but she had already done everything she could to her house: 'the *spirit* of her society is lost, and business she cannot have, for both her Houses in Town and Country are so compleat she has not a chair or table to amuse herself with attiring'.[18] Some widows found a London house, or the work done on it, therapeutic. The duchess of Ancaster was said to have made many alterations to her house in Berkeley Square, 'to take off from the melancholy Idea's it must naturally bring to her mind'.[19]

While alterations to their houses occupied and distracted many women, for Mrs Montagu the pleasure was in the finished house, or the anticipation of it, not in its construction.[20] Her new town-house project enabled her to satisfy her desire to be surrounded by pretty, tasteful things at this late point of her life. 'In so little while', she told her sister-in-law, 'I shall never see anything belonging to me that is not pretty, except when I behold myself in the looking glass.'[21] The splendid new house was not simply a machine for entertaining, therefore, and the evidence afforded by Mrs Montagu's letters warns against viewing the town house as solely, or perhaps even primarily, fulfilling that role. Anecdote can therefore be used to temper other sorts of evidence. Mrs Montagu thought her new house had taken years off her, 'from its chearfulness, and from its admirable conveniences and comforts', which made her less afraid of growing old. 'A good Winter habitation', she wrote in 1781, 'like a good friend is a comfort in all seasons and circumstances, and most particularly felt in bad seasons, bad health, bad spirits'; while the following year she declared a 'good House' to be 'a great comfort in old age and among the few real facilities that money will procure'.[22]

To what extent, however, can personal remarks relating to specific instances and circumstances be used to recreate a generic 'client perspective'? In this instance there is other anecdotal evidence that a

[17] *Letters of Mary Lepel, Lady Hervey with a Memoir, and Illustrative Notes* (1821), p. 261, Lady Hervey to Rev. Edmund Morris, 25 Sept. 1759.

[18] British Library, Holland House papers, Add. MS 51354, Sarah Lennox to Lady Susan O'Brien, 9 Mar. 1779.

[19] Badminton, Glos., Badminton muniments, FmK 1/3/20, letter no. 15, Lady Charlotte Finch to Dowager Duchess of Beaufort, n.d.

[20] See British Library, Montagu correspondence, Add. MS 40663, fol. 97, letter to Mrs Robinson, 19 Dec. [1779].

[21] British Library, Montagu correspondence, Add. MS 40663, fol. 104, Mrs Montagu to Mrs Robinson, 4 Dec. [1781].

[22] British Library, Montagu correspondence, Add. MS 40663, fol. 104, Mrs Montagu to Mrs Robinson, 1 Dec. [1781]; fol. 110, Mrs Montagu to Mrs Robinson, 17 Jan. [1782]; fol. 112, Mrs Montagu to Mrs Robinson, 2 Mar. 1782.

tastefully and comfortably furnished house, primed for city life, some-times superseded the inducements that persuaded or obliged people to take it in the first place, itself becoming the reason for being in town. For example, Lady Holland hoped that the duke of Leinster's 'pretty house in Arlington Street would tempt him to come to London' in 1768.[23]

Broader study of anecdotal evidence can therefore enlighten and reward the architectural historian. But there is another problem inherent in the anecdotal material itself. A shortcoming of any research that relies heavily on eighteenth-century family papers is that it tends, necessarily, to be limited to studies of the upper and perhaps upper-middle classes, whose papers have been preserved, archived and cata-logued, or published. In turn, this restriction limits the classes of house that can be studied, and findings derived from anecdotal evidence, and family papers generally, cannot therefore claim to be representative of anything beyond their own referents. Yet even though they cannot be generalised to other classes of person or house, such findings can broaden the range and detail of our understanding of attitudes towards architecture, provided that we acknowledge their limits.

Another bias often inherent in the material, as hinted earlier, is a gender bias. Anecdotal evidence draws attention to the diversity of players interested in a house, not just occupants, but visitors and other observers, but how far can we generalise from the comments of women, which dominate the sources? If the researcher relies on references to the London house in private papers, then women's letters, especially to other women, and their diaries, tend to reap greater and quicker rewards than do men's, for two reasons. First, women's correspondence in this period is almost exclusively private, even if it discusses public affairs, and concerns their own and others' domestic and personal concerns. On the other hand, although men had private cor-respondence, it is not always archived separately from their official correspondence, and even so is often as much concerned with public affairs as private. So, any given number of men's letters is unlikely to yield the same amount of pertinent information as the equivalent number of women's letters. This inherent bias in the sources makes the problem of generalising from the particular more acute – how representative are women's views and actions? Any insight into what men wanted from a home is often lacking altogether, or reported by women, which would not matter if we knew that attitudes to houses were not gender-specific, but makes it harder to establish if they were.

This predicament is part of the greater problem of defining and

---

[23] *Correspondence of Emily, Duchess of Leinster (1731–1814)*, ed. Brian Fitzgerald (3 vols.) (Dublin, 1949–57), I, 544, Lady Holland to duchess of Leinster, 6 Oct. [1768].

articulating the link between anecdote and architecture. Having stepped away from the built or visual evidence and created a context for it, it is often hard to return and point to any direct correspondence between text and object. We can tell what women wanted from a house, yet we do not see too easily how it translated into specific instructions for an architect, or into built form. The anecdotal evidence is often unrelated to an identified house, or to one whose form and finish have been recorded. With the exception, therefore, of a few cases where building, client and circumstances are all well documented, it serves best in reconstructing a range of motives and situations to enhance our understanding of behaviour and reasoning in respect of the town house in this period.[24]

Despite the 'pastime' element evident in some women's decoration of their houses, most architectural projects are a means to an end for a client, not an end in themselves. We take houses as interesting, or not, for the history of architecture, but perhaps thereby overlook their importance in the history of their occupants or their time. It is possible, with the help of anecdotal evidence, to view houses not just as entities in themselves, with their own histories, in which successive occupants were actors, but as functional objects in the histories of those occupants. The two approaches are not mutually exclusive, but complementary. Elizabeth Montagu's letters tell us little about the architecture and finish of her London homes, but plenty about her attitude towards them. Evidence not directly related to architecture provides information about the wider context in which the town house operated. It can humanise the built evidence, setting the house or house type in the broader context of people's ongoing lives, concerns and aspirations. The difficulty of making the direct link between anecdote and architecture is no excuse for leaving our stuffed fish isolated in his glass case.

[24] See Colin Campbell, 'Understanding Traditional and Modern Patterns of Consumption in Eighteenth-Century England: A Character-Action Approach', in *Consumption and the World of Goods*, ed. John Brewer and Roy Porter (1993), 40–57 (44) for an argument that, in the absence of any specific articulation of consumer motives, the researcher can use such sources as diaries, letters and autobiographies to plot a range of potential meanings.

Transactions of the RHS 13 (2003), pp. 329–43 © 2003 Royal Historical Society
DOI: 10.1017/S0080440103000192   Printed in the United Kingdom

HOUSES AS MUSEUMS: THE CASE OF THE YORKSHIRE WOOL TEXTILE INDUSTRY

By S.A. Caunce

ABSTRACT. Oakwell Hall, Birstall, Red House, Gomersal, and Bagshaw Museum, Batley, are three historic properties which lie at the heart of the old Yorkshire woollen manufacturing district, west of Leeds, where factory production emerged out of a dual economy that combined farming and making. Each effectively represents a key stage in that evolution. Here we examine how the real history of such houses, focusing especially on Red House, which epitomises the dynamic era when its owners helped build up domestic manufacturing to global success, could pay dividends in connecting people to the real social and economic history of their area.

Museum collections, by definition, are normally displayed and stored within buildings. Although rarely outstanding in architectural terms, these are often houses with their own histories, and Mark Girouard has showed how the study of country houses can make accessible many different approaches to understanding the past.[1] Other houses can be used just as effectively, but drawing attention to a building, its location and its outbuildings often in practice threatens its function as a simple container, wherein 'mobile' collections can be displayed and interpreted according to their own logic or the curator's perception of it. In a museum setting they are therefore often deliberately neutralised, instead of becoming the prime artefact in the collection. If promoted as historic houses, they are usually treated as part of an abstract architectural movement, or interpreted as symbols of an often ahistorical heritage unless they are truly outstanding.

For two centuries, moreover, scholarly history has relied upon documents to separate itself from myth-making and hero worship, but it is now sophisticated and self-confident enough to embrace a rapidly expanding range of sources, which should include material culture. With documents no longer generating the old certainty, confidence in our overall understanding of the distant past surely increases when

[1] M. Girouard, *Life in the English Country House: A Social and Architectural History* (New Haven and London, 1978).

different types of evidence support congruent analyses. Archaeologists have shown that eclectic approaches can produce results that even two decades ago would have seemed like fantasy. Most of these relate to new ways of investigating material remains, and they have shown how effectively past societies can be studied through museum collections. Natural historians depend heavily upon the examination and classification of specimens held in museums, and concern has been expressed that current neglect of collections will be disastrous for science. Such collections dominate the related study of the fossil past, and a leading geologist once remarked, 'the best geologist is the one who has seen most rocks!', so here again they are essential, just as art galleries are for art historians.[2]

Unfortunately, social and economic historians often see history museums and historic buildings as the natural terrain of antiquarians, and now perceive added threats from the booming heritage industry, where evidence-based truthfulness gives way to telling simple, popular stories. Since expertise in linking evidence from material culture to analytical history is lacking, works of mainstream history rarely cite a museum or a collection among their sources, even in such object-oriented subjects as technology. A self-reinforcing cycle of mutual incomprehension and missed opportunities thus seems to exist between academics and those who manage historic houses. However, successful television programmes like *House Detectives* show that non-academic people can enjoy fact-based approaches to buildings, even when long-standing beliefs are challenged. Museums and historians could similarly come together without making museums into daunting temples of esoteric knowledge or threatening critical standards. Historians would thereby communicate with a wider audience, including many not actively searching for real history. The elucidation of the potential of houses, their surroundings and their place in the landscape and community, would be an ideal vehicle for starting this process, and conflicts between this potential and their role as functional buildings must be overcome. This paper deals with a case study of three historic properties all now operated by Kirklees Metropolitan Council, based in Huddersfield and separated by only a few miles. It is drawn from my time as a museum curator in West Yorkshire, and illustrates both the difficulties and potential of this approach.

Red House Museum, Gomersal, is the main focus. A twelve-roomed, apparently Georgian house, it was originally purchased and opened to the public because of associations with Charlotte Bronte and her novel *Shirley*.[3] Oakwell Hall, Birstall, is a more architecturally

---

[2] Quoted in E. H. Shackleton, *Lakeland Geology* (Clapham, Yorkshire, 1973), 9.
[3] C. Bronte, *Shirley* (1842).

striking, stone gabled house dating from 1598, located a mile away, which has lesser Bronte links. Bagshaw Museum, Batley, is about two miles from both, but was never seen as having anything in common with them. It is based in The Woodlands, a classic Victorian gothic manufacturer's house built in 1876 by George Sheard, a local industrialist. None was particularly well visited or convincing as educational institutions before Kirklees assumed responsibility for them all in 1974 during local government reorganisation. Significant resources were committed to improve the dilapidated interiors and displays, but the tension between their possibilities as historic houses and as museums was always present, and questions were asked as to why they were open as museums at all, given continuing low attendances. Oakwell Hall's potential was transformed when the colliery that stood on its front doorstep was closed and cleared away, and the site was transformed into a country park, but this denied the fundamentally industrial character of the area and overshadowed the other two.

Fitting them into a wider museum service, while promoting a truly local, accurate and meaningful history within them, was the goal, but personnel changes led to sudden changes in direction. A general lack of historical insight among both those who took the real decisions and the local public made this a largely heritage-driven, often opportunistic exercise. Local particularism complicated matters, for Kirklees is an uneasy and unnatural amalgamation of fiercely independent and mutually suspicious towns. The name Kirklees, for instance, derives from a locality outside the council's boundaries, since baffling all residents was preferred to offending many of them by implying the dominance of any one town. It does include, however, a substantial part of the area devoted from the eighteenth century to the production of woollen, as opposed to worsted, yarn and cloth, and almost all the events in Yorkshire Luddism occurred within it. The immediate area around the houses experienced a disproportionate share of the dramatic events which still grip people's imagination, and Charlotte Bronte had explicitly incorporated Red House and Oakwell into *Shirley* for this reason.

The question is, can the houses contribute significantly as houses and sites to understanding the past of this distinctive place, and to conveying some aspects of it to the people of today who live there? It is now recognised that modern manufacturing, especially in Britain, began in rural areas like this, not towns, and we need to understand the real dynamics of economic systems which combined living, farming and manufacturing on one site. The proto-industrial model claimed to do this in the 1970s and 80s, but those who examine the key manufacturing districts of northern England directly rather than through the lens of theory have never accepted its accuracy.[4] It actually describes best those areas that began to develop, but then stalled, or even de-industrialised. Now, both Oakwell Hall and Red House lay within the early modern township of Gomersal, one of eight which constituted the typically large Pennine parish of Birstall. Birstall was a dynamic part of the woollen industry that as late as 1806 consisted of a mass of self-consciously independent producers and merchants.

Ingenious research has given insight into how the domestic system worked, especially surveys by Dickenson and Gregory, and Hudson's illuminating analysis of business methods.[5] However, family enterprises answerable to no one but themselves created few business records, and historians have exaggerated by default the contribution of those few who did leave something behind.[6] However, a surprising percentage of both the landscape and physical infrastructure survives from pre-industrial times, because the hilly terrain encouraged periodic fresh starts rather than a constant redevelopment of key sites, and possession of land and buildings did give typical family enterprises an incentive to preserve documents relating to them. Books like those produced for the Royal Commission on Historical Monuments and Thornes's survey of West Yorkshire's industrial archaeology have demonstrated how rich the potential of this approach is, yet they produced few significant effects.[7] These three houses actually symbolise three stages in a very distinctive and globally important historical development path for the woollen industry, which laid down the foundations on which worsted and cotton built, and also remained a vital part of British indus-trialisation. Oakwell Hall was the head of the sprawling medieval manor of Gomersal. Red House was the home of the Taylor family, who made and traded cloth.[8] The Woodlands is a relic of the factory system that eventually replaced domestic manufacturing.

---

[4] Thus, A. Randall, *Before the Luddites: Custom, Community and Machinery in the Woollen Industry, 1776–1809* (Cambridge, 1991), 7 and 22–3; and P. Hudson, *Genesis of Industrial Capital: A Study of the West Riding Wool Textile Industry, c. 1725–1850* (Cambridge, 1986), ch. 3, both argue against the case made in F. Mendels, 'Proto-industrialization: The First Phase of the Industrialization Process', *Journal of Economic History*, 32 (1972), 241–61.

[5] M.J. Dickenson, 'The West Riding Worsted and Woollen Industries, 1679–1770: An Analysis of Probate Inventories and Insurance Policies' (PhD thesis, University of Nottingham, 1974); D. Gregory, *Regional Transformation and Industrial Revolution: A Geography of the Yorkshire Woollen Industry* (1982); Hudson, *Genesis*.

[6] R.G. Wilson, *Gentlemen Merchants: The Merchant Community in Leeds, 1770–1830* (Manchester, 1971); J. Smail, *The Origins of Middle Class Culture: Halifax, Yorkshire, 1660–1780* (Ithaca, 1985), see especially ch. 3.

[7] Royal Commission on Historical Monuments of England, *Rural Houses of West Yorkshire* (HMSO, 1986), and R. Thornes, *West Yorkshire: A Noble Scene of Industry*, West Yorkshire Archaeology Service (Wakefield, 1981).

[8] *The Minutes of Evidence Taken before the Select Committee Appointed to Consider the State of the Woollen Manufacture*, Parliamentary Papers 1806, Vol. 3, pp. 378–83.

Rural industry evolved out of an earlier socio-economic system, and Oakwell Hall and its site illuminate this process. The manor of Gomersal, typically for the Pennines, covered several townships, one of which was named Gomersal.[9] Good arable land, with only a scanty population, lay only a few miles away, beyond Leeds, whereas corn could only be grown in small pockets hereabouts. Settlement, farming and rents all inevitably reflected this, and Gomersal township included three separate townfields associated with hamlets at Birstall (a subsidiary hamlet despite giving its name to the parish), at Great Gomersal (where Red House is located) and at Little Gomersal (another subsidiary hamlet). In between lay pasture, moorland and some long-established, self-contained farmsteads. Manorialism had depended on tenant farmers paying rents and providing labour, thereby enabling lords to support a superior lifestyle. Medieval rent rolls of Pennine manors were inevitably low despite their size, and they usually were combined with others to produce adequate lordly incomes, leading to absenteeism. Archaeology suggests that from the thirteenth century Oakwell declined to become a neglected outstation, without even a house fit for a steward between *c.* 1400 and 1583.

The confusing, sometimes chaotic, institutional and practical landscape around Oakwell was typical of the textile area, where most people were without ready access to churches, or habituation to deferential attitudes to resident social superiors, and this probably helped create the conditions suited to domestic manufacturing.[10] Yet the manor of Gomersal had mineral resources, for another hamlet was Birstall Smithies, an early centre of coal mining and metal working as its name suggests. Also, it was not really isolated, for the medieval track of the ancient, strategic route from York to Chester passed through it. This made manufacturing for sale a possibility, and since early taxation lists show local people rated almost universally on the lowest level of incomes, they had little reason to idealise a peasant way of life. In nearby Halifax parish, on rougher land, the local historian Watson commented in 1775 that he did not believe a single family then lived entirely by farming.[11] Thus, a new type of tenant emerged, involved in textiles and desiring a modest holding simply as a base for business operations and as insurance against hard times. Absentee lords encouraged such men by making small farms available to them to increase the total rent roll, and milking their right to provide and charge

[9] G. and N. Cookson, *Gomersal: A Window on the Past*, Kirklees Cultural Services (Huddersfield, 1992), is a thorough, rounded and impeccably evidence-based history of the township. See ch. 2 for the manor of Gomersal.

[10] S. Caunce, 'Complexity, Community Structure, and Competitive Advantage within the West Yorkshire Woollen Industry', *Business History*, 39 (1997), 26–43.

[11] J. Watson, *The History and Antiquities of the Parish of Halifax* (1775), 8–9.

for the fulling mills that were an essential part of making woollen cloth.

Thus, whereas the proto-industrial model of the origins of manufacturing assumed that it was overcrowding and poverty that forced reluctant peasants into becoming weavers, here population growth followed the new order, which really made people's lives better in the long term, and the houses from the past testify to this. Proto-industrialisation also assumes the dominance of town-based merchants who wished to overthrow the old order. The Yorkshire system in contrast invigorated agrarian life, and the privileged classes profited from joining in rather than resisting.[12] There was a general upwelling of initiative, with the tiny market centres that existed, especially Leeds, becoming co-ordinating centres. Merchants competed with each other, and evidence suggests that they preferred to take no responsibility for manufacturing, since the costs of it then fell upon the clothiers. Some merchants, including the Taylors, resided in manufacturing communities and identified with them.

This process might have been threatened in Gomersal in the late sixteenth century when the Batt family bought the manor. Henry Batt built, probably in 1583, the first version of the venerable, mullioned and partly timbered Oakwell Hall that we see today, and thus re-constituted the manor as a single, if large, administrative unit with a resident lord at its heart.[13] The Batts were rising local lawyers with a poor reputation for honesty, and their building of the hall consciously presented them as nascent gentry, rather than engaging in conflict with that class. They could not afford simply to play the squire, however, for they had fewer resources than the nearby Armytages of Clifton and the Tempests of Tong, who both did keep manufacturing out of their domains. The Batts stood or fell by the commercial success of their investment in Gomersal manor. They needed to share in the prosperity that manufacturing was bringing, not to stifle it. There even seems to have been a willingness to sell off parts of the manor, and the Taylors were among many who became freeholders as a result.

The Batt's first version of Oakwell Hall lasted only a short time, for it was substantially altered shortly after 1611 in an apparently retrograde conversion from two storeys throughout into a central, open hall, almost surrounded by a gallery, connecting two-storeyed wings. This must have embodied a conscious decision to reinforce the attempt to obliterate the Batts's origins, further demonstrating their desire to join the old order, on their own terms, rather than to destroy it. We cannot know

[12] S. Caunce, 'Communities in Economic Development: Lessons From the Past', in *Community Economic Development*, ed. G. Haughton (Regional Studies Association, 1999).
[13] Cookson, *Gomersal*, 13–14.

if they would ultimately have been successful because their finances were destroyed by their royalist sympathies in a fiercely parliamentarian area in the Civil War, and the manor entered a cycle of neglect and sale soon after the Restoration. By 1750 the manor as a meaningful unit was in terminal decline, though residual rights would still be valuable a century later. So completely did it disintegrate that the actual boundaries are now very unclear, but manufacturing flourished within them.

That brings us to Red House and its part in the rising domestic textile industry. Richard Taylor bought a house with a garden, a croft and other lands in Great Gomersal sometime in the mid-sixteenth century. It is unlikely the family were natives, so they may have moved precisely to further trading and manufacturing instincts. In any event, in 1577 more land was purchased by his son Thomas, a chapman or minor merchant, thereby creating an agricultural holding running up the western slope of the Gomersal ridge, over its crest, which is almost 500 feet above sea level, and down the other side. It is striking how tenaciously the Taylors clung to this stem holding, though many other plots of land passed through their hands. Though split several times in wills, it was always reunited in the next generation, and it was farmed at least to the mid-nineteenth century, long after any economic need to do so had ceased.

The death of William Taylor, who called himself a yeoman, in January 1688/9 creates a window into the family's situation as they prospered, for his will and inventory survive.[14] Two south-facing houses are described, one old and the other described as new. The latter, which is credibly attributed within the family to a construction date of 1660, formed the basis of the present Red House despite many alterations. Together they created one long building running away from a lane parallel to and below the crest of the ridge. Now the A651 from Heckmondwike to Bradford, it then gave access to fields and moorland to the north, but to the south it connected to the York to Chester highway mentioned earlier, just a quarter of a mile away. The paradox of apparent isolation co-existing with real access to the outside world is thus clear at Red House in the seventeenth century.

The inventory relates to the old house, which centred around a traditional housebody with a chamber above it and also three parlours (two with beds in) and a buttery. Clothmaking gear was scattered round the house, and a range for coal fires reflected the ready availability of this fuel. The 'house chamber' contained:

[14] Documents relating to the Taylor family are held by the Yorkshire Archaeological Society (hereafter YAS), MD292 and MD311, and the West Yorkshire Archive Service, KC52 and KX100–49. This is from YAS MD311/11. Copies of some are held at Red House. The most complete study of the family is M. Ferrett, *The Taylors of the Red House*, Kirklees Cultural Services (Huddersfield, 1987).

One bed and bedding	1 − 0 − 0
one chest	2 − 0
one hustlement	10 − 0
Item Oats wheat barleys beanes	8 − 10 − 0
Item hay	3 − 0 − 0
Loome and materiall belonging	2 − 10 − 0

This bed was of reasonable quality, even though it was the least valuable of the four in the house, and the presence of the hustlement to give privacy and protection from draughts suggests it was in use, so here we see domestic arrangements, the varied produce of the land and the manufacture of cloth, all in intimate contact. Two spinning wheels were in the little parlour, along with furniture appropriate to a yeoman existence. Three bibles were listed, but no other books. Outside there was a tenter (a frame for stretching cloth while it dried) as well as farm equipment, while a little horse suited to a clothier's needs was valued alongside four cattle. Two fine cloths and two of middling quality were appraised at £20 collectively. Total assets of £78.1.0d, plus a £7 debt owing, show a clothier several steps up from the typical hand-to-mouth man dependent on selling one cloth to buy the materials to make another. However, the family had not distanced itself from manual work, there is nothing to suggest trading on a grand scale, and nothing in the furniture or equipment suggests a man concerned with the cultural norms of anywhere but his place of birth.

In 1713 a second inventory was made on the death of William's second son John, who inherited the business, and this shows us both the layout of the new house and apparent changes in attitudes. The estate was now valued at £181.10.6d, or £170.16s if debts are deducted. Only one loom was listed, almost certainly outside the house, with a coarse cloth being woven on it, but several pairs of gears suggest the presence of other looms somewhere. Equipment and stores were now kept either in the old house or in outbuildings scattered around a foldstead, a cross between a true farmyard and a clothworking complex. The old house apparently had its own foldstead, and was inhabited by another branch of the family. Two barns are recorded, a 'swinecote' or pigsty, workshops, and a newly erected outkitchen whose ground floor was used for brewing beer for the household, while on the first floor fourteen finished cloths were stored with sundry equipment. An old and a new cloth finishing shop provided substantial facilities for shearing and pressing. At the top of the foldstead was a 'little house' or toilet, and beyond, in its own garth or enclosure, was the draw well, a very large and deep affair which was rediscovered in 1983. A reliable source of clean water was essential to a business like this, and Gomersal's location above a natural sandstone aquifer was ideal for this purpose.

The emphasis on finishing indicates merchant status, since ordinary clothiers never undertook it. The types of cloth listed, and the lack of dyeing equipment, suggest that the Taylors traded white broadcloth at the new Leeds White Cloth Hall, a typical activity for the area.

Beyond the well was a croft, probably a vegetable garden and orchard, and then came three long thin fields in a line. The first formed a tentercroft, and so would have been covered with fencelike frames, indicating that clothiers used land for non-agricultural purposes. They all seem to have been arable land that had formed several strips on the extreme southern edge of the former Gomersal townfield, which would explain their odd shape.[15] Much of this field remains in agricultural use today. Moreover, the deeds recording the fields' acquisition mention that they were 'to be holden of the Chief lordes of the ffee thereof by services therefore due and of right accustomyd', demonstrating the dismemberment of the old manorial structures to make way for a newer economy, but also the lack of a clean break.[16] Gomersal's townfield apparently disappeared rapidly as clothmaking succeeded, leaving clothiers free to allocate their time as they saw fit. The Taylor's livestock list only includes one sheep, confirming, along with one or two other records, that wool was bought in from east Yorkshire and Lincolnshire. Sheep suited to this part of the Pennines had fleeces too coarse to make saleable cloth, and this has always really been cattle country. They also had a range of farm gear, from wains to a plough. This, along with the storage of grain in the house, confirms a serious commitment to arable since the practice of graving, or digging fields with a spade and a mattock, survived well into the nineteenth century locally.

The new house, where John lived and died, is itself a symbol and a record of their rising status, and the attitudes that went with it. All local houses had been timbered, new ones were now stone-built, but Red House was made of bricks (the name was apparently coined only in the 1880s, but it has been used throughout here for convenience). There is brick earth nearby, and the variable colour and texture of the bricks in the oldest surviving walls suggest local manufacture. A handful of other relatively early brick buildings exist nearby, and the inspiration for them all probably lies in the area's mercantile links with Leeds and lowland Yorkshire.[17] The bond is completely irregular on the surviving old walls, which were an archaic brick and a half thick (fourteen inches),

---

[15] Cookson, *Gomersal*, ch. 5, see esp. map on p. 61. This developed initial research into the field patterns done by myself while curator at Red House in the 1980s.

[16] YAS MD 311/21.

[17] Thus, an acquitance dated 14 June 1596 acknowledges the cancellation of a debt owed to Richard Birkehead, a husbandman of Knedlyngton in the East Riding of Yorkshire, by James Taylor. YAS MD 311.

with quoins at those corners that survive. The utterly plain appearance (lacking even a string course) and uncertain constructional use of the new material indicate an inexperienced local builder, though bricks were generally used in chimney stacks.[18] The present east wall seems older than the rest, so it may reflect the original appearance of the whole house. Its windows have stone surrounds, a feature seen in another local house built in 1690. The internal walls are mostly as strong as the external ones, something that would prove significant later. At the rear, a very small cellar (well away from the site of the old house) is entered through a trap door, and may predate the house as it extends beyond the present boundary. It has stone walls, while another cellar in front of it has the remains of a mullioned window of a crude type consistent with a date of 1660. No definitive explanation of these features is possible.

Mostly, Red House remained part of local tradition, with three gables each fronting a double-pile cell.[19] The single-storey housebody was furnished predictably, and cooking equipment stood around a coal-burning range. A 'pewter dresser' with drawers held eighteen dishes and twelve plates, and there was a milk house and buttery which, in typical Yorkshire fashion, contained linen, silver plate and the eating utensils, including wooden trenchers, as well as dairy utensils. There was, however, a dining room where the family could opt out of life in the housebody, which cannot have been large. The north parlour was the only room besides the housebody to have a fireplace, and with a mirror and a china cabinet it had some pretensions despite containing two beds. The house had two other mirrors, and a carpet in one chamber. Most chambers contained beds but little else, apart from chests and such workaday items as kneading troughs and a meal ark, with meal in.

The Taylors were thus both steadily prospering and wealthier than average for the area, but still far from gentry status. They seem to have valued education and had a strong religious bent, for on at least two occasions the eldest son actually went into the church, including John's elder brother James. A picture of a genuinely mixed economy emerges, which supported quite a colony of people on the evidence of the ten beds scattered round the new house in 1713. The majority were probably used by more than one person, so John's wife and seven children were

---

[18] There were brickworks in Gomersal in the nineteenth century, one of which the Taylors had an interest in, and two fields the Taylors owned at Hunsworth were called the Upper and Lower Sinderhills in 1840, often a sign of previous brickmaking. On the bricklaying, see R. Brunskill and A. Clifton-Taylor, *English Brickwork* (1977).

[19] M.W. Barley, *The English Farmhouse and Cottage* (Stroud, 1987), describes this as the archetypal local style. See also E. Mercer, *English Vernacular Houses*, Royal Commission on Historical Manuscripts (1975).

presumably complemented by several servants and apprentices, and this was something farming alone could never have achieved. There is evidence of intermittent attempts to operate the holding on some form of joint basis, with the core holding split by a will and arrangements made for amicable operations. Thus, John's will shows that there was a communicating door in 1713 between the two houses, and he specified which house should have the use of a parlour on one side of it.[20]

Among John's large family were two sons, and again the younger, Joshua, carried on the family business, to such effect that he seems to have demolished the old house, and this seems to mark a conscious transition to merchant status. The front of the new house was also removed except for its eastern corner, an operation made possible by the cellular construction. A symmetrical façade with five windows upstairs, and four and a central door downstairs, replaced it, though still with extraordinarily plain brickwork of the old thickness. Sash windows may have been installed. The ridge poles of the gables were cut back and a continuous, front-facing slope of slates leaned against them as if there was a hipped roof. This new fashionable front contrasted sharply with the traditional, gabled rear, where the construction of a new cell as an extension of the new house over part of the old site added an extra gable. The house as we see it today was largely created in this exercise.

Inside, the housebody vanished and the central cell became an imposing but small and unheated entrance hall, and a gallery at first floor level showed the same desire as at Oakwell Hall to impress visitors. What must have been a milk-house, with a built-in stone table at its centre, remained however, cut out from the rear of the hall. In the western parlour, a symmetrical central fireplace flanked by alcoves showed a concern for fashion, and the room was heightened at the expense of the bedroom above. The new extension allowed two connected service rooms to be isolated at the rear, including a separate kitchen. Yet outside the front door still lay the yard of a working establishment, and remains of dye vats quite near the house which may date from this time have been discovered. Dyeing was a noxious process and this confirms that visitors would have been in no doubt that this family earned its living.

Both the separation between life and work and the commitment to Red House deepened as the family's status rose, despite the tensions this created. Another John Taylor and his son, another Joshua, were both astute, thrusting and successful business men who maintained the family's reputation for individuality. John erected a large new mill

---

[20] Will of John Taylor, copy held by Kirklees Archives, Huddersfield, and Red House.

complex around 1785 a mile away at Hunsworth, the nearest available site with water power. This was emphatically not a factory, but a fulling mill open to all for the payment of a standard fee now the manorial monopoly had been broken. It was gradually extended as new machinery was invented, but always for the use of clothiers, thus keeping the domestic system on which the Taylors' livelihood depended dynamic and competitive.[21] Cloth finishing mostly seems to have moved to Hunsworth, and a small coal mine was sunk to provide fuel for the steam engine installed there soon after they became available.[22] However, a large barn, described as 'lately erected' in 1773, appeared at the top of Red House's grounds, combining a cow house and stable on the ground floor in typical local style with a cloth inspection and packing area upstairs, while various mortgages still show the existence of a smoothing shop, a warehouse, a pressing shop and a drying house. John also built his own, very small and plain dissenting chapel close to the house.

Joshua spoke Italian and French, and had paintings and books from Europe in the house, and yet preferred to speak broad Yorkshire. He despised the gentry and the church of England, but had a strong commitment to community. He lived through the Luddite disturbances, but does not seem to have been actively involved except that Charlotte Bronte, the friend of his daughter, was so impressed by the Taylors that she made the whole family, renamed, symbolically, the Yorkes, central to her version in *Shirley*. This is why we know so much about Joshua, his wife and children, and the house itself is clearly described. Her version of the great Luddite attack on Rawfolds Mill, actually about a mile south of Red House, was set at Hunsworth since she knew it well. Joshua stood at the heart of an extensive manufacturing network of domestic production of standard heavy woollen cloth and by 1826 his estate, including all realisable assets, was worth an estimated £30,000. His counting house, also the office of a bank that the family had run for a quarter of a century, was probably in the warehouse. A vault underneath served as a safe, and it has also been rediscovered. The close connection between trade and the land thus persisted as the family became more mercantile than manufacturing in orientation. Weaving seems to have ended, though nearby Broadyards, a house and outbuildings erected by yet another John Taylor in the early nineteenth

---

[21] S. Caunce, 'Not Sprung from Princes: The Nature of Middling Society in Eighteenth-century West Yorkshire', in *The Making of the British Middle Class? Studies in Regional and Cultural History since 1750*, ed. D. Nicholls (Stroud, 1998), 244–5 and 247.

[22] This figure should not be taken literally, but indicates that the family were acknowledged to be wealthy by local standards. George Rae, in his authoritative contemporary manual, *The Country Banker*, 9th edn (1902), 6–9, states that such figures are usually exaggerated.

century, had a small purpose-built weaving shop which employed twelve hands in 1851.

By the mid-century, however, the family was in decline. The bank collapsed during the financial storm of 1825–6, and though Joshua's creditors told him to continue trading and so pay them back gradually, the business was never the same again. The domestic system was becoming a backwater and the factories seem to have been started by a different type of individual. Hunsworth became a dye-works, and was allowed to get completely out-dated. The Taylors inherited and were able to use a spurious title of 'lords of the manor of Great Gomersal', supported the Conservative party and aped the gentry, and in this they were again typical of their class as the nineteenth century progressed. No real physical changes occurred at Red House, but farming ended and the foldsteads became an ornamental garden, which is how visitors see it today. A cartshed with open-fronted bays replaced the warehouse at some date, removing most of the remaining connections with the cloth trade at Red House. By 1893 an almost free-standing, stone-built mock-gothic tower had been added to the east end, for no clear reason. Dr Richard Waring Taylor became the last of the family to reside and work at Red House, as a doctor, since he sold the whole property in 1920, ending Taylor connections with Gomersal. Two years later, both the sitting and dining rooms were extended, with extremely large windows inserted in the new end walls. The final stages in development and change have come under public ownership, when various minor internal adaptations have been made, unmade and remade, including the recent rebuilding of the back wall to stop it collapsing, perhaps under the strain of so many visitors' feet. Thus, the house we see when we visit Red House Museum has changed and developed continuously since its first erection, and to try to point to any one phase as definitive is both impossible and misleading. In this, it reflects the dynamic nature of the family that built and altered it, and the sense of change made clear to visitors.

This brings us to The Woodlands, the house that sprang from the factory system. Batley was the last of the woollen towns to cohere and industrialise, because its poor water supply prevented powered operations until steam power became practical.[23] It became a very poor, heavily polluted town reliant on the shoddy trade, which recycled worn out wool garments for mixing with fresh wool for spinning. The Woodlands was quite unlike Oakwell Hall and Red House since there was no human history at all to the site, and there was no hint of a connection with industry except through any planning and paperwork

[23] The rocks of the area form aquifers that absorb much of the rainfall, making wells like those at Red House very reliable, but militating against stream formation.

that Sheard, a woollen manufacturer of a very different type from the Taylors, may have done at home. Although only a mile from the centre of the town, the site was so isolated that he cut himself off from his work. Its mock-gothic design owes nothing to vernacular styling, while its internal layout and decoration show aspirations to an approved middle-class lifestyle whose basics were determined in the metropolitan south. However, the style was so prevalent locally that it effectively became a quasi-vernacular for his class, and here the owner apparently made his own interpretation rather than relying on architects and interior designers. After Sheard's death it was sold at auction for £5 in 1902 to Batley Council, who wanted to add the grounds to a new public park. No one else would buy it. Another wealthy local manufacturer, Walter Bagshaw, decided to turn it into a miniature British Museum for the town at his own expense, and it opened as such in 1909. It has suffered most from the clash between its inherent nature and its new functions.

It could be presented as a symbol of the success of local capitalism, where the millowner took the place of the squire as the wealthy leader of local society, drawing his income from the labour of others if not from agricultural rents. However, if that is accurate, it was a partial, short-lived victory, and many of the comparisons implicit within it are actually superficial and misleading. Sheard was certainly not the master of the local community, and while his elite lasted longer than his house, it was not by much, for Batley today is not run by their descendants, and textiles have almost vanished. A lord of the manor apparently had no choice but to draw his rents and dues from a fixed area, but the essence of real capitalism is that money can be transferred anywhere and to any activity. In practice Oakwell's lords had not been resident until the Batts, and they mostly encouraged change. Sheard could indeed be seen as one of the last of the clothiers, still operating within an industry he did not and could not influence much, dependent on merchants for his connections with global markets. However, his house does show a very different attitude to community from that of the Taylors. Trying to show how complex history is is a worthy goal, and a house like this provides a chance to do so.

Over the past two decades these three houses have been displayed much more sensitively, and linked more firmly to their own pasts than ever before, which have been progressively recovered through a combination of work by staff and outsiders. At Red House, this has the added dimension of cutting back the sense that Charlotte Bronte's limited connection with the house was more important than anything the Taylors did themselves, without giving up the power of the Bronte connection to draw people. The opening up of the outbuildings as exhibition space has been a great success, and publications by Ferrett and the Cooksons have made Gomersal's real past accessible as never before. Yet more could still be done within the museum to relate the house itself to the family, and to show that it dates from many periods, all of which it still reflects. The actual presentation of the house as a pocket country house still subliminally contradicts the messages about the Taylor family business, and belies the facts of the majority of the family's existence. Similarly, Oakwell is largely allowed to function simply as one of the many stone-built seventeenth-century houses of that part of the Pennines rather than given its real context. The Woodlands has spent much of its time as a museum covered up internally so as not to draw attention away from very conventional displays, though in recent years more has been done to make it visible in its own right to visitors. All of them, and the landscape of which they are part, have much to offer the researcher in search of real understanding of a key period, as this essay demonstrates.

In this special case there is the additional dimension that linking them together can create, for many opportunities are lost when they are presented as three separate houses. This is not meant to be combative, for until recently the history that would have justified this approach was unknown. It is now available, however, and visitors are much more used to looking at historic properties. All houses are artefacts, products and mirrors of circumstances as well as aesthetics, and parts of human landscapes which are complex and interconnected. Bringing this out adds extra dimensions to most museums which possess such assets. When the available documents, and *Shirley*, are used in conjunction with this physical record, instead of considered separately, the houses acquire a status they could never have otherwise. The landscape surrounding these three is full of fossil elements but is not fossilised, and it certainly played a key part in developing my own understanding of the way the woollen industry really worked. Properly presented and understood, these houses and this landscape, in conjunction with other local places representative of the transition from domestic to factory production, have serious claims to world heritage site status, if that is not dependent upon size, grandeur and the obvious.

Transactions of the RHS 13 (2003), pp. 345–57 © 2003 Royal Historical Society
DOI: 10.1017/S0080440103000204   Printed in the United Kingdom

THE POLITICS OF COLLECTING:
THE EARLY ASPIRATIONS OF THE NATIONAL
TRUST, 1883–1913

By Melanie Hall

ABSTRACT. The early National Trust reflected current concerns about national identies. Small-scale buildings, acquired 1895–1910, demonstrate a desire to monumentalise English political, religious (Anglican) and literary traditions for English-speaking peoples at home and abroad, particularly in America. Its active, though overlooked, founders include Liberal politicians such as James Bryce (Britain's ambassador to Washington). Its buildings had antiquarian appeal but seeing them only in terms of their architectural history or regional characteristics overlooks conscious attempts to use architecture as historical evidence for a vision of an English life and social order, as both that order at home and England's status abroad altered.

The Trust appeals for its support not only to all lovers of their country, but also to those who, by race or language are brought up in English traditions, or to whom the historic associations of England are dear. It is hoped the work of the Trust will find support among the English-speaking people throughout the whole world; that the many who look to England as the parent of their own institutions will take the opportunity of helping to preserve her many charms for the enjoyment of the entire race.[1]

As Charles Robert Ashbee, an exponent of the Arts and Crafts movement and an active member of the National Trust's Council, prepared for a fund-raising publicity trip to America in October 1900, he considered 'The Aims and Work of the Trust'. For Ashbee and his fellow Council members, one of the primary aims was to help cement a union of English-speaking people that rested on sentiment, rather than upon material interest, on common social, political and religious traditions, on historical memories and on English literature. Such ideas about Englishness and Empire had held a strong attraction for English

[1] 'The National Trust, Its Aims and Work', quoted in C.R. Ashbee, Journal, 181, Oct. 1900. Ashbee Papers, King's College, Cambridge. All items from the Ashbee Journal quoted with the kind permission of Felicity Asbee.

middle-class Liberal intellectuals for several decades. Cambridge historian J.R. Seeley described the Empire as 'a vast English nation', in his influential *Expansion of England*, which appeared in 1883 and was reprinted numerous times. He predicted that once distance was diminished by science, ' "Greater Britain" would become a reality and would "belong to the stronger class of political unions".'[2] Such ideas form a significant, but overlooked – or even suppressed – strand of thinking underpinning the formation of the National Trust for Places of Historic Interest and Natural Beauty (hereafter the National Trust or the Trust), and the buildings which it acquired between its founding in 1895 and 1910, while its founders were still active, reflect this desire to monumentalise English political, religious and literary traditions. Although these buildings undoubtedly had antiquarian appeal, to see them only in terms of their architectural history or regional characteristics, as has hitherto been the case, is to overlook the National Trust's conscious use of architecture as historical evidence for its vision of English life and social order in its attempt to engage the sentiment of English-speaking people as both that social order at home and England's status abroad altered.

The National Trust has become, in David Cannadine's words, 'the most important and successful voluntary society in modern Britain'.[3] Arguably, it is the most successful voluntarist preservation organisation anywhere. Its membership is over 2 million. It is the second largest landholder in the country, with some 600,000 acres. It owns over 200 historic houses, ranging from country houses to a workhouse; at least 60 villages and hamlets; over 8,000 paintings, a significant collection of decorative art and more than one million books. Its history and collection deserves to be better understood, along with its approach to collecting and interpretation of its architectural holdings. Nevertheless, as Cannadine points out in his essay for the volume commissioned by the Trust for its centenary celebrations, the organisation has been little considered by anyone outside its own employ.[4] Cannadine provided 'a brief survey of a very broad subject', and 'a preliminary attempt to locate the Trust in the broader context of modern British history, in the hope of illuminating both subjects'.[5] The Trust's early years are

[2] J.R. Seeley, *The Expansion of England* (1883), 75. Similar ideas were expressed at the University of Oxford; see, for example, W.M. Ramsay, 'The Imperial Peace', Romanes Lecture, 1913, *Oxford Lectures on History, 1904–1923* (Freeport, New York, 1969), 1–28.

[3] David Cannadine, 'The First Hundred Years', in *The National Trust: The Next Hundred Years*, ed. Howard Newby (1995), 11–31.

[4] R. Fedden, *The Continuing Purpose: A History of the National Trust, its Aims and Work* (1968); J. Gaze, *Figures in a Landscape* (1988); Merlin Waterson, *The National Trust: The First Hundred Years* (1994); Graham Murphy, *Founders of the National Trust* (1987); Jennifer Jenkins and Patrick James, *From Acorn to Oak Tree: The Growth of the National Trust 1895–1994* (1994).

[5] Cannadine, 'The First Hundred Years', 11 and 27.

usually seen in terms of its land holdings, rather than its buildings, and three principal founders, rather than its founding Council. Its founding triumvirate has been accepted as Octavia Hill, the noted housing reformer; Sir Robert Hunter, honorary solicitor to the Commons Preservation Society (founded in 1865 and dedicated to saving common land from enclosure) and Solicitor to the Post Office, and Canon Hardwicke Rawnsley, an Anglican clergyman working to preserve the Lake District. These three, sometimes with the addition of the first duke of Westminster, are represented as high-minded individuals whose concern was to protect open spaces and who subscribed to an invented tradition of Englishness predicated on the countryside.[6] The presupposition that preservation is equated with an inward-looking nationalism has permeated studies of the subject in most countries. Such an approach obscures the nineteenth-century cultural context in which the international preservation movement began, when states defined themselves not only in terms of commonalties but also in juxtaposition to one another. Vernacular buildings (as originals, composites or reproductions) were often shown at international exhibitions and worlds' fairs. Historic preservation and, in particular, the preservation of vernacular buildings and crafts represented a common response to industrialisation and urbanisation which simultaneously enabled countries to express regional differences while comparing similar traditions. These 'invented communities' expressed not only national, but colonial identities. Such exhibitions help to form the cultural background of the early work of the National Trust.

The fledgling Trust's mission was to collect buildings not merely of aesthetic, but of 'historic interest'.[7] Between 1895 and 1913 it acquired two medieval clergy houses at Alfriston in Sussex (the half-timbered and thatched parish priest's house of around 1350 with later additions, bought in 1896 for £10 was the Trust's first building) and Muchelney, Somerset; the gatehouse of the College of Priests in Westbury-on-Trym, near Bristol, where John Wycliff had been a prebend; the Chantry Chapel, Buckingham; the court house, Long Crendon, Buckinghamshire; a guild hall, the Joiners' Hall in Salisbury, Wiltshire; Winster market house (dating from *c.* 1700, with a later upper storey), Derbyshire; the fourteenth-century manor house and the former post office in Tintagel, Cornwall – near Barras Nose where King Arthur was supposed to have had his castle (made famous by Tennyson), acquired in 1903; a minor country house, Barrington Court, Somerset; and the poet Coleridge's house, Nether Stowey, Somerset. These

[6] Alun Howkins, 'The Discovery of Rural England', in *Englishness, Politics and Culture 1880–1920*, ed. Robert Colls and Philip Dodd (Beckenham, 1996), 62–88.

[7] 'The National Trust, Its Aims and Work', *c.* 1895, Acc 42/19. National Trust (hereafter NT) Archive, London.

original holdings have since been represented through the telescope of the Trust's later achievements, rather than in the context of its early aspirations. In particular, the success of the Country Houses Scheme of the 1930s and 1940s has contributed to the perception that the Trust's buildings were collected for aesthetic reasons. The Trust's early holdings were an embarrassment, dismissed as reflecting the antiquarian and vernacular interests of the Society for the Protection of Ancient Buildings (founded in 1877 by William Morris), with which the Trust initially co-operated, and forming merely a prelude to the serious work of collecting country houses and hob-nobbing with the aristocracy. Interpretation, focusing on architectural history and family genealogy, has obliterated any reference to politics. However, when taken as a group rather than as individual specimens, the initial collection of buildings clearly reveals an interest in traditional forms of social organisation and governance, as well as English literature, language and religious traditions. Together, the collection represents the church in England, the guild system, the country's legal legacy, together with the old order of the squirearchy and pre-industrial revolution trade. There were undoubtedly reasons more powerful than an antiquarian interest in architectural history for such a collection policy.

The Trust's founding Council provides a more coherent representation of its epistemic community than do the 'three founders' alone; indeed, it is misleading to think of only three founders. Of its initial forty-five Council members, fifteen were either Liberal MPs or Liberal members of the House of Lords, including the leader of the new County Council Association. Representatives of Britain's main universities, the museum establishment, the country's literary and artistic elite, as well as botanists and geologists were present. Also, notably, a representative of the newly formed New England preservation organisation, the Trustees of Public Reservations, was nominated.[8] This group suggests a unifying concept of English values that encompassed educational, religious, literary, artistic and landscape traditions and, crucially, those traditions of governance which were very much in the public mind during the eleven years (1884–95) it took to get the Trust off the ground. The pattern is more strongly affirmed when campaigns to save buildings with which the Trust engaged are added: Trinity Almshouses, Mile End, London; the poet and hymnist William Cowper's house; Dr Johnson's birthplace, Lichfield; and houses reputedly owned by Shake-

---

[8] NT, *Report of the Provisional Council* (1895), i, 7; NT, *Report of the Council* (1896), i. The Trustees of Public Reservations nominated Prof. Charles Sprague Sargent, the director of Harvard University's Arnold Arboretum, to the Trust's Council, records of the Standing Committee of Public Reservations, 28 Oct. 1895, Trustees of Reservations Archive, Beverley, MA.

speare's family in Stratford-upon-Avon.[9] Its support for the saving of two others, the homes of W.M. Turner and Lord Leighton, denote their interest in artistic traditions.[10] Significantly, they also contributed to the campaign to save historian Thomas Carlyle's London house, 53 Cheyne Walk.[11]

Carlyle offers a key as to why these people should be interested in saving historic buildings. His promotion of the usefulness of tangible evidence to bring history to life helped to kick-start the movement to preserve historic houses in Britain, America and continental Europe. His famous essay, *On Heroes, Hero-Worship and the Heroic in History* (1841) had spot-lit several notable men whose homes were subsequently saved as material examples of emulatory lives in an era keen to domesticate history. Shakespeare, John Knox and Goethe, all mentioned by Carlyle, all had house museums dedicated to them within twenty-two years, as had the American revolutionary leader, George Washington, whom Carlyle mentioned by type, if not in person. The founding of the National Trust represents a second wave of this activity. Although its campaigns and collection still evince interest in history's individuals, added to this was a concern with historic institutions. Simultaneously, the formation of the Trust reflects a wider concern to push preservation activities beyond individual voluntarist group interests and to institutionalise and provide for the movement a national and an international context.

The 'official' catalysts for the Trust's inception have been given as the fight led by Canon Rawnsley, aided by the Commons Preservation Society, against a proposed railway from Buttermere to Braithwaite in the Lake District in 1883, together with the suggestion that diarist John Evelyn's London garden be given to the Kyrle Society (run by Octavia Hill's sister, Miranda) in 1884 and the resulting recognition by Robert Hunter and Octavia Hill of the usefulness of a land-holding company or trust to procure such properties.[12] Undoubtedly, these were among the crises that helped to kick-start preservation's institutionalisation, but a far, far more dangerous threat to the countryside at large and to historic buildings was posed by proposals to reform county governance. A bill, put forward by Sir William Vernon Harcourt (MP, Liberal) as early as 1883, though modified, was enacted by Salisbury's Conservative

[9] NT, *Interim Report of the Executive Committee* (1896), 5, 7.

[10] NT, *Interim Report of the Executive Committee* (1896), Appendix A; 'Ancient Houses, Stratford-upon-Avon', Society for the Protection of Ancient Buildings (hereafter SPAB) Archive, London.

[11] NT, *Interim Report of the Executive Committee* (1896), Appendix A.

[12] Eleonore F. Rawnsley, *Canon Rawnsley: An Account of His Life* (Glasgow, 1923), 49–55. Hill to Hunter 22 Aug. 1884, Dorothy Hunter papers, 1260/4/10, Surrey History Centre, Woking.

government in 1888. The Local Government Acts were revolutionary. Since Tudor times, England's counties had been administered by a plethora of voluntary groups and communities, from the Parish Vestry to the Court of Quarter Sessions. The Acts aimed to streamline this process and increase local government control. Enabling county councils to co-operate across borders to facilitate housing, reservoir and road development, the Acts threatened to change the countryside far more than the railways. Inevitably, those buildings that had housed the former agencies would become redundant. It was surely Harcourt's proposal that prompted (Sir) Robert Hunter to act, supported by a fellow-member of the Commons Preservation Society, James Bryce (MP, Liberal). Sometimes overlooked as a shadowy figure, Hunter was Solicitor to the Post Office and had made his reputation in preservation through his knowledge of British common law and its application to the preservation of common land. He had acted as voluntary solicitor to the campaigning Commons Preservation Society, founded by Shaw Lefevre whom Hunter had helped to redraft Sir John Lubbock's Ancient Monuments Bill (MP, Liberal, SPAB) with Leonard Courtney (MP, Liberal, SPAB) at the Treasury, to achieve the 1882 Ancient Monuments Protection Act. In September 1884, Hunter proposed the creation of a voluntary land-holding preservation association in an address to the Association for the Promotion of Social Science (chaired that year by Shaw Lefevre), an organisation concerned with government reform and community life.[13] Bryce had Hunter's paper published for circulation around the Commons Preservation Society membership with reper-cussions that reached New England – and resulted in the founding of the Trustees of Public Reservations.[14] Nothing happened to Hunter's suggestion (in England) for another ten years, apparently due to lack of support from and loyalty to Shaw Lefevre.[15] Harcourt, who had proposed the bill, attended the Trust's founding meeting in 1894.[16] Both Lubbock and Courtney sat on the Trust's Provisional Council, as did the new chairman of the County Councils Association, Sir John Hibbert (MP, Liberal).[17] Present, too, was Lord Rosebery, Liberal prime minister (1894–5), then actively monumentalising British parliamentary traditions in sculpture, commissioning the statue of Oliver Cromwell from Sir

[13] Robert Hunter, 'A Suggestion for the Better Preservation of Open Space', *Transactions of the National Association for the Promotion of Social Science* (1885), 753–5.

[14] Robert Hunter, *A Suggestion for the Better Preservation of Open Spaces: A Paper Read at the Annual Congress of the National Association for the Promotion of Social Science, Held at Birmingham, in September 1884* (Commons Preservation Society, 1884).

[15] 'Synopsis of Events Leading to the Genesis and Foundation of the National Trust', Acc 2/6, NT Archive.

[16] NT, *Report of the Provisional Council* (1895), i.

[17] *Ibid.*, and NT, *Report of the Council* (1896).

Hamo Thornycroft (SPAB), which stands outside the House of Commons.[18] Bryce also attended.

By the 1890s, not only change at home, but also concerns with Britain's influence abroad, helped to focus support for the formation of a preservation organisation that could act on a national scale and saw itself as representing national interests. National identities, currently fashionable as a topic of discussion today, were also a topic of debate in 1900 to which the Trust contributed. Among the broader political questions then affecting Britain was its relationship with its dependent territories, together with Home Rule for Ireland. In retrospect, Britain can be seen to have been at the apogee of Empire by 1900, yet its relationship with current and former colonies encompassed a complex web of political, legal, educational, literary and linguistic, religious and family ties. The émigré population of the colonies was around twelve million and the Trust included this group in its definition of 'the nation'. In his 1870 inaugural lecture John Ruskin, Slade Professor of Fine Art at Oxford (1869–79 and 1883–4), one of the early promoters of preservation and acknowledged as an intellectual mentor to both Octavia Hill (whose early housing work he helped to fund) and Rawnsley (one of the so-called 'Hincksey Boys' at Oxford whom Ruskin had been encouraged to undertake social work), had urged that 'Colonists [be taught] that their chief virtue is ... fidelity to their country, and that, though they live in a distant plot of land, they are no more to consider themselves therefore disenfranchised from their native land than the sailors of her fleet do.'[19]

Oxford University (and, specifically, Balliol College where Rawnsley studied) maintained strong connections with the colonies, particularly between 1883 and 1895 when approximately one fifth of its graduates worked in the Colonial Service. Several ways of institutionalising this relationship were established; for example, in 1902, Cecil Rhodes (former governor of Cape Colony) endowed scholarships at Oxford for potential leaders from the Anglo-Saxon world. In such ways English cultural influence, or what was popularly termed 'Anglo-Saxon values' (and, indeed, 'Anglo-Saxons'), might be exported and regenerated. These were not merely abstract ideas to the forty-five founder members of the Trust, ten of whom were Oxford graduates. Of the remaining Trust Council members, at least five had studied at Cambridge. As the Executive Committee noted in 1896, 'England, without the places of historic interest or natural beauty that are continuously being threatened, would be a poorer country and less likely to attract and hold the

---

[18] Hamo Thornycroft correspondence with Lord Rosebery, 1898–9, Thornycroft papers, C 283, 535–54, Henry Moore Institute, Centre for the Study of Sculpture, Leeds.

[19] Richard Symonds, *Oxford and Empire: The Last Lost Cause?* (Oxford, 1991), 25–6.

affections of her sons who, far away, are colonising the waste places of the Earth.'[20] Bryce, Regius Professor of Law (1870–93) and Rosebery, both Oxford men and both on the Trust's elected Council, were members of the Imperial Federation League and Bryce, in particular, was the foremost advocate of Anglo-American unity.[21] At the political level, successive governments hosted Colonial Conferences held mostly in London between 1887 and 1911 in an attempt to make the association between Dominions and the United Kingdom more openly voluntary and multi-lateral in character. It therefore comes as no surprise when, in 1897, the Trust's executive committee secretary 'suggested a conference in London at the time of the visit of the Colonial Premiers for the Queen's Reign Celebration'.[22] The executive committee expressly hoped that representatives of the Massachusetts Trustees of Public Reservations might be able to attend. At the same committee meeting C.R. Ashbee, Arts and Craftsman and architect, suggested that lecture tours to America be arranged to promote the Trust's work there. Ashbee was a Cambridge man and of the two older English universities, Cambridge tended to attract American students, since John Harvard had studied at Emmanuel College. The Harvard link was one that the Trust intended to foster.

The fledgling National Trust was a remarkably small organisation with some 250 members and limited financial resources. Britain lagged behind other countries in preservation initiatives, as activists were aware, and the organisation needed support from wherever it could be found. One significant source was America, where a state-sponsored landscape preservation movement was already established, and particularly in New England where Trust founders had individual and institutional links. Colonial sons – and daughters – had their own reasons for wishing to commemorate their inheritance of English political traditions. By the end of the nineteenth century the vast wave of immigration to America threatened the established political and architectural character of the historic city of Boston, a port of entry. Voluntarist groups endeavoured to preserve such threatened buildings as the Old State House. Also known as the Old Colony House, this building had been the seat of British colonial administration and was saved by the Boston Antiquarian Club (later, the Bostonian Society) in 1880–1. Thus, an almost overwhelming culture of change that threatened fragile Anglophil traditions led Boston Brahmins to bolster their own position by stressing their connection with the colonial past, as

---

[20] NT, *Interim Report of the Executive Committee* (1896), 12–13.
[21] See Hugh Tulloch, *James Bryce's American Commonwealth: The Anglo-American Background* (Woodbridge, 1988).
[22] Executive Committee Minutes, 16 Mar. 1897, NT Archive.

well providing a reminder to immigrants of Massachusetts's history of stable government. The Trust was thus not the first organisation to memorialise in stone English traditions of governance. The preservation of the Old State House doubtless helped 'to aid the historian in his work' as the Boston Society protested.[23] It doubtless also helped to influence the preservation ambitions of James Bryce, who had already made several visits to that city, staying with his friend, Harvard's president Charles W. Eliot, while working on his influential two-volume *The American Commonwealth* (London and New York, 1888).[24] It was Bryce who acquainted Charles Eliot jr with Hunter's proposal for a land-holding preservation organisation which resulted in Eliot's formation in 1890 of the Trustees of Public Reservations. It is Bryce who helps to provide the intellectual framework for the Trust's collecting policy.[25] Seeing the United States as a successful continuum of Anglo-Saxon traditions of government, he re-orientated Britain's popular perception away from the American War of Independence to the common colonial past. Additionally, Bryce's ties with Harvard proved pivotal to the development of Anglo-American preservation links around 1900, while his appointment as British ambassador to Washington (1907–13) gave him the opportunity to build the relationship in stone.

American interest helped to spur English preservationist action. In 1895–6, 'descendants of the Pilgrim Fathers' were hosted by the Trust's executive committee on a visit to 'their old homes'.[26] It was noted that, 'in America, there is a strong and growing feeling for the preservation of those features of *this* country which, whether from association or from inherent beauty, go to make it interesting and inspiring'.[27] Knowledge of American, as well as British, tourist routes seems to have been a contributory factor influencing the fledgling Trust's purchase decisions. It was unable to afford property in London, but all of its properties were commutable from London. Many of their early holdings are in the West Country, in East Anglia and in Derbyshire, all areas from which Americans were known to have emigrated or which were already

[23] Michael Holleran, *Boston's 'Changeful Times', Origins of Preservation and Planning in America* (Baltimore and London, 1998), 106, quoting William H. Whitmore.

[24] Bryce visited both Longfellow and the Revere House in 1870. Bryce to Henry Wadsworth Longfellow, 28 Aug. 1870, Longfellow papers, bMS AM 1340.2 (819), Houghton Library, Harvard University, Cambridge, MA. Bryce stayed regularly with the Eliots from 1882, Lord Harcourt was another of the Harvard president's guests; Mrs Grace H. Eliot, 'Company Received' Notebook, 1884, 25 Sept. 1884, Alexander Yale (hereafter AY) Goriansky papers, Boston, MA.

[25] Charles Eliot's Journal in Europe 1885–6, 22 July 1886, AY Goriansky papers. A copy of Hunter's published lecture (Hunter, 1884) is among the Charles Eliot papers, CE NAB 6010, Loeb Design Library, Harvard University, Cambridge, MA.

[26] NT, *Interim Report of the Executive Committee* (1896), 12–13.

[27] *Ibid.* Author's italics.

popular with Americans doing the 'giro of England'. A guestroom was provided at Tintagel's Old Post Office, and a guest book might prove revealing.[28] The Trust had sound reasons for looking to American tourists. In the year ending April 1853 Shakespeare's birthplace had attracted 1,898 English visitors; the second largest national group, of 306, came from the United States. By 1909, of the 42,246 visitors to Shakespeare's birthplace, 18,541 were from Britain and 9,790 from United States.[29] American literary tourists, and New Englanders in particular, made the pilgrimage to Wordsworth's Dove Cottage in the Lake District (saved in 1891).[30] Americans also generously subscribed to the campaign to save Thomas Carlyle's house in 1895.[31]

Thus, the Trust's Council had financial as well as sentimental reasons for hoping that 'once it could point to useful work done, it will be able to secure efficient support from beyond as well as from this side of the Atlantic'.[32] It was arranged that Hardwicke Rawnsley and C.R. Ashbee would make fact-finding lecture tours to America, in 1899 and 1900 respectively. Their aim, in the words of the Council Report, was to 'arouse a lively interest in the beauties of the common house of the Anglo-Saxon race'.[33] Or, as Ashbee put it, to encourage 'the generous assistance you have given us ... in preserving the great international monuments in the mother country'.[34] Rawnsley delivered fifteen lectures and addresses, focusing on the 'literary associations' of the Lake District.[35] Attempts were made to foster institutional links with American academic, preservation and civic organisations; forty-three corresponding members had been recruited from other institutions by 1901 and an American Sub-committee was established.[36]

In 1900, Ashbee was charged with fund-raising for 'the formation of a Club House and Bureau of Historical Information, available to all its members from all parts of the English-speaking world'.[37] In conjunction

---

[28] Detmar Blow, 'A Report on the Old Post Office, Tintagel', 23 Feb. 1897, quoted in H.D. Rawnsley, *A Nation's Heritage* (1920), Appendix A, 158–60.

[29] Levi Fox, *The Shakespeare Birthplace Trust: A Personal Memoir* (Norwich, 1997), 31.

[30] Dove Cottage Visitors Book 1891–3, the Wordsworth Trust Archive, Centre for British Romanticism, Dove Cottage, Grassmere, Cumbria.

[31] *Boston Globe*, 23 Apr. 1896, included in Ashbee Journal, opp. 80.

[32] NT, *Interim Report of the Executive Committee* (1896), 13.

[33] NT, *Annual Report* (1899), 15.

[34] Ashbee to the editor, *Boston Globe*, 23 Apr. 1896, included in Ashbee Journal, opp. 80.

[35] NT, *Annual Report* (1900), pp. 10, 15. E. Rawnsley (1923), 139. Council Minutes, 11 Dec. 1899, NT Archive.

[36] Council Minutes, 11 June 1900, NT Archive. C.R. Ashbee, 'Report to the Council of the National Trust for the Preservation of Places of Historic Interest and Natural Beauty, on his visit to the United States in the Council's Behalf, October 1900–February 1901', 23, Appendix 1, NT Archive.

[37] Ashbee Journal, 100 (Oct. 1900).

with the London County Council, the Trust hoped 'to secure the old Henry VIII palace ... by Temple Bar', as 17 Fleet Street was then believed to be, as a venue for all those who 'are anxious to study the beautiful and historic spots in the British Isles in the course of their travels in the Mother Country'.[38] On the popular front Ashbee's tour was a failure in the practice of public diplomacy. Despite help from the British embassy in Washington and the intervention of his wife, he was dogged by bad press coverage.[39] A complex character, Ashbee had hoped to garner support for an English mode of Arts and Crafts activity, as well as for the Trust and other preservation initiatives in London. Of his eight lectures, only one was nominally on the work of the National Trust; most took as their theme the threat of 'modern commercialism' and 'a lesson in citizenship' modelled on an idealised English (Elizabethan) aristocracy.[40] Naive and chauvinistic, Ashbee was unprepared for the contribution of women in American preservation and seemed irritated by American patriotism, which conflicted with his mission to bring together 'the English-speaking people as a whole ... To safeguard the historic associations of the race and preserve the amenities of life.'[41] For Ashbee, the 'principle of patriotism' was a 'love of the past' and a 'love of beauty' which he saw as the great heritage of 'the English-speaking people' of 'America, or the British Colonies'.[42] Some months later, the Trust's Council was alarmed to read a self-published book of his lectures, *American Sheaves and English Seed Corn* and requested that Ashbee 'omit from the title of his proposed work all reference to the National Trust'; additionally, they refused any proceeds from its sale and the episode contributed to Ashbee's resignation from the organisation.[43]

Nevertheless, the two tours helped to foster a mutually supportive sense of common cause among the preservation-minded in America (particularly on the east coast) and England with tangible repercussions in both countries. A short-lived branch of the National Trust was established in America (1901–4), helping to stimulate state-wide preservation organisations.[44] Though a Fleet Street venue for visiting

---

[38] *Ibid.* 17 Fleet Street, popularly thought to be King Henry or Prince Henry's lodgings, was obtained by the London County Council in 1898.

[39] Ashbee Journal, 288–315, includes clippings from Chicago press for Dec. 1900.

[40] 'Report by Mr C.R. Ashbee to the Council of the National Trust..., on his visit to the United States on the Council's Behalf, October 1900 to February 1901' (London, Essex House Press) Mar. 1901.

[41] C.R. Ashbee, *American Sheaves and English Seed Corn* (1901), 5.

[42] *Ibid.*, 9, 10.

[43] Executive Committee Minutes, 11 Nov., 9 Dec. 1901, 14 Jan. 1902, NT Archive. Additionally, Ashbee had an altercation with Octavia Hill over his use of Long Crendon Court House.

[44] In New York in 1901, the American Scenic and Historic Preservation Society was

American researchers failed to materialise, a similar scheme to provide a resting place for Harvard graduates in Stratford, Harvard House, did come off in 1907, but through the efforts of the popular novelist Marie Corelli rather than the Trust (whom Corelli thought ineffective), supported by James Bryce, then ambassador to Washington, Harvard's president Charles W. Eliot and America's ambassador to the court of St James, Whitelaw Reid.[45] Bryce was elected to its board in 1914.[46] Similarly, the Trust was involved with discussions in 1903 to save Sulgrave Manor, the Washington family's ancestral home in North-amptonshire, although the Trust itself was too small to take the project on.[47] Nothing happened until 1913 by which time, as Eliot agreed with Bryce, 'there is increasing good feeling between England and the United States'.[48] So, when the American William B. Howland, then Editor of *The Outlook*, 'suggested in England in connection with the Centenary Celebration of the 100 years Peace the purchase of Sulgrave Manor as a shrine in England to be visited by American travellers', a 'Sulgrave Committee of the Whole to Celebrate the Tercentenary Landing of the Pilgrim Fathers' was established with branches in England and America.[49] Among the British activists were Bryce and Lord Curzon, both of whom were active in the National Trust, though the Trust was not involved; the Americans were led by the National Association of Colonial Dames. Sulgrave Manor was purchased in 1914 and, although the First World War intervened in the celebrations, it remains 'a place of pilgrimage for Americans in England, and as a symbol of the kinship of the two peoples'.[50]

Between 1883 and 1913 the National Trust emerged as a society that aspired to institutionalise the saving of buildings and landscapes, crossing county and even national borders, a significant development of the

---

evolved from the state-level Trustees of Scenic and Historic Places and Objects, which society had been a corresponding member of the Trust since 1900, had hosted both Rawnsley and Ashbee and had as its mission the protection of scenic places and historic sites. Council Minutes, 9 Apr. 1900, NT Archive.

[45] Letters from Charles W. Eliot to James Bryce, 1871–1922, C.W. Eliot to James Bryce, 1 May 1907, Bryce papers, MSS Bryce USA 1, fol. 88, Bodleian Library, Oxford. *Boston Evening Transcript*, 17 Oct. 1909. Marie Corelli, 'The Rescue of "Harvard House", Stratford-upon-Avon', *Harvard Graduates Magazine*, Sept. 1907, 25–30. Teresa Ransom, *The Mysterious Miss Marie Corelli: Queen of Victorian Bestsellers* (Stroud, 1999), 145–68.

[46] Marie Corelli, Percy S. Brentnall and Bertha Vyver, *Harvard House, Stratford-upon-Avon, Guide Book* (c. 1920).

[47] Executive Committee Minutes, 12 Jan. 1903, NT Archives.

[48] Charles W. Eliot to James Bryce (copy), 31 May 1910, C.W. Eliot papers, UAI5.150/394, Pusey Library, Cambridge, MA.

[49] Public Record Office (hereafter PRO), FO 371/10647 (1925); FO 395/294, N.45 001379/00137.

[50] Memo signed R.R. Craigie, 7 Oct. 1925 outlining the terms under which Sulgrave Manor was purchased, PRO, FO 371/10647 (1925).

existing voluntarist structure through which individual buildings were saved. As part of its early educational mission the Trust consciously attempted to use architecture as historical evidence for a vision of English life and social order which it hoped would cement a union of English-speaking people that rested on sentiment, rather than upon material interest, upon common religious traditions, political ideals and historical memories, and upon English language and literature. Stimulated by county council reform, fuelled by American interest and inspired by a high-minded cultural idealism, the Trust's early activities received the support of Liberal politicians. However, it was not a very large conservation body and was subject to financial limitations and the efforts and enthusiasms of its various active members, mainly located in rural England. While aspiring to bolster an Anglo-American relationship as well as to provide political legitimacy for and, perhaps, to generate interest in local government reforms, the Trust was not effective enough to co-operate with Americans to save sites such as Sulgrave Manor or even Harvard House. Those activists, such as Bryce, who had promoted more overtly political objectives pursued them through other channels. Nevertheless, the Trust's early aspirations resulted in a significant utilisation of architecture and history at the turn of the twentieth century.

Transactions of the RHS 13 (2003), pp. 359–76 © 2003 Royal Historical Society
DOI: 10.1017/S0080440103000216   Printed in the United Kingdom

THE CONSERVATION MOVEMENT: A CULT OF
THE MODERN AGE*

By Miles Glendinning

ABSTRACT. In this polemical paper, I argue that, although conservation has generally presented itself as an *anti*-modern phenomenon, it is actually very modern indeed; the rise of the conservation movement has been a key element in the modern transformation of the built environment. The paper assesses how this situation has come about, drawing on the turn-of-century ideas of Alois Riegl, and argues that this modern concept of the monument has had a positive, creative side and a negative, even destructive side. In a concluding section, I explore the problems that conservation faces today as a result of that 'committed' stance.

My text is Psalm 49, verses 11–13:

> Their inward thought is, that their houses shall continue for ever, and their dwelling places to all generations; they call their lands after their own names./Nevertheless man being in honour abideth not; he is like the beasts that perish./This their way is their folly; yet their posterity approve their sayings.

In this essentially polemical paper, I intend to make only one main point – although at some length and in several different ways. My point is that, although conservation has generally presented itself as an *anti*-modern phenomenon, it is actually very modern indeed; the rise of the conservation movement has been a central supporting part of the transformation of the built environment in the modern age. Most of the paper is devoted to an explanation of how this has come about. I will argue that this modern concept of the monument has had a positive, creative side and a highly negative, even destructive side; but it has invariably been actively engaged as a participant in the pursuit of modernity. In a concluding section, I shall explore some of the

---

*This paper is a substantially revised and expanded version of a lecture given at the Institute of Historic Buildings Conservation Annual School, Strathclyde University, on Friday 16 June 2000, and reproduced in the 2001 issue of *Context* (the newsletter of the IHBC).

problems that conservation faces as a result of that incessantly 'committed' stance.

Now I should say, as a preliminary point of definition, that when I use the word 'modern', I am not referring just to the Modern Movement in architecture, nor even just to the twentieth century or the post-1945 period. I am using the word 'modern' to denote the general climate that prevailed from the eighteenth century onwards, in the wake of the Enlightenment; the idea that society and the natural world are no longer mysteries handed down by God, but are phenomena which are intelligible, and even controllable, by human beings. People began to believe they could direct events in accordance with a historical plan; and in that post-Enlightenment drive to control and order, the built environment played a central role. In architecture, conservation has usually been seen as a rejection of that modern ideal of intelligibility and controllability. But I wish to argue that it exemplifies it.

That is because in the built environment, as in many other areas of culture, modernity has had a double nature, an internal tension that gave it its energy. On the one hand, there has been a straightforward, dynamic modernity, with its overt drive for 'Progress', and for control through change and newness. But on the other, there has been 'traditionalism', a concept which has tried to harness change and re-cement identity by appealing to the authority of traditions – including historic monuments. Traditionalism often pretended to be anti-modern but in fact, it was just as modern. It was just as self-conscious and activist, just as reliant on concepts of historical change and the human ability to control events, unlike the unselfconscious timelessness of pre-modern tradition and religion; often its 'traditions' were invented ones. These two contrasting aspects of modernity were mutually dependent. At first, from the late eighteenth century, the ideal of Progress became bound up with the drive for material advancement through individualistic, laissez-faire capitalism, and correspondingly the traditionalist response was largely confined to nostalgic evocations of a pre-industrial lost golden age. But during the late nineteenth and early twentieth centuries, both aspects were affected by the trend towards collectivist, authoritarian ideologies, especially socialism and nationalism. Dynamic modernity's desire to transform, and its obsession with material progress, were energised especially by socialism. Traditionalist modernity became more bound up with competitive nationalism. Finally, in the late twentieth century, these totalitarian ideas collapsed, and the capitalist, laissez-faire model of modernity reasserted itself on a far greater scale. All these shifts have faithfully been reflected by the conservation movement but in my view that activist position is no longer sustainable: the conservation movement can best safeguard its future by scaling down its interventive aspirations, and re-orientating itself towards reflecting, rather than trying actively to dominate, the processes of evolution at work in the built environment.

The origins of the monument idea

The history of innovation in the idea of the monument, at any rate until the twentieth century, is largely a European story. Its beginnings are bound up with the emergence of modern historical consciousness. This was separate from religion; it allowed people to be self-consciously backward and forward looking, to look on 'history' as an autonomous concept in its own right, something which could inspire them in its own right. The first self-conscious 'conservation' began in the Renaissance. At that stage, a 'monument' meant only one thing: a literal commemoration, usually by a statue or inscription. And as early as the late fifteenth century, there was already a debate in Rome about how to treat these remains of classical statues, which uncannily presaged the modern clashes between active restoration and conservative repair. From the eighteenth century onwards, two things happened which had the effect of breaking open that narrow concept of the monument. First, its architectural scope began to extend, to include whole buildings and environments. And secondly, its social scope began to widen, as it became bound up with collectivist ideals. Now, instead of God, human concepts such as the nation or class solidarity were raised up as objects of veneration and piety.[1] Now the monument began to be seen as something 'sacred', which could be used to oppose the blind onrush of commercially driven modernisation.

The decisive starting point in this process of the sacralisation of the monument was the French Revolution, whose emphasis on equality and emancipation gave rise both to unifying and divisive types of idealism. On the one hand, its concept of universal fraternity freed people from the old stuffy international cultures of antiquity and 'Christendom', dominated by popes and Roman emperors, and instead popularised the idea of a general common humanity; the effect of this on the development of the monument idea was to encourage the assumption that there was a common human responsibility for historic relics, transcending social or national divisions. On the other hand, and ultimately more important to the growth of conservation, there was the rival doctrine of nationalism. This sprang from the combined impact of equality and liberty in allowing each nation's culture to be given equal weight – a concept also greatly reinforced by the contemporary writings of Johann Gottfried Herder. During the nineteenth century, this emancipatory idea of the nation gradually took on sharper

[1] Early conservation: J. Jokilehto, *A History of Architectural Conservation* (Oxford, 1999).

overtones of competitivenesss. Each nation tried to be internally classless and united, while externally striving to outdo all others in its cultural excellence. Monuments began to be seen as a testimony of the culture and continuity of the entire nation, and so as the responsibility of the state, which started to create posts and organisations to ensure that this 'national heritage' could be properly handed on to future citizens. In France, the Commission des Monuments was founded in 1790, followed two years later by a law to safeguard historic objects and buildings. Under the influence of Napoleonic expansionism, these ideas were copied in many other countries over the following decades. In Prussia, 1815 saw a royal order to initiate state care of monuments. The further step of the creation of a permanent inspectorate general of historic monuments in France in 1830 was followed by the foundation of similar state commissions in Belgium in 1835, Spain in 1844, Russia in 1869 and the Netherlands in 1874. The situation in Scotland, and Britain, was a little different, owing to the greater strength of private and capitalist interests, and the feeling that the heritage was not a matter in which the state should intervene.

History versus age: the trend from restoration to conservation

During the early nineteenth century, this growing nationalist climate across Europe became bound up with the evolving debate between restoration and conservation approaches to the monument. What happened, as we all know, was a gradual shift in popularity from the restoration to the repair approach. This paralleled the shift in new architecture from trying to symbolise the nation using specific historic styles, to the use of subtler and more abstract methods. The idea of 'restoring' individual monuments to an ideal stylistic 'authenticity' gave way to an insistence on preserving the existing old fabric from demolition and from restoration. In general, nations were now competing on a broader and broader front, through their claims of classless 'community'. 'Authenticity' was still an aim, but this was now taken to refer not to stylistic accuracy but to the collective social spirit as shown in the cumulative fabric. Despite all its traditionalist rhetoric, this expanding concept of the monument was linked strongly to the emergence of modern collectivist society. 'Nation' and 'tradition' became more and more closely identified.

In the first phase of the nineteenth-century national-heritage concept, that is the era of restoration, the competition was especially focused on great cathedrals, and on the issue of which country invented Gothic. The most ambitious 'restoration' project was in fact a completion project, for Cologne Cathedral, started from 1841 after prolonged propagandising by Schinkel and Zwirner, and completed in 1890 in its present form, with its two huge west towers. Cologne, the fountainhead of German architectural nationalism, showed that the restoration era was actually concerned with creating something new rather than with protecting something old. That fact emerged even more clearly in contemporary France, where the era of restoration was dominated by the work of Viollet-le-Duc. His rationalistic reliance on the idea of 'scientific' progress made the modernity of restoration explicit: in 1866, in his *Dictionnaire*, Viollet argued that 'The term restoration and the thing itself are both modern. To restore a building is not to preserve it...it is to reinstate it in a condition of completeness which may never have existed at any given time.'

By that time, within France, the writings of Victor Hugo had begun to point away from this relatively narrow concern with great set-pieces; he wrote in 1831 that the most important monuments were the buildings of society as a whole. But it was in Britain, the only country that had so far really experienced massive urbanisation and industrialisation, that this sacralisation of the monument was carried much further, and combined with a decisive rejection of monument restoration as a whole, and a new and intense focus on the material substance of old buildings as something which itself had an intrinsic moral status. The early establishment of rural 'Improvement' and urban industrial growth in Britain had been associated not only with planned Progress but also with rampant commercial capitalism. In reaction to this commercialisation, a utopian traditionalism emerged, which embraced the entire built environment, and linked it in to a vision for society as a whole. At first, predictably, it was expressed mainly in religious form: A.W.N. Pugin, from the late 1830s, argued for the revival of pre-modern 'Catholic England' through a 'total' Gothic built environment. But soon a 'secular sacredness' became dominant. John Ruskin extended that utopianism to the field of monuments, within which he set out a critique of cathedral restorations, reinforced with extreme ethical force. Ruskin's writings pointed to a secular alternative to eternity, talking of 'stones' as if they were part of the natural world: 'When we build, let us think that we build for ever...that a time to come when those stones will be held sacred because our hands have touched them.' Buildings were the testaments of their first builder to later generations, like Roman ancestral shrines; the key monuments were not religious set-pieces but ordinary 'homes', out of which the whole nation's identity was built. As the moral authority of monuments lay in their substance, as 'things' rather than ideas, 'restoration' therefore constituted an immoral violation of ancestral piety: 'that which they laboured for...in those buildings they intended to be permanent, we have no right to obliterate'...' Architecture is always destroyed causelessly.' In his 1877 manifesto of the newly founded Society for the Protection of Ancient Buildings, William Morris extended these ideas to embrace the entire stock of 'old' buildings; to him, a monument was 'anything which can be looked on as artistic, picturesque, historical, antique,or substantial; any work...over which educated, artistic people would think it worth while to argue at all'.[2]

Across Europe, the debate between the 'Viollet' restoration ideology and this 'Ruskin' conservationism continued during the late nineteenth and early twentieth centuries. But that debate was rapidly overtaken and left behind by wider developments in the monument concept. Ruskin's most significant legacy was not his anti-restoration argument in its own right, but the fact that old buildings were now accepted as a highly charged ground of collective identity, about which the most sweepingly subjective and utopian assertions could be made, especially in support of nationalist ideals, and in opposition to the liberal capitalism which began to spread across Europe and North America – the first international 'globalisation' movement. From the late nineteenth century onwards, that collectivist, nationalist monument ethos flourished most strongly not in Britain and France but in the German-speaking lands. There, it was underwritten by powerful philosophical arguments, which jettisoned the last remnants of absolute or religious dogmas. According to writers like Nietzsche and Heidegger, human beings now had to generate their own values; and a premium was put on dogmatic, authoritative statements to support those values. In place of God, they saw secular excellence, especially in art, as a new kind of hyper-reality – something which would give an insight into a deeper truth.

Within this framework, it was not individual old buildings, whether restored or conserved, which were seen as having the deepest meaning for this new national community, but the entire older built environment, the historic cities and towns – the city-monuments, as one might call them. And the stigmatising of restoration, by implication, displaced interest away from the cathedrals towards the buildings of secular society. This wider, socialised view of the monument was also, at the turn of the century, brought into a more collaborative relationship with the planners of *new* environments. In the books of the German architect Paul Schultze-Naumburg, for example, the simple classicism of the pre-industrial 'Biedermeier' era was contrasted in a Pugin manner with pictures of fussy contemporary eclectic buildings.[3] The common enemy was the laissez-faire chaos of nineenth-century capitalism. Both city-monuments and 'planned' modernity had their part to play in rectifying this chaos.

[2] John Ruskin, *The Seven Lamps of Architecture* (Orpington, 1880 edition), 197; Society for the Protection of Ancient Buildings, *Manifesto*, 1877.
[3] Paul Schultze-Naumburg, *Kulturarbeiten* (2nd edn, Munich, 1904), I, 190.

The cult of *Heimatschutz*

The point of transition to the new secular community ethos of the monument was marked in the greatest of all 'conservation texts': *Der Moderne Denkmalkultus* – the Modern Cult of the Monument – written in 1903 by the Austrian theorist Alois Riegl. Riegl's book summed up all the existing values of the monument and pointed to the twentieth-century future. The wording of his title was carefully chosen, and emphasised that the monument was an idea of the modern age, which set out to some extent to replace religion with humanistic values. In his book, Riegl tried to separate and define the constituent values of this 'cult of the monument'. The main division, he argued, was between a group of 'present day values', which roughly corresponded to Vitruvius's criteria of architecture (i.e. practical use, or *utilitas*, artistic value, or *venustas*, firmness, or *firmitas*), and, on the other hand, a grouping of values concerned solely with the past. The latter had undergone their own process of evolution from the 'commemorative value' of the statues and inscriptions of the pre-modern epoch, to the 'historic value' of the restoration age, and finally to the 'age-value' of his own day, which valued the entire historic built environment, rather than any particular buildings, for its role as a testimony to the general culture of a nation.

In Riegl's view, historic value had acted as a 'battering ram' for age-value, which he predicted would now become the dominant monument concept of the twentieth century. That was indeed what happened – but not in the way he foresaw. His own definition of age-value was very subtle and humanistic, and of a generally international socialist orientation, emphatically *not* linked to intransigent and authoritarian demands for preservation; whereas the use that was generally made of the concept of age-value in the twentieth century was far cruder and more exaggerated.[4]

What happened was that its overarching scope and social-utopian force proved to be natural allies or supports for the twentieth-century state, with its aspirations to 'total' control based on national community, and its concern to defend or lay claim to its 'national soil'. The city-monument idea became integrated with the growing concerns of town planning, by helping to support its claims of harmony and co-ordination. Especially influential here were the writings of the Austrian town-planning pioneer Camillo Sitte, who had argued in 1889 that modern classical cities could be inspired by what he saw as the artistic planning of medieval towns. In Austria, Riegl's ideas were developed into a fully fledged state preservation system by Max Dvorak. His *Katechismus der*

[4] Alois Riegl, *Der Moderne Denkmalkultus* (Vienna, 1903); English part-translation in *Oppositions* (Autumn 1982) (Rizzoli, New York).

Denkmalpflege of 1916 (written, significantly, in wartime) extended the scope of preservation to interiors, landscapes, vernacular traditional buildings, nature, the whole field of culture, not just buildings. The entire environment could be potentially protected, just as all could be potentially planned or mobilised. The name for this vast concept was *Heimatschutz*: 'protection of the homeland'.

All over Europe, movements of modern social nationalism began to emerge, drawing inspiration from the supposed coherence of folk culture. In Britain, detached from the continental tensions over land, these ideas were less pronounced, although in Edinburgh, in the 1890s, Patrick Geddes set out a doctrine of urban social evolution that exploited the city-monument concept as an inspiration for cultural regeneration: the Old Town of Edinburgh, and its symbiotic relationship with the classical New Town, would serve as an inspiration for a humanistic process of social evolution. For Geddes, the monument-movement was something not of the past but of the future, although his ideas were developed between the wars into a more orthodox traditionalist preservationism by the marquess of Bute and Ian Lindsay, the pioneers of Scottish 'listing'.[5]

But it was in Germany that the most vigorous steps were taken to link *Heimatschutz* to a full and active system of community nationalism in the built environment, designed to re-embed and stabilise a society that had been turned upside down by industrial urbanisation. Advocacy of protection for city-monuments would run alongside a system of planning which aimed to abolish dense inner city *Mietskaserne* tenements and promote large-scale land colonisation. Although many German states around 1900 passed pioneering laws to protect historic towns, and every year from 1900 there was a grand pan-German 'Monument Day' convention, the main emphasis was still on inventorisation. Here the key figure was Georg Dehio, founder of the famous blue guidebook series. His world view was one of secularised piety, with the nation replacing God as a focus: the monument was, he argued in 1905, *ein Stück unseres nationalen Daseins* – a piece of our national existence.[6]

Total monument – total war

As I have already suggested, this modern cult of the monument had its dark as well as its creative side; and now we have to trace the growth of that dark side. In the struggle over land in Europe, Riegl's humanism was supplanted by a nationalistic politicisation and polar-

---

[5] Geddes: M. Glendinning, A. MacKechnie and R. MacInnes, *A History of Scottish Architecture* (Edinburgh, 1996), ch. 7.
[6] Stefan Muthesius, *Polska* (Koenigstein and Taunus, 1994), 8–17.

isation of the monument idea. Each country made the maximal assertion of its own values, in a psychological-existential rather than rational sense. Between the wars, the city-monument concept was integrated with the modernising and competitive policies of totalitarian regimes. For example, one German painting of 1940 showed the historic town of Limburg an der Lahn with a new, Roman-style autobahn bridge in the background. The all-embracing scope of *Heimatschutz* was combined with forceful 'special' claims under the aegis of 'art-geography'. These ultimately took on an absurdly circular character: for example, Wilhelm Pinder, the early mentor of Nikolaus Pevsner, claimed in his 1944 book, *Special Achievements of German Art*, that 'In the end, actually, the whole of German art is one single special achievement.'[7]

The logical consequence of this politicisation of the 'mass national heritage' was the implication of monuments themselves in mass warfare and destruction. The First World War, with its massive damage in north-eastern France and southern Belgium, did not significantly break from the nineteenth-century story of towns destroyed by field artillery; despite the rapidly rising temperature of rhetoric, there were attempts by both sides to protect monuments, including the appointment of the conservationist Paul Clemen as a cultural protection officer by the German occupation army in Belgium. To the east, there were higher temperatures already: a guidebook to Marienburg Castle in 1917 boasted of 'the fight for the cultural work of the Teutonic Knights for the Ostmark'. And after the war, the Polish–German relationship developed into an explosive confrontation of rival national heritages.[8] The rise in German antagonism to Poland could be measured in descriptions of the Krakow altarpiece by the painter Veit Stoss: in 1918, it was praised for its 'inexhaustible plenitude, most noble humanity', whereas Pinder in 1933 hailed Stoss's 'fundamentally German temperament, consuming itself in fighting, expressing itself in the passionate creation of forms'. The new Polish state also found time to demolish the most prominent relic of Russian rule in Warsaw, an almost brand new Orthodox Cathedral completed in 1912.

A particular focus of such tensions across interwar Europe was the heightened awareness of borderlands, following the land transfers of Versailles. The planting of war cemeteries in such zones gave an opportunity for the older type of commemorative 'monument' to make a temporary comeback. In that sense, again, the British position was a rather different one, with a sharper geographical division between 'overseas' and 'home'; significantly, the Scottish National War Memor-

[7] *Reichsautobahn*, ed. R. Stommer (Marburg, 1982), 108; Muthesius, *Polska*.

[8] Muthesius, *Polska*; 'razing' of Warsaw: A. Ciborowski and S. Jankowski, *Warsaw Rebuilt* (Warsaw, 1962), 15.

ial, with its incredible concentration of emotional symbolism, was housed in a converted old rubble building perched directly on the bare rock of Edinburgh Castle.[9] On the Continent, the sharpest of the new architectural and heritage borderland zones ran through Upper Silesia. Previously a neglected area when it was all part of Germany, now it became a focus of feeling of threatened *Heimat*: in 1938 a Breslau writer hailed Silesian historic architecture as an artistic 'combat zone against the east', a 'gangway of attack for the forces of German form'. After the actual attack of the forces of German form in 1939, what followed was the systematic wrecking and plunder of the Polish cultural patrimony, culminating in the dynamiting of the Royal Palace in Warsaw in 1944, as a deliberate attempt at cultural decapitation. Following the Warsaw rising, in October 1944, Hitler ordered historic central Warsaw to be 'razed to the ground', through a methodical campaign, burning libraries and archives, blowing up statues and even ploughing up parks.

But of course, by 1944, this destruction was taking place not in a vacuum but within a well-established 'total war'. And this was a war in which the greatest devastation of monuments was by now being carried out not *by* Germany but *against* Germany. Here we encounter a double irony: on the one hand, that the precocious German championing of total urban heritage was now being followed by an almost total destruction of that same German urban heritage; and on the other hand, that it was geographically detached Britain, whose chief contribution to monument theory was the Ruskin–Morris insistence on total preservation and reverence for ancient substance, which, in alliance with the United States, was now destroying more European monuments than everyone else put together.

How far did these attacks amount to a deliberate 'cultural bombing' (as opposed to tactical air attacks in support of army campaigns), and how did they relate to the concern for *Heimatschutz* and the city-monument? The first deliberate mass bombing of a historic city was the Royal Air Force attack which incinerated over 80 per cent of the timber-built Hanseatic old town of Lübeck on Palm Sunday, 28 March 1942. This attack by over 200 heavy bombers was ordered by the South African chief of Bomber Command, Air Marshal Arthur Harris, as an experiment, to test whether bombing timber-framed buildings could start an inferno large enough to be used as an aiming point for later waves of bombers: 'I wanted my crews to be well blooded, as they say in fox hunting, to have a taste of success for a change.' 'Bomber' Harris's motive seems merely to have been one of philistine utilitarianism; but

---

[9] See for instance Wilhelm Kreis, *Soldatengraeber und Gedenkstaetten* (Munich, 1944); Glendinning *et al.*, *Scottish Architecture*, ch. 8.

the emotional hold of the *Heimatschutz* philosophy in Germany led to public outrage at the destruction of Lübeck, and calls for revenge targeted against the English architectural heritage. On 14 April, Hitler issued an order for the deliberate bombing of historic cities, the so-called Baedeker raids named after the guidebooks used to select the targets. The first hit Exeter, Bath and York, where the Guildhall was gutted: the German radio announced that 'Exeter was a jewel; we have destroyed it.'[10]

That, however, was an exaggeration. The fact that the German air force only had light tactical bombers meant that these retaliations could only be pinpricks, compared to what was coming in the opposite direction. For example, as the attackers headed for Bath, a massive formation of RAF bombers crossed their path heading for another Hanseatic city, Rostock, where three-quarters of the medieval Old Town was flattened. At a meeting three days later, Hitler raged against the destruction of Rostock, and Goebbels recorded that 'he shares my opinion absolutely that cultural centres, health resorts and civilian centres must be attacked now. There is no other way of bringing the English to their senses. They belong to a class of human beings with whom you can only talk after you have first knocked out their teeth.' But – quite apart from the fact that 'Bomber' Harris was not himself an Englishman – most of the historic teeth knocked out in this competition were German ones. In May 1942, in Operation Millennium, over 1,000 bombers rained incendiaries on Cologne, predictably using the Cathedral and the Old Town as their aiming point, and destroyed over 13,000 houses. In July 1943, in 'Operation Gomorrah' (the name itself says much), the week-long fire raid on Hamburg, over one third of all buildings in the city were destroyed, including most of the historic centre and its churches, and the university library with its 800,000 volumes.[11]

The mounting devastation of the German heritage by the British and, to a lesser extent) American air forces was raised in a parliamentary debate on 9 February 1944, by the bishop of Chichester. Reviving the older monument justification of universal European values, something that had been almost swamped in the tidal wave of nationalistic hatred, the bishop pleaded for a more discriminating approach, to try to save the remaining German city-monuments: 'In the fifth year of the war it must be apparent to any but the most complacent and reckless how far the destruction of European culture has already gone. We ought to

---

[10] M. Gilbert, *Second World War* (1989), 314, 328–9, 446–8; B. Collier, *The Defence of the United Kingdom* (1957), 121–3, 304–11; H.W. Koch, 'The Strategic Air Offensive against Germany', *Historical Journal*, 34 (1991), 117–41; *Kriegsschicksaele deutscher Architektur* (n.d.), vols. I and II.

[11] Gilbert, *Second World War*, 319.

think once, twice and three times before destroying the rest.'[12] By 1945, the bishop's warning proved all too prescient, as Bomber Harris, running out of bigger targets, turned his attentions to smaller historic centres. For example, in March 1945, there was a mass attack on Rothenburg ob der Tauber, one of the most renowned picture-postcard small towns in Europe – rather like trying to wipe out St Andrews or Stratford-on-Avon.

In the wake of this destruction the monument idea, in most parts of Europe, became generally and decisively detached from nationalist propagandising. The special, and influential, exception to this rule was Poland, whose post-war moral authority allowed it to become the pioneer of a novel approach to reconstruction: the rebuilding of destroyed towns in facsimile form. In 1944, it was decided to build a replica of the entire Old Town of Warsaw. This was not to be a literal restoration of its 1939 condition, but a Viollet-style attempt to recreate an idealised eighteenth-century Warsaw, decorated with the fanciful 'Soz-Realizm' motifs of the forties and fifties. It was supported by an extreme nationalist rhetoric: for example, the director of the Polish National Museum described it in 1966 as 'the last victorious act in the fight with the enemy...the finishing touch of our unbending struggle with enemy violence'.[13] Concluded in 1981 with the completion of a facsimile of the Royal Palace, the exacting art-historical standards gave the reconstruction a unique international appeal. But there was also a more ambiguous side to Polish post-war restoration, in the cases of formerly German cities annexed by Poland in 1945, such as Gdańsk/Danzig and Wrocław/Breslau. Here the anachronistic application of the modern cohesive nation-state concept to the Middle Ages led to bizarre biases and anomalies. In general, the decision was taken to 'restore' only the buildings and environments of the centuries of Polish domination of those towns. The remaining ruins were largely cleared and the historic building materials shipped to Warsaw for use there. But this restoration policy was only inconsistently applied. For example, the seventeenth-century buildings of Elbląg/Elbing were at first not restored, although dating from a 'Polish' rather than 'German' period in the town's history.

In Western Europe, this nationalist propaganda became a thing completely of the past. Instead, a new type of dynamic rhetoric came to the fore, concerned rather with socialist progress, but in a form which safeguarded the key role of the heritage. The 1940s to 1960s saw a revival of a different strand of the turn-of-century modern monument

---

[12] *Hansard*, 9 Feb. 1944.
[13] 'Unbending struggle': National Trust for Historic Preservation, *Historic Preservation Today* (Charlottesville, 1966).

idea: the alliance between conservation and modern city planning against the 'chaos' of the nineteenth-century industrial-capitalist environment. Fuelled by the huge social-democratic expansion of the powers of the state in planning and building, there began a forceful campaign of massive urban extensions and redevelopments, complete with exhortatory and warlike rhetoric ('battle against the slums', 'housing crusade'), and involving a continuation of massive destruction of the urban fabric as well as large-scale building of International Modern blocks and towers. The 'target', the environments of the nineteenth century, were seen not as heritage but as the opposite of heritage. Generally, despite the radical difference in appearance between new and old, the relationship between social-democratic modernity led by the state, and conservation, was a collaborative one. In Scotland, for example, government conservation activity and 'listing', although hesitant at first, was dealt with from 1962 as an integrated part of the Scottish Development Department, a newly created ministry intended to promote state-led modernisation. This collaborative approach was exemplified in the work of architect-planners such as the Scottish designer Robert Matthew, former chief London municipal architect and regional planner, who drew constantly on Geddes's formula of modern 'conservative surgery' in schemes such as his Edinburgh University redevelopment in George Square (from 1960). The established categories and periods of heritage (generally, eighteenth-century and earlier buildings) were treated with respect, as a counterpart to the new developments, while war-damaged historic towns like Caen or Nürnberg were rebuilt in a compromise-modern style, retaining the steep roofs and general profile but without the medieval details.[14]

The victory of conservation: from social democracy to global capitalism

But when the fortunes of the Modernist, social-democratic reconstruction drive took a downturn in Western Europe from the late 1960s, and conservation emerged as a victorious opposition force, what seemed unexpected was the fact that the association between conservation and the state bureaucracy continued, and was even strengthened. It seemed unexpected because a more general questioning of the Enlightenment values of historical progress was underway. Yet, in fact, that continuity was entirely predictable, given the history we have traced of the close interrelation between the monument idea and modernising 'action'. Conservation continued to be drawn towards the pursuit of power and control. The architectural discrediting of the Modern Movement's

[14] Muthesius, Polska; J.-J. Bertaux, *Renaissance d'une ville* (Caen, 1994), 28.

campaign for radical rebuilding had elevated conservation to a status of dominance, as the only major combatant left on the field. That victory was directly bound up with the defeat of planned social building; for the first time, monuments and new buildings were plunged into open confrontation. Yet the effect, after an initial phase of anti-establishment activism, was to increase even further the interventive and controlling activity of the state. And then, in a second stage of evolution, from the 1970s, that machinery became static and ossified. Conservation became a sheep in wolf's clothing: as with the language of revolution in the Soviet Union under Stalin and his successors, an institutionalised status was given to the highly politicised 'shock' language inherited from Ruskin and Morris and from the twentieth-century epoch of total war – loss, threat, destruction, vandalism, rape, protect, save, tragic, scandalous and so forth – all used to cloak the work of a bureaucracy.

This new orthodoxy extended the scope of modern controllability far further than even the Modern Movement, by claiming it could inventorise and 'protect' the entire built environment – including, ultimately, the environments of the Modern Movement itself – for ever. The social structure of this new establishment was just as elitist and dominated by experts as the modernist technocratic planning it replaced. Everywhere across Western Europe, there was a move from the old creative traditionalism to a new fundamentalism, which claimed it could fix and 'stop' dynamic human cultures through preserved material culture objects. The era of *Heimatschutz* had been extreme in its rhetoric heritage, but more modest in its powers of preservation. It had emphasised the 'total', but not active 'control'. Now, state conservation activity was expanded in most countries into huge, open-ended government 'listing' programmes, coupled with development controls by a range of local and national state bodies. These added up to a quantitative, routinised bureaucratic procedure which differed little from the production drives of modern housing and planning. And the buildings it was interested in were also increasingly 'modern', as the scope of heritage became more focused on the nineteenth and twentieth centuries. The whole movement was becoming self-containedly 'modern' from start to finish.

One possible explanation, however illogical, for the extremism of this triumphalist phase of conservation, was the awareness in people's minds of the risk of nuclear holocaust, a threat which worsened after the late 1950s. After 1989, of course, that threat vanished, yet the state conservation movement had become so entrenched and bureaucratised that it continued to spread of its own accord. At any rate, no trace remained in Western Europe of the old competitive and boastful language of national pride in relation to monuments, and the link between heritage and warfare seemed to have been broken for good – in contrast to the 'cultural bombing' of architectural landmarks (albeit not carried out by a nation-state) which apparently formed an element in the 'September 11th' attacks on the United States.

Equally important for the continued confidence and intransigence of conservation was the fact that it had come under the influence of a new kind of 'total' modernity: the framework of resurgent global capitalism, with its demands that the built environment should be commercialised and commodified, especially through the 'branding' of buildings, areas or entire cities through an 'iconic', image-led approach. A fresh alliance emerged between monuments and new city development. Within new architecture, the dominant trend was a 'signature' Modernism, in the service of capital rather than the community. Equally, old buildings could provide the 'icons' around which a new 'mixed use' urban development could be hung. For example, in the Holyrood area of Edinburgh, two artistic-individualistic gesture-buildings by signature designers – the Scottish Parliament by Enric Miralles and the tent-like 'Dynamic Earth' theme park by Michael Hopkins – sit alongside the 'heritage icon' of a seventeenth-century mansion, Queensberry House, gaily remodelled with brightly tiled orange roofs like a toy fisherman's cottage.

This alliance between heritage and new building highlights the deeper reality of identity in the built environment of the twenty-first century. That is, the insatiable demand of global capitalism to commodify everything, including civic and national identity, into an element in marketplace competition. 'National heritage' is now just a mask for global commodification. Heritage islands are dotted within the mass-produced sprawl of Clone City, alongside the equally shallow images of the new Retro-MoMo signature architecture. The reality of international capitalism is papered over with images of national cultural autonomy. Ruskin's strictures about the lack of authenticity in 'restored' cathedrals could equally apply to this entire identity-structure of 'national heritage', as well as to individual set-pieces such as the Miralles parliament, itself like a theme-park pavilion in its 'upturned-boat' metaphors of 'Scottishness'.[15]

Could this new alliance between heritage and the politico-economic powers-that-be of modernity amount to a fundamental revitalisation of the monument idea – allowing it to draw its strength from twenty-first-century capitalism just as it drew its strength from nineteenth- and twentieth-century nationalism and socialism? The answer to that is likely to be no. The reason is that the marketplace, unlike the 'Heimat',

---

[15] M. Glendinning and D. Page, *Clone City* (Edinburgh, 1999); Ruskin, *Seven Lamps*, 194 and 196.

requires no hortatory baggage to fuel it. Pugin, Geddes and their followers were far closer to the mark when they saw it as the big enemy of the heritage, rather than its friend. Where previously the monument stood in a creative or destructive tension with modernity, now there is no intellectual connection at all. In a sense, this is history as farce, following history as tragedy – and of course, in that this marketing competition is preferable to competition by bombing campaigns, it is clearly an improvement. It is a kind of new internationalism, replacing violent nationalism. But it not only lacks the overarching ideals of the old universalisms: it lacks any intellectual sensibility at all. It may be that the gap between conservation's claims to all-embracing control and the reality of its servitude to market forces is too vast to bridge. But if the monument concept is to be anything more than a marketing image in the twenty-first century, it will have to develop a more critical attitude to the forces of global capitalism. And that will mean relinquishing its hold on the levers of power. It cannot have it both ways any longer: the choice is between the action and power of modernity on the one hand, and intellectual and critical integrity on the other.

If the choice falls on the latter – as I hope it will – the conservation movement will have to take a more realistic view of its relation to the march of time and the inevitability of change and decay. It will have to address the fundamental question of how monuments are to be related to the processes of change, at a time when the modern myth of human control of history has been shattered. But in a way, that loss hardly matters any more. The fact that we can now create our communities by choice means that the search for identity has lost its urgent, existential dimensions and has reduced in importance. Identity can become something more provisional, accepting the limits to our power of comprehension and control.

With the ending of the Enlightenment concept of History as a driving force, the role of old buildings can change radically. The Ruskinian and nationalist concept of the monument as a *material* testimony to the continuity of the nation, an eternal physical legacy of the founding fathers, to be treated with pseudo-religious piety – this concept becomes meaningless. The way in which the *Heimatschutz* propaganda led within a matter of decades to the material obliteration of the old towns it exalted shows, in itself, that the concept of living national heritage is mischevious nonsense. If we accept instead the fact that all buildings, like nations, are ephemeral social constructions, and that the built environment is a testament to change rather than something of enduring materiality, we can begin to look on old buildings with a new lightness. Perhaps there is no longer any necessary connection between their material substance and their 'meaning'. As *substance*, they can be merged into the general building stock as something for use today; as *ideas*, what they can tell us is something special, but it is mainly about change, about the relationship of place and change.

In this retreat from aggressive, dominant conservationism, we could do worse than begin by returning to the 'oppositional' critiques of the nineteenth-century figures, who, like us, faced a market-driven chaos that could hardly be defined, still less controlled. That does not, of course, amount to a fundamentalist quest for a return to pre-Enlightenment unselfconscious tradition, as advocated by the openly anti-modern Victorian utopianists of the Pugin–Morris tradition: far more relevant are the critiques of writers such as Geddes, who accepted the inevitability of modernity but sought to moderate its effects. Geddes's writings emphasised the symbolic role that the monument, especially the city-monument, could play in the cycle of forgetfulness and renewal. In his words, 'the ideals and the achievements of one day and generation and city are ever melting away, and passing out of sight of the next'...'we have no continuing city'...'Upon all these degrees of dying, all these faint and fading steps between immortality and oblivion, we may arrange what we call our historic cities. Obviously in the deeper and more living sense the city exists only in actualising itself; and thus to us it is that the ideal city lies ever in the future. Yet it is the very essence of this argument that an ideal city is latent in every town.'[16]

This more fluid and modest conception of the city-monument differs radically from today's calls for the open-ended spread of conservation across the entire built environment, just as it also differs from the aggressive newness of today's image-modernism. Demands for mass conservation, in the context of twenty-first-century Western Europe, are clearly an anachronistic absurdity. We cannot carry on 'protecting' and controlling for ever as if we are God. The monument idea has been one of the modern age's most powerful and alluring substitutes for religious mystery and eternity – but it has now been taken to an extreme which has exposed its ultimate emptiness. Yet a monument-movement which acknowledges the ultimate impossibility of pre-servation, the fact that all buildings must fall down in the end, is ultimately a self-cancelling or self-contradicting idea.

Here I would like to return, as always in the most fundamental issues of conservation theory, to Alois Riegl. I want to return to him not because he was infallible but because his prediction that age-value would be the dominant concept in the twentieth century was not quite accurate. What happened instead was a monstrous perversion by others of his definition of age-value, and only *now*, in the twenty-first century,

---

[16] Patrick Geddes, *Civics: As Applied Sociology*, II (1905), 159 (in 1979 Leicester reprint edition).

are we at last in a position to realise it. The central feature of Riegl's definition was that age-value was seen as a matter not of oldness preserved, but of natural decay and passing away. While today, the rhetoric of 'sustainability' and the analogy with nature is used as an argument for stronger preservation controls, Riegl argued that 'nature's unhampered processes will lead to the complete destruction of a monument' and that 'the cult of age-value...stands in ultimate opposition to the preservation of monuments'; thus, 'from the standpoint of age-value one need not worry about the eternal preservation of monuments, but rather one should be concerned with the constant representation of the cycle of creation, and this purpose is fulfilled even when future monuments have supplanted those of today'.[17]

If the cult of the strong monument is now obsolete, what can replace it? It is not the purpose of this paper to argue for a libertarian agenda, for a 'bonfire of controls' or for 'good architects to be given their head'. Arguably, what we need is more, rather than less, planning – but planning of a less rigid kind than the present system of listing and conservation controls. Today's conservation movement is an unsatisfactory half-way house between extremes. The most valuable aspect of the system of listed building consent is that it compels a pause for thought, an opportunity for the intellectualisation of change, within the development process. That opportunity should be extended to all buildings and environments, however banal or recent – while discarding, in compensation, the controlling force implicit in the totalitarian (mis-)conception of age-value.

Only now with all the force of old-fashioned modern Progress spent, can the cult of age-value, emancipated from the concern to preserve old material substance, become a truly universal movement. Only now can it celebrate its own ultimate powerlessness and transience, pointing towards the 'greater context' that unites everyone. In the words of Patrick Geddes: 'The songs of militant nationality may lose their power, the psalmody of Zion no more stir the sons as it was wont to do the fathers, yet gentler voices may reappear, older voices win a reading:

> In Iona of my heart, Iona of my love,
> Instead of the voice of monks shall be lowing of cattle,
> But ere the world come to an end,
> Iona shall be as it was.[18]

[17] Riegl, *Denkmalkultus*.
[18] Geddes, 'The Scots Renaissance', *The Evergreen* (Spring 1895).

Transactions of the RHS 13 (2003), pp. 377–92 © 2003 Royal Historical Society
DOI: 10.1017/S0080440103000228   Printed in the United Kingdom

OF SHELLS AND SHADOWS: A MEMOIR ON AUSCHWITZ

By Robert Jan van Pelt

ABSTRACT. In Auschwitz Germans killed more than a million Jews and 70,000 mainly Roman Catholic Poles. As a result, Auschwitz is a site holy to both peoples who have conflicting views as to what is historically and religiously important, and how the site should be managed. In 1996 the author led a group of architects to create a masterplan for the future of the former annihilation camp. It became the basis of an international agreement in 1997.

In the late 1980s Debórah Dwork and I began work on Auschwitz. By that time, Auschwitz had become one of the most powerful and universal myths of the post-modern age – an age which philosophers such as Adorno, Habermas and Jonas have described as an age 'after Auschwitz'. Staunch Heideggerians, seeking to justify their master's inability to confront the Holocaust, had declared Auschwitz to be an unthinkable realm shrouded in silence. Many concurred: Auschwitz had been defined as an unintelligible world, a strange universe, that cannot be explained. Banished from the world of description, analysis and conclusion, Auschwitz had become a myth in which the assumed universality of its impact obscures the contingencies of its beginning and operation. It had become a myth.

Dwork and I wrote *Auschwitz: 1270 to the Present* in response to the challenge of present-day mythification which, in the words of the survivor David Rousset, understood the concentration camp world as a 'dead planet laden with corpses'.[1] In our book, we rejected these simple descriptions mired in metaphor and symbolism. 'Auschwitz is the most significant memorial site of the Shoah, and it is also the most significant memorial site of Polish suffering under German rule', we wrote. 'Every aspect of the camp is an object of contention and conflicting interpretation, even its shape and location.'[2] The analysis that followed explored these problems in some detail. The main issue,

[1] David Rousset, *The Other Kingdom*, trans. Ramon Guthrie (New York, 1947), 168–9.
[2] Robert van Pelt and Debórah Dwork, *Auschwitz: 1270 to the Present* (New Haven and London, 1996), 359.

we argued, was the fact that the tourist facilities and the main exhibition of the Auschwitz-Birkenau State Museum were located in Auschwitz I, which had survived the war more or less intact. The relatively small compound with its solid, two-storey brick buildings offered a convenient home for these functions. A large, eerie landscape of ruins, Birkenau offered few facilities, and therefore it was maintained as a memorial landscape.

The problem, we argued, was that Auschwitz I derived its historical significance from its use by the Germans to subjugate the Poles into serfdom, and that by locating the exhibition and facilities there, this aspect of the history of the camp was foregrounded. This is a problem especially when Jewish visitors from abroad visit the camp, looking for the central site of the Holocaust of the Jews. They often do not know that Auschwitz I and Birkenau are distinct sites, and have difficulty understanding what happened where. The recollections of the American Konnilyn Feig may stand for the experience of many. When she first visited Auschwitz, she did not know that Birkenau was a separate place. She found Auschwitz I 'tidy, contained, sterile, clipped, professional, detached, and small...It is truly like visiting just another museum.' Yet some exhibitions still touched her: the rooms full of hair, of tooth-brushes, shaving brushes, spectacles, dentures and artificial limbs were overwhelming. 'From them, I learned.' Nevertheless, she felt some-thing was wrong: 'Although I felt the degradation and the horror, I could not place it in the context of that neat orderly little camp.'[3] She did not know that all those things exhibited in the barracks of Auschwitz I were actually recovered a mile and a half down the road – in Birkenau.

Unlike many others, who think that they have seen all of Auschwitz after inspecting the gas chamber and ovens of crematorium I at the end of the tour through the Stammlager, Feig did discover Birkenau, if only by accident.

We left Auschwitz when it was dark, but a full orange Polish moon stood in the sky. Wrong turn, and suddenly, silhouetted starkly against the sky, the strangest, eeriest sight I had ever seen. No one was around. It was silent. We got out, walked to the gates, and then peered through the fences. I did not know what I was looking at, but it frightened me to my depths – a young American girl standing with a friend in Poland in the deserted countryside, at Birkenau. I felt an overwhelming sense of evil – not horror, as in the Auschwitz warehouses, but evil. God, it was awful. I stood with my eyes wide

[3] Konnilyn G. Feig, *Hitler's Death Camps: The Sanity of Madness* (New York and London, 1981), 335–6.

and my mouth open, speechless. I had no idea what it was, but I felt evil, and that moment, that time, has never left me.[4]

By the time we wrote our book, the Auschwitz-Birkenau State Museum had made a valiant effort to make Birkenau more accessible. A shuttle ran between Auschwitz and Birkenau, and an excellent and aesthetically unobtrusive system of signs, placed throughout Birkenau, was created to inform the visitor about the war-time function of the various compounds, buildings and ruins.

But many problems remained. We noted that in Auschwitz I the legitimate desires of Roman Catholic Poles to commemorate compatriots who were murdered there often offended the sensibilities of Jewish visitors who, like Konnylin Feig, were insufficiently aware that most Jews were murdered 'down the road'. And Birkenau too provided occasion for irritation and conflict. One of the over 900,000 Jewish victims of Birkenau was the Carmelite nun Sister Benedicta of the Cross, née Edith Stein. Born in a Jewish family, Edith Stein was a convert to Roman Catholicism. Her death would have remained a tragic footnote in the history of Birkenau if not for Pope John-Paul II's decision in 1979 to initiate her beatification. As a result, the place where she was murdered, the so-called 'Field of Ashes', became a place of Christian pilgrimage.

The Polish government was not unaware that there were serious problems in Auschwitz. Recognising the complexity of the legacy of the camp, the prime minister, Tadeusz Mazowiecki, took the time-honoured option of politicians and established a commission in the autumn of 1989 to transform the memorial camp into a site acceptable to all concerned. The commission faced a nearly impossible task, and to co-opt as many people as possible appointed a myriad of sub-committees and working-groups. One of these was a group of Jewish intellectuals who were asked to advise the Polish Commission on the Future of Auschwitz. 'We were set up', the British philosopher, Gillian Rose, observed. 'Enticed to preen ourselves as *consultants*, in effect, our participation was staged.'[5] As an international conference on 'The Future of Auschwitz: Should the Relicts be Preserved?' held in the summer of 1993 revealed, the commission faced a nearly impossible task. So it enticed another group of experts – we amongst them – to preen themselves as consultants. The exhibits in Auschwitz I are deteriorating rapidly, and the physical remains of Auschwitz-Birkenau are falling apart. The museum conservators therefore posed very practical questions on the conference agenda: What should be done with the hair, the suitcases, the brushes? Should the disintegrating barbed wire in Birkenau be replaced?

[4] *Ibid.*, 337.
[5] Gillion Rose, *Love's Work* (1995), 8.

The participants quickly found themselves caught in the web of the many contradictory functions and meanings of Auschwitz. It is a destination of mass tourism (in 1989 alone 700,000 people from eighty-nine countries visited the camp), a Polish museum to preserve the physical remains of the Germans' crimes and to educate future generations and a place of pilgrimage, a cemetery for mourners. Inseparable and entangled, these three functions collide at every spot.

That a lot of impassioned nonsense was adduced at the conference by otherwise clear-thinking scholars and conservators is a reflection of the conundrum posed by Auschwitz. Everyone rode his or her hobby-horse. Jean-Claude Pressac, who wrote an important book about the gas chambers and the crematoria,[6] proposed rebuilding crematorium III to counter those who denied the Holocaust. The American scholar of monuments, James Young, by contrast, proposed that the site 'age gracefully', an adverb which, as the American conservator James Frantz observed, does not feel quite right. Yaffa Eliach, who through the hundreds of photographs she painstakingly collected has created a powerful memorial to the people of her hometown in the Ejszyski Tower in the United States Holocaust Memorial Museum, urged that a greater place be given to the victims. Optimistically assessing the museum's ability to create and maintain an extensive and sophisticated electronic infrastructure, she suggested the installation of video terminals all over the site. At the push of a button, one could hear and see survivor testimony *in situ*.

The Auschwitz-Birkenau State Museum staff listened respectfully to the foreign guests' suggestions, and then presented their own plans to construct a memorial consisting of slabs of glass inscribed with the names of the people who died in the camp complex. These slabs – hundreds of them – were to be installed in the Central Sauna. With the best of intentions, but with poor judgement, the museum authorities in Auschwitz proposed to repeat the mistakes of their predecessors, who had changed the prisoner reception building in the main camp to accommodate the demands of the tourist industry. If executed, the planned memorial would obliterate a unique architectural record of the National Socialist system for dehumanization: the interior of the Central Sauna building. This was German industry at its most effective; the designer of the building took pride in the fact that it worked 'like a conveyer belt'.[7]

[6] Jean-Claude Pressac, *Auschwitz: Technique and Operation of the Gas Chambers* (New York, 1989).
[7] Letter Karl Bischoff to WVHA/C:1, 4 June 1943. Archive Auschwitz-Birkenau State Museum, BW 1/3, 106.

Dwork and I proposed moving the presentation of the Shoah from Blocks 4 and 5 of Auschwitz I to Birkenau, where the Jews were murdered. Auschwitz I, we believe, should focus on the significance of the camp in the history of Polish–German relations. We argued that the present resurgence of the kind of ethnic troubles that contributed to Germany's annexation of Danzig, Pomerania, Posen and eastern Upper Silesia in 1939 provides a powerful impetus to refocus the exhibition in the *Stammlager* which should explain Himmler's policies as Reich Commissioner for the Consolidation of the German Nation in the annexed territories. We also argued that the present visitor reception centre should be stripped of its tourist services and preserved as a major relic of the German regime. Most important, Auschwitz I was to be recognised as a central site for Poles in particular and Christians in general; the didactic labels and informational plaques ought not to merge the separate histories of Auschwitz I and Birkenau. It was important to articulate clearly that the genocide of the Jews and the mass murder of gypsies and Soviet prisoners-of-war took place at Birkenau, and the lack of a memorial museum suppressed that fact. At the time of the conference, visitors entered the camp through the well-known gate and hurried along the tracks to the monument at the end of the axis. This discouraged exploration of the rest of the site. We believed it would be helpful to give visitors a sense of the sheer scale of the place and of the megalomaniac ambition of the Germans. Our proposal included a permanent exhibition to present the history of the *Shoah* on the site of 'Canada' because of its specific role, its location between the three gas chamber sites and its moral significance.

On leaving the exhibition the visitors would proceed by the waste water treatment plant to the ruins of crematorium III, the monument and the ruins of crematorium II. Only then would they follow the railway tracks, but in counter-movement to the arriving cattle cars in the 1940s. This, we argued, would be consistent with the dominant ideology of our project which derived directly from my first encounter with *Night and Fog*: we cannot experience the fate of the victims; at best, we can be witnesses to their suffering.

On my return to Canada, I became increasingly uncomfortable with the proposals made in the conference, including our own. It seemed that we had fallen victim to the usual situation that, once a problem (such as, for example, a 'Jewish Problem') has been formulated, a solution (such as, for example, a 'Final Solution') must be found. Was it really necessary to tinker with Auschwitz? Should we not we just acknowledge the radical 'otherness' of the place, and allow it to be? It was not difficult to formulate a philosophical perspective on this issue. In trying to deal with the site, we had implicitly assumed that there was still a continuity between past and future. Yet had not Auschwitz severed past and future into disparate realms of time? I was well aware that, at least since 1951 when Theodor Adorno stated that 'to write a poem after Auschwitz is barbaric', the term 'after Auschwitz' had become a linguistic marker of a historical rupture.[8] Following Adorno, the philosopher Hans Jonas explained, the single name of Auschwitz serves 'as a blindingly concentrating lens' to gather the widely dispersed reality of the Holocaust. 'Auschwitz', he said, 'marks a divide between a "before" and an "after", where the latter will be forever different from the former.'[9] And Jürgen Habermas stated that 'Auschwitz' had changed the world because there the fundamental solidarity of all human beings had been destroyed. Therefore 'Auschwitz altered the conditions for the continuation of historical life contexts – and not only in Germany.'[10]

If Auschwitz were such a rupture, why preserve the landscape and the structures? At that time I reread Jorge Semprun's *The Long Voyage* (1964). Semprun was a veteran of the Spanish Civil War when he was arrested in France for activities in the Resistance. He was sent to Buchenwald, to be liberated by the Americans in 1945, and return to a society which, unlike himself, was not only utterly unchanged, but also proved to be resistant to any change. He realised that, as a survivor from the camp, he did not share any more the same reality with those who had not been there and who refused to reflect on their lives *as if* they had been there. When he tried to communicate 'what it was like', Semprun realised that it was beyond communication. 'This evening I no longer know whether I dreamed all that, or whether I've been dreaming since the whole thing has ceased to exist.'[11] And Semprun also realised that the reality of Buchenwald was not only impossible to transmit to others in the present, but that even during his imprisonment he had been incapable of knowing this. Buchenwald, in short, had forged a unity between reality and unreality.

To Semprun, the only possibility way of resolving the contradiction between the opposing realities would be the disappearance of all 'objective' traces of the camp and its history.

[8] Theodor Adorno, 'Kulturkritik und Gesellschaft', in *Kulturkritik und Gesellschaft*, I: *Prismen* (Frankfurt am Main, 1977), 33.

[9] Hans Jonas, 'The Concept of God after Auschwitz', in *Echoes from the Holocaust: Philosophical Reflections on a Dark Time*, ed. Alan Rosenberg and Gerald E. Meyers (Philadelphia, 1988), 292.

[10] Jürgen Habermas, 'Historical Consciousness and Post-Traditional Identity', in *The New Conservatism: Cultural Criticism and the Historians' Debate*, trans. Shierry Weber Nicholson (Cambridge, 1989), 251.

[11] Jorge Semprum, *The Long Voyage*, trans. Richard Seaver (Toronto and Montreal, 1964), 143.

I was saying, only a few weeks ago I was saying to myself that I would like to see that: the grass and the bushes, the roots and brambles encroaching as the seasons go by, beneath the persistent Ettersberg rains, the winter snow, beneath the brief, rustling April sun, endlessly, obstinately encroaching, with that excessive obstinacy of natural things, among the cracks in the disjointed wood and the powdery crumbling of the cement that would split and yield to the thrust of the beech forest, unceasingly encroaching on this human countryside on the flank of the hill, this camp constructed by men, the grass and the roots repossessing the place where the camp had stood. The first to collapse would be the wooden barracks, those of the main camp, painted a pretty green, blending in easily, soon drowned by the invading tide of grass and shrubs, then later the two-storey cement buildings, and then at last, surely long after all the other buildings, years later, remaining standing the longest, like the remembrance, or rather the evidence, the special symbol of that whole, the massive square chimney of the crematorium, till the day when the roots and brambles shall also overcome that tenacious resistance of death rising among the waves of green covering over what was an extermination camp, and those shadows of dense black smoke, shot through with yellow, that perhaps still linger over the countryside, that smell of burning flesh still hovering over this countryside, when all the survivors, all of us, have long since disappeared, when there will no longer be any real memory of this, only the memory of memories related by those who will never really know (as one knows the acidity of a lemon, the feel of wool, the softness of a shoulder) what all this really was.[12]

Semprun offered a perspective which I found increasingly attractive. Thus I came to the conclusion that, in response to the question 'Should the Relics be Preserved?' the answer ought to be 'No!'

Yet circumstances and pride would push me in another direction. In the wake of the conference the future of Auschwitz became front page news in America when a businessman proposed to redevelop an existing store close to the entrance of Auschwitz I into a shopping mall. Polish–Jewish tension at Auschwitz became an occasion for official embarrassment in the commemoration ceremonies for the fiftieth anniversary of the liberation of Auschwitz. President Lech Walesa refused to acknowledge the Holocaust at the official observances scheduled for 26 and 27 January 1995. Outraged by his high-handed marginalisation of Jewish suffering, 1,500 Jews assembled for a separate ceremony in Birkenau. Thirty miles away at the official ceremony in

[12] *Ibid.*, 190.

Cracow, Walesa lamented the Germans' attempts to destroy Poland's 'intellectual and spiritual strength'. He failed to mention the Jews. Tensions between Jews and Poles increased as the day progressed, and only thanks to personal intervention by Elie Wiesel did Walesa acknowledge the next day in his speech at Auschwitz the special suffering of Jews in Auschwitz. All was duly reported in foreign papers. For the Poles the commemoration was a public-relations disaster.[13]

A year later Walesa faced re-election, and his opponent Alexander Kwasniewski made Walesa's mishandling of the commemoration, and the international uproar it had caused, into an election issue: seeking entry into NATO, Poland could ill afford to alienate what they perceived to be an important American constituency. Kwasniewski won, and shortly after his inauguration, he ordered his chancellery to prepare the *Program Oswiecimski* – a proposal that was to provide a framework for the future development of the site acceptable to both Poles and Jews. The chancellery turned for advice to the municipal government of Oswiecim and the staff of the Auschwitz-Birkenau State Museum and, on the basis of existing proposals, they hastily cobbled together the requested *Program Oswiecimski*. Endorsed by the chancellery, President Kwasniewski presented it to Miles Lerman, Chairman of the United States Holocaust Memorial Council, during his visit to Washington on 9 July 1996.

In order to prepare a response that represented the views of the leaders of international organisations with a stake in the future of Auschwitz, Lerman convened the leaders of the American Gathering of Jewish Holocaust Survivors, the American Jewish Committee, the Anti-Defamation League, the Ronald S. Lauder Foundation, Yad Vashem, the World Jewish Congress and the United States Holocaust Memorial Museum, in the Auschwitz Proposal Review Committee. This committee invited Dwork and me to comment on the *Program Oswiecimski*. We had shortly before published our book on Auschwitz, and knew the issues addressed in the *Program Oswiecimski* from our ten-year-long involvement with the history and topography of the site. Given our experiences with the 1993 conference, and the conclusions we had drawn in its wake, we should have said: 'Thank you, but no thank you.' But we did not, and accepted the challenge.

We presented our initial response at a meeting of the Auschwitz Proposal Review Committee on 21 November 1996. The central problem with the Polish proposal, we argued, was the absence of any overall strategy. It would be very difficult to reach a Polish–Jewish consensus about the future of Auschwitz and Birkenau without a strategy or 'Master Plan' – a concept which, when we presented it, we

[13] Van Pelt and Dwork, *Auschwitz*, 372.

admitted to be somewhat inappropriate, but which quickly caught the imagination of everyone around the table. We argued that the *Program Oswiecimski*, an ill-considered tinkering with the site without proper consultation with interested groups, would provide a recipe for disaster and conflict. We suggested that the process of formulating a comprehensive strategy would demand clarity about certain key issues. Poles, Jews and others would have to ask themselves: 'What is important to us, and why?' A 'Master Plan', with its urban and architectural design guidelines, was to provide a useful tool of dialogue because the identified 'space' would emerge as a common plane on which all could see the different issues, tensions and conflicts in relationship to each other.

We proposed that the urban development of Oswiecim and Brzezinka and the consequent encroachment on the UNESCO Protective Zone converged with the historical misunderstandings and conflicts between Poles and Jews into an issue of spatial design and management. For example: the present location of most visitor facilities and the resulting protocol of visitation suggests that a visit to Birkenau, where four of the five crematoria stood, is less important than a visit to Auschwitz. Therefore the present museological arrangement *inadvertently* suggested that Polish suffering deserves more attention than Jewish suffering. We argued therefore that relocating the visitor centre from its present location in Auschwitz to a site between Auschwitz and Birkenau would go far to address this issue.

In order to demonstrate how the problem of urban encroachment and the misinterpretation engendered by the present visitor protocol could be understood in terms of space and therefore should be resolved with space management, we submitted to the committee a *Preliminary Proposal for a Conceptual Master Plan for the Auschwitz-Birkenau State Museum*.[14] This *Preliminary Proposal* was based on the idea that the basis for any further discussion on the Polish proposal should be a common effort to identify and describe the historical character and significance of the various precincts and structures of the Auschwitz-Birkenau State Museum and its surroundings. On this basis it should be possible to propose an intelligent and responsible system of site and visitor management. Specifically, the *Preliminary Proposal* suggested that Auschwitz and Birkenau become one museum district with clearly defined boundaries to ensure the continued preservation of both camps amidst a dynamically growing community. Furthermore it proposed a new visitor centre half-way between the two camps, in order to present Auschwitz and Birkenau as sites equally worthy of pilgrimage. Finally

---

[14] The *Preliminary Proposal* was drafted by Robert Jan van Pelt and Valerio Rynnimeri, in consultation with Debórah Dwork.

it called for the development of the economic and tourist infrastructure of the communities of Oswiecim and Brzezinka to ensure successful management of the increased pressure of tourism on the memorial sites.

In hindsight the *Preliminary Proposal* was irresponsible – one of the many urban visions testifying to the hubris of architects and planners who think they can shape life through a few lines on a white sheet of paper. But somehow all in the room were caught up in this belief that one could 'solve' the 'Auschwitz problem' with a few sheets of paper. The committee accepted our analysis and, stating that our proposal 'incorporates essential elements for a future proposal and could serve as a fruitful basis for discussions',[15] called in its Response to *Program Oswiecimski* for the creation of such a Master Plan by Poles, Israeli and North American Jews. The *Preliminary Proposal for a Conceptual Master Plan* was included as an appendix to the Response.

The Polish government replied promptly. Marek M. Siwiec, Secretary of State in the Chancellery of the President of the Republic of Poland noted with delight that 'comparing the Government Program with the concept proposed by Prof. Debórah Dwork and Prof. Robert Jan van Pelt, we can see many common elements that can be developed jointly',[16] and invited us to present the full argument of the two documents in Poland at the end of February 1997.

We had very little time – less than six weeks in fact – and in an atmosphere of extreme urgency I and the committee took no time to reflect on Debórah's query whether we ought not to step back and reconsider the whole approach. In a parody of the difference between male and female attitudes to power, the men were caught in a frenzy to use this unique opportunity to make a real difference, and we set out to create a project that would impress the Poles. Only half-convinced, Debórah supported us. And thus I established a design collaborative at the University of Waterloo School of Architecture, operating in collaboration with the Center for Holocaust Study at Clark University, to produce a plan that would make the most of the opportunity offered.[17]

---

[15] 'Response to *Program Oswiecimski*: Requirements for a Future Plan', signed on 21 Nov. 1996 by representatives of the American Gathering of Jewish Holocaust Survivors, American Jewish Committee, Anti-Defamation League, Ronald S. Lauder Foundation, United States Holocaust Memorial Museum, World Jewish Congress and Yad Vashem, clause 11; collection author.

[16] Letter Marek Siwiec to Miles Lerman, 9 Jan. 1997, 2; copy collection author.

[17] The collaborative consisted of five partners (Robert Jan van Pelt, chair, Debórah Dwork, Donald McKay, Dereck Revington and Valerio Rynnimeri), six graduate associates (Douglas Birkenshaw, Jed Braithwaite, Beth Kapusta, Neil Kaye, Katherine Anne Mullin and Geoffrey Thün) and six student associates (Omer Arbel, Paul Blaser, Andrew Chatham, Margaret Graham, Ariella Kanner and Jeffrey Pidsaney).

The new report, to be entitled a *Strategy for the Auschwitz-Birkenau State Museum*, was to identify in some detail the civic, cultural, environmental and economic circumstances of Auschwitz and Birkenau, and propose in text and drawings a new relation to adjacent residential, commercial, industrial and agricultural areas of Oswiecim and Brzezinka. The *Strategy* was to reiterate the central principles of the earlier proposal: a unified museum district with clearly defined boundaries, a new visitor centre half-way between the two camps, the closure of Leszcynska Street to through traffic and a new approach from the Visitor Reception Centre to Birkenau, and a new perspective on the development of the economic and tourist infrastructure of the communities of Oswiecim and Brzezinka. It differed from the earlier work in offering a substantial analysis of the failure of the two Unesco Protective Zones in preserving the historical precincts of the memorial camps at Auschwitz and Birkenau. We found that the boundaries of these zones had been established with little regard for the form of the natural landscape or the structure of the built-up areas of Oswiecim and Brzezinka, and that the zones had been established without archaeological precision, leaving historically important sites and structures outside its boundaries.

> Ill-drawn boundaries (and resulting encroachment), inappropriate land use, and omission of significant sites and artifacts, combine with the huge scale of the site, and the isolation of museum facilities in one camp to compromise the presentation of both Auschwitz and Birkenau as two parts of a single domain of genocide and martyrdom. As such, disposition of the camps and their history exacerbate the points of friction brought about by the mutual misunderstandings among members of different national, ethnic, religious, and political groups visiting the site.[18]

The *Strategy* stipulated that in a future Master Plan the issue of preservation must be of central importance, and should govern the future management of the site. We decided, however, against a single policy of preservation for artifacts on the site, as this would not only imply massive dislocation of various non-museological activities now occurring within the historic precinct of Auschwitz and Birkenau, but also impose an unrealistic financial burden on future generations. Hence we proposed that a future policy of preservation should be based on a hierarchy of historical importance distinguishing between critical sites or artifacts (places of genocide and martyrdom), important sites or artifacts (SS and other German facilities) and significant sites or artifacts

---

[18] Auschwitz Birkenau Collaborative, *Strategy for the State Museum of Auschwitz-Birkenau, Report Presented to the Honorable Aleksander Kwasniewski, President of Poland, March 5, 1997*, 6; collection author.

(sites that provide a sense of the comprehensive character of the German concentration camp). Critical sites were only to serve purposes of commemoration; important sites were to serve museological functions; and significant sites could be used for other appropriate purposes.

We adopted the triad of critical/important/significant in order to create a simple matrix that would force us, and in the future our Polish partners, to define our values and, consequently, our negotiating position. Issues or sites designated by any party as 'critical' were to remain in principle non-negotiable, and be preserved in their entirety; issues and sites designated as 'significant' could become the object of concession and compromise, and be adapted to facilitate the life of the surrounding community; 'important' issues were those we felt were worth a good fight.

In our deliberations we decided that preservation should not only concentrate on historically important sites and artifacts but also on the landscape as an ecological hierarchy. Again we applied the hierarchy of critical/important/significant. We defined critical landscapes as places of genocide and martyrdom, while important landscapes were to be those agricultural, recreational and park lands adjacent to the camps that define the connection between the approach to, and the most important views from, the critical landscapes. Finally the ecological catchment area of the critical landscapes was to be defined as significant. We proposed that historical landscapes should not be changed, while all change in land use and all construction within the important landscapes should be subject to development and design controls. Change in land use and construction in significant landscapes should, in turn, be done in consultation with the Polish Government Pleni-potentiary for the Government Strategic Plan for Oswiecim, and a new Board of trustees.

In the *Strategy* we reiterated important principles of the earlier *Preliminary Proposal*, such as the idea to erect a new visitor infrastructure centred on a new Visitor Reception Centre, with bus arrivals, the central parking area, general visitor services and an orientation centre. The new centre was to be built half-way between the two camps. We proposed two shuttle lines: the first was to connect the visitors from the new centre to the scattered, historically important sites, while the second was to connect the centre back to the town of Oswiecim.

The site of Auschwitz-Birkenau is one of the most important cultural-historical precincts in the world, and we anticipated that it would become an increasingly important destination of cultural tourism, changing from a day-trip destination into an occasion for longer stays. In the *Strategy* we identified sites that ought, over time, to be developed to provide a comprehensive cultural environment. We suggested that industrial and commercial enterprises adjacent to this zone should become subject to special controls, while existing agricultural uses between Auschwitz and Birkenau should become subject to various restrictions.

Unlike the various earlier 'protective', 'exclusion' and 'quiet' zones, which were relatively insensitive to the intensely varied local conditions around the two camps, we set out to formulate a realistic set of seven tailor-made operating policies for the protection and management of the camps and their surrounding areas. Reviewing the failure of earlier attempts to enforce the 1962 so-called 'Quiet Zone', the 1977 'Protective Zone', the 1979 'Unesco Zone' and the 1984 'Exclusion Zone' we proposed that the new policies were to be implemented and enforced by a separate planning authority for the regulated area, operating under instructions from the government Plenipotentiary for the implementation of the *Program Oswiecimski* and a new Board of Trustees. We came to the conclusion that the success of the Auschwitz-Birkenau State Museum as a tourist destination depended on the symbiosis between a well-managed museum and a prosperous community.

It took one month to bring *The Strategy for the Auschwitz-Birkenau State Museum* to completion. The *Strategy* consisted of two posters, each showing four analytical plans, a conceptual urban plan and four images of the new Visitor Reception Centre. It included a very large, carefully crafted, Canadian Maple site model of the area surrounding the proposed Visitor Reception Centre, and a thirty-two-page illustrated report, summarising in text and colour and black-and-white images, and eight coloured maps the reasoning behind the proposal.

The panels, model and reports were despatched to Poland, and arrived in time for three days of substantial dialogue in the President's Palace in Warsaw. From there we moved to Oswiecim, to present our ideas to the town council. That presentation led to what diplomats politely call a 'frank and open exchange of ideas'. Some local politicians supported our efforts, but others adopted a xenophobic rhetoric which compared our efforts to the German plans for the area in the 1940s. Yet in the end all sides agreed that the *Strategy* had raised some important issues, and consequently a 10-point *Declaration concerning Principles for Implementation of Program Oswiecimski*, initialled in Warsaw on 5 March 1997 in the presence of President Kwasniewski by Polish and Jewish leaders, confirmed that the final version of the *Program Oswiecimski* must

include an urban Master Plan for the State Museum of Auschwitz-Birkenau that will serve as a basis for a future proposal. The presence of a mutually-agreeable Master Plan, which incorporates all the pertinent principles contained in this agreement, will create a common language and concrete reference point to evaluate, develop and implement a future proposal.

The signatories of this Declaration, in cooperation with the International Council of the State Museum of Auschwitz-Birkenau, will appoint the most competent experts to jointly develop a Master Plan. Such a Master Plan shall be completed by 31 December 1998.

This Master Plan shall take into account: the physical linkage of both sites; the adherence to and preservation of the Protection Zones; and the encouragement of the economic growth of the surrounding communities.[19]

The next day the major Polish daily, the *Rzeczpospolita*, approvingly quoted the mayor of Oswiecim who called the agreement a 'historic day for both the Polish and Jewish people'.[20]

Having made my small mark on the history of Auschwitz, I began a process of disengagement. This was aided by an increasing sense that the way in which the Auschwitz-Birkenau State Museum was to operate the site was of little ultimate importance to Jews, even if the *New York Times* were to suggest otherwise. This shift in position was informed by my reconsideration of Jewish tradition. I recalled how Jews celebrate Passover because 'In every age man must see himself as if he himself went out of Egypt' (*Mishnah Pessahim*, 10, 5). Few, however, feel obliged to visit the shores of the Sea of Reeds (Red Sea). At the end of the Seder we exult: 'Next Year in Jerusalem!', but we do not need to be in Jerusalem to tell the story and share the matzot. What is important is the belief – or hope – that Jerusalem will be ready to receive us next year. Psychologists tells us that a strongly developed sense of home allows adolescents to go out into the great world, and begin a process of individuation. In the same way the strong memory and anticipation of Jerusalem had allowed Jews to live in the diaspora. Like the Jerusalem of the Passover Seder, I now began to see Auschwitz as a site one does *not* need to visit in order to teach and remember, but at the same time it was a site *that must remain available*. To be assured, to rest secure, that such a visit were to be possible, was more important than the visit itself. And if visited, the story told years after the event would also be more important than the actual encounter with the place.

This approach fitted my own experience: my first visit to Auschwitz in 1989 had been a disappointment, and in the final analysis the experience was only worthwhile because of the fifteen years of spiritual preparation and the slow metamorphosis of memory in the years which

---

[19] *Declaration concerning Principles for Implementation of Program Oswiecinski*, signed in Warsaw on 5 Mar. 1997 by Marek Siwiec, Lech Nikolski, Miles Lerman, Israel Gutman, Wladyslaw Bartoszewski, Jerzy Wroblewski and Andrzej Telka; copy collection author.

[20] 'Widoczny postep', *Rzeczpospolita*, 6 Mar. 1997, 2.

followed that first visit. I came to realise that a visit to Auschwitz can only be a disappointment, because at present the site does not permit us to imagine what the place was like between 1940 and 1945. As I stood at the intersection of roads where the selection took place, I realised that I could not imagine what selection was like. As I walked through a musty smelling barrack, I realised that I could not imagine what it was like crowded with frightened, starved and sick people. All that was left were shells and shadows.

This led me to re-examine the central idea that had informed the *Preliminary Proposal* and *The Strategy for the Auschwitz-Birkenau State Museum*: the construction of a new visitor reception centre. I came to realise that the simple act of building the centre left the most important issues unresolved. Visitors arrive at Auschwitz with their own preconceptions, fears and objectives, and so no building can truly 'receive' them. Understood primarily as a reception centre, even the most brilliantly conceived and executed building designed by an outstanding architect could not but fail the visitor, but it could, perhaps, transcend its limitations if it were an exit from Auschwitz. If the question that was to inform the building could be reformulated from 'What should be the first thing one sees when arriving in Auschwitz?' to 'What would be an appropriate image before leaving for one's car or bus?', the nature of the visit itself is now clearly accepted within the context of the visitor's unique situation. In seeing the entrance gate as an exit to a site which, during its years of operation, had no exit except through the chimneys, we could declare, 'Yes, you will leave and live, and yes we hope that you will re-enter the world as a changed person.'

The true purpose of a visitor reception centre *at Auschwitz* would be to help people define for themselves what could and should be done to prevent a future Auschwitz. The brief for the building should not be how to process unruly tourists into docile pilgrims who visit the sites appropriate to their religious and national backgrounds (Jews first to Birkenau, Poles first to Auschwitz I), but to impress on all of them that it should be impossible to leave Auschwitz and carry on as if nothing happened, as if nothing does happen, in the world in which we live. At present, the exit from the museum goes through a one-way metal gate, and most people do not know what to do. They have a choice between the cafeteria or the little shops that line the parking lot. How different, and more powerful, is the exit from the museum at Yad Vashem in Jerusalem, where tourists walk along the shaded Avenue of the Righteous on their way to the parking lot. That exit gives direction. It is unique to Yad Vashem. But it offers, quite literally, direction. And it would be a model for us to consider.

In short, when visitors leave the building next to the Auschwitz parking lot, they should know what to do, know where to go, know what to be. It might seem like a small difference, but it makes all the difference in the world to the visitor about to re-enter that everyday world which was so radically changed by the existence of the death camps.

ROYAL HISTORICAL SOCIETY: REPORT OF COUNCIL. SESSION 2002–2003

Officers and Council

- At the Anniversary Meeting on 22 November 2002, K.C. Fincham, MA, PhD, succeeded Dr. P. Mandler as Honorary Secretary; the remaining Officers of the Society were re-elected.
- The Vice-Presidents retiring under By-law XVII were Professor D.N. Cannadine, Professor P.A. Stafford, Professor J.A. Tosh and Mrs. S. Tyacke, CB. Professor H.T. Dickinson, MA, PhD, DLitt. and C.J. Kitching, PhD, FSA were elected to replace them.
- The Members of Council retiring under By-law XX were Dr. W.R. Childs, Professor M.L. Dockrill, Professor V.I.J. Flint and Professor J.L. Miller. In accordance with By-law XXI, amended, Professor G.A. Hosking, MA. PhD. FBA., R.S. Mackenney, MA. PhD. and Professor D.M. Palliser, MA. DPhil. were elected in their place.
- Dr. W.R. Childs was elected for a further term of one year in place of Professor T.A. Reuter, who had died mid-term during the session and Professor V.I.J. Flint was elected for a further term of one year in place of Professor C.M. Andrew, who had resigned mid-term.
- The Election of Officers Subcommittee convened during the year proposed that Professor M.J. Daunton succeed Professor J.L. Nelson as President from November 2004. Professor Daunton consented to Council's request that his name be put forward to the Society's Anniversary Meeting on 21 November 2003 to become President-elect for one year with effect from that date.
- haysmacintyre were appointed auditors for the year 2002–2003 under By-law XXXIX.
- Cripps Portfolio continue to manage the Society's investment funds.

Activities of the Society during the Year

At this particularly challenging time, the Society continued to speak vigorously on behalf of the historical profession and of historical research to government, to the nation's research bodies, funding councils and other scholarly groups.

- Among the major responses submitted this year by the Society have been:

- ○ The White Paper on 'The Future of Higher Education'
- ○ HEFCE's invitation to contribute to the joint funding bodies' review of research assessment in higher education
- ○ The British Academy's Review of the impact of the arts and social sciences on society and the economy
- The worrying implications of the White Paper led the Honorary Secretary to represent the Society in an informal alliance of eleven Learned Societies which expresses concern, privately and publicly, at the government's plans to concentrate research in a small number of elite institutions.
- The changing character of research funding for research and postgraduate training as the Arts and Humanities Research Board changes into a Research Council has been closely monitored by the Society, and its views expressed through a series of meetings and seminars. The Society welcomes the AHRB's intention to establish a number of ring-fenced doctoral awards each year, to protect important but vulnerable areas of research, and the President has submitted a proposal for one to be devoted to 'research in historical fields requiring languages other than English'.
- Close relations with the History at the Universities Defence Group were maintained. The President and Honorary Secretary have had regular meetings with the co-convenors of HUDG, and Council has been briefed by the HUDG steering committee, which has enabled the two bodies to co-ordinate their approaches to national and local developments.
- The Society has maintained its close interest in the teaching of history in the schools, working alongside the Historical Association. The President and Dr Childs attended an Historical Association Conference on 28 September 2002, to discuss the structure of the current AS/A2 examination. Dr Childs and Professor R.D. McKitterick have participated in a study of the comparability of A Level and the International Baccalaureate Diploma. The President and Professor Dickinson have represented the Society at meetings of the History Subject Group on the Qualifications and Curriculum Authority.
- In Spring 2003 the President and Honorary Secretary represented the Society on the panel of judges for the National Awards for Teaching in Higher Education, a new scheme to recognise innovation, leadership and excellence in the teaching of history.
- In April 2003 the Historical Manuscripts Commission and the Public Record Office joined forces to create The National Archives. In November 2002 the Society hosted a highly successful meeting of stakeholders and speakers from the two institutions to discuss the implications of this amalgamation.

- In October 2002 the Society combined with the Historical Manuscripts Commission to organise the first of a regular series of
seminars in memory of Professor Gerald Aylmer (President 1984-
1988). Over a hundred participants addressed the implications of
*The Missing Link – Specialist Repositories in England: A Map of Develop-
ment and Funding Needs*, a report produced by the Society of
Archivists.

- The Society is represented on all the English Regional Archives
Councils, and this year has re-activated this 'Archives Group' of its
representatives, who are to contribute to a meeting of archivists
and historians for the 2nd Gerald Aylmer seminar in October 2003.

- The Society continued to administer the British National Committee
of the International Committee of Historical Sciences (or, to use its
familiar French acronym, CISH). In September 2002 the President
and Honorary Secretary-elect attended a General Assembly of
CISH in Amsterdam, to discuss the themes for the 20th Quin-
quennial Congress, which will be held at the University of New
South Wales, Sydney, on 3–9 July 2005. The President was elected
as a member of the central nominating committee, and preparations
are now underway to find participants for the approved list of
topics and funding to support them.

- The free on-line Bibliography of British and Irish History
(www.rhs.ac.uk/bibwel.html) was launched in July 2002, and has
rapidly established itself as an indispensable research tool for
historians. Dr I.W. Archer, General Editor, and his team have
secured enhancement funding for three years from the Arts and
Humanities Research Board and are collaborating with other
bibliographical projects, such as London Past On-Line, whose site
went live in May 2003, and have entered into a partnership with
Irish historians led by Dr J.R. Hill, who have obtained funding
from the Irish Research Council so that *Writings on Irish History* can
be made available on-line. In view of the success of the website,
and mindful of future funding applications, in July 2003 Council
reluctantly resolved to cease publishing the *Annual Bibliography* after
the completion of the volume for 2002.

- The Society aims to maintain and improve its links with postgraduate students in history, encouraging them to apply for bursaries
and to consider the advantages of membership. In 2003 a newsletter
was despatched to all those registered for higher degrees in the
UK, which from 2004 will be sent electronically, and a copy will
be posted on the Society's website.

- The increasing number of public roles that the Society performs, and
the broadening constituency that it represents, led to a fundamental
review in the autumn of 2002 of its structures and proceedings.

The committee structure has been reorganised, with the intention of encouraging Council to be pro-active in its decision-making, and to consider longer-term strategic issues, rather than being merely responsive to demands from government and funding bodies on proposals for change.

- The Society's website is currently being redesigned, so that it becomes more attractive, easier to navigate, and more informative about the many roles that the Society fulfils. New features include 'News and Initiatives' which contains, for example, the Society's response to the government's White Paper on higher education.

- All these activities have been possible only because of the dedication and expert support provided by Joy McCarthy, the Executive Secretary, and Amy Warner, Administrative Assistant. Council and the Society's Officers express gratitude for their hard work throughout the year.

Meetings of the Society

- Five papers were given in London this year and two papers were read at locations outside London. Welcome invitations were extended to the Society to visit the history departments at the Universities of Aberystwyth, the University of Greenwich and Oxford Brookes University. The trip to Aberystwyth included a conducted tour of the National Archives of Wales as well as demonstrations by staff at the Royal Commission on Ancient and Historic Monuments Wales of their latest initiatives. The visit to Greenwich was an opportunity to admire the University's magnificent setting, and that to Oxford Brookes University included lunch in 'the most expensive Council house in the country', the former residence of Robert Maxwell, and a tour of their refurbished library. Members of Council met with the departments to discuss issues of interest to historians before the papers were delivered. As always, the Society received a warm welcome and generous hospitality from the universities concerned and is very grateful to them for their kindness. Future visits are planned to include the University of Newcastle upon Tyne on 24th October 2003, Royal Holloway, University of London on 26th March 2004, the University of Kent at Canterbury on 30th April 2004 and the University of the West of England, together with the British and Empire Commonwealth Museum, Bristol, on the 22nd and 23rd October 2004.

- The Colin Matthew Memorial Lecture for the Public Understanding of History – previously known as the Gresham Lecture – was given on 7th November 2002 to an appreciative audience by Professor Marianne Elliott at Staple Inn Hall, High Holborn, London on

'Robert Emmet: the Making of a Legend'. These lectures are given in memory of the late Professor Colin Matthew, a former Literary Director and Vice-President of the Society. The lecture in 2003 will be on Thursday 6th November when Professor Brian Harrison, Editor of the *New Dictionary of National Biography* will speak on ' "A slice of their lives": The DNB's editors, 1882-1999' . The lecture in 2004 will be on Wednesday 3rd November by Dr. Gareth Griffiths, Director of the British Empire and Commonwealth Museum, Bristol.

● Future conferences would include: i) a joint conference with The National Maritime Museum on the 'Age of Exploration' to be held in September 2003; ii) an annual seminar to commemorate the Society's former President Professor Gerald Aylmer; iii) a one-day conference, 'What can historians contribute to public debate?', to be held in London on 22 November 2003; iv) a study day, 'Can we construct a history of trust?', to be held in London on 7 February 2004; v) a joint conference was planned with the North American Conference on British Studies and the British Association for American Studies, 'Crosstown Traffic: Anglo-American Cultural Exchange since 1865', to be held at the University of Warwick on 4–6 July 2004; vi) a conference on 'History and Music' to be held at CRASSH, Cambridge, in early 2005; vii) a joint conference with the Centre for English Local History, University of Leicester to mark the 50th Anniversary of W.G. Hoskins' *Making of the English Landscape* would be held in July 2005; and viii) a conference to mark the Tercentenary of the Union with Scotland would be held in 2007.

● Council decided to go ahead on an experimental basis in 2003 with the proposal for two new committees, Teaching Policy and Research Policy. To accommodate them, Research Support Committee would meet in parallel with either or both of the policy committees and Membership Committee would move onto a virtual basis (but with the option to meet in parallel with one of the two policy committees).

Prizes

The Society's annual prizes were awarded as follows:

● The Alexander Prize was not awarded in 2003.

● The David Berry Prize for 2002, for an essay on Scottish history, was awarded to Dr Dauvit E. Broun of the Department of Scottish History, University of Glasgow for his essay 'The Absence of Regnal

Years for the Dating clause of Charters of Kings of Scots, 1195–1222'.

The judge's citation read:

'This essay is an accomplished study of a tricky and much-discussed problem in the diplomatic of Scottish royal documents of the twelfth and thirteenth centuries. What raises it to the level of a significant contribution to Scottish history is the way it extracts findings about the politics and political ideas of rulers, counsellors, elites both ecclesiastical and secular in general, and charter-writers in particular, from the diplomatic material. These findings are original and convincing. They amount to a demonstration that some Scots in the course of these centuries were wrestling successfully with the problem of finding a language, technical, legal and symbolic, for asserting Scottish independence. I therefore have no hesitation in recommending that this submission be awarded the David Berry Prize.'

- The Whitfield Prize for a first book on British history attracted 22 entries. The generally high quality of the entries was again commended by the assessors.

The prize for 2002 was awarded to:

Ethan H. Shagan, *Popular Politics and the English Reformation* [Cambridge University Press]

The judges wrote:

'The author set himself the goal of exploring the 'process by which the Reformation entered English culture through the back door, not dependent upon spectacular epiphanies but rather exploiting the mundane realities of political allegiance, financial investment and local conflict'. It is a classic theme of English historiography, here addressed with trenchantly deployed scholarship to argue that 'the Reformation thus created owed as much to the dynamics of popular engagement as to the dynamics of elite enforcement'. Sharply focussed on the twenty years following the primordial 'act of State' of 1534, addressing the wealth of alternative revisionisms which others have proposed, the argument is sustained in clear and lively prose as a two-way conversation with both sixteenth-century witnesses and twentieth-century advocates. It should prove a stimulus, not to consensus, but to revitalized debate.

The assessors also wish to commend as proxime accessit, James J. Nott, *Music for the People: popular music and dance in Interwar Britain* (Oxford University Press):

This invigorating study of the popular music industry and its audience, its changing genres and vehicles of gramophone, radio, cinema and dance halls, rests on a notably resourceful exploitation of source-material and on admirably ingenious approaches to the slippery matter of how to gauge 'popularity' – while maintaining a steadily beady eye on the question of commercialism vis-à-vis the myth of 'authentic' working-class culture.'

• Thanks to the continuing generous donation from The Gladstone Memorial Trust, the third Gladstone History Book Prize for a first book on a subject outside British history was awarded. The number of entries this year was 17.

The prize for 2002 was awarded jointly to Guy Rowlands for his book, *The Dynastic State and the army under Louis XIV: Royal Service and Private Interest, 1661–1701*, published by Cambridge University Press and to David M. Hopkin, *Soldier and Peasant in French popular culture, 1766-1870*, The Boydell Press, for the Royal Historical Society; Woodbridge/Rochester NY, USA.

The judges wrote:

'David Hopkin's, *Soldier and Peasant in French popular culture, 1766-1870* is a fine and original analysis of the representation of the soldier and of peasants' attitudes towards the military in Lorraine, Alsace, Champagne and Franche Comté in the post-Revolutionary era. Hopkin makes a convincing case for peasant attitudes in this region being of particular consequence in this period, for it was a border region and the site of a great deal of military activity and it provided a large number of recruits for the army. The 'Frenchness' of people in the area is obviously an issue and toward the end of the book Hopkin suggests that military service became an engine for national integration, and played a crucial role in the peasants' understanding of what it meant to be French.

If one might expect a pro-soldier bias in Lorraine, the evidence Hopkin produces soon demonstrates the contrary. Peasants even in Lorraine did not identify with soldiers: they looked on them as leading a disreputable and very unpeasant-like way of life, drinking, whoring, gambling, marauding. They probably also envied their travelling and knowledge of the world, their freedom from petty local hierarchies and rigid moral norms. Hopkin suggests that the division between 'peasant' and 'Frenchman' posited by Eugen Weber may be partly a division between 'peasant' and 'soldier'.

Overall, it is vigorously written, lucid, well argued, based on abundant evidence and deals with a subject of real importance. In the general issues of methods and evidence, especially about how the historian can document the attitudes and thinking of peasants, it is a very important contribution to learning. It is the work of an excellent historian and a pleasure to read.

Guy Rowlands', *The Dynastic State and the Army under Louis XIV*, aims to place the army at the centre of both French society and the French state in the seventeenth century. It pulls together the multiple influences shaping the military forces during the reign of Louis XIV and demonstrates how the French army became a paradigm of the standing army for contemporaries and historians alike. It places itself securely in its historiographical context, both of military histories of early modern Europe, particularly of the French army, and of kingship and government. It moves far beyond them, however, by concentrating on the functioning and administration of the land forces at the disposal of Louis XIV and placing them in their social context. He also extends his enquiry into the 1690s. Thus it continues, for a slightly later period, the revisionism in the relationship between military change and state formation undertaken by scholars such as Roger Mettam and David Parrott.

The book is substantial (362 pp. of quite small print) and impressive in the range of sources, published and unpublished, institutional and personal. It is argued with great energy, and an imaginative engagement with the lives of the host of men, great and small, whose careers and family connections Rowlands has found documented in the archives, their behaviour, personal and political conduct and family relationships. The pages are full of individuals, from the Le Tellier family down to the wretched subalterns trying desperately to make their way. Above all it is a strong and sustained argument from first to last , providing not only a reinterpretation of the development of the French army but more crucially of the 'dynastic state' of France and its rulers. Altogether, for the significance of its claims, the lucidity of its writing and the solidity of the supporting evidence, this is an outstanding first book.'

- In order to recognise the high quality of work now being produced at undergraduate level in the form of third-year dissertations, the Society is continuing, in association with *History Today* magazine, an annual prize for the best undergraduate dissertation. Departments are asked to nominate annually their best dissertation and a joint committee of the Society and *History Today* select in the autumn the national prizewinner from among these nominations. The prize also recognizes the Society's close relations with *History Today* and the important role the magazine has played in disseminating scholarly research to a wider audience.

First prize was awarded to Paul Shirley [UCL] for his essay ' "Tek Force Wid Force!" Marronage, Resistance and Freedom Struggles in the Experience of North American Émigré Blacks in the Bahamas, 1783–1789';

Second prize was awarded Anthony Craig Lockley [University of Manchester] for his essay 'Propaganda and Intervention at Archangel 1918–1919';

Third prize was awarded to Anna Chapman [University of East Anglia] for her essay 'Piety, Patronage and Politics: An Exploration of Fact and Fiction in the Early Legend of St. Edmund'.

Articles by prize-winners presenting their research have appeared or will appear shortly in *History Today* editions in 2003.

At the kind invitation of the Keeper, all entrants and their institutional contacts were invited to a celebratory lunch and a behind the scenes visit to the Public Record Office in January 2003. Over thirty candidates and tutors attended.

- Frampton and Beazley Prizes for A-level performances were awarded, following nominations from the examining bodies:

Frampton Prizes:
  o Edexcel Foundation incorporating the London Examination Board:
    Ella Davies, Redlands High School, Bristol
  o Oxford, Cambridge and RSA Board:
    Laura Venning, Somervale School, Bath
  o Welsh Joint Education Committee:
    Katie Fisher, Penglais School, Aberystwyth

Beazley Prizes:
  o Northern Ireland Council for the Curriculum Examinations and Assessment:
    Deborah F. Toner, St. Louis Grammar School, Ballymena, County Antrim
  o Scottish Examination Board:
    Scott G. Manson, Mearns Castle High School, Glasgow

Publications

- *Transactions*, Sixth Series, Volume 12 was published during the session, and *Transactions*, Sixth Series, Volume 13 went to press, to be published in November 2003.
- In the Camden, Fifth Series, *Travel, Trade and Power in the Atlantic, 1765–1884*, ed. W.A. Speck/B. Wood and M. Lynn (Vol. 19), *Letters from Arnold Stephenson Rowntree to Mary Katherine Rowntree, 1910–1918*, ed. I. Packer (vol. 20) and *British Envoys to Germany, 1816–1866, Vol. II: 1830–1847*, ed. M. Moesslang, S. Freitag and P. Wende (Vol. 21) were published during the year. *Religion, Politics and Society in Sixteenth-Century England*, eds. S. Adams, I. Archer, G.W. Bernard, F. Kisby, M. Greengrass and P. Hammer (Vol. 22) New Style 'Miscellany XXVI', *Lollards of Coventry, 1486–1522*, eds. S. McSheffrey and N. Tanner (vol. 23) went to press for publication in 2003–2004.
- The Society's *Annual Bibliography of British and Irish History, Publications of 2001*, was published by Oxford University Press during the session,

and the *Annual Bibliography of British and Irish History, Publications of 2002* went to press, to be published in 2003.

- The *Studies in History* second series continued to produce exciting volumes. The following volumes were published, or went to press, during the session:

  - *The Allotment Movement in England, 1793–1873* by Jeremy Burchardt;
  - *Kingship and Crown Finance under James VI and I, 1603–1625* by John Roland Cramsie;
  - *Great Britain, Germany and the Soviet Union: Rapallo and after, 1922–1934* by Stephanie Salzmann;
  - *Social Investigation in Rural England, 1876–1914* by Mark Freeman;
  - *The Labour Party and the Planned Economy, 1931–1951* by Richard Toye; and
  - *Lordship and Medieval Urbanisation: Coventry 1045–1355* by Richard Goddard.

- As in the two previous subscription years, volumes in the *Studies in History* series were offered to the membership at a favourably discounted price. 275 accepted the offer for volumes published during the year, and orders for further copies of the volumes to be published in the year 2003–2004 were received.
- The Society acknowledges its gratitude for the continuing subvention from the Economic History Society to the *Studies in History* series, and is delighted to announce a similar subvention to be received from the Past and Present Society.
- The Society was continuing to investigate the possible re-publication of former Presidential lectures, particularly those of Sir Richard Southern.

Papers Read

- At the ordinary meetings of the Society the following papers were read:

  - 'Writing Fornication: Medieval Layrwite and its Historians'
    Professor Judith Bennett (4th July 2002: Prothero Lecture)
  - 'Resistance, Reprisal and Community in Occupied France, 1941–1944'
    Dr. Robert Gildea (18th October 2002 at the University of Aberystwyth)
  - 'Revolutionary Worlds in Southeast Asia, 1914–1941'
    Dr. Tim Harper (24th January 2003)

○ 'The Legacy of the Nineteenth-Century Bourgeois Family and the Wool Merchant's Son'
   Professor Leonore Davidoff (14th February 2003 at the University of Greenwich)

○ '*Pristina libertas*: liberty and the Anglo-Saxons revisited'
   Dr. Julia Crick (14th March 2003)

○ 'Tropical Views and Visions: Images of the Tropical World, c.1750–1850'
   Professor Felix Driver (2nd May 2003 at Oxford Brookes University)

○ 'Dividing Up Great Time: From Middle Ages to Modernity and on to Postmodernity?'
   Professor P.J. Corfield (23rd May 2003)

● At the Anniversary meeting on 22nd November 2002, the President, Professor Janet L. Nelson, delivered an address on 'England the Continent in the Ninth Century: I. Vikings and Others'.

Finance

● Because world-wide political and economic uncertainty continued to afflict stockmarkets, and hence the value of our investments, financially this was another difficult year for the Society. Between July 2002 and June 2003 the value of the Society's investments fell by £106,834 or 5.31 per cent, from £2,011,500 to £1,904,666. Total income received fell very slightly. In this environment a close watch was kept on expenditure, to the extent that a small operating surplus of £8,352 was recorded, as against a deficit of £20,040 in the previous year.

● Council records with gratitude the benefactions made to the Society by:

○ Mr. L.C. Alexander
○ The Reverend David Berry
○ Professor Andrew Browning
○ Professor C.D. Chandaman
○ Professor G. Donaldson
○ Professor Sir Geoffrey Elton
○ Mr. E.J. Erith
○ Mr. P.J.C. Firth
○ Mrs. W.M. Frampton
○ Mr. A.E.J. Hollaender
○ Professor C.J. Holdsworth
○ Professor P.J. Marshall
○ Mr. E.L.C. Mullins

- ○ Sir George Prothero
- ○ Dr. L. Rausing
- ○ Professor T.F. Reddaway
- ○ Miss E.M. Robinson
- ○ Miss J.C. Sinar
- ○ Professor A.S. Whitfield

Membership

- ● Council was advised and recorded with regret the deaths of 1 Honorary Vice-President, 7 Fellows, 1 Life Fellow, 23 Retired Fellows, 4 Corresponding Fellows, 3 Associates and 1 Member. These included

  Mr. E.A. Bird – Associate
  Mr. P.D. Brown – Fellow
  Mr. J.M. Bruce – Retired Fellow
  Professor A.E. Campbell – Retired Fellow
  Professor J.W. Cell – Fellow
  Professor C. Cipolla – Corresponding Fellow
  Lord Dacre of Glanton – Life Member
  Mrs. A.M. Erskine – Retired Fellow
  Dr. H.E.S. Fisher – Retired Fellow
  Dr. B.J. Greenhill – Retired Fellow
  Mr. W.J. Grisbrooke – Retired Fellow
  Sir John Habakkuk – Honorary Vice-President and former
      President
  Mr. P.C. Hancock – Member
  Dr. J.E.C. Hill – Retired Fellow
  Dr. G.A.M. Hills – Fellow
  Professor E. Hopkins – Retired Fellow
  Mr J.L. Kirby – Retired Fellow
  Professor Dr. K. Kluxen – Corresponding Fellow
  Professor J.R. Lander – Retired Fellow
  Professor P.E. Lasko – Retired Fellow
  Miss V.C.M. London – Retired Fellow
  The Rev. A.J. Loomie – Retired Fellow
  Dr. M.J.C. Lowry – Fellow
  Dr. J.F. McCaffrey – Retired Fellow
  Rev. Dr. T.J. McKenna – Associate
  Professor A.C. Miller – Retired Fellow
  Professor R. Mitchison – Retired Fellow
  Dr. P.R. Newman – Retired Fellow
  Miss H.E. Peek – Retired Fellow

Mr. J.O. Prestwich – Retired Fellow
Professor T.A. Reuter – Fellow and Member of Council
Dr. J.M. Roberts – Retired Fellow
Professor N. Rubinstein – Retired Fellow
Mrs. E. Russell – Associate
Professor T. Sakata – Fellow
Mr. B.W. Spencer – Retired Fellow
Professor J.A. van Houtte – Corresponding Fellow
Dr. D.W.T.C. Vessey – Retired Fellow
Mr. V.E. Watts – Fellow
Professor A.J.G. Wyse – Corresponding Fellow

- 96 Fellows and 23 Members were elected. 6 new Honorary Vice-Presidents and 6 Corresponding Fellows were invited to accept election. The membership of the Society on 30th June 2003 numbered 2705, comprising 1848 Fellows, 520 Retired Fellows, 18 Life Fellows, 12 Honorary Vice-Presidents, 91 Corresponding Fellows, 80 Associates and 136 Members.
- The Society exchanged publications with 15 Societies, British and foreign.

Representatives of the Society

- Dr. M. Smith agreed to succeed Professor R.A. Griffiths as the Society's representative on the Court of Governors of the University of Wales, Swansea.

- Dr. R. Mackenney agreed to represent the Society on the University of Stirling Conference and

- Professor N. Thompson agreed to represent the Society on the Court of the University of Wales Swansea.

- Dr. C.J. Kitching agreed to represent the Society on the National Council on Archives.

- The representation of the Society upon various bodies was as follows:

  o Dr. Julia Crick on the Joint Committee of the Society and the British Academy established to prepare an edition of Anglo-Saxon charters;

○ Professor N.P. Brooks on a committee to promote the publication of photographic records of the more significant collections of British Coins;

○ Professor G.H. Martin on the Council of the British Records Association;

○ Mr. P.M.H. Bell on the Editorial Advisory Board of the *Annual Register*;

○ Professor C.J. Holdsworth on the Court of the University of Exeter;

○ Professor D. d'Avray on the Anthony Panizzi Foundation;

○ Professor M.C. Cross on the Council of the British Association for Local History; and on the British Sub-Commission of the Commission International d'Histoire Ecclésiastique Comparée;

○ Professor L.J. Jordanova on the Advisory Council of the reviewing committee on the of the Export of Works of Art;

○ Professor W. Davies on the Court of the University of Birmingham;

○ Professor R.D. McKitterick on a committee to regulate British co-operation in the preparation of a new repertory of medieval sources to replace Potthast's *Bibliotheca Historica Medii Aevi*.

○ Professor J. Breuilly on the steering committee of the British Centre for Historical Research in Germany;

○ Dr. W.R. Childs at the Court at the University of Sheffield;

○ Dr. J. Winters on the History Data Service Advisory Committee;

○ Dr. R.A. Burns on the user panel of the RSLP Revelation project 'Unlocking research sources for 19th and 20th century church history and Christian theology';

○ Professor J.A. Tosh on the History Advisory Panel of the Subject Centre for History, Classics and Archaeology.

● Council received reports from its representatives.

Grants

● The Royal Historical Society Centenary Fellowship for the academic year 2002–2003 was awarded jointly to Eva De Visscher studying for a doctorate at the University of Leeds and working on a thesis entitled 'The Jewish-Christian dialogue in 12th century exegesis: The Hebrew and Latin sources of Herbert of Bosham's commentary on the Psalter' and Elizabeth Vlossak studying at Cambridge and working on a thesis entitled 'The Nationalisation of women in Alsace, 1871–1940'.

● The Society's Peter Marshall Fellowship will be awarded for the academic year 2003–2004.

- A grant of £2,000 to the Historical Association was made during the year. This was towards the publication of their Careers in History leaflet circulated to school and college students who take GCSE and A-level examinations.
- The Society's Research Support Committee continued to provide grants to postgraduate students for attendance at training courses or conferences, and funding towards research within and outside the United Kingdom. Funding is also available to organizers of workshops and conferences to encourage the participation of junior researchers. Grants during the year were made to the following:

Training Bursaries

○ Catherine ARMSTRONG, University of Warwick
Elizabethan and English Renaissance Area of the '33rd Annual Popular Culture Association Conference', held in New Orleans, Louisiana, USA, 16th–19th April 2003.
○ Michael Francis BROWN, University of York
'The North American Conference on British Studies in Conjunction with the Southern Conference on British Studies, Annual Meeting 2002', held in Baltimore, USA, 8th–10th November 2002.
○ Fabio CHISARI, De Montfort University, Leicester
'VIII Congress of the International Society for the History of Physical Education and Sport: Sport and Education in History', held in Urbino, Italy, 9th–13th July 2003.
○ Louisa CROSS, University of Dundee
'Prints and Pocket Books from the collection of Harry Matthews.' Study Day at the Museum of London, held at the Museum of London, 29th March 2003.
○ Sally CRUMPLIN, University of St Andrews
'International Medieval Congress: Power and Authority', held at the University of Leeds, 14th–17th July 2003.
○ Luke DAVIDSON, University of York
'Death in the Eighteenth-Century': Bloomington Eighteenth-Century Workshop, held at the University of Indiana, Bloomington, USA, 21st–24th May 2003.
○ Raquel DELGADO-MOREIRA, Imperial College London
'Canadian Society for the History and Philosophy of Science 2003 Meeting', to be held at the University of Dalhousie, Halifax, Canada, 29th–31st May 2003.
○ Catherine EAGLETON, Cambridge University
'International Medieval Conference', held in Kalamazoo, Michigan, USA, 8th–11th May 2003.
○ Tanya Gwynneth EVANS, Goldsmiths, University of London

'Northeast Conference on British Studies', held at Yale University, USA, 18th–19th October 2002.

○ Hannah GREIG, Royal Holloway, University of London
'Northeast Conference on British Studies', held at Yale University, USA, 18th–19th October 2002.

○ Francesca LOCATELLI, School of Oriental and African Studies, University of London
African Studies Association Annual Meeting 2002, 'Africa in the Information and Technology Age', held in Washington DC, USA, 5th–8th December 2002.

○ Pawel MACIEJKO, St. Hugh's College, Oxford
'34th Annual Conference of the Association for Jewish Studies', held in Los Angeles, California, 15th–17th December 2002.

○ Karen MILLER, University of Aberdeen
'Thirty-eighth International Congress on Medieval Studies at Western Michigan University', held at Western Michigan University, Kalamazoo, Michigan, USA, 8th–11th May 2003.

○ Lavinia MITTON, London School of Economics
'Association of British Historians Annual Conference', to be held at the University of Cambridge, 30th–31st May 2003.

○ Tim REINKE-WILLIAMS, University of Warwick
Elizabethan and English Renaissance Area of the '33rd Annual Popular Culture Association Conference', held in New Orleans, Louisiana, USA, 16th–19th April 2003.

○ Theo RICHES, King's College London
'Thirty-eighth International Congress on Medieval Studies', held at Western Michigan University, Kalamazoo, Michigan, USA, 8th–11th May 2003.

○ Matthew Owen ROBERTS, University of York
'North American Conference on British Studies', held in Baltimore, USA, 8th–10th November 2002.

○ Joanna ROYLE, University of Glasgow
'Christina of Markyate: a Typology of Female Sanctity?' held in St Albans, 2nd–3rd August 2003.

○ Elizabeth SCHOALES, University of Wales, Lampeter
'12th International Congress of Celtic Studies' held at the University of Wales, Aberystwyth, 24th–30th August 2003.

○ Paula STILES, University of St Andrews
'The World of Eleanor of Aquitaine: Literature and Society in Southern France between the Eleventh and Thirteenth Centuries', 8th–10th April 2003.

○ Joseph STREET, University of Sheffield
'Southern Historical Association Annual Conference', held in Baltimore, USA, November 2002.

O   Selina TODD, University of Sussex
    'Social History Society Annual Conference', held at Leicester
    University, 3rd–5th January 2003.

[22]

Research Fund: Research within the United Kingdom

O   Amanda BEAM, University of Stirling
    Visits to Edinburgh, London and Paris, May 2003.
O   Hayden BELLENOIT, Oxford University
    Visits to the Records of the Church Mission Society and Bir-
    mingham University Library, June – November 2003.
O   Katherine BERESFORD, University College London
    Visits to Public Record Office, Kew, and archives in Kent and
    Northampton, October - December 2002.
O   Olga BORYMCHUK, St Hugh's College, Oxford
    Visits to archives in London, Brighton, Hull and Warwick, 20th
    January–1st April 2003.
O   Sally CRUMPLIN, University of St Andrews
    Visits to the Bodleian Library, Oxford; Cambridge University
    Library; Lincoln's Inn Library and the British Library, June
    2003.
O   Janet DEATHERAGE, University of St Andrews
    Visits to archives in West Sussex, 12th–17th May 2003.
O   Janet DICKINSON, University of Southampton
    Visits to the British Library, London, November 2002–March 2003.
O   John HALLAM, University of Leicester
    Visits to the Public Record Office, Kew and Oxford and Cambridge
    Universities, March 2003–February 2004.
O   Clare HARDING, University of Birmingham
    Visits to the Public Record Office, Kew; Bodleian/Rhodes House
    Libraries, Oxford; Labour History Archive, Manchester; British
    Library of Political and Economic Sciences, London and the School
    of Oriental and African Studies, London, March–June 2003.
O   Khondker Iftekhar IQBAL, Fitzwilliam College, Cambridge
    Visits to the British Library and SOAS Library, London, 30th
    October–30th December 2002.
O   Michael LYON, Stirling University
    Visits to Dundee University Archives, 7th–11th April 2003.
O   Patricia MELDRUM, University of Stirling
    Visits to libraries in Aberdeen, Glasgow, Edinburgh, Dundee and
    London and to various churches in Scotland, March 2002–March
    2003.
O   Avril MORRIS, University of Leicester

Visits to the British Library, Lambeth Palace Library and the Society of Antiquaries Library, London, March–October 2003.

o   Kieran McGOVERN, University of Birmingham
Visits to the Public Record Office; the Public Record Office Northern Ireland; Bodleian Library, Oxford; Linen Hall, Belfast and the British Library.

o   David WILLCOX, Kent University
Visits to the University of Sussex, Marylebone Information Service, and the British Library, July and August 2003.

[15]

Research Fund: Research outside the United Kingdom

o   Ariadna ACEVEDO-RODRIGO, University of Warwick
Visits to Archives in Mexico, 17th May to 21st July 2003.

o   Laura Jane COLE, University of Sheffield
Visit to Archives Nationales, Paris, October 2002–May 2003.

o   Anna CROZIER, Wellcome Trust Centre, UCL
Visits to the Kenya National Archives, Nairobi, Kenya, 27th–19th September 2003.

o   Adam DAVIS, University of Luton
Visits to the National Archives and the Alexander Turnbull Library, Wellington, New Zealand, 2nd–30th June 2003.

o   Larissa DOUGLASS, University of Oxford
Visits to Archives in Prague and Vienna, July and August 2003.

o   Catherine EAGLETON, Jesus College, Cambridge
Visits to the Adler Planetarium, Chicago; the Smithsonian Museum, Washington; Yale University Library, New Haven, Connecticut; Houghton Library, Harvard University, Cambridge, Massachusetts; the Columbia University Library, New York and the Metropolitan Museum of Art, New York, 1st–7th May 2003 and 11th–30th May 2003.

o   Johanna GIBSON, Dundee University
Visits to the Archive of the Foreign Policy of Russia, Moscow and Russian State Archive of the Navy, St Petersburg, 15th January 2004–15th April 2004.

o   Mary HUNTER, University College London
Visits to Archives in Paris and Toulouse, July and August 2003.

o   Alexandra KESS, University of St. Andrews
Visits to the Bibliothèque Nationale de France, Paris and the Bibliotheque Municipale, Lyon, France, September 2002–September 2003.

o   Simone LAQUA, University of Oxford
Visit to Münster, Germany, October 2003–May 2004.

○ Richard James LA SPINA, Royal Holloway, University of London
Visits to Madrid, Barcelona, Cadiz, Toledo, Lisbon and Naples.

○ Arianna LISSONI, School of Oriental and African Studies, University of London
Visits to the Mayibuye Centre, University of the Western Cape, Cape Town and the University of Witwatersrand, Johannesburg, South Africa.

○ Francisco LOPEZ MARTIN, London Guildhall University
Visit to the Naval Musuem and the Army Museum, Istanbul, September 2002.

○ Pawel MACIEJKO, St Hugh's College, Oxford
Visits to Moravsky Zemsky Archiv, Brno, Czech Republic, 15th March–30th March 2003.

○ Alexandra MELITA, Royal Holloway, University of London
Visits to Libraries and Archives in Venice, 7th–13th July 2003.

○ Tatsuya MITSUDA, University of Cambridge
Visits to Archives in Vienna, Berlin and Paris, 18th August–26th September 2003.

○ James MORRISON, University of Birmingham
Visit to the National Archives of Canada, May 2003.

○ Diego MUSITELLI, University of Manchester
Visit to the Centre des Archives D'Outre Mer, Aix-en-Provence, France, July–September 2003.

○ Ivan POLANCEC, University College London
Visits to the Vatican Archives Rome, Italy and Bibliothèque Nationale, Paris, France, 1st April–15th April 2003.

○ Jens-Ulrich POPPEN, London School of Economics
Visit to Iberian Peninsula, December 2002–February 2003.

○ Asaf SINIVER, University of Nottingham
Visits to the National Archives, the Library of Congress, the National Security Archives and the George Washington Library, Washington D.C., July–August 2003.

○ Paula STILES, University of St Andrews
Visits to various archives in Spain, either March 2003 or May 2003.

○ Elke STOCKREITER, School of Oriental and African Studies, University of London
Visits to Zanzibar National Archives, Zanzibar and the Tanzania National Archives, Dar es Salaam, Tanzania, The Public Record Office, London and the Bodleian Library, Oxford, July 2003–June 2004.

○ Flora TSILAGA, King's College London
Visits to the Archive of the United Nations Relief and Rehabilitation Administration, New York, USA, March–May 2003.

○ Benedikta VON SEHERR-THOSS, Worcester College, Oxford
    Visits to German State Archive, Koblenz, and Archive of the
    German Foreign Office, Berlin, Germany.
○ Thomas WALES, University of Edinburgh
    Visits to archives in the United States of America, 21st–30th July
    2003.
○ Carl Peter WATTS, University of Birmingham
    Visits to the LBJ Library, Austin, Texas and the Bentley Library,
    University of Michigan, Ann Arbor, USA, 28th December–27th
    January 2003.
○ Christopher WRIGHT, Royal Holloway, University of London
    Visits to archives in Italy, October 2003–April 2004.

[28]

Royal Historical Society Conferences Workshop Fund

○ 'Elizabeth I and the Expansion of England', to be held at the
    National Maritime Museum, Greenwich, 4th–6th September 2003
    (Nigel RIGBY).

Workshop Fund

○ 'Interrogating Hearsay: Rumours and Gossip in Historical Per-
    spective, 1500–2003', to be held at the University of Essex, 26th July
    2003 (D. BORG-MUSCAT, M. McLAUGHLIN, C. SCHRODER).
○ 'Consecrated Women: Towards the history of women religions of
    Britain and Ireland' held at the Institute of Historical Research, 11
    October 2003 (Caroline BOWDEN).
○ 'Four Empires and Enlargement. States, Societies and Individuals:
    Transfiguring Perspectives and Images of Central and Eastern
    Europe', to be held at the School of Slavonic and East European
    Studies, UCL, 6th–8th November 2003 (Daniel BRETT).
○ '1603: The Historical and Cultural Consequences of the Accession
    of James I', held at the University of Hull, 27th–28th June 2003
    (Glenn BURGESS).
○ 'Magical Practice and Belief, 1800 – present', held at the University
    of Bristol, 25th–6th April 2003 (Alison BUTLER).
○ 'British Society for Eighteenth Century Studies Annual Conference',
    held at St. Hugh's College, Oxford, 3rd–5th January 2002 (Kimberly
    CHRISMAN CAMPBELL).
○ 'Broadening Narratives: Alternative Sources for Anglo-Saxon His-
    tory', held at the Royal Society of Antiquaries, organised by the
    Charles Homer Haskins Society, 13th September 2003 (David
    CROUCH).

o 'The Chamberlains of Birmingham', held at the University of Birmingham, 27th–28th June 2003 (Nicholas CROWSON and Peter MARSH)

o 'The History of the Future: Visions for the Past', held at the University of Leicester, 16th–19th July 2003 (Nicholas CULL).

o 'Texts, Ma(r)kers, Markets' held at the University of York, 24th–26th July 2003 (Matthew DAY).

o 'Family, *Familia* and Feud: Society and Culture in the North of England from the Anglo-Scottish Wars to the Reformation' held at the University of Durham, 4th–6th July 2003 (Claire ETTY).

o 'Tenth Thirteenth Century England Conference' to be held at the University of Durham, 1st–3rd September 2003 (Robin FRAME).

o 'Memory' to be held at the Institute of Historical Research, 11th July 2003 (Jane HAMLETT).

o 'Society for the Study of French History, Annual Conference, Nottingham 2003: France, Centres and Peripheries', held at the University of Nottingham, 10th–11th April 2003 (Michael JONES).

o 'Scotland's World:Perspectives on Scotland's Place in World History', held at the University of Glasgow, 27th–29th March 2003 (Sara Karly KEHOE).

o 'Kings, Clerics and Warlords: Channels of Power in Medieval Europe', held at the Royal Museum, Edinburgh, 31st May 2003 (Sergi MAINER).

o 'Queer Matters', to be held at King's College London, 28th–30th May 2004 (Robert MILLS).

o 'Understanding Urban Wales', to be held at the University of Wales, Swansea, 9th–10th September (Louise MISKELL).

o '2nd International Legal History Conference: Mapping the Law in the Middle Ages and Early Modern Period', held at the University of Exeter, 3rd–5th April 2003 (Anthony MUSSON).

o 'Conference of the International Federation for Research in Women's History' held at Queen's University, Belfast, 11th–14th August 2003 (Mary O'DOWD).

o 'Immigration, History and Memory in Britain' to be held at the University of Leicester, 6th–7th September 2003 (Panikos PANAYI).

o Postgraduate Conference in the History of Science, Technology and Medicine, held at Imperial College London and University College London , 4th–6th November 2002 (Jessica REINISCH)

o 'Tartan Arthur: The Scots and Medieval Arthurian Legend', held at the University of Nottingham, 21st June 2003 (Nicola ROYAN).

o 'American Cinema and Everyday Life', held at University College London, 26th–28th June 2003 (Melvyn STOKES).

o 'Palmerston Congress', held at the University of Southampton, 11th–13th July 2003 (Miles TAYLOR).

o 'British Rocketry Oral History Project, 2003' held at Charterhouse School, 10th–12th April 2003 (Dave WRIGHT).

[26]

ORS Awards

o Izabella ORLOWSKA, SOAS, London.
o Katherine CHAMBERS, St John's College, Cambridge.

[2]

THE ROYAL HISTORICAL SOCIETY
FINANCIAL ACCOUNTS
FOR THE YEAR ENDED 30 JUNE 2003

haysmacintyre
Chartered Accountants
Registered Auditors
London

LEGAL AND ADMINISTRATIVE INFORMATION

THE ROYAL HISTORICAL SOCIETY
REPORT OF THE COUNCIL OF TRUSTEES
FOR THE YEAR ENDED 30 JUNE 2003

The members of Council present their report and audited accounts for the year ended 30 June 2003.

PRINCIPAL ACTIVITIES AND REVIEW OF THE YEAR

The Society exists for the promotion and support of historical scholarship and its dissemination to historians and a wider public. This year, as in previous years, it has pursued this objective by an ambitious programme of publications – a volume of Transactions, three volumes of edited texts in the Camden Series and further volumes in the Studies in History Series have appeared, by the holding of meetings in London and at universities outside London at which papers are delivered, by the sponsoring of the joint lecture for a wider public with Gresham College, by distributing over £24,000 in research support grants to 98 individuals, and by frequent representations to various official bodies where the interests of historical scholarship are involved. It is Council's intention that these activities should be sustained to the fullest extent in the future.

RESULTS

The Society experienced a difficult year with total funds decreasing from £2,077,185 in June 2002 to £1,941,366 in June 2003, a decrease of £135,819. This was entirely due to a down turn in the stock-market since the Society produced a modest surplus of £8,352 (2002:minus £20,040) from its operating activities.

Membership subscriptions income was largely consistent with the previous year as subscription rates remained at the level set at the Society's Anniversary Meeting on 26 November 1999. The increase in investment income £138,092 (2002:£112,231) resulted as a consequence of re-structuring the investment portfolio in line with the investment policy detailed below. During the year £36k was added to the portfolio.

Income from royalties has decreased from £29,283 to £20,584. Book revenue fell due in part to lower sales of the Guides and Handbooks and to lower sales of the Camden Fifth Series volumes.

Income from conferences was Nil compared with £7,928 in 2002 due to the fact that no conferences with a charge took place during the year. This is reflected by a proportionate reduction in conference expenditure.

Grants for awards were reduced by £17,000 principally due to changes in the funding of the British History Bibliographies project grant.

FIXED ASSETS

Information relating to changes in fixed assets is given in notes 2 and 3 to the accounts.

INVESTMENTS

The Society has adopted a "total return" approach to its investment policy. This means that the funds are invested solely on the basis of seeking to secure the best total level of economic return compatible with the duty to make safe investments, but regardless of the form the return takes.

The Society has adopted this approach to ensure even-handedness between current and future beneficiaries, as the focus of many investments moves away from producing income to maximising capital values. In the current investments climate, to maintain the level of income needed to fund the charity, would require an investment portfolio which would not achieve the optimal overall return, so effectively penalising future beneficiaries.

The total return strategy does not make distinctions between income and capital returns. It lumps together all forms of return on investment – dividends, interest, and capital gains etc, to produce a "total return". Some of the total return is then used to meet the needs of present beneficiaries, while the remainder is added to the existing capital to help meet the needs of future beneficiaries.

The Society's investments are managed by Cripps Portfolio, who report all transactions to the Honorary Treasurer and provide six monthly reports on the portfolios, which are considered by the Society's Finance Committee which meets three times a year. In turn the Finance Committee reports to Council.

The Society closely monitors its investments, with its main portfolio being assessed against a bespoke benchmark and its smaller Whitfield and Robinson portfolios against the standard APCIMS balanced benchmark.

RISK ASSESSMENT

The Trustees are satisfied that they have considered the major risks to which the charity is exposed, that they have taken action to mitigate or manage those risks and that they have systems in place to monitor any change to those risks.

GRANT MAKING

The Society awards funds to assist advanced historical research. It operates several separate schemes, for each of which there is an application form. The Society's Research Support Committee considers applications at meetings held 6 times a year. In turn the Research Support Committee reports to Council. A list of awards made is provided in the Society's Annual Report.

RESERVES POLICY

The Council have reviewed the Society's need for reserves in line with the guidance issued by the Charity Commission. They believe that the Society requires approximately the current level of unrestricted general funds of £1.8m to generate sufficient total return, both income and capital, to cover the Society's expenditure in excess of the other sources of income on an annual basis to ensure that the Society can run efficiently and meet the needs of beneficiaries.

The Society's restricted funds consist of a number of different funds where the donor has imposed restrictions on the use of the funds which are legally binding. The purposes of these funds are set out in note 16.

STATEMENT OF TRUSTEES' RESPONSIBILITIES

Law applicable to charities in England and Wales requires the Council to prepare accounts for each financial year which give a true and fair view of the state of affairs of the Society and of its financial activities for that year. In preparing these accounts, the Trustees are required to:

- select suitable accounting policies and apply them consistently;
- make judgements and estimates that are reasonable and prudent;
- state whether applicable accounting standards have been followed, subject to any material departures disclosed and explained in the accounts;
- prepare the accounts on the going concern basis unless it is inappropriate to presume that the Society will continue in business.

The Council is responsible for ensuring proper accounting records are kept which disclose, with reasonable accuracy at any time, the financial position of the Society and enable them to ensure that the financial statements comply with applicable law. They are also responsible for safeguarding the assets of the Society and hence for taking reasonable steps for the prevention and detection of error, fraud and other irregularities.

MEMBERS OF THE COUNCIL

At the Anniversary Meeting on 22 November 2002, K C Fincham succeeded Dr P Mandler as Honorary Secretary; the remaining Officers of the Society were re-elected.

The Vice-Presidents retiring under By-law XVII were Professor D.N. Cannadine, Professor P.A. Stafford, Professor J.A. Tosh and Mrs. S. Tyacke. Professor H.T. Dickinson and Dr C.J. Kitching were elected to replace them.

The Members of Council retiring under By-law XX were Dr. W R Childs, Professor M L Dockrill, Professor V I J Flint and Professor J L Miller. In accordance with By-law XXI, amended, Professor G A Hosking, Dr R S Mackenney and Professor D M Palliser were elected in their place. Dr. W R Childs was elected for a further term of one year in place of Professor T A Reuter, who had died mid-term during the session and Professor V I J Flint was elected for a further term of one year in place of Professor C M Andrew, who had resigned mid-term.

APPOINTMENT OF TRUSTEES

In accordance with By-law XVII, the Vice-Presidents shall hold office normally for a term of three years. Two of them shall retire by rotation, in order of seniority in office, at each Anniversary Meeting and shall not be eligible for re-election before the Anniversary Meeting of the next year. In accordance with By-law XIX, the Council of the Society shall consist of the President, the Vice-Presidents, the Treasurer, the Secretary, the Librarian, the Literary Directors and twelve Councillors. The President shall be *ex-officio* a member of all Committees appointed by the Council; and the Treasurer, the Secretary, the Librarian and the Literary Directors shall, unless the Council otherwise determine, also be *ex-officio* members of all such Committees. In accordance with By-law XX, the Councillors shall hold office normally for a term of four years. Three of them shall retire by rotation, in order of seniority in office, at each Anniversary Meeting and shall not be eligible for re-election before the Anniversary Meeting of the next year.

STANDING COMMITTEES 2003

The Society was operated through the following Committees during 2003:

Finance Committee	Dr S R Ditchfield	
	Mr P J C Firth	– non Council Member
	Professor P Mathias	– non Council Member
	Professor R J McKitterick	– Chair
	The six Officers as above	
Membership Committee	Dr J E Burton	
	Professor H Meller	
	Professor R J A R Rathbone	– Chair
Publications Committee	Dr J E Burrton	
	Professor C D H Jones	– Chair
	Dr R S Mackenney	
	Professor F O'Gorman	
	The six Officers as above	
Research Support Committee	Dr M Finn	
	Professor P J Corfield	– Chair
	Professor V I J Flint	
General Purposes Committee	Dr M Finn	
	Professor G A Hosking	
	Professor L J Jordanova	– Chair
	Professor D M Palliser	
	The six Officers as above	
Teaching Policy Committee	Dr W R Childs	
	Dr S R Ditchfield	
	Professor H T Dickinson	– Chair
	Professor H E Meller	
	The six Officers as above	
Research Policy Committee	Dr C J Kitching	– Chair
	Professor J A Green	
	Professor G A Hosking	
	Professor R J A R Rathbone	
	The six Officers as above	

Studies in History	Professor D S Eastwood	– Convenor
Editorial Board	Professor M Braddick	– non Council Member
	Dr S J Gunn	– non Council Member
	Dr J E Hunter	– Economic History Society
	Professor C D H Jones	– non Council Member
	Professor M Mazower	– non Council Member
	Professor M. Taylor	– non Council Member
	Dr S Walker	– non Council Member
	Dr A Walsham	
	A Literary Director	
	Honorary Treasurer	
Election of Officers	Professor C D H Jones	– Convenor
Subcommittee:	Dr W R Childs	
[President and Literary	A Literary Director	
Director]	Honorary Treasurer	
	Honorary Secretary	

AUDITORS

A resolution proposing the appointment of auditors will be submitted at the Anniversary Meeting.

By Order of the Board

Honorary Secretary
.... 2003

INDEPENDENT REPORT OF THE AUDITORS
FOR THE YEAR ENDED 30 JUNE 2003

We have audited the financial statements of The Royal Historical Society for the year ended 30 June 2003 which comprise the Statement of Financial Activities, the Balance Sheet, and the related notes. These financial statements have been prepared under the historical cost convention (as modified by the revaluation of certain fixed assets) and the accounting policies set out therein.

This report is made solely to the charity's trustees, as a body, in accordance with the regulations made under the Charities Act 1993. Our audit work has been undertaken so that we might state to the charity's trustees those matters we are required to state to them in an auditor's report and for no other purpose. To the fullest extent permitted by law, we do not accept or assume responsibility to anyone other than the charity and the charity's trustees as a body, for our audit work, for this report, or for the opinions we have formed.

RESPECTIVE RESPONSIBILITIES OF TRUSTEES AND AUDITORS

The Trustees' responsibilities for preparing the Annual Report and the financial statements in accordance with applicable law and United Kingdom Accounting Standards are set out in the Statement of Trustees' Responsibilities.

We have been appointed as auditors under section 43 of the Charities Act 1993 and report in accordance with regulations made under section 44 of that Act. Our responsibility is to audit the financial statements in accordance with relevant legal and regulatory requirements and United Kingdom Auditing Standards.

We report to you our opinion as to whether the financial statements give a true and fair view and are properly prepared in accordance with the Charities Act 1993. We also report to you if, in our opinion, the Trustees' Report is not consistent with the financial statements, if the charity has not kept proper accounting records or if we have not received all the information and explanations we require for our audit.

We read the other information contained in the Trustees' Report and consider whether it is consistent with the audited financial statements. We consider the implications for our report if we become aware of any apparent misstatements or apparent material inconsistencies with the financial statements.

BASIS OF AUDIT OPINION

We conducted our audit in accordance with United Kingdom Auditing Standards issued by the Auditing Practices Board. An audit includes examination, on a test basis, of evidence relevant to the amounts and disclosures in the financial statements. It also includes an assessment of the significant estimates and judgements made by the Trustees in the preparation of the financial statements, and of whether the accounting policies are appropriate to the charity's circumstances, consistently applied and adequately disclosed.

We planned and performed our audit so as to obtain all the information and explanations which we considered necessary in order to provide us with sufficient evidence to give reasonable assurance that the financial statements are free from material misstatement, whether caused by fraud or other irregularity or error. In forming our opinion we also evaluated the overall adequacy of the presentation of information in the financial statements.

OPINION

In our opinion the financial statements give a true and fair view of the state of the charity's affairs as at 30 June 2003 and of its incoming resources and application of resources in the year then ended and have been properly prepared in accordance with the Charities Act 1993.

haysmacintyre
Chartered Accountants
Registered Auditors

Southampton House
317 High Holborn
London
WC1V 7NL

THE ROYAL HISTORICAL SOCIETY

STATEMENT OF FINANCIAL ACTIVITIES
FOR THE YEAR ENDED 30 JUNE 2003

	Notes	Unrestricted Funds £	Restricted Funds £	Total Funds 2003 £	Total Funds 2002 £
INCOMING RESOURCES					
Donations, legacies and similar incoming Resources	7	6,161	–	6,161	5,277
Activities In Furtherance Of The Charity's Objects					
Grants for awards		345	3,768	4,113	6,490
Conferences		–	–	–	7,928
Subscriptions		57,646	–	57,646	56,101
Royalties		20,584	–	20,584	29,283
Activities To Generate Funds					
Investment income	3	132,871	5,221	138,092	112,231
Other		964	–	964	11,743
TOTAL INCOMING RESOURCES		218,571	8,989	227,560	229,053
RESOURCES EXPENDED					
Cost of Generating Funds					
Investment manager's fee		10,996	857	11,853	17,034
Charitable Expenditure					
Grants for awards	8	38,967	3,750	42,717	59,860
Conferences and Receptions		8,363	–	8,363	22,742
Publications		58,039	–	58,039	63,243
Library		11,219	–	11,219	12,153
Support costs		67,424	5,719	73,143	60,237
Management and administration		13,874	–	13,874	13,824
TOTAL RESOURCES EXPENDED	9	208,882	10,326	219,208	249,093
NET INCOMING/(OUTGOING) RESOURCES		9,689	(1,337)	8,352	(20,040)
OTHER RECOGNISED GAINS AND LOSSES					
Unrealised (loss) on investments	3	(136,393)	(7,778)	(144,171)	(239,067)
NET MOVEMENT IN FUNDS		(126,704)	(9,115)	(135,819)	(259,107)
Balance at 1 July 2002		£1,916,729	£160,456	£2,077,185	£2,336,292
Balance at 30 June 2003		£1,790,025	£151,341	£1,941,366	£2,077,185

THE ROYAL HISTORICAL SOCIETY

BALANCE SHEET AS AT 30TH JUNE 2003

	Notes	£	2003 £	£	2002 £
FIXED ASSETS					
Tangible assets	2		463		390
Investments .	3		1,906,197		2,011,500
			1,906,660		2,011,890
CURRENT ASSETS					
Stocks .	4	30,430		30,471	
Debtors	5	7,506		29,405	
Cash at bank and in hand		25,671		30,492	
		63,607		90,368	
LESS: CREDITORS					
Amounts due within one year .	6	(28,901)		(25,073)	
NET CURRENT ASSETS			34,706		65,295
NET ASSETS			£1,941,366		£2,077,185
REPRESENTED BY:	17				
Unrestricted – General Fund			1,790,025		1,916,729
Restricted – E M Robinson Bequest	16		92,950		98,321
Restricted – A S Whitfield Prize Fund	16		37,229		39,169
Restricted – BHB 2 (Andrew Mellon Fund)	16		6,792		12,511
Restricted – P J Marshall Fellowship	16		3,768		–
Restricted – The David Berry Essay Trust	16		10,602		10,455
			£1,941,366		£2,077,185

Approved by the Council on 21 November 2003

President:

Honorary Treasurer:

The attached notes form an integral part of these financial statements.

THE ROYAL HISTORICAL SOCIETY

NOTES TO THE ACCOUNTS FOR THE YEAR ENDED 30 JUNE 2003

1. ACCOUNTING POLICIES

   (a) *Basis of Preparation*

   The financial statements have been prepared in accordance with the Statement of Recommended Practice 2000 "Accounting and Reporting by Charities" and with applicable accounting standards issued by UK accountancy bodies. They are prepared on the historical cost basis of accounting as modified to include the revaluation of fixed assets including investments which are carried at market value.

   (b) *Depreciation*

   Depreciation is calculated by reference to the cost of fixed assets using a straight line basis at rates considered appropriate having regard to the expected lives of the fixed assets. The annual rates of depreciation in use are:

   Furniture and equipment   10%
   Computer equipment   25%

   (c) *Stock*

   Stock is valued at the lower of cost and net realisable value.

   (d) *Library and archives*

   The cost of additions to the library and archives is written off in the year of purchase.

   (e) *Subscription income*

   Subscription income is recognised in the year it became receivable with a provision against any subscription not received.

   (f) *Investments*

   Investments are stated at market value. Any surplus/deficit arising on revaluation is   included in the Statement of Financial Activities. Dividend income is accounted for when the Society becomes entitled to such monies.

   (g) *Publication costs*

   Publication costs are transferred in stock and released to the Statement of Financial Activities as stocks are depleted.

   (h) *Donations and other voluntary income*

   Donations and other voluntary income is recognised when the Society becomes legally entitled to such monies.

   (i) *Grants payable*

   Grants payable are recognised in the year in which they are approved.

   (j) *Funds*

   Unrestricted : these are funds which can be used in accordance with the charitable objects at the discretion of the trustees.

   Restricted: these are funds that can only be used for particular restricted purposes defined by the benefactor and within the objects of the charity.

   (k) *Allocations*

   Wages and salary costs are allocated on the basis of the work done by the Executive Secretary and the Administrative Secretary.

   (l) *Pensions*

   Pension costs are charged to the SOFA when payments fall due. The Society contributes 10% of gross salaries to the personal pension plans of one of the employees.

2. TANGIBLE FIXED ASSETS

	Computer Equipment £	Furniture and Equipment £	Total £
Cost			
At 1 July 2002	29,742	1,173	30,915
Additions	618	–	618
At 30 June 2003	30,360	1,173	31,533
Depreciation			
At 1 July 2003	29,352	1,173	30,525
Charge for the year	545	–	545
At 30 June 2003	29,897	1,173	31,070
Net book value			
At 30 June 2003	£463	£–	£463
At 30 June 2002	£390	£–	£390

All tangible fixed asset are used in the furtherance of the Society's objects.

3. INVESTMENTS

	General Fund £	Robinson Bequest £	Whitfield Prize Fund £	David Berry Essay Trust £	Total £
Market value at 1 July 2002	1,851,870	113,187	44,913	1,530	2,011,500
Additions	416,170	3,529	22,143	–	441,842
Disposals	(379,768)	(619)	(22,587)	–	(402,974)
Net realised/unrealised (loss)/ gain on investments . .	(136,394)	(5,906)	(1,871)	–	(144,171)
Market value at 30th June 2003	£1,751,878	£110,191	£42,598	£1,530	£1,906,197
Cost at 30th June 2003 . .	£1,662,558	£86,688	£43,084	£1,530	£1,793,860

	2003 £	2002 £
UK Equities	931,917	1,033,987
UK Government Stock and Bonds	834,084	823,429
Overseas equities	17,398	18,861
Uninvested Cash	122,798	135,223
	£1,906,197	£2,011,500
Dividends and interest on listed investments	137,880	111,725
Interest on cash deposits	212	506
	£138,092	£112,231

4. STOCK

	2003 £	2002 £
Transactions Sixth Series	3,617	3,866
Camden Fifth Series	14,284	11,664
Guides and Handbooks	1,281	2,571
Camden Classics Reprints	11,248	12,370
	£30,430	£30,471

5. DEBTORS

	2003 £	2002 £
Other debtors	5,209	19,398
Prepayments	2,297	10,007
	£7,506	£29,405

6. CREDITORS: Amounts due within one year

	2003 £	2002 £
Trade creditors	2,773	4,705
Sundry creditors (Note 8)	5,573	3,937
Subscriptions received in advance	11,452	9,557
Accruals and deferred income	9,103	6,874
	£28,901	£25,073

7. DONATIONS AND LEGACIES

	2003 £	2002 £
A Browning Bequest	180	96
G R Elton Bequest	4,342	4,176
Donations via membership	410	516
Gladstone Memorial Trust	600	–
Sundry income	629	489
	£6,161	£5,277

8. GRANTS FOR AWARDS

	Unrestricted Funds £	Restricted Funds £	Total 2003 £	Total 2002 £
Alexander Prize	253	–	253	625
Sundry Grants	700	–	700	200
Research support grants (note 12)	26,227	–	26,227	20,404
Historical Association	2,000	–	2,000	2,500
Centenary fellowship	8,225	–	8,225	4,875
A-Level prizes	500	–	500	600
A S Whitfield prize	–	1,125	1,125	1,050
E M Robinson Bequest				
– Grant to Dulwich Picture Library	–	2,375	2,375	4,750
Gladstone history book prize	1,062	–	1,062	1,000
P J Marshall Fellowship	–	–	–	6,500
BHB project grant	–	–	–	17,106
David Berry Prize	–	250	250	250
	£38,967	£3,750	£42,717	£59,860

GRANTS PAYABLE

	2003 £	2002 £
Commitments at 1 July 2002	3,937	20,087
Commitments made in the year	42,717	59,610
Grants paid during the year	(41,081)	(75,760)
Commitments at 30 June 2003 (Note 6)	£5,573	£3,937

9. DIRECT CHARITABLE EXPENDITURE

	Staff Costs £	Depreciation £	Other Costs £	Total £	2002 £
Cost of Generating Funds					
Investment manager's fee .	–	–	11,853	11,853	*17,034*
Charitable Expenditure					
Grants for awards (Note 8)	–	–	42,717	42,717	*59,860*
Conferences	2,298	–	6,065	8,363	*22,742*
Publications	16,470	–	41,569	58,039	*63,243*
Library	3,065	–	8,154	11,219	*12,153*
Support costs	32,886	545	39,712	73,143	*60,237*
Management and administration	–	–	13,874	13,874	*13,824*
TOTAL RESOURCES EXPENDED	£54,719	£545	£163,944	£219,208	*£249,093*

STAFF COSTS

	2003 £	2002 £
Wages and salaries	46,528	*40,938*
Social Security costs	4,542	*3,889*
Other pension costs	3,649	*3,684*
	£54,719	*£48,511*

The average number of employees in the year was 2 (2002: 2)
There were no employees whose emoluments exceeded £50,000 in the year.

10. COUNCILLORS' EXPENSES
During the year travel expenses were reimbursed to 30 Councillors attending Council meetings at a cost of £5,565 (2002: £6,012).

11. AUDITOR'S REMUNERATION

	2003 £	2002 £
Audit fee	6,698	*6,404*
Other services	493	*470*

12. GRANTS PAID
During the year Society awarded grants to a value of £26,227 (2002: £20,404) to 98 (2002: 83) individuals (Note 8).

13. LEASE COMMITMENTS
The Society has the following annual commitments under non-cancellable operating leases which expire:

	2003 £	2002 £
Within 1–2 years	–	*–*
Within 2–5 years	7,281	*7,281*
	£7,281	*£7,281*

14. LIFE MEMBERS
The Society has ongoing commitments to provide membership services to 19 Life Members at a cost of approximately £42 each per year.

15. UNCAPITALISED ASSETS
The Society owns a library the cost of which is written off to the Statement of Financial Activities at the time of purchase.

This library is insured for £150,000 and is used for reference purposes by the membership of the Society.

16. RESTRICTED FUNDS

	Balance at 1 July 02 £	Incoming Resources £	Outgoing Resources £	Investment (Losses) £	Balance at 30 June 03 £
(i) E M Robinson Bequest	98,321	3,529	(2,993)	(5,907)	92,950
(ii) A S Whitfield Prize Fund	39,169	1,295	(1,364)	(1,871)	37,229
(iii) BHB/A.Mellon Fund	12,511	–	(5,719)	–	6,792
(iv) P J Marshall Fellowship	–	3,768	–	–	3,768
(v) David Berry Essay Trust	10,455	397	(250)	–	10,602
	£160,456	£8,989	£(10,326)	£(7,778)	£151,341

(i) *E M Robinson Bequest*
Income from the E M Robinson bequest is used to provide grants to the Dulwich Picture Gallery.

(ii) *A S Whitfield Prize Fund*
The A S Whitfield Prize Fund is used to provide an annual prize for the best first monograph for British history published in the calendar year.

(iii) *BHB/A Mellon Fund*
The British History Bibliographies project funding is used to provide funding for the compilation of bibliographies in British and Irish History.

(iv) *P J Marshall Fellowship*
The P J Marshall Fellowship is used to provide a sum sufficient to cover the stipend for a one-year doctoral research fellowship alongside the existing Royal Historical Society Centenary Fellowship at the Institute of Historical Research in the academic year 2003–2004.

(v) *The David Berry Essay Trust*
The David Berry Essay Trust is to provide an annual prize for the best essay on a subject dealing with Scottish history.

17. ANALYSIS OF NET ASSETS BETWEEN FUNDS

	General Fund £	E.M. Robinson Bequest Fund £	A.S. Whitfield Prize Fund £	BHB/ Andrew Mellon Fund £	David Berry Essay Trust £	PJ Marshall Fellowship £	Total £
Fixed assets	463	–	–	–	–	–	463
Investments	1,751,878	110,191	42,598	–	1,530	–	1,906,197
	1,752,341	110,191	42,598	–	1,530	–	1,906,660
Current assets							
Stocks	30,430	–	–	–	–	–	30,430
Debtors	7,506	–	–	–	–	–	7,506
Cash at bank and in hand	5,789	–	–	6,792	9,322	3,768	25,671
	43,725	–	–	6,792	9,322	3,768	63,607
Less: creditors	(6,041)	(17,241)	(5,369)	–	(250)	–	(28,901)
Net current assets	37,684	(17,241)	(5,369)	6,792	9,072	3,768	34,706
Net assets	£1,790,025	£92,950	£37,229	£6,792	£10,602	£3,768	£1,941,366